AN INTRODUCTION TO THE ROCK-FORMING MINERALS

W. A. DEER F.R.S.
Professor of Mineralogy & Petrology, Cambridge University

R. A. HOWIE
Professor of Mineralogy, University of London, King's College

J. ZUSSMAN
Professor of Geology, Manchester University

LONGMAN

LONGMAN GROUP LIMITED
London
Associated companies, branches and representatives
throughout the world

Distributed in the U.S.A. by Halsted Press,
a Division of John Wiley & Sons, Inc.

First Published 1966
Tenth Impression 1977

ISBN 0 582 44210 9 (paper)

Set in 9 pt. on 10 pt. Monotype Modern Extended type
Printed in Great Britain by
Richard Clay (The Chaucer Press) Ltd,
Bungay, Suffolk.

CONTENTS

Part 1 ORTHO- AND RING SILICATES

OLIVINE GROUP Olivine, tephroite–knebelite, monticellite . . 1
HUMITE GROUP 11
ZIRCON 13
SPHENE 17
GARNET GROUP, VESUVIANITE (idocrase) 21
SILLIMANITE, MULLITE, ANDALUSITE, KYANITE . . . 34
TOPAZ 45
STAUROLITE, CHLORITOID 49
DATOLITE, SAPPHIRINE 56
Larnite, Merwinite, Spurrite, Eudialyte, Rosenbuschite . . . 58
EPIDOTE GROUP 61
LAWSONITE, PUMPELLYITE 70
MELILITE GROUP 72
Rankinite, Tilleyite, Låvenite, Catapleiite 77
BERYL, CORDIERITE, TOURMALINE 80
AXINITE 97

Part 2 CHAIN SILICATES

PYROXENE GROUP Enstatite–orthoferrosilite, diopside–hedenbergite, johannsenite, augite–ferroaugite, pigeonite, aegirine, aegirineaugite, spodumene, jadeite 99
WOLLASTONITE, PECTOLITE, RHODONITE, BUSTAMITE, PYROXMANGITE 140
AMPHIBOLE GROUP Anthophyllite–gedrite, cummingtonite–grunerite, tremolite–ferroactinolite, hornblende, basaltic hornblende, kaersutite, barkevikite, glaucophane–riebeckite, richterite, katophorite, eckermannite–arfvedsonite 148
Aenigmatite, Astrophyllite 191

Part 3 SHEET SILICATES

MICA GROUP Muscovite, paragonite, glauconite, phlogopite, biotite, lepidolite, zinnwaldite, margarite, clintonite–xanthophyllite . . 193
STILPNOMELANE 222
PYROPHYLLITE, TALC 225
CHLORITE 231
SERPENTINE 242

CLAY MINERALS Kaolinite group (kandites), illite, montmorillonite group (smectites), vermiculite 250
APOPHYLLITE 275
PREHNITE 277

Part 4 FRAMEWORK SILICATES

FELDSPAR GROUP Alkali feldspars 281
      Plagioclase 318
      Barium feldspars (celsian, hyalophane) . . 339
SILICA MINERALS Quartz, tridymite, cristobalite . . . 340
NEPHELINE GROUP Nepheline, kalsilite 356
PETALITE, LEUCITE 366
SODALITE GROUP Sodalite, nosean, haüyne 375
      Helvite, danalite, genthelvite 380
CANCRINITE–VISHNEVITE, SCAPOLITE 381
ANALCITE, ZEOLITE GROUP 389

Part 5 NON-SILICATES

OXIDES Periclase, cassiterite, corundum, haematite, ilmenite, rutile, anatase, brookite, perovskite, spinel group (spinel series, magnetite series, chromite series) 403
HYDROXIDES Brucite, gibbsite, diaspore, boehmite, goethite, lepidocrocite, limonite 434
SULPHIDES Pyrites, pyrrhotite, chalcopyrite, sphalerite, galena . 445
SULPHATES Barytes, celestine, gypsum, anhydrite . . . 462
CARBONATES Calcite, magnesite, rhodochrosite, siderite, dolomite, ankerite, huntite, aragonite, strontianite, witherite . . . 473
PHOSPHATES Apatite, monazite 504
HALIDES Fluorite, halite 511

APPENDIX 1 Calculation of a chemical formula from a mineral analysis 515
APPENDIX 2 Molecular weights for use in calculation of mineral formulae from chemical analyses 518

INDEX 519

ACKNOWLEDGEMENTS

For permission to redraw diagrams we are indebted to the following:

Linus Pauling and the National Academy of Sciences for a diagram from *Proc. Nat. Acad. Sci. U.S.A.*; H. H. Hess, O. F. Tuttle, N. L. Bowen, A. E. J. Engel, C. G. Engel, R. F. Fudali and the Geological Society of America Inc. for diagrams from *G.S.A. Bull.* and various *Memoirs*; John Wiley & Sons Ltd. for diagrams from *Researches in Geochemistry* (ed. Abelson); The Carnegie Institution of Washington for a diagram from their *Year Book 1955*; H. Strunz and Akademische Verlagsgesellschaft Geest & Portig K.-G. for diagrams from *Mineralogische Tabellen* (third edition); W. H. Freeman & Co. for diagrams from W. F. de Jong's *General Crystallography: A Brief Compendium* (1959); The University of Chicago Press for diagrams from the *Journal of Geology*; The Editor for diagrams from the *American Journal of Science*; W. H. Taylor, R. M. Barrer, and The Royal Society for diagrams from *Proc. Roy. Soc. of London*; Cambridge University Press for a diagram from R. C. Evans' *An Introduction to Crystal Chemistry*; The Royal Swedish Academy of Sciences for a diagram from *Arkiv. Kemi. Min. Geol.*; R. M. Barrer and The Faraday Society for a diagram from *Trans. Faraday Soc.*; Springer-Verlag for a diagram from *Die Naturwissenschaften*; Carnegie Institution of Washington for diagrams from the *Annual Report of the Director of the Geophysical Laboratory*; The Editor for diagrams from *Zeitschrift für Kristallographie*; Allen & Unwin Ltd. for a diagram from *The Determination of the Feldspars in Thin Section* by K. Chudoba; Consejo Superior de Investigaciones Cientificas for a diagram from *Tercera Reunión Internacional sobre Reactividad de los Sólidos*; The Clarendon Press for diagrams from *Journal of Petrology*; Munksgaard for diagrams from *Acta Crystallographica*; Masao Atoji, E. J. W. Verwey and the American Institute of Physics for diagrams from *J. Chem. Phys.*; Pergamon Press Ltd. for diagrams from *Geochimica et Cosmochimica Acta*; and P. M. Bell and the Editor for a diagram from *Science* (© 1963 by the American Association for the Advancement of Science).

PREFACE

The authors began about ten years ago to write a text book for university students, but this aim was gradually relinquished as the text grew into the five volumes of *Rock-Forming Minerals*. We have now reverted to our original purpose by condensing the latter work into this single volume, which is intended to provide a short account of the more important minerals encountered in many undergraduate courses in mineralogy and petrology. We have attempted to present the basic data which are essential to the understanding of minerals, especially in relation to the environment of their formation.

The study of minerals is commonly presented largely as a listing of optical and physical properties which can be used for mineral identification. While this is without doubt an essential aspect of the subject, the study of minerals, particularly in relation to petrology, requires also the detailed consideration of crystal structure, chemistry and paragenesis, and we make no apologies for the prominence we have given these topics.

To those familiar with the five volumes of *Rock-Forming Minerals* the present volume will be seen to be based essentially on the pattern of the earlier work. Thus the more common minerals are each considered under the headings: Structure, Chemistry, Optical and Physical Properties, Distinguishing Features and Paragenesis. Sections on chemistry show typical compositions and illustrate the major atomic replacements which occur in the various minerals. In the sections on optical and physical properties, the variations of these properties with chemistry are discussed and are in many cases presented graphically.

We have tried to make the text useful also as a laboratory manual by giving tabulated data and optic orientation sketches at the head of each mineral section, and by including the paragraphs on distinguishing features.

Selected references are given for most minerals, and have been chosen, not so much in order to augment the data presented, but rather to draw attention to the various types of information available relating to particular minerals. Moreover, by drawing the attention of the student to some of the original data on which this work is based, it is hoped to stimulate a deeper interest in the study of minerals.

Minerals of lesser importance are given a shorter treatment. All the minerals dealt with in *Rock-Forming Minerals* are included in the present work, and in addition mullite, some of the rarer but typical minerals of calc-silicate rocks, and the accessory minerals of nepheline-syenites and related rocks have been included.

The earlier spelling of felspar has been changed to feldspar in accordance with the 1962 recommendation of the New Minerals and Mineral Names Commission of the International Mineralogical Association.

A description of the method of calculating structural formulae from mineral analyses is given in Appendix 1.

W. A. DEER
R. A. HOWIE
J. ZUSSMAN

October 1965

ABBREVIATIONS AND SYMBOLS

A	Angstrom units (10^{-8} cm)
a	cell edge in the x direction
a_{rh}	rhombohedral cell edge
a_{hex}	hexagonal cell edge
anal.	analysis
b	cell edge in the y direction
Bx_a	acute bisectrix
c	cell edge in the z direction
calc.	calculated
D	specific gravity
D	(in association with λ) sodium (yellow) light (589 mμ)
d	interplanar spacing
d.t.a.	differential thermal analysis
H	hardness (Mohs' scale)
mμ	millimicron
M.A.	*Mineralogical Abstracts*
max.	maximum
min.	minimum
m. eq./g	milliequivalents per gram (cation exchange capacity)
n	refractive index (for a cubic mineral)
O.A.P.	optic axial plane
P	pressure
R	metal ions
$r < v$ (or $r > v$)	the optic axial angle in red light is less than (or greater than) that in violet light
rh	rhombohedral
T	temperature
2V	the optic axial angle
x, y, z	the crystal axes
Z	number of formula units per unit cell
α, β, γ	least, intermediate and greatest refractive indices; the vibration directions of the fast, intermediate and slow ray; also these rays
α, β, γ	angles between the positive directions of the y and z, x and z, and x and y crystal axes
δ	birefringence
λ	wavelength
ε	extraordinary ray, refractive index
ω	ordinary ray, refractive index

PART 1

ORTHO- AND RING SILICATES

OLIVINE GROUP

The minerals of the olivine group all possess orthorhombic symmetry and a structure consisting of independent $[SiO_4]$ tetrahedra linked by divalent atoms in octahedral coordination. Minerals of the group show complete diadochy between the atomic pairs Mg and Fe^{+2}, and Fe^{+2} and Mn, i.e. between forsterite, Mg_2SiO_4, and fayalite, Fe_2SiO_4, and between fayalite and tephroite, Mn_2SiO_4. The other members of the group are monticellite, $CaMgSiO_4$, glaucochroite, $CaMnSiO_4$, and kirschsteinite, $CaFeSiO_4$. Compositions intermediate between monticellite and glaucochroite, and between the latter two minerals and olivines of the Mg_2SiO_4–Fe_2SiO_4–$MnSiO_4$ series, are unknown. Larsenite, $PbZnSiO_4$, is not isostructural with the olivine group, nor does the compound Ca_2SiO_4 possess an olivine structure.

Olivine $\hfill (Mg,Fe)_2[SiO_4]$

ORTHORHOMBIC (+)(−)

Forsterite	Fayalite
Mg_2SiO_4	Fe_2SiO_4

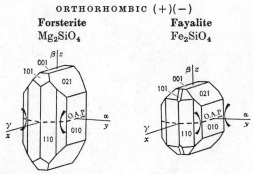

α 1·635–1·827†
β 1·651–1·869
γ 1·670–1·879
δ 0·035–0·052, 2V$_\gamma$ 82°–134°
$\alpha = y, \beta = z, \gamma = x$, O.A.P. (001)

† Values of refractive indices, birefringence, optic axial angle and density refer to end-members forsterite, Mg_2SiO_4, and fayalite, Fe_2SiO_4, between which there is continuous variation.

Dispersion: $r > v$.   D 3·22–4·39.   H 7–6½.

Cleavage: {010}, {100} imperfect in Mg-rich members, moderate in Fe-rich members.

Twinning: {100}, {011}, {012} not common.

Colour: Green, lemon-yellow, greenish yellow, yellow-amber; Mg-rich members colourless, Fe-rich members pale yellow in thin section.

Pleochroism: Fe-rich members $\alpha = \gamma$ pale yellow, β orange yellow. Gelatinizes in HCl.

STRUCTURE

The olivine structure consists of individual [SiO$_4$] tetrahedra linked by (Mg,Fe) atoms each of which has six nearest oxygen neighbours. The oxygens are arranged in approximate hexagonal packing and lie in sheets parallel with the (100) plane (Fig. 1). The [SiO$_4$] tetrahedra point alter-

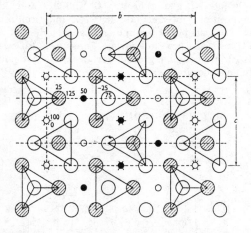

Fig. 1. *Olivine structure parallel to* (100) *plane. Si atoms are at the centres of the tetrahedra and are not shown. Small open circles* ○ *Mg atoms at* $x = 0$; *small solid circles* ● *Mg atoms at* $x = \frac{1}{2}$; * *centre of symmetry (after Bragg, W. L. & Brown, G. B.,* 1926, Zeit. Krist., *vol.* 63, *p.* 538).

nately either way in both the x and y directions; half the (Mg,Fe) atoms are located at centres of symmetry and half on reflection planes. The replacement of Mg by Fe^{+2} ions is accompanied by a linear increase in the cell parameters (Fo$_{100}$ a 4·756, b 10·195, c 5·981 Å; Fo$_0$ a 4·817, b 10·477, c 6·105 Å), and olivine compositions may be readily determined from X-ray powder diffraction data.

CHEMISTRY

Olivines vary in composition from Mg_2SiO_4, forsterite, to Fe_2SiO_4, fayalite, there being complete diadochy between Mg and Fe^{+2} in the structure (Table 1). The names forsterite and fayalite are restricted to the compositions Fo_{100-90} and Fo_{10-0} respectively; the nomenclature of the intermediate members of the series is given in Fig. 3. Ni is commonly present in magnesium-rich olivines, and small amounts of Mn and Ca are present in both magnesium- and iron-rich members. Minute octahedra and plates oriented parallel to (001) and (100) planes, which probably represent small amounts of exsolved ferric and chromic oxide, are the likely source of the small amounts of Cr (in magnesium-rich varieties) and Fe^{+3} shown by many olivine analyses.

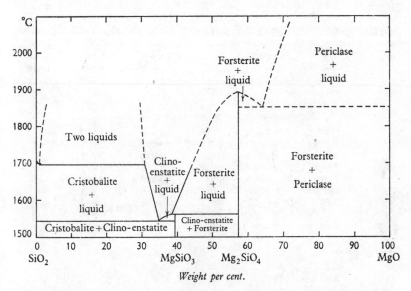

Fig. 2. *Phase diagram of the system MgO–SiO₂ (after Bowen, N. L. &*
Schairer, J. F., 1935, Amer. Journ. Sci., ser. 5, vol. 29, p. 197).

Mg_2SiO_4 melts at 1890°C, Fe_2SiO_4 at 1205°C, and the (Mg,Fe) olivines illustrate the effect on melting temperatures in a diadochic series of replacing an ion of smaller by one of larger radius (Mg^{+2} 0·66 Å, Fe^{+2} 0·74 Å). Cation–oxygen bonds are weaker for the larger cation, thus as more of the larger ions enter the structure there is a progressive reduction in the melting points of intermediate compositions. The first olivines to crystallize from a melt of specific composition are more Mg-rich than those of later crystallization, and in consequence the larger Fe^{+2} ions are concentrated in the residual liquids. In the olivine series the heats of solution

Table 1. OLIVINE ANALYSES

	1.	2.	3.	4.	5.	6.
SiO_2	41·07	39·87	34·04	30·56	30·15	25·59
TiO_2	0·05	0·03	0·43	0·72	0·20	0·61
Al_2O_3	0·56	0·00	0·91	0·09	0·07	6·53
Fe_2O_3	0·65	0·86	1·46	0·10	0·43	31·44
FeO	3·78	13·20	40·37	60·81	65·02	4·64
MnO	0·23	0·22	0·68	3·43	1·01	—
MgO	54·06	45·38	20·32	3·47	1·05	15·83
CaO	0·00	0·25	0·81	1·13	2·18	1·30
Na_2O	—	0·04	—	—	—	0·31
K_2O	—	0·01	—	—	—	0·28
H_2O^+	0·05	0·33	0·09	—	—	9·09
H_2O^-	0·00	0·10	—	—	—	3·74
Total	100·45	100·30	99·11	100·31	100·11	99·36
α	—	1·6626	1·742	1·809	1·827	—
β	—	—	—	1·842	1·869	1·816
γ	—	1·6990	—	1·862	1·879	—
$2V\gamma$	—	90°	103°	128°	132°	—

NUMBERS OF IONS ON THE BASIS OF 4 OXYGENS

	1.	2.	3.	4.	5.	6.
Si	0·979	0·997	0·990	0·996	1·002	—
Al	0·016	—	0·032	0·004	0·003	—
Ti	0·001	0·001	0·009	0·018	0·005	—
Fe^{+3}	0·012	0·016	0·032	0·004	0·011	—
Mg	1·920	1·692	0·881	0·169	0·052	—
Fe^{+2}	0·075	0·276	0·983	1·659	1·808	—
Mn	0·005	0·005	0·017	0·094	0·028	—
Ca	—	0·007	0·025	0·039	0·078	—
$[Y]^6$	2·03	2·00†	1·98	1·99	1·99	—

Atomic ratios

	1.	2.	3.	4.	5.	6.
Mg	96·2	86·0	47·3	8·8	2·8	—
Fe^{+2}	3·8	14·0	52·7	91·2	97·2	—

1. Forsterite, metamorphosed limestone, Finland (Sahama, Th. G., 1953, *Ann. Acad. Sci. Fennicae*, 3. Geol. Geogr., No. 31, p. 1).
2. Chrysolite, allivalite, Rhum (Brown, G. M., 1956, *Phil. Trans. Roy. Soc. London*, Ser. B., vol. 240, p. 1. Includes P_2O_5 0·01, Cr_2O_3 trace).
3. Hortonolite, olivine gabbro, Muck (Tilley, C. E., 1952, *Amer. Journ. Sci.*, Bowen vol., p. 529).
4. Fayalite, porphyritic obsidian, Pantelleria (Carmichael, I. S. E., 1962, *Min. Mag.*, vol. 33, p. 86).
5. Fayalite, fayalite ferrogabbro, East Greenland (Deer, W. A. & Wager, L. R., 1939, *Amer. Min.*, vol. 24, p. 18).
6. Iddingsite, trachybasalt, Gough Island (Gay, P. & Le Maitre, R. W., 1961, *Amer. Min.*, vol. 46, p. 92).

  † Includes Na 0·007, K 0·002.

(Fo_{100} $-95,380$ cal./mole, Fo_0 $-81,330$ cal./mole) are a linear function of the molar composition, indicating that during the replacement Mg $\rightleftharpoons$ Fe^{+2} perfect thermal equilibrium is maintained, and that the heat of isomorphous mixing is zero.

Both Mg_2SiO_4 and $MgSiO_3$ are stable phases in the $MgO-SiO_2$ system (Fig. 2). Under conditions of equilibrium crystallization from liquids containing between 43 and 61 per cent SiO_2, the early formed forsterite reacts at about 1550°C with the liquid to form a $MgSiO_3$ pyroxene (clinoenstatite or protoenstatite, see p. 109). An analogous reaction does not occur in the $FeO-SiO_2$ system and fayalite and tridymite form a eutectic at 1178°C. Fayalite melts incongruently with the separation of small amounts of metallic iron.

Forsterite has been synthesized in many dry systems and has also been obtained from stoichiometric mixtures of its oxides in the presence of water vapour at temperatures above 500°C and pressures between 2000 and 40,000 lb/in^2. Forsterite is in equilibrium with brucite, serpentine and vapour at temperatures of approximately 400°C (Fig. 79). The reaction

$$2Mg(OH)_2 + Mg_6Si_4O_{10}(OH)_8 \rightleftharpoons 4Mg_2SiO_4 + 6H_2O$$
$$\text{brucite} \qquad \text{serpentine} \qquad\qquad \text{forsterite}$$

is reversible, and forsterite crystallized at high temperature from an anhydrous melt can be serpentinized (formation of brucite + serpentine); in the more iron-rich olivines serpentinization occurs at lower temperatures, e.g. at the composition Fo_{90} serpentinization takes place at 340°C at a water vapour pressure of 15,000 lb/in^2.

Olivine is very susceptible to hydrothermal alteration, to the effects of low grade metamorphism, and to weathering. The common alteration products are serpentine, iddingsite, bowlingite, chlorite, amphibole, talc, carbonates and iron oxides. These products may be fine-grained and intimately mixed and are sometimes difficult or impossible to identify precisely by optical methods; this has led to the common use of the omnibus names serpentine, iddingsite and bowlingite. The serpentine-type product has a restricted range of chemical composition and consists of one or more polymorphs of $Mg_3Si_2O_5(OH)_4$, e.g. chrysotile, antigorite; it is commonly associated with talc and carbonate:

$$3Mg_2SiO_4 + H_2O + SiO_2 \rightarrow 2Mg_3Si_2O_5(OH)_4$$
$$\text{olivine} \qquad\qquad\qquad \text{serpentine}$$

$$2Mg_3Si_2O_5(OH)_4 + 3CO_2 \rightarrow Mg_3Si_4O_{10}(OH)_2 + 3MgCO_3 + 3H_2O$$
$$\text{serpentine} \qquad\qquad \text{talc} \qquad \text{magnesite}$$

The compositions of both iddingsite and bowlingite show considerable variation and their detailed constitution is not known. The iddingsite product is red-brown to orange-brown in colour and has a high refringence ($\beta \simeq 1{\cdot}76$ to $1{\cdot}89$); goethite and haematite have both been positively identified but the silicate constituent of iddingsite commonly appears to be embryonic in structure and variable in composition. The process of iddingsitization is a continuous transformation in the solid state brought about by the diffusion of hydrogen atoms into the olivine structure where they become attached to oxygens and so release Mg, Fe^{+2} and Si and allow their replacement by Fe^{+3}, Al and Ca ions. Bowlingite, the name generally used to describe the green alteration product of olivine, consists principally of chlorite and goethite.

OPTICAL AND PHYSICAL PROPERTIES

The refractive indices vary linearly with composition and both α and γ indices increase by approximately 0·002 per unit mol. per cent Fe_2SiO_4 (Fig. 3). The optic axial angle likewise varies systematically and increases

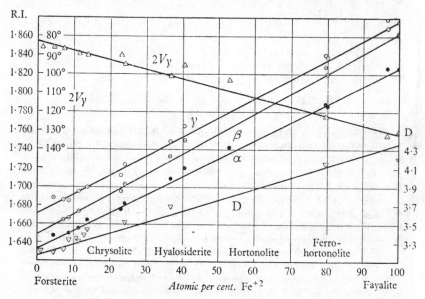

Fig. 3. *Relation of the optical properties and density to chemical composition in the (Mg,Fe)-olivines. End-member values for* $2V_\gamma$ *(Henriques, A., 1958, Arkiv Min. Geol., vol. 2, p. 305); refractive indices (Bowen, N. L. & Schairer, J. F., 1935, Amer. Journ. Sci., ser. 5, vol. 29, p. 197); and density (Bloss, F. D., 1952, Amer. Min., vol. 37, p. 966).*

from $2V_\gamma$ 82° for the magnesium end-member to $2V_\gamma$ 134° for the iron end-member, changing sign at approximately Fa_{13}. Cleavage in the more magnesium-rich members is usually very imperfect but in the more iron-rich minerals the {010} cleavage, and sometimes also the {100} cleavage, is well developed. A banded structure due to the presence of deformation lamellae parallel to (100) occurs in the olivines of some ultrabasic rocks.

Zoned olivines, in which the rim is more iron-rich than the core, are rare in plutonic rocks but are not uncommon in olivines of basic alkali hypabyssal rocks, e.g. theralite, teschenite and crinanite. Zoning is most readily detected by observing the polarization colours in a single grain; for normal zoning, from magnesium-rich core to iron-rich margin the birefringence decreases from the centre to the periphery in sections perpendicular to α, and increases in sections perpendicular to either β or γ.

DISTINGUISHING FEATURES

Olivines are distinguished by their higher birefringence, larger 2V, poorer cleavage and common alteration from diopside and augite, and by their higher refringence and birefringence from monticellite and the humite group minerals; when cleavage or twinning is present in either chondrodite or clinohumite these may further be distinguished by their oblique extinction. Fayalite and the more iron-rich olivines are distinguished from epidote by the yellow-green pleochroism, larger optic axial angle and oblique extinction of the latter.

PARAGENESIS

Pure forsterite is unknown in igneous rocks and the composition of dunite and peridotite olivines respectively is approximately Fo_{92} and Fo_{88}. Olivines in the compositional range Fo_{85} to Fo_{40} are very common constituents in gabbros, dolerites and basalts; olivines in this compositional range also occur in trachybasalts and trachytes as well as in theralites and teschenites. More iron-rich olivines are less common but occur in iron-rich dolerites, ferrogabbros and granophyres. Fayalite is a relatively common constituent in quartz-bearing syenites in which it is often associated with hedenbergite and arfvedsonite, but is comparatively rare in granites; it is also present in small amounts in some acid and alkaline volcanic rocks (e.g. pitchstone), and is an important constituent of fayalite ferrogabbro.
The most magnesium-rich olivines occur in thermally metamorphosed impure limestones and dolomites where their formation is due to the reaction:

$$2CaMg(CO_3)_2 + SiO_2 \rightarrow Mg_2SiO_4 + 2CaCO_3 + 2CO_2$$
$$\text{dolomite} \qquad\qquad \text{forsterite}$$

Fayalite also occurs in thermally metamorphosed sediments but is a more common constituent of regionally metamorphosed iron-rich sediments (eulysites and collobrièrites) in which it is associated with hedenbergite, iron-rich orthopyroxene, grunerite and almandine. Olivines, particularly in metamorphosed basic rocks, may be surrounded by reaction rims which are variously described as coronas, kelyphitic borders or corrosion mantles. The zonal sequence between the olivine and the outer rim differs in individual examples but the commoner sequences are:

olivine–orthopyroxene–(amphibole + spinel)–plagioclase

olivine–orthopyroxene–garnet–plagioclase

REFERENCES

GAY, P. and LE MAITRE, R. W. (1961). Some observations on 'Iddingsite', *Amer. Min.*, vol. 46, p. 92.

JOHNSTON, R. (1953). 'The olivines of the Garbh Eilean Sill, Shiant Isles', *Geol. Mag.*, vol. 90, p. 161.

MURTHY, M. V. N. (1958). 'Coronites from India and their bearing on the origin of coronas', *Bull. Geol. Soc. Amer.*, vol. 68, p. 23.

ROSS, C. S., FOSTER, M. D. and MYERS, A. T. (1954). 'Origin of dunites and of olivine-rich inclusions in basaltic rocks', *Amer. Min.*, vol. 39, p. 693.

WILKINSON, J. F. G. (1956). 'The olivines of a differentiated teschenite sill near Gunnedah, New South Wales', *Geol. Mag.*, vol. 93, p. 441.

Tephroite
Knebelite

$Mn_2[SiO_4]$

$(Mn,Fe)_2[SiO_4]$

ORTHORHOMBIC $(-)$

α 1·770–1·815
β 1·807–1·853
γ 1·817–1·867
δ 0·040–0·051
$2V_\alpha$ 70°–44°
$\alpha = y, \beta = z, \gamma = x$, O.A.P. (001)
Dispersion: $r > v$. D 3·78–4·25. H 6–6½.
Cleavage: {010} moderate, {001}, imperfect.
Twinning: {011} uncommon.

Colour: Tephroite, olive-green, bluish green, grey; pale green in thin section; knebelite, brown-black, grey-black, colourless or pale yellow in thin section.

Pleochroism: Tephroite, α brownish red, β reddish, γ greenish blue in thick sections only; knebelite, feeble with α pale yellow, γ pale blue.

The substitution of Mn in the manganese olivines for the Fe^{+2} in fayalite gives rise to larger cell parameters (e.g. tephroite a 4·9, b 10·6, c 6·25 Å). There is a complete series of compositions from Mn_2SiO_4 to Fe_2SiO_4 but Mg is present only in small to moderate amounts and the absence of minerals containing larger quantities is probably related to the small amounts of Mg available in the crystallization environment of the tephroite–knebelite minerals. Small replacements of (Fe,Mn) by Zn occur in some tephroites; a Zn-rich olivine (ZnO 10·68 weight per cent; 0·26 Zn atoms to 4 oxygens) has been named roepperite. There is also a rare calcium–manganese olivine, $CaMnSiO_4$, glaucochroite.

Tephroite and knebelite are distinguished from the magnesium-rich olivines by smaller optic axial angles and higher refractive indices, and from the iron-rich olivines by lower refractive indices. Tephroite and knebelite have higher refractive indices and birefringence than monticellite. The paragenesis of the manganese-rich olivines is distinctive and they normally occur in association with other manganese minerals, particularly in iron–manganese ore deposits and their associated skarns.

Monticellite

CaMg[SiO$_4$]

ORTHORHOMBIC (−)

α 1·639–1·654
β 1·646–1·664
γ 1·653–1·674
δ 0·012–0·020
2V$_α$ 72°–82°
α = y, β = z, γ = x, O.A.P. (001)
Dispersion: r > v. D 3·08–3·27. H 5½.
Cleavage: {010} poor.
Twinning: {031}.
Colour: Colourless or grey; colourless in thin section.

Monticellite (unit cell a 4·815, b 11·08, c 6·37 Å, Z = 4) has an olivine-type structure, in which the Ca ions occupy the octahedral positions situated on reflection planes parallel to (001); the Mg ions occupy the octahedral positions located at symmetry centres. There is some substitution of (Ca,Mg) by Fe^{+2} but most monticellites do not depart significantly from the ideal composition CaMgSiO$_4$. The iron analogue CaFeSiO$_4$, kirschsteinite, is known only from artificial sources but a magnesium-rich kirschsteinite has been described from a melilite nephelinite lava.

The optical properties of monticellite do not exhibit a wide range (kirschsteinite has considerably higher refractive indices and birefringence, and a markedly lower 2V than monticellite), and it is distinguished from the Mg–Fe–Mn olivines by its lower birefringence, and from diopside by being negative with large 2V and having a poorer cleavage.

The commoner paragenesis of monticellite is in metamorphosed and metasomatized siliceous dolomitic limestones at contacts with both basic and acid igneous rocks. Monticellite occurs more rarely in some basic and ultrabasic rocks, e.g. alnöite, and in this paragenesis is present usually as rims surrounding magnesium olivine.

REFERENCES

SAHAMA, TH. G. and HYTÖNEN, K. (1957). 'Kirschsteinite, a natural analogue of synthetic iron monticellite, from the Belgian Congo', Min. Mag., vol. 31, p. 698.

TILLEY, C. E. (1951). 'The zoned contact skarns of the Broadford area, Skye: a study of boron-fluorine metasomatism in dolomites', Min. Mag., vol. 29, p. 621.

HUMITE GROUP

$$Mg(OH,F)_2 \cdot 1\text{–}4Mg_2[SiO_4]$$

Chondrodite	Humite	Clinohumite

	Norbergite	Chondrodite	Humite	Clinohumite
	$Mg(OH,F)_2 \cdot Mg_2SiO_4$	$Mg(OH,F)_2 \cdot 2Mg_2SiO_4$	$Mg(OH,F) \cdot 3Mg_2SiO_4$	$Mg(OH,F)_2 \cdot 4Mg_2SiO_4$
	ORTHORHOMBIC	MONOCLINIC	ORTHORHOMBIC	MONOCLINIC
α	1·563–1·567	1·592–1·615	1·607–1·643	1·629–1·638
β	1·567–1·579	1·602–1·627	1·619–1·653	1·641–1·643
γ	1·590–1·593	1·621–1·646	1·639–1·675	1·662–1·674
δ	0·026–0·027	0·028–0·034	0·029–0·031	0·028–0·041
$2V_\gamma$	44°–50°	71°–85°	65°–84°	73°–76°
$\alpha{:}z$	—	22°–31°	—	9°–15°
		$\gamma=y$, O.A.P. $\perp(010)$	$\gamma=y$, O.A.P. (001)	$\gamma=y$, O.A.P. $\simeq(100)$
Dispersion:	$r>v$	$r>v$, strong	$r>v$	$r>v$, strong
D	3·15–3·18	3·16–3·26	3·20–3·32	3·21–3·35
H	6½	6½	6	6
Cleavage:	—	{100} poor	{100} poor	{100} poor

Twinning: {001} simple, lamellar, common in chondrodite and clinohumite.

Colour: Brownish, yellow, dark orange, red; colourless, pale yellow, yellow in thin section.

Pleochroism:

α	pale yellow	pale yellow	pale–dark yellow	golden, reddish yellow
β	pale yellow	colourless	colourless	pale orange-yellow
γ	colourless	colourless	colourless	pale orange-yellow

The ratio of the unit cell dimensions $b:c$ is the same for each of the humite group minerals; the $a:c$ and $a:b$ ratios change in a progressive manner from norbergite to clinohumite. The structures of the humite group minerals are related to that of forsterite, and consist of layers having an atomic arrangement as in olivine alternating with layers of brucite–sellaite, $Mg(OH,F)_2$, composition; both layers are parallel to the (100) plane (Fig. 4). The thickness of the $Mg(OH,F)_2$ layer is the same in all members of the group, but the ratio of the olivine to the $Mg(OH,F)_2$ layers varies from unity in norbergite to 4 : 1 in clinohumite. The replacement of Mg by Fe^{+2} is limited in the humite group minerals, and compositions analogous to the fayalitic olivines are unknown. Some humite group minerals, in contrast to the olivines, contain relatively large amounts of titanium (up to 5·4 weight per cent TiO_2). Norbergite and chondrodite have been synthesized in solid state reactions by heating olivine (Fo_{90}) and MgF_2 at atmospheric pressure.

The refractive indices and densities of the humite minerals increase progressively from norbergite to clinohumite, but due to variable $Mg \rightleftharpoons Fe^{+2}$ and $F \rightleftharpoons OH$ replacements there is a considerable overlap in the values of

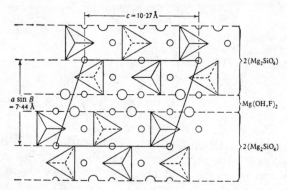

Fig. 4. *Chondrodite structure showing the arrangement of layers of Mg_2SiO_4 and $Mg(OH,F)_2$ composition. Projection on (010) plane. Smaller circles magnesium, larger circles (OH,F) (after Taylor, W. H. & West, J., 1928, Proc. Roy. Soc. London, A, vol. 117, p. 517).*

refractive indices and of densities, and neither property, except the indices of norbergite, can be used to identify with certainty individual members of the group.

Colourless and faintly coloured members of the series are distinguished from magnesium-rich olivine by their lower refringence and smaller 2V. The pleochroism of some of the coloured varieties of the humite group is similar to that of staurolite but their absorption is $\gamma < \alpha$ in contrast to $\gamma > \alpha$ for staurolite.

Minerals of the humite group have a very limited paragenesis, and their occurrence is, with rare exceptions, restricted to metamorphosed and metasomatized limestones and dolomites, and to skarns associated with ore deposits at contacts with acid plutonic rocks.

Zircon

Zr[SiO₄]

TETRAGONAL (+)

$$\omega \ 1{\cdot}923\dagger{-}1{\cdot}960$$
$$\epsilon \ 1{\cdot}968\dagger{-}2{\cdot}015$$
$$\delta \ 0{\cdot}042\dagger{-}0{\cdot}065$$

Dispersion: Very strong. D 4·6†–4·7. H 7½.

Cleavage: {110} imperfect, {111} poor.

Twinning: Rare, on {111}. Some zoning may occur.

Colour: Reddish brown, yellow, grey, green or colourless; colourless to pale brown in thin section.

Pleochroism: Very weak: thick sections may show absorption $\omega < \epsilon$.
Slowly attacked by hot concentrated H_2SO_4.

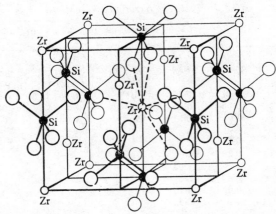

Fig. 5. *The structure of zircon. The eight bonds from each zircon atom to neighbouring oxygens are shown only at the centre of the figure (after Bragg, W. L., 1937, Atomic Structure of Minerals, Cornell Univ. Press).*

STRUCTURE

In the zircon structure (Fig. 5) each silicon atom is surrounded by a tetrahedral group of four oxygen atoms at a distance of 1·61 Å, while each zirconium atom lies between four oxygen atoms at 2·15 Å and four at a distance of 2·29 Å. It has cell dimensions $a \simeq 6{\cdot}60$, $c \simeq 5{\cdot}98$ Å; Z = 4.

† These values are for relatively fresh material: metamict varieties may have properties outside this range.

Although zircon is fairly resistant to normal chemical attack, altered varieties are not uncommon, the mineral eventually becoming converted to an isotropic form with a lower density. This metamict state in zircon may be due, at least in part, to the presence of radioactive atoms. In particular, the decay of uranium and thorium often occurring in zircon may cause displacement of atoms by recoil nuclei, and this and the high temperatures produced in the path of the nuclear particles may bring about the gradual breakdown of the structure. There is thus a considerable range of properties observable in zircon, from the fresh or normal zircon to the fully metamict type, giving rise to varietal names such as malacon, cyrtolite, etc. A three-fold division is commonly made, into normal zircon with high specific gravity, birefringence, and refractive indices, and low or metamict zircon (malacon) with a low specific gravity of about 4, and those with intermediate properties which are termed intermediate zircon.

CHEMISTRY

Zircons always contain some hafnium: the HfO_2/ZrO_2 ratio varies but is normally about 0·01, rising to 0·04 in zircons in granite. A cluster of zircon

Table 2. ZIRCON ANALYSES

	1.	2.	NUMBERS OF IONS ON THE BASIS OF 16 (O)		
				1.	2.
SiO_2	32·51	27·13	Si	4·013	3·586 3·94‡
$ZrO_2 + HfO_2$	67·02	51·68	Zr + Hf†	3·941⎤	3·257⎤
TiO_2	—	tr.	Al	0·030⎟	0·075⎟
Al_2O_3	0·21	0·48	Fe^{+3}	0·007⎬4·01	0·044⎬4·19§
Fe_2O_3	0·08	0·45	Mg	—⎟	—⎦
R.E.	0·04	10·51	Ca	0·030⎦	
MnO	—	tr.			
MgO	0·01	tr.			
CaO	0·22	tr.			
ThO_2	—	1·03			
P_2O_5	—	3·37			
H_2O^+	0·03	3·12			
H_2O^-	—	0·32			
Total	100·12	99·84			
ω	1·950	—			
ϵ	2·008	—			
D	4·658	3·957			

1. Dark red-brown zircon, North Burgess, Ontario (Palache, C. & Ellsworth, H. V., 1928, *Amer. Min.*, vol. 13, p. 384).
2. Greyish green to greyish brown zircon, with allanite, fergusonite and thorogummite in pegmatite, Hayamadake, Fukushima Pref., Japan (Hasegawa, S., 1957, *Sci. Rep. Tohoku Univ.*, ser. 3, vol. 5, p. 345. Includes UO_2 1·75: R.E. = Ce_2O_3 0·37, Y_2O_3 10·14).

† The molecular weight of ($ZrO_2 + HfO_2$) has been taken as 126 in these calculations.
‡ Includes P 0·349.
§ Includes U 0·052, Ce 0·018, Y 0·713 and Th 0·031.

from Norway, however, has been found to contain 22 to 24 per cent HfO_2, with an Hf/Zr ratio of about 0·6, and a zircon from Karibib, south-west Africa, has been reported with 31 per cent HfO_2. Some forms of metamict zircon can be shown to consist of mixtures in various proportions of SiO_2, cubic ZrO_2 and baddeleyite (monoclinic ZrO_2).

Two analyses of zircon are given in Table 2. Iron is often present but various other elements sometimes reported in considerable amounts, such as Sn, Nb, Ta, etc., are more probably present in inclusions of other minerals : the latter are frequent in zircon and the different types may sometimes be useful in heavy mineral assemblages for distinguishing zircons from different sources. Yttria is commonly present and this can be related to the isostructural relationship of xenotime (YPO_4) and zircon. The altered variety cyrtolite contains appreciable water and this may imply the substitution $(OH)_4 \rightleftharpoons SiO_4$. For age determinations the Th/U ratio or the ratios of the various lead isotopes to each other or to those of uranium are determined.

Zircon can be synthesized by sintering ZrO_2 and SiO_2 in air at high temperatures. It may be synthesized hydrothermally by heating gelatinous ZrO_2 and SiO_2 with water in steel bombs at 150° to 700°C. In the system ZrO_2–ThO_2–SiO_2–H_2O the limit of solid solution of $ThSiO_4$ in $ZrSiO_4$ is less than 3 mol. per cent at about 800°C and 1500 atmospheres. Most metamict varieties of zircon can be converted to normal zircon by heating to between 1000° and 1450°C, which gives material with the X-ray pattern of zircon and with an increased specific gravity, though the latter is never quite as high as that for normal fresh zircon.

OPTICAL AND PHYSICAL PROPERTIES

The optical properties and specific gravity of zircon vary not only with the small amount of iron and similar elements which may enter the structure but also with the degree of alteration or metamictization (see above). The birefringence is approximately inversely proportional to the intensity of radioactivity :

	D	ω	ϵ	δ	Radio-activity
Normal zircon	4·6–4·7	1·924–1·934	1·970–1·977	0·036–0·053	Low
Intermediate	4·2–4·6	1·903–1·927	1·921–1·970	0·017–0·043	Medium
Metamict zircon	3·9–4·2	1·782–1·864	1·827–1·872	0–0·008	High

The metamict variety may show an appreciably biaxial character.

Zircon may be colourless or of varying shades of brown, yellow, green or even blue (usually after heat treatment), but in thin section it is typically colourless to pale brown, and may be weakly pleochroic in very thick sections. The dispersion is high and only slightly less than that of diamond. Gem varieties have received various names, jargoon being the colourless, slightly smoky or pale yellow zircon, while hyacinth is the orange and reddish brown transparent type. The low, or metamict, zircon is typically leaf green to olive or brownish green in colour.

DISTINGUISHING FEATURES

The straight extinction, high refractive indices and high birefringence of zircon are fairly characteristic and the often observable tetragonal form is an additional aid to identification. Cassiterite and rutile have higher refractive indices and birefringence and are more typically reddish brown in thin section or in grains.

PARAGENESIS

Zircon is a common accessory mineral of igneous rocks, particularly in the plutonic rocks and especially those plutonic rocks relatively rich in sodium. It is generally present as small early formed crystals often enclosed in later minerals, but may form large well developed crystals in granite pegmatites and particularly in those of nepheline-syenites. When enclosed by biotite or amphibole or other coloured silicates it sometimes gives rise to pleochroic haloes due to its content of radioactive elements. The size and morphological character of zircons, particularly their length/breadth ratio, may be closely similar throughout a body of magmatic granite, and it has been suggested that lack of such a relationship may indicate that an intrusive is complex. A study of zircon shapes has also revealed, however, that some rounding of zircon can take place in igneous rocks by magmatic resorption and that appreciable corrosion of the grains may be due to metasomatism.

Zircon is a common accessory mineral in many sediments, often surviving more than one cycle of weathering and sedimentation. It may be of use in correlating sandstones by their heavy mineral content, its distinctive features of colour, zoning, habit or inclusions enabling the zircons of one horizon to be distinguished from those of another horizon nearby. In metamorphic rocks zircon is less common but it often resists even high grade metamorphism, during which it may develop overgrowths.

REFERENCES

POLDERVAART, A. (1955). 'Zircon in rocks. 1. Sedimentary rocks', *Amer. Journ. Sci.*, vol. 253, p. 433.
——— (1956). 'Zircon in rocks. 2. Igneous rocks', Ibid, vol. 254, p. 521.
TILTON, G. R., DAVIS, G. L., WETHERILL, G. W., and ALDRICH, L. T. (1957). 'Isotopic ages of zircon from granites and pegmatites', *Trans. Amer. Geophys. Union*, vol. 38, p. 360.

Sphene

Ca Ti[SiO₄](O,OH,F)

MONOCLINIC (+)

α 1·843 1·950
β 1·870–2·034
γ 1·943–2·110
δ 0·100–0·192
2V$_γ$ 17°–40°
α : z ≃ 40°, O.A.P. (010).
Dispersion: r > v, strong. D 3·45–3·55. H 5.
Cleavage: {110} good.
Twinning: Single twins with twin plane {100}:
occasional lamellar twinning on {221}.
Colour: Colourless, yellow, green, brown or black; colourless, yellow or typically brown in thin section.
Pleochroism: Coloured varieties may be moderately pleochroic, e.g. α pale yellow, β brownish yellow, γ orange-brown.
Decomposed by H_2SO_4.

STRUCTURE

The structure of sphene contains independent silicon–oxygen tetrahedra (Fig. 6) with groups of [CaO₇] and [TiO₆]. The unit cell has a 6·56, b 8·72,

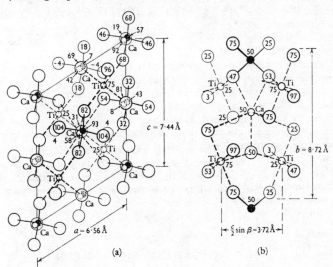

Fig. 6. (a) *The structure of sphene projected on* (010). (b) *Part of the structure around a two-fold axis projected on a plane normal to x, showing coordination of Ca and Ti atoms (after Bragg, W. L.,* 1937, Atomic Structure of Minerals, *Cornell Univ. Press*).

c 7·44 Å, β 119° 43'; $Z = 4$. In this unit cell containing 20 oxygen atoms one in five of these oxygens can be replaced by (OH,F).

CHEMISTRY

Three sphene analyses are given in Table 3, where they have been recalculated on the basis of 20 (O,OH,F) per unit cell. Calcium may be partially replaced by strontium and barium, or by the rare earths and thorium, the high valencies of the latter being balanced by the entry of trivalent iron and aluminium into the titanium position. Keilhauite (yttrotitanite) is one such variety with up to about 12 per cent $(Y,Ce)_2O_3$: anal. 2 represents a sphene moderately rich in yttrium and cerium, while that of anal. 3 has minor thorium. Grothite is a variety of sphene with relatively high Al and Fe^{+3} in which the rare earths are comparatively low. The Ti group also may be partially replaced by Sn, Nb and Ta, with possible compensation by way of Na replacing Ca. Almost all sphenes probably have at least some replacement of (OH) by F. The principal substitutions are thus:

Calcium: Na, rare earths, Mn, Sr, (Ba).

Titanium: Al, Fe^{+3}, Fe^{+2}, Mg, Nb, Ta, V, (Cr).

Oxygen: OH, F, (Cl).

Sphene has been prepared artificially by fusing its component oxides: it melts congruently at 1382°C.

Alteration products of sphene include anatase, often together with quartz, or occasionally rutile.

OPTICAL AND PHYSICAL PROPERTIES

Data are insufficient to allow the relationship between the optical properties and chemical composition to be fully determined, but in general a decrease in Ti causes the refractive indices and birefringence to decrease and 2V to increase: thus the grothite varieties containing Fe^{+3} and Al usually have lower refractive indices and higher values of 2V. The colour of sphene may be correlated with the iron content, the green and yellow varieties being low in iron while the brown or black sphenes may have 1 per cent or more of Fe_2O_3: rare earths may cause an orange hue, though this is often dominated by the iron coloration.

DISTINGUISHING FEATURES

The rhombic or sphenoidal cross-section of sphene is characteristic. Its extreme refringence, birefringence and dispersion distinguish it from monazite and its monoclinic symmetry enables it to be distinguished from cassiterite. Often, complete extinction does not occur.

Table 3. SPHENE ANALYSES

	1.	2.	3.			NUMBERS OF IONS ON THE BASIS OF 20 (O,OH,F)		
					1.	2.	3.	
SiO_2	30·44	29·32	30·35	Si	4·040	3·931 }4·00	3·936 }4·00	
TiO_2	39·66	35·26	35·44	Al	—	0·161	0·329	
ZrO_2	0·11	tr.	—	Fe^{+3}	—	0·136	0·245	
Nb_2O_5	0·34	—	—	Mg	—	0·072	0·020	
Ta_2O_5	0·01	—	—	Ti	3·960	3·555	3·457	
V_2O_5	0·10	—	—	Nb	0·024 }4·01	— }3·97	— }3·99	
R.E.	0·37	4·51	1·06	Ta	—	—	—	
Al_2O_3	0·00	1·02	2·15	V	0·009	—	—	
Fe_2O_3	0·00	1·34	2·50	Fe^{+2}	0·016	0·118	—	
FeO	0·14	1·05	—	Zr	—	—	—	
MnO	0·05	0·03	0·25	Mn	0·008	0·003	0·027	
MgO	0·00	0·36	0·10	Na	0·096	0·036		
CaO	27·20	25·72	26·46	R.E.	0·016 }4·02	0·257 }4·01‡	0·027 }3·74§	
BaO	0·005	0·04	0·00	Ca	3·904†	3·695	3·677	
Na_2O	0·37	0·14	—	K	—	0·012	0·003	
K_2O	0·00	0·07	0·02	F	0·256 }0·75	—	0·274 }1·08	
F	0·61	—	0·67	OH	0·496	0·572	0·804	
H_2O^+	0·56	0·64	0·93					
H_2O^-	0·08	0·18	0·17					

	1.	2.	3.
	"100·26"	99·74	100·38
$O \equiv F$	0·26	—	0·28
Total	"100·00"	99·74	100·10

	1.	2.	3.
α	1·94	1·90	1·912
β	—	—	1·917
γ	2·095	2·04	2·08
$2V_\gamma$	23°	(2E69°−71°)	36°
γ:z	53°	35°–36°	—
D	3·54	3·55	3·54

1. Light reddish brown sphene, nepheline-syenite, Kola Peninsula, U.S.S.R. (Sahama, Th. G., 1946, *Bull. Comm. géol. Finlande*, vol. 24, no. 138, p. 88; includes SrO 0·32: rare earths are La_2O_3 0·04, Ce_2O_3 0·12, Pr_2O_3 0·02, Nd_2O_3 0·08, Sm_2O_3 0·02, Gd_2O_3 0·02, $Dy_2O_3 < 0·01$, $Er_2O_3 < 0·01$, Y_2O_3 0·05).
2. Black sphene (red in thin chips), pegmatite, Quoscescer, N.E. of Harar, Abyssinia (Morgante, S., 1943, *Periodico Min. Roma*, vol. 14, p. 13; includes P_2O_5 0·06: rare earths are Ce_2O_3 2·98, Y_2O_3 1·53).
3. Sphene, beach sand, Wainui inlet, N.W. Nelson, New Zealand (Hutton, C. O., 1950, *Bull. Geol. Soc. Amer.*, vol. 61, p. 635; includes ThO_2 0·28: rare earths are Ce_2O_3 0·03, La_2O_3 0·85, Y_2O_3 0·18).

† Includes Sr 0·024.
‡ Includes Ba 0·002 (rare earths are Ce 0·147, Y 0·110).
§ Includes Th 0·008 (rare earths are Ce 0·001, Y 0·003, La 0·020).

PARAGENESIS

Sphene is a widespread accessory mineral of igneous rocks, and in many intermediate and acid plutonic rocks it is the dominant titanium-bearing mineral: it may be particularly abundant in nepheline-syenites (e.g. Table 3, anal. 1). It also occurs in low temperature Alpine-type veins where it may be associated with adularia, albite and epidote. In metamorphic rocks it occurs chiefly in gneisses and schists rich in ferromagnesian minerals, and it is fairly common in metamorphosed impure calc-silicate rocks and in skarns. In some sedimentary rocks sphene is found as detrital grains (anal. 3); where it is abundant it is possibly of authigenic origin.

REFERENCES

JAFFE, H. W. (1947). 'Re-examination of sphene (titanite)', *Amer. Min.*, vol. 32, p. 637.

SAHAMA, TH. G. (1946). 'On the chemistry of the mineral titanite', *Bull. Comm. géol. Finlande*, vol. 24, no. 138, p. 88.

GARNET GROUP

CUBIC

	$n\dagger$	D	$a(\text{Å})$	
Pyrope	1·714	3·582	11·459	$Mg_3Al_2Si_3O_{12}$
Almandine	1·830	4·318	11·526	$Fe_3^{+2}Al_2Si_3O_{12}$
Spessartine	1·800	4·190	11·621	$Mn_3Al_2Si_3O_{12}$
Grossular	1·734	3·594	11·851	$Ca_3Al_2Si_3O_{12}$
Andradite	1·887	3·859	12·048	$Ca_3(Fe^{+3}, Ti)_2Si_3O_{12}$
Uvarovite	1·86‡	3·90‡	12·00	$Ca_3Cr_2Si_3O_{12}$
Hydrogrossular	1·734–	3·594–	11·85–	$Ca_3Al_2Si_2O_8(SiO_4)_{1-m}(OH)_{4m}$
	1·675	3·13	12·16	

Dispersion: Weak. H 6–7½.

Cleavage: None; {110} parting sometimes present (?); subconchoidal fracture.

Twinning: Complex and sector twinning, and zoning, may be visible in birefringent varieties.

Colour: Red, brown, black, green, yellow, pink or white; colourless, pink, yellow or brown in thin section.

Soluble with difficulty in HF. Hydrogrossular soluble in HCl or HNO_3.

The minerals of the garnet group are particularly characteristic of metamorphic rocks but are also found in some igneous types and as detrital grains in sediments. The group is sub-divided into the species listed above, which represent the end-members of the isomorphous series. A garnet corresponding in composition to any one end-member is rare, however, and the name is assigned according to the dominant 'molecular' type present. The garnets may be divided into two series—pyralspite (*py*rope, *al*mandine, *spes*sartine) and ugrandite (*u*varovite, *gros*sular, *and*radite) : fairly complete and continuous variation in composition occurs within these two series, but there appears to be no continuous variation between pyralspite and ugrandite.

STRUCTURE

The unit cell of garnet contains eight formula units. In it the silicon–oxygen tetrahedra exist as independent groups linked to octahedra of the trivalent ions, while the divalent metal ions are situated in the interstices

† Grossular, spessartine, andradite and uvarovite may show appreciable birefringence.

‡ With these exceptions the values tabulated are those obtained for pure synthetic end-member garnets.

within the Si-Al network, each divalent ion being surrounded by eight oxygens (Fig. 7).

The length of the cell edge within the garnet group is of considerable use as a diagnostic feature and is one which is readily obtained. Its determination need only entail the measurement of the positions of the three strong high-angle reflections 10,4,0, 10,4,2 and 880. Assuming that the cell edge is an additive function of the molecular proportions of the end-members of

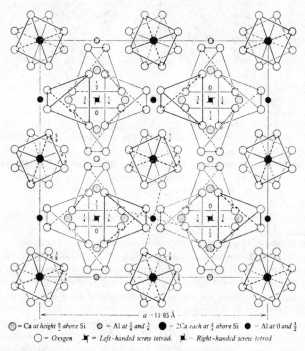

Fig. 7. *Projection on (001) of the structure of grossular garnet (after Strunz, H., 1957, Mineralogische Tabellen, 3rd edit. Leipzig).*

the garnet group, formulae may be constructed enabling the cell edge to be related to the number and type of metal ions in the particular garnet molecule. If in the pyralspite series it is assumed that the R^{+2} ions have radii between 0·780 and 0·823 kX, the R^{+3} ions an average radius of 0·571 kX and the R^{+4} ions 0·413 kX, then $a = 10·629 + 1·560R^{+2}$. For grossular and andradite, assuming average radii R^{+2} 1·01 kX and R^{+4} 0·413 kX, $a = 10·695 + 2·000R^{+3}$. A combined form of equation covering the five main garnet molecules is given by $a = 9·125 + 1·560R^{+2} + 2·000R^{+3}$.

CHEMISTRY

In addition to the 6 normal end-member garnet molecules it must be considered theoretically possible to have a total of 16 such species, each of the divalent metals Ca, Mg, Fe and Mn combining with each of the four trivalent metals Al, Fe, Mn and Cr. Some of the unusual combinations have in fact been reported, and in particular the composition $3MnO \cdot Fe_2O_3 \cdot 3SiO_2$ (calderite) may occur in manganese ores such as those in South-West Africa. Substitutions which can take place in the garnet structure include the possible replacement of a small proportion of the Si atoms by P or perhaps by Ti, though the latter may also replace Al. In the hydrogarnets there is replacement of SiO_2 by $2H_2O$, with vacant Si spaces in the structure. Chemical analyses of 7 typical garnets of various compositions are given in Table 4, where they have been recalculated on the basis of 24 (O) and also into the molecular percentages of their end-member components.

Pyrope garnets containing more than about 75 per cent of the pyrope molecule are unknown and the typical pyrope of high grade metamorphic rocks contains around 40 to 70 per cent of this molecule (anal. 4), the other components being chiefly almandine and subsidiary grossular. Chromium remains low, even in those pyropes from chromium-rich environments such as peridotites. Pyrope has been synthesized from kaolin, SiO_2, MgO and $MgCl_2$, the best conditions for its formation being 30,000 atmospheres and 900°C. At 36 kilobars pressure pyrope melts congruently at about 1775°C; in the pressure range 25 to 36 kilobars, however, there are at least three incongruent melting reactions over the range 1600°–1775°C. Retrograde changes affecting pyrope may cause its breakdown to a mixture of hornblende, plagioclase and iron ore, often in the form of a light green kelyphitic intergrowth, or to a fibrous amphibole and green biotite. Pyrope is typically pinkish red, ranging from an almost crimson colour to a purplish shade with increasing amounts of the almandine molecule. The clear varieties have been used as a gem: the similarity in colour has led to some specimens being known as 'ruby', e.g. Cape ruby from South African kimberlites and peridotites.

Almandine is the commonest end-member molecule in the garnet group, and almandine garnets generally also contain appreciable amounts of the pyrope and spessartine molecules. Calcium and ferric iron are typically low. Almandines containing more than 30 mol. per cent of the ugrandite molecule have been reported from eclogites and from glaucophane schists in California. A common alteration product is chlorite. Almandine has been synthesized from kaolin, Fe_2O_3, SiO_2 and $FeCl_2 \cdot 4H_2O$, the best conditions for its formation being 10,000 atmospheres at 900°C. Almandine is commonly deep red to brownish black, and in thin section is colourless to pinkish red. All members of the garnet group show a strong force of crystallization and commonly develop dodecahedral and icositetrahedral forms : almandines occurring in mica schists frequently show good examples of these.

Spessartine garnets have a range of composition from approximately 90 per cent to 40 per cent of the spessartine molecule and analyses of a

Table 4. GARNET ANALYSES

	1.	2.	3.	4.	5.	6.	7.
SiO_2	38·03	37·03	38·69	41·52	35·84	35·88	34·48
TiO_2	—	0·04	0·55	tr.	0·03	—	0·03
Al_2O_3	22·05	8·92	18·17	23·01	20·83	1·13	19·87
Cr_2O_3	—	—	—	0·22	—	27·04	—
Fe_2O_3	0·88	18·34	5·70	1·22	0·65	2·46	0·61
FeO	29·17	2·25	3·78	12·86	1·78	—	0·85
MnO	1·57	1·09	0·64	0·33	33·37	0·03	0·02
MgO	6·49	0·83	0·76	16·64	2·48	0·04	2·07
CaO	1·80	30·26	31·76	4·71	5·00	33·31	37·40
H_2O^+	—	0·48	0·13	}0·16	—	}0·18	4·65
H_2O^-	—	0·16	0·06		—		0·23
Total	99·99	99·40	100·24	100·67	99·98	100·07	100·24

	1.	2.	3.	4.	5.	6.	7.
n	1·793	1·827	1·7692	1·750	1·787	1·85(±)†	1·702
D	4·08	3·77	3·688	3·782	4·12	3·75	3·35
$a(Å)$	11·529	—	11·844	—	11·653	—	—

NUMBERS OF IONS ON THE BASIS OF 24 (O)

	1.	2.	3.	4.	5.	6.	7.
Si	5·951 }6·00	6·043	5·966 }6·00	5·999 }6·00	5·808 }6·00	5·964 }6·00	5·043 }6·18
Al	0·049	—	0·034	0·001	0·192	0·036	1·133†
Al	4·019	1·716	3·268	3·912	3·786	0·186	3·416
Cr	0·102 }4·12	— }3·97	— }3·99	0·026 }4·07	— }3·87	3·554 }4·05	— }3·49
Fe^{+3}	—	2·253	0·662	0·132	0·080	0·308	0·070
Ti	—	0·005	0·064	—	0·004	—	0·003
Mg	1·513	0·201	0·175	3·580	0·598	0·010	0·452
Fe^{+2}	3·818 }5·84	0·307 }5·95	0·487 }5·99	1·552 }5·90	0·241 }6·29	— }5·95	0·104 }6·42
Mn	0·203	0·151	0·083	0·040	4·581	0·004	0·002
Ca	0·302	5·292	5·248	0·730	0·868	5·934	5·858

	1.	2.	3.	4.	5.	6.	7.
Almandine	65·4	5·2	8·1	26·1	4·0	—	
Andradite	2·7	56·9	18·2	3·3	2·2	7·7	
Grossular	2·5	32·0	69·4	8·9	11·2	2·4	
Pyrope	25·8	3·4	2·9	60·3	7·9	0·2	
Spessartine	3·6	2·5	1·4	0·7	74·7	0·1	
Uvarovite	—	—	—	0·7	—	89·6	

1. Almandine, quartz–biotite gneiss, Adirondack Mts., New York (Engel, A. E. J. & Engel, C. G., 1960, *Bull. Geol. Soc. Amer.*, vol. 71, p. 1).
2. Reddish brown andradite, metasomatic fissures in thermally metamorphosed andesite, Shap, Westmorland (Firman, R. J., 1957, *Quart. Journ. Geol. Soc.*, vol. 113, p. 205).
3. Brownish red grossular, anorthite–clinozoisite–corundum–garnet gneiss, Sittampundi complex, Madras (Subramaniam, A. P., 1956, *Bull. Geol. Soc. Amer.*, vol. 67, p. 317).
4. Pyrope, eclogite, Rodhaugen, Sandmore, Norway (Eskola, P., 1921, *Vid. Skrift.* I, *Mat.-nat. Kl.*, vol. 1, no. 8).
5. Golden yellow spessartine, rhodonite–spessartine–pyrrhotite rock, calcsilicate hornfels, Meldon, Devonshire (Howie, R. A., 1965, *Min. Mag.* vol. 34 (Tilley vol.), p. 249).
6. Uvarovite, uvarovite–tremolite–tawmawite–pyrrhotite vein, Outokumpu, Finland (Eskola, P., 1933, *Compt. Rend. Soc. géol. Finlande*, no. 7, p. 26).
7. Hydrogrossular, rodingite, Champion Creek, New Zealand (Hutton, C. O., 1943, *Trans. Roy. Soc. New Zealand*, vol. 73, p. 174; includes Na_2O 0·02, K_2O 0·01).

† For green light.
‡ OH/4.

phosphate-bearing spessartine from Western Australia report up to 43·10 per cent MnO : in the latter mineral some replacement of the SiO_4 group by PO_4 may occur. The other garnet molecules commonly occurring in spessartine are almandine and to a lesser extent pyrope. Grossular generally is present only in small amounts, though peach-tan garnets from Nevada contain roughly equal amounts of spessartine and grossular, indicating an inter-mixing between the pyralspite and ugrandite series, e.g. one such garnet has a mol. composition $Sp_{42.8}Gro_{41.4}Alm_{12.4}And_{3.4}$. Appreciable replacement of Mn by Y may occur in some spessartines from pegmatites, sometimes amounting to over 2 per cent Y_2O_3. Spessartine is fairly readily synthesized from its component oxides; using SiO_2, $Al(OH)_3$, $Al(NO_3)_3 \cdot 6H_2O$ and MnO_2, the best conditions have been reported to be 900°C and 10,000 atmospheres, though it can be produced at as low as 410°C and 200 to 1500 bars pressure, using $MnCO_3$, Al_2O_3 and SiO_2. It varies in colour from black to red, brown and yellowish orange, but may undergo surface alteration and oxidation to a mixture of black manganese oxides and hydroxides.

Grossular very close to the end-member in composition can occur, e.g. with 96·8 per cent of the grossular molecule, and being in the ugrandite series the predominant substitutional molecule is andradite (e.g. anal. 3) with which it forms a continuous series, or more rarely uvarovite. Indeed many so-called uvarovites are in reality grossular with an appreciable but subordinate uvarovite component. Despite the existence of the grossular–hydrogrossular series there is no evidence that the grossular typical of thermal metamorphism contains appreciable amounts of water. Anhydrous grossular can be synthesized from glass of the appropriate composition at 800°C and water-vapour pressures of 2000 bars; using a reaction mixture of kaolin, SiO_2, CaO and $CaCl_2$ the best conditions were reported to be 900°C and 20,000 atmospheres. In the system grossular–$3CaO \cdot Al_2O_3 \cdot 6H_2O$, anhydrous grossular has been produced at 500°C and is probably stable with water to 400°C: at 15,000 lb/in² and above 850°C it decomposes to wollastonite + gehlenite + anorthite. The colour of grossular is determined largely by the amount of iron and manganese present. The cinnamon-coloured variety has been called cinnamon stone: hessonite is another name used for the yellowish and brownish red varieties. Appreciable chromium imparts a vivid green colour to the mineral.

Andradite containing over 94 per cent of the andradite molecule is known: the other common component in andradite garnets is the grossular molecule, e.g. anal. 2 of the well-known garnet from Shap shows it to consist of andradite 56·9 per cent and grossular 32·0 per cent. A few rare examples have been reported intermediate in composition between andradite and spessartine, for which the name spandite has been proposed. Melanite is the name given to the dark brown or black variety of andradite containing usually between 1 and 5 per cent TiO_2, while in the schorlomite variety of andradite TiO_2 is even more abundant and may amount to approximately 20 per cent. The role of Ti in these garnets remains problematical: there is too much Ti for it all to be considered as replacing Si, whereas if it is placed in the R^{+3} group substituting for Fe^{+3} (ionic radii 0·68 and 0·64 Å respectively), the Al can be divided, as is usual in silicate structures, between the Si and the R^{+3} positions. There is, however, some infra-red evidence to show that TiO_4 tetrahedra play the same structural role as the SiO_4 tetrahedra. A zirconium-bearing variety of andradite with ZrO_2 3·7 per cent has been described, and kimzeyite is a zirconium garnet (ZrO_2 29·9 per cent) but is so low in silica (9·6 per cent) as to be quite different from the normal silicate garnets. A vanadiferous variety, goldmanite, has also been described, with 18·3 per cent V_2O_3. Andradite has been synthesized hydrothermally from glasses and from its powdered component oxides: using wollastonite, Fe_2O_3 and $FeCl_3$, the best conditions were reported to be 20,000 atmospheres and 900°C. The colour of andradite ranges from black to red, brown, yellow and green: it is often yellowish in thin section. The Ti-bearing varieties melanite and schorlomite are very dark brown to black. The transparent green variety is known as demantoid, topazolite is a honey-yellow variety, and a light brown variety has been called allochroite.

Uvarovite chiefly occurs (e.g. anal. 6) as a dominant garnet molecule in association with grossular and andradite, and forms a continuous series with these molecules. It can be synthesized from its powdered component oxides by heating to 525°C at 110 atmospheres. Uvarovite is typically dark green to a vivid emerald green.

Hydrogrossular has been taken as the name for members of the series $3CaO \cdot Al_2O_3 \cdot 3SiO_2$–$3CaO \cdot Al_2O_3 \cdot 6H_2O$ with a composition between grossular and hibschite (plazolite), $3CaO \cdot Al_2O_3 \cdot 2SiO_2 \cdot 2H_2O$. Minerals in this compositional range have also been called hydrogarnet, grossularoid and garnetoid. Garnets in the compositional range between hibschite and the silica-free compound $3CaO \cdot Al_2O_3 \cdot 6H_2O$ are not known to occur naturally. Anal. 7 (Table 4) has been recalculated on the basis of 24 oxygens and with one quarter of the (OH) value allocated to the Z group, assuming the replacement to be $Si \rightleftharpoons 4H$. The complete series from close to grossular to $3CaO \cdot Al_2O_3 \cdot 6H_2O$ has been synthesized by the hydrothermal treatment of glasses of appropriate composition below approximately 500°C and 2000 atmospheres. Although the natural hydrogarnets are all hydrogrossular, the existence of the hydropyrope molecule forming a series with hydrogrossular has been demonstrated in synthetic studies, and hydrospessartine has also been postulated.

OPTICAL AND PHYSICAL PROPERTIES

Garnet is often thought of as the isotropic mineral *par excellence*, but although almandine and pyrope are usually completely isotropic, spessartine may be weakly anisotropic, and the ugrandite series frequently shows marked anisotropism. Small crystals of andradite, grossular and uvarovite may be isotropic but weak birefringence is rather characteristic of large crystals of these species, all of which may also show a complex series of twins probably due to internal strain in the crystals. The type of twinning varies, often appearing as sector twins composed of 6, 12 or 24 pyramids with vertices meeting at the centre of the crystal: these sectors may be slightly biaxial. In the ugrandite series distinct zoning may also occur: zoning and twinning is shown particularly well in the andradite of some contact metamorphic skarn deposits and examples are known with a 2V of approximately 90° and a birefringence of 0·006.

The synthesis of the five major end-member garnet molecules has enabled the refractive indices, specific gravities and cell edges of the end-member components to be established, and various diagrams have been constructed relating variation in physical properties with change in chemical composition within the garnet group. Of the three common physical measurements (D, n, a) that of specific gravity (D) is the least reliable because of the frequent occurrence in garnet of small inclusions of quartz or other minerals. Diagrams have been constructed, however, in which the refractive index and cell edge are taken as independent variables and used as ordinate and abscissa, while the chemical compositions of the end-member molecules and the specific gravity are plotted as functions of the two variables (Figs. 8 and 9). Using these diagrams it is possible to estimate compositions in terms of the three-component or four-component composition fields. Thus, for example, if a garnet of unknown composition has a 11·550 Å, n 1·770, D 3·380, its composition may be estimated by reference in Fig. 8 to the triangle Pyr–Alm–Gro as mostly $Pyr_{45}Alm_{55}$ (found by drawing a line through the apex Gro and the given point to cut the Pyr–Alm base of the triangle at $Pyr_{45}Alm_{55}$), modified by about 17 per cent Gro, i.e. $Pyr_{37}Alm_{46}Gro_{17}$: the contour lines show that such a garnet would have D 3·894. Similarly in Fig. 8 the composition could also be $Pyr_{66}Alm_{34} + 13$ per cent And, or $Pyr_{57}Alm_{30}And_{13}$, which has D 3·808. From Fig. 9 the same point may also represent a garnet with composition $Pyr_{38}Alm_9Sp_{53}$ with D 3·950. The measured value D 3·880 lies 0·84 of the way from $Pyr_{57}Alm_{30}And_{13}$ to $Pyr_{37}Alm_{46}Gro_{17}$, and the composition may therefore be estimated as $Pyr_{40}Alm_{44}Gro_{14}And_2$ (found by adding 0·84 $Pyr_{37}Alm_{46}$-Gro_{17} and 0·16 $Pyr_{57}Alm_{30}And_{13}$): alternatively (Fig. 9) the composition may be $Pyr_{47}Alm_{20}Sp_{27}And_6$. In addition any other data available such as the MnO or FeO content or a knowledge of the mineral associations or paragenesis may be used to estimate more completely and less ambiguously the composition of the garnet. The use of such diagrams is based on the assumption that the physical properties represented are additive functions of the molecular proportions of the end-members, and that components other than the five common end-member garnet molecules are relatively insignificant. A linear relationship between cell edge and composition and between refractive index and composition has been demonstrated for the almandine–pyrope series and for the grossular–pyrope series, and a similar relationship has been demonstrated for specific gravity in the spessartine–almandine and almandine–pyrope series: it is thus probable that the additive relationship applies throughout this group.

In the hydrogrossular series the presence of $(OH)_4$ replacing Si results in lower specific gravities and refractive indices but in an increase in cell edge. The artificial end-member $3CaO \cdot Al_2O_3 \cdot 6H_2O$ has n 1·605, a 12·56 A, D 2·52.

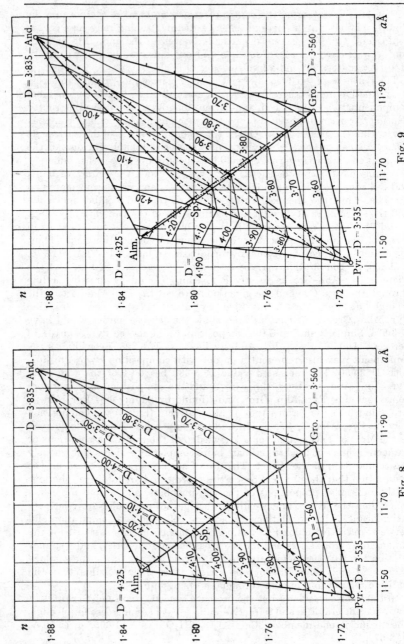

Fig. 9

Fig. 8

Determinative charts for garnets (after Winchell, H., 1958, Amer. Min., vol. 43, p. 595).

DISTINGUISHING FEATURES

The high relief and isotropic or weakly birefringent nature of garnet is characteristic, with, in the birefringent varieties, zoning or sector twinning. Minerals of this group generally are less strongly coloured in thin section than the spinels, and lack the {111} cleavage sometimes seen in the latter. Within the garnet group the various species are best distinguished by their refractive indices, specific gravities and cell edges, in conjunction, if possible, with partial chemical data, e.g. for FeO or MnO. Hydrogrossular has a lower refractive index than any of the natural anhydrous garnets.

PARAGENESIS

Garnet is especially characteristic of metamorphic rocks as well as being found in some granites and pegmatites and acid volcanic rocks. As it is fairly resistant to abrasion and to chemical attack it is often found in detrital sediments.

Pyrope occurs in certain ultrabasic rocks such as the mica peridotites, kimberlites and associated serpentinites and is also found in the sands and gravels derived from the outcrops of such ultrabasic bodies. The Bohemian garnets of gem quality are pyrope and occur in the debris of a basaltic breccia derived from a peridotite. The garnets of eclogites (e.g. Table 4, anal. 4) vary in composition within the pyrope–almandine range: they invariably have a higher FeO : MgO ratio than the parent rock and the associated pyroxenes.

Almandine is the typical garnet of the garnetiferous schists resulting from the regional metamorphism of argillaceous sediments, and as such it is used as a zonal mineral in regions of progressive metamorphism of these rocks. It may be developed partly from the chlorite of the lower grades, but in higher grades it may also be produced from the breakdown of mica to give garnet and potassium feldspar and from the reaction of staurolite with quartz to give garnet together with kyanite or sillimanite. There appears to be a general pattern of substitutions in the garnet molecule during progressive metamorphism, with (FeO + MgO) substituting for (CaO + MnO) with increasing metamorphic grade. In the rocks of the granulite facies the garnet is typically almandine or more rarely almandine–pyrope: in the eclogite facies the typical garnet is in the almandine–pyrope series with almandine often just dominant. Almandine also occurs in some aureoles of thermal or contact metamorphism which typically also contain white mica but which lack potassium feldspar. In plutonic igneous rocks almandine may result from contamination of granitic material by argillaceous impurities: it is also known as phenocrysts in volcanic rocks and in some examples it is believed that the almandine is neither metamorphic nor metasomatic but was present in the original magma before its extrusion or ejection.

Spessartine is the commonest garnet in granitic pegmatites, where it is often a spessartine–almandine garnet: the yttrium-bearing spessartines are restricted to this paragenesis. Spessartine also occurs in some skarn deposits and in Mn-rich assemblages, with rhodonite, tephroite, etc., of metasomatic origin (e.g. anal. 5) associated either with adjacent igneous intrusions or with a more widespread regional metasomatism. It is also known from veins in metamorphosed greywacke type sediments and the spessartine molecule is often present in significant amount in almandine from igneous and metamorphic rocks, especially those of thermal aureoles.

Grossular is especially characteristic of both thermally and regionally metamorphosed impure calcareous rocks, and also occurs in rocks which have undergone calcium metasomatism. It is found, for example, in metamorphosed marls and calcareous shales, and may also result from the replacement of earlier formed wollastonite. Grossular is also known from zeolite-bearing vesicles in metamorphosed basaltic lavas and is sometimes found with diopside or scapolite resulting from pneumatolysis associated with granite pegmatites. It also occurs in association with serpentinite and has been described from a highly metamorphosed layered complex (anal. 3) possibly resulting from the alteration of anorthite.

Andradite typically occurs in contact or thermally metamorphosed impure calcareous sediments and particularly in the metasomatic skarn deposits often associated with such metamorphism. This involves the addition of Fe_2O_3 and SiO_2:

$$3CaCO_3 + Fe_2O_3 + 3SiO_2 \rightarrow Ca_3Fe_2Si_3O_{12} + 3CO_2$$
$$\text{calcite} \qquad\qquad\qquad\qquad \text{andradite}$$

If FeO also is introduced, hedenbergite may form in addition to andradite, and if insufficient silica is available magnetite may result

$$4CaCO_3 + 2Fe_2O_3 + 2FeO + 5SiO_2 \rightarrow$$
$$Ca_3Fe_2Si_3O_{12} + CaFeSi_2O_6 + Fe_3O_4 + 4CO_2$$

giving the typical andradite–hedenbergite–magnetite skarn assemblage. Andradite also occurs as the result of metasomatism connected with the thermal metamorphism of calcic igneous rocks such as andesite (e.g. anal. 2). The topazolite and demantoid varieties occur mainly in serpentinite and chlorite schist. Melanite and schorlomite, the Ti-bearing varieties of andradite, occur in an entirely different paragenesis, being found in alkaline igneous rocks such as nepheline-syenite and ijolite and their volcanic equivalents, phonolite, nephelinite, etc. They are also known, however, from skarn deposits.

Uvarovite is the rarest of the six common anhydrous garnet species, and although the uvarovite molecule is known in association with grossular, garnets with uvarovite as the dominant molecule are of restricted occurrence and are found chiefly in serpentinite, often in association with chromite, and in metamorphosed limestones and skarn ore-bodies (e.g. anal. 6). In such calcareous rocks the production of uvarovite appears to depend on the pre-existence of chromite in associated serpentinites.

Hydrogrossular is probably more common than hitherto realized: it occurs in metamorphosed marls, and in altered gabbroic rocks and rodingites (anal. 7) where a redistribution of calcium has taken place. It is also found where metasomatic introduction of calcium has occurred or where water and alumina have been introduced into a calc-silicate assemblage.

REFERENCES

BLOXAM, T. W. (1959). 'Glaucophane-schists and associated rocks near Valley Ford, California', *Amer. Journ. Sci.*, vol. 257, p. 95.

COES, L. (1955). 'High-pressure minerals', *Journ. Amer. Ceram. Soc.*, vol. 38, p. 298.

FLEISCHER, M. (1937). 'The relation between chemical composition and physical properties in the garnet group', *Amer. Min.*, vol. 22, p. 751.

HOWIE, R. A. and SUBRAMANIAM, A. P. (1957). 'The paragenesis of garnet in charnockite, enderbite, and related granulites', *Min. Mag.*, vol. 31, p. 565.

KNORRING, O. VON (1951). 'A new occurrence of uvarovite from northern Karelia in Finland', *Min. Mag.*, vol. 29, p. 594.

LEE, D. E. (1962). 'Grossularite-spessartite garnet from the Victory mine, Gabbs, Nevada', *Amer. Min.*, vol. 47, p. 147.

MILTON, C., INGRAM, B. L. and BLADE, L. V. (1961). 'Kimzeyite a zirconium garnet from Magnet Cove, Arkansas', *Amer. Min.*, vol. 46, p. 533.

OLIVER, R. L. (1956). 'The origin of garnets in the Borrowdale Volcanic Series and associated rocks, English Lake District', *Geol. Mag.*, vol. 93, p. 121.

PABST, A. (1931). 'The garnets in the glaucophane-schists of California', *Amer. Min.*, vol. 16, p. 327.

SKINNER, B. J. (1956). 'Physical properties of end-members of the garnet group', *Amer. Min.*, vol. 41, p. 428.

STURT, B. A. (1961). 'The composition of garnets from pelitic schists in relation to the grade of regional metamorphism', *Journ. Petr.*, vol. 3, p. 181.

Vesuvianite (Idocrase) $\quad$ $Ca_{10}(Mg,Fe)_2Al_4[Si_2O_7]_2[SiO_4]_5(OH,F)_4$

TETRAGONAL $(-)$

$$\epsilon \quad 1\cdot700-1\cdot746$$
$$\omega \quad 1\cdot703-1\cdot752$$
$$\delta \quad 0\cdot001-0\cdot008$$

Dispersion: strong. D $3\cdot33-3\cdot43$. H 6–7.

Cleavage: {110} poor, {100} and {001} very poor.

Colour: Yellow, green, brown, more rarely red or blue; colourless to pale yellow, green or brown in thin section.

Varieties with low birefringence may show anomalous interference colours in brilliant blues or browns. Optically positive and biaxial varieties are also known.

The structure of vesuvianite (unit cell a 15·6, c 11·8 Å, Z = 4) is closely related to that of grossular garnet, the c dimension of vesuvianite being similar in length to the cube edge of grossular: certain parts of the structure are common to both minerals. In vesuvianite each Si is surrounded tetrahedrally by four oxygens, and of the nine Si atoms in the formula four form Si_2O_7 groups and the other five form independent SiO_4 groups.

Although the ideal formula has been taken to be $Ca_{10}(Mg,Fe)_2 Al_4Si_9O_{34}$ $(OH,F)_4$ considerable variation from this formula is shown by vesuvianite analyses, particularly with respect to the distribution of Mg and Al. An alternative formula of $X_{19}Y_{13}Z_{18}(O,OH,F)_{76}$, where $X = Ca(Na,K,Mn)$, $Y = (Al,Fe^{+3},Fe^{+2},Mg,Ti,Zn,Mn)$, $Z = Si$, has been claimed to fit the analytical results better. In addition to the major constituents in the above formulae, MnO, TiO_2, and more rarely BeO, ZnO, CuO and Cr_2O_3, may amount to over 1 per cent. Normal vesuvianite and a (Mg,Fe)-free variety have been synthesized.

The refractive indices of vesuvianite in general increase with increasing amounts of titanium and iron. The birefringence falls with increasing (OH) content and some varieties are virtually isotropic; optically positive varieties are also known, e.g. wiluite. Vesuvianite with such low birefringence may be positive for one wavelength and negative for another and may exhibit anomalous birefringence colours. The colour of vesuvianite is mainly controlled by the amount and state of oxidation of the iron present: the Cu-bearing variety cyprine is blue or greenish blue. A compact grass-green vesuvianite has been called californite.

The tetragonal form, high relief and low birefringence of vesuvianite are characteristic, though the distinction from grossular garnet may be difficult.

Vesuvianite occurs principally in contact metamorphosed limestones, and is associated with garnet, diopside, wollastonite, etc. It is common in skarns and is also found in regionally metamorphosed limestones. It is also known from nepheline-syenite and related rocks, as well as in veins and pockets in basic and ultrabasic rocks.

Sillimanite Al_2SiO_5

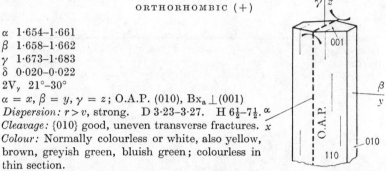

ORTHORHOMBIC (+)

α 1·654–1·661
β 1·658–1·662
γ 1·673–1·683
δ 0·020–0·022
2V$_\gamma$ 21°–30°
$\alpha = x$, $\beta = y$, $\gamma = z$; O.A.P. (010), Bx$_a \perp$(001)
Dispersion: $r > v$, strong. D 3·23–3·27. H $6\frac{1}{2}$–$7\frac{1}{2}$.
Cleavage: {010} good, uneven transverse fractures.
Colour: Normally colourless or white, also yellow,
brown, greyish green, bluish green; colourless in
thin section.
Pleochroism: In thick sections coloured varieties may be pleochroic with
α pale brown or pale yellow, β brown or greenish, γ dark brown or blue.

STRUCTURE

Sillimanite (a 7·44, b 7·59, c 5·75 Å ; Z = 4) has a structure consisting of
chains of aluminium–oxygen octahedra parallel to the z axis (Fig. 10).
Within the chains, octahedra of 6 oxygen ions around Al share edges with

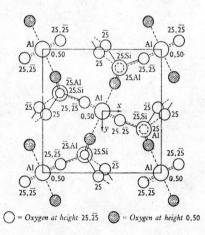

$\bigcirc$ = *Oxygen at height* 25,$\overline{25}$ ⬤ = *Oxygen at height* 0,50

Fig. 10. *The structure of sillimanite projected along z (after Hey, J. S. &
Taylor, W. H.*, 1931, Zeit. Krist., *vol.* 80, *p.* 428).

neighbouring octahedra on either side. The lateral linkage between octahedral chains is made by a chain of alternating Si and Al tetrahedra. The Al in sillimanite is thus half in octahedral coordination and half in tetrahedral coordination. The chains of octahedra in the three Al_2SiO_5 polymorphs are illustrated in Fig. 11.

CHEMISTRY

The composition is fairly constant and relatively close to Al_2SiO_5. The commonest ion replacing Al in the structure is Fe^{+3} (Table 5, p. 43): the small amounts of other elements sometimes reported probably represent impurities. Water may be present, as when it is entrapped and absorbed in the fine fibrous mass of crystals in the variety fibrolite. Sillimanite can be

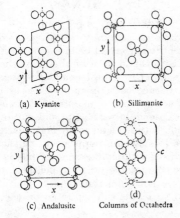

(a) Kyanite   (b) Sillimanite

(c) Andalusite   (d) Columns of Octahedra

Fig. 11. *The chains of octahedral groups in the three forms of* Al_2SiO_5 *(after Hey, J. S. & Taylor, W. H., 1931, Zeit. Krist., vol.* 80, *p.* 428).

synthesized from its component oxides at high temperatures and pressures: the phase diagram for the Al_2SiO_5 minerals (Fig. 13, p. 40) shows the triple point between andalusite, sillimanite and kyanite to lie at about $300° \pm 50°C$ and 8 ± 0.5 kilobars. On heating above 1545°C natural sillimanite is unstable and is converted to mullite + liquid. Alteration products of sillimanite include muscovite and sericite, pyrophyllite, kaolinite and montmorillonite. By inversion under conditions of stress or rising pressure it may be converted to kyanite.

OPTICAL AND PHYSICAL PROPERTIES

Sillimanite commonly occurs in long prismatic crystals or as a fibrous mat of fine crystalline material, although more equidimensional crystals are sometimes found. The relief is moderately high and the refractive indices vary only slightly; the birefringence is comparatively strong, though the normal retardation is not always observed in finely fibrous material. The {010} cleavage is not always noticeable in thin section: in cross sections showing the dominant {110} form the extinction is symmetrical with respect to the crystal boundaries.

DISTINGUISHING FEATURES

The positive (length-slow) elongation and higher birefringence distinguish sillimanite from andalusite. Apatite is length-fast and has weaker birefringence, while kyanite has higher refractive indices and a greater 2V. The distinction of sillimanite from mullite is difficult and is best made with the aid of cell dimensions or infra-red absorption curves.

PARAGENESIS

Sillimanite is the high temperature polymorph of Al_2SiO_5 and is found both in the higher grades of thermally metamorphosed argillaceous rocks, as in sillimanite–cordierite gneiss and biotite–sillimanite hornfels (where it is often derived from the breakdown of biotite or by the inversion of earlier formed andalusite), and in the highest grade of regional metamorphism of similar rocks, as in micaceous sillimanite schist or the coarser quartz–sillimanite gneiss. Much of the sillimanite of regional metamorphism is derived from the breakdown of muscovite and biotite but it may also be produced by reaction between staurolite and quartz. The polymorphic transition of kyanite to sillimanite appears to be sluggish and local persistence of kyanite in the sillimanite zone of metamorphism is not uncommon. Where regional metamorphism of pelitic rocks has been followed by thermal metamorphism, sillimanite and andalusite may be found in oriented intergrowth, as in the sillimanite gneiss enclosed in the Ross of Mull granite.

REFERENCE

HEY, J. S. and TAYLOR, W. H. (1931). 'The co-ordination number of aluminium in the alumino-silicates'. *Zeit. Krist.*, vol. 80, p. 428.

Mullite

$3Al_2O_3 \cdot 2SiO_2$

ORTHORHOMBIC (+)

α 1·640–1·670
β 1·642–1·675
γ 1·651–1·690
δ 0·012–0·028
2V, 45°–61°
$\alpha = x, \beta = y, \gamma = z$; O.A.P. (010)
Dispersion: $r > v$. D 3·15–3·26. H 6–7.
Cleavage: {010} distinct.
Colour: Normally colourless or white, also yellow,
pink or red; colourless or pinkish in thin section.
Pleochroism: $\alpha = \beta$ colourless, γ pinkish.

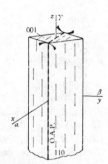

Mullite has a structure consisting of chains of Al octahedra parallel to the z axis, cross-linked by tetrahedra containing both Si and Al. The structure thus resembles that of sillimanite, and mullite cell dimensions (a 7·53–7·59, b 7·67–7·73, c 2·884–2·903 Å) are only slightly larger than those of sillimanite (in sillimanite c is doubled). It may be regarded as a disordered phase intermediate between two ordered phases, sillimanite and andalusite, with partial replacement of Si by Al and a shift of some tetrahedral cations into open sites.

Both natural and synthetic mullites show some deviations of composition from $3Al_2O_3 \cdot 2SiO_2$ with 60 mol. per cent Al_2O_3; natural mullites and synthetic experiments reaching equilibrium indicate a limit of alumina at about 63 mol. per cent Al_2O_3, but synthetic mullite of composition $2Al_2O_3 \cdot SiO_2$ or about 67 mol. per cent Al_2O_3 has also been produced. Fe^{+3} and Ti may appreciably replace Al (e.g. Table 5, p. 43, anal. 5), and natural iron-mullites with up to almost 6 per cent Fe_2O_3 are known.

The refractive indices of mullite are raised slightly by the increasing solid solution of Al_2O_3 and are raised further by the substitution of Fe^{+3} and Ti, the γ value for an iron-mullite with Fe_2O_3 5·93, TiO_2 0·55 being 1·690. The distinction of mullite from sillimanite is best made by cell dimensions from single-crystal X-ray photographs or by infra-red absorption spectra.

Mullite is found typically in pelitic xenoliths (buchites) in basic igneous rocks. The type occurrence in Mull (Table 5, anal. 5) is in a fused Jurassic shale xenolith in the tholeiitic portion of a composite sill, and iron-mullite has been described from a thermally metamorphosed lateritic lithomarge. It is also a very common refractory product.

REFERENCE

AGRELL, S. O. and SMITH, J. V. (1960) 'Cell dimensions, solid solution, polymorphism and identification of mullite and sillimanite', *Journ. Amer. Ceram. Soc.*, vol. 43, p. 69.

Andalusite

Al_2SiO_5

ORTHORHOMBIC $(-)$

α 1·629–1·649
β 1·633–1·653
γ 1·638–1·660
δ 0·009–0·011
$2V_\alpha$ 73°–86°
$\alpha = z$, $\beta = y$, $\gamma = x$, O.A.P. (010).
Dispersion: $r < v$. D 3·13–3·16. H $6\frac{1}{2}$–$7\frac{1}{2}$.
Cleavage: {110} good, {100} poor; (110) : (1$\bar{1}$0) = 89°.
Twinning: Rare, on {101}.

Colour: Usually pink, but may be white or rose-red; also grey, violet, yellow, green or clouded with inclusions; in thin section normally colourless, but may be pink or green.

Pleochroism: In coloured varieties weak, with α rose-pink, β and γ greenish yellow.

STRUCTURE

Andalusite (*a* 7·78, *b* 7·92, *c* 5·57 Å; Z = 4) has chains of aluminium–oxygen groups parallel to the *z* axis. The chains are formed by octahedral

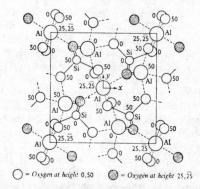

Fig. 12. *The structure of andalusite projected along z (after Hey, J. S. & Taylor, W. H., 1931, Zeit. Krist., vol. 80, p. 428).*

groups sharing edges with neighbours and they are linked laterally by Si between 4 tetrahedrally arranged oxygen atoms alternating with Al between 5 oxygen atoms (Fig. 12): the Al octahedra are somewhat irregular.

CHEMISTRY

The mineral is relatively pure Al_2SiO_5, and the only other ions present in noteworthy amounts are ferric iron and manganese; the replacement of Al by Fe^{+3} is generally small and in most andalusites Fe_2O_3 is less than 2 per cent. The manganese-rich variety manganandalusite may contain up to 7 per cent Mn_2O_3. A green variety of andalusite, viridine, contains appreciable ferric iron and manganese (e.g. Table 5, p. 43, anal. 3) and viridine with up to 9·6 per cent of Fe_2O_3 and 7·6 per cent Mn is known. Andalusite can be synthesized from kaolinite, or from $Al_2O_3 + SiO_2$, at 450°–650°C and water-vapour pressure 10,000–30,000 lb/in². The phase diagram for the Al_2SiO_5 composition (Fig. 13) shows the triple point between andalusite, sillimanite and kyanite to lie at about $300° \pm 50°$C and 8 ± 0.5 kilobars. Andalusite may alter rather easily to sericite, the variety chiastolite being particularly liable to this type of alteration along the lines of carbonaceous inclusions. Other alteration products include sillimanite and kyanite (by inversion with rising temperature or pressure), e.g. the 'chiastolite' hornfels of Carn Chuinneag where the andalusite has been replaced by brush-like aggregates of kyanite or pseudomorphs of kyanite and shimmer aggregate, pinite, corundum, spinel and feldspar.

OPTICAL AND PHYSICAL PROPERTIES

The refractive indices and specific gravity are increased by the entry of ferric iron and manganese into the structure. The colour and pleochroism are related chiefly to the Fe and Mn contents, the pink and red varieties containing Fe whereas the green crystals contain Mn. For the green variety viridine the optic sign becomes positive and the pleochroism may become marked and vary from yellow to emerald green. The chiastolite variety shows a regular arrangement of carbonaceous impurities, often forming a cruciform pattern when viewed in cross-section. The impurities may be concentrated at the centre of each crystal, representing the initial growth stage when the structure was unable to free itself from inclusions, and along the diagonals representing the trace of the prism edges as the crystal grew, the foreign matter being brushed aside to the edges by crystal growth which was most effective in directions perpendicular to the prism faces. On heating to between 1450° and 1500°C andalusite is converted to mullite, and is used as such in refractories.

DISTINGUISHING FEATURES

The almost square cross-section, high relief, low birefringence, and length-fast prismatic crystals are characteristic. The pleochroic varieties may be distinguished from orthopyroxene by the length-slow character and higher birefringence of the latter mineral.

PARAGENESIS

Andalusite is found typically in the argillaceous rocks of contact aureoles around igneous intrusions, where it is often associated with cordierite. In the early stages of such metamorphism it occurs as anhedral grains but rapidly acquires a prismatic outline, pushing aside enclosed foreign matter to form the chiastolite pattern: in a more advanced grade the andalusite becomes clear of inclusions. Under conditions of higher temperature and pressure it may become unstable and invert to its polymorphs sillimanite or kyanite (see Fig. 13). Andalusite and cordierite schists are found occasionally in regionally metamorphosed areas where there appears to have been a deficiency or relaxation of shearing stress, as in the Banff area of North-East Scotland. Andalusite is of rare occurrence in granites, probably having been formed as a result of contamination, although the occurrence of pseudomorphs of andalusite in quartz veins in pegmatites has

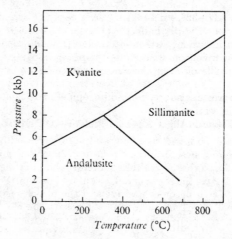

Fig. 13. *Experimentally determined phase diagram for* Al_2SiO_5 *(after Bell, P. M., 1963, Science, vol. 139, p. 1055).*

sometimes been taken to suggest a pegmatitic or hydrothermal origin for this mineral. It is found in large crystals with corundum in pegmatites in Yosemite National Park, where it resulted from the reaction of the magmatic material with the pelitic wall rock. Andalusite is a fairly common detrital mineral in some sandstones.

REFERENCES

BELL, P. M. (1963) 'Aluminium silicate system: experimental determination of the triple point', *Science*, vol. 139, p. 1055.

HEINRICH, E. W. and COREY, A. F. (1959) 'Manganian andalusite from New Mexico', *Amer. Min.*, vol. 44, p. 1261.

ROSE, R. L. (1957) 'Andalusite and corundum-bearing pegmatites in Yosemite National Park, California', *Amer. Min.*, vol. 42, p. 635.

Kyanite

Al_2SiO_5

TRICLINIC (−)

α 1·712–1·718
β 1·721–1·723
γ 1·727–1·734
δ 0·012–0·016
$2V_\alpha$ 82°–83°
γ' : z on (100) = 27°–32°, on (010) = 5°–8° ;
α' : x on (001) = 0°–3° : Bx_a nearly $\perp$(100).

Dispersion: $r > v$, weak. D 3·53–3·65. H 5½–7, variable.

Cleavage: {100} perfect, {010} good, {001} parting. (001) : z = 85°.

Twinning: Lamellar on (100), twin axis $\perp$(100) or $\parallel y$ or z ; multiple on {001}.

Colour: Blue to white, also grey, green, yellow, pink or black ; colourless to pale blue in thin section.

Pleochroism: Weak ; in thick sections α colourless, β violet-blue, γ cobalt-blue.

STRUCTURE

Kyanite (a 7·10, b 7·74, c 5·57 Å, α 90° 5½′, β 101° 2′, γ 105° 44½′ ; Z = 4) has a structure in which the oxygen atoms are arranged in a slightly distorted close-packed cubic array. As in andalusite and sillimanite, there are chains of Al–O octahedra and these chains are linked together by the remaining Si, Al and O ions, Si being coordinated by 4 oxygen ions, and Al by 6 oxygen ions (Fig. 14). The Si lying between 4 oxygens thus gives a structure with independent SiO_4 tetrahedra. Kyanite, with a volume of 15·3 Å³ per oxygen ion, has the closest packing of the aluminosilicates.

CHEMISTRY

Like the other aluminosilicates, kyanite approximates closely to Al_2SiO_5 (Table 5) with apparently only a very limited amount of Fe^{+3} able to enter the structure : Cr is sometimes present in moderate amounts. The small amounts of Ti reported may be due to inclusions of rutile which frequently occur in kyanite, and recent work has shown that in pure material the alkali content never exceeds 0·06 per cent. Synthetic kyanite has been reported to be produced readily at 900°C and 20,000 atmospheres. The phase diagram for the Al_2SiO_5 composition (Fig. 13, p. 40) shows the triple point between kyanite, andalusite and sillimanite to lie at about 300° ± 50°C and 8 ± 0·5 kilobars. On heating to about 1300°C kyanite is converted to mullite and a glass. Alteration products include pyrophyllite, muscovite and sericite. It may also invert to sillimanite or andalusite by a change in the pressure–temperature conditions, the kyanite of regional metamorphism, for instance, being converted to andalusite within the aureole of a later granite.

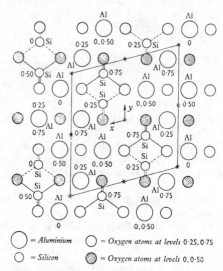

Fig. 14. *The structure of kyanite projected along z (after Náray-Szabó, St., Taylor, W. H. & Jackson, W. W., 1929, Zeit. Krist. vol. 71, p. 117).*

OPTICAL AND PHYSICAL PROPERTIES

The relief is very distinctly high for a mineral which is normally colourless in thin section, while the birefringence is moderate giving rise to higher first-order colours for sections of normal thickness. The optic axial plane is almost perpendicular to {100}, and is inclined at approximately 30° to {010} or the z axis. The extinction position nearest to z corresponds to the slow ray, and the extinction angle varies from around 30° to zero: in basal sections it is almost zero. The colour is variable from colourless to blue, and is often unevenly distributed. The hardness varies from face to face and according to crystallographic direction. Kyanite when calcined is used in refractory products and is the most important of the aluminosilicates in this respect as it sometimes occurs in relatively large workable deposits.

DISTINGUISHING FEATURES

Kyanite has a higher relief than the other aluminosilicates: its birefringence is less than that of sillimanite but greater than that of andalusite while it also differs from the latter in being length-slow. The maximum

Table 5. SILLIMANITE, ANDALUSITE, KYANITE AND MULLITE ANALYSES

	1.	2.	3.	4.	5.
SiO_2	36·70	36·74	35·71	37·46	29·04
TiO_2	—	0·01	0·17	0·03	0·79
Al_2O_3	62·73	62·70	58·38	61·52	69·63
Fe_2O_3	0·63	0·36	2·21	0·71	0·50
FeO	—	0·05	—	—	—
Mn_2O_3	—	—	3·67	0·006	—
MgO	—	0·03	—	0·03	—
CaO	—	0·02	—	0·02	—
Na_2O	—	—	—	0·03	0·18
K_2O	—	0·07	—	0·01	0·06
H_2O^+	—	0·15	—	}0·05	—
H_2O^-	—	0·01	—		—
Total	100·06	100·14	100·14	99·87	100·20
α	—	1·631	1·649	1·713	1·651
β	—	1·637	1·652	1·720	—
γ	—	1·642	1·660	1·728	1·668
2V	(+)	—	59°–69°(+)	83°(−)	—
D	3·209	—	3·19	3·63	—

NUMBERS OF IONS ON THE BASIS OF 20 OXYGENS (13 FOR MULLITE)

Si		3·966		3·972		3·933		4·057		2·057	
Al	7·992⎞		7·994⎞		7·579⎞		7·855⎞		5·826⎞		
Fe^{+3}	0·052		0·030		0·183		0·058		0·027		
Mg	—		0·005		—		0·005		—		
Ti	—		0·001		0·014		0·003		0·042		
Fe^{+2}	— │8·04	0·005 │8·05	— │8·08	— │7·93	— │5·9	
Mn^{+3}	—		—		0·308		—		—		
Na	—		—		—		0·006		0·025		
Ca	—		0·003		—		0·002		—		
K	—⎠		0·009⎠		—⎠		0·001⎠		0·006⎠		

1. Colourless prisms of sillimanite, sillimanite–biotite gneiss, Romaine, Quebec (Walker, T. L. & Parsons, A. L., 1923, *Univ. Toronto Studs.*, *Geol. Ser.*, no. 16, p. 29).
2. Andalusite, kyanite–andalusite–sillimanite schist, Goat Mountain, Boehls Butte quadrangle, Idaho (Hietanen, A., 1956, *Amer. Min.*, vol. 41, p. 1).
3. Green viridine, Mt. Ragged, Western Australia (Prider, R. T., 1960, *Indian Min.*, vol. 1, p. 42).
4. Light blue kyanite, kyanite quartzite, Hållsjöberget, Varmland, Sweden (Henriques, Å., 1957, *Arkiv. Min. Geol.*, vol. 2, p. 271).
5. Pale lilac-pink mullite, buchite, Seabank Villa, Mull, Scotland (Bowen, N. L., Greig, J. W. & Zies, E. G., 1924, *Journ. Wash. Acad. Sci.*, vol. 14, p. 183).

extinction angle of around 30° is distinctive and is obtained on sections giving a negative biaxial figure with a large 2V. In detrital grains kyanite may often be recognized by the step-like features caused by its good cleavage.

PARAGENESIS

Kyanite occurs typically as a mineral of regional metamorphism of pelitic or more rarely psammitic rocks. It is commonly used as a zonal mineral in pelitic assemblages, kyanite developing after staurolite and before sillimanite with increasing grade of metamorphism. Kyanite may be derived also from pyrophyllite, from the dehydration of paragonite with the addition of quartz, and from the inversion of andalusite in areas where a regional metamorphism is superimposed on a normal thermal metamorphism. It has also been recorded in thermal aureoles, together with staurolite, where it may be due to an element of shear during the emplacement of the igneous body. Kyanite, in addition to its occurrence in metamorphosed pelitic rocks, may be found in some eclogites and kyanite amphibolites. It has also been recorded in some 'pegmatitic veins', though these are more probably quartz–kyanite segregation veins, and it is fairly common as a detrital mineral in sedimentary rocks.

REFERENCES

HENRIQUES, Å. (1957) 'The alkali content of kyanite', *Arkiv. Min. Geol.*, vol. 2, p. 271.

MACKENZIE, W. S. (1949) 'Kyanite-gneiss within a thermal aureole', *Geol. Mag.*, vol. 86, p. 251.

TAYLOR, W. H. and JACKSON, W. W. (1928) 'The structure of cyanite Al_2SiO_5', *Proc. Roy. Soc. London*, A, vol. 119, p. 132.

Topaz

$Al_2[SiO_4](OH,F)_2$

ORTHORHOMBIC (+)

α 1·606–1·629
β 1·609–1·631
γ 1·616–1·638
δ 0·008–0·011
$2V_\gamma$ 48°–68°
$x = \alpha, y = \beta, z = \gamma$, O.A.P. (010).
Dispersion: $r > v$. D 3·49–3·57. H 8.
Cleavage: {001} perfect.
Colour: Variable—colourless, white, yellow, light shades of grey, green, red or blue; colourless in thin section.
Pleochroism: Coloured varieties may show pleochroism in thick sections, e.g. α yellow, γ pink.
Only slightly attacked by H_2SO_4.

STRUCTURE

Topaz has a unit cell† with a 4·650, b 8·800, c 8·394 Å, Z = 4. The structure consists of tetrahedral SiO_4 groups together with linked octahedral groups around aluminium (Fig. 15): four of the six anions around

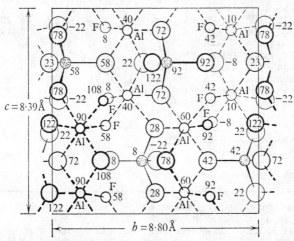

Fig. 15. *The structure of topaz. Superimposed oxygen atoms are displaced as also are fluorine atoms (after Bragg, W. L., 1937, Atomic Structure of Minerals, Cornell Univ. Press).*

† Morphological data refer to a cell with halved c dimension.

each Al are oxygens belonging to the SiO_4 groups, the others being fluorine or hydroxyl ions.

CHEMISTRY

The composition is fairly constant, the only major variation being in the ratio of fluorine to hydroxyl ions. Several analyses (e.g. Table 6, anal. 1) show a fluorine content close to the theoretical maximum of 20·7 per cent. The replacement of F by (OH), however, is limited and anal. 3 shows one of the highest (OH) values reported.

Topaz has been synthesized by the thermal hydrolysis of AlF_3 and SiO_2, topaz being formed between 750° and 850°C. It has also been produced by heating a mixture of Na_2SiF_6, amorphous Al_2O_3 and water to 500°C for 9 days with a pressure of 4000 bars. Topaz liberates fluorine on heating to

Table 6. TOPAZ ANALYSES

	1.	2.	3.		NUMBERS OF IONS ON THE BASIS OF 24 (O,OH,F) 1.	2.	3.
SiO_2	31·93	31·94	33·00	Si	3·905⎫4·00	3·922⎫4·00	4·037
Al_2O_3	56·26	55·80	56·76	Al	0·095⎭	0·078⎭	—
Fe_2O_3	—	0·32	tr.	Al	8·017	7·980⎫	8·186
FeO	—	0·07	—	Fe^{+3}	—	0·029	—
MgO	—	0·07	—	Fe^{+2}	—	0·007⎬8·04	—
CaO	—	0·13	—	Mg	—	0·014	—
F	20·37	17·24	13·23	Ca	—	0·014⎭	—
H_2O^+	0·19	1·57	2·67	F	7·884⎫8·04	6·688⎫7·97	5·122⎫7·30
H_2O^-	—	0·03	0·04	OH	0·156⎭	1·281⎭	2·178⎭
	108·75	107·18	105·70				
$O \equiv F$	8·58	7·27	5·57				
Total	100·17	99·91	100·13				
α	1·607₂	1·616	1·629				
β	1·610₄	1·618	1·631				
γ	1·617₆	1·625	1·638				
$2V_\gamma$	67°	61°	48°				
D	3·565	3·55	3·509				

1. Colourless topaz, rhyolite, Thomas Range, Utah (Penfield, S. L. & Minor, J. C., Jr., 1894, *Zeit. Krist.*, vol. 23, p. 321).
2. Colourless topaz, topaz–quartz rock, Belowda Beacon, Roche, Cornwall (Deer, W. A., Howie, R. A. & Zussman, J., 1962, *Rock-forming minerals*, vol. I, Longmans; includes TiO_2 0·01).
3. Fine-grained topaz in quartz vein, near granite, Chesterfield Co., South Carolina (Pardee, J. T.. Glass, J. J. & Stevens, R. E., 1937, *Amer. Min.*, vol. 22, p. 1058).

850–900°C and mullite is produced. Natural alteration products include fluorite, kaolinite, sericite and hydromuscovite.

OPTICAL AND PHYSICAL PROPERTIES

As the optic axial plane is parallel to (010) and the positive acute bisectrix is normal to (001), the plane of the cleavage, an interference figure is obtainable on cleavage flakes. The optic axial angle decreases with increasing replacement of F by (OH), as does the specific gravity, while the refractive indices increase with increasing (OH), see Fig. 16.

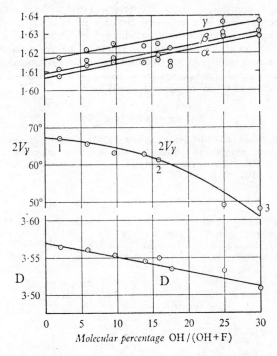

Fig. 16. *The variation in the refractive indices, optic axial angle and specific gravity of topaz.*

The colour of topaz is very variable, ranging from water-clear colourless crystals through yellow and delicate shades of wine-red, light blue and light green. The rose-coloured variety (Brazilian 'ruby') is rare but can be produced by careful heating of the yellow type. Microscopic cavities are sometimes found in topaz, usually filled with a liquid: one such liquid, brewsterlinite, has a refractive index of 1·13 and has been supposed to be liquid CO_2.

DISTINGUISHING FEATURES

The high relief, weak birefringence, positive optic sign, prismatic form and moderate 2V are characteristic of topaz. It differs from andalusite in having a smaller 2V and in having γ parallel to z.

PARAGENESIS

Topaz occurs chiefly in acid igneous rocks, such as granites, granite pegmatites and rhyolites, and is often found in veins and cavities in such rocks (Table 6, anals. 1, 3). It is usually associated with late-stage pneumatolytic action and is a common constituent of greisen. Associated minerals may include quartz (particularly in topaz–quartz rock or topazfels: e.g. anal. 2), fluorite, tourmaline, beryl, cassiterite, and muscovite or zinnwaldite. It may be found as a heavy mineral in detrital sediments near areas of acid intrusive rocks and is known also from emery deposits produced by the metamorphism of bauxite.

REFERENCES

PARDEE, J. T., GLASS, J. J. and STEVENS, R. E. (1937) 'Massive low-fluorine topaz from Brewer mine, South Carolina', *Amer. Min.*, vol. 22, p. 1058.
RUSSELL, A. (1924). 'Topaz from Cornwall, with an account of its localities', *Min. Mag.*, vol. 20, p. 221.

Staurolite

$(Fe^{+2},Mg)_2(Al,Fe^{+3})_9O_6[SiO_4]_4(O,OH)_2$

MONOCLINIC (pseudo-orthorhombic) $(+)$

α 1·739–1·747
β 1·745–1·753
γ 1·752–1·761
δ 0·012–0·014
$2V_\gamma$ 82°–90°
$\alpha = y,\ \beta = x,\ \gamma = z$, O.A.P. (100).
Dispersion: $r > v$, weak. D 3·74–3·83. H $7\frac{1}{2}$.
Cleavage: {010} moderate.
Twinning: {023}, {232} interpenetration, rarely seen in thin section.
Colour: Dark brown, reddish brown, yellow-brown; pale golden yellow in thin section.
Pleochroism: α colourless, β pale yellow, γ golden yellow.

STRUCTURE

The structure of staurolite is based on a unit cell, $a \simeq 7.9$, $b \simeq 16.7$, $c \simeq 5.6$ Å, $\beta \simeq 90.0°$, containing 48 oxygens in cubic close packing. The arrangement of $[AlO_6]$ and $[SiO_4]$ groups in chains parallel to the z axis is similar to the arrangement in kyanite, and the repeat distance d_{001} is similar in both minerals. The unit cell contains $Fe_4^{+2}(Al,Fe^{+3})_{18}Si_8\text{-}O_{46}(OH)_2$ and the structure consists of layers, parallel to (010), of $4Al_2SiO_5$ (kyanite arrangement) alternating with layers of composition $Al_2Fe_4O_8H_2$ (Fig. 17). Staurolite analyses invariably show that there are more than two hydroxyl ions in the unit cell; the electrostatic neutrality is maintained by balancing deficiencies in the number of Si and Fe^{+2} ions, which are less than the ideal 8 and 4 ions respectively.

CHEMISTRY

The composition of the common ferroan staurolites varies only within narrow limits and there is no significant variation in the replacement of Fe^{+2} by Mg. The analytical data do not fit precisely the simple formula $Fe(OH)_2 \cdot 2Al_2SiO_5$, nor the unit cell content of $H_2Fe_4^{+2}Al_{18}Si_8O_{48}$ as indicated by recent structure investigations. Calculations of staurolite analyses on the basis of 48 (O,OH) indicate that more than two oxygens in the unit cell are associated with hydrogen as hydroxyl ions. High values of (Al,Fe^{+3}) are generally associated with low values of (Fe^{+2},OH) and it is likely that (Fe^{+2},H^+) may be replaced by Al or Fe^{+3}. Rare zincian and cobaltoan staurolites are known in which Fe^{+2} is partially replaced by Zn or Co(Ni).

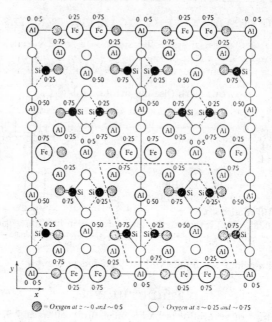

Fig. 17. *The structure of staurolite. Two unit cells are shown projected on (001); kyanite unit cell is outlined by dotted lines (after Náray-Szabó, I. & Sasvári, K., 1958, Acta Cryst., vol. 11, p. 862).*

Table 7. STAUROLITE ANALYSES

	1.	2.	NUMBERS OF IONS TO 48 (O, OH)	1.	2.
SiO_2	27·22	28·64	Si	7·539	8·043
TiO_2	0·56	0·56	Al	17·687⎫	16·602⎫
Al_2O_3	54·16	50·14	Ti	0·116⎬18·11	0·118⎬16·90
Fe_2O_3	1·47	0·84	Fe^{+3}	0·306⎭	0·179⎭
FeO	12·31	7·18	Mg	0·965⎫	1·439⎫
ZnO	—	7·44	Fe^{+2}	2·851⎬3·87	1·686⎬4·71
MnO	0·23	0·16	Zn	—⎪	1·542⎪
MgO	2·34	3·44	Mn	0·053⎭	0·039⎭
H_2O	1·98	1·92	OH	3·659	3·598
Total	100·27	100·32			

1. Staurolite, staurolite–mica schist (Juurinen, A., 1956, *Ann. Acad. Sci. Fennicae,* ser. A, III (Geol. Geogr.), no. 47).
2. Zincian staurolite, with chalcocite and quartz (Juurinen, A., 1956, Ibid).

OPTICAL AND PHYSICAL PROPERTIES

The optical properties of staurolite show only small variations and are affected as much by variation in Fe^{+2}/Fe^{+3} ratios as by the limited $Mg \rightarrow Fe^{+2}$ replacement. Commonly occurring in well formed porphyroblasts, the crystals are prismatic in habit and show six-sided basal sections with the forms {110} and {010}. Inclusions, particularly of quartz, are very common and the mineral often has a sponge-like appearance. The morphology, twinning and optical properties of staurolite show orthorhombic symmetry. Staurolite is slowly attacked by H_2SO_4, but is insoluble in cold HF.

DISTINGUISHING FEATURES

Staurolite can usually be distinguished by its colourless to golden yellow pleochroism, straight extinction, high refringence and moderate birefringence from other minerals having a yellow colour in thin section: vesuvianite is uniaxial and has a lower birefringence. Melanite garnet is isotropic, and iron-rich olivines have higher refringence, higher birefringence and negative optic sign.

PARAGENESIS

Staurolite is a common constituent of medium grade regionally metamorphosed argillaceous sediments. Although typically developed in rocks rich in alumina, staurolite occurs also in some metamorphosed grits and carbonate rocks. In its lower temperature stability range staurolite is often associated with chloritoid, the amount of staurolite increasing, and the amount of chloritoid decreasing in the rocks of higher metamorphic grade. Although there is usually little textural evidence of the direct formation of staurolite from chloritoid, it has been shown experimentally that chloritoid breaks down at a pressure of 10,000 bars above 675°C, to staurolite, almandine, hercynite and vapour.

During the progressive regional metamorphism of pelitic sediments staurolite generally develops before kyanite but the two minerals commonly occur together. With increasing metamorphic grade, however, staurolite is replaced by kyanite and almandine, or less commonly by sillimanite and almandine. It is replaced by sericite and chlorite under conditions of retrograde metamorphism. Staurolite is resistant to chemical weathering and is a common resistate mineral in clastic sediments.

REFERENCES

JUURINEN, A. (1956) 'Composition and properties of staurolite', *Ann. Acad. Sci. Fennicae*, ser. A, III (Geol. Geogr.), No. 47.

NÁRAY-SZABÓ, I. and SASVÁRI, K. (1958) 'On the structure of staurolite, $HFe_2-Al_9Si_4O_{24}$', *Acta Cryst.*, vol. 11, p. 862.

WILLIAMSON, D. H. (1953) 'Petrology of chloritoid and staurolite rocks north of Stonehaven, Kincardineshire', *Geol. Mag.*, vol. 90, p. 353.

Chloritoid $(Fe^{+2},Mg,Mn)_2(Al,Fe^{+3})Al_3O_2[SiO_4]_2(OH)_4$

MONOCLINIC, TRICLINIC $(+)$ or $(-)$

α 1·713–1·730
β 1·719–1·734
γ 1·723–1·740
δ 0·006–0·022
$2V_\gamma$ 45°–68°†
$\gamma : z$ 2°–30°
$\alpha = y$, O.A.P. $\perp$ (010) monoclinic polymorph
$\beta \simeq y$, O.A.P. $\simeq$ (010) triclinic polymorph
Dispersion: $r > v$, strong (anomalous interference colours). D 3·51–3·80. H 6½.

Cleavage: {001} perfect, planes of other cleavages uncertain but probably (hhl) moderate, (h0l) parting.

Twinning: {001} simple, lamellar: common.

Colour: Dark green, colourless to green in thin section.

Pleochroism: α pale grey-green to green, β slaty blue to indigo, γ colourless to pale yellow.

STRUCTURE

The chloritoid structure can be described in terms of two octahedral layers, one a brucite-type layer of composition $(Fe^{+2}Mg)_4Al_2O_4(OH)_8$, the other a corundum-type layer of composition Al_6O_{16} (Fig. 18). These sheets alternate in the direction perpendicular to the (001) plane and are linked by layers of $[SiO_4]$ tetrahedra, also parallel to the basal plane, and by hydrogen bonds. The silicon and oxygen atoms do not form a continuous sheet $[Si_2O_5]_\infty$ in composition as in the micas, but occur as individual $[SiO_4]$ tetrahedra, and the ideal structural formula may be expressed $(Fe^{+2},Mg)_2Al(OH)_4Al_3O_2[SiO_4]_2$, or to illustrate the linkage of the oxide and hydroxide layers by silicon atoms, as $(Al_3O_8)Si_2(Fe^{+2},Mg)_2AlO_2(OH)_4$. Compared with micas having comparable amounts of (Fe^{+2},Mg), this arrangement results in larger a and b cell dimensions.

The cell dimensions of the monoclinic polymorph of chloritoid are $a \simeq 9.5$, $b \simeq 5.5$, $c \simeq 18.2$ Å, $\beta \simeq 102°$, and there are four formula units per cell. The triclinic polymorph has the same a and b dimensions, and β and γ ($\simeq 90°$) angles; the c parameter, however, is approximately half

† The optic axial angles of most chloritoids fall within these values, but the full range of the optic axial angle about γ is from 36° to 125°

(9·16 Å) that of the monoclinic polymorph and the unit cell contains two formula units. The monoclinic cell can be related to the triclinic cell by twinning, either about a two-fold rotation axis, or a two-fold screw axis, parallel to the *b*-axis (Halferdahl, 1961). This relationship between the monoclinic and triclinic chloritoid structures accounts for the development, in some rocks, of parallel growths of the two polymorphs.

CHEMISTRY

The compositions of most chloritoids do not depart significantly from the empirical formula, $H_2(Fe^{+2},Mg)Al_2SiO_7$. The substitution of Fe^{+2} by Mg is very much limited in comparison with the wide range of this replacement

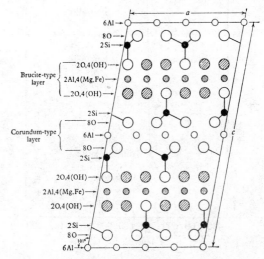

Fig. 18. *Chloritoid structure projected on* (010) *plane (after Brindley, G. W. & Harrison, F. W.,* 1952, Acta Cryst., *vol.* 5, *p.* 698).

in the iron–magnesium micas; in most chloritoids the replacement does not exceed 30 atomic per cent and the known limit is 42 per cent. Replacement of Fe^{+2} by Mn is present in some chloritoids (0–17 atomic per cent), and the manganese-rich variety is known as ottrelite. Substitution of Al by Fe^{+3} also occurs but is limited to 14 atomic per cent. Chloritoid dehydration curves show that the loss of water begins at approximately 400°C and is complete at 800°C. The dehydration is accompanied by the oxidation of $Fe^{+2} \rightarrow Fe^{+3}$ and the reaction may be expressed by the following equation:

$$4\{Fe_2^{+2}Al(OH)_4Al_3O_2[SiO_4]_2\} + 2O_2 \rightarrow 4\{Fe_2^{+3}AlO_3Al_3O_2[SiO_4]_2\} + 8H_2O$$

Chloritoid has been synthesized, from mixtures of kaolinite, γ-alumina and either siderite or ferrous oxalate, at about 10 kilobars and temperatures up to 675°C. Above 675°C and with pressure above 10 kilobars both synthetic and natural chloritoid break down to staurolite, almandine, hercynite and vapour. At pressures below approximately 7 kilobars and temperatures below 675°C the breakdown products are iron-cordierite, hercynite and vapour (Fig. 19).

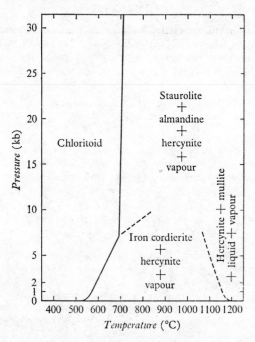

Fig. 19. *Univariant curves for the reactions chloritoid⇌iron cordierite + hercynite + vapour, chloritoid ⇌ almandine + staurolite + hercynite + vapour, staurolite + almandine⇌iron cordierite + hercynite + vapour, and iron cordierite⇌mullite + liquid (after Halferdahl, L. B., 1961, Journ. Petr., vol. 2, p. 49).*

OPTICAL AND PHYSICAL PROPERTIES

The optical orientation of chloritoid is very variable; in some cases the orientation differs even in grains from the same rock. In most chloritoids, however, γ is the acute bisectrix and the majority are therefore optically positive. Likewise α is the commonest vibration direction to lie in the (001) plane, and in the monoclinic polymorphs α is almost always parallel to y and the optical axial plane $\perp$(010); exceptionally $\beta = y$, and the optic axial plane parallel to (010). In most triclinic polymorphs β is closer to (001) than α, but the orientation of α and β with respect to the x and y crystal axes in triclinic chloritoid usually cannot be determined because it is not possible to identify crystallographic directions other than the (001) plane. In addition the dispersion is so high in chloritoid that in most orientations the crystals do not extinguish between crossed nicols unless viewed in monochromatic light.

The substitution of Fe by Mg results in a small decrease in refractive indices but their correlation with the atomic ratio Mg : $(Fe^{+2} + Fe^{+3} + Mn + Mg)$ is not sufficiently precise to be of determinative value. Repeated twinning, in which the composition plane is parallel to the (001) cleavage, is common. Many chloritoids also show a well developed hour-glass structure which is visible either because inclusions are concentrated within the hour-glass or because it has a colour difference from the rest of the crystal.

DISTINGUISHING FEATURES

The chloritoid-pleochroic scheme, high relief, common lamellar twinning, and strong dispersion are usually sufficiently diagnostic for its identification. Varieties with low birefringence and anomalous interference colours can be distinguished from chlorites by higher refractive indices. Clintonite has a smaller optic axial angle and negative sign, green biotites and stilpno-melanes have a higher birefringence and single cleavage.

PARAGENESIS

Chloritoid is a relatively common constituent of aluminium- and ferric iron-rich regionally metamorphosed pelitic sediments. In these rocks chloritoid often first develops as small porphyroblasts in the biotite zone, reaches its maximum development in the garnet zone, then rapidly diminishes in amount in the staurolite zone, and is absent in higher grade rocks. In such regionally metamorphosed rocks the chloritoid crystals are commonly randomly oriented indicating that the shearing stress has had no general effect on the orientation of the chloritoid crystals.

Chloritoid also forms in non-stress environments, e.g. in quartz and quartz–carbonate veins, and in sericitized and ankeritized lavas. Although the stability fields of the two polymorphs of chloritoid are unknown it appears likely that the monoclinic form develops during conditions of greater stress and temperature, and the triclinic forms in an environment in which stress is not an important factor.

REFERENCES

HALFERDAHL, L. B. (1961) 'Chloritoid: Its composition, X-ray and optical properties, stability and occurrence', *Journ. Petr.*, vol. 2, p. 49.

HARRISON, F. W. and BRINDLEY, G. W. (1957) 'The crystal structure of chloritoid', *Acta. Cryst.*, vol. 10, p. 77.

Datolite

CaB[SiO$_4$](OH)

MONOCLINIC (−)

α 1·622–1·626
β 1·649–1·654
γ 1·666–1·670
δ 0·044–0·046
2V$_\alpha$ 72°–75°
$\gamma : z = 1°–4°$, O.A.P. (010).
Dispersion: $r > v$, weak. D 2·96–3·00. H 5–5$\frac{1}{2}$.
Cleavage: None.
Twinning: None.
Colour: Generally colourless or white, may be tinted in pale shades of yellow, green or pink; colourless in thin section.

Insoluble in HCl, but may gelatinize. Gives intense yellowish green colour to a flame, particularly if moistened with H$_2$SO$_4$.

Datolite is an orthosilicate, with a 4·84, b 7·60, c 9·62 Å, β 90° 09′, Z = 4. Its structure consists of superimposed complex sheets of linked oxygen and O,OH tetrahedra around silicon and boron atoms respectively: the SiO$_4$ and B(O,OH)$_4$ tetrahedra alternate forming rings of four and eight tetrahedra. Chemically it shows little variation from the ideal formula. The optical properties also are relatively constant. Datolite crystals have a characteristic glassy appearance: the moderately high birefringence distinguishes it from danburite and topaz, and the greenish coloration in a flame test is diagnostic of boron.

Datolite most commonly occurs in cavities and veins in hypabyssal and volcanic basic igneous rocks. It is almost always a secondary mineral and may be associated with calcite, prehnite, zeolites and axinite. It is also known from skarns at limestone–granite or limestone–dolerite contacts and has been reported from serpentinite and hornblende schist.

Sapphirine $(Mg,Fe)_2Al_4O_6[SiO_4]$

MONOCLINIC $(-)(+)$

α 1·701–1·725
β 1·703–1·728
γ 1·705–1·732
δ 0·005–0·007
$2V_\alpha$ 50°–114°
$\gamma : z$ 6°–9°, $\beta = y$, O.A.P. (010).
Dispersion: $r < v$, strong. D 3·40–3·58. H 7½.
Cleavage: {010}, {001}, {100} poor.
Twinning: {010}, {100} repeated, uncommon.
Colour: Light blue or green; colourless, blue or pinkish orange in thin section.
Pleochroism: α colourless, pale reddish, yellowish green, pale yellow; β sky-blue, lavender-blue, bluish green, pale lime-green; γ blue, sapphire-blue, dark blue, pale pinkish orange.

Details of the sapphirine structure (cell parameters a 9·77, b 14·54, c 10·06 Å, β 100° 20'; $Z = 8$) are not known, and there is some uncertainty as to the most appropriate formula. The majority of analyses of sapphirine contain less Si and more Al than is shown in the formula above, and the average content, on the basis of 80 oxygens per unit cell, is Si 7·0, Al 34·0. The number of divalent cations is commonly less than that of the ideal cell content and it is possible that some $Al,Al \rightleftharpoons Mg,Si$ type replacement occurs; the maximum substitution of Mg by Fe^{+2} is approximately 20 per cent. Pure magnesium sapphirine has been synthesized by sintering appropriate oxide mixtures at 1450°C.

Sapphirine is distinguished from corundum by its biaxial character and lower refractive indices, from cordierite by higher refractive indices, from kyanite by poorer cleavages and lower birefringence, and from sodium-rich amphiboles and zoisite by poorer cleavage.

Sapphirine is a comparatively rare mineral, and occurs characteristically in high grade, aluminium-rich, silicon-poor, regional and contact metamorphic rocks. At Cortland, New York, sapphirine occurs in emery deposits where they are cut by quartz veins; it has been formed by reaction between a spinel and silica. Common associates of sapphirine are spinel, cordierite, corundum, orthopyroxene, sillimanite, biotite, calcium plagioclase, potassium feldspar, anthophyllite and kornerupine.

REFERENCE

KEITH, M. and SCHAIRER, J. F. (1952). 'The stability field of sapphirine in the system $MgO–Al_2O_3–SiO_2$', *Journ. Geol.*, vol. 60, p. 181.

58

Larnite

Ca$_2$[SiO$_4$]

MONOCLINIC ($+$)

α 1·707
β 1·715
γ 1·730
δ 0·023
2V$_\gamma$ moderate
α:z = 13°–14°
D 3·28.

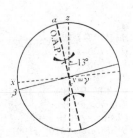

Cleavage: {100}, distinct.
Twinning: Lamellar twinning on {100}, common.
Colour: White; colourless in thin section.

Larnite is distinguished from rankinite by its higher birefringence and lamellar twinning; it usually has higher birefringence than merwinite; spurrite is optically negative.

Larnite occurs at dolerite–limestone contacts as at Scawt Hill, near Larne, Northern Ireland, and at Ardnamurchan: it is also known from metamorphosed calcitic amygdales in a volcanic plug in Mull. (Bredigite is the high-temperature, orthorhombic, pseudo-hexagonal polymorph of Ca$_2$SiO$_4$.)

Merwinite

Ca$_3$Mg[Si$_2$O$_8$]

MONOCLINIC ($+$)

α 1·702–1·710
β 1·710–1·718
γ 1·718–1·726
δ 0·008–0·023
2V$_\gamma$ 52°–76°
γ = y; α:z = 36°
Dispersion: r > v, weak. D 3·15–3·31. H 6.
Cleavage: {010}, perfect.
Twinning: lamellar twinning common, twin axis z, composition plane {110}; also twins on {100}.
Colour: White; colourless in thin section.

Merwinite is distinguished from tilleyite and spurrite by its lower birefringence, from larnite by its lower refractive indices and usually by its lower birefringence, and from rankinite by its lamellar twinning and larger extinction angle.

Merwinite occurs at gabbro–limestone contacts as at Crestmore, California, and the Little Belt Mountains, Montana.

Spurrite

$2Ca_2[SiO_4] \cdot CaCO_3$

MONOCLINIC (−)

α 1·637–1·641
β 1·672–1·676
γ 1·676–1·681
δ 0·039–0·040
$2V_\alpha$ 35°–41°
$\gamma:x \simeq 0°$, $\alpha = y$, $\beta:z = 33°$.
Dispersion: $r > v$, weak. D 3·01. H 5.
Cleavage: {001}, distinct; {001} poor.
Twinning: Lamellar twinning on {001}.
Colour: White; colourless in thin section.

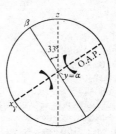

The structure of spurrite consists of isolated SiO_4 tetrahedra and CO_3 triangles, linked together by Ca atoms.

It may be distinguished from merwinite, rankinite and larnite by being optically negative with a much smaller 2V.

Spurrite occurs at gabbro–limestone contacts as on the island of Muck, Inner Hebrides, and at Scawt Hill, Northern Ireland. It is also found in northern Coahuila, Mexico, where rhyolite plugs have solidified within limestone.

Eudialyte (Eucolite)

$(Na,Ca,Fe)_6Zr[(Si_3O_9)_2](OH,F,Cl)$

TRIGONAL (+) (−)

ω 1·593–1·643
ϵ 1·597–1·634
δ 0·000–0·010

D 2·8–3·1. H 5–6.
Cleavage: {0001} good, {11$\bar{2}$0} poor.
Colour: Pink, carmine, reddish brown, red, yellow; usually colourless in thin section. Thick sections are pleochroic with ω colourless to yellow, ϵ pink. Absorption $\omega < \epsilon$ is independent of the optic sign.

Gelatinizes with HCl.

Eudialyte is optically positive, eucolite optically negative. Both varieties may occur in zoned crystals, the intermediate zone of which is isotropic.

It is distinguished from catapleite, lavenite and rosenbuschite by much lower birefringence and from the two latter minerals by lower refringence. Anomalously birefringent garnets have higher refringence.

It occurs chiefly as a late crystallizing primary mineral in nepheline pegmatites and nepheline-syenites, particularly in foyaite. Commonly associated with other zirconium-rich minerals, catapleiite, låvenite, rosenbuschite, and with astrophyllite.

Rosenbuschite $(Ca,Na,Mn)_3(Zr,Ti,Fe^{+3})[SiO_4]_2(F,OH)$

TRICLINIC (+)

α 1·678–1·680
β 1·687–1·688
γ 1·705–1·708
δ 0·027–0·028
$2V_\gamma$ 68°–78°, $\alpha \simeq z$, $\gamma : \perp (100)$ 28°
Dispersion: $r > v$, weak.
D 3·31–3·38. H 5–6.
Cleavage: {100} perfect, {1$\bar{2}$0}, {010} poor.
Colour: Pale orange, grey; colourless or very pale yellow in thin section.
Pleochroism: α colourless, very pale yellow; β very pale yellow; γ pale yellow.
   Soluble in HCl.

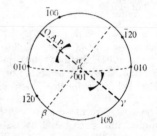

It is distinguished from låvenite by lower refractive indices and optically positive character and commonly also by its characteristic occurrence in close packed parallel or divergent fibres and needles.

   Rosenbuschite occurs as an accessory mineral in nepheline-syenite, but is a more frequent constituent of nepheline-syenite pegmatites. It also occurs as an essential constituent of the lakarpite (arfvedsonite–albite–nepheline-syenite) and pulaskite of the Norra Kärr complex, Sweden.

EPIDOTE GROUP

Members of the epidote group crystallize in both the orthorhombic and monoclinic systems. All members have a structure consisting of chains of AlO_6 and $AlO_4(OH)_2$ octahedra linked by independent SiO_4 and Si_2O_7 groups. Zoisite, the orthorhombic member, shows only minor replacement of Al by Fe^{+3}, but a wide range of substitutions is present in the monoclinic members. The group formula is:

$$X_2Y_3Z_3(O,OH,F)_{13}$$

in which $X = Ca, Ce^{+3}, La^{+3}, Y^{+3}$, Th, $Fe^{+2}, Mn^{+2}, Mn^{+3}$; $Y = Al, Fe^{+3}, Mn^{+3}, Fe^{+2}, Mn^{+2}$, Ti, and $Z = Si$. The main features of the composition of the members of the series are expressed by the following formulae:

Zoisite
Clinozoisite} $Ca_2Al \cdot Al_2O \cdot OH \cdot Si_2O_7 \cdot SiO_4$

Epidote $Ca_2Fe^{+3}Al_2O \cdot OH \cdot Si_2O_7 \cdot SiO_4$

Piemontite $Ca_2(Mn^{+3}, Fe^{+3}, Al)_3O \cdot OH \cdot Si_2O_7 \cdot SiO_4$

Allanite $(Ca, Mn^{+2}, Ce)_2(Fe^{+2}, Fe^{+3}, Al)_3O \cdot OH \cdot Si_2O_7 \cdot SiO_4$

Zoisite $Ca_2Al \cdot Al_2O \cdot OH[Si_2O_7][SiO_4]$

ORTHORHOMBIC (+)

α 1·685–1·705
β 1·688–1·710
γ 1·697–1·725
δ 0·004–0·008
$2V_\gamma$ 0°–60°

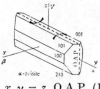 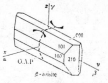

α-zoisite $\alpha = y$, $\beta = x$, $\gamma = z$, O.A.P. (100).
β-zoisite $\alpha = x$, $\beta = y$, $\gamma = z$, O.A.P. (010).

Dispersion: $r > v$ (α-zoisite), $r < v$ (β-zoisite).   D 3·15–3·27.   H 6.

Cleavage: {100} perfect, {001} imperfect.

Twinning: None.

Colour: Grey, green, brown (thulite, pink); colourless in thin section (thulite, pink-yellow).

Pleochroism: (Thulite) α pale pink (rose), dark pink; β nearly colourless, bright pink; γ pale yellow, yellow.

The zoisite cell parameters, b 5·45, c 10·13 Å, are approximately equal to b and c ($b \simeq 5·6$, $c \simeq 10·20$ Å) for epidote, and the zoisite a parameter, 16·19 Å, is approximately equal to $2a \sin \beta$ (16·20 Å) for epidote. This relationship is comparable with that between the ortho- and clino-pyroxenes and between the orthorhombic and monoclinic amphiboles, and zoisite can be regarded as consisting of a 'twinned' epidote structure. There is little variation in the chemical composition and the maximum occupation of octahedral positions by Fe^{+3} is 3 per cent; in the pink manganese-bearing variety, thulite, the replacement of Ca by Mn^{+2} does not exceed 2 per cent. In contrast, the optical properties show considerable variation and the optic axial plane in some zoisites (α-zoisite) is parallel to (100), and in others (β-zoisite) it is parallel to (010). Anomalous blue interference colours are displayed by some specimens.

Zoisite is distinguished from clinozoisite by parallel extinction, from epidote by lack of colour (except thulite) and weaker birefringence, from vesuvianite by biaxial character, positive sign and perfect cleavage, from sillimanite by weaker birefringence, and from apatite by biaxial character and positive sign.

Zoisite is a typical constituent of medium grade regionally meta-morphosed rocks of marly composition and in such granulites and schists it is usually associated with garnet, sodic plagioclase, biotite and hornblende. It is an occasional thermal metamorphic product in impure limestones, and occurs in some hornblende-bearing eclogites. Zoisite is a common product, together with sodium-rich plagioclase, sericite and calcite, of the hydro-thermal alteration (saussuritization) of calcic plagioclase.

REFERENCE

KENNEDY, W. Q. (1949) 'Zones of progressive regional metamorphism in the Moine Schists of the Western Highlands of Scotland', *Geol. Mag.*, vol. 86, p. 43.

Clinozoisite	Epidote	Piemontite
Ca₂Al·Al₂O·	CaFe⁺³Al₂O·	Ca₂(Mn,Fe⁺³,Al)₂AlO·

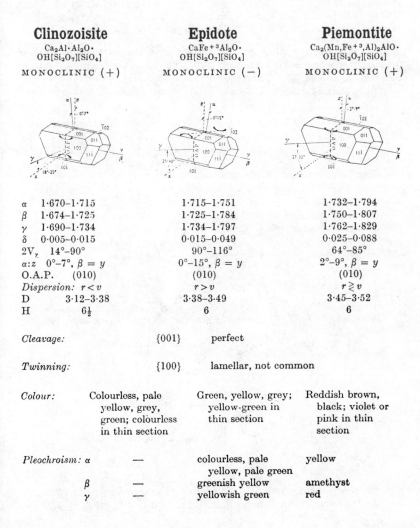

	Clinozoisite	Epidote	Piemontite
α	1·670–1·715	1·715–1·751	1·732–1·794
β	1·674–1·725	1·725–1·784	1·750–1·807
γ	1·690–1·734	1·734–1·797	1·762–1·829
δ	0·005–0·015	0·015–0·049	0·025–0·088
$2V_\gamma$	14°–90°	90°–116°	64°–85°
$\alpha{:}z$	0°–7°, $\beta = y$	0°–15°, $\beta = y$	2°–9°, $\beta = y$
O.A.P.	(010)	(010)	(010)
Dispersion:	$r < v$	$r > v$	$r \gtrless v$
D	3·12–3·38	3·38–3·49	3·45–3·52
H	6½	6	6

Cleavage:	{001}	perfect
Twinning:	{100}	lamellar, not common

Colour:	Colourless, pale yellow, grey, green; colourless in thin section	Green, yellow, grey; yellow-green in thin section	Reddish brown, black; violet or pink in thin section
Pleochroism: α	—	colourless, pale yellow, pale green	yellow
β	—	greenish yellow	amethyst
γ	—	yellowish green	red

STRUCTURE

The structure (unit cell $a \simeq 8\cdot9$, $b \simeq 5\cdot6$, $c \simeq 10\cdot3$ Å, $\beta \simeq 115°\ 30'$; $Z = 2$) consists of continuous chains of AlO_6 and $AlO_4(OH)_2$ octahedra parallel to the y axis, which are bridged by single $[SiO_4]$ and double $[Si_2O_7]$ tetrahedral groups (Fig. 20). Iron atoms and/or further aluminiums in octahedral coordination outside the chains, and calcium ions, the latter surrounded irregularly by eight oxygens, complete the framework.

CHEMISTRY

The replacement of Al by Fe^{+3} in the clinozoisite–epidote minerals does not significantly exceed one atom per formula unit, i.e. their compositions lie between $Ca_2Al_3Si_3O_{12}(OH)$ and $Ca_2Fe^{+3}Al_2Si_3O_{12}(OH)$. A wider range is exhibited by the manganese epidotes and their compositions fall within the field

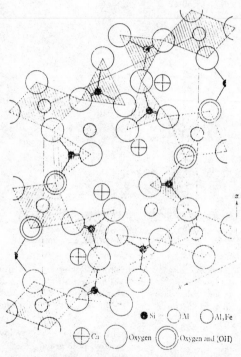

Fig. 20. *Schematic diagram of epidote structure projected on (010) (after Ito, J., Morimoto, N. & Sadanaga, R., 1954, Acta Cryst., vol. 7, p. 53).*

$Ca_2Fe^{+3}Al_2Si_3O_{12}(OH)$–$Ca_2Mn^{+3}Al_2Si_3O_{12}(OH)$–$Ca_2Mn_2^{+3}AlSi_3O_{12}(OH)$. Rare compositional varieties include the lead and strontium-rich hancockite, approximate composition $(Ca_{1.1}Mn_{0.2}Sr_{0.2}Pb_{0.5})Fe^{+3}Al_2Si_3O_{12}$ (OH), and the chrome-bearing tawmawite which contains 6·8 weight per cent Cr_2O_3 (equivalent to 0·4 Cr atoms per formula unit).

Table 8. EPIDOTE GROUP ANALYSES

	1.	2.	3.	4.	5.
SiO_2	39·16	39·08	36·92	36·63	30·32
TiO_2	0·001	—	tr.	0·21	0·04
ThO_2	—	—	—	—	1·70
Al_2O_3	33·50	30·96	22·25	17·21	15·89
Fe_2O_3	1·75	4·13	15·21	6·85	3·77
Mn_2O_3	—	—	—	17·78	—
Y_2O_3	—	—	—	—	1·85
Ce_2O_3	—	—	—	—	7·44
La_2O_3	—	—	—	—	14·74
FeO	0·00	0·42	0·57	—	10·81
MnO	0·014	0·01	0·75	—	6·06
MgO	0·00	0·01	tr.	0·85	0·32
CaO	25·02	23·32	23·11	18·98	4·28
H_2O^+	0·57	1·86	1·16	1·75	2·13
H_2O^-	0·06	0·01	0·16	—	0·24
Total	100·40	99·80	100·13	100·26	99·59
α	1·700	1·710	1·727	1·772‡	—
β	1·700	1·712	1·755	1·813	—
γ	1·705	1·716	1·768	1·860	--
δ	0·005	0·006	0·041	0·088	—
$2V_\gamma$	25°	14°–20°	—	79°	—
$\alpha:z$	—	50°–60°	—	9°	—
D	3·364	3·37	3·43	—	3·943

NUMBERS OF IONS ON THE BASIS OF 13 (O,OH)

ion	1.	2.	3.	4.	5.
Si	3·018	3·002	2·998	2·986	2·943
Al	—	—	0·002	0·014	0·057
(Σ)	*}3·02*	*}3·00*	*}3·00*	*}3·00*	*}3·00*
Al	3·044	2·804	2·128	1·640	1·762
Fe^{+3}	0·102	0·238	0·929	0·420	0·275
Mn^{+3}	—	—	—	0·927	—
(Σ)	*}3·17†*	*}3·04*	*}3·06*	*}2·99*	*}2·04*
Mn^{+3}	—	—	—	0·175	—
Mg	—	0·001	—	0·103	0·046
Ti	—	—	—	0·013	0·003
Fe^{+2}	—	0·026	0·039	—	0·878
Mn^{+2}	0·001	—	0·052	—	0·498
Y^{+3}	—	—	—	—	0·096
Ca	2·066	1·920	2·011	1·658	0·445
Th^{+4}	—	—	—	—	0·037
Ce^{+3}	—	—	—	—	0·265
La^{+3}	—	—	—	—	0·528
(Σ)	*}2·07*	*}1·95*	*}2·10*	*}1·95*	*}0·93 / }1·87*
OH	0·293	0·952	0·628	0·950	1·380

1. Zoisite, amphibolite, Tanganyika (Game, P. M., 1954, *Min. Mag.*, vol. 30, p. 458; includes Cr_2O_3 0·33).

† Includes Cr 0·020.
‡ Newly determined by R. G. J. Strens.

3 + I.R.F.M.

2. Clinozoisite, vein in amphibolite, Eire (Johnston, R. W., 1949, *Min. Mag.*, vol. 28, p. 505).

3. Epidote, vein in pegmatite, Japan (Yokoyama, K., 1957, *Sci. Rep. Tohoku Univ.*, 3rd Ser., vol. 5, p. 373).

4. Piemontite, pegmatite, India (Bilgrami, S. A., 1956, *Min. Mag.*, vol. 31, p. 236).

5. Allanite, pegmatite, Japan (Hasegawa, S., 1957, *Sci. Rep. Tohoku Univ.*, 3rd Ser., vol. 5, p. 345).

OPTICAL AND PHYSICAL PROPERTIES

The variation of the refractive indices of the clinozoisite–epidote minerals shows a relatively good correlation with the replacement of Al by Fe^{+3} in

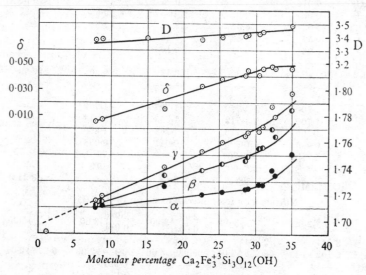

Fig. 21. *Variation of the refractive indices, birefringence and density with Fe^{+3} content in the clinozoisite–epidote minerals.*

the range 7 to 30 mol. per cent $Ca_2Fe^{+3}Al_2Si_3O_{12}(OH)$ (Fig. 21). In the manganese-rich members there is a similar fair correlation for compositions in which the replacement of Al by (Mn^{+3},Fe^{+3}) does not exceed one atom per formula unit, but piemontites with higher (Mn^{+3},Fe^{+3}) contents show considerably lower refractive indices than those extrapolated from the data of epidotes less rich in (Mn^{+3},Fe^{+3}). It is possible that this break in the linearity of the variation is related to the replacement of Al in the AlO_6 and $AlO_4(OH)_2$ chains, in addition to the replacement of the Al outside these structural units. Replacement of Al by Fe^{+3} is accompanied by an increase in the optic axial angle but this optical property is particularly sensitive to changes in composition in the iron-poor members of the series, and it cannot be used as a precise indication of the magnitude of the Al $\rightleftharpoons$ Fe^{+3} substitution. Colour and pleochroism are closely related to the replacements Al $\rightleftharpoons$ Fe^{+3} and Al $\rightleftharpoons$ Mn^{+3}; in particular the characteristic pleochroism of piemontite is exhibited by minerals containing quite small amounts of Mn^{+3} (e.g. 0·06 Mn^{+3} atoms per formula unit). Clinozoisite may show anomalous interference colours.

DISTINGUISHING FEATURES

The name clinozoisite is used for positive monoclinic (Fe^{+3},Al) members of the series; they may also be distinguished from epidote by their lower birefringence and lack of pleochroism. Clinozoisite is distinguished from zoisite by its oblique extinction in prism zone sections; it differs from melilite and vesuvianite in its biaxial character. Epidote is distinguished from hornblende by its greater refringence and birefringence, single good cleavage and characteristic greenish yellow to yellowish green pleochroism, and from clinopyroxene by its single cleavage, negative optic sign and pleochroism. Piemontite is distinguished by its distinctive pleochroic scheme. The epidote minerals are generally characterized by well-developed striations parallel to y.

PARAGENESIS

Epidote minerals occur principally in regionally metamorphosed rocks, and their formation, which marks the threshold of the change from the greenschist to the epidote–amphibolite facies, may be represented by the reaction:

$$3(OH)_8(Mg,Fe)_5Al_2Si_3O_{10} + 10CaCO_3 + 21SiO_2 \rightleftharpoons$$
chlorite

$$2Ca_2Al_3Si_3O_{12}(OH) + 3Ca_2(Mg,Fe)_5Si_8O_{22}(OH)_2 + 10CO_2 + 8H_2O$$
clinozoisite   actinolite

Epidote is produced during the retrograde readjustments associated with dynamic metamorphism, particularly of the basic igneous rocks. Although the formation of epidote is favoured by shearing stress and low temperature it also crystallizes in the absence of stress, e.g. as a product of the hydrothermal alteration (saussuritization) of plagioclase feldspar, along joints and fissures, and in amygdales and vugs. The formation of piemontite is similar to, but less common than, that of the clinozoisite–epidote minerals. Its crystallization takes place at a lower grade and it occurs in rocks belonging to the glaucophane schist and greenschist facies. The most manganese-rich piemontites are associated with manganese deposits and are of metasomatic origin.

REFERENCES

ITO, J., MORIMOTO, N. and SADANAGA, R. (1954) 'On the structure of epidote', *Acta Cryst.*, vol. 7, p. 53.

MIYASHIRO, A. and SEKI, Y. (1958) 'Enlargement of the composition field of epidote and piemontite with rising temperature', *Amer. Journ. Sci.*, vol. 256, p. 422.

Allanite $\qquad$ $(Ca,Ce)_2(Fe^{+2},Fe^{+3})Al_2O \cdot OH[Si_2O_7][SiO_4]$

MONOCLINIC $(-)(+)$

α 1·690–1·791
β 1·700–1·815
γ 1·706–1·828†
δ 0·013–0·036
$2V_\alpha$ 40°–123°
$\alpha:z$ 1°–42°
$\beta = y$, O.A.P. (010).
Dispersion: $r > v$. D 3·4–4·2.‡ H 5–6½.
Cleavage: {001} imperfect, {100}, {110} poor.
Twinning: {100} not common, {001} rare.
Colour: Light brown to black, brownish; yellow or brown in thin section.
Pleochroism: α reddish brown, light brown; β brownish yellow, brown; γ greenish brown, very dark red brown.

Allanite (the name orthite is sometimes used as a synonym) is the only member of the epidote group in which Fe^{+2} is an essential component. The ferrous iron replaces Al and there is a balancing substitution of Ca by trivalent Ce or other rare earth ions, particularly La and Y. The unit cell, a 8·98, b 5·75, c 10·23 Å, β 115° 00′, is a little larger than for the clinozoisite-epidote series. Radioactive components are usually present in allanite and range from 0·35 to 2·23 weight per cent ThO_2, and from 30 to 650 p.p.m. of U. Allanite occurs commonly in the metamict state due to the partial destruction of its crystalline structure by alpha particle bombardment from the disintegration of the radioactive components in the mineral.

The replacement of Al by Fe^{+2}, and that of Ca by rare earth ions are accompanied by an increase in refractive indices. The degree of metamictization is also an important influence on both birefringence and refringence and the latter value for some isotropic varieties is as low as 1·54. The wide density range shown by allanite can also be correlated with the degree of metamictization and alteration, the low density minerals having high water contents. The alteration and hydration of allanite is accompanied by expansion, and the mineral is commonly surrounded by anastomosing cracks which radiate into the adjacent minerals.

Non-metamict varieties are distinguished from other epidote minerals by their brownish colour and from the metamict varieties by the latter's isotropic character and the presence of anastomosing cracks. Non-metamict allanite is distinguished from brown amphiboles by the single cleavage and

† Some metamict allanites are isotropic with n 1·54 to 1·72.
‡ Density of metamict allanites may be as low as 2·8 g/cm³.

straight extinction in sections parallel to the elongation. Isotropic varieties are distinguished from melanite garnet by lower refractive index.

Allanite is a characteristic accessory mineral in many granites, granodiorites, monzonites and syenites; it occurs in larger amounts in some limestone skarns and in pegmatites.

Lawsonite

$CaAl_2(OH)_2[Si_2O_7]H_2O$

ORTHORHOMBIC (+)

α 1·665
β 1·674
γ 1·685
δ 0·020
$2V_\gamma$ 76°--87°
$\gamma = y$, O.A.P. (100).
Dispersion: $r > v$, very strong. D 3·05--3·12. H 6.
Cleavage: {100}, {010} perfect, {101} imperfect.
Twinning: {101} single, lamellar; common.
Colour: Colourless, white, bluish; colourless to bluish green in thin section.
Pleochroism: α blue, pale brownish yellow; β yellowish green, deep bluish green; γ colourless, yellowish.

The structure of lawsonite ($a \simeq 8\cdot8$, $b \simeq 13\cdot2$, $c \simeq 5\cdot8$ Å, Z = 4) consists of chains parallel to the z axis, of $AlO_4(OH)_2$ octahedral groups, each of which shares an edge with two neighbouring groups, as in the Al_2SiO_5 minerals (cf. sillimanite c 5·75 Å; lawsonite $c \simeq 5\cdot8$ Å). The chains of octahedral $Al(O,OH)_6$ are linked by Si_2O_7 groups; Ca atoms and H_2O molecules occupy holes and not channels in the structure. Only minor replacements occur and the composition of lawsonite does not depart appreciably from that of the ideal formula $H_4CaAl_2Si_2O_{10}$. Lawsonite is converted to hexagonal $CaAl_2Si_2O_8$ on heating at 650°C and to anorthite at higher temperatures.

The optical properties show little variation, and lawsonite is distinguished from zoisite by its stronger birefringence, two perfect cleavages, the common presence of twinning and the absence of anomalous interference colours; from prehnite by its lower birefringence, higher refringence and better cleavage; from scapolite by its biaxial character and from andalusite by its higher birefringence, refringence and positive optic sign.

Lawsonite is restricted to low-temperature metamorphic parageneses and is most commonly present in glaucophane-bearing schists. Common associates are chlorite, albite, pumpellyite and glaucophane.

REFERENCE

DAVIS, G. A. and PABST, A. (1960) 'Lawsonite and pumpellyite in glaucophane schist, North Berkeley Hills, California', *Amer. Journ. Sci.*, vol. 258, p. 689.

Pumpellyite $Ca_4(Mg,Fe^{+2})(Al,Fe^{+3})_5O(OH)_3[Si_2O_7]_2[SiO_4]_2.2H_2O$

MONOCLINIC (+)

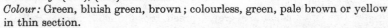

α 1·674–1·702
β 1·675–1·715
γ 1·688–1·722
δ 0·012–0·022
$2V_\gamma$ 26°–85°
$\alpha:x$ 4°–32°
$\beta = y$, O.A.P. (010).
Dispersion: r < v.   D 3·18–3·23.   H 6.
Cleavage: {001}, {100} moderate.
Twinning: {001}, {100} common.
Colour: Green, bluish green, brown; colourless, green, pale brown or yellow in thin section.
Pleochroism: α colourless, pale yellowish brown, pale greenish yellow; β bluish green, pale green, brownish yellow; γ colourless, pale yellowish brown, brownish yellow.

The structure of pumpellyite (unit cell a 8·81, b 5·94, c 19·14 Å, β 97·6°, Z = 2) has not been determined, but in view of its crystallographic similarities with epidote and lawsonite and their comparable a and b cell dimensions it is probable that the pumpellyite structure contains $Al(O,OH)_6$ octahedral and Si_2O_7 and SiO_4 tetrahedral groups. Calculations of pumpellyite analyses, on the basis of 28 (O,OH,H_2O), are not at variance with the presence of such structural units, and are compatible with the formula given above. Small replacements of Ca by Na, (Mg,Fe^{+2}) by Mn, and (Al,Fe^{+3}) by Ti are commonly present in pumpellyite. The optical properties of pumpellyite show considerable variation, and higher refractive indices, optic axial angles and birefringences, and stronger green, brown or yellow absorption colours are related to higher total iron contents (i.e. $Mg \rightleftharpoons Fe^{+2}$, and $Al \rightleftharpoons Fe^{+3}$ replacements).

Weakly coloured varieties are difficult to distinguish from clinozoisite, but such pumpellyites have lower refractive indices and high birefringence. The more iron-rich varieties are distinguished from epidote by their characteristic blue-green β absorption colour and positive sign. Pumpellyite is distinguished from zoisite by inclined extinction in (010) sections, from lawsonite by higher refractive indices, poorer cleavage and weaker pleochroism, and from penninite by higher refringence and birefringence.

Pumpellyite occurs principally in low-grade regionally metamorphosed schists, and is characteristically developed in rocks of the glaucophane schist facies. Its common mineral associates are albite, clinozoisite, epidote, chlorite, lawsonite, glaucophane, actinolite, prehnite and calcite.

MELILITE GROUP

Gehlenite	**Melilite**	**Åkermanite**
$Ca_2[Al_2SiO_7]$	$(Ca,Na)_2[(Mg,Fe^{+2},Al,Si)_3O_7]$	$Ca_2[MgSi_2O_7]$
TETRAGONAL $(-)$	TETRAGONAL $(+)(-)$	TETRAGONAL $(+)$

ω	1·669	1·624–1·666	1·632
ϵ	1·658	1·616–1·661	1·640
δ	0·011	0·001–0·013	0·008
D	3·038	2·95–3·05	2·944
H	5–6	5–6	5–6

Cleavage: {001} moderate, {110} poor.

Twinning: {100}, {001}.

Colour: Gehlenite, colourless, greyish green, brown; melilite, honey-yellow, brown, green-brown; åkermanite, greyish green, brown. All members of the group are colourless in thin section. Thick sections of melilite may be pleochroic with ω golden brown, ϵ colourless to faint yellow. Melilite may show anomalous interference colours.

STRUCTURE

The structure of the melilite group minerals is based on a tetragonal lattice which in åkermanite (Fig. 22) has Mg atoms located at the corners

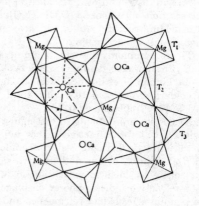

Fig. 22. *Melilite structure projected on* (001): *longer Ca–O distance long broken lines* ———, *shorter CaO–O distance short broken lines* – – – (*after Warren, B. E.,* 1930, Zeit. Krist., *vol.* 74, *p.* 131, *and Smith, J. V.,* 1953, Amer. Min., *vol.* 38, *p.* 643).

and face centres of the unit cell ($a = 7 \cdot 8$, $c \simeq 5 \cdot 0$ Å, $Z = 2$) and Si atoms at the centres of [SiO$_4$] tetrahedra joined in pairs to form Si$_2$O$_7$ groups. The structure consists of [SiO$_4$], [AlO$_4$] and [MgO$_4$] tetrahedra arranged in a sheet-like pattern parallel to (001). The sheets are held together by Ca–O linkages; the calcium coordination polyhedron is strongly distorted, four of the Ca–O distances being $\simeq 2 \cdot 4$ and the other four $\simeq 2 \cdot 7$ Å. The mean cation–oxygen distances are not identical for all the tetrahedrally co-ordinated positions; that of T$_1$ (Fig. 22) is $1 \cdot 87$ Å and those of T$_2$ and T$_3$ are $1 \cdot 63$ Å.

In åkermanite the Mg atoms most probably occupy the larger T$_1$ tetra-hedra, while in gehlenite both T$_1$ and T$_2$,T$_3$ tetrahedra are occupied by Al and Si atoms; the limiting cases of ordering are (a) one Al in T$_1$, and one Al and one Si in T$_2$ and T$_3$, (b) one Si in T$_1$ and two Al in tetrahedra T$_2$ and T$_3$. Intermediate stages of ordering are possible, and the probable

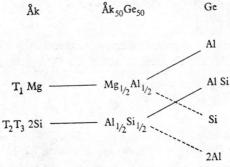

Fig. 23. *Possible substitutions in the åkermanite–gehlenite series (after Smith, J. V., 1953, Amer. Min., vol. 38, p. 643).*

arrangements of atoms in the åkermanite–gehlenite series, between the two extreme cases of ordering, are shown in Fig. 23. If no substitution occurs between Mg and Si the distribution of atoms, with Al replacing Mg, and the corresponding replacement of Si by Al in the other tetrahedra, is shown by full lines in Fig. 23. A possible alternative gehlenite structure, the sub-stitutional derivative of which is shown by the dotted lines in the figure, in which each tetrahedron contains only one type of atom, may be more stable. Such a structure requires a change in the mode of substitution at some composition in the series, i.e. from MgSi$_2$ $\rightleftharpoons$ Al,AlSi to MgSi$_2$ $\rightleftharpoons$ Si,AlAl.

CHEMISTRY

Akermanite and gehlenite melt congruently at 1454°C and 1590°C respectively, and form a solid solution series with a minimum melting temperature at 1385°C at the composition Åk$_{72}$Ge$_{28}$. Crystallization in the åkermanite–gehlenite system thus proceeds from either åkermanite-rich or gehlenite-rich compositions to the minimum freezing point. Natural melilites, however, contain appreciable amounts of iron and sodium (Table 9, anal. 1): the replacement of (Ca,Mg,Al) by (Na,Fe^{+2},Fe^{+3}) causes a marked lowering of the melting temperature, and residual liquids of melilite crystallization become enriched in both iron and sodium. The extent to which sodium enters the melilite structures is not precisely known, and earlier claims of the synthesis of a sodium melilite, $NaCaAlSi_2O_7$, have been questioned by Christie (1962), who has shown that the solubility of $Na_2Si_3O_7$ in gehlenite, i.e. the replacement $CaAl \rightleftharpoons NaSi$, is probably limited to 15 per cent.

The melilite minerals are unstable at temperatures below about 500°C for åkermanite and 600°C for gehlenite in the presence of water vapour pressures in the range 4·8 kilobars to 6·7 kilobars. The decomposition products under these conditions are hydrogrossular, vesuvianite, xonotlite $(Ca_6Si_6O_{17}(OH)_2)$, and clinopyroxene, $(Ca,Mg)_2Si_2O_6$. Natural alteration products of melilite include garnet, calcite, vesuvianite, diopside, and a fibrous brownish material cebollite, $Ca_5Al_2Si_3O_{14}(OH)_2$.

Table 9. MELILITE ANALYSES

| | 1. | 2. | | NUMBERS OF IONS ON THE BASIS OF 14 (O) | | | |
				1.		2.	
SiO_2	42·81	32·60	Si	3·921		2·991	
TiO_2	0·12	0·00	Al	0·711		1·957	
Al_2O_3	6·59	18·10	Ti	0·008		—	
Fe_2O_3	1·90	0·95	Fe^{+3}	0·131	6·03	0·064	6·03
FeO	3·06	0·92	Mg	1·021		0·944	
MnO	0·08	0·02	Fe^{+2}	0·234		0·070	
MgO	7·48	6·91	Mn	0·006		0·001	
CaO	33·27	40·08	Na	0·666		0·032	
Na_2O	3·75	0·18	Ca	3·265	3·97	3·940	4·00
K_2O	0·33	0·21	K	0·038		0·024	
H_2O^+	0·43	0·48					
H_2O^-	0·00	0·00					
Total	99·82	100·45					
ϵ	1·637	1·654					
ω	1·630	1·656					

1. Melilite, melilite basalt, Hawaii (Neuvonen, K. J., 1952, *Bull. Comm. géol. Finlande*, vol. 26, No. 158, p. 1).
2. Massive gehlenite, New Mexico (Neuvonen, K. J., ibid).

OPTICAL AND PHYSICAL PROPERTIES

The replacement of Al,Al by MgSi is accompanied by a decrease in both the ω and ϵ refractive indices. The rate of decrease of ω is much greater than that of ϵ, and the birefringence decreases from 0·011 for pure gehlenite to zero ($\omega = \epsilon \simeq 1\cdot65$) at approximately 52 mol. per cent åkermanite; solid solutions of this composition are thus isotropic. Similar rates of decrease in the indices persist in the compositional range $Ge_{50}Ak_{50}$–Ak_{100} and the åkermanite-rich members of the series are optically positive (Fig. 24). The replacement of Ca by Na, and to a smaller extent by K, in both gehlenite- and åkermanite-rich melilites results in a lowering of the refractive indices. Melilites are sometimes zoned and may show anomalous blue interference colours; the minerals are commonly tabular in form with well developed {001} faces.

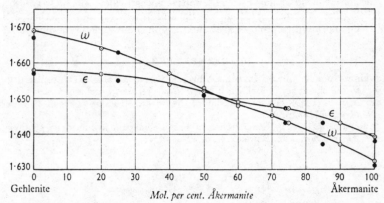

Fig. 24. *Refractive indices of the synthetic åkermanite–gehlenite series. Open circles, data from Ferguson, J. B. & Buddington, A. F., 1920, Amer. Journ. Sci., 4th ser., vol. 50, p. 131; solid circles data from Neuvonen, K. J., 1952, Bull. Comm. géol. Finlande, vol. 26, No. 158, p. 1.*

DISTINGUISHING FEATURES

Gehlenite-rich melilites may be distinguished from åkermanite-rich varieties by the optic sign; small values for the birefringence indicate intermediate compositions. The melilites are distinguished from zoisite by their uniaxial optical character, from vesuvianite by lower refractive indices, and from apatite by their simple tabular habit.

PARAGENESIS

Åkermanite occurs in thermally metamorphosed siliceous limestones and dolomites. The reaction

$$CaMgSi_2O_6 + CaCO_3 \rightleftharpoons Ca_2MgSi_2O_7 + CO_2$$
$$\text{diopside} \qquad\qquad\qquad \text{åkermanite}$$

occurs at a relatively high metamorphic grade. At higher temperatures, however, åkermanite is unstable in the presence of calcite and reacts with the carbonate to form merwinite and larnite:

$$Ca_2MgSi_2O_7 + CaCO_3 \rightleftharpoons Ca_3MgSi_2O_8 + 2Ca_2SiO_4 + CO_2$$
$$\text{åkermanite} \qquad\qquad \text{merwinite} \qquad \text{larnite}$$

In the highest grade of thermally metamorphosed impure carbonate rocks, åkermanite and spurrite may react to form larnite and merwinite:

$$Ca_2MgSi_2O_7 + 2Ca_2SiO_4 \cdot CaCO_3 \rightleftharpoons 2Ca_2SiO_4 + Ca_3MgSi_2O_8 + CO_2$$
$$\text{åkermanite} \qquad \text{spurrite} \qquad\qquad \text{larnite} \qquad \text{merwinite}$$

In many thermally metamorphosed impure limestones, Al as well as Si is present, and the melilite mineral is often closer in composition to gehlenite than to åkermanite.

Melilite is a common constituent of feldspathoidal rocks formed by the reaction of basic magmas with carbonate rocks (Tilley, 1952). It is also a constituent of some nepheline basalts and leucitites, and together with olivine and monticellite occurs abundantly in some varieties of alnöite.

REFERENCES

CHRISTIE, O. H. J. (1962) 'On sub-solidus relations of silicates. III. A contribution to the chemistry of melilites', *Norsk. Geol. Tidsskrift*, vol. 42, p. 1.

SMITH, J. V. (1953) 'Re-examination of the crystal structure of melilite', *Amer. Min.*, vol. 38, p. 643.

TILLEY, C. E. (1952) 'Some trends of basaltic magma in limestone syntexis', *Amer. Journ. Sci.*, Bowen vol., p. 529.

Rankinite

$Ca_3[Si_2O_7]$

MONOCLINIC $(+)$

α 1·640–1·642
β 1·643–1·644
γ 1·650
δ 0·008–0·010
$2V_\gamma$ 63°–64°
$\alpha:x = 15°$; $\beta = y$.
D 2·96. H 5½.
Cleavage: None [on (100) in slag material].
Colour: White; colourless in thin section.

Rankinite may be distinguished from spurrite, tilleyite, larnite and merwinite by its lack of lamellar twinning and from spurrite and tilleyite by its much lower birefringence.

Rankinite occurs at contacts between limestone and basic igneous rocks, as at Scawt Hill, Northern Ireland, and Ardnamurchan: it is also known from metamorphosed calcitic amygdales in a volcanic plug in Mull.

Tilleyite

$Ca_3[Si_2O_7] \cdot 2CaCO_3$

MONOCLINIC $(+)$

α 1·605–1·617
β 1·626–1·635
γ 1·651–1·654
δ 0·035–0·046
$2V_\gamma$ 85°–89°
$\alpha:z = 24°–26°$; $\beta = y$.
$\gamma:\{20\bar{1}\}$ cleavage trace $\simeq 12°$.
Dispersion: $r < v$. D 2·84.
Cleavage: $\{20\bar{1}\}$ perfect; $\{100\}$ and $\{010\}$ poor.
Twinning: Often lamellar, with $\alpha:$ twin plane = 23°–24°.
Colour: White; colourless in thin section.

The structure of tilleyite contains isolated Si_2O_7 and CO_3 groups, linked by Ca atoms.

It may be distinguished from merwinite, rankinite, and larnite by its higher birefringence, and from spurrite by its positive optic sign and larger 2V.

Tilleyite occurs at gabbro–limestone contacts, as at Crestmore, California, at Carlingford, Ireland, and on the island of Muck, Inner Hebrides.

Låvenite

$(Na,Ca,Mn,Fe^{+2})_3(Zr,Nb,Ti)[Si_2O_7](OH,F)$

MONOCLINIC (−)

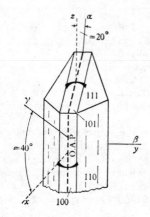

α 1·690–1·704
β 1·707–1·725
γ 1·720–1·745
δ 0·030–0·047
$2V_\alpha$ 73°–85°; $\gamma : x$ 40°–41°; $\beta = y$, O.A.P. (010).
Dispersion: $r < v$, weak. D 3·4–3·53. H 6.
Cleavage: {100} good. *Twinning:* {100} lamellar.
Colour: Colourless, yellow, brown; colourless to yellow in thin section. Stronger yellow with increasing Ti and Mn.
Pleochroism: α colourless, β colourless, γ very pale yellow, golden, brownish yellow. Absorption $\gamma > \beta > \alpha$.
   Soluble in HCl.

Låvenite is distinguished from other common accessory minerals of nepheline-syenites by its high refringence and birefringence.

It is chiefly found in nepheline-syenite pegmatites but also as an accessory mineral associated with astrophyllite, catapleite and rosenbuschite in nepheline-syenite.

Catapleiite

$(Na,Ca)_2Zr[Si_3O_9]\cdot 2H_2O$

MONOCLINIC (pseudohexagonal) (+)

α 1·582–1·591
β 1·582–1·592
γ 1·600–1·627
δ 0·018–0·036
$2V_\gamma$ 0°–30°; $\gamma : z$ 3°; O.A.P. (010).
Dispersion: $r < v$, moderate.
D 2·75–2·9. H 6.
Cleavage: {100} perfect, {101} poor.
Twinning: {201}.
Colour: Colourless, grey, blue (Na-rich variety), pale yellow to red brown (Ca-rich variety); colourless in thin section.
   Gelatinizes in HCl.

Catapleiite is distinguished from eudialyte by its higher birefringence and from most other common accessory minerals of nepheline-syenites by its lack of colour in thin section.

The occurrence of catapleiite is restricted to alkaline rocks and it is a relatively common accessory mineral in nepheline-syenite pegmatites. It is, however, rarely found as a primary mineral and usually occurs as an alteration product of eudialyte.

Beryl

$Be_3Al_2[Si_6O_{18}]$

HEXAGONAL (−)

ϵ 1·557–1·599
ω 1·560–1·602
δ 0·004–0·009

Dispersion: Weak. D 2·66–2·92. H 7½–8.
Cleavage: {0001} imperfect.
Twinning: Rare; on {31$\bar{4}$1}, {11$\bar{2}$0} and {40$\bar{4}$1} (?)
Colour: Colourless, white, bluish green, greenish yellow, yellow, blue, rose; usually colourless in thin section.
Pleochroism: In thick sections, weakly pleochroic: e.g. emerald may show ω yellowish green, ϵ sea green.

STRUCTURE

The dominant features in the structure ($a \simeq 9\cdot21$, $c \simeq 9\cdot20$ Å, Z = 2) are the hexagonal rings of six Si–O tetrahedra (Fig. 25), these rings forming

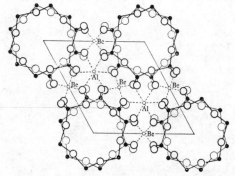

Fig. 25. *The structure of beryl projected on the basal plane* (0001), *showing the rings on the upper plane and* (*in fainter line*) *those halfway down the cell* (*after Bragg, W. L.*, 1937, Atomic Structure of Minerals, *Cornell Univ. Press*).

hollow columns parallel to the *z* axis of the crystal. Within the rings two of the oxygen atoms in each SiO_4 group are shared by SiO_4 groups on either side, thus giving the metasilicate ratio. Between the rings lie the Al and Be atoms, each Al coordinated with an octahedral group of six oxygen atoms, and each Be surrounded by four oxygen atoms on a distorted tetrahedron. In these positions they link the oxygens of neighbouring Si_6O_{18} rings both laterally and vertically. The structure is thus like a honeycomb; no atomic centre is nearer than 2·55 Å to the centres of the open channels. Alkali beryls are known, however, with appreciable amounts of Na and Cs, and these larger ions must evidently occupy the otherwise vacant channels, the positive charges contributed by them being balanced by cation substitutions elsewhere in the structure. The water commonly reported in beryl analyses may also be located in these channels.

CHEMISTRY

Although normally regarded as $Be_3Al_2Si_6O_{18}$, beryl usually contains some alkalis and in certain varieties the total alkali content may rise to

Table 10. BERYL ANALYSES

	1.	2.	3.	4.		1.	2.	3.	4.
						NUMBERS OF IONS ON THE BASIS OF 36 (O)			
SiO_2	65·14	64·16	61·88	59·52	Si	11·997	11·865	12·059	11·965
TiO_2	0·06	—	0·01	0·05	Ti	0·008	—	0·001	0·008
Al_2O_3	18·20	18·73	17·10	10·63	Al	3·950	4·083	3·928	2·520
Cr_2O_3	—	—	—	0·09	Fe^{+3}	0·090	0·040	0·012	0·314
Fe_2O_3	0·65	0·28	0·08	2·08	Be	5·671	5·766	4·935	6·032
FeO	0·28	—	—	2·24	Mg	0·137	—	0·064	0·647
BeO	12·82	12·98	10·54	12·49	Li	—	0·060	0·471	0·186
MnO	—	—	—	0·29	Fe^{+2}	0·043	—	—	0·376
MgO	0·50	—	0·22	2·16	Na	0·144	0·456	0·944	0·452
CaO	tr.	—	0·44	0·11	Ca	—	—	0·092	0·024
Na_2O	0·40	1·27	2·50	1·16	K	0·012	0·098	—	0·041
K_2O	0·05	0·39	—	0·16	Cs	—	0·033	0·343	0·572
Li_2O	—	0·08	0·60	0·23					
Cs_2O	—	0·42	4·13	6·68	Σ	10·06	10·54	10·79	11·25†
H_2O^+	1·98	1·44	2·26	1·62	Σ=sum of metal ions other than Si				
H_2O^-	0·23	0·02	0·16	—					
Total	100·31	99·77	99·92	99·88					
ϵ	1·572	1·577	1·586	1·599					
ω	1·577	1·583	1·592	1·608					
D	2·70	2·725	2·78	2·921					

1. Pale green beryl, Charleston, New Zealand (Hutton, C. O. & Seelye, F. T., 1945, *Trans. Roy. Soc., New Zealand*, vol. 75, p. 160).
2. Clear vitreous beryl, Varuträsk pegmatite, Sweden (Quensel, P., 1937, *Geol. För. Förh. Stockholm*, vol. 59, p. 269).
3. Pink beryl, inner zone of granite pegmatite (Sosedko, T. A., 1957, *Mem. All-Union Min. Soc.*, vol. 86, p. 495).
4. Bluish alkali beryl, pegmatite, Mohave Co., Arizona (Schaller, W. T., Stevens, R. E. & Jahns, R. H., 1962. *Amer. Min.*, vol. 47, p. 672: includes Sc_2O_3 0·10, P_2O_5 0·27).

† Includes Cr 0·014, Sc 0·017, Mn 0·049.

around 5 to 8 per cent. As well as Na and Li the larger alkali ions K and Cs are found but Rb is less common. In these alkali beryls, Li substitutes for Al in octahedral positions, and Al replaces some Be in tetrahedral positions: the additional positive charge is then supplied by the large alkali cations in the structural channels. Thus beryl can be considered as an isomorphous series between $Be_3 \cdot Al_2 \cdot Si_6O_{18}$ and $(Na,Cs)Be_2Al \cdot AlLi \cdot Si_6O_{18}$ (Schaller *et al*, 1962). The latter authors have also postulated the existence of a third end-member, 'femag' beryl, of composition $(Na,K,Cs) \cdot Be_3 \cdot R^{+3}R^{+2} \cdot Si_6$-$O_{18}$, to take into account the iron, magnesium, etc. found in some analyses of carefully purified beryl (e.g. Table 10, anal. 4): thus R^{+3} would be Al, Fe^{+3}, Cr and Sc, and R^{+2} would be Fe^{+2}, Mn and Mg. The green colour of the emerald variety is usually associated with Cr. Even gem quality beryls may contain appreciable H_2O^+, but although it has been suggested that some Si may be replaced by (OH), as in hydrogrossular, it is more probable that the water is of zeolitic nature and is accommodated in the structural channels.

Beryl can be synthesized hydrothermally from a mixture of SiO_2, Al_2O_3 and $BeCO_3$ at 400 to 2000 bars pressure and 400° to 850°C. Emeralds have been synthesized in an autoclave, using seed crystals in a weakly alkaline solution, with BeO, Al_2O_3, SiO_2 and a little Cr_2O_3; local deficiency of Al_2O_3 may give phenakite (Be_2SiO_4) inclusions. It has been reported that the time taken to synthesize an emerald crystal large enough to yield a 1 carat stone is about one year.

Alteration products of beryl include kaolinite, muscovite, bavenite, bertrandite, phenakite, epididymite, and milarite.

OPTICAL AND PHYSICAL PROPERTIES

The major factor affecting the properties of beryl is the alkali content. As shown in Fig. 26 an increase in the alkali content is accompanied by an increase in the refractive indices, and also in the specific gravity. The optical and physical properties of beryl (including cell parameters) have been correlated with the composition by Schaller *et al* (1962): the entry of constituents other than SiO_2, BeO and Al_2O_3 increases the birefringence and the *a* cell parameter, whereas *c* remains fairly constant. The lowest refractive indices appear to be those of some synthetic beryls: for common beryl the values may be taken as ϵ 1·564–1·584, ω 1·570–1·590, δ 0·006, D 2·67–2·76. Beryl is normally uniaxial, but biaxial (orthorhombic) crystals have been reported, with 2V up to 17°.

The colour of beryl is commonly white to pale green or yellowish green and it is generally opaque. Clear transparent types are classed as aquamarine when having a pale green, yellowish green or bluish green colour, while the emerald variety has a vivid grass green colour. Amber or golden yellow gem beryl is sometimes known as heliodor and the pink variety has been named morganite. Pleochroism may be noticeable in thickish sections: emerald has ω yellowish green, ϵ sea green; blue beryl has ω light blue or colourless, ϵ blue.

DISTINGUISHING FEATURES

Beryl may be confused with quartz, but can be distinguished by having higher refractive indices, negative sign and length-fast orientation. Apatite has considerably higher refractive indices and is less hard, being scratched by a knife.

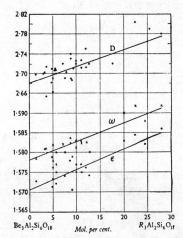

Fig. 26. *Variation in the refractive indices and specific gravity of beryl.*

PARAGENESIS

Common beryl and aquamarine characteristically occur in vugs and druses in granite and in granite pegmatites : associated minerals may include quartz, feldspar, muscovite, lepidolite, topaz, tourmaline, spodumene, cassiterite, columbite and tantalite. The occurrence of beryl in granite pegmatites is related to the small size of the Be ion, which, being too small to substitute in most silicate structures, is concentrated in the residual magmatic fluids. It has been suggested that it occurs in aluminium-rich rocks while helvite, $(Mn,Fe,Zn)_8Be_6Si_6O_{24}S_2$, is deposited in aluminium-poor rocks (Holser, 1953). Beryl also occurs in some nepheline-syenites and in mica schists and marbles. Emeralds, as opposed to aquamarines, are almost restricted to a metamorphic paragenesis, typically in biotite schist, though the principal modern source of emeralds, at Muzo, Colombia, is in calcite veins in bituminous limestone.

REFERENCES

HOLSER, W. T. (1953) 'Beryllium minerals in the Victorio Mountains, Luna County, New Mexico', *Amer. Min.*, vol. 38, p. 599.

SCHALLER, W. T., STEVENS, R. E. and JAHNS, R. H. (1962) 'An unusual beryl from Arizona', *Amer. Min.*, vol. 47, p. 672.

WEBSTER, R. (1955) 'The emerald', *Journ. Gemm.*, vol. 5, p. 185.

Cordierite

$Al_3(Mg,Fe^{+2})_2[Si_5AlO_{18}]$

ORTHORHOMBIC (pseudohexagonal) $(-)$ $(+)$

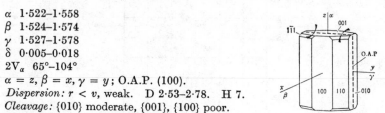

α 1·522–1·558
β 1·524–1·574
γ 1·527–1·578
δ 0·005–0·018
$2V_\alpha$ 65°–104°
$\alpha = z, \beta = x, \gamma = y$; O.A.P. (100).
Dispersion: $r < v$, weak. D 2·53–2·78. H 7.
Cleavage: {010} moderate, {001}, {100} poor.
Twinning: {110}, {130} simple, lamellar, cyclic, common; {021}, {101} rare.
Colour: Greyish blue, lilac-blue, dark blue; colourless or very pale blue in thin section.
Pleochroism: Iron-rich cordierite, α colourless; γ violet; magnesium-rich cordierite in thick section, α pale yellow or green, β pale blue, γ pale blue, violet or violet-blue.

STRUCTURE

Most natural specimens of composition $Al_3(Mg,Fe^{+2})_2[Si_5AlO_{18}]$ are of the low-temperature polymorph. This polymorph is orthorhombic, pseudo-

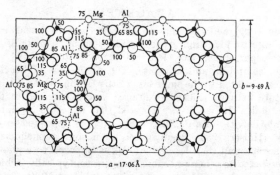

Fig. 27. *Cordierite structure projected on* (001). *Figures give heights in percentages of the c translation (after Byström, A., 1942, Arkiv. Kemi Min. Geol., vol. 15B, p. 1).*

hexagonal ($a \simeq 9·7, b \simeq 17·1, c \simeq 9·4$ Å; Z = 4; the pseudohexagonal nature of the unit cell is shown by the relationship $b \simeq a \sqrt{3}$). The high-temperature form is hexagonal ($a \simeq 9·8, c \simeq 9·3$ Å) and is isostructural with beryl, $Be_3Al_2Si_6O_{18}$. The structure of both polymorphs consists of six-membered hexagonal rings of linked $(Si,Al)O_4$ tetrahedra. The $[Si_5AlO_{18}]$ rings are joined to others above and below, and to adjacent rings, by two oxygens of each tetrahedron being linked to one Al in 4-fold coordination, and one Mg in 6-fold coordination, one oxygen forming the link to the $[Si_5AlO_{18}]$ ring above, and the other the link to the ring below (Fig. 27). In the high-temperature, hexagonal, polymorph the distribution of Si and Al atoms among the ring sites must be completely random. In the low-temperature polymorph the six-membered rings are distorted, and this distortion is probably related to the ordering of Si and Al atoms in the ring sites. The distortion is present in varying degrees in different crystals of the low-temperature polymorph; the magnitude of the distortion can be estimated by the separation of three peaks in the X-ray powder pattern.

Table 11. CORDIERITE ANALYSES

| | 1. | 2. | 3. | | NUMBERS OF IONS ON THE BASIS OF 18 OXYGENS | | |
					1.	2.	3.
SiO_2	49·46	47·69	46·69	Si	4·984	4·964	4·931
TiO_2	0·01	tr.	0·34	Al	1·016	1·036	1·069
Al_2O_3	33·58	32·52	32·00	Al	2·974	2·954	2·915
Fe_2O_3	0·14	0·63	0·39	Ti	0·000	—	0·027
FeO	2·12	8·04	12·04	Fe^{+3}	0·010	0·048	0·030
MnO	0·08	0·04	0·09	Mg	1·811	1·172	0·930
MgO	12·06	7·56	5·91	Fe^{+2}	0·179	0·700	1·063
CaO	0·03	0·52	0·18	Mn	0·007	0·003	0·008
Na_2O	0·14	0·53	0·28	Na	0·026	0·106	0·050
K_2O	0·30	0·42	0·16	Ca	0·003	0·058	0·020
H_2O^+	1·71	1·85	1·95	K	0·038	0·055	0·020
H_2O^-	0·10	0·55	—				
Total	99·73	100·35	100·03	Z	6·00	6·00	6·00
				$[Y]^4$	2·98	3·00	2·97
α	1·530	1·538	1·548	$[XY]^6$	2·06	2·09	2·10
β	1·535	1·542	1·554				
γ	1·538	1·547	1·558	100 Mg/	91	63	47
				(Mg+Fe)			
$2V_\alpha$	84·5°	96°	72°–78°				
D	2·583–	2·64	—				
	2·603						

1. Cordierite, kyanite–andalusite–sillimanite–cordierite schist, Idaho (Hietanen, A., 1956, *Amer. Min.*, vol. 41, p. 1).
2. Cordierite, argillaceous hornfels, Aberdeenshire (Stewart, F. H., 1942, *Min. Mag.*, vol. 26, p. 260).
3. Cordierite, cordierite–garnet–biotite–plagioclase–orthoclase–quartz hornfels, Angus, Scotland (Chinner, G. A., 1962, *Journ. Petr.*, vol. 3, p. 316).

CHEMISTRY

In most cordierites the octahedrally coordinated positions in the structure are occupied predominantly by magnesium, and cordierites containing more than one Fe^{+2} atom per formula unit are rare. Compared with associated ferromagnesian minerals, such as biotite, garnet and spinel, cordierites are preferentially enriched in magnesium relative to iron. The Al content does not vary significantly and the ratio Al:Si in the six-membered rings of the structure consistently approximates to 1:5. Many cordierite analyses show an appreciable content of H_2O^+ which in most cases cannot be attributed to alteration, but which is probably present as H_2O molecules located in the large channels parallel to the z axis. Potassium and sodium atoms are invariably present and are probably also accommodated in these channels.

High-temperature cordierite has been synthesized from anhydrous mixtures of its oxides, and hydrothermally from glass of $Mg_2Al_4Si_5O_{18}$ composition in the presence of excess water, the latter synthesis taking place at temperatures as low as 450°C. At pressures up to 5000 bars and temperatures in the range 450° to 525°C cordierite breaks down to amesitic chlorite and pyrophyllite:

$$2Mg_2Al_4Si_5O_{18} + 6H_2O \rightarrow \underset{\text{chlorite}}{Mg_4Al_4Si_2O_{10}(OH)_8} + \underset{\text{pyrophyllite}}{2Al_2Si_4O_{10}(OH)_2}$$
$$\underset{\text{cordierite}}{}$$

Magnesium cordierite melts incongruently at 1465°C to mullite and a liquid; the high-temperature iron cordierite, $Fe_2Al_4Si_5O_{18}$, melts incongruently at 1210°C to mullite, tridymite and a liquid. Iron cordierite is one of the breakdown products of natural chloritoid at 200 bars and a temperature as low as 600°C.

Cordierite is commonly altered; the most frequent alteration product is greenish pinite which consists of a fine felty mixture of muscovite with some chlorite or serpentine mineral and iron oxides. The pinite alteration product may be colourless, or greenish, bluish or yellow in colour.

OPTICAL AND PHYSICAL PROPERTIES

The majority of cordierites are optically negative with $2V_\alpha$ between 65° and 85°; values beyond this range as well as optically positive cordierites, however, are not uncommon. Although the replacement of Mg by Fe^{+2} is accompanied by a steady increase in refractive indices, the latter are also dependent on the thermal history of the individual crystals, i.e. they are related to the degree of structural disorder. The refractive indices of cordierites thus give only a general indication of their chemical composition unless the structural state of the individual crystal is known (Fig. 28).

Cordierite is commonly twinned and the twinning may be simple, lamellar or cyclic. In the latter the composition planes radiate from a central point at intervals of 30°, 60° or 120°. In basal sections of (110) twins the angles between the β and γ vibration directions and the trace of the composition plane are 60° and 30° respectively; in similar sections of

(130) twins the angles between the β and γ directions and the trace of the composition plane are respectively 30° and 60°. In concentric twins the twin lamellae are arranged parallel to or at angles of 30° and 60° to the hexagonal outline of the basal section (Fig. 29). The more complex twins are generally restricted to minerals of high temperature paragenesis, and the more simply twinned cordierite to lower temperature parageneses. Small crystals of zircon and apatite commonly occur as inclusions in cordierite, and they are frequently surrounded by an intense pleochroic halo, the outer part of which is deep yellow and the inner part less strongly coloured.

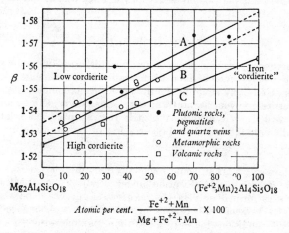

Fig. 28. *Variation of β-refractive indices with composition of cordierites from plutonic rocks, pegmatites, and quartz veins (A), metamorphic rocks (B), and volcanic rocks (C).*

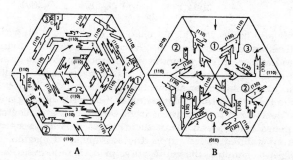

Fig. 29. *Concentric twinning in cordierite. A. Concentric hexagonal pattern on a trilling, all twin planes are similar and inclined to each other at angles of 60°. B. Star-shaped concentric pattern on a sixling (after Venkatesh, V., 1954, Amer. Min., vol. 39, p. 636).*

DISTINGUISHING FEATURES

Cordierite when colourless and unaltered resembles quartz, but it can usually be distinguished by the large negative optic axial angle. Cordierite can also be distinguished from both quartz and feldspar by the characteristic dusting of the mineral by fine opaque material, by pleochroic haloes around included zircons and apatites, and by the typical micaceous, pinite, alteration products. Cordierite showing well developed lamellar twinning on {110} is difficult to distinguish from plagioclase, and in the absence of pleochroic haloes it may be necessary to use thick sections to display the pleochroism.

PARAGENESIS

The commonest paragenesis of cordierite is in thermally metamorphosed rocks, particularly those derived from argillaceous sediments. Cordierite crystallizes at an early stage in the metamorphism, commonly associated with andalusite and biotite, and initially forms poorly defined and ovoid crystals crowded with inclusions of the recrystallized material of the original sediment. It persists in the hornfelses of higher grade, in which its common associates are sillimanite, potassium feldspar, muscovite, corundum or spinel.

Cordierite also occurs in some regionally metamorphosed rocks but in contrast to its early crystallization under conditions of thermal metamorphism it is formed only in the high grade gneisses. The absence of garnet and the presence of cordierite in such rocks may be associated with abnormal PT conditions (i.e. stress less than maximum), or to a regional metamorphism followed by a period of thermal metamorphism, i.e. by reactions of the type:

$$8Al_2SiO_5 + 2K(Mg,Fe^{+2})_3AlSi_3O_{10}(OH)_2 + 7SiO_2 \rightarrow$$
$$\text{kyanite} \qquad\qquad \text{biotite}$$
$$3(Mg,Fe)_2Al_4Si_5O_{18} + 2KAl_3Si_3O_{10}(OH)_2$$
$$\text{cordierite} \qquad\qquad \text{muscovite}$$

Cordierite also occurs in a highly characteristic association with anthophyllite. This association occurs in a variety of geological environments and in a wide range of rock compositions; in most examples, however, the formation of the cordierite–anthophyllite pair was associated with either magnesium metasomatism or autometasomatism.

Cordierite is found in some igneous rocks. Cordierite-bearing norites are commonly considered to be derived from gabbroic magma contaminated by argillaceous material; in many such norites it is not xenocrystal in origin but crystallized directly from the contaminated magma. Likewise in the cordierite granites, the cordierite is of both xenocrystal and pyrogenetic origin. Cordierite also occurs in some granite pegmatites; in this paragenesis it is usually present in large well shaped grains which are occasionally of gem quality. Micropegmatitic intergrowths of iron-rich cordierite and quartz occur in some pegmatites, their constant ratio (cordierite : quartz $\simeq$ 43 : 57) and the regular orientation of the inter-growth are indicative of the simultaneous crystallization of the two minerals and demonstrate that the cordierite is not of replacement origin.

REFERENCES

MIYASHIRO, A. (1957) 'Cordierite–indialite relations', *Amer. Journ. Sci.*, vol. 255, p. 43.

SCHREYER, W. and SCHAIRER, J. F. (1961) 'Compositions and structural states of anhydrous Mg-cordierites : A re-investigation of the central part of the system $MgO–Al_2O_3–SiO_2$', *Journ. Petr.*, vol. 2, p. 324.

Tourmaline $\qquad$ Na(Mg,Fe,Mn,Li,Al)$_3$Al$_6$[Si$_6$O$_{18}$](BO$_3$)$_3$(OH,F)$_4$

TRIGONAL $(-)$

	Dravite NaMg$_3$Al$_6$B$_3$· Si$_6$O$_{27}$(OH,F)$_4$	Schorl Na(Fe,Mn)$_3$Al$_6$B$_3$· Si$_6$O$_{27}$(OH,F)$_4$	Elbaite Na(Li,Al)$_3$Al$_6$B$_3$· Si$_6$O$_{27}$(OH,F)$_4$
ϵ	1·610–1·632	1·625–1·650	1·615–1·630
ω	1·635–1·661	1·655–1·675	1·640–1·655
δ	0·021–0·026	0·025–0·035	0·017–0·024
D	3·03–3·15	3·10–3·25	3·03–3·10

Dispersion: Weak. H 7.

Cleavage: {11$\bar{2}$0} and {10$\bar{1}$1} very poor.

Twinning: Rare, on {10$\bar{1}$1} and {40$\bar{4}$1} (?)

Colour: Extremely variable: schorl commonly black, blue-yellow in thin section; elbaite blue, green, yellow, red or colourless, colourless in thin section; dravite black to brown, yellow to colourless in thin section.

Pleochroism: Variable in intensity, normally very strong; absorption always $\omega > \epsilon$.

Only slightly attacked by HF: decomposed by fusion with alkali carbonates or bisulphates. Crystals have polar symmetry and generally show a strong pyroelectric effect.

STRUCTURE

Tourmaline has a rhombohedral unit cell with $a \simeq 9·5$ Å, α 66°, or on hexagonal axes a 15·84–16·03, c 7·10–7·25 Å. In the structure of dravite the magnesium ions are surrounded octahedrally by oxygen and (OH) ions: the three octahedra immediately surround the 3-fold axis and each octahedron shares an edge with each of its two neighbours. The six silicon atoms are each surrounded tetrahedrally by four oxygen atoms (Fig. 30), each tetrahedron sharing two of its oxygens with the neighbouring tetrahedra to form a six-membered ring of composition Si$_6$O$_{18}$: the Al ions are coordinated to six oxygen atoms in a very distorted octahedron. The Al, B and Na ions serve in different ways to tie together the central core of the structure of composition Mg$_3$(OH)$_4$Si$_6$O$_{21}$. From the variation in cell parameters two series, between dravite and schorl and between elbaite and schorl, can be distinguished.

CHEMISTRY

The chemistry of tourmaline is complex and until recently its basic formula was uncertain. Structural determinations, however, make it reasonably certain that the formula is $NaR_3Al_6B_3Si_6O_{27}(OH)_4$. In this formula Na may be partially replaced by K or by Ca if valency conditions are satisfied: R can be predominantly Fe^{+2} as in schorl, Mg as in dravite, or (Al+Li) as in the elbaite series; other ions which may enter this position are Mn, as in the variety tsilaisite (e.g. Table 12, anal. 5), and Fe^{+3} or Cr subject to valency balance. There is no appreciable substitution of Al for Si in tourmaline: in the hydroxyl position part of the (OH) is often replaced by F, particularly in the elbaite series (Table 12, anals. 4, 5). There is a complete range of composition between the magnesium and iron-rich

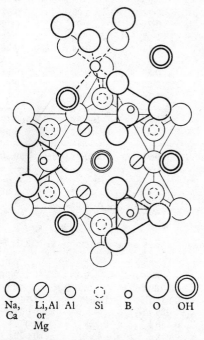

◯	⊘	◦	⟡	ₒ	◯◯	◎
Na, Ca	Li,Al or Mg	Al	Si	B	O	OH

Fig. 30. *The structure of tourmaline (in part) projected on (0001), (after Ito, T. & Sadanaga, R., 1951, Acta Cryst., vol. 4, p. 385). One Si_6O_{18} and three BO_3 groups are traced by thin and thick full lines respectively: bonds around Al are represented by broken lines.*

members, and between the iron-rich and the lithium tourmalines, though intermediate members in the latter range are less common. The magnesium and lithium tourmaline molecules, however, are almost immiscible. The magnesium-rich tourmalines, or dravites, are typically brown in colour and the iron-rich schorl variety is black. In the elbaite series there is a wide range of colour from the colourless or white variety achroite, to pink rubellite containing divalent manganese and with a low iron content, the green

Table 12. TOURMALINE ANALYSES

	1.	2.	3.	4.	5.
SiO_2	35·96	33·78	36·36	38·06	35·61
TiO_2	0·14	0·41	tr.	0·02	0·13
B_2O_3	10·73	10·70	10·30	10·88	10·04
Al_2O_3	30·85	33·80	40·48	41·78	38·64
Fe_2O_3	—	0·20	—	0·03	0·79
FeO	0·76	15·11	3·64	—	0·33
MnO	—	0·25	1·05	0·45	4·52
MgO	13·67	0·74	0·09	0·02	0·61
CaO	2·41	0·21	0·67	0·72	0·85
Na_2O	1·63	1·92	2·20	2·48	3·30
K_2O	0·09	0·11	0·44	0·25	0·42
Li_2O	—	—	1·27	1·55	0·30
F	—	0·98	0·10	0·92	0·76
H_2O^+	4·16	2·22	3·64	3·02	3·53
H_2O^-	—	0·19	0·08	—	—
	100·40	100·62	100·32	100·19	99·83
$O \equiv F$	—	0·41	0·04	0·39	0·30
Total	100·40	100·21	100·28	99·80	99·53
ϵ	1·616	1·633	1·623	1·6205	—
ω	1·637	1·668	1·644	1·6391	—
D	3·050	3·218	3·096	3·025	—

NUMBERS OF IONS ON THE BASIS OF 31 (O,OH,F)

	1.	2.	3.	4.	5.
Si	5·759	5·789	5·841	6·001	5·822
B	2·965	3·163	2·855	2·960	2·833
Al	5·826	6·000	6·000	6·000	6·000
Al	—	0·826	1·664	1·766	1·440
Fe^{+3}	—	0·026	—	0·004	0·097
Mg	3·262	0·189	0·021	0·004	0·148
Ti	0·017	0·052	—	0·002	0·016
Li	—	—	0·821	0·983	0·197
Fe^{+2}	0·101	2·165	0·488	—	0·045
Mn	—	0·036	0·143	0·060	0·626
Na	0·506	0·636	0·685	0·758	1·045
Ca	0·414	0·039	0·115	0·122	0·149
K	0·018	0·024	0·090	0·049	0·088
	4·32	3·99	4·03	3·75	3·85
OH	4·444	2·537	3·900	3·175	3·851
F	—	0·531	0·050	0·458	0·393
		3·07	3·95	3·63	4·24

1. Brown dravite, dolomite marble, Gouverneur, New York State (Kunitz, W., 1929, *Chemie der Erde*, vol. 4, p. 208).
2. Schorl, Yuzhakova, Urals (Slivko, M. M., 1955, *The study of tourmalines of certain localities in the U.S.S.R.* Publ. Lvov Univ.).

3. Light green tourmaline, pegmatite vein in aplite, Meldon, Okehampton, Devon (Deer, W. A., Howie, R. A. & Zussman, J., 1962, *Rock-forming minerals*, vol. I, Longmans).
4. Pink rubellite, Varuträsk pegmatite, Sweden (Quensel, P. & Gabrielson, O., 1939, *Geol. För. Förh. Stockholm*, vol. 61, p. 63; includes Rb_2O 0·01).
5. Green tsilaisite (Slivko, M. M., 1959, *Min. Mag. Lvov Geol. Soc.*, vol. 13, p. 139).

tourmaline verdelite containing appreciable ferrous iron (a high proportion of iron in the ferric state gives a yellowish green colour), and the blue tourmaline or indicolite whose colour appears to be related to both iron and manganese. Colour-zoning is common and may run parallel to the prism faces or to the basal plane.

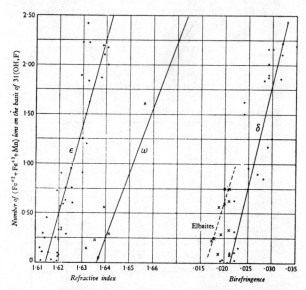

Fig. 31. *Optical properties of tourmaline in relation to the number of* $(Fe^{+2} + Fe^{+3} + Mn)$ *ions on the basis of* 31 (O,OH,F).

Tourmaline has been synthesized from its component oxides in water at 400°–500°C: its stability field in concentrated solutions is wholly in the weakly alkaline range, though for very dilute solutions it is stable in weakly acid conditions.

Alteration products of tourmaline include muscovite, biotite or lepidolite micas, and also chlorite and cookeite, $LiAl_4(Si,Al)_4O_{10}(OH)_8$.

OPTICAL AND PHYSICAL PROPERTIES

The refractive indices, birefringence and specific gravity of a number of analysed tourmalines are plotted in Figs. 31 and 32 against the number of

$(Fe^{+2} + Fe^{+3} + Mn)$ ions on the basis of 31 (O,OH,F) ions. The iron and manganese content of tourmaline controls the refractive indices and specific gravity, and the birefringence also increases with rising iron content. For the iron-poor tourmalines these properties do not distinguish the lithium from the magnesium tourmalines, though the former tend to have a lower birefringence (Fig. 31).

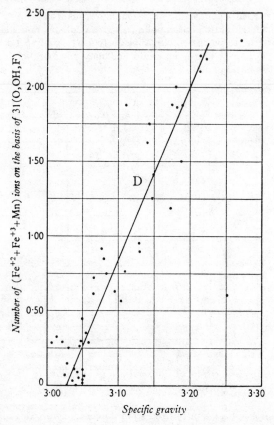

Fig. 32. *The specific gravity of tourmaline in relation to the number of* $(Fe^{+2} + Fe^{+3} + Mn)$ *ions on the basis of* 31 (O,OH,F).

The pleochroism is variable in intensity, but in the iron-bearing tourmalines it is normally very strong. The absorption is always $\omega > \epsilon$, with the result that maximum absorption occurs when the z axis is lying perpendicular to the vibration direction of the polarizer: in ordinary light the contribution by the ω ray to the transmitted intensity reaches 10 per cent only in the middle of the wavelength spectrum, hence the use of tourmaline to provide plane polarized light, as in tourmaline tongs. The iron tourmalines typically show pleochroism from yellow, brown or blue to pale yellow or yellowish green; the magnesium tourmalines often show yellow to pale yellow pleochroism, and the lithium tourmalines or elbaites are generally colourless in the ϵ direction and show a paler shade of their body-colour in the direction of maximum absorption. The absorption for the ω ray for pink tourmaline corresponds closely to that given by manganous sulphate and that of green tourmaline the absorption curve of ferrous ammonium sulphate (the absorption of potassium permanganate and potassium manganate are entirely different)

DISTINGUISHING FEATURES

Tourmaline can be distinguished under the microscope by its marked pleochroism: this differs from that of biotite or the common amphiboles in showing maximum absorption when the elongation of the crystal is perpendicular to the vibration plane of the polarizer. The straight extinction, uniaxial character, relatively high relief and moderate birefringence are also diagnostic. Distinction between different varieties of tourmaline is easiest by reference to the refractive indices or birefringence to indicate the amount of the schorl molecule present, in conjunction with consideration of the colour or pleochroism to help distinguish between the elbaite and the dravite series.

PARAGENESIS

Tourmaline is typically a mineral of granite pegmatites, pneumatolytic veins, and of some granites: it is also commonly found in metamorphic rocks as a product of boron metasomatism or as the result of recrystallization of detrital grains from the original sediment. In granitic rocks the tourmalines belong to the schorl–elbaite series and are generally fairly iron-rich, the typical tourmaline-bearing granites of south-west England having black prismatic crystals visible in hand specimen and showing yellow or bluish yellow pleochroic tourmaline in thin section. In certain pegmatites and late-stage granitic vein material the lithium tourmalines are developed, often showing a variation in colour and composition corresponding to their position in the pegmatite. In the Varuträsk pegmatite both black and coloured tourmalines occur in the original zonal pegmatitic phase, while rubellite (Table 12, anal. 4) and the zoned tourmalines are mainly restricted to the sodium replacement unit in the so-called pneumatogenic stage. In the pneumatolytic stage of alteration, tourmalinization may occur by the introduction of boron which attacks the normal granitic minerals. Thus the well known rock type luxullianite is regarded as the product of the arrested pneumatolytic modification by boric emanations from a porphyritic alkali granite: in this rock the biotite has been attacked first to give yellow tourmaline, and subsequently the feldspar has been replaced by a blue or blue-green tourmaline. Some yellow tourmaline may be primary in origin but, after a period of corrosion, serves as a nucleus for radially disposed acicular secondary tourmaline, giving the so-called tourmaline 'suns'. The quartz is not replaced, and if tourmalinization goes to completion a tourmaline–quartz rock results. In pneumatolytic igneous assemblages minerals associated with tourmaline may include topaz, lepidolite, petalite, spodumene, cassiterite, fluorite, apatite, columbite, etc.

The magnesian tourmalines or dravites are usually found in metamorphic or metasomatic assemblages. They are known from basic igneous rocks where they may be associated with axinite and datolite, the boron having been metasomatically introduced; they have been recorded, locally making up most of the rock, in spilosites and adinoles. Elsewhere in metamorphic rocks the tourmaline may represent the recrystallization of detrital grains present in the original sediment, as in some Dalradian psammitic rocks. The small amounts of boron found in argillaceous sedimentary rocks is not present as tourmaline but appears to have been derived from sea water and to be held by adsorption.

Tourmaline is a common mineral in detrital sediments, different types being found depending on the source. Authigenic tourmaline is known from limestones and as secondary growths on well rounded detrital tourmaline grains in sandstones.

REFERENCES

BRADLEY, J. E. S. and BRADLEY, O. (1953) 'Observations on the colouring of pink and green zoned tourmaline', *Min. Mag.*, vol. 30, p. 26.

DONNAY, G. and BUERGER, M. J. (1950) 'The determination of the crystal structure of tourmaline', *Acta Cryst.*, vol. 3, p. 379.

QUENSEL, P. (1957) 'The paragenesis of the Varuträsk pegmatite including a review of its mineral assemblage', *Arkiv. Min. Geol.* vol. 2, p. 9.

STAATZ, M. H., MURATA, K. J. and GLASS, J. J. (1955) 'Variation of composition and physical properties of tourmaline with its position in the pegmatite', *Amer. Min.*, vol. 40, p. 789.

Axinite

$(Ca, Mn, Fe^{+2})_3Al_2BO_3[Si_4O_{12}]OH$

TRICLINIC $(-)$

α 1·674–1·693
β 1·681–1·701
γ 1·684–1·704
δ 0·009–0·011
$2V_\alpha$ 63°–80°
α approximately $\perp(\bar{1}11)$
Dispersion: $r < v$. D 3·26–3·36. H 6½–7.
Cleavage: {100} good; {001}, {110} and {011} poor.
Twinning: Rare, twin axis [3$\bar{3}$4]?
Colour: Typically lilac-brown, manganoan axinite yellowish; colourless, or vary pale shades of violet or yellow in thin section.
Pleochroism: Weak or absent, but in thick sections α light brown, β violet, γ light yellow or colourless.

A flame test will give the pale green colour due to boron, especially on moistening with H_2SO_4. Manganese may also be detectable.

The basic feature of the structure of axinite (a 7·15, b 9·16, c 8·96 Å, α 88° 04′, β 81° 36′, γ 77° 42′; Z = 2) is a ring of four SiO_4 tetrahedra (composition Si_4O_{12}): separate Si_4O_{12} rings and BO_3 groups are bound together by Fe^{+2}, Al and Ca ions. The Si_4O_{12} rings lie parallel to each other and almost parallel to (010): four of these groups are joined by a double octahedron, Al_2O_{10}, and another four by a double octahedron, $Fe_2O_8(OH)_2$. Chemically, iron and manganese show an approximately reciprocal variation, and in some manganese-rich axinite (tinzenite) manganese also partially replaces calcium. MnO contents of 4 to 5 per cent. are common and the manganese-rich varieties may contain up to 21 per cent MnO.

There are insufficient data to establish the variation in optics with a varying Fe^{+2} : Mn ratio, though the manganese-rich varieties have the highest refractive indices. The normal axinites have a purplish hue on a light to dark brown background whereas the manganese-rich varieties are yellow or sometimes orange-red. The well developed axe-shaped crystals, and in thin section the high relief combined with low birefringence, large 2V and generally at least one cleavage, are characteristic.

Axinite occurs chiefly in contact metamorphic aureoles, generally where metasomatic introduction of boron into altered calcareous sediments or into basic igneous rocks has taken place, particularly where the latter have undergone alteration with the formation of calcite before the metamorphism. Associated minerals may include prehnite, zoisite, datolite, tourmaline, actinolite and calcite.

PART 2

CHAIN SILICATES

PYROXENE GROUP

INTRODUCTION

The pyroxene group includes both orthorhombic and monoclinic minerals. The orthorhombic sub-group consists essentially of the compositional series $MgSiO_3$–$FeSiO_3$ while the monoclinic sub-group includes members having a wide range of chemical composition. A large number of the mono-

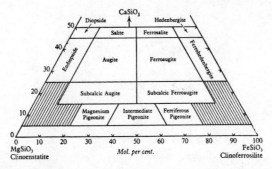

Fig. 33. *Nomenclature of clinopyroxenes in the system* $CaMgSi_2O_6$–$CaFeSi_2O_6$ –$Mg_2Si_2O_6$–$Fe_2Si_2O_6$ *(After Poldervaart, A. & Hess, H. H., 1951, Journ. Geol., vol. 59, p. 472).*

clinic pyroxenes can, as a first approximation, be considered as members of the four component system $CaMgSi_2O_6$–$CaFeSi_2O_6$–$MgSiO_3$–$FeSiO_3$ and the nomenclature used to describe such pyroxenes is illustrated in Fig. 33.

A wide range of ionic substitutions is present in the monoclinic pyroxenes; there is complete replacement of Mg by Fe^{+2} and of Fe^{+2} by Mn, i.e. between $CaMgSi_2O_6$ and $CaFeSi_2O_6$ and between $CaFeSi_2O_6$ and $CaMnSi_2O_6$. In other pyroxenes, however, substitutions are limited, and for example there is very little replacement of either Li or Al in spodumene, $LiAlSi_2O_6$. The general formula of the pyroxene group may be expressed

$$X_{1-p}Y_{1+p}Z_2O_6$$

where $X = Ca,Na$; $Y = Mg,Fe^{+2},Mn,Li,Ni,Al,Fe^{+3},Cr,Ti$; $Z = Si,Al$. In the orthopyroxene series $p \simeq 1$ and the content of trivalent ions is small; in the monoclinic pyroxenes the value of p varies from zero, e.g. diopside, $CaMgSi_2O_6$, to one, e.g. spodumene, $LiAlSi_2O_6$. The wide range of replacements in the Y ions commonly involves substitution of ions of different charge and is accompanied by compensatory replacements of either the X or Z ions; the substitution must be such that the sum of the charges of the XYZ ions is twelve.

The compositions of the principal pyroxene minerals and the order in which they are here considered is as follows

Orthorhombic pyroxenes
     Enstatite–Orthoferrosilite $(Mg,Fe^{+2})_2Si_2O_6$

Monoclinic pyroxenes
     Diopside–Hedenbergite–Johannsenite $Ca(Mg,Fe^{+2},Mn)Si_2O_6$
     Augite–Ferroaugite $(Ca,Na,Mg,Fe^{+2},Mn,Fe^{+3},Al,Ti)_2(Si,Al)_2O_6$
     Pigeonite $(Mg,Fe^{+2},Ca)(Mg,Fe^{+2})Si_2O_6$
     Aegirine–Aegirine-augite $NaFe^{+3}Si_2O_6$–$(Na,Ca)(Fe^{+3},Fe^{+2},Mg)Si_2O_6$
     Spodumene $LiAlSi_2O_6$
     Jadeite $NaAlSi_2O_6$

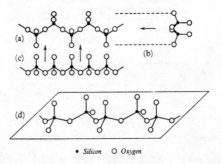

• *Silicon*   O *Oxygen*

Fig. 34. *Idealized illustration of a single pyroxene chain $(SiO_3)_n$ as seen in three projections (a) on (100), (b) along the z direction, (c) along the y direction, and (d) in perspective (after Bragg, W. L., 1937, Atomic Structure of Minerals, Cornell Univ. Press, and Jong, W. F. de, 1959, General Crystallography, Freeman, San Francisco).*

STRUCTURE

The essential feature of the structure of all pyroxenes is the linkage of SiO_4 tetrahedra by sharing two of the four corners to form continuous chains of composition $(SiO_3)_n$, see Fig. 34. The repeat distance along the length of the chain is approximately 5·3 Å and this defines the c parameter of the unit cell. The chains, which are linked laterally by cations (Ca,Mg, Fe,Na,Al), may have various dispositions relative to one another, and it is the grossly different arrangements of chains that lead to the main sub-division of pyroxenes into clino- and orthopyroxenes which are monoclinic and orthorhombic respectively. The cell parameters of the clinopyroxene diopside (a 9·73, b 8·91, c 5·25 Å, β 105° 50′) and the orthopyroxene enstatite ($a \simeq 18·23$, b 8·81, c 5·19 Å) are typical of the two sub-groups. The b and c parameters are similar while a (orthopyroxene) $\simeq 2a \sin \beta$ (clinopyroxene).

Pyroxenes having a composition that can be expressed in terms of $CaMgSi_2O_6$–$CaFeSi_2O_6$–$MgSiO_3$–$FeSiO_3$ can be divided into two structural groups. One group, which ranges in composition from diopside–heden-bergite to $CaMgSi_2O_6$–$CaFeSi_2O_6$ with up to about 25 mol. per cent (Mg,Fe)SiO_3 (Fig. 35) has monoclinic symmetry, and all members of the group are structurally similar to diopside. The compositions of the members of the other group lie near the $MgSiO_3$–$FeSiO_3$ join and have a maximum content of about 15 mol. per cent $CaSiO_3$. In this group those with more

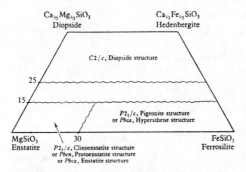

Fig. 35. *Illustration of structural relationships among pyroxenes in the diopside–hedenbergite–enstatite–ferrosilite field.*

than approximately 30 per cent $FeSiO_3$ are monoclinic in the high-temperature form (pigeonite) and are orthorhombic in the low-temperature form. The more magnesium-rich members of this group ($FeSiO_3$ less than about 30 per cent) can exist in three polymorphic forms. These have the structures of enstatite, protoenstatite (both orthorhombic) or clinoenstatite (monoclinic); only the orthorhombic polymorphs are known to occur in rocks.† The structures of the two calcium-poor monoclinic phases, pigeonite and clinoenstatite, differ from that of the diopside-type clinopyroxenes. A small number of pyroxenes have compositions intermediate between the calcium-rich and calcium-poor groups; their structures, however, have not been fully investigated and it is possible that they exist only metastably. Pyroxenes, the compositions of which are outside the diopside–heden-bergite–ferrosilite–enstatite field, all have the clinopyroxene structure.

† Clinoferrohypersthene can occur, however, as lamellae in augite (Binns, R. A., Long, J. V. P. & Reed, S. J. B., *Nature*, 1963, vol. 198, p. 177).

In *diopside* the $[SiO_3]_n$ chains are linked laterally by Ca and Mg ions in the manner shown in Fig. 36. The Mg ions (M_1 positions) are octahedrally coordinated by oxygens which themselves are linked to only one silicon. The larger Ca ions (M_2 positions) are surrounded by 8 oxygens two of which are shared by neighbouring tetrahedra in the chains. The Mg atoms lie principally between the apices of SiO_3 chains, whereas Ca atoms lie principally between their bases. There is no displacement of neighbouring chains in the y direction but neighbouring chains are staggered in the z direction so that a monoclinic cell results.

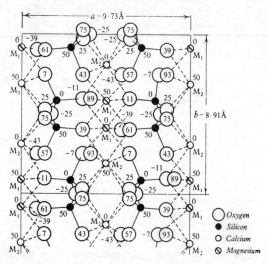

Fig. 36. *Idealized structure of diopside as viewed along the z direction. Atoms overlying one another have been slightly displaced (after Warren, B. E. & Bragg, W. L., 1928, Zeit. Krist., vol. 69, p. 168).*

There is a close relationship between the cell parameters and compositions of pyroxenes in the diopside–hedenbergite–clinoenstatite–ferrosilite field. The c parameter variation is small, but the b parameter is very sensitive to changes in the Mg : Fe ratio. The a and β parameters together vary strongly with both the Ca : Mg and Ca : Fe ratios, and the $a \sin \beta$, as well as the b, parrmeter is diagnostically useful.

The structure of *clinoenstatite* is similar to that of diopside but differences occur because sites M_1 and M_2, occupied by Mg and Ca in diopside, are filled by Mg in clinoenstatite. Both cation sites have six-fold coordination and this causes some distortion of the $[SiO_3]$ chains, and results in the non-equivalence of neighbouring chains.

In *enstatite* and the other *orthorhombic pyroxenes* the $[SiO_3]$ chains are linked laterally by Mg or (Mg,Fe) atoms which are in positions comparable with those of Mg and Ca in diopside. Since both Mg and Fe are smaller ions than Ca the stacking of the chains differs from that in diopside and is such as to produce an orthorhombic cell with approximately double the a dimension of diopside.

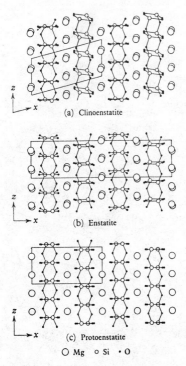

(a) Clinoenstatite

(b) Enstatite

(c) Protoenstatite

◯ Mg ○ Si • O

Fig. 37. *The structures of (a) clinoenstatite, (b) enstatite, and (c) protoenstatite projected on (010): the unit cells are outlined (after Morimoto, N., 1959, Carnegie Inst. Washington, Ann. Rep. Dir. Geophys. Lab., 1958–59, p. 197).*

In the high temperature polymorph, *protoenstatite*, the chains as in diopside are crystallographically equivalent. The chains are, however, fully extended and the c parameter of protoenstatite is greater than that of any other member of the pyroxene group. The structures of clinoenstatite, orthoenstatite and protoenstatite are illustrated in Fig. 37; the sequence of successive planes of Mg atoms in the direction of the x axis can be represented as ABABAB... for clinoenstatite, AABBAABB... for enstatite and AAAA... for protoenstatite.

The structure of *pigeonite* is similar to that of diopside; in pigeonite, however, there are insufficient Ca ions to fill the M_2 sites and the rest of the M_2 sites are occupied by Fe rather than by Mg ions (e.g. a pigeonite of composition $Ca_{0.24}$ $Mg_{0.52}$ $Fe_{1.24}$ Si_2O_6 has $Ca_{0.24}Fe_{0.76}$ in M_2 and $Mg_{0.52}$-$Fe_{0.48}$ in M_1 sites). The M_2 position remains one of six-fold coordination but

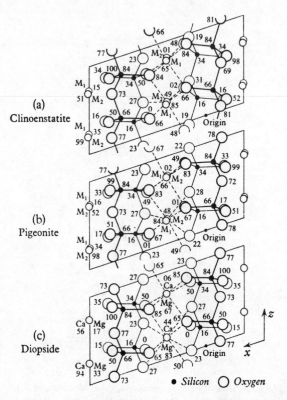

Fig. 38. *The structure of (a) clinoenstatite, (b) pigeonite, and (c) diopside projected on (010) (after Morimoto, N., Appleman, D. E. & Evans, H. T. 1959, Carnegie Inst. Washington, Ann. Rep. Dir. Geophys. Lab., 1958–59, p. 193).*

the coordination of M_2 is reduced from eight to seven by substitution of Fe for Ca ions (Fig. 38). The change in the coordination of the M_2 position is accompanied by some distortion of the chain configuration which results in the non-equivalence of neighbouring chains. In addition the cations in M_1 and M_2 do not lie on diad axes as they do in diopside and the space group becomes $P2_1/c$ compared with $C2/c$ of diopside.

Table 13. PYROXENE ANALYSES

	1.	2.	3.	4.	5.
SiO_2	57·73	50·08	45·95	54·09	48·34
TiO_2	0·04	0·64	0·10	0·28	0·08
Al_2O_3	0·95	1·23	0·90	1·57	0·30
Fe_2O_3	0·42	2·34	0·31	0·74	1·50
Cr_2O_3	0·46	—	—	2·03	—
FeO	3·57	27·85	41·65	1·47	22·94
MnO	0·08	0·85	5·02	0·09	3·70
NiO	0·35	—	—	0·03	—
MgO	36·13	15·78	3·49	16·96	1·06
CaO	0·23	1·44	1·43	21·10	21·30
Na_2O	—	0·05	—	1·37	0·14
K_2O	—	0·02	—	0·15	0·03
H_2O^+	0·52	—	0·65	0·22	0·46
H_2O^-	0·04	0·00	0·09	0·08	—
Total	100·52	100·28	99·59	100·64	99·85
α	—	1·707	1·755	—	1·7225
β	—	—	1·763	> 1·66	1·7300
γ	1·670	1·722	1·773	—	1·7505
$2V_\gamma$	$72\frac{1}{4}°$	130°	83°	70°–75°	$62\frac{1}{2}°$
D	3·249	—	3·88	—	3·535

NUMBERS OF IONS ON THE BASIS OF 6 OXYGENS

	1.	2.	3.	4.	5.
Si	1·972 ⎫2·00	1·937 ⎫2·00	1·972 ⎫2·00	1·961 ⎫2·00	1·988 ⎫2·00
Al	0·028 ⎭	0·056 ⎭	0·028 ⎭	0·039 ⎭	0·012 ⎭
Al	0·010 ⎫	—	0·018 ⎫	0·029 ⎫	0·006 ⎫
Ti	0·001	0·019	0·003	0·008	0·002
Fe^{+3}	0·010	0·068	0·010	0·020	0·046
Cr	0·012	—	—	0·058	—
Mg	1·839	0·910	0·223	0·917	0·065
Ni	0·010 ⎬1·99	— ⎬1·98	— ⎬2·00	0·001 ⎬2·01†	— ⎬1·99
Fe^{+2}	0·102	0·901	1·495	0·045	0·789
Mn	0·002	0·028	0·183	0·003	0·129
Ca	0·008	0·060	0·066	0·820	0·939
Na	—	0·004	—	0·096	0·011
K	— ⎭	0·001 ⎭	— ⎭	0·007 ⎭	0·001 ⎭
Mg	93·9	46·9	12·4	50·8	3·3
Fe	5·7	50·0	83·9	3·8	49·0
Ca	0·4	3·1	3·7	45·4	47·7

1. Enstatite, pyroxenite, North Carolina (Hess, H. H., 1952, *Amer. Journ. Sci.*, Bowen vol., p. 173).
2. Ferrohypersthene, hypersthene–diopside–plagioclase hornfels, Oslo district, Norway (Muir, I. D. & Tilley, C. E., 1958, *Geol. Mag.*, vol. 95, p. 403).
3. Orthoferrosilite, thermally metamorphosed iron-rich rock, Manchuria (Tsuru, K. & Henry, N. F. M., 1937, *Min. Mag.*, vol. 24, p. 527).
4. Chrome diopside, kimberlite, S. Africa (Holmes, A., 1937, *Trans. Geol. Soc. S. Africa*, vol. 39, p. 379; includes ZrO_2 0·12, V_2O_3 0·07, SrO 0·01, CO_2 0·26, Ca tr., S tr.).
5. Hedenbergite, California (Wyckoff, R. W. G., Merwin, H. E. & Washington, H. S., 1925, *Amer. Journ. Sci.* 4th Ser., vol. 10, p. 389).

† Includes Zr 0·002, V 0·002.

Table 13. PYROXENE ANALYSES—*continued*

	6.	7.	8.	9.	10.
SiO_2	52·92	46·61	49·68	48·90	52·84
TiO_2	0·50	1·18	0·56	0·12	0·22
Al_2O_3	2·80	3·47	0·78	3·86	0·44
Fe_2O_3	0·85	0·90	3·29	4·65	1·06
Cr_2O_3	0·88	—	—	—	—
FeO	5·57	20·18	18·15	25·35	16·89
MnO	0·15	1·11	0·59	0·51	0·56
NiO	0·10	—	—	—	—
MgO	16·40	7·27	16·19	6·87	23·51
CaO	19·97	17·24	9·90	7·96	4·06
Na_2O	0·35	1·04	0·65	0·58	0·19
K_2O	0·01	0·27	0·15	0·20	0·00
H_2O^+	0·10	0·42	0·10	0·57	—
H_2O^-	0·07	0·04	0·00	0·35	0·22
Total	100·67	99·73	100·04	99·92	99·99
α	1·6818	1·710	1·709	—	—
β	1·6865	1·716	—	—	—
γ	1·7085	1·736	1·738	—	—
$2V_\gamma$	49°	52°	28°–30°	—	—
D	—	3·49	—	—	—

NUMBERS OF IONS ON THE BASIS OF 6 OXYGENS

	6.		7.		8.		9.		10.	
Si	1·929	2·00	1·859	2·00	1·905		1·941	2·00	1·955	
Al	0·071		0·141		0·034	2·00	0·059		0·018	2·00
Al	0·049		0·021		—		0·121		—	
Ti	0·014		0·035		0·016		0·004		0·006	
Fe^{+3}	0·024		0·026		0·094		0·139		0·030	
Cr	0·026		—		—		—		--	
Mg	0·891		0·432		0·925		0·406		1·296	
Ni	0·003	1·99	—	2·05			—	1·92		2·02
Fe^{+2}	0·170		0·673		0·582	2·04	0·842		0·523	
Mn	0·005		0·037		0·019		0·017		0·017	
Ca	0·780		0·737		0·407		0·338		0·161	
Na	0·024		0·080		0·048		0·046		0·014	
K	0·000		0·014		0·008		0·010		0·000	
Mg	47·6		22·8		45·6		23·3		63·9	
Fe	10·7		38·6		34·3		57·3		28·1	
Ca	41·7		38·6		20·1		19·4		8·0	

6. Chromian augite, gabbro, Bushveld Complex (Hess, H. H., 1949, *Amer. Min.*, vol. 34, p. 621).

7. Ferroaugite, syenite, South-West Africa (Simpson, E. S. W., 1954, *Trans. Geol. Soc. S. Africa*, vol. 57, p. 126).

8. Sub-calcic augite, basalt, Japan (Kuno, H., 1955, *Amer. Min.*, vol. 40, p. 70).

9. Sub-calcic ferroaugite, andesite, Japan (Kuno H. & Inoue, T., 1949, *Proc. Japan Acad.*, vol. 25, p. 128).

10. Magnesian pigeonite, andesite, Japan (Kuno, H. & Nagashima, K., 1952, *Amer. Min.*, vol. 37, p. 1000).

Table 13. PYROXENE ANALYSES—*continued*

	11.	12.	13.	14.
SiO_2	49·72	51·92	64·89	59·38
TiO_2	0·85	0·77	—	0·04
Al_2O_3	0·90	1·85	26·74	25·82
Fe_2O_3	1·72	31·44	0·57	0·45
Cr_2O_3	—	—	—	0·01
FeO	27·77	0·75	0·04	tr.
MnO	0·98	—	0·01	0·00
NiO	—	—	—	—
MgO	12·69	—	0·00	0·12
CaO	3·80	—	0·00	0·13
Na_2O	0·23	12·86	0·05	13·40
K_2O	0·12	0·19	0·16	0·02
H_2O^+	1·27	0·17	0·48	0·22
H_2O^-	0·08	—	0·06	0·16
Total	100·13	99·95	100·12	99·75
α	1·7137	1·770	1·661	1·654
β	1·7137	1·812	1·666	1·657
	1·7417	1·830	1·676	1·666
$2V_y$	0°–12°	—	—	70°
D	3·44	—	3·163	3·43

NUMBERS OF IONS ON THE BASIS OF 6 OXYGENS

	11.		12.		13.		14.	
Si	1·968	} 2·00	1·986	} 2·00	2·026	} 2·03	1·998	} 2·00
Al	0·032		0·014		—		0·002	
Al	0·010		0·069		0·984		1·022	
Ti	0·025		0·022		—		0·001	
Fe^{+3}	0·051		0·905		0·014		0·012	
Cr	—		—		—		0·000	
Mg	0·749		—		—		0·006	
Ni	—	} 1·97	—	} 1·98	—	} 1·90†	—	} 1·92
Fe^{+2}	0·919		0·024		0·001		—	
Mn	0·033		—		—		—	
Ca	0·161		—		—		0·005	
Na	0·018		0·953		0·002		0·874	
K	0·006		0·008		0·006		0·001	
Mg	39·2		—		—		—	
Fe	52·4		—		—		—	
Ca	8·4		—		—		—	

11. Pigeonite, andesite, Scotland (Hallimond, A. F., 1914, *Min. Mag.*, vol. 17, p. 97).
12. Aegirine, riebeckite–albite granite, Nigeria (Greenwood, R., 1951, *Bull. Geol. Soc. Amer.*, vol. 62, p. 1151).
13. Wine-yellow spodumene, pegmatite, Sweden (Quensel, P., 1938, *Geol. För. Förh. Stockholm*, vol. 60, p. 201; includes Li_2O 7·12).
14. White jadeite, serpentinite, California (Coleman, R. G., 1955, *Amer. Min.*, vol. 40, p. 312).

† Includes Li 0·894.

Enstatite–Orthoferrosilite

$(Mg,Fe^{+2})[SiO_3]$

ORTHORHOMBIC $(+)(-)$

α 1·650–1·768
β 1·653–1·770
γ 1·658–1·788
δ 0·007–0·020
$2V_\alpha$ 50°–125°
$\alpha = y$, O.A.P. (100)

Enstatite $(+)$ Hypersthene $(-)$

Dispersion: $r > v$†, weak to strong. D 3·21–3·96. H 5–6.
Cleavage: {210} good; {100}, {010} partings. (210) : (2$\bar{1}$0) $\simeq$ 88°.
Colour: Magnesium-rich members colourless, grey, green, yellow, brown; colourless in thin section. Iron-rich members green or dark brown; reddish or greenish in thin section.
Pleochroism: Enstatite none, other compositions variable weak to strong: α pink, pale reddish brown, purple-violet, smoky brown; β yellow, pale greenish brown, pale reddish yellow, pale brown; γ green, pale green, smoky green.

Two crystallographic orientations have been used in describing the orthorhombic pyroxenes. In the one adopted here (a 18·23, b 8·81, c 5·19 Å) the largest dimension is taken as a, thus the optic axial plane is (100) and the prismatic cleavage {210}. The nomenclature used to describe the compositional variation of the series is shown in Fig. 41; the divisions between enstatite and bronzite, and between eulite and orthoferrosilite are at Fs_{12} and Fs_{88}, compositions at which there is a change in the optic sign.

MgSiO$_3$ and the magnesium-rich members of the series occur in at least three polymorphic forms, the low-temperature orthorhombic enstatite (the form almost universally found in rocks), the high-temperature protoenstatite which also has orthorhombic symmetry, and clinoenstatite. Members of the clinoenstatite–clinoferrosilite series have from time to time been reported as natural minerals, but in almost all cases the material has subsequently been shown to be an orthopyroxene solid solution. Enstatite (En_{100}) is stable to 985°C, and above this temperature inverts to protoenstatite (Fig. 39). The inversion temperature is, however, pressure sensitive, and the inversion curve has a slope of 84°/kilobar. Protoenstatite can be quenched and studied at room temperature, but on cooling it usually undergoes a metastable inversion to clinoenstatite which thus forms in the

† The dispersion measured over α changes from $r < v$ to $r > v$ at approximately Fs_{15}, and from $r > v$ to $r < v$ at Fs_{50}, thus at 2V 90° and $2V_\alpha$ 50° there is no dispersion.

stability field of enstatite. Protoenstatite is the stable $MgSiO_3$ polymorph between 985°C and 1385°C; the polymorphic relationships at higher temperatures are uncertain. Protoenstatite solid solution $En_{76}Di_{24}$ melts incongruently to forsterite and a more siliceous liquid at 1386°C, while pure protoenstatite melts incongruently to forsterite and liquid at 1557°C.

CHEMISTRY

Ions other than Mg and Fe^{+2} are invariably present in the orthopyroxenes and these commonly include Ca, Mn, Ni, Fe^{+3}, Cr, Al and Ti; in most specimens, however, the sum of these constituents does not exceed ten mol. per

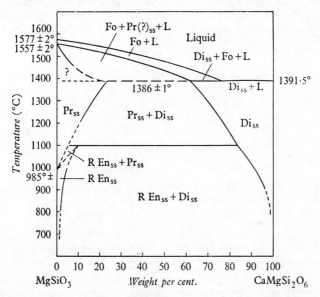

Fig. 39. *Equilibrium relations along the join* $MgSiO_3$–$CaMgSi_2O_6$. *Fo forsterite; Pr_{ss} protoenstatite solid solutions; R En_{ss} orthopyroxene solid solutions; Di_{ss} diopside solid solutions; L liquid (after Boyd, F. R. & Schairer, J. F., 1964, Journ. Petr., vol. 5, p. 275).*

cent. Chromium and nickel occur mainly in the magnesium-rich orthopyroxenes of igneous rocks. High contents of manganese are found in iron-rich orthopyroxenes of igneous rocks as well as in a wide range of compositions in the orthorhombic pyroxenes of metamorphic rocks (e.g. Table 13, anal. 3); high contents of aluminium occur mainly in orthopyroxenes of high grade metamorphic rocks, e.g. pyroxene granulites. In most analyses the content of CaO is not greater than 1·5 weight per cent (equivalent to approximately 0·06 Ca ions per formula unit, i.e. $(Mg,Fe^{+2})_{97}Ca_3)$.

Solid solution between enstatite (and protoenstatite) and diopside is not complete at solidus temperatures. The relationships in the system $MgSiO_3$–$CaMgSi_2O_6$ are illustrated in Fig. 39, which shows that on the protoenstatite side of the system the solvus curve intersects the solidus at the composition $En_{76}Di_{24}$ at 1386°C (i.e. the maximum solubility of diopside in protoenstatite is 24 weight per cent). The solubility decreases rapidly as the temperature falls and is 5 per cent $CaMgSi_2O_6$ at 1100°C, the temperature of the inversion enstatite ($En_{90}Di_{10}$) ⇌ protoenstatite ($En_{95}Di_5$). Below 1100°C the solubility of diopside in protoenstatite decreases still further and is zero at 985°C, the inversion temperature of protoenstatite (En_{100}) to enstatite. At 985°C the maximum solubility of diopside in enstatite is 5 weight per cent but decreases at lower temperatures and is only 2 per cent at 800°C. In many magnesium-rich orthopyroxenes (Fs_{10}–Fs_{30}) of plutonic rocks the bulk of the $Ca(Mg,Fe)Si_2O_6$ initially in

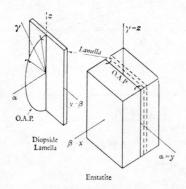

Fig. 40. *The optical and crystallographic directions for enstatite and included diopside lamellae (after Hess, H. H., 1960, Geol. Soc. Amer., Mem. 80).*

solid solution at the temperature of crystallization is exsolved on cooling. The exsolved material forms lamellae of a calcium-rich monoclinic pyroxene as thin parallel-sided continuous sheets, or as rows of flattened blebs, in the (100) plane of the orthorhombic host (*pyroxenes of Bushveld type*), Fig. 40. Similar lamellae occur in the more iron-rich (> Fs_{30}) orthopyroxenes of plutonic rocks; these pyroxenes are inverted pigeonites (see p. 129) and the exsolved plates of the calcium-rich monoclinic pyroxene are oriented parallel to a plane which represents (001) of the original pigeonite (*pyroxenes of Stillwater type*). The calcium content (≃ 4 weight per cent CaO) of the latter is about three times greater than that of the Bushveld type pyroxenes.

Magnesium-rich orthopyroxenes are an early crystallization product of basic magmas; the $(Mg,Fe)SiO_3$ pyroxene which crystallizes from more iron-rich differentiates of basic magmas is a monoclinic pigeonite which on slow cooling later inverts to an orthopyroxene. This relationship has usually been considered to result from the crystallization of the magnesium-rich orthopyroxene at magmatic temperatures below those of the enstatite $\rightleftharpoons$ monoclinic pyroxene inversion, which had been determined as 1140°C for the pure magnesium end-member, and as 955°C for a composition of approximately 88 mol. per cent $FeSiO_3$. This conclusion is, however, not justified in view of the metastable character of the magnesium-rich members of the clinoenstatite–clinoferrosilite series.

In the synthetic system $MgO–SiO_2–H_2O$, enstatite crystallizes at temperatures above 650°C at water vapour pressures greater than 5000 lb/in², and is stable in the presence of water vapour below approximately 850°C; the pressure–temperature curve of the reaction

$$\underset{\text{talc}}{(OH)_2Mg_3Si_4O_{10}} + \underset{\text{forsterite}}{Mg_2SiO_4} \rightleftharpoons \underset{\text{enstatite}}{5MgSiO_3} + H_2O$$

is shown in Fig. 79 (p. 229).

Orthopyroxenes are sometimes altered to serpentine and where alteration is complete the pseudomorphs show a characteristic bronze-like metallic lustre or schiller and are known as bastite. Alteration to a pale green amphibole, commonly referred to as uralite, also occurs.

OPTICAL AND PHYSICAL PROPERTIES

There is very good correlation between the optical properties and chemical composition of the orthopyroxene series (Fig. 41). The γ refractive index increases by approximately 0·00125 for each atomic per cent $(Fe^{+2} + Fe^{+3} + Mn)$. Deviations from this linear variation are mainly due to variable contents of Al, which in amounts between 0·070 and 0·140 atoms per formula unit increase the γ index by 0·005 at the composition Fs_0; this effect diminishes to zero for the most iron-rich members of the series. The rate of increase of the α index is less than that of the γ index and the birefringence increases progressively with increasing $(Fe^{+2} + Fe^{+3} + Mn)$. Because many crushed fragments of orthopyroxenes lie on a {210} cleavage plane the γ index can be measured with greater ease and accuracy than the α and β indices, and this is the most precise optical method of determining the Fs content of an orthorhombic pyroxene.

The optic axial angles of the members of the orthopyroxene series vary continuously and symmetrically with increasing replacement of Mg by Fe^{+2}. Enstatite, Fs_{0-12}, is optically positive ($2V_\gamma$ 55°–90°), in the bronzite and hypersthene range of composition $2V_\gamma$ increases to approximately 130° at Fs_{50}, then decreases and is 90° at Fs_{88} at which composition the series is again optically positive.

Many orthorhombic pyroxenes, but particularly those of bronzite and hypersthene composition, display a characteristic α pink, γ green pleochroism. The presence and intensity of the pleochroism is not simply related to the iron or aluminium content of individual orthopyroxenes but depends upon the simultaneous substitutions of Fe^{+3} in Y sites and Al in both Y and Z sites. The orthorhombic pyroxenes of volcanic rocks are commonly zoned and have magnesium-rich cores and more iron-rich margins.

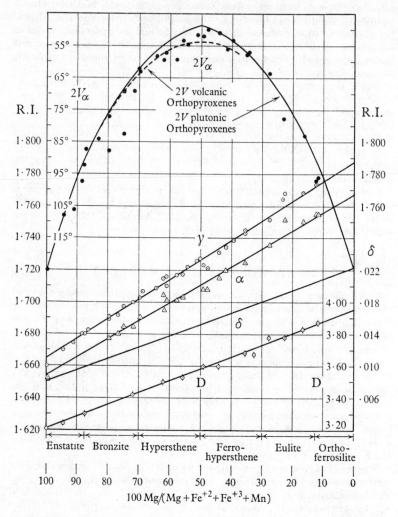

Fig. 41. *The relationship of the optical and physical properties to the chemical composition of the orthorhombic pyroxenes.*

DISTINGUISHING FEATURES

Many orthopyroxenes can be distinguished from clinopyroxenes by their characteristic pink to green pleochroism. In the absence of pleochroism they are distinguished from clinopyroxenes by their lower birefringence and their straight extinction in all [001] zone sections. Furthermore, bronzite, hypersthene, ferrohypersthene and eulite are all optically negative. Orthopyroxenes are distinguished from sillimanite by the presence of {210} and the absence of {010} cleavage, as well as by the smaller optic axial angles of sillimanite; they are distinguished from andalusite by the positive sign of the magnesium-rich, and the greater birefringence of the more iron-rich, orthopyroxenes.

PARAGENESIS

Magnesium-rich orthopyroxenes are common constituents of some ultrabasic rocks, e.g. pyroxenites, harzburgites, lherzolites and picrites, in which they are commonly associated with forsteritic olivine, diopsidic augite and magnesium spinel; they are also common constituents in the olivine-rich inclusions in basalts. Orthopyroxenes occur also in the cumulate rocks of many layered intrusions, e.g. Bushveld, Stillwater and Skaergaard; in the latter the early formed orthopyroxene is $Fs_{18.5}$ in composition, is progressively richer in iron in the later cumulates and is $\simeq Fs_{60}$ (inverted pigeonite) at the two-pyroxene boundary. More iron-rich orthopyroxenes are rare in igneous rocks but occur in some highly differentiated rocks in dolerite sills, and in some granites. Orthorhombic pyroxene is the essential ferromagnesian constituent of norites and in many of these rocks its formation is associated with the assimilation of aluminium-rich sediments by basic magma. The main effect of this reaction is to increase the amount of orthopyroxene and the anorthite content of the plagioclase at the expense of calcium-rich pyroxene:

$$Ca(Mg,Fe)Si_2O_6 + Al_2SiO_5 \rightarrow (Mg,Fe)SiO_3 + CaAl_2Si_2O_8$$
$$\text{salite} \qquad\qquad\qquad\qquad \text{hypersthene} \quad \text{anorthite}$$

Orthorhombic pyroxene is the most characteristic and important ferromagnesian mineral in the rocks of the charnockite series, and is a typical mineral of the granulite facies. It also occurs in medium grade thermally metamorphosed argillaceous rocks in which, together with cordierite, it is largely derived from the chlorite of the original sediment:

$$(OH)_8(Mg,Fe^{+2})_4Al_4Si_2O_{10} + 5SiO_2 \rightarrow 2(Mg,Fe^{+2})SiO_3$$
$$\text{chlorite} \qquad\qquad\qquad\qquad\qquad \text{orthopyroxene}$$
$$+ (Mg,Fe^{+2})_2Al_4Si_5O_{18} + 4H_2O$$
$$\text{cordierite}$$

Its presence, however, in argillaceous hornfelses is generally indicative of higher metamorphic grades, in which it is derived from the breakdown of biotite:

$$(OH)_2K(Mg,Fe^{+2})_3AlSi_3O_{10} + 3SiO_2 \rightarrow 3(Mg,Fe)SiO_3 + KAlSi_3O_8 + H_2O$$
$$\text{biotite} \qquad\qquad\qquad\qquad \text{hypersthene} \quad \text{orthoclase}$$

Eulite and orthoferrosilite are characteristic constituents, associated with fayalite, hedenbergite, grunerite and almandine–spessartine garnet, of eulysite, a regionally metamorphosed iron-rich sediment.

REFERENCES

GREEN, D. H. (1964) 'The petrogenesis of the high-temperature peridotite in the Lizard area, Cornwall', *Journ. Petr.*, vol. 5, p. 135.

HESS, H. H. (1952) 'Orthopyroxenes of the Bushveld type, ion substitution and changes in unit cell dimensions', *Amer. Journ. Sci.*, Bowen vol., p. 173.

KUNO, H. (1954) 'Study of orthopyroxenes from volcanic rocks', *Amer. Min.*, vol. 39, p. 30.

Diopside–Hedenbergite
Johannsenite

$Ca(Mg,Fe)[Si_2O_6]$
$Ca(Mn,Fe)[Si_2O_6]$

MONOCLINIC (+)

Diopside–Hedenbergite

α 1·664–1·726 (1·732)†
β 1·672–1·730
γ 1·694–1·751 (1·757)†
δ 0·031–0·024
$2V_\gamma$ 50°–62°
$\gamma:z$ 38°–48°
$\beta = y$, O.A.P. (010)
Dispersion: $r > v$, weak to strong.
D 3·22–3·56. H 5½–6½.

Johannsenite

1·703–1·716
1·711–1·728
1·732–1·745
0·028–0·029
68°–70°
46°–48°
$\beta = y$, O.A.P. (010)
$r > v$, moderate.
D 3·44–3·55. H 6.

Cleavage: {110} good; {100}, {010}, {001} partings. (110) : (1$\bar{1}$0) $\simeq$ 87°.
Twinning: {100}, {001} simple and multiple, common.
Colour: diopside, white, pale green, dark green; colourless in thin section.
Hedenbergite, brownish green, dark green, black; pale green, yellow-green;
brownish green in thin section. Johannsenite, clove-brown, grey, green;
colourless in thin section.
Pleochroism: Salite, ferrosalite and hedenbergite may show weak pleo-
chroism in pale greens, greenish-brown, bluish green and yellow-green.

CHEMISTRY

In natural pyroxenes there is a complete series of compositions between
diopside and hedenbergite. Solid solution along the $CaMgSi_2O_6$–$MgSiO_3$
and $CaFeSi_2O_6$–$FeSiO_3$ joins of the pyroxene quadrilateral, however, is
limited to approximately 35 and 40 wt. per cent $MgSiO_3$ and $FeSiO_3$ respectively. Similar amounts of solid solution of $(Mg,Fe)SiO_3$ in $Ca(Mg,Fe)Si_2O_6$,
i.e. between diopside–hedenbergite and augite–ferroaugite, are common in
the pyroxenes of basic rocks. Aluminium is present in most diopside-
hedenbergites but the replacement of Si by Al does not usually exceed 10
per cent. Chromium is characterisitically present (e.g. Table 13, anal. 4) in
the diopsides and endiopsides (see Fig. 33, p. 99) of basic and ultrabasic
rocks, but Ni is rarely present in more than trace amounts. The content of
Mn is small (< 0·25 wt. per cent MnO) in the magnesium-rich members of
the series but often occurs in larger amounts in the more iron-rich members
(e.g. hedenbergites contain up to 4 per cent. MnO). The majority of the
johannsenite minerals approximate closely in composition to $CaMnSi_2O_6$;

---

† Values for synthetic hedenbergite.

ferroan johannsenites, however, containing 1·0 Ca, 0·5 Mn and 0·5 Fe ions per formula unit are known and there is little doubt that solid solution between $CaFeSi_2O_6$ and $CaMnSi_2O_6$ is complete.

The maximum solubility of $MgSiO_3$ in $CaMgSi_2O_6$ is 37 wt. per cent (see Fig. 39) and occurs at 1386°C, the temperature at which melting begins in this series of conjugate pyroxenes. The solubility decreases at lower temperatures and at 750°C there is only 5 per cent $MgSiO_3$ in solid solution

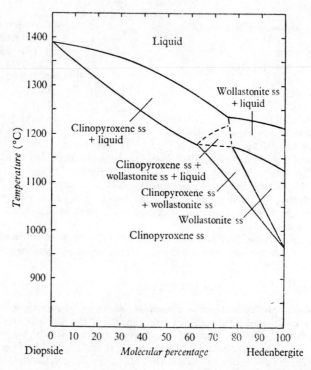

Fig. 42. *Phase diagram of the join diopside–hedenbergite (after Turnock, A.C., 1962, Carnegie Inst. Washington, Ann. Rep. Dir. Geophys. Lab., 1961–62, p. 81).*

with diopside. A break in the slope of the solvus boundary occurs between 1050 and 1100°C due to the inversion protoenstatite ⇌ enstatite.

The early work by Bowen *et al* (1933) on the system CaO–FeO–SiO_2 showed that hedenbergite is not stable at liquidus temperatures and undergoes an inversion at 965°C to an iron-rich wollastonite solid solution. A more recent investigation of the $CaMgSi_2O_6$–$CaFeSi_2O_6$ system (Fig. 42) has shown that it has a binary character only for compositions having between 0 and approximately 60 mol. per cent of the hedenbergite component. In the iron-rich part of the system a wollastonite solid solution crystallizes at liquidus temperatures and subsequently inverts to an iron-rich member of the diopside–hedenbergite series at subsolidus temperatures.

In the system $CaSiO_3$–$FeSiO_3$, hedenbergite forms a solid solution series which extends to compositions containing approximately 80 per cent $FeSiO_3$. With greater amounts of $FeSiO_3$, incongruent decomposition occurs with the crystallization of fayalitic olivine and tridymite.

OPTICAL AND PHYSICAL PROPERTIES

The variation of refractive indices with composition of the members of the diopside–hedenbergite series shows large discrepancies compared with the assumed linear variation between the two synthetic end-members (Fig. 43). It has been shown experimentally that the entry both of Al and Fe^{+3} into the diopside structure is accompanied by increases in the refractive indices, and the discrepancies shown by natural members of the series are due mainly to their varying contents of Al and Fe^{+3}. The optic axial angles of the members of the series do not show major variation and $2V_\gamma$ is between 56° and 62° for most of these minerals. Between diopside and hedenbergite the extinction angle $\gamma : z$ increases from 38° to 48°, the variation, however, is erratic and extinction angles are of little practical diagnostic value.

DISTINGUISHING FEATURES

The members of the diopside–hedenbergite series cannot in all cases be distinguished from clinopyroxenes of augite and ferroaugite composition, but in general they have larger 2V's than those of augite and ferroaugite with comparable refractive indices. They are distinguished from the orthopyroxenes by higher birefringence, oblique extinction in prismatic section and, except for enstatite and orthoferrosilite, by being optically positive. Diopside is distinguished from wollastonite by having only two cleavages, and by higher refringence and birefringence. Ferrosalite and hedenbergite are distinguished from rhodonite by higher birefringence, lower 2V, and by the two cleavages of the pyroxene.

PARAGENESIS

Members of the diopside–hedenbergite series occur in a variety of metamorphic rocks, and the more magnesium-rich varieties are particularly characteristic constituents of thermally metamorphosed calcium-rich sediments. Diopside forms, following tremolite, relatively early in the crystallization sequence of the progressive thermal metamorphism of siliceous dolomites:

$$Ca_2Mg_5Si_8O_{22}(OH)_2 + 3CaCO_3 + 2SiO_2 \rightarrow 5CaMgSi_2O_6 + 3CO_2 + H_2O$$
$$\text{tremolite} \qquad\qquad\qquad\qquad\qquad \text{diopside}$$

Common assemblages are diopside–forsterite or diopside–forsterite–calcite; the latter assemblage is unstable at higher temperatures and is replaced by monticellite:

$$CaMgSi_2O_6 + Mg_2SiO_4 + 2CaCO_3 \rightarrow 3CaMgSiO_4 + 2CO_2$$
$$\text{diopside} \qquad \text{forsterite} \qquad \text{calcite} \qquad \text{monticellite}$$

Hedenbergite occurs in both thermally and regionally metamorphosed

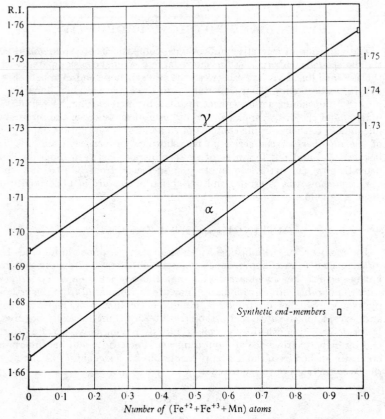

Fig. 43. *The relationship between the refractive indices and composition in the diopside–hedenbergite minerals.*

iron-rich sediments, and together with grunerite and fayalite is a characteristic constituent of eulysite. Diopside, salite, ferrosalite and hedenbergite are all typical skarn minerals, and hedenbergite in particular is associated with Pb and Zn metasomatism.

Diopside occurs in some picrites and basalts, whereas salite is the typical pyroxene in hypabyssal rocks derived from alkali basalt magmas, e.g. in the picrite and picrodolerite of the Garbh Eilean sill, Shiant Isles, and in the teschenite of the Black Jack Sill, New South Wales. The clinopyroxene in olivine-rich nodules in basalts is commonly an endiopside. Hedenbergite occurs in quartz-bearing syenites, and also in some fayalite granites (e.g. the ring complexes of northern Nigeria) and granophyres. Ferrohedenbergite is a major constituent of the fayalite ferrogabbros of the Skaergaard intrusion; in some of these ferrogabbros the mineral crystallized first as a wollastonite solid solution which later inverted to ferrohedenbergite.

REFERENCES

BOWEN, N. L., SCHAIRER, J. F. and POSNJAK, E. (1933) 'The system CaO–FeO–SiO$_2$', *Amer. Journ. Sci.*, 5th Ser., vol. 26, p. 193.

HESS, H. H. (1949) 'Chemical composition and optical properties of common clinopyroxenes, Part I', *Amer. Min.*, vol. 34, p. 621.

MURRAY, R. J. (1954) 'The clinopyroxenes of the Garbh Eilean sill, Shiant Isles', *Geol. Mag.*, vol. 91, p. 17.

WILKINSON, J. F. G. (1956) 'Clinopyroxenes of alkali-basalt magma', *Amer. Min.*, vol. 41, p. 724.

Augite–Ferroaugite $(Ca,Na,Mg,Fe^{+2},Mn,Fe^{+3},Al,Ti)_2[(Si,Al)_2O_6]$

MONOCLINIC $(+)$

α 1·662–1·735
β 1·670–1·741
γ 1·688–1·761
δ 0·018–0·033
$2V_\gamma$ 25°–83°†
$\gamma:z$ 35°–48°; $\beta = y$, O.A.P. (010)

Dispersion: $r > v$, weak to strong. D 2·96–3·52. H 5–6.

Cleavage: {110} good; {100}, {010} partings. (110) : (1$\bar{1}$0) $\simeq$ 87°.

Twinning: {100} simple, multiple, common; {001} multiple.

Colour: Pale brown, brown, purplish brown, green, black; colourless, pale brown, pale purplish brown, pale greenish brown or pale green in thin section. Omphacite and fassaite varieties pale to dark green in colour; colourless to pale green in thin section.

Pleochroism: More strongly coloured varieties show weak to moderate pleochroism; titanaugite moderate to strong pleochroism: α pale greenish, pale brownish, green, greenish yellow; β pale brown, pale yellow-green, violet; γ pale green, greyish green, violet.

The subdivision of the augitic pyroxenes into augite, ferroaugite, sub-calcic augite and subcalcic ferroaugite is an arbitrary one (see Fig. 33), and there is continuous variation in their chemistry and optical properties, as well as with those of the diopside–hedenbergite series. The compositions of the omphacitic and fassaitic pyroxenes lie outside the $CaMgSi_2O_6$–$CaFeSi_2O_6$ --$MgSiO_3$–$FeSiO_3$ field; in omphacite substantial replacement of Ca by Na and (Mg,Fe^{+2}) by Al, and in fassaite the substitution of (Mg,Fe^{+2})Si by (Al,Fe^{+3})Al is present. Clinopyroxenes containing a high content of Ti, and characterized by their violet-purple pleochroism, are termed titanaugites.

CHEMISTRY

The great majority of pyroxenes contain between 2 and 4 per cent Al_2O_3 (equivalent to between 0·1 and 0·2 Al ions per formula unit) and in most of these minerals Si + Al is sufficient to satisfy the numerical requirements of the Z group. In rare cases it is necessary to allot Ti also to tetrahedral positions in order, on the basis of 6 oxygens per formula unit, to bring the Z group to 2 atoms. Common augite contains relatively small amounts of Ti (0·5 to 0·8 TiO_2 per cent), but in titanaugite the typical content is between 3 and 6 per cent TiO_2, equivalent to about 1 in 10 of the Y positions.

† Values of 2V greater than $\simeq 50°$ are uncommon except for fassaite (2V 51°–62°) and omphacite (2V 58°–83°) varieties.

Chromium is an important minor constituent in the magnesium-rich augites (e.g. Table 13, anal. 6); in contrast the largest contents of Mn occur in the ferroaugites. Alkalis, largely Na_2O, generally amount to between 0·5 and 0·8 per cent. In omphacite, however, sodium is an essential constituent and it may occupy as much as half the X positions, the charge balance being maintained by Al in Y positions; thus the main replacements in omphacite may be expressed as $Ca(Mg,Fe^{+2}) \rightleftharpoons Na,Al$. The chief characteristics of the composition of fassaite are the high content of Ca ($CaO \simeq 25$ per cent, equivalent to approximately one Ca ion per formula unit), a high Al content, and a high ferric/ferrous iron ratio. Monovalent ions are not present in appreciable amounts and the charge balance is maintained by the coupled substitution $(Mg,Fe^{+2})Si \rightleftharpoons (Al,Fe^{+3})Al$.

The relationships of the boundary pairs in the system $CaMgSi_2O_6$–$CaFeSi_2O_6$–$MgSiO_3$–$FeSiO_3$ are known both from experimental investigation (i.e. $CaMgSi_2O_6$–$MgSiO_3$, pp. 109–110; $MgSiO_3$–$FeSiO_3$; $CaFeSi_2O_6$–$FeSiO_3$, p. 117) and from natural minerals (e.g. diopside–hedenbergite). The extent to which the immiscibility gap in the synthetic diopside–protoenstatite system extends into the augite and subcalcic augite fields is estimated from natural minerals to reach to at least $Ca_{20}Mg_{55}Fe_{25}$ and possibly $Ca_{20}Mg_{50}Fe_{30}$. Similarly the decomposition reactions, which in the $CaFeSi_2O_6$–$FeSiO_3$ system give rise to the crystallization of fayalitic olivine and tridymite from compositions more iron-rich than 80 per cent $FeSiO_3$, extend into the four component system, and there is a gap in pyroxene compositions in the iron-rich sector comparable with that in the magnesium-rich part of the system.

The pyroxenes of lavas, particularly the subcalcic augites and subcalcic ferroaugites of the quickly cooled groundmass of basalts and andesites, show a wide range of $(Mg,Fe) \rightleftharpoons Ca$ substitution. The extent of this substitution in the more iron-rich pyroxenes, compared with those of the $MgSiO_3$–$CaMgSi_2O_6$ series, may be related to the higher Fe^{+3} content of the former. Some subcalcic augites, however, are unmixed on a cryptoperthitic scale, and it is thus possible that their more extensive compositional range is due to the crystallization of metastable solid solutions.

The compositions of clinopyroxenes which have crystallized under slow cooling plutonic conditions show a more restricted range of solid solution, and the usual limit of $(Mg,Fe)_2Si_2O_6$ initially in solid solution in $Ca(Mg,Fe)Si_2O_6$ is less than 40 mol. per cent. On cooling, much of the $(Mg,Fe)_2Si_2O_6$ held in solid solution at the temperature of crystallization is exsolved either as pigeonite or orthopyroxene.

Two pyroxenes, one calcium-rich and one calcium-poor, commonly form at an early stage in the fractional crystallization of tholeiitic magma. During the initial period of crystallization the composition of the augite is $\simeq Ca_{45}Mg_{45}Fe_{10}$, while the calcium-poor phase is an orthorhombic pyroxene $\simeq Ca_4Mg_{77}Fe_{19}$ in composition. As differentiation proceeds on further cooling, both pyroxenes become richer in the Fe component but in most intrusions the pyroxenes do not become more iron-rich than $Ca_{35}Mg_{35}Fe_{30}$ and $Ca_{10}Mg_{45}Fe_{45}$ respectively before crystallization is complete. Although with more extreme fractionation the calcium-rich pyroxene becomes even richer in iron, the calcium-poor phases cease to crystallize and subsequent pyroxene crystallization is represented solely by a calcium-rich ferroaugite. Continued crystallization of the latter takes place with increasing amounts of both the iron and calcium components and the late-stage clinopyroxenes approximate to hedenbergite in composition. The limit to the compositional field in which two pyroxene phases

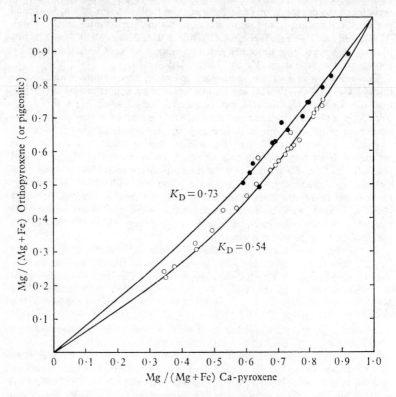

Fig. 44. *Graphical expression of the distribution of Mg and* Fe^{+2} *between coexisting calcic pyroxene and orthopyroxene (or pigeonite) from metamorphic rocks, curve* $K_D = 0.54$; *crystallized from silicate melt, curve* $K_D = 0.73$ *(after Kretz, R., 1963, Journ. Geol., vol. 71, p. 779).*

crystallize together is termed the two-pyroxene boundary. The relationships in the more iron-rich part of the $CaMgSi_2O_6$–$CaFeSi_2O_6$–$MgSiO_3$–$FeSiO_3$ quadrilateral have not been investigated and the absence of natural iron-rich pigeonite cannot be explained on the basis of experimental data. It is, however, possible that its absence may result from a shift in the liquidus minimum of the pigeonite–augite cotectic towards the calcium-rich side of its intersection with the solvus to a point where the liquidus minimum passes beyond the intersection with the solvus.

When the compositions of coexisting calcium-rich and calcium-poor pyroxenes of igneous rocks are plotted on a $CaSiO_3$–$MgSiO_3$–$FeSiO_3$ diagram the projections of the joins of the pairs of pyroxenes, as first noted by Hess (1941), intersect the $MgSiO_3$–$CaSiO_3$ side of the triangle at positions corresponding to between 75 and 85 per cent $CaSiO_3$. The tie-line intersections of metamorphic pyroxene pairs do not depart significantly from those of plutonic assemblages, and it is probable that the general relationship observed by Hess holds for all calcium-rich–calcium-poor pyroxene pairs that have crystallized under equilibrium conditions. Thus by this method of plotting coexisting pyroxene pairs it is not possible to distinguish igneous from metamorphic assemblages.

A more useful pyroxene relationship appears to lie in the ferrous iron–magnesium distribution, the distribution coefficient K being defined as

$$K_{(Mg-Fe)} = [X^o_{Mg}(1 - X^c_{Mg})]/[(1 - X^o_{Mg})X^c_{Mg}]$$

where the superscripts o and c refer to Ca-poor and Ca-rich pyroxene respectively and X is the mol. fraction. It has been demonstrated by Kretz (1963) that the distribution coefficient K appears to be constant for varying iron–magnesium ratios for a given set of equilibrium conditions but changes as a function of pressure and temperature. Thus for a series of granulite facies rocks (Madras charnockite series) the coexisting pyroxenes have K 0·54, while for an igneous differentiation series (Skaergaard intrusion) the value of K is approximately 0·73: the general difference between K for metamorphic and igneous pyroxenes is shown graphically in Fig. 44.

The augites of basic plutonic rocks of tholeiitic affinities commonly enclose lamellae of an orthopyroxene parallel to the (100) plane (Fig. 45) or lamellae of pigeonite parallel to the (001) plane of the augite host. In those pyroxenes in which pigeonite was exsolved, the pigeonite itself may have later inverted to orthorhombic pyroxene giving rise to a second set of lamellae parallel to the (100) plane of the augite.

Augite is frequently altered to a uralitic amphibole, either as a single crystal or as an aggregate of small prismatic crystals. The alteration usually begins at the periphery or along the cleavages, and in the early stages the alteration may be accompanied by an irregular bleaching of the crystal resulting in the formation of patchy areas of colourless pyroxene flecked with small plates of amphibole. Chlorite is also a common alteration product of augite; less common products include epidote and carbonates.

OPTICAL AND PHYSICAL PROPERTIES

There is a systematic relationship between the optical properties and chemical composition of the diopside–hedenbergite–enstatite–ferrosilite pyroxenes. The variation of the β refractive index for pyroxenes in which the optic axial plane is parallel to (010), and the variation of the α index for those in which the optic axial plane is perpendicular to (010) are plotted, together with the variation in 2V, in Fig. 46. As the β vibration is parallel to y for pyroxenes in which the optic plane is (010), and the α vibration is parallel to y for pyroxenes in which the optic plane is perpendicular to (010), and as β and α are coincident at 2V = 0, the two indices can be used to construct a continuous set of curves. These curves are constructed for pyroxenes containing normal amounts of the minor constituents, Al, Fe^{+3}, Ti, Cr, Mn and Na (these expressed as per cent oxides are: Al_2O_3 3, Fe_2O_3 1·5, Na_2O 0·4, TiO_2 0·4, MnO 0·3 but higher in the more iron-rich pyroxenes, Cr_2O_3 1·1 in the magnesium-rich augites but negligible in minerals more

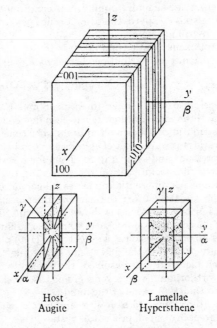

Host
Augite

Lamellae
Hypersthene

Fig. 45. *Lamellae of orthopyroxene parallel to* (100) *in magnesium-rich augite host (after Poldervaart, A. & Hess, H. H.,* 1951, Journ. Geol., *vol.* 59, *p.* 472).

iron-rich than $(CaMg)_{87}Fe_{13}$). The effect of the minor constituents on the refractive indices depends not only on their absolute amount but also on their position in the pyroxene structure; thus Al, Ti and Fe^{+3} in tetrahedral coordination increase the optic axial angle and lower the refractive index, whereas in octahedral coordination the same ions have the opposite result. Because of these factors compositions estimated from the optical properties may differ by as much as 5 per cent of the Ca, Mg or Fe^{+2} content from their true value.

Crushed fragments of the monoclinic pyroxenes include tablets lying parallel to the prismatic cleavage {110} and a smaller number of tablets parallel to the {100} parting. The latter are easy to recognize by their low birefringence and their orientation can be checked by observing the inter-ference figure which will show an off-centre optic axis figure. If on rotating the stage until the isogyre is east–west the brush divides the field exactly, then the optic axial plane is normal to the section and the β vibration direction is north–south.

Zoning is not uncommon in augites of quickly chilled rocks; oscillatory, hourglass and sector zoning is a characteristic feature of titanaugite.

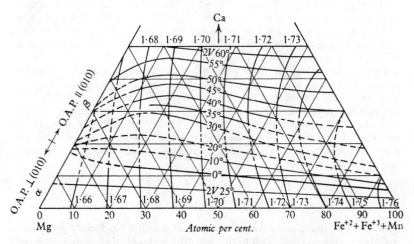

Fig. 46. *Variation of the optical properties with chemical composition of clinopyroxenes included in the system* $CaMgSi_2O_6$–$CaFeSi_2O_6$–$Mg_2Si_2O_6$ –$Fe_2Si_2O_6$ (*After Hess, H. H., 1949, Amer. Min., vol. 34, p. 621, and Muir, I. D., 1951, Min. Mag., vol. 29, p. 690*).

DISTINGUISHING FEATURES

Because of the continuous chemical variation between diopside, heden-bergite, augite and ferroaugite it is not always possible to identify precisely these minerals on the basis of their optical properties. In general augite is distinguished from diopside by smaller birefringence, higher refractive indices and stronger dispersion, and the more (Mg,Fe)-rich augites and ferroaugites have smaller optic axial angles than salite and ferrosalite; ferroaugites have smaller optic axial angles and smaller extinction angles than hedenbergite. Titanaugites can usually be distinguished by their stronger colour and characteristic pleochroism, with a violet colour in the γ vibration direction; sodian augites have a stronger green absorption colour, and higher optic axial angles and extinction angles than augite with more normal contents of sodium. Augite is also distinguished from aegirine-augite and aegirine by the strong colour, higher birefringence, higher $\gamma : z$ extinction angles and higher optic axial angles of the latter minerals. Magnesium-rich augites are difficult to distinguish from both omphacite and fassaite but these pyroxenes may sometimes be distinguished by their smaller birefringence combined with their pale green colour.

Augite is distinguished from spodumene and jadeite by higher extinction angle and refractive indices, from johannsenite by lower optic axial angle, and from the orthorhombic pyroxenes by higher birefringence, lower optic axial angle and by the negative optical character of many orthopyroxenes; moreover in the latter the extinction angle is straight in all sections of the [001] zone. Augite is distinguished from wollastonite by the presence of two cleavages only, higher refractive indices and birefringence; wollastonite has inclined extinction in all [001] zone sections. Rhodonite is similarly distinguished from augite except that there is an overlap with the refractive indices of the more iron-rich augites.

Fassaite is difficult to distinguish from omphacite but generally has a smaller optic axial angle, higher refractive indices, a larger extinction angle and stronger birefringence. Omphacite is distinguished from diopside by larger optic axial angle, and from jadeite by its stronger colour, higher refractive indices, smaller extinction angles and stronger pleochroism. In rocks in which omphacite is associated with hornblende it is distinguished from the amphibole by its pale colour and weaker pleochroism as well as by the pyroxene cleavage.

PARAGENESIS

Augite, ferroaugite, subcalcic augite and subcalcic ferroaugite occur mainly in igneous rocks, and pyroxenes of this compositional range are the essential ferromagnesian minerals of gabbros, dolerites and basalts. In rocks of tholeiitic affinities they are usually associated with either orthopyroxene or pigeonite, thus in the early cumulates of the Skaergaard intrusion the compositions of the associated clino- and orthopyroxenes are respectively $Ca_{42}Mg_{48}Fe_{10}$ and $Ca_4Mg_{78}Fe_{18}$. In later cumulates, clinopyroxene, $Ca_{35}Mg_{37}Fe_{28}$, is associated with pigeonite, $Ca_9Mg_{45}Fe_{46}$ (Fig. 47); with further differentiation the pyroxene crystallization passes from the two-pyroxene to the one-pyroxene field; the ferroaugites formed at this stage contain increasing amounts of calcium, and this latter trend is continued by pyroxenes of ferrohedenbergite composition (see p. 122). In contrast, the clinopyroxenes crystallized from alkali basalt magmas are salitic in composition and are never associated with either pigeonite or orthopyroxene.

In many basalts the first pyroxenes to crystallize are close to diopside in composition, but as crystallization proceeds the content of calcium gradually decreases and the pyroxenes first become augite and later subcalcic augite in composition. Although most subcalcic augites and subcalcic ferroaugites occur in volcanic rocks (Table 13, anals. 8, 9), such compositions, mainly as peripheral zones around more calcium-rich cores, are found in the pyroxenes of some more slowly cooled intrusive rocks, e.g. the Mount Arthur dolerite complex, East Griqualand.

Omphacitic pyroxene and pyrope–almandine are the two essential constituents of eclogite. This assemblage is chemically equivalent to normal basic igneous rocks such as gabbro and olivine gabbro. Experimental data suggest that the assemblage may be stable below 700°C at pressures above 10,000 bars, and it is possible that the variation in the composition of omphacite is related to the specific *PT* environment of the metamorphism, i.e. less severe conditions give rise to omphacites containing smaller amounts of Na and Al. The clinopyroxenes of granulites, like those of eclogites, are associated with almandine–pyrope garnet, but in contrast to the eclogite

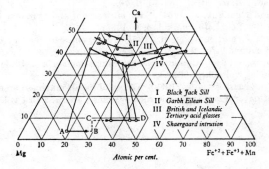

Fig. 47. *Trends of pyroxene crystallization. I differentiated teschenite sill, Gunnedah, New South Wales; II Garbh Eilean sill, Shiant Isles; III British and Icelandic Tertiary acid glasses; IV Skaergaard intrusion. Line A–B crystallization trend of primary orthopyroxenes. Line C–D crystallization trend of inverted pigeonites. Tie-lines are shown for 4 coexisting pyroxene pairs from rocks of the Skaergaard intrusion.*

assemblage, granulite clinopyroxenes are associated also with plagioclase. The compositions of the clinopyroxenes of eclogites and granulites are markedly different, and in particular reflect the different effects of pressure and temperature on the position of aluminium in the pyroxene structure. Thus in the omphacite of eclogites the Al is located mainly in the six-fold coordinated positions (*Y* sites), while in the granulite clinopyroxenes much of the Al occupies the four-fold coordinated *Z* sites. These contrasted clinopyroxene compositions can be expressed in terms of their jadeite and Tschermak components (calculated according to the convention adopted by Yoder and Tilley, 1962); thus the molecular ratio Jd : Ts $> \frac{4}{5}$ for eclogite clinopyroxenes, while Jd : Ts $< \frac{1}{2}$ for granulite clinopyroxenes. Fassaite is an aluminium-rich pyroxene in which the greater part of the aluminium also occupies four-fold coordinated positions and, like the granulite clinopyroxenes, it contains little sodium. It occurs typically in quartz-free environments and is most commonly found associated with spinel and calcite in metamorphosed limestones.

REFERENCES

BROWN, G. M. (1957) 'Pyroxenes from the early and middle stages of fractionation of the Skaergaard magmas', *Min. Mag.*, vol. 31, p. 511.

────── and VINCENT, E. A. (1963) 'Pyroxenes from the late stages of fractionation of the Skaergaard intrusion, east Greenland', *Journ. Petr.*, vol. 4, p. 175.

HESS, H. H. (1941) 'Pyroxenes of common mafic magmas, Part II', *Amer. Min.*, vol. 26, p. 573.

KRETZ, R. (1963) 'Distribution of magnesium and iron between orthopyroxene and calcic pyroxene in natural mineral assemblages', *Journ. Geol.*, vol. 71, p. 773.

KUNO, H. (1955) 'Ion substitution in the diopside–ferropigeonite series of clinopyroxenes', *Amer. Min.*, vol. 40, p. 70.

MUIR, I. D. and TILLEY, C. E. (1964) 'Iron enrichment and pyroxene fractionation in tholeiites', *Geol. Journ.*, vol. 4, p. 143.

POLDERVAART, A. and HESS, H. H. (1951) 'Pyroxenes in the crystallization of basaltic magma', *Journ. Geol.*, vol. 59, p. 472.

WHITE, A. J. R. (1964) 'Clinopyroxenes from eclogites and basic granulites', *Amer. Min.*, vol. 49, p. 883.

YODER, H. S. and TILLEY, C. E. (1962) 'Origin of basalt magmas: an experimental study of natural and synthetic rock systems', *Journ. Petr.*, vol. 3, p. 363.

Pigeonite

$(Mg,Fe^{+2},Ca)(Mg,Fe^{+2})[Si_2O_6]$

MONOCLINIC $(+)$

α 1·682–1·722
β 1·684–1·722
γ 1·705–1·751
δ 0·023–0·029
$2V_\gamma$ 0°–30°
$\gamma : z$ 37°–44°
$\alpha = y$, O.A.P. $\perp$(010); more rarely $\beta = y$, O.A.P. (010)
Dispersion: $r \gtrless v$, moderate. D 3·30–3·46. H 6.
Cleavage: {110} good; {100}, {010}, {001} partings; (110) : (1$\bar{1}$0) $\simeq$ 87°.
Twinning: {100} or {001}, simple or lamellar, common.
Colour: Brown, greenish brown, black; colourless, pale brownish green, pale yellow-green in thin section.
Pleochroism: Often absent but may be weak to moderate with α colourless, pale green, yellowish green or smoky brown; β pale brown, pale brownish green, brownish pink or smoky brown; γ colourless, pale green or pale yellow.

CHEMISTRY

Pigeonites are calcium-poor monoclinic pyroxenes and contain some 10 per cent of the $CaSiO_3$ component (see Fig. 33). This corresponds to $\simeq 0·2$ Ca atoms per formula unit and is approximately three times the amount of calcium that can be accommodated in the orthorhombic pyroxene structure. The Al content of pigeonites does not in general exceed 2 per cent of the metal ions and in many pigeonites there is insufficient Al to bring the Si + Al atoms up to the ideal 2 atoms per formula unit; in these minerals it is possible that some Fe^{+3} and Ti atoms occupy tetrahedral positions (Table 13, anal. 10). The major variation in pigeonite compositions is due to the replacement $Mg \rightleftharpoons Fe^{+2}$. The pigeonites first to crystallize from most saturated basaltic magmas have an $Mg : Fe^{+2}$ ratio $\simeq$ 70 : 30; with fractional crystallization, the pigeonite becomes progressively richer in iron until an $Mg : Fe^{+2}$ ratio of $\simeq$ 35 : 65 is reached, at which composition pigeonite ceases to crystallize from the magma and subsequent pyroxene crystallization is represented by a calcium-rich monoclinic phase, either ferroaugite or ferrohedenbergite.

In volcanic and some other quickly quenched rocks the original composition of the pigeonite is preserved and represents the equilibrium conditions at the time of crystallization. Under plutonic conditions, however, pigeonite exsolves some of the excess calcium ions as calcium-rich augite (Fig. 48) along planes parallel to (001). It then later inverts to an orthorhombic pyroxene and the inversion is accompanied by the exsolution of a second generation of augite lamellae parallel to the (100) plane of the ortho-pyroxene.

The amount to which the stability field of protoenstatite extends into the more iron-rich portion of the pyroxene composition quadrilateral has not been determined. Nevertheless there is no evidence for regarding pigeonite as a metastable form comparable with clinoenstatite. On the other hand, by analogy with the relationships between protoenstatite and enstatite, if pigeonite was derived by inversion from a protoenstatite

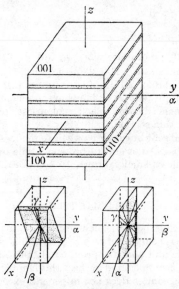

Host Pigeonite   Lamellae Augite

Fig. 48. *Augite lamellae parallel to* (001) *in pigeonite* (*after Poldervaart, A. & Hess, H. H.*, 1951, Journ. Geol., *vol.* 59, *p.* 472).

structure it would be likely to have a smaller, and not as noted above, a greater calcium content than associated hypersthenes. It is thus likely that there is a first-order transition between protoenstatite and pigeonite at a composition of about $En_{70}Fs_{30}$.

OPTICAL AND PHYSICAL PROPERTIES

Pigeonites are characterized optically by low values of the optic axial angle which are always less than 30° and generally are below 25°. The optic axial plane may be either parallel with or perpendicular to (010); the majority of pigeonites display the latter orientation. The effect of the replacement of Mg by Fe^{+2} on the β refractive index is shown in Fig. 46 (see p. 125), from which the Ca content can also be estimated provided the optic axial angle and the β index are both measured. It is difficult to locate precisely the α, β and γ directions on those pigeonites which are sensibly uniaxial. A procedure for the determination of the optic axial angle and extinction angle in pigeonites is given by Turner (1940). Zoning is a common feature in pigeonites and crystals in which the central part has the optic axial plane $\perp$ (010), and the outer zone has (100) as the optic axial plane, are not infrequent.

DISTINGUISHING FEATURES

Pigeonite is distinguished from orthorhombic pyroxene by the lower birefringence and straight extinction in all [001] zone sections of the latter mineral. In small grains pigeonite may be confused with olivine but the higher birefringence of the latter is usually sufficiently diagnostic. In plutonic rocks inverted pigeonites are identified by the presence of augite lamellae located along the (001) plane of the original pigeonite and, in twinned crystals, by the herring-bone pattern of the lamellae.

PARAGENESIS

Uninverted pigeonite occurs only in quickly chilled rocks and it is restricted to lavas and other rocks formed by rapid crystallization. The crystals are rarely found as phenocrysts and are characteristically present as microphenocrysts and smaller grains in the groundmass of volcanic rocks, particularly those of andesitic and dacitic composition. Inverted pigeonites are common in basic plutonic rocks of tholeiitic affinities, e.g. Bushveld, Stillwater and Skaergaard complexes.

REFERENCES

BOWN, M. G. and GAY, P. (1957) 'Observations on pigeonite', *Acta Cryst.*, vol. 10, p. 440.

KUNO, H. (1955) 'Ion substitution in the diopside–ferropigeonite series of clinopyroxenes', *Amer. Min.*, vol. 40, p. 70.

TURNER, F. J. (1940) 'Note on dermination of optic axial angle and extinction angle in pigeonite', *Amer. Min.*, vol. 25, p. 821.

Aegirine (Acmite) $NaFe^{+3}[Si_2O_6]$
Aegirine-augite $(Na,Ca)(Fe^{+3},Fe^{+2},Mg)[Si_2O_6]$

MONOCLINIC

Aegirine $(-)$ Aegirine-augite $(-)(+)$

	Aegirine	Aegirine-augite
α	1·750–1·776	1·700–1·750
β	1·780–1·820	1·710–1·780
γ	1·800–1·836	1·730–1·800
δ	0·040–0·060	0·030–0·050
$2V_\alpha$	60°–70°	70°–110°

$\alpha : z$ 0°–10° (β obtuse); O.A.P. (010) $\alpha : z$ 0°–20° (β acute); O.A.P. (010)
Dispersion: $r > v$, moderate to strong.
D 3·55–3·60.   H 6.   D 3·40–3·55.   H 6.
Cleavage: {110} good, {100} parting. (110) : (1Ī0) $\simeq$ 87°.
Twinning: {100} simple and lamellar, common.
Colour: Aegirine, dark green to greenish black; pale to dark green and yellowish green in thin section. Acmite, reddish brown, dark green to black; light brown to yellow or greenish yellow in thin section. Aegirine-augite, dark green to black, green, yellow-green or brown; pale green, green and yellowish green in thin section.
Pleochroism: Aegirine α emerald-green, deep green, β grass-green, deep green, γ brownish green, yellowish brown. Aegirine-augite, α bright green, deep green, brownish green, β yellowish green, γ yellow, greenish brown, brownish green.

The names aegirine and acmite are both used to describe pyroxenes close to $NaFe^{+3}Si_2O_6$ in composition. The term aegirine is applied to those crystals of this composition which are green to black in colour, and are bluntly terminated by faces of the form {111}; in thin section aegirine is strongly pleochroic. Acmite is the name applied to the brown variety of $NaFe^{+3}Si_2O_6$ which shows pointed terminations of the forms {221} and {661}, and which, in thin section, is only weakly pleochroic. The name aegirine-augite is used to describe the green strongly pleochroic pyroxenes, with high $\gamma : z$ extinction angles, which are intermediate in composition between aegirine and augite. The compositional division between aegirine and aegirine-augite is placed at 70 mol. per cent $NaFe^{+3}Si_2O_6$. At this composition the extinction angle, $\alpha : z$, is zero; in minerals with between $Fe^{+3}_{0.7}$ and $Fe^{+3}_{1.0}$ atoms per formula unit the α vibration direction lies in the obtuse angle β, in minerals with less than $Fe^{+3}_{0.7}$ the α vibration direction lies in the acute angle β. The name aegirine-augite can be conveniently used to describe pyroxenes containing between $Fe^{+3}_{0.7}$ and about $Fe^{+3}_{0.2}$ per formula unit.

CHEMISTRY

The main variations in the chemical composition of the aegirine–aegirine-augite series result from the replacement $NaFe^{+3} \rightleftharpoons Ca(Mg,Fe^{+2})$. Aluminium is not an important constituent; in aegirine in particular, the replacement of Si by Al is negligible, and the small amounts of Al present replace Fe^{+3} in octahedral coordination. Some aegirine-augites contain relatively large quantities of vanadium (e.g. 3·98 per cent V_2O_3) and aegirines may contain appreciable amounts of zirconium and cerium. Aegirine is readily synthesized from the appropriate molecular proportions of SiO_2, Fe_2O_3 and $Na_2CO_3 \cdot H_2O$ fused with NaCl, and it melts incongruently at 990°C with the formation of haematite and liquid.

OPTICAL PROPERTIES

The refractive indices of the aegirine–aegirine-augite series vary linearly with composition (Fig. 49), and for those members of the series rich in Fe^{+3} the indices approximate closely to those of the synthetic aegirine–diopside solid solutions ($Ae_{100}Di_0$ α 1·776, γ 1·836; $Ae_{48}Di_{52}$ α 1·727, γ 1·769). Correlation between composition and refractive indices of the Fe^{+3}-poor members of the natural and synthetic series is less precise due to $Mg \rightleftharpoons Fe^{+2}$ replacement in natural minerals. The extinction angle $\alpha : z$ (in obtuse angle β) is 10° for the pure $NaFe^{+3}Si_2O_6$ end-member, the angle decreases to zero at a composition of approximately $Fe^{+3}_{0.7}$, and with further replacement of Fe^{+3} by $(MgFe^{+2})$ the extinction angle (in acute angle β) increases and at a composition of about $Fe^{+3}_{0.2}$ is 20°. Aegirines and aegirine-augite commonly show colour zoning, and varying pleochroism and extinction angles; the zoning, which may be of hour-glass pattern, is usually from a more augite-rich core to a more aegirine-rich margin. Aegirine may occur in stout prismatic crystals, slender needles elongated parallel to the z axis, or more rarely in bundle-like or felted aggregates of minute fibres.

DISTINGUISHING FEATURES

Aegirine is distinguished from other pyroxenes by its small $\alpha : z$ extinction angle, high refringence and birefringence, negative optic axial angle and strong pleochroism, and aegirine-augites by their high $\gamma : z$ extinction angles, large 2V and characteristic strong pleochroism. Aegirine and aegirine-augite resemble some alkali amphiboles: in basal and near basal sections the

pyroxene cleavage angle is diagnostic and in prismatic sections the pleochroism is sufficiently characteristic to distinguish them from arfvedsonite
and riebeckite. The length-fast optical character of aegirine and aegirine-
augite distinguishes them from other amphiboles. Aegirine and aegirine-
augite have refractive indices, birefringence, $\alpha : z$ extinction angles, optic
axial angles, colour and pleochroism comparable with those of iron-rich
epidotes: they have stronger absorption, however, which reduces the
apparent birefringence, and can generally be distinguished from epidote by

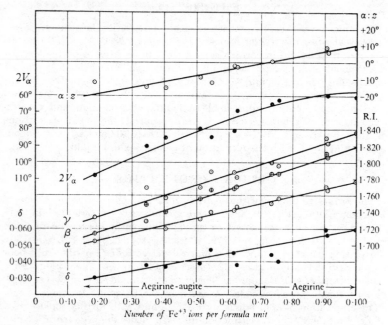

Fig. 49. *The relation between the optical properties and the number of Fe^{+3}
ions per formula unit in aegirine and aegirine-augite.*

the higher birefringence colours of the latter mineral. In sections showing
one cleavage and small extinction angles the optic axial plane is parallel to
the cleavage in aegirine and normal to the cleavage in epidote.

PARAGENESIS

Aegirine and aegirine-augite occur most commonly as the later products
of crystallization of alkaline magmas; they are typical constituents
commonly intergrown with arfvedsonitic amphiboles, of quartz syenites,
syenites, and nepheline-syenites as well as a wide variety of ultra-alkaline
rocks. Aegirine occurs in some alkali granites (e.g. Table 13, anal. 12) and

here is usually associated and intergrown with riebeckitic amphibole. Aegirine-augite is found in some regionally metamorphosed rocks and in such crystalline schists its associates include glaucophane, crossite and riebeckite.

REFERENCES

GROUT, F. F. (1946) 'Acmite occurrences in the Cuyuma Range, Minnesota' *Amer. Min.*, vol. 31, p. 125.

SABINE, P. A. (1950) 'The optical properties and composition of acmitic pyroxenes', *Min. Mag.*, vol. 29, p. 113.

WHITE, A. J. R. (1962) 'Aegirine-riebeckite schists from south Westland, New Zealand', *Journ. Petr.*, vol. 3, p. 38.

Spodumene

$LiAl[Si_2O_6]$

MONOCLINIC (+)

α 1·648–1·663
β 1·655–1·669
γ 1·662–1·679
δ 0·014–0·027
$2V_\gamma$ 58°–68°
$\gamma : z$ 22°–26°
$\beta = y$, O.A.P. (010).

Dispersion: $r < v$. D 3·03–3·22. H 6½–7.
Cleavage: {110} good, {100}, {010} partings. (110) : (1$\bar{1}$0) $\simeq$ 87°.
Twinning: {100} common.
Colour: Colourless, greyish white, pale amethyst, pale green, yellowish, emerald-green (hiddenite), lilac (kunzite); usually colourless in thin section.
Pleochroism: Hiddenite α green, γ colourless; kunzite α purple, γ colourless.

The chemical composition of spodumene does not show any great varia-tion from the ideal formula $LiAlSi_2O_6$. There is no replacement of Si by Al, and an interesting characteristic of the composition of spodumene is a small but consistent amount of Si present in excess of two atoms per formula unit, which may represent small amounts of SiO_2 originally in solid solution in the high temperature polymorph, β-spodumene. The replacement of Al by Fe^{+3} is generally small; there is, however, more replacement of the monovalent ion, and the substitution of Li by Na may be significant in amount.

There is little variation in the optical properties of spodumene but minerals in which some Li is replaced by Na have a lower α refractive index than those minerals closer to $LiAlSi_2O_6$ in composition; the γ index is not affected by this substitution and the more sodium-rich spodumenes have a higher birefringence. The green colour of the hiddenite variety of spodumene is due to small amounts of chromium, and the pink colour of kunzite is due to the presence of a relatively high concentration of Mn but more especially to a low Fe : Mn ratio.

Spodumene is distinguished from other monoclinic pyroxenes except some aegirine-augites by the small extinction angle, and from aegirine-augites by the pleochroic scheme and higher refractive indices of the latter.

Spodumene is a characteristic mineral of the lithium-rich granite pegma-tites (e.g. anal. 13, p. 107) in which it is typically associated with quartz, albite, lepidolite, beryl and tourmaline.

REFERENCE

CLAFFY, E. W. (1953) 'Composition, tenebrescence and luminescence of spodumene minerals', *Amer. Min.*, vol. 38, p. 919.

Jadeite

$NaAl[Si_2O_6]$

MONOCLINIC (+)

α 1·640–1·658
β 1·645–1·663
γ 1·652–1·673
δ 0·012–0·013
$2V_\gamma$ 67°–70°
$\gamma : z$ 33°–40°
$\beta = y$, O.A.P. (010)
Dispersion: $r > v$, moderate. D 3·24–3·43. H 6.
Cleavage: {110} good, (110) : (1$\bar{1}$0) $\simeq$ 87°.
Twinning: {100}, {001} simple, lamellar.
Colour: Colourless, white, green, greenish blue; colourless in thin section.

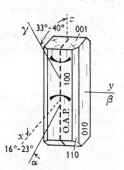

The tough compact form of jadeite is one of the two varieties of *jade*; the other, nephrite, is a tremolitic or actinolitic amphibole.

CHEMISTRY

In jadeite there is no replacement of Si by Al and little substitution of Al by Fe^{+3}, and many jadeite analyses do not depart significantly from the ideal composition $NaAlSi_2O_6$ (e.g. Table 13, anal. 14). Pyroxenes having a composition intermediate between jadeite and diopside, however, are known, but the range of the replacement of (Ca,Mg,Fe^{+2}) by (Na,Al) is uncertain. Jadeite has a composition intermediate between that of nepheline and albite but the pyroxene does not crystallize at normal pressures in the binary system $NaAlSiO_4$–$NaAlSi_3O_8$ (see Fig. 136, p. 360). The stability fields of jadeite and nepheline + albite at pressures between 10,000 and 25,000 bars and at temperatures between 600° and 1200°C are shown in Fig. 50. On heating in the nepheline + albite stability field natural jadeite breaks down to these two minerals; similarly on heating in the jadeite stability field, a mixture of albite and nepheline begins to form jadeite:

$$2NaAlSi_2O_6 \rightleftharpoons NaAlSiO_4 + NaAlSi_3O_8$$
$$\text{jadeite} \qquad \text{nepheline} \qquad \text{albite}$$

OPTICAL AND PHYSICAL PROPERTIES

The range of optical properties of jadeite is relatively narrow. The variation in refractive indices does not show any marked correlation with the replacement of Al by Fe^{+3}, but some jadeites in which this substitution is relatively large display anomalous interference colours and very strong dispersion of the optic axes ($r > v$).

DISTINGUISHING FEATURES

Jadeite is distinguished by lower refractive indices from all other pyroxenes except spodumene, from which it is distinguished by lower bire-fringence and higher extinction angles. In addition jadeite is distinguished from omphacite and fassaite by its lower birefringence, and from aegirine by the absence of colour, higher extinction angles and lower birefringence. It is distinguished from actinolite by its pyroxene cleavage, larger extinction angle and lack of colour.

PARAGENESIS

Jadeite is a comparatively uncommon pyroxene which occurs, always in association with albite, in rocks of low metamorphic grade, and particularly in those of the glaucophane schist facies. Its relative rarity here, however,

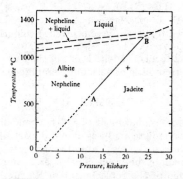

Fig. 50. *Equilibrium curve for the reaction albite + nepheline = 2 jadeite. AB, experimentally determined curve from transformation of synthetic glass of jadeite composition (after Robertson, E. C., Birch, F. & MacDonald, G. J. F., 1957, Amer. Journ. Sci., vol. 255, p. 115).*

indicates some modification of the normal PT environment of this facies, and in view of the reduction in the molar volume accompanying the reaction albite $\rightarrow$ jadeite + quartz, it is possible that jadeite-bearing rocks develop under conditions characterized by higher confining pressures than are typical of the glaucophane schist facies. Jadeite, associated with glauco-phane, lawsonite, sericite, chlorite and albite, occurs in some Californian metagreywackes in which the original bedding planes are preserved. Much of the albite is replaced by jadeite which contains inclusions of both law-sonite and quartz; the latter is probably a by-product of the replacement reaction albite $\rightarrow$ jadeite + quartz, while the lawsonite may represent the anorthite content of the original plagioclase:

$$\underset{\text{plagioclase}}{NaCaAl_3Si_5O_{16}} + 2H_2O \rightarrow \underset{\text{jadeite}}{NaAlSi_2O_6} + \underset{\text{lawsonite}}{CaAl_2Si_2O_7(OH)_2 \cdot H_2O} + \underset{\text{quartz}}{SiO_2}$$

Gabbros under similar conditions of regional metamorphism give rise to jadeite–pumpellyite-rich assemblages.

REFERENCES

BLOXAM, T. W. (1956) 'Jadeite-bearing metagraywackes in California', *Amer. Min.*, vol. 41, p. 488.

MCKEE, B. (1962) 'Widespread occurrence of jadeite, lawsonite and glaucophane in central California', *Amer. Journ. Sci.*, vol. 260, p. 596.

ROBERTSON, E. C., BIRCH, F. and MACDONALD, G. J. F. (1957) 'Experimental determination of jadeite stability relations to 25,000 bars', *Amer. Journ. Sci.*, vol. 255, p. 283.

Wollastonite

Ca[SiO$_3$]

TRICLINIC ($-$)

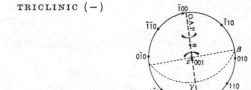

α 1·616–1·640
β 1·628–1·650
γ 1·631–1·653
δ 0·013–0·014
2V$_\alpha$ 38°–60°.
$\alpha:z = 30°$–44°, $\beta:y = 0°$–5°, O.A.P. approx. (010).
Dispersion: $r > v$.   D 2·87–3·09.   H 4½–5.
Cleavage: {100} perfect, {001} and {$\bar{1}$02} good; on (010) sections (100) : (001) = 84½°, (100) : ($\bar{1}$02) = 70°.
Twinning: Common; twin axis [010], composition plane {100}.
Colour: Usually white, sometimes colourless, grey or very pale green colourless in thin section.

STRUCTURE

There are three structural modifications of CaSiO$_3$: pseudowollastonite (β-CaSiO$_3$), the high-temperature form, is triclinic (pseudo-orthorhombic). Parawollastonite and wollastonite are both referred to as the low-temperature form (α-CaSiO$_3$): their structures are closely related but that of parawollastonite is monoclinic whereas wollastonite is triclinic (a 7·94, b 7·32, c 7·07 Å, α 90° 02′, β 95° 22′, γ 103° 26′; Z = 6). The wollastonites are not structurally related to the pyroxene group but have a different type of infinite-chain structure, with three tetrahedra per unit cell arranged parallel to y, this repeat unit consisting of a pair of tetrahedra joined apex to apex as in the [Si$_2$O$_7$] group, alternating with a single tetrahedron with one edge parallel to the chain direction (Fig. 51). The monoclinic parawollastonite is related to the triclinic wollastonite by a simple packing modification.

CHEMISTRY

Although normally fairly pure CaSiO$_3$, wollastonite can accept considerable amounts of Fe and Mn replacing Ca. Natural iron wollastonites have been reported from the contact metamorphism and metasomatism of impure limestones (Table 14, anal. 3). Wollastonite can be synthesized readily from its component oxides, or from hydrous gels via xonotlite, Ca$_6$(Si$_6$O$_{17}$)(OH)$_2$, which breaks down on heating to yield wollastonite. It forms a solid solution series in the system CaSiO$_3$–FeSiO$_3$, and can contain up to 76 per cent FeSiO$_3$ at high temperature: this wollastonite inverts at a lower temperature to a member of the hedenbergite–clinoferrosilite series.

Table 14. Wollastonite analyses

| | 1. | 2. | 3. | | Numbers of ions on the basis of 18 (O) | | |
					1.	2.	3.
SiO_2	51·56	50·53	50·00	Si	5·976 ⎫	5·883 ⎫	5·985
Al_2O_3	0·15	0·67	—	Al	0·021 ⎬ 6·01	0·093 ⎬ 6·00	—
Fe_2O_3	0·21	0·30	0·00	Fe^{+3}	0·018 ⎭	0·027 ⎭	—
FeO	0·08	0·18	9·29	Mg	0·045 ⎫	0·105 ⎫	— ⎫
MnO	0·06	0·02	1·22	Fe^{+2}	0·007	0·018	0·930
MgO	0·26	0·61	—	Mn	0·006 ⎬ 5·99	0·002 ⎬ 6·09	0·123 ⎬ 6·03
CaO	47·73	47·01	38·86	Na	0·004	0·018	
Na_2O	0·02	0·24	—	Ca	5·928	5·895	4·981
K_2O	0·00	0·12	—	K	— ⎭	0·055 ⎭	— ⎭
H_2O^+	0·03	0·22	—				
H_2O^-	0·02	0·10	—				
Total	100·12	100·00	99·82				

	1.	2.	3.
α	1·618	1·617	1·640
β	1·628	1·630	—
γ	1·631	1·632	1·653
$2V_\alpha$	—	36°–38°	60°
D	2·922	2·871	3·09

1. White parawollastonite, associated with vesuvianite, blue calcite and diopside, Crestmore, California (Deer, W. A., Howie, R. A. & Zussman, J., 1963, *Rock-forming minerals*, vol. 2, Longmans).
2. Wollastonite, limestone–granodiorite contact, Adamello, Italy (Schiavinato, G., 1946, *Mem. Inst. Geol. Univ. Padova*, vol. 15, no. 5; recalc. to 100 per cent after subtracting 0·96 per cent $CaCO_3$).
3. White iron-wollastonite, around chert nodules in dolomite metamorphosed by granite, Skye (Tilley, C. E., 1948, *Amer. Min.*, vol. 33, p. 736; includes 0·45 insol. in HCl).

This inversion is believed to have taken place in the fayalite ferrogabbros of the Skaergaard intrusion, giving rise to small interlocking grains of pyroxene. Wollastonite often occurs as a result of the reaction of quartz and calcite in metamorphosed limestones: the univariant P_{CO_2}–T curve for the reaction $CaCO_3 + SiO_2 \rightleftharpoons CaSiO_3 + CO_2$ is given in Fig. 177, p. 482. The reaction wollastonite + calcite ⇌ spurrite + carbon dioxide has also been investigated experimentally: at 5000 lb/in^2 CO_2 pressure the reaction takes place at about 1000° C. The P–T curve for the reaction wollastonite + monticellite ⇌ åkermanite lies between 700° and 750°C in the pressure range 30,000–60,000 lb/in^2, i.e. the P–T curve for this reaction is nearly parallel to the pressure axis. The inversion wollastonite–pseudowollastonite takes place at 1120°C but this temperature is raised to 1368°C by the solid solution of 21 per cent diopside in wollastonite.

OPTICAL AND PHYSICAL PROPERTIES

Typical values for the various structural modifications of $CaSiO_3$ are:

	α	β	γ	δ	$\alpha{:}z$	$\beta{:}y$	Sign
Wollastonite	1·618	1·630	1·632	0·014	39°	4°	(−)
Parawollastonite	1·618	1·630	1·632	0·014	38°	0°	(−)
Pseudowollastonite	1·610	1·611	1·654	0·044	9°	—	(+)

The introduction of iron increases the refractive indices and the optic axial angle of wollastonite; see, for example, Bowen *et al* (1933).

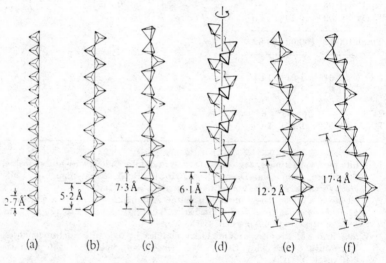

Fig. 51. *Schematic diagram of possible arrangements of chains of linked SiO_4 tetrahedra of composition $(SiO_3)_n$, parallel to the y axes: (a) 1 tetrahedron repeat, (b) 2 tetrahedra (pyroxene), (c) 3 tetrahedra (wollastonite), (d) 4 tetrahedra, (e) 5 tetrahedra (rhodonite) and (f) 7 tetrahedra (pyroxmangite) (after Liebau, F., 1959, Acta Cryst., vol. 12, p. 177).*

DISTINGUISHING FEATURES

Wollastonite differs from tremolite and pectolite in its weaker birefringence and its variable sign of elongation $(\beta\|y)$: diopside, with which it is often associated, has higher relief, higher 2V and is optically positive. The three cleavages of wollastonite may also be noticeable. The distinction between wollastonite and parawollastonite is best made by single-crystal X-ray photographs.

PARAGENESIS

Wollastonite is a common mineral of metamorphosed impure limestones, while parawollastonite, although it may occur in the same paragenesis, is rarer. Wollastonite may occur in contact altered calcareous sediments where the Si is metasomatically introduced, and also in the invading igneous rock as a result of contamination. In most of these occurrences it is the result of the reaction $CaCO_3 + SiO_2 \rightarrow CaSiO_3 + CO_2$ (Fig. 177): in some circumstances the CO_2 pressure may be effectively reduced, either by dilution by another volatile component or by the escape of CO_2 through fissures, and under these conditions wollastonite may form at somewhat lower temperatures than those indicated. In the progressive metamorphism of siliceous dolomites the early stages of the sequence are talc–tremolite–diopside–forsterite–wollastonite–periclase–monticellite.

Wollastonite also occurs in some alkaline igneous rocks, as in the Alnö alkaline complex, Sweden, the ijolitic alkaline rocks of Kenya and in wollastonite phonolites. Pseudowollastonite has only once been reported as a natural occurrence, in pyrometamorphosed rocks in south-west Persia, where sediments have been baked by the burning of hydrocarbons in prehistoric times.

REFERENCES

BOWEN, N. L., SCHAIRER, J. F. and POSNJAK, E. (1933). 'The system CaO–FeO–SiO$_2$', *Amer. Journ. Sci.*, ser. 5, vol. 26, p. 193.

HARKER, R. I. and TUTTLE, O. F. (1956) 'Experimental data on the P_{CO_2}-T curve for the reaction: calcite + quartz ⇌ wollastonite + carbon dioxide', *Amer. Journ. Sci.*, vol. 254, p. 239.

Pectolite

$Ca_2NaH[SiO_3]_3$

TRICLINIC (+)

α 1·595–1·610†
β 1·605–1·615
γ 1·632–1·645
δ 0·030–0·038
$2V_y$ 35°–63°
$\alpha : z = 10°–19°$, $\beta : x$ 10°–16°
$\gamma : y = 2°$; O.A.P. near (100)
Dispersion: $r > v$, weak. D 2·86–2·90†. H $4\frac{1}{2}$–5.
Cleavage: {100} and {001}, perfect.
Twinning: Rare, twin axis y, composition plane approximately (100).
Colour: Colourless or white; colourless in thin section.

The structure of pectolite (a 7·99, b 7·04, c 7·02 Å, α 90° 03′, β 95° 17′, γ 102° 28′; Z = 2) is based on single Si–O chains in a sequence of alternate single and double tetrahedral groups similar to that found in wollastonite. The Ca atoms are coordinated by oxygen octahedra sharing edges to form a lath-like strip, while the Na atoms have trigonal pyramidal coordination and these pyramids also share edges with those of the Ca octahedra.

Although pectolite is typically found with a composition close to $Ca_2NaHSi_3O_9$, divalent manganese can replace calcium in the structure and there is an isostructural series from pectolite to manganoan pectolite (schizolite) and serandite (the Mn end-member analogue of pectolite). Mg and Fe may also be present and some Al can enter the Z group along with Si. Pectolite has been synthesized by heating SiO_2, CaO, H_2O and NaOH in a closed vessel at 180°C for $3\frac{1}{2}$ days. It may undergo alteration to stevensite, $Mg_3Si_4O_{10}(OH)_2$, by reaction with $MgH_2(CO_3)_2$ and water.

The entry of iron and manganese increases the refractive indices and specific gravity and lowers the birefringence and optic axial angle. Pectolite may be distinguished from wollastonite by its considerably greater birefringence and by its length-slow character.

Pectolite typically occurs as a hydrothermal mineral in cavities and joint planes in basic igneous rocks. It is also found as a primary mineral in some alkaline igneous rocks such as tinguaite and nepheline-syenite, and in some mica peridotites and in calcium-rich metamorphic rocks and skarns.

REFERENCE

SCHALLER, W. T. (1955) 'The pectolite–schizolite–serandite series,' *Amer. Min.*, vol. 40, p. 1022.

† Highly manganoan pectolite has properties outside these ranges.

Rhodonite

(Mn,Ca,Fe)[SiO$_3$]

TRICLINIC (+)

α 1·711–1·738
β 1·716–1·741
γ 1·724–1·751
δ 0·011–0·014
2V$_γ$ 61°–76°
$α:x \simeq 5°, β:y \simeq 20°, γ:z \simeq 25°$.†
Dispersion: $r < v$. D 3·55–3·76. H 5½–6½.
Cleavage: {110} and {1$\bar{1}$0} perfect, {001} good; (110):(1$\bar{1}$0) = 92½°.†
Twinning: Lamellar twinning with composition plane (010), not common.
Colour: Rose-pink to brownish red; colourless to faint pink in thin section.
Pleochroism: Weak; in thick sections α yellowish red, β pinkish red, γ pale
yellowish red.

The structure of rhodonite (a 7·66, b 12·27, c 6·68 Å, $α$ 86·0°, $β$ 93·2°,
$γ$ 111·1°; Z = 10) contains chains of SiO$_4$ tetrahedra, of composition
(SiO$_3$)$_n$, parallel to y, the repeat unit of which has 5 tetrahedra (see Fig. 51,
p. 142). The structure is closely related to that of wollastonite (3 tetrahedra
periodicity) and pyroxmangite (7 tetrahedra periodicity).

Rhodonite is never pure MnSiO$_3$ but always contains some calcium.
There is not a continuous isomorphous series between rhodonite and bustamite, however, and it seems likely that rhodonite cannot contain more than
about 20 per cent CaSiO$_3$. Ferrous iron may replace Mn to a considerable
extent, and zinc can also enter the structure to give the rare zinc-rich variety
fowlerite. Rhodonite can be synthesized from MnO$_2$ and SiO$_2$ in an atmosphere with low partial pressure of oxygen to keep the manganese in the
divalent state: it melts incongruently at 1291°C to tridymite and a liquid,
and the rhodonite–tephroite eutectic is at 1251°C and 38·3 weight per cent
SiO$_2$. Alteration products include pyrolusite and rhodochrosite.

The entry of Ca (and Mg) into the rhodonite structure decreases the
refractive indices and specific gravity and tends to increase the optic axial
angle, whereas the effect of the replacement of Mn by Fe is small. The pink
colour (sometimes masked by blackish alteration products) and inclined
extinction help to distinguish rhodonite as a triclinic manganese silicate:
it differs from bustamite in its positive optic sign and from pyroxmangite
in having a larger 2V and smaller birefringence.

It occurs in many manganese ore bodies and is usually associated with
metasomatic activity.

† Optical data and cleavages are given according to the old choice of unit cell:
cell parameters refer to later choice of axes. The planes ($\bar{1}\bar{1}$0), (00$\bar{1}$) and (1$\bar{1}$0) of
the old cell correspond to (100), (010) and (001) respectively in the newer orienta-
tion.

Bustamite

$(Mn,Ca,Fe)[SiO_3]$

TRICLINIC (−)

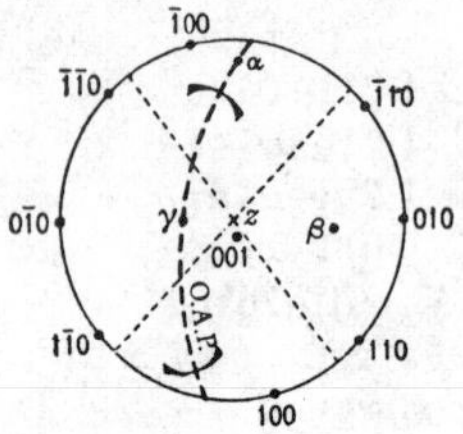

α 1·662–1·692
β 1·674–1·705
γ 1·676–1·707
δ 0·014–0·015
$2V_{\alpha}$ 30°–44°
O.A.P. and α approx. $\perp$(100).†
$\alpha : x \simeq 15°, \beta : y \simeq 35°, \gamma : z \simeq 30°–35°$
Dispersion: $r < v$, weak to strong. D 3·32–3·46. H $5\frac{1}{2}$–$6\frac{1}{2}$.
Cleavage: {100} perfect, {110} and {1$\bar{1}$0} good, {010} poor.† (110) : (1$\bar{1}$0) = 95°.
Twinning: Simple twins with composition plane (110), not common.
Colour: Pale pink to brownish red; colourless to yellowish pink in thin section.
Pleochroism: Weak; in thick sections $\alpha = \gamma$ orange, β rose.

The structure of bustamite (*a* 15·46, *b* 7·18, *c* 13·84 Å, α 89° 34 , β 94° 53′, γ 102° 47′; Z = 24) is similar to that of wollastonite, but with approximately doubled *a* and *c* parameters.

The chemical composition shows considerable variation in the amounts of Mn, Ca and Fe^{+2} (MnO being typically beween 25 and 40 per cent, CaO 25 to 12 per cent and FeO varying from almost nil to over 8 per cent). Mg is generally low and Zn is only found in material from a zinc-rich environment as at Franklin, New Jersey. Solid solution with rhodonite is limited and there is an apparent discontinuity in optical properties at around 65 per cent (FeO + MnO)/(FeO + MnO + CaO); there is probably complete solid solution between bustamite and wollastonite. Brownish manganese oxide alteration products frequently form on the surface and obscure the pink colour.

The refractive indices and specific gravity increase with increasing Mn and Fe, while the birefringence varies only slightly and the optic axial angle may decrease. Sections perpendicular to the acute bisectrix show γ at 29°–30° to the trace of the cleavage. Bustamite is often brownish pink but less pink than rhodonite and may have a fibrous character. It differs from rhodonite and pyroxmangite in its negative optic sign, lower refractive indices and smaller specific gravity: its 2V is less than that of rhodonite and its birefringence less than that of pyroxmangite.

Bustamite is a mineral typical of manganese ore bodies, usually resulting from metamorphism with associated metasomatism, and it often occurs in skarn deposits.

† Optical data and cleavages are given according to the old choice of unit cell; cell parameters refer to later choice of axes (see p. 145).

Pyroxmangite

$(Mn,Fe)[SiO_3]$

TRICLINIC (+)

α 1·726–1·748
β 1·728–1·750
γ 1·744–1·764
δ 0·016–0·020
$2V_\gamma$ 35°–46°
O.A.P. approximately $\perp(1\bar{1}0)$†
Dispersion: $r > v$, moderate. D 3·61–3·80. H 5½–6.
Cleavage: {110} and {1$\bar{1}$0} perfect, {010} and {001} poor.† $(110):(1\bar{1}0)=92°$, $(010):(110)=45°$, $(001):z=64°$.
Twinning: Lamellar on {010}, simple on {001}; not common.
Colour: Pink, but normally covered with brown or black oxidation products; colourless to faint lilac in thin section.

The structure of pyroxmangite (a 7·56, b 17·45, c 6·67 Å, α 84·0°, β 94·3°, γ 113·7°; Z = 14) contains chains of linked SiO_4 tetrahedra, of composition $(SiO_3)_n$, parallel to the y axis, with 7 tetrahedra in the repeat distance of the chain (see Fig. 51, p. 142). Layers of chains alternate with layers of cations parallel to (110) and the structure is similar to that of rhodonite (5 tetrahedra repeat) and wollastonite (3 tetrahedra repeat).

Chemically, pyroxmangite is typically fairly pure $(Mn,Fe)SiO_3$, with FeO varying from almost nil to about 25 per cent. CaO and MgO are generally present in small amounts, though CaO is less abundant than in rhodonite and it is possible that whereas one in five cation positions in rhodonite may be occupied by Ca, in pyroxmangite this may be limited to one in seven. Brownish alteration products consisting of manganese oxide and hydroxide are generally present on the cleavage surfaces, etc: this material has been described as skemmatite or ferrian wad.

The variation in optics with change in Mn/Fe ratio is not very pronounced, though there is a slight increase in refractive indices with increasing iron content, and a small decrease in the optic axial angle. The entry of appreciable amounts of Ca or Mg lowers the refractive indices. The pinkish colour in hand specimen, often with brownish black surface alteration, the distinct cleavages and the inclined extinction are characteristic. Pyroxmangite differs from rhodonite in its smaller 2V and higher birefringence and from bustamite by its positive optic sign.

Pyroxmangite is a mineral typical of manganiferous metasomatic or metamorphic rocks and is found in association with such minerals as spessartine, tephroite, rhodochrosite, etc.

† Optical data and cleavages are given according to the old choice of unit cell; cell parameters refer to later choice of axes (see p. 145).

AMPHIBOLE GROUP

INTRODUCTION

Members of the amphibole group of minerals occur in a wide range of P,T-environments and are common constituents of both igenous and metamorphic rocks. Among igneous rocks they are found in all the major groups ranging from ultrabasic to acid and alkaline types, but are particularly common constituents of the intermediate members of the calc-alkali series. Amphiboles occur characteristically in the plutonic rocks and in general are relatively unimportant minerals of the volcanic rocks. Amphi-

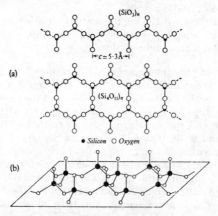

Fig. 52. (a) *Comparison of amphibole band* $(Si_4O_{11})_n$ *and pyroxene chain* $(SiO_3)_n$, (b) *perspective view of the double chain, or band, which occurs in the structures of all amphiboles (after Jong, W. F. de, 1959, General Crystallography, Freeman, San Francisco).*

boles crystallize in a large variety of regionally metamorphosed rocks formed under conditions ranging from the greenschist to lower granulite facies. They occur less commonly in the environment of thermal metamorphism but nevertheless are not uncommon in thermally metamorphosed limestones, dolomites and other calcium-rich sediments.

STRUCTURE

The essential feature of the structures of all amphiboles is the presence of $(Si,Al)O_4$ tetrahedra linked to form chains which have double the width of those in pyroxenes and have the composition $(Si_4O_{11})_n$ (Fig. 52 a and b).

These double chains or bands repeat along their length at intervals of approximately 5·3 Å, and this defines the c parameter of the unit cell; they are separated, and bonded to each other laterally, by planes of cations as shown in Fig. 53, but there are in addition some hydroxyl ions in the positions marked OH. An alternative view of the structure is that it contains 'talc-like' strips, made up by five cations (Mg, Fe, etc., octahedrally co-ordinated in sites M_1, M_2, M_3) sandwiched between two inward pointing bands of tetrahedra; these units are linked, back to back, by larger cations (Ca,Na,K) in the sites M_4, and in some cases by an additional large cation

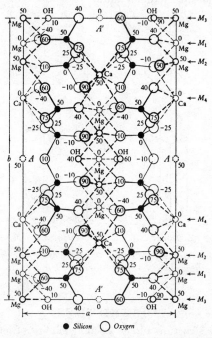

● *Silicon* ○ *Oxygen*

Fig. 53. *The structure of tremolite* $Ca_2Mg_5Si_8O_{22}(OH)_2$ *projected along the z direction. In this figure superimposed oxygens and hydroxyls have been shifted (after Bragg, W. L., 1937, The Atomic Structure of Minerals, Cornell Univ. Press).*

at the site A. The sizes of the cations at M_1, M_2, M_3 and M_4 determine the way in which they are surrounded by oxygens of the Si_4O_{11} bands, and this in turn determines the positions of the bands relative to one another. In most cases the stacking of bands is such as to produce a monoclinic cell similar to that in tremolite (a 9·84, b 18·05, c 5·275 Å, β 104·7°; Z = 2).

For amphiboles in which the content of larger (Ca,Na,K) ions is low, the modes of stacking of neighbouring bands can result in an orthorhombic cell (e.g. anthophyllite which has Z = 4 and cell size $a \simeq 18\cdot6$, $b \simeq 18\cdot0$,

$c \simeq 5 \cdot 3$ Å). The relationships between the monoclinic and orthorhombic amphibole and pyroxene cells are shown in Fig. 54, and it is seen that:

c orthorhombic $\simeq c$ monoclinic
b orthorhombic $\simeq b$ monoclinic
a orthorhombic $\simeq 2\,a \sin \beta$ monoclinic.

In tremolite, $Ca_2Mg_5Si_8O_{22}(OH)_2$, and anthophyllite, $Mg_7Si_8O_{22}(OH)_2$, positions A and A' are not occupied, but in some amphiboles these positions are either partially or completely occupied. Such amphiboles contain more than $2(Ca,Na,K)$ ions per formula unit.

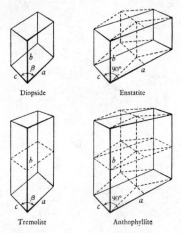

Fig. 54. *The relationship between unit cell dimensions of diopside, enstatite, tremolite and anthophyllite (after Warren, B. E. & Modell, D. I., 1930, Zeit. Kryst., vol. 75, p. 161).*

CHEMISTRY

The amphibole structure admits great flexibility of ionic replacement, and the minerals of the group exhibit an extremely wide range of chemical composition (Table 15). The composition of the simplest calcium-rich amphibole, tremolite, may be expressed by the formula $Ca_2Mg_5Si_8O_{22}(OH)_2$, the Ca atoms occupying the larger positions of between 6- and 8-fold coordination in the structure. In considering the chemistry of the amphiboles it has been generally accepted that the X positions (M_4, Fig. 53) may be occupied by Ca, Na and K atoms, and the Y positions (M_1, M_2, M_3) by the smaller cations Mg,Fe^{+2},Fe^{+3} and Al. Although structural investigations indicate that the occupation of these structural positions by the larger and smaller ions respectively is not always strictly fulfilled, the conception nevertheless is valuable as a basis for discussing amphibole chemistry. In many amphiboles Si is replaced by Al (this substitution being limited to approximately 2 Al atoms per formula unit), and the whole or a proportion

Table 15. AMPHIBOLE ANALYSES

	1.	2.	3.	4.	5.	6.
$)_2$	58·48	44·89	51·53	47·54	51·40	42·05
$)_2$	0·03	0·67	0·31	—	0·74	1·48
$_2O_3$	0·57	17·91	5·02	0·20	3·88	14·69
$_2O_3$	0·58	0·67	0·82	0·71	3·90	3·21
O	7·85	13·31	16·91	47·25	14·91	6·30
O	0·27	0·37	0·22	2·14	0·33	0·04
O	29·25	18·09	20·84	0·04	11·22	14·91
O	0·14	0·40	1·34	0·00	10·17	12·83
$_2O$	0·08	1·45	0·65	0·29	1·67	2·01
O	0·02	0·05	0·00	0·11	0·09	0·65
O^+	2·60	2·02	2·15	1·55	1·90	1·53
$_2O^-$	0·20	0·00	0·64	—	0·04	0·09
	—	—	—	0·01	—	0·5
	100·20	99·87	100·43	99·84	100·25	100·29
≡ F,Cl	—	—	—	—	—	0·21
tal	100·20	99·87	100·43	99·84	100·25	100·08
	—	1·649	1·643	1·686	1·650	1·648
	—	1·656	1·650	1·709	1·663	1·660
	1·632	1·669	1·663	1·729	1·670	1·670
α	80°	—	105°	85°	65°	85°
	3·01	3·15	3·10	3·597	—	3·16

NUMBERS OF IONS ON THE BASIS OF 24 (O,OH,F,Cl)

	1.	2.	3.	4.	5.	6.
	7·885 } 7·98	6·325 } 8·00	7·364 } 8·00	7·968 } 8·00	7·543 } 8·00	6·099 } 8·00
	0·090	1·675	0·636	0·032	0·457	1·901
	—	1·301	0·209	0·008	0·215	0·611
+3	0·003	0·071	0·033	—	0·082	0·161
	0·058	0·070	0·087	0·088	0·430 } 5·05	0·350 } 5·12
+2	5·876 } 6·90†	3·799 } 7·32	4·438 } 7·20	0·010 } 7·15	2·453	3·224
	0·885	1·569	2·022	6·626	1·830	0·764
	0·031	0·044	0·027	0·304	0·040	0·005
	0·020	0·396	0·180	0·093	0·474 } 2·09	0·564 } 2·68
	0·020	0·060	0·205	—	1·599	1·994
	0·004	0·008	—	0·024	0·018	0·120
	2·338 } 2·34	1·898 } 1·90	2·049 } 2·05	1·732 } 1·74	1·861 } 1·86	1·480 } 1·71
	—	—	—	0·007	—	0·229

Anthophyllite, serpentinite, outer Hebrides (Guppy, E. M., 1956, *Mem. Geol. Surv. Gt. Britain*; includes Cr_2O_3 0·04, NiO 0·01, CO_2 0·08).

Gedrite, kyanite–garnet gedritite, Idaho (Hietanen, A., 1959, *Amer. Min.*, vol. 44, p. 539; includes P_2O_5 0·04).

Cummingtonite, oligoclase–biotite schist, Scotland (Collins, R. S., 1942, *Min. Mag.*, vol. 26, p. 254).

Grunerite, U.S.A. (Bowen, N. L. & Schairer, J. F., 1935, *Amer. Min.*, vol. 20, p. 543).

Actinolite, albite–stilpnomelane–actinolite schist, New Zealand (Hutton, C. O., 1940, *Dept. Sci. and Ind. Res. New Zealand, Geol. Mem.*, No. 5).

Hornblende, ultrabasic rock, India (Howie, R. A., 1955, *Trans. Roy. Soc. Edinburgh*, vol. 62, p. 725).

Includes Cr 0·054, Ni 0·001.

Table 15. AMPHIBOLE ANALYSES—*continued*

	7.	8.	9.	10.	11.	12.
SiO_2	44·99	48·10	37·49	45·17	39·68	40·88
TiO_2	1·46	0·10	0·86	2·11	7·12	0·22
Al_2O_3	11·21	11·05	10·81	7·68	12·81	11·04
Fe_2O_3	3·33	0·67	7·52	14·30	4·04	7·56
FeO	13·17	1·65	25·14	2·81	8·79	17·41
MnO	0·31	—	0·95	0·41	0·16	1·32
MgO	10·41	20·60	1·34	13·44	11·22	5·92
CaO	12·11	12·50	9·77	11·18	11·06	10·46
Na_2O	0·97	2·54	2·06	1·35	3·37	3·75
K_2O	0·76	1·24	1·91	1·09	1·04	0·78
H_2O^+	1·48	0·71	2·01	0·19	0·78	1·16
H_2O^-	0·04	0·11	—	0·06	0·15	—
F	—	1·90	—	0·35	0·33	—
	100·41	101·17	99·86	100·14	100·55	100·50
$O \equiv F,Cl$	—	0·80	—	0·14	0·14	—
Total	100·41	100·37	99·86	100·00	100·41	100·50
α	1·650	1·613	1·697	1·675	1·685	1·691
β	1·672	1·618	1·713	1·715	—	—
γ	1·681	1·635	1·714	1·735	1·736	1·707
$2V_\alpha$	(+)	119·5°	16°	—	66°–74°	—
D	—	3·069	—	3·246	—	3·418

NUMBERS OF IONS ON THE BASIS OF 24 (O,OH,F,Cl)

	7.		8.		9.		10.		11.		12.	
Si	6·669	8·00	6·760	8·00	6·074	8·00	6·728	8· 0	5·937	8·00	0·377	3·0
Al	1·331		1·240		1·926		1·272		2·063		1·623	
Al	0·629		0·592		0·138		0·076		0·197		0·407	
Ti	0·163		0·011		0·105		0·236		0·801		0·025	
Fe^{+3}	0·370	5·13	0·071	5·18	0·917	5·02	1·602	5·30	0·454	5·07	0·886	5·1
Mg	2·300		4·315		0·323		2·984		2·501		1·376	
Fe^{+2}	1·633		0·194		3·408		0·350		1·100		2·271	
Mn	0·039		—		0·131		0·051		0·020		0·174	
Na	0·278		0·693		0·648		0·390		0·976		1·134	
Ca	1·923	2·35	1·882	2·80	1·696	2·74	1·784	2·38	1·773	2·95	1·748	3·0
K	0·144		0·221		0·395		0·208		0·198		0·156	
OH	1·462	1·46	0·667	1·51	2·174	2·17	0·190	0·36	0·778	0·93	1·208	1·2
F	—		0·845		—		0·165		0·156		—	

7. Hornblende, tonalite, Idaho (Larsen, E. S. & Schmidt, R. G., 1958, *U.S. Geol. Surv. Bu* 1070-A; includes P_2O_5 0·17).
8. Pargasite, metamorphosed limestone, Finland (Laitakari, A., 1921, *Bull. Comm. géol. Finland* No. 54).
9. Ferrohastingsite, nepheline-syenite, Sweden (Quensel, P., 1914, *Bull. Geol. Inst. Upsala*, vol. **1** p. 146).
10. Basaltic hornblende, latite, Colorado (Larsen, E. S., Irving, J., Gonyer, F. A. & Larsen, E. **S** 3rd., 1937, *Amer. Min.*, vol. 22, p. 889).
11. Kaersutite, cognate xenolith in trachyte (Aoki, K., 1959, *Sci. Rept. Tohoku Univ.*, ser. 3, vol. p. 261).
12. Barkevikite, nepheline-syenite, Norway (Kunitz, W., 1930, *Neues Jahrb. Min.*, Abt. A., vol. p. 171).

Table 15. AMPHIBOLE ANALYSES—*continued*

	13.	14.	15.	16.	17.	18.
O_2	57·73	52·41	53·80	48·51	57·10	48·41
iO_2	—	0·45	0·10	1·32	0·35	1·32
l_2O_3	12·04	0·61	1·37	6·60	6·19	1·81
$_2O_3$	1·16	14·37	1·89	4·09	8·01	11·25
O	5·41	14·82	0·00	9·48	2·69	23·81
nO	—	1·46	8·69	0·19	0·34	0·75
gO	13·02	5·07	18·45	14·79	9·13	0·06
O	1·04	1·33	5·43	5·60	0·31	1·18
a_2O	6·98	4·94	5·63	6·01	9·77	7·37
$_2O$	0·68	2·10	1·72	2·20	2·38	1·52
$_2O^+$	2·27	2·02	1·91	1·47	0·50	0·94
$_2O^-$	—	0·10	—	—	0·08	0·13
	—	0·30	0·36	—	2·69	2·95
	100·33	99·98	99·88	100·26	101·28	101·50
$\equiv$ F,Cl	—	0·13	0·16	—	1·13	1·24
tal	100·33	99·85	99·72	100·26	100·15	100·26
	1·606	1·686	1·622	1·639	1·636	—
	—	—	1·635	1·658	1·644	—
	1·627	—	1·641	1·660	1·649	—
α	—	—	66½°	38°	75°	—
	3·085	—	3·08	—	3·16	—

NUMBERS OF IONS ON THE BASIS OF 24 (O,OH,F,Cl)

	13.	14.	15.	16.	17.	18.
Si	7·789	7·924	7·748	7·119	8·021	7·618
Al	0·211	0·076	0·232	0·881	—	0·334
Σ	8·00	8·00	7·98	8·00	8·02	7·95
Al	1·704	0·032	—	0·259	1·025	—
Ti	—	0·051	0·011	0·145	0·037	0·156
Fe^{+3}	0·118	1·634	0·206	0·452	0·847	1·332
Mg	2·618	1·142	3·961	3·235	1·911	0·014
Fe^{+2}	0·611	1·874	—	1·164	0·316	3·134
Mn	—	0·187	1·061	0·024	0·040	0·100
Σ	5·05	4·92	5·24	5·28	4·89‖	4·74
Na	1·826	1·448	1·572	1·708	2·660	2·248
Ca	0·150	0·215	0·838	0·880	0·046	0·199
K	0·117	0·406	0·315	0·412	0·425	0·304
Σ	2·09	2·07	2·74‡	3·00	3·13	2·75
(OH)	2·043	2·036	1·834	1·440	0·469	0·988
	—	0·143	0·163	—	1·193	1·468
Σ	2·04	2·18	2·01§	1·44	1·66	2·46

Glaucophane, glaucophane schist, Switzerland (Kunitz, W., 1930, *Neues Jahrb. Min.*, Abt. A., vol. 60, p. 171).

Riebeckite, aegirine–riebeckite syenite, Korea (Miyashiro, A. & Miyashiro, T., 1956, *Journ. Fac. Sci. Tokyo Univ.*, vol. 10, p. 1).

Richterite, metamorphosed limestone, Sweden (Sundius, N., 1945, *Geol. För. Förh. Stockholm*, vol. 67, p. 266; includes BaO 0·30, Cl 0·04, SO₃ 0·19).

Magnesiokatophorite, theralite, Montana (Wolff, J. E., 1939, *Bull. Geol. Soc. Amer.*, vol. 49, p. 1569).

Eckermannite, nepheline-syenite, Sweden (Sundius, N., 1945, *Årsbok, Sveriges Geol. Undersök.*, vol. 39, No. 8; includes Li₂O 1·15, ZnO 0·59).

Arfvedsonite, arfvedsonite–aegirine syenite, east Greenland (Deer, W. A., Howie, R. A. & Zussman, J., 1963 *Rock Forming Minerals*, vol. 2, p. 368, Longmans).

Includes Ba 0·017.
Includes Cl 0·010.
Includes Li 0·650, Zn 0·061.

of the A sites, vacant in the tremolite structure, are commonly occupied by Na and K atoms. The general formula of the calcium-rich amphiboles can therefore be expressed:

$$X_{2-3}Y_5Z_8O_{22}(OH)_2$$

where $X = Ca,Na,K,Mn$; $Y = Mg,Fe^{+2},Fe^{+3},Al,Ti,Mn,Cr,Li,Zn$; $Z = Si,Al$. The hydroxyl ions may be partially or wholly replaced by F and Cl and, particularly in the case of basaltic hornblende and kaersutite, by oxygen.

Although the above formula and the probable atomic occupants of the X and Y positions cover the majority of the amphibole minerals, in the orthorhombic amphiboles and in the cummingtonite–grunerite series the X positions are occupied by Mg and Fe^{+2}.

Although the replacement $Mg \rightleftharpoons Fe$ is of prime importance in consideration of the optical and physical properties of amphiboles, and their parageneses, this is a comparatively simple substitution which involves no charge unbalance, and which can be described by a simple nomenclature using the prefixes magnesio- or ferro-. Four other important substitutions may, however, occur in the amphiboles, i.e. $Al \rightleftharpoons Si$, $(Mg,Fe) \rightleftharpoons Al$, Na $\rightleftharpoons Ca$, and the introduction of Na(K) into the A site. More than one substitution of this type must occur in a given amphibole in order to maintain charge balance, and the range of amphibole compositions can be expressed in terms of various end-members as indicated in Table 16. This table has been simplified by ignoring the possible substitutions of Fe^{+2} and other divalent ions for Mg, and of Fe^{+3} and other trivalent ions for Al in Y sites.

The end-members tremolite, common hornblende, and tschermakite involve increasing substitutions in the Y and Z positions of the type $MgSi \rightleftharpoons AlAl$.

The edenite and pargasite formulae can be regarded as derived from tremolite and common hornblende respectively by the addition of Na in the A site and the substitution of Al for Si. The end-members common hornblende, tschermakite, edenite and pargasite, and intermediate compositions can be collectively termed hornblendes. End-members 3–7 inclusive are termed the calcium amphiboles since the X site is occupied almost exclusively by Ca; Ca also predominates over Na when the X and A sites are considered together.

The remaining amphiboles in Table 16 are termed alkali amphiboles, since in these Na predominates over Ca. The richterite and katophorite formulae may be regarded as derived from tremolite and common hornblende respectively by the substitution of Na for Ca in X accompanied by the addition of Na in the A site. The occurrence of an amphibole end-member (with the suggested name mboziite) related in this way to tschermakite, has recently been reported.

Glaucophane and eckermannite are related to tremolite and pargasite by the complete replacement of Ca_2 by Na_2, and this is compensated by the replacement of Mg_3Al_2 for Mg_5 and Si_8 for Si_6Al_2 respectively.

Certain other coupled substitutions can be imagined but do not seem to occur in amphiboles. For example, no amphibole end-member has NaCa in

Table 16. Cation distribution in magnesium end-members of the amphibole minerals

	A	X	Y	Z		
1. Cummingtonite (Anthophyllite)	—	Mg_2	Mg_5	Si_8		
2. Gedrite	—	Mg_2	Mg_3Al_2	Si_6Al_2		
3. Tremolite	—	Ca_2	Mg_5	Si_8	⎫	
4. Common Hornblende	—	Ca_2	Mg_4Al	Si_7Al	⎬ H	Calcium
5. Tschermakite	—	Ca_2	Mg_3Al_2	Si_6Al_2	O R N	Amphiboles
6. Edenite	Na	Ca_2	Mg_5	Si_7Al	B L E N D E S	
7. Pargasite	Na	Ca_2	Mg_4Al	Si_6Al_2		
8. Richterite	Na	NaCa	Mg_5	Si_8	⎫	
9. Katophorite	Na	NaCa	Mg_4Al	Si_7Al	⎬	
10. Mboziite	Na	NaCa	Mg_3Al_2	Si_6Al_2		Alkali Amphiboles
11. Glaucophane	—	Na_2	Mg_3Al_2	Si_8		
12. Eckermannite	Na	Na_2	Mg_4Al	Si_8	⎭	

The above table has been simplified by ignoring substitutions of Fe^{+2} for Mg, Fe^{+3} for Al in Y sites, K for Na, and other similar substitutions. The $Mg \rightleftharpoons Fe^{+2}$ substitution can be dealt with in nomenclature by use of prefixes magnesio- or ferro-, or in other cases, e.g. glaucophane and riebeckite, by the use of individual names.

X and nothing in A, although formulae such as $NaCa \cdot Mg_4Al \cdot Si_8$ or $NaCa \cdot Mg_3Al_2 \cdot Si_7Al$ are possible.†

The formulae in Table 16 represent ideal compositions which are rarely matched by natural amphiboles, and some of the formulae used in the following pages to designate individual members of the amphibole group are based on actual compositions as well as on considerations of theoretical substitutions. The arrangement adopted here is as follows:

(i) Anthophyllite–cummingtonite sub-group ($Ca + Na \simeq 0$).

Anthophyllite, gedrite, ferrogedrite, holmquistite, cummingtonite, grunerite.

(ii) Calcium amphibole sub-group ($Ca \gg Na$).

Tremolite, ferroactinolite, common hornblende, edenite, ferroedenite, tschermakite, ferrotschermakite, pargasite, ferrohastingsite, basaltic hornblende, kaersutite, barkevikite.

(iii) Alkali amphibole sub-group ($Na \gg Ca$).

Glaucophane, magnesioriebeckite, riebeckite, richterite, katophorite, magnesiokatophorite, eckermannite, arfvedsonite.

† It may be that NaCa also does not occur in X when A is occupied and that the formulae of the richterite sub-group should be written $Ca \cdot Na_2$ etc. instead of $Na \cdot NaCa$.

Anthophyllite
Gedrite

$(Mg,Fe^{+2})_7[Si_8O_{22}](OH,F)_2$

$(Mg,Fe^{+2})_5Al_2[Si_6Al_2O_{22}](OH,F)_2$

ORTHORHOMBIC $(-)(+)$

α 1·596–1·694
β 1·605–1·710
γ 1·615–1·722
δ 0·013–0·028
$2V_\gamma$ 78°–111°
Dispersion: $r \gtrless v$.
D 2·85–3·57.
H 5½–6.

Anthophyllite   Gedrite

Cleavage: {210} perfect; {010}, {100} imperfect: (210): (2$\bar{1}$0) $\simeq$ 54½°.
Twinning: None.
Colour: White, grey, green, clove-brown, yellow-brown, dark brown; colourless to pale green or yellow in thin section.
Pleochroism: Feeble to moderate, absorption $\gamma = \beta > \alpha$; or $\gamma > \beta = \alpha$; commonly $\alpha = \beta$ pale grey-brown, γ brown-grey to clove-brown.

CHEMISTRY

The major variations in the composition of the anthophyllite–gedrite minerals are associated with the replacements $Mg \rightleftharpoons Fe^{+2}$ and $(Mg,Fe^{+2})Si \rightleftharpoons AlAl$. In most specimens the substitution of Si by Al, on the basis of 24(O,OH), is either less than 0·5 or greater than 1·5 Al atoms per formula unit, and it is because of the rarity of minerals containing intermediate amounts of Al that it is convenient to retain the names anthophyllite and gedrite for Al-poor and Al-rich varieties respectively (Table 15, anals. 1, 2). Most anthophyllites are magnesium-rich, and the replacement of Mg by Fe^{+2} is limited to compositions having approximately 40 per cent of the $Fe_7Si_8O_{22}(OH)_2$ component. Gedrites containing more than 80 per cent $Mg_5Al_4Si_6O_{22}(OH)_2$ are not found, but the replacement of Mg by Fe^{+2} in the aluminium-rich members of this subgroup extends to almost pure ferrogedrite, $Fe_5Al_4Si_6O_{22}(OH)_2$.

There is a small compositional overlap between anthophyllite and the monoclinic (Mg,Fe) amphibole, cummingtonite, for minerals of the two series containing between 30 and 40 per cent $Fe_7Si_8O_{22}(OH)_2$. This relationship may be due to the inversion curves of the orthorhombic and monoclinic forms of $(Mg,Fe)_7Si_8O_{22}(OH)_2$ being truncated at the low-temperature end by the stability field for talc, and at the high-temperature end by the breakdown of anthophyllite to an orthopyroxene, quartz and vapour (Fig. 55). The pure Mg end-member has been synthesized from appropriate

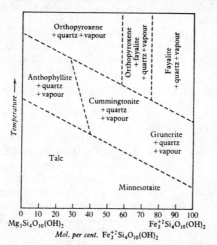

Fig. 55. *Hypothetical temperature–composition diagram for the join $Mg_3Si_4O_{10}(OH)_2–Fe_3^{+2}Si_4O_{10}(OH)_2$ showing the principal phases in the system $MgO–FeO–SiO_2–H_2O$ (after Boyd, F. R., 1959, in* Researches in Geochemistry, *Wiley, New York).*

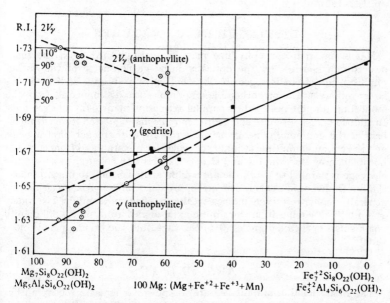

Fig. 56. *Relation between the optical properties and chemical composition for anthophyllite and gedrite.*

proportions of MgO and cristobalite and is stable between 667° and 745°C at P_{H_2O} 1000 bars.

Holmquistite, $Li_2(Mg,Fe^{+2})_3(Al,Fe^{+3})_2[Si_8O_{22}](OH)_2$, is a rare Li-rich orthorhombic amphibole, the composition of which can be derived from that of anthophyllite through the coupled substitution $Mg_4 \rightleftharpoons Li_2(Al,Fe^{+3})_2$.

OPTICAL AND PHYSICAL PROPERTIES

The substitution of Mg by Fe^{+2} and of Mg,Si by Al,Al raises the refractive indices of the anthophyllite–gedrite minerals. As the presence of both Fe^{+2} and $[Al]^4$ are accompanied by an increase in the indices the variation of this property cannot be represented by a single curve, and in Fig. 56 separate curves are given for anthophyllites and gedrites. Magnesium-rich anthophyllites are optically negative; $2V_\alpha$ increases with the replacement of Mg by Fe^{+2} and the more iron-rich anthophyllites are optically positive. The refractive indices of the synthetic Mg end-member are α 1·587, β 1·602, γ 1·613. Gedrites, except for compositions close to $Fe_5Al_4Si_6O_{22}(OH)_2$, have large optic axial angles and are optically positive. Holmquistite differs from the other orthorhombic amphiboles by its light blue to violet colour, and by its yellowish to bluish-violet pleochroism. The anthophyllite minerals vary in habit from fibrous and asbestiform to bladed and prismatic. The fibres of anthophyllite asbestos do not have great tensile strength and are of less economic importance than the amosite and crocidolite fibres (see pp. 162, 182).

DISTINGUISHING FEATURES

Magnesium-rich anthophyllites may be distinguished from the magnesium-rich gedrites by the optically negative character of the anthophyllites, and from ferrogedrites by the higher refractive indices of the latter minerals. The orthorhombic amphiboles are distinguished from the monoclinic amphiboles by their parallel extinction in all [001] zone sections. In addition, anthophyllite and gedrite may be distinguished from the members of the cummingtonite–grunerite series by the stronger birefringence and the common multiple twinning of the latter minerals and from common hornblende by its twinning and stronger absorption colours. In zoisite the cleavage is parallel to (010), the optic axial angle is small to moderate and the birefringence is weaker. The orthopyroxenes have pyroxene cleavages, generally higher refractive indices, weaker birefringence and for a considerable range of composition their optic axial angles are smaller. Sillimanite has a small optic axial angle, (010) cleavage, and the prism angle is close to 90°.

PARAGENESIS

The orthorhombic amphiboles are unknown in igneous rocks; anthophyllite and gedrite, however, occur in a wide range of rocks of metamorphic and metasomatic origin. Thus the well known anthophyllite–cordierite-bearing gneisses of the Orijärvi region of Finland are considered by Eskola to have originated by the metasomatic introduction of magnesium and iron from granodioritic magma into acid volcanic rocks. Other Finnish petrologists, however, have suggested that the formation of the anthophyllite–cordierite assemblage is related to a metamorphic concentration of magnesium and iron and loss of water in the crests and troughs of minor folds in argillaceous sediments, and is compatible with their origin from chlorite–quartz schists according to the reaction:

$$\underbrace{5Mg_3Si_2O_5(OH)_4 + 6Mg_2Al_2SiO_5(OH)_4}_{\text{clinochlore}} + 23SiO_2 \rightarrow$$

$$\underset{\text{anthophyllite}}{3Mg_7Si_8O_{22}(OH)_2} + \underset{\text{cordierite}}{3Mg_2Al_4Si_5O_{18}} + 19H_2O$$

Anthophyllite is commonly developed, often with an asbestiform habit, during the regional metamorphism of ultrabasic rocks, and in this paragenesis is usually associated with talc, e.g. in anthophyllite–talc schists. Other parageneses include its occurrence as rims surrounding orthopyroxene formed during the retrograde metamorphism of earlier thermally metamorphosed rocks, and as a hornfels constituent within the metamorphic aureoles of intermediate intrusives.

Holmquistite typically occurs at the contact of lithium-rich pegmatites with country rocks, and its origin, commonly from hornblende, is always associated with lithium metasomatism.

REFERENCES

FYFE, W. S. (1962) 'On the relative stability of talc, anthophyllite and enstatite', *Amer. Journ. Sci.*, vol. 260, p. 460.

GREENWOOD, H. J. (1963) 'The synthesis and stabilty of anthophyllite', *Journ. Petr.*, vol. 4, p. 317.

RABBIT, J. C. (1948) 'A new study of the anthophyllite series', *Amer. Min.*, vol. 33, p. 263.

Cummingtonite
Grunerite

$(Mg,Fe^{+2})_7[Si_8O_{22}](OH)_2$

$(Fe^{+2},Mg)_7[Si_8O_{22}](OH)_2$

MONOCLINIC $(+)(-)$

α 1·635–1·696
β 1·644–1·709
γ 1·655–1·729
δ 0·020–0·045
2V$_\gamma$ 65°–96°
$\gamma:z$ 21°–10°
$\beta = y$, O.A.P. (010)
Dispersion: $r \gtrless v$, weak. D 3·10–3·60.
H 5–6.

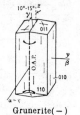

Cummingtonite(+)   Grunerite(−)

Cleavage: {110} good; (110) : (1$\bar{1}$0) $\simeq$ 55°.
Twinning: {100} simple, lamellar, very common.
Colour: Dark green, brown; colourless to pale green in thin section.
Pleochroism: Magnesium-rich cummingtonite non-pleochroic: iron-rich cummingtonite $\alpha = \beta$ colourless, γ pale green; grunerite $\alpha = \beta$ very pale yellow or brown, γ pale brown.

CHEMISTRY

The composition of the monoclinic (Mg,Fe)-amphiboles extends from minerals containing approximately 30 per cent of the $Fe_7Si_8O_{22}(OH)_2$ component to the $Fe_7Si_8O_{22}(OH)_2$ end-member. The name cummingtonite is used to describe minerals containing between 30 and 70 per cent $Fe_7Si_8O_{22}(OH)_2$, and grunerite for the more iron-rich members (Table 15, anals. 3, 4). The replacement of (Mg,Fe) by Mn is generally small but manganese-rich cummingtonites occur, in which up to two of the seven XY sites are occupied by Mn, e.g. in the high grade metamorphic, Pre-Cambrian, Wabush Iron Formation, Labrador. The content of calcium in the cummingtonite–grunerite series is usually small (i.e. Ca occupies about 3 per cent of the XY sites), and it is unlikely that a complete range of composition occurs between them and the hornblende series.

Cummingtonites in the range 85 to 40 mol. per cent $Mg_7Si_8O_{22}(OH)_2$ have been synthesized at a water vapour pressure of 1000 bars at temperatures above 800°C; attempts to synthesize more magnesium-rich and more iron-rich varieties have been unsuccessful. The synthesis of the monoclinic fluor-(Mg,Fe)-amphibole series, $Mg_7Si_8O_{22}F_2$–$Fe_7Si_8O_{22}F_2$, however, has been achieved by heating (Mg,Fe) pyroxenes with NaF.

OPTICAL AND PHYSICAL PROPERTIES

The refractive indices vary linearly with composition and the γ index increases approximately 0·001 per mol. per cent $Fe_7Si_8O_{22}(OH)_2$ (Fig. 57).

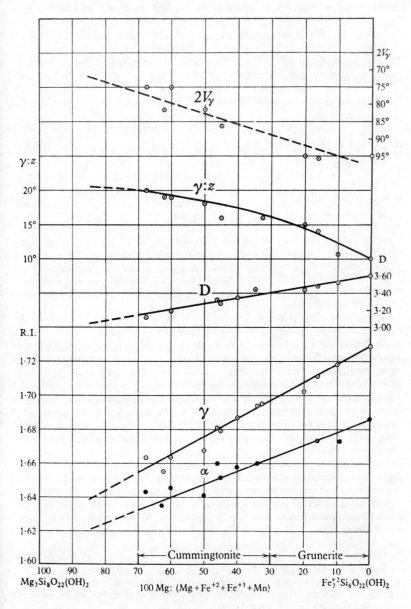

Fig. 57. *The variation of the optical properties and density with composition in the cummingtonite–grunerite series.*

The extinction angle $\gamma:z$ shows a fair correlation with composition, and although not so precise as the γ index it can be used to estimate the approximate position of members within the series. The manganese-rich cummingtonites are commonly light green and non-pleochroic.

The characteristic habit of the cummingtonite–grunerite minerals is acicular or fibrous; asbestiform varieties are common, and amosite and montasite are names given respectively to the harsher more iron-rich and softer more magnesium-rich fibres of economic importance.

DISTINGUISHING FEATURES

Cummingtonite is distinguished from tremolite and actinolite by higher refractive indices and by its optically positive character, and from anthophyllite by the straight extinction in all [001] zone sections of the latter mineral. Grunerite is distinguished from ferroactinolite by higher refractive indices and birefringence. The most valuable diagnostic feature of the cummingtonite–grunerite minerals is the very characteristic multiple twinning on (100), the twin lamellae of which are usually very narrow. The division of the series between cummingtonite and grunerite is taken at the change in optic sign; extinction angles lower than $\gamma:z$ 15° also serve to distinguish grunerite from cummingtonite.

PARAGENESIS

Cummingtonite is most commonly found in amphibolites derived by regional metamorphism from basic igneous rocks. In such rocks it is associated with common hornblendes either as individual crystals or in crystals sharply zoned by the calcium amphibole, a relationship that supports the compositional evidence that there is not complete miscibility under the PT conditions of normal metamorphism, between the cummingtonite–grunerite and the calcium amphibole minerals. Cummingtonite is not uncommon in hybrid rocks of intermediate composition and in such rocks is the middle member of the reaction series: orthopyroxene → cummingtonite → hornblende. Cummingtonite occurs as a mineral of primary crystallization in some dacites.

Grunerite is a characteristic mineral of metamorphosed iron-rich siliceous sediments. Where the metamorphism has been predominantly of a regional nature the characteristic assemblage is magnetite–grunerite–quartz; in rocks which have undergone both thermal and regional metamorphism grunerite is commonly associated with fayalite, hedenbergite and almandine.

REFERENCES

BOWEN, N. L. and SCHAIRER, J. F. (1935) 'Grunerite from Rockport, Massachusetts, and a series of synthetic fluor-amphiboles', *Amer. Min.*, vol. 20, p. 543.
BOYD, F. R. (1959) 'Hydrothermal investigations of amphiboles' in *Researches in Geochemistry*, Wiley, New York, p. 377.
KLEIN, C. (1964) 'Cummingtonite–grunerite series: a chemical, optical, and x-ray study', *Amer. Min.*, vol. 49, p. 963.

Tremolite–Ferroactinolite

$$Ca_2(Mg,Fe^{+2})_5[Si_8O_{22}](OH,F)_2$$

MONOCLINIC (−)

α 1·599–1·688
β 1·612–1·697
γ 1·622–1·705
δ 0·027–0·017
$2V_\alpha$ 86°–65°
$\gamma : z$ 21°–10°
$\beta = y$, O.A.P. (010)

Dispersion: r < v, weak. D 3·02–3·44. H 5–6.

Cleavage: {110} good; {100} parting; (110):(1$\bar{1}$0) $\simeq$ 56°.

Twinning: {100} simple, lamellar, common; {001} lamellar, rare.

Colour: Tremolite colourless or grey, actinolite pale to dark green, ferro-actinolite dark green to black; colourless, pale green, deep green in thin section.

Pleochroism: Tremolite non-pleochroic; actinolite and ferroactinolite strength of pleochroism related to iron content, with α pale yellow, yellowish green, β pale yellow-green, green, γ pale green, deep greenish blue.

CHEMISTRY

There is probably a continuous range of compositions between the tremolite–ferroactinolite and the hornblende series; because, however, of the extremely wide range of composition of the calcium amphiboles it is convenient to consider separately the aluminium-poor tremolite–ferro-actinolites. The division between this and the hornblende series, taken at a Si⇌Al replacement of 0·5 atoms per formula unit, is however, an arbitrary one.

Members of the tremolite–ferroactinolite series in which the replacement of Mg by Fe is greater than 50 per cent are most uncommon. Rare man-ganoan varieties in which one of the five Y sites is occupied by Mn occur, but in most tremolites and actinolites the content of MnO does not exceed 0·3 weight per cent (equivalent to less than 1 per cent of the Y sites).

Tremolite and fluor-tremolite, $Ca_2Mg_5Si_8O_{22}F_2$, have both been synthe-sized and the stability field of hydroxy-tremolite has been determined in the water vapour pressure range 400 to 2000 bars at temperatures between 400° and 900°C (Fig. 58). The breakdown products are enstatite, diopside, quartz, and vapour; the reaction is reversible and tremolite has been crystallized from the breakdown products:

$$\underset{\text{tremolite}}{Ca_2Mg_5Si_8O_{22}(OH)_2} \rightleftharpoons \underset{\text{enstatite}}{3MgSiO_3} + \underset{\text{diopside}}{2CaMgSi_2O_6} + \underset{\text{quartz}}{SiO_2} + H_2O$$

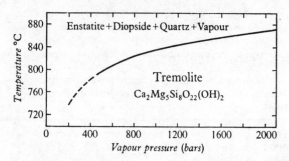

Fig. 58. *The univariant equilibrium curve for the reaction tremolite⇌
enstatite + diopside + quartz + vapour (after Boyd, F. R., 1954, Carnegie
Inst. Washington, Ann. Rep. Dir. Geophys. Lab., 1953–54, p. 109).*

OPTICAL AND PHYSICAL PROPERTIES

The variations in the refractive indices of the members of the tremolite–
ferroactinolite series are mainly related to the replacement of Mg by Fe.
They are, however, also affected by the substitution of Si by Al, and of OH
by F and in consequence estimates of Mg and Fe end-member contents
(Fig. 59) of individual minerals based on refractive indices may be in error
by as much as 15 mol. per cent.

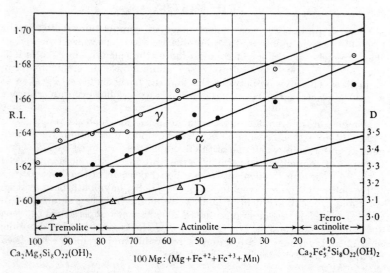

Fig. 59. *The relation between chemical composition and refractive indices and
density of the tremolite-ferroactinolite series.*

DISTINGUISHING FEATURES

The more magnesium-rich members of the series are distinguished from cummingtonite by their negative optical character and lower refractive indices, while the more iron-rich minerals have smaller optic axial angles and a lower birefringence than the more iron-rich members of the cummingtonite–grunerite series. Multiple twinning is less common and is generally not on the fine scale so characteristic of cummingtonite and grunerite. Distinction of the actinolite–ferroactinolite series from the orthorhombic amphiboles may be made by the straight extinction of the latter in all [001] zone sections. Tremolite and the more magnesium-rich actinolites, because of the lack of colour or very pale green colour, are not difficult to distinguish from hornblende. The optical properties of the more iron-rich actinolites are commonly transitional to those of the common hornblendes: extinction angles ($\gamma : z$) between 10° and 15° are, however, indicative of ferroactinolite. Tremolite is distinguished from wollastonite by higher birefringence and optic axial angle and by the presence of the amphibole cleavage.

PARAGENESIS

Tremolite and actinolite are essentially metamorphic minerals and occur in both contact and regionally metamorphosed rocks. In thermally metamorphosed impure dolomites, tremolite forms early by reaction between dolomite and quartz:

$$5CaMg(CO_3)_2 + 8SiO_2 + H_2O \rightarrow Ca_2Mg_5Si_8O_{22}(OH)_2 + 3CaCO_3 + 7CO_2$$
$$\text{dolomite} \quad \text{quartz} \qquad\qquad \text{tremolite} \qquad\quad \text{calcite}$$

At higher grades of metamorphism tremolite is unstable and if SiO_2 is still available after the above reaction the tremolite reacts with calcite to form diopside:

$$Ca_2Mg_5Si_8O_{22}(OH)_2 + 3CaCO_3 + 2SiO_2 \rightarrow 5CaMgSi_2O_6 + 3CO_2 + H_2O$$
$$\text{tremolite} \qquad\qquad \text{calcite} \quad \text{quartz} \qquad \text{diopside}$$

In contrast, where there is an excess of dolomite relative to quartz, the early formed tremolite reacts with the dolomite to give forsterite and calcite:

$$Ca_2Mg_5Si_8O_{22}(OH)_2 + 11CaMg(CO_3)_2 \rightarrow 8Mg_2SiO_4 + 13CaCO_3 + 9CO_2 + H_2O$$
$$\text{tremolite} \qquad\qquad \text{dolomite} \qquad \text{forsterite} \qquad \text{calcite}$$

Tremolite and actinolite also occur in regionally metamorphosed carbonate rocks and they are characteristic minerals in low grade regionally metamorphosed ultrabasic rocks such as tremolite–talc, and tremolite–carbonate–antigorite schists.

Actinolite, in association with epidote and chlorite, is a typical mineral of the greenschist facies. In this paragenesis it sometimes occurs in parallel intergrowths with hornblende, or in crystals sharply rimmed by hornblende, relationships which are indicative of a miscibility gap between actinolite and hornblende in such a P,T environment. At higher grades the miscibility gap disappears and hornblende becomes the stable amphibole.

Actinolite is also a constituent of some glaucophane schists, and here is associated particularly with albite, chlorite, epidote, pumpellyite, lawsonite and stilpnomelane (e.g. Table 15, anal. 5). Actinolite is a common product of the retrograde metamorphism of basic rocks, but with increasing grade of metamorphism its content of aluminium increases and in the biotite and garnet zones the amphibole becomes hornblendic in composition.

In many basic rocks pyroxene is altered marginally to a pale green amphibole to which the name uralite is often given. This amphibole is commonly considered to be actinolitic in composition and to be derived by the pneumatolytic action of the residual water-enriched magmatic fluids on the earlier crystallized pyroxenes (see also p. 174).

REFERENCES

COMEFORO, J. E. and KOHN, J. A. (1954) 'Synthetic asbestos investigations. I. Study of synthetic fluor-tremolite', *Amer. Min.*, vol. 39, p. 537.
MIYASHIRO, A. (1958) 'Regional metamorphism of the Gosaisyo–Takanuki district in the central Abukuma Plateau', *Journ. Fac. Sci. Univ. Tokyo*, Sec. II, vol. 11, p. 219.

Hornblende $(Na,K)_{0-1}Ca_2(Mg,Fe^{+2},Fe^{+3},Al)_5[Si_{6-7}Al_{2-1}O_{22}](OH,F)_2$

MONOCLINIC $(-)(+)$

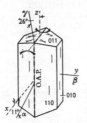
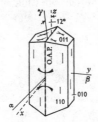

Common Hornblende	Pargasite	Ferrohastingsite
α 1·615–1·705	1·613	1·702
β 1·618–1·714	1·618	1·729
γ 1·632–1·730	1·635	1·730
δ 0·014–0·026	0·022†	0·028†
$\gamma:z$ 13°–34°	26°	12°
$2V_\alpha$ 95°–27°	120°	$\simeq$ 10°
$\beta = y$, O.A.P. (010)	$\beta = y$, O.A.P. (010)	$\beta = y$, O.A.P. (010)
Dispersion: $r \gtrless v$	$r > v$, weak.	$r < v$, moderate to strong
D 3·02–3·45	3·05	3·50
H 5–6	5–6	5–6

Cleavage: {1̄10} good; {100}, {001} partings; (110): (1̄10) $\simeq$ 56°.

Twinning: {100} simple, lamellar, common.

Colour: Common hornblende, green, dark green, black; pale green, green, light yellow-brown to brown in thin section. Pargasite, light brown, brown; colourless, very light brown, bluish green in thin section. Ferrohastingsite, dark green, black; yellow, brown-green, dark green in thin section.

Pleochroism: Common hornblende, variable in greens, yellow-green, bluish green and brown; absorption $\gamma \geq \beta > \alpha$ or $\beta > \gamma > \alpha$. Pargasite, α colourless, greenish yellow, $\beta = \gamma$ light brown, bluish green. Ferrohastingsite, α yellow, greenish brown, yellowish green; β deep greenish blue, brownish green, dark olive green; γ deep olive green, smoky blue-green, very dark green.

CHEMISTRY

It is convenient to consider the hornblende minerals as consisting of three compositional series. The first, of edenite–ferroedenite composition,

† Smaller and larger birefringences have been reported for some minerals with compositions intermediate between pargasite and ferrohastingsite.

$NaCa_2(Mg,Fe^{+2})_5AlSi_7O_{22}(OH)_2$, can be regarded as derived from the tremolite composition by the entry of Na into the A sites together with a balancing replacement of one Si by one Al, i.e. $NaAl \rightleftharpoons Si$. The second series can similarly be considered to be derived from tremolite by the replacement of Si by Al and a balancing substitution of Mg by Al, the A sites remaining vacant, i.e. $Al,Al \rightleftharpoons Mg,Si$; the approximate limit to which this replacement occurs is represented by $Ca_2(Mg,Fe^{+2})_3Al_2Al_2Si_6O_{22}(OH)_2$, for which compositions the names tschermakite and ferrotschermakite are used. The combination of both substitutions, $NaAl_3 \rightleftharpoons MgSi_2$, gives the composition $NaCa_2(Mg,Fe^{+2})_4AlAl_2Si_6O_{22}(OH)_2$, the magnesium and iron

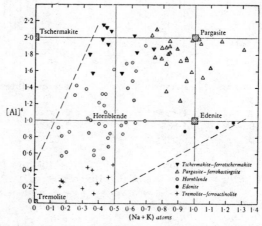

Fig. 60. *The chemical variation of the calcium-rich amphiboles expressed as the numbers of (Na,K) and [Al]⁴ atoms per formula unit.*

end-members of which are known respectively as pargasite and ferro-hastingsite (Table 15, p. 152). Compositions approaching those of the edenite and tschermakite end-members are rare, and the compositions of the majority of the hornblendic amphiboles are intermediate between the two end-member series, tremolite–ferroactinolite and pargasite–ferrohastingsite (Figs. 60, 61). Within the group as a whole the diadochy of Mg and Fe^{+2} is complete; but in the edenitic and tschermakitic hornblendes the replacement of Mg by Fe^{+2} is less extensive. In the great majority of hornblendes the replacement of Si by Al does not exceed two atoms per formula unit, and the limit of the $Si \rightleftharpoons Al$ substitution is approximately 2·5 atoms. The content of Fe^{+3} is greater in the more iron-rich hornblendes but very rarely exceeds a 1 : 1 ratio with Fe^{+2}. Sodium is the dominant alkali ion and only in very few hornblendes is the content of potassium greater than that of sodium.

Some hornblende analyses show more $H_2O +$ than is required to give two

(OH,F,Cl) ions per formula unit; this may represent extra hydrogen ions which are associated with oxygens as (OH) replacing O, but is commonly due to water absorbed on fine-grained material. In other hornblendes the number of monovalent anions is apparently less than two per formula unit; in some the low value may be due to the omission of the determination of fluorine and chlorine in the analysis. Both these anions are important constituents in many amphiboles and in some pargasite–ferrohastingsites the replacement of OH by F is as much as one atom per formula unit.

A wide range of both hydroxy and fluor-hornblende compositions have been synthesized by the dry and hydrothermal methods and by solid state

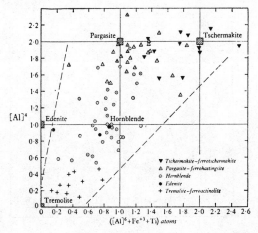

Fig. 61. *The chemical variation of the calcium-rich amphiboles expressed as numbers of $([Al]^6 + Fe^{+3} + Ti)$ and $[Al]^4$ atoms per formula unit.*

reactions. The temperature–vapour pressure diagram for pargasite composition (Fig. 62) shows that this amphibole breaks down between 840° and 1025°C at vapour pressures of between 250 and 800 bars (curve A) to the following anhydrous crystalline phases and vapour:

$$2NaCa_2Mg_4Al_3Si_6O_{22}(OH)_2 \rightarrow 3CaMgSi_2O_6 + 2Mg_2SiO_4$$
$$\text{pargasite} \qquad\qquad\qquad \text{diopside} \qquad \text{olivine}$$
$$+ 2NaAlSiO_4 + CaAl_2Si_2O_8 + MgAl_2O_4 + 2H_2O$$
$$\text{nepheline} \qquad \text{anorthite} \qquad \text{spinel}$$

Curve B marks the beginning of melting of these anhydrous phases in the presence of vapour, and the stable phases are diopside, forsterite and spinel. At vapour pressures greater than 800 bars pargasite melts incongruently along curve C to diopside, forsterite, spinel, liquid and vapour. Comparison of the breakdown curve of pargasite with that of tremolite (see Fig. 58) shows that the range of temperature in which a calcium-rich amphibole is stable is increased by the substitution of Si by Al and by the

6*

introduction of sodium into the amphibole structure. When silica in excess of that required to saturate the undersaturated breakdown products olivine and nepheline is added to the melt, the phase assemblage above 900°C and 1000 bars vapour pressure is diopside, enstatite, labradorite and quartz:

$$NaCa_2Mg_4Al_3Si_6O_{22}(OH)_2 + 4SiO_2 \rightarrow CaMgSi_2O_6 + 3MgSiO_3$$

pargasite   diopside   enstatite

$$+ \underbrace{NaAlSi_3O_8 + CaAl_2Si_2O_8}_{labradorite} + H_2O$$

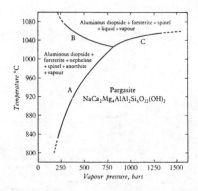

Fig. 62. *The stability field of pargasite (after Boyd, F. R., 1956, in* Researches in Geochemistry, *Wiley, New York).*

OPTICAL AND PHYSICAL PROPERTIES

The substitution of Mg by Fe^{+2} exercises the major control on the refractive indices of the hornblende minerals (see Figs 63, 64), but an appreciable effect is also exerted by the amount of Al in tetrahedral coordination; the effect of octahedrally coordinated Al on the refractive indices does not differ appreciably from that of Mg. The replacements of Mg by Fe^{+2} and of Si by Al are both accompanied by higher indices but, owing to the uncertainty as to the magnitude of the effect of each of these substitutions, correlation between the chemical composition and the refractive indices is rarely precise.

The optic axial angle of the calcium amphiboles varies widely but in the common hornblendes and in the pargasite–ferrohastingsite series the larger angles are found in the magnesium-rich members; for ferrohastingsites $2V_\alpha$ varies between 10° and 50°. The extinction angle, $\gamma : z$, even of minerals of comparable composition, may show considerable variation and this property is of little diagnostic value. The absorption scheme is variable but the strongest absorption is coincident with either the γ or β vibration direction,

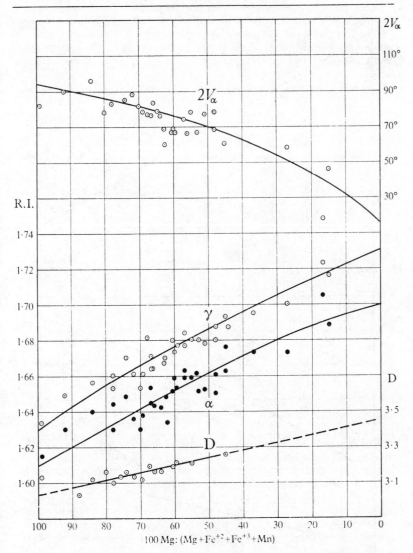

Fig. 63. *The relation between chemical composition and optical properties and density of common hornblendes.*

and in all hornblendes absorption is least in the α direction. Zoned hornblendes occur in some igneous rocks; the zoning is marked by changes in absorption colours, and the crystals normally consist of a magnesium-rich core and an iron-rich periphery.

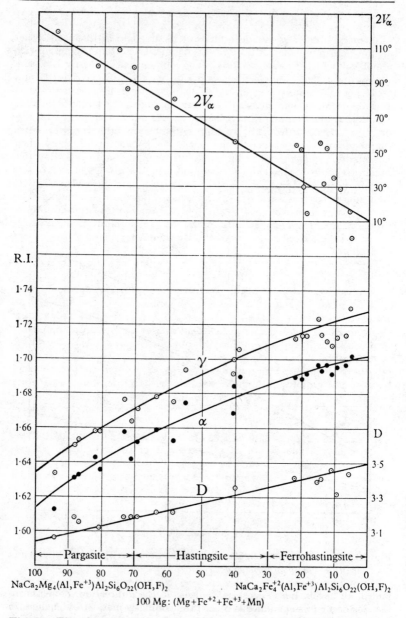

Fig. 64. *The relation between chemical composition and optical properties and density of the pargasite–ferrohastingsite amphiboles.*

DISTINGUISHING FEATURES

Common hornblende cannot in all cases be distinguished from the other calcium-rich amphiboles. It is, however, distinguished from magnesian-rich tremolites by higher refractive indices and moderate to strong pleochroism, and from actinolite and ferroactinolite by larger optic axial angle and birefringence. Common hornblende is distinguished from pargasite by its optically negative character and from ferrohastingsite by larger optic axial angle and extinction angle; in general, it cannot with certainty be distinguished optically from the edenitic and tschermakitic varieties. Both cummingtonite and grunerite can generally be distinguished by their characteristic multiple twinning on (100); cummingtonite is further distinguished from the calcium-rich amphiboles, except pargasite, by its optically positive character, whilst grunerite has higher refractive indices and stronger birefringence. Basaltic hornblende, kaersutite and barkevikite are all distinguished by intense absorption and pleochroism. Ferrohastingsite is distinguished from arfvedsonite by the weaker pleochroism and orientation of the optic axial plane parallel to the symmetry plane of the former mineral.

PARAGENESIS

Hornblendes are particularly characteristic minerals of intermediate plutonic rocks but also occur as products of primary crystallization in ultrabasic and basic rocks, as well as in rocks of acid and alkali composition. This wide range of igneous parageneses gives rise to a correspondingly large variation in the composition of the hornblendes and there is a continuous series from the more magnesium-rich hornblendes $(Mg : Fe^{+2} \simeq 3 : 1)$ of the gabbros to the iron-rich ferrohastingsites $(Mg : Fe^{+2} \simeq 5 : 95)$ of nepheline-syenites and granites. The typical hornblende of the diorites and other intermediate rocks of the calc-alkaline series has a $Mg : Fe^{+2}$ ratio of approximately $1 : 1$, and a moderate content of aluminium ($\simeq 1\cdot5$ Al per formula unit).

In some basic igneous rocks, and particularly in troctolites and olivine gabbros, hornblende occurs as a component of the symplectic coronas between olivine and plagioclase. In the typical corona sequence, hornblende, usually in vermicular intergrowth with spinel, forms the outer zone in contact with the plagioclase. The reaction which gives rise to the formation of the corona may be expressed:

$$14(Mg,Fe^{+2})_2SiO_4 + \underbrace{2NaAlSi_3O_8 \cdot 4CaAl_2Si_2O_8}_{} + 2H_2O \rightarrow 14(Mg,Fe^{+2})SiO_3$$

$$\text{olivine} \qquad \text{labradorite} \qquad\qquad\qquad\qquad \text{orthopyroxene}$$

$$+ 2NaCa_2(Mg,Fe^{+2})_5AlSi_7O_{22}(OH)_2 + 4(Mg,Fe)Al_2O_4$$

$$\text{edenite} \qquad\qquad\qquad \text{spinel}$$

Hornblende is one of the most common constituents of regionally metamorphosed rocks, and is stable under a wide range of P,T conditions from the greenschist to the lower part of the granulite facies. Hornblende and plagioclase are the main, and sometimes the sole, constituents of hornblende schists, hornblende gneisses and amphibolites, rocks which constitute the main bulk of the amphibolite facies. Progressive change in composition with increasing grade is shown by the hornblende in some metamorphic terrains. Thus the hornblendes from the chlorite to the garnet zone in the south-west Highland epidiorites are increasingly rich in aluminium. In other areas (e.g. the central Abukuma Plateau, Japan), however, the change from the lower grade actinolitic amphibole to the common hornblende of the higher grade rocks is abrupt, and the change to the formation of the aluminium-rich hornblende is shown by its development as sharply defined peripheral zones around actinolitic cores.

Tschermakitic amphiboles occur in rocks of high metamorphic grade, e.g. kyanite amphibolites. They are also common in altered eclogites, and in this paragenesis are derived from omphacite in the early stages of the retrograde metamorphism. At a later stage the garnet is replaced by hornblende–plagioclase symplectites, the hornblende of which is often in optical continuity with that derived from the omphacite.

The occurrence of common hornblendes and pargasites very rich in magnesium is restricted to metamorphosed impure dolomitic limestones (Table 15, anal. 8); more iron-rich pargasites occur in regionally metamorphosed skarns and are commonly associated with hydroxyl-, fluorine- or boron-metasomatism.

The hornblende in many igneous rocks is secondary in origin and derived from primary pyroxene. The secondary character of the hornblende is not obvious in all cases but is apparent where its development is related to joints and other smaller less regular fractures which facilitated the movement of solutions. Some secondary amphiboles are tremolites or cummingtonites but the difficulty of identifying the composition of the more fibrous amphibole varieties has led to the common use of the name *uralite*, a term first applied to minerals with the habit of pyroxene and the structure of an amphibole, but now frequently used to describe a secondary fibrous light blue-green amphibole of undetermined composition. The alteration of pyroxenes to fibrous amphiboles is described as uralitization and the formation of these secondary hornblendes is generally ascribed to the action of hydrothermal solutions which may be associated with the late stage crystallization of igneous rocks, or may be a post consolidation process unrelated to the igneous activity from which the rocks were derived; in the latter case the uralitization may be associated with either regional, thermal or metasomatic metamorphism.

REFERENCES

BORLEY, G. D. (1963) 'Amphiboles from the Younger Granites of Nigeria, Part I. Chemical classification', *Min. Mag.*, vol. 33, p. 358.

ENGEL, A. E. J. and ENGEL, C. G. (1962) 'Hornblendes formed during progressive metamorphism of amphibolites, northwest Adirondack Mountains, New York', *Bull. Geol. Soc. Amer.*, vol. 73, p. 1499.

SHIDÔ, F. and MIYASHIRO, A. (1959) 'Hornblendes of basic metamorphic rocks', *Journ. Fac. Sci. Univ. Tokyo*, Sec. II, vol. 12, p. 85.

SUNDIUS, N. (1946) 'The classification of the hornblendes and the solid solution relations in the amphibole group', *Årsbok Sveriges Geol. Undersök*, vol. 40, No. 4.

Basaltic Hornblende

$$(Ca,Na)_{2-3}(Mg,Fe^{+2})_{3-2}(Fe^{+3},Al)_{2-3}O_2[Si_6Al_2O_{22}]$$

MONOCLINIC $(-)$

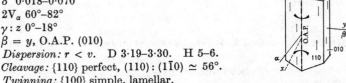

α 1·662–1·690
β 1·672–1·730
γ 1·680–1·760
δ 0·018–0·070
$2V_\alpha$ 60°–82°
$\gamma : z$ 0°–18°
$\beta = y$, O.A.P. (010)
Dispersion: $r < v$. D 3·19–3·30. H 5–6.
Cleavage: {110} perfect, (110):(1$\bar{1}$0) $\simeq$ 56°.
Twinning: {100} simple, lamellar.
Colour: Brown to black; brown to dark brownish red in thin section.
Pleochroism: α pale yellow, yellow; β dark chestnut brown, dark brown; γ dark brown, dark reddish brown.

The essential chemical features of the basaltic hornblendes are their high $Fe^{+3} : Fe^{+2}$ ratio and low hydroxyl content. In terms of general hornblende chemistry they include hastingsitic and tschermakitic, as well as common hornblende compositions. The latter can be transformed to basaltic hornblende by heating in air at 800°C. The change is brought about by the loss of hydrogens from the hydroxyl ions, the valence electrons of the oxygens previously supplied by the hydrogen coming from adjacent iron atoms and converting them to the ferric state. The transformation is reversible and by heating in hydrogen, hydrogen can be reintroduced into the structure and the ferric iron reduced. Hornblende has two structural hydrogens per formula unit, and the oxidation of the ferrous iron by loss of hydrogen is thus limited to two ions. Thus the composition of ferrohastingsite may be expressed $NaCa_2Fe_4^{+2}Fe^{+3}Al_2Si_6O_{22}(OH)_2$ and that of basaltic ferrohastingsite $NaCa_2Fe_2^{+2}Fe_3^{+3}O_2Al_2Si_6O_{22}$.

The conversion of common hornblende to basaltic hornblende on heating at about 800°C is accompanied by an increase in refractive indices and birefringence, a decrease in the extinction angle, and a change in the absorption colours and pleochroism from greens to browns.

Many basaltic hornblendes show peripheral resorption effects, and the crystal margins are dusty with fine grains of black iron ore, or sometimes with reddish brown grains of haematite; the hornblende may be completely replaced by iron oxide or by pyroxene.

Basaltic hornblende is distinguished from other amphiboles except kaersutite (p. 176), barkevikite (p. 177), and katophorite (p. 186) by its intense yellow to dark brown or dark reddish brown pleochrosim. It is distinguished from aenigmatite by the smaller optic axial angle, higher refractive indices and more intense γ absorption colour of the latter mineral.

Basaltic hornblendes occur in a large variety of volcanic rocks varying in composition from basalts to trachytes, and are particularly characteristic constituents of andesites, latites (Table 15, anal. 10, p. 152), basanites and tephrites, and their corresponding tuffs. Most basaltic hornblendes probably crystallized initially as common hornblendes and were oxidized after eruption during the later stages of the consolidation of lava.

REFERENCE

BARNES, V. E. (1930) 'Changes in hornblende at above 800°C', *Amer. Min.*, vol. 15, p. 393.

Kaersutite $\qquad$ $Ca_2(Na,K)(Mg,Fe^{+2},Fe^{+3})_4Ti[Si_6Al_2O_{22}](O,OH,F)_2$

MONOCLINIC $(-)$

α 1·670–1·689
β 1·690–1·741
γ 1·700–1·772
δ 0·019–0·083
$2V_\alpha$ 66°–82°
$\gamma:z$ 0°–19°
$\beta = y$, O.A.P. (010)
Dispersion: $r > v$. D 3·2–3·28. H 5–6.
Cleavage: {110} perfect; {100}, {001} partings; (110):(1$\bar{1}$0) $\simeq$ 56°.
Twinning: {100} simple, lamellar, common.
Colour: Dark brown to black; yellow-brown, brown, reddish brown and occasionally greenish brown in thin section.
Pleochroism: α brownish yellow, light yellow brown, pale yellow; β reddish, reddish brown; γ dark reddish brown, greenish brown.

Kaersutite is characterized chemically by a very high titanium content (5 to 10 weight per cent TiO_2; equivalent to 0·5 to 1·0 atoms per formula unit). Kaersutites, like basaltic hornblendes, are magnesium-rich and the substitution of Mg by $(Fe^{+2} + Fe^{+3})$ is limited approximately to 1·5 atoms. Unlike basaltic hornblende the $Fe^{+3}:Fe^{+2}$ ratio is low to moderate and is similar to the ferric–ferrous iron ratios characteristic of barkevikite. The amount of hydroxyl and fluorine varies from the low values typical of basaltic hornblende to $2(OH + F)$: there is, however, no apparent relationship between the numbers of monovalent anions and the $Fe^{+3}:Fe^{+2}$ ratios. In a few kaersutites the number of Si + Al atoms is a little less (between 1 and 2 per cent) than the ideal 8 per formula unit, and it is possible, as in some pyroxenes, that titanium occupies these tetrahedral positions.

Kaersutites, except those with relatively high $Fe^{+3}:Fe^{+2}$ ratios are distinguished from basaltic hornblende by the nearly equal absorption in the β and γ directions; barkevikite and katophorite have a small optic axial angle, and aenigmatite has a smaller optic axial angle, higher refractive indices and more intense γ absorption. Titanaugite has a higher extinction angle and a paler and more violet absorption colour as well as the pyroxene cleavage.

Kaersutite is a typical constituent of alkaline volcanic rocks, and occurs as phenocrysts in trachybasalts, trachyandesites, trachytes (Table 15, anal. 11) and alkali rhyolites; in the more silica-rich rocks it occurs also as a groundmass constituent. Reaction rims of kaersutite around olivine phenocrysts, and the partial or complete replacement of titanaugite by kaersutite, are commonly found in trachybasalts; the kaersutite of these rocks is invariably surrounded by opacite margins of magnetite. Kaersutite occurs in camptonite dykes, and it is an abundant constituent of some monzonites.

REFERENCE

AOKI, K. (1963) 'The kaersutites and oxykaersutites from alkalic rocks of Japan and surrounding areas', *Journ. Petr.*, vol. 4, p. 198.

Barkevikite $Ca_2(Na,K)(Fe^{+2},Mg,Fe^{+3},Mn)_5[Si_{6.5}Al_{1.5}O_{22}](OH)_2$

MONOCLINIC $(-)$

α 1·685–1·691
β 1·696–1·700
γ 1·701–1·707
δ 0·014–0·018
$2V_\alpha \simeq 40°–50°$
$\gamma : z$ 11°–18°
$\beta = y$, O.A.P. (010)

Dispersion: $r > v$, weak to strong. D 3·35–3·44. H 5–6.
Cleavage: {110} perfect; {100}, {001} partings; (110) : (1$\bar{1}$0) $\simeq$ 56°.
Twinning: {100} simple.
Colour: Black, brownish yellow to dark brown in thin section.
Pleochroism: α light yellow, light brownish yellow, β reddish brown, γ dark or very dark brown. Absorption $\gamma > \beta > \alpha$.

The main chemical characteristics of the barkevikitic amphiboles are their high contents of $Fe^{+2}+Fe^{+3}$ and relatively low $Fe^{+3} : Fe^{+2}$ ratios; both features are in marked contrast to the basaltic hornblendes. The content of alkali ions is higher than in basaltic hornblendes in which the numbers of $(Na+K)$ ions per formula unit are comparable with those in common hornblendes. The chief chemical differences between barkevikite and kaersutite are the higher content of iron in barkevikite and the much higher contents of titanium in kaersutite. Barkevikites have a comparatively high content of manganese ($\simeq$ 1 per cent MnO).

The range in optical properties of barkevikite is small, and the refractive indices and optic axial angle are comparable with those of hastingsite and ferrohastingsite having similar Mg : $(Mg + Fe^{+2} + Fe^{+3} + Mn)$ ratios, but it is distinguished from the latter by its characteristic yellow to very dark brown pleochroism. Barkevikite is distinguished from both basaltic hornblende and kaersutite by its smaller 2V. The mineral commonly occurs in well developed prismatic crystals showing terminal faces and elongation parallel to z.

The paragenesis of barkevikite is restricted to alkaline rocks, and it occurs in theralites, essexites, nepheline-syenites (Table 15, anal. 12) and foyaites as well as in some ultra-alkaline rocks, e.g. in the jacupirangite of the Alnö complex, Sweden. Other parageneses include its occurrence in trachytes, phonolites and tephrites at Rungwe, Lake Nyasa, and in dolerites of the Morotu district, Sakhalin.

REFERENCE

WILKINSON, J. F. G. (1961) 'Calciferous amphiboles, oxyhornblende, kaersutite and barkevikite', *Amer. Min.*, vol. 46, p. 340.

Glaucophane
Riebeckite

$$Na_2Mg_3Al_2[Si_8O_{22}](OH)_2$$
$$Na_2Fe_3^{+2}Fe_2^{+3}[Si_8O_{22}](OH)_2$$

MONOCLINIC

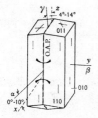 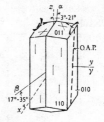

Glaucophane (−)

α 1·606–1·661†

β 1·622–1·667

γ 1·627–1·670

δ 0·008–0·022

$\gamma : z$ 4°–14°; $2V_\alpha$ 50°–0°

$\beta = y$, O.A.P. (010)

Dispersion: $r < v$ (crossite $r \lessgtr v$)

D 3·08–3·30.   H 6.

Cleavage: {110} good, (110) : (1$\bar{1}$0) $\simeq$ 58°

Twinning: {100} simple, lamellar.

Colour: Grey, lavender-blue; lavender-blue to colourless in thin section.

Pleochroism: α colourless
      β lavender-blue
      γ blue

Riebeckite (−) (+)

1·654–1·701‡

1·662–1·711

1·668–1·717

0·006–0·016

$\alpha : z$ 3°–21°; $2V_\alpha$ 40°–90°

$\gamma = y$, O.A.P. $\perp$(010)

$r \lessgtr v$, strong

D 3·02–3·43.   H 5.

{110} good, (110) : (1$\bar{1}$0) $\simeq$ 56°

{100} simple lamellar.

Dark blue, black; dark blue to yellow-green in thin section.

prussian blue

indigo-blue

yellowish green

CHEMISTRY

Pure magnesium glaucophanes are unknown and some replacement of Mg by Fe^{+2} and of Al by Fe^{+3} is always present in natural minerals. The substitution of Mg by Fe^{+2} is limited and there are no amphiboles of ferroglaucophane composition. There is, however, a complete range of the Al $\rightleftharpoons Fe^{+3}$ substitution between minerals close to $Na_2Mg_3Al_2Si_8O_{22}(OH)_2$ and $Na_2Mg_3Fe_2^{+3}Si_8O_{22}(OH)_2$ in composition, i.e. from glaucophane through crossite to magnesioriebeckite (Fig. 65); solid solution is also complete between magnesioriebeckite and riebeckite.

† Higher values refer to crossite.

‡ Lower values refer to magnesioriebeckite.

Glaucophane has been synthesized and its P, T stability field has been determined. In the vapour pressure range of 200 to 1500 bars glaucophane breaks down at temperatures between 850° and 875°C to solid phases and vapour:

$$Na_2Mg_3Al_2Si_8O_{22}(OH)_2 \rightarrow Mg_2SiO_4 + MgSiO_3 + 2NaAlSi_3O_8 + H_2O$$

glaucophane   forsterite   enstatite   albite

Above 1500 bars vapour pressure and a temperature of 875°C glaucophane melts incongruently to forsterite, enstatite, liquid and vapour (Fig. 66).

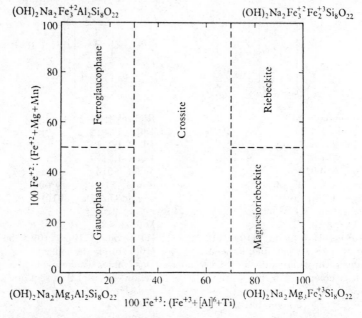

Fig. 65. *The variation in the chemical composition, expressed as* $100\ Fe^{+3}$: $(Fe^{+3} + [Al]^6 + Ti)$ *ratios, and nomenclature of the glaucophane–crossite–riebeckite amphiboles.*

Riebeckite and magnesioriebeckite have also been synthesized. At a vapour pressure of 200 bars the breakdown temperature of magnesioriebeckite is approximately 75°C higher than that of glaucophane, but magnesioriebeckite melts incongruently at a much lower vapour pressure, i.e. 250 bars. Riebeckite melts incongruently at a lower temperature and a lower vapour pressure than magnesioriebeckite. The experimental data are in accord with the paragenesis of the natural minerals; glaucophane is stable at higher vapour pressures but lower temperatures than either magnesioriebeckite or riebeckite. At still lower pressures and/or higher

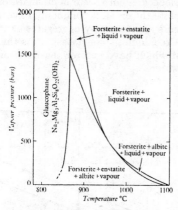

Fig. 66. P_{vapour}–T *diagram of the composition* $Na_2O \cdot 3MgO \cdot Al_2O_3 \cdot 8SiO_2$ *with excess water (after Ernst, W. G., 1961, Amer. Journ. Sci., vol. 259, p. 735).*

temperatures the stable compositions appear to be magnesioriebeckite and riebeckite.

OPTICAL AND PHYSICAL PROPERTIES

Members of the glaucophane–riebeckite series display a very considerable range of optical properties; both main replacements, $Mg \rightleftharpoons Fe^{+2}$ and $Al \rightleftharpoons Fe^{+3}$, have a marked effect on the refractive indices, and the latter substitution is accompanied in addition by large changes in optic axial angles, and by a change in orientation of the optic axial plane. In the magnesioriebeckite–riebeckite series the substitution is Fe^{+2} for Mg. In the glaucophane–crossite series $Fe^{+2}Fe^{+3}$ replaces Mg,Al and, as the effect of $[Al]^6$ does not differ appreciably from that of Mg, the increase in the refractive indices is more rapid than it is in the magnesioriebeckite–riebeckite minerals (Fig. 67).

In glaucophane the optic axial plane is (010) and the obtuse bisectrix γ makes a small angle with the z axis. Increasing replacement of Al by Fe^{+3} is first accompanied by a reduction in 2V which becomes zero in minerals close to crossite in composition, and then opens out in the plane perpendicular to (010) in minerals in which the $Fe^{+3} : [Al]^6$ ratio is greater than unity. The replacement in riebeckite of Fe^{+2} by Mg is accompanied by a reduction in the optic axial angle and an increase in the extinction angle (magnesioriebeckite $2V_\alpha$ 40° to 50° and $\beta : z$ 15° to 30°).

The pleochroism of riebeckite is variable but in most minerals the absorption colour parallel to β is indigo-blue; the absorption is either $\alpha > \beta > \gamma$ or $\alpha > \gamma \geqslant \beta$. Zoned crystals are common and often consist of a glaucophane-rich core rimmed by either crossite or magnesioriebeckite.

Glaucophane and riebeckite both occur in prismatic crystals and columnar aggregates; in riebeckite the crystals commonly have a needle-like appearance. Riebeckite occurs also in mossy aggregates as well as in fibrous and asbestiform habits. Crocidolite, 'blue asbestos', is the blue, highly fibrous variety, the fibres of which have greater tensile strength but lower heat resistance than chrysotile.

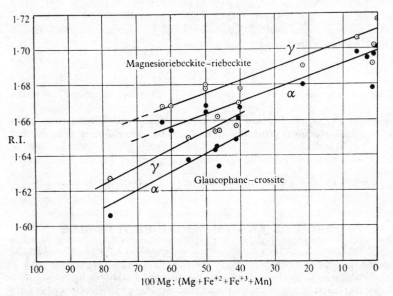

Fig. 67. *The relation between chemical composition and refractive indices in the glaucophane–crossite and magnesioriebeckite–riebeckite series.*

DISTINGUISHING FEATURES

The pale blue colour and less intense pleochroism of glaucophane is usually sufficiently characteristic to distinguish it from both magnesioriebeckite and riebeckite. Glaucophane is also distinguished from riebeckite by lower refractive indices, smaller optic axial angle and positive elongation. It is distinguished from arfvedsonite, eckermannite and riebeckite in having the optic plane parallel to (010). Glaucophane may be difficult to distinguish from crossite but the latter has a smaller optic axial angle, the optic axial plane is generally perpendicular to (010), and the dispersion of the bisectrices is stronger than in glaucophane. Glaucophane may be confused with tourmaline but the latter is uniaxial and shows stronger absorption parallel to the elongation. Riebeckite is distinguished from arfvedsonite by smaller extinction angles and pleochroism, the arfvedsonite pleochroic scheme usually including a brownish colour not shown by riebeckite; moreover arfvedsonite rarely shows complete extinction in white light.

PARAGENESIS

Glaucophane-bearing rocks are usually located in folded geosynclinal terrains and are commonly associated with greenschists and epidote amphibolites; glaucophane and crossite do not form except under the P,T conditions of the glaucophane schist facies (e.g. Table 15, anal. 13). Although some glaucophane-bearing schists are rich in Na_2O, many contain no more Na_2O than typical greenschists and the chemical equivalence of the two rocks is illustrated by the equation:

$$2Na_2Mg_3Al_2Si_8O_{22}(OH)_2 + 2H_2O \rightleftharpoons 4NaAlSi_3O_8 + Mg_6Si_4O_{10}(OH)_8$$
$$\text{glaucophane} \qquad\qquad \text{albite} \qquad\qquad \text{antigorite}$$

Glaucophane, associated with lawsonite, is abundant in some Californian metagreywackes, and in these rocks it has been derived from chloritic material and by alteration of jadeite. The formation of glaucophane from pyroxene also occurs during the retrograde metamorphism of eclogite, and in this paragenesis it may be associated with pumpellyite as well as lawsonite. The temperatures and pressures necessary for the formation of glaucophane schists are probably not substantially different from those under which greenschists are formed. In view, however, of the higher density of the minerals of the glaucophane schists it is likely that for a given temperature, a higher pressure is essential for their formation.

Riebeckite is the only member of this subgroup of alkali amphiboles to have an igneous paragenesis. It occurs in granites, quartz syenites, syenites (e.g. Table 15, anal. 14) and nepheline-syenites but is a much commoner constituent of the oversaturated than of the undersaturated rocks; riebeckite also occurs in microgranites and in acid volcanic rocks.

The best known occurrences of crocidolite are in South Africa and Western Australia where it occurs in seams conformable with the bedding of the ironstone. The composition of the crocidolite is closely comparable with that of the ironstone, and the crystallization of the amphibole, initially in the form of massive riebeckite, occurred with little or no addition of material and under conditions of moderate temperature and pressure consequent on the burial of the ironstones to moderate depths. The transformation of the riebeckite to the fibrous crocidolite may result from the instability of the massive riebeckite during a period when the ironstones were subjected to shearing stress. Riebeckite is found in a few low grade regionally metamorphosed schists; an intermediate member of the magnesioriebeckite–riebeckite series occurs as an authigenic mineral in rocks of the Green River formation, U.S.A.; associated minerals are acmite and shortite ($Na_2CO_3 \cdot 2CaCO_3$).

REFERENCES

CILLIERS, J. J. LE R., FREEMAN, A. G., HODGSON, A. and TAYLOR, H. F. W. (1961). 'Crocidolite from the Koegas-Westerberg area, South Africa,' *Econ. Geol.*, vol. 56, p. 1421.

ERNST, W. G. (1960) 'The stability relations of magnesioriebeckite', *Geochim. et Cosmochim. Acta*, vol. 19, p. 10.

—— (1963) 'Petrogenesis of glaucophane schists', *Journ. Petr.*, vol. 4, p. 1.

MIYASHIRO, A. and BANNO, S. (1958) 'Nature of glaucophanitic metamorphism', *Amer. Journ. Sci.*, vol. 256, p. 97.

PHEMISTER, J., HARVEY, C. O. and SABINE, P. A. (1950) 'The riebeckite-bearing dikes of Shetland', *Min. Mag.*, vol. 29, p. 359.

Richterite–Ferrorichterite

$$Na_2Ca(Mg,Fe^{+3},Fe^{+2},Mn)_5[Si_8O_{22}](OH,F)_2$$

MONOCLINIC (−)

α 1·605–1·685
β 1·618–1·700
γ 1·627–1·712†
δ 0·015–0·029
$2V_\alpha$ 66°–87°
$\gamma : z$ 15°–40°
$\beta = y$, O.A.P. (010)

Dispersion: $r < v$ strong. D 2·97–3·45. H 5–6.
Cleavage: {110} perfect; {100}, {001} partings. (110) : (1$\bar{1}$0) ≃ 56°.
Twinning: {100} simple, lamellar.
Colour: Brown, yellow, brownish red, pale to dark green; colourless, pale yellow, yellow, violet in thin section.
Pleochroism: Very variable, usually in pale yellow, orange and reddish tints, sometimes violet and blue (e.g. ferrian varieties winchite and chiklite). Anomalous interference colours shown by some varieties. Absorption variable but generally $\beta > \gamma > \alpha$.

Some richterite–ferrorichterite amphiboles contain more calcium and less sodium than the ideal composition, and the series as a whole shows more extensive solid solution with the calcium amphiboles, particularly the tremolite–ferroactinolites, than do the members of either the glaucophane–riebeckite or the eckermannite–arfvedsonite series. Most richterites are magnesium-rich and have a high $Fe^{+3} : Fe^{+2}$ ratio. A rare ferririchterite in which the X and A atoms are Na_2Ca, and which contains only four Y group atoms, namely $2(Mg,Fe^{+2},Mn)$ and $2Fe^{+3}$, is of unusual interest in that the valency balance is maintained by the substitution of 3 divalent by 2 trivalent atoms in the Y group.

The most extensive substitution in richterite is that of Mg by (Al,Fe^{+3}). This replacement is associated with higher refractive indices, higher extinction angles, greater depth of colour and stronger dispersion. Because, however, of their wide chemical variation correlation of the optical properties and composition is not precise.

Richterite occurs in thermally metamorphosed limestones (e.g. Table 15, anal. 15) and in skarns; it is also found as a hydrothermal product and in veins in alkaline igneous rocks.

† Maximum values refer to ferririchterite. The refractive indices of Mg-rich richterites are normally in the range α 1·605–1·624, γ 1·627–1·641.

Magnesiokatophorite–Katophorite

$$Na_2Ca(Mg,Fe^{+2})_4Fe^{+3}[Si_7AlO_{22}](OH,F)_2$$

MONOCLINIC $(-)$

α 1·639–1·681
β 1·658–1·688
γ 1·660–1·690
δ 0·007–0·021
$2V_\alpha$ 0°–50°
$\alpha : z$ 36°–70°
$\beta = y$, O.A.P. (010) for magnesiokatophorite
$\gamma = y$, O.A.P. $\perp$ (010) for katophorite

Katophorite

Dispersion: $r < v$, strong (magnesiokatophorite). $r > v$, strong (katophorite). D 3·20–3·50. H 5.
Cleavage: {110} perfect, {010} parting; (110) : (1$\bar{1}$0) $\simeq$ 56°.
Twinning: {100}.
Colour: Rose-red, dark red-brown; bluish black in iron-rich varieties; yellow, reddish brown, bluish green in thin section.
Pleochroism: α yellow, yellow-red, pale brown; β greenish brown, brownish red, deep brown; γ reddish yellow, deep purple-red-brown, greenish brown α pale yellow, β bluish green, γ dark green to black for some iron-rich varieties. Absorption $\gamma < \beta > \alpha$ for magnesiokatophorite, $\gamma > \beta > \alpha$ for katophorite.

Katophorites are the only alkali amphiboles except mboziite which show substantial replacement of Si by Al. The Fe^{+3} : $[Al]^6$ ratio is high and in this respect the composition of katophorite resembles that of arfvedsonite; the latter mineral, however, contains only about half as much calcium.

As for the glaucophane–riebeckite and the eckermannite–arfvedsonite series, the optic axial plane is parallel to (010) in the magnesium-rich and perpendicular to (010) in the iron-rich members; the composition at which the change in optical orientation occurs is not known with certainty. The extinction angle, $\alpha : z$, is high in all members of the series, but the higher values occur in the iron-rich minerals.

Katophorite is distinguished from other members of the amphibole group of minerals, except barkevikite, kaersutite and basaltic hornblende, by the characteristic yellow, reddish yellow and brownish absorption colours. Katophorite is distinguished from aenigmatite (cossyrite) by its less intense absorption colours and lower refractive indices.

Magnesiokatophorite and katophorite are comparatively rare amphiboles which occur mainly in the more basic alkaline rocks.

Eckermannite–Arfvedsonite $\quad$ Na$_3$(Mg,Fe^{+2})$_4$Al[Si$_8$O$_{22}$](OH,F)$_2$

MONOCLINIC $(-)(+)$

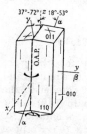

Eckermannite† $(-)$

α 1·612–1·638
β 1·625–1·652
γ 1·630–1·654
δ 0·009–0·020‡
2V$_α$ 80°–15°
α : z 53°–18°
β = y, O.A.P. (010)
Dispersion: r > v, very strong
D 3·00–
H 5–6

Arfvedsonite† $(-)$

1·674–1·700
1·679–1·709
1·686–1·710
0·005–0·012‡
0°–50° (data uncertain)
0°–30° (anomalous extinction)
γ = y, O.A.P. ⊥(010)
r < v, very strong
–3·50
5–6

Cleavage: {110} perfect, {010} parting; (110) : (1$\bar{1}$0) $\simeq$ 56°.
Twinning: {100}, simple, lamellar.
Colour: Eckermannite, dark bluish green; pale bluish green in thin section.
Arfvedsonite, greenish black, black; yellowish green, brownish green, grey-green or grey-violet in thin section.
Pleochroism: Eckermannite: α bluish green, β light bluish green, γ pale or very pale yellowish green; absorption α > β > γ. Arfvedsonite: α greenish blue, deep blue-green, bluish green to indigo; β lavender-blue to brown-yellow, pale orange-yellow, greyish violet; γ greenish yellow to blue-grey, bluish or greenish yellow, light yellowish green; absorption variable.

CHEMISTRY

The compositions of the members of the eckermannite–arfvedsonite series only rarely correspond closely to the ideal formula, Na$_3$(Mg,Fe^{+2})$_4$-Al[Si$_8$O$_{22}$](OH,F)$_2$. Most of the minerals contain appreciable amounts of

† Magnesioarfvedsonites are intermediate in composition and optical properties between eckermannite and arfvedsonite.

‡ Higher values of birefringence have been reported for some magnesioarfvedsonites.

calcium, and in many there is a moderate replacement of Si by Al and their composition is more accurately represented by the formula $Na_{2.5}Ca_{0.5}$-$(Mg,Fe^{+2},Fe^{+3},Al)_5[Si_{7.5}Al_{0.5}O_{22}](OH,F)_2$. Eckermannite from the type locality contains appreciable lithium, and lithium in smaller quantities is present in other members of the series. The magnitude of the (Mg,Fe^{+2}) $\rightleftharpoons Fe^{+3}$ replacement shows considerable variation, and in minerals with a high content of Fe^{+3} the valency balance is maintained by a reduction in the number of Y atoms, i.e. in minerals with $\simeq 2Fe^{+3}$ atoms the number of Y atoms is $\simeq 4.5$.

OPTICAL AND PHYSICAL PROPERTIES

Although data on the optical properties are relatively few there are sufficient to show a moderate correlation between the refractive indices and chemical composition (Fig. 68). The optic axial plane is parallel to the symmetry plane in the magnesium-rich and perpendicular to (010) in the more iron-rich members of the series. This change in orientation of the optic axial plane, which occurs at a composition of about 70 per cent of the magnesium end-member, has been adopted as the division between eckermannite and magnesioarfvedsonite. The division between magnesio-arfvedsonite and arfvedsonite is arbitrarily taken at 30 per cent of the eckermannite molecule.

The extinction angle $\alpha : z$ in eckermannite is usually greater than $40°$; extinction is commonly 'flamy' and variable even within a single crystal. Magnesioarfvedsonites have moderate to large extinction angles of between $20°$ and $35°$; the extinction angle $\alpha : z$ in arfvedsonite is usually very small (Fig. 68). Arfvedsonites are often anomalous in that (010) sections do not exhibit complete extinction even in monochromatic light. After heating at temperatures above 700°C such minerals show normal extinction and it is possible that the anomalous extinction is due to the presence of a fine intergrowth of two amphiboles. The determination of the optical properties of the more iron-rich members of the series is difficult due to their strong absorption, strong dispersion and anomalous extinction.

DISTINGUISHING FEATURES

Eckermannite is distinguished from cummingtonite by its lower refractive indices and smaller birefringence and extinction angles, from tremolite by its smaller birefringence, larger extinction angle and pleochroism, and from common hornblende by its characteristic $\alpha > \beta > \gamma$ absorption. Arfved-sonite is distinguished from all other amphiboles except riebeckite, some crossites and katophorites by the orientation of the optic axial plane per-pendicular to the symmetry plane. It is also distinguished from these amphiboles by its lower birefringence and characteristic pleochroism. The pleochroism of ferrohastingsite is less intense and its birefringence greater. Glaucophane has lower refractive indices and less intense absorption. Arfvedsonite is distinguished from tourmaline by the stronger absorption parallel to the elongation, by its amphibole cleavages and its biaxiality.

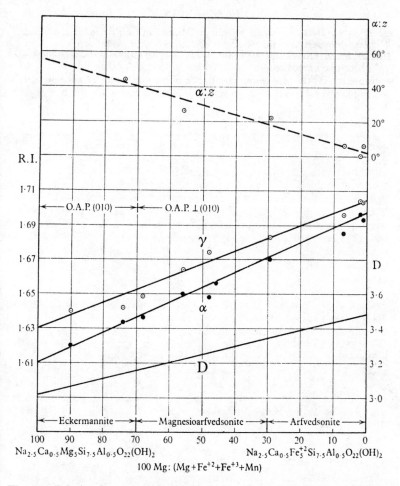

Fig. 68. *Relation between optical properties and density and chemical com-position of the eckermannite–arfvedsonite series.*

PARAGENESIS

Arfvedsonite (e.g. Table 15, anal. 18) is a characteristic constituent of alkaline plutonic rocks and occurs in both quartz-bearing and in nepheline-syenites. It is commonly associated, sometimes in parallel intergrowths, with aegirine or aegirine-augite and is usually a product of late crystalliza-tion. Eckermannite occurs in a pectolite–aegirine–eckermannite–nepheline-syenite at Norra Kärr, southern Sweden (anal. 17).

REFERENCES

ERNST, W. G. (1962) 'Synthesis, stability relations and occurrence of riebeckite and riebeckite-arfvedsonite solid solutions', *Journ. Geol.*, vol. 70, p. 689.

SAHAMA, TH. G. (1956) 'Optical anomalies in arfvedsonite from Greenland', *Amer. Min.*, vol. 41, p. 509.

SUNDIUS, N., (1945) 'The composition of eckermannite and its position in the amphibole group', *Årsbok, Sveriges Geol. Undersök.*, vol. 39, No. 8.

Aenigmatite

$Na_2Fe_5^{+2}TiSi_6O_{20}$

TRICLINIC (+)

$\alpha \simeq 1\cdot81$
$\beta \simeq 1\cdot82$
$\gamma \simeq 1\cdot88$
$\delta \simeq 0\cdot07$
$2V_\gamma \simeq 32°$, O.A.P. near $(1\bar{1}0)$
$\gamma' : z \simeq 45°$ on (010), $\gamma' : z \simeq 4°$ on (100)
Dispersion: $r < v$. D $\simeq 3\cdot8$. H $5\frac{1}{2}$.
Cleavage: {010} and {100} perfect. Cleavage angle 66°
Colour: Black; brown to black in thin section.
Pleochroism: α reddish or yellowish brown, β brown, γ dark brown.

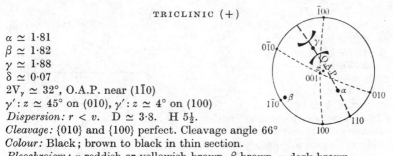

Aenigmatite was once thought to be a variety of amphibole but recent investigations suggest that pyroxene-type chains are present in the structure. Its crystals may exhibit simple or repeated twinning, the latter occurring mainly in specimens with volcanic parageneses.

The composition of aenigmatite may vary a little from the ideal formula by the presence of some K and Ca replacing Na, and by Mg, Mn, Fe^{+3} and Al replacing other ions. Varieties rich in Fe^{+3} have been referred to as cossyrite, although this name is also used synonymously with aenigmatite.

Aenigmatite is distinguished from basaltic hornblende and other dark brown amphiboles by its extremely high refractive indices and very intense γ absorption. Its 2V is smaller than that of most amphiboles.

Aenigmatite occurs in alkaline volcanic rocks such as pantellerites, phonolites and trachytes, and also in plutonic rocks, as for example in nepheline- and sodalite-syenites, alkali syenites and granites.

Astrophyllite

$(K,Na)_3(Fe,Mn)_7Ti_2[Si_4O_{12}]_2(O,OH,F)_7$

TRICLINIC (+)

α 1·676–1·691
β 1·703–1·726
γ 1·731–1·759
$\delta \simeq 0·06$
$2V_\gamma$ 70°–88°, α approx $\perp(001)$,
$\gamma \simeq x, \beta : y \simeq 13°$
Dispersion: $r > v$ strong. D 3·3–3·4. H $3\frac{1}{2}$.
Cleavage: {001} perfect, {010} moderate.
Colour: Bronze to golden yellow; orange-brown to yellow in thin section.
Pleochroism: α orange red, β yellow, γ lemon-yellow.

Astrophyllite occurs as tabular crystals with positive elongation. Its structure contains continuous sheets of $(Fe,Mn)O_6$ octahedra which are sandwiched between two sheets composed of chains of Si–O tetrahedra joined by Ti–O octahedra. These composite sheets are separated by alkali ions.

There appears to be a complete solid solution series between astrophyllite and kupletskite, the iron and manganese end-members respectively.

Astrophyllite is more brittle than biotite and differs also in having the obtuse bisectrix and the highest absorption perpendicular to the perfect cleavage. Staurolite has poorer cleavage and the ottrelite variety of chloritoid has lower birefringence.

Astrophyllite occurs in nepheline-syenites and alkali granites and associated pegmatites, as for example in Kola, U.S.S.R.

PART 3
SHEET SILICATES

MICA GROUP

INTRODUCTION

The mica minerals as a whole show considerable variation in chemical and physical properties, but all are characterized by a platy morphology and perfect basal cleavage which is a consequence of their layered atomic structure. Of the micas, muscovite, phlogopite and lepidolite are of considerable economic importance. The following sections deal with the most common micas: muscovite, paragonite, glauconite, lepidolite, phlogopite, biotite and zinnwaldite, and also with the brittle micas margarite, clintonite and xanthophyllite. For the most part each of these is a distinct mineral which does not form a complete solid solution series with any of the others, but phlogopite and biotite are separated merely for convenience in dealing with otherwise so large a group.

STRUCTURE

The basic structural feature of mica is a composite sheet in which a layer of octahedrally coordinated cations is sandwiched between two identical layers of linked $(Si,Al)O_4$ tetrahedra. Two of these tetrahedral sheets [of composition $(Si,Al)_2O_5$] are illustrated in Fig. 69. On the left is a sheet in which all tetrahedra are pointing upwards as may be seen from the 'elevation' drawing below it, and on the right is a sheet of tetrahedra which point downwards. The two sheets are superimposed and are linked by a plane of cations as shown in Figs. 70 and 71. Additional hydroxyl ions (marked A in Fig. 70), together with the apical oxygens of the inward pointing tetrahedra, complete the octahedral coordination of the sandwiched cations. Alternatively the structure may be regarded as having a central brucite layer $Mg_3(OH)_6$ (in phlogopite) or gibbsite layer $Al_2(OH)_6$ (in muscovite), in which four out of six (OH) ions are replaced by apical oxygens of the tetrahedral layers (two on each side). The remaining (OH) ions are then situated at the centres of hexagons formed by the tetrahedral vertices. The central Y ions determine the positions of the two tetrahedral sheets so that they are displaced relative to one another by $a/3$ in the [100] direction. The composite layers have a symmetry plane PP', and are repeated on a rectangular network with dimensions approximately 5·3

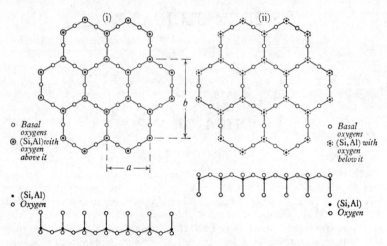

Fig. 69. (i). *Mica structure. Plan of tetrahedral layer* $(Si, Al)_4 O_{10}$ *with tetrahedra pointing upwards, and end view of layer looking along y axis.*

(ii). *Mica structure. Plan and elevation of tetrahedral layer with tetrahedra pointing downwards.*

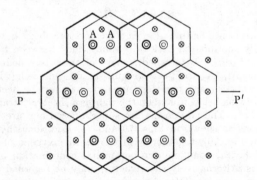

⊗ *Octahedrally coordinated cations; mainly* MgAl *or* Fe

○ *Additional hydroxyl ions*

O *X ions below bottom layer* (K, Na, Ca)

○ *X ions above upper layer* (K, Na, Ca)

Thick lines :- bottom $(Si, Al)_2 O_5$ *layer*

Thin lines :- upper $(Si, Al)_2 O_5$ *layer*

Fig. 70. *Mica structure. Plan of* (i) *and* (ii) *of Fig.* 69 *superimposed and linked by a layer of cations.*

× 9·2 Å. In the micas these layers have a net negative charge which is balanced by planes of X ions (K, Na, etc.) lying between them, and the repeat distance perpendicular to the sheets is approximately 10 Å or a multiple of 10 Å. The X ions are in twelve-fold coordination since they lie centrally on the line joining the centres of hexagons formed by the basal oxygens of tetrahedral layers, and no lateral displacement is introduced in going from the basal oxygens of one composite sheet to the corresponding oxygens of its neighbour. The hexagons may be superimposed, however, in six different ways. Thus one hexagon may be related to the next by rotation through 0° or by a multiple of 60°, and this, combined with the stagger of $a/3$ introduced by the Y layer, determines the location of corresponding atoms in successive cells. Various sequences of layer rotations are possible,

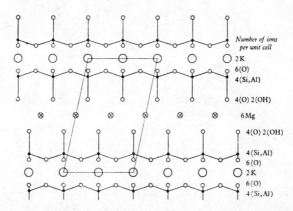

Fig. 71. *Mica structure. Elevation of Fig.* 69 (i) *and* (ii) *superimposed and linked by a plane of octahedrally coordinated cations. Composite layers are shown linked by potassium ions, and the simplest unit cell is outlined. View is along y axis.*

and when repeated regularly these build up unit cells with 1, 2, 3 or more layers (Fig. 72). The most common stacking sequences lead to either one- or two-layered monoclinic cells (symbols 1M, $2M_1$), a different two-layered monoclinic cell ($2M_2$), or a three-layered trigonal cell (3T). Disordered crystals are not uncommon.

The above description of the fundamental mica layer is somewhat idealized; in the true mica structure the tetrahedra are twisted so that the $(Si,Al)_2O_5$ sheets have di-trigonal instead of hexagonal symmetry.

The cell parameters of micas are influenced by the various ionic substitutions; thus di-octahedral and tri-octahedral micas (see below) can in general be distinguished by the position of the 060 reflection in an X-ray powder pattern. For the former $d_{060} \simeq 1·50$ and for the latter $d_{060} \simeq 1·53-1·55$ Å.

CHEMISTRY

The general formula which describes the chemical composition of micas is $X_2Y_{4-6}Z_8O_{20}(OH,F)_4$ where

X is mainly K, Na or Ca but also Ba, Rb, Cs, etc.
Y is mainly Al, Mg or Fe but also Mn, Cr, Ti, Li, etc.
Z is mainly Si or Al but perhaps also Fe^{+3} and Ti.

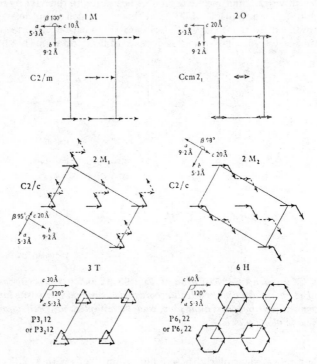

Fig. 72. *The six simple ways of stacking mica layers in an ordered manner. The arrows are the inter-layer stacking vectors. Full line vectors show the layer stacking in one unit cell, whereas broken line vectors show the positions of layers in the next unit cell. The base of the unit cell is shown by thin lines, and the space group and lattice parameters are listed by the side of the diagram in each case (after Smith, J. V. & Yoder, H. S., 1956, Min. Mag., vol. 31, p. 209).*

The micas can be subdivided into di-octahedral and tri-octahedral classes in which the number of Y ions is 4 and 6 respectively. A further subdivision can be made according to the nature of the principal X constituent. In the common micas X is largely K or Na but in the so-called 'brittle micas' X is largely Ca; further subdivisions of the common micas are made according to the principal constituents in the categories X, Y and Z, and these are depicted with approximate formulae in Table 17. More precise representation of formulae will be found later in the relevant sections. For the di-octahedral common micas, substitution of silicon for aluminium in tetrahedral coordination is generally balanced electrostatically by equivalent substitution of divalent ions for aluminium in octahedral sites.

Table 17. APPROXIMATE CHEMICAL FORMULAE OF MICAS

Di-octahedral

		X	Y	Z
Common Micas	Muscovite	K_2	Al_4	Si_6Al_2
	Paragonite	Na_2	Al_4	Si_6Al_2
	Glauconite	$(K, Na)_{1.2-2.0}$	$(Fe, Mg, Al)_4$	$Si_{7-7.6}Al_{1.0-0.4}$
Brittle Micas	Margarite	Ca_2	Al_4	Si_4Al_4

Tri-octahedral

		X	Y	Z
Common Micas	Phlogopite	K_2	$(Mg, Fe^{+2})_6$	Si_6Al_2
	Biotite	K_2	$(Mg, Fe, Al)_6$	$Si_{6-5}Al_{2-3}$
	Zinnwaldite	K_2	$(Fe, Li, Al)_6$	$Si_{6-7}Al_{2-1}$
	Lepidolite	K_2	$(Li, Al)_{5-6}$	$Si_{6-5}Al_{2-3}$
Brittle Micas	Clintonite and Xanthophyllite	Ca_2	$(Mg, Al)_6$	$Si_{2.5}Al_{5.5}$

The minerals talc and pyrophyllite are closely related structurally to the micas but differ in having no X ions and no Al in Z positions.

A chemical feature which most micas have in common is their water content; analyses, except for those with high fluorine content, show approximately 4–5 per cent H_2O^+. Both di- and tri-octahedral micas are found in fine-grained 'clay mica' form, often with higher water content and other characteristic features discussed elsewhere (p. 261).

Table 18. MICA ANALYSES

	1.	2.	3.	4.
SiO_2	45·24	48·42	49·29	40·95
TiO_2	0·01	0·87	0·12	0·82
Al_2O_3	36·85	27·16	3·17	17·28
Fe_2O_3	0·09	6·57	21·72	0·43
FeO	0·02	0·81	3·19	2·38
MnO	0·12	—	tr.	tr.
MgO	0·08	tr.	3·85	22·95
CaO	0·00	tr.	0·74	0·00
Na_2O	0·64	0·35	0·12	0·16
K_2O	10·08	11·23	6·02	9·80
F	0·91	tr.	—	0·62
H_2O^+	4·12	4·31	7·21	4·23
H_2O^-	0·46	0·19	4·60	0·48
	100·24	99·91	100·35	100·13
$O \equiv F$	0·38	—	—	0·26
Total	99·86	99·91	100·35	99·87
α	—	—	1·592	1·546
β	1·586	—	—	1·588–1·590
γ	1·589	—	1·614	1·590
$2V_\alpha$	46°	—	10°	0°–13°
D	—	—	2·580	2·78

NUMBERS OF IONS ON THE BASIS OF 24 (O,OH,F)

	1.		2.		3.‡		4.	
Si	6·050	8·00	6·597	8·00	7·634	8·00	5·724	8·00
Al	1·950		1·403		0·366		2·276	
Al	3·860		2·959		0·213		0·562	
Ti	—		0·089		0·014		0·084	
Fe^{+3}	0·093		0·672		2·532		0·340	
Fe^{+2}	0·002	4·26†	0·091	3·81	0·413	4·06	0·276	6·04
Mn	0·014		—		—		—	
Mg	0·022		—		0·889		4·776	
Ca	—		—		0·123		—	
Na	0·166	1·98§	0·092	2·04	0·036	1·35	0·034	1·78
K	1·720		1·952		1·190		1·746	
F	0·385	4·06	—	3·92	—	4·00	0·278	4·22
OH	3·676		3·916		4·00		3·946	

1. Rose-muscovite, pegmatite, New Mexico (Heinrich, E. W. & Levinson, A. A., *Amer. Min.*, 1953, vol. 38, p. 25; includes Rb_2O 0·93, Cs_2O 0·20, Li_2O 0·49).
2. Muscovite, low grade psammitic schist, Inverness-shire (Lambert, R. St J., 1959, *Trans. Roy. Soc. Edinburgh*, vol. 63, p. 553).
3. Glauconite, sandstone, Otago, New Zealand (Hutton, C. O. & Seelye, F. T., .1941, *Amer. Min.*, vol. 26, p. 593; includes P_2O_5 0·32).
4. Phlogopite, marble, New Zealand (Hutton, C. O., 1947, *Trans. Roy. Soc. New Zealand*, vol. 76, p. 481; includes BaO 0·03).

† Includes 0·264 Li.
§ Includes 0·080 Rb, 0·012 Cs.
‡ Nos. of ions calculated on basis of 20 (O) and 4 (OH).

Table 18. MICA ANALYSES—*continued*

5.	6.	7.	8.	9.	
39·14	37·17	35·98	35·03	49·80	SiO_2
4·27	3·14	2·35	2·56	0·00	TiO_2
13·10	14·60	18·06	20·38	25·56	Al_2O_3
12·94	3·75	1·47	1·08	0·08	Fe_2O_3
5·05	26·85	21·56	20·41	0·00	FeO
0·14	0·06	0·13	0·02	0·38	MnO
12·75	4·23	7·40	7·11	0·22	MgO
1·64	0·17	0·15	0·17	0·00	CaO
0·70	0·15	0·42	0·96	0·40	Na_2O
6·55	8·25	9·09	8·62	9·67	K_2O
1·11	0·85	0·09	—	6·85	F
2·41	1·35	3·28	3·60	0·38	H_2O^+
0·58	—	0·23	0·07	0·50	H_2O^-
100·38	100·57	100·21	100·01	102·96	
0·46	0·36	—	—	2·89	$O \equiv F$
99·92	100·21	100·21	100·01	100·07	Total
1·594	1·610	—	—	—	α
1·671	1·676	1·644	1·640	—	β
1·672	1·677	—	1·640	—	γ
10°–25°	5°	—	—	36°	$2V_\alpha$
2·862	—	—	—	2·898	D

NUMBERS OF IONS ON THE BASIS OF 24 (O,OH,F)

5.		6.		7.		8.		9.		
5·790	8·00	5·972	8·00	5·545	8·00	5·339	8·00	6·750	8·00	Si
2·210		2·028		2·455		2·661		1·250		Al
0·074		0·736		0·827		1·001		2·834		Al
0·474		0·379		0·272		0·293		—		Ti
1·440	5·44	0·454	6·20	0·170	5·77	0·124	5·64	0·008	6·17†	Fe^{+3}
0·625		3·608		2·780		2·602		—		Fe^{+2}
0·017		0·007		0·017		0·003		0·044		Mn
2·811		1·013		1·700		1·615		0·044		Mg
0·260		0·029		0·025		0·027		—		Ca
0·199	1·70	0·046	1·77	0·126	1·94	0·282	1·99	0·106	2·02‡	Na
1·236		1·691		1·787		1·676		1·674		K
0·519	2·90	0·431	1·88	0·043	3·42	—	3·66	2·936	3·28	F
2·378		1·446		3·373		3·660		0·344		OH

5. Biotite, quartz latite, Colorado (Larsen, E. S., Jr., Gonyer, F. A. & Irving, J., 1937, *Amer. Min.*, vol. 22, p. 898).

6. Biotite, granite, Southern California (Larsen, E. S., Jr. & Draisin, W., 1950, *Int. Geol. Congr. Rep. 18th Session, Gt. Britain*, Pt. 3, p. 66).

7. Biotite, low grade garnet–mica schist, Inverness-shire (Lambert, R. St J., 1959, *Trans. Roy. Soc. Edinburgh*, vol. 63, p. 553).

8. Biotite, garnet–sillimanite–mica schist, Angus, Scotland (Snelling, N. J., 1957, *Geol. Mag.*, vol. 94, p. 297).

9. Lepidolite, Varuträsk pegmatite, Sweden (Berggren, T., 1941, *Geol. För. Förh.*, vol. 68, p. 262; includes Li_2O 5·95, Rb_2O 1·97, Cs_2O 1·20).

† Includes Li 3·244.   ‡ Includes Rb 0·172, Cs 0·070.

OPTICAL AND PHYSICAL PROPERTIES

The optical properties of micas cover a wide range but all have negative sign and have α approximately perpendicular to their perfect (001) cleavage. Most are biaxial, with 2V moderate for di-octahedral and generally small for trioctahedral micas; relatively few specimens appear to be strictly uniaxial. Birefringence is generally very weak in the plane of cleavage flakes but strong in transverse sections; pleochroism is strong in coloured micas and the absorption is greatest for vibration directions parallel to the cleavage. In thin sections, relief relative to the mounting medium is low for lepidolite and phlogopite but moderate to high for other micas. The di-octahedral micas generally have their optic axial planes perpendicular to (010) while others (with the exception of certain biotites which have the $2M_1$ structure) have the optic axial plane parallel to (010). All micas may show twinning on the 'mica twin law' with composition plane {001} and twin axis [310], and well formed crystals often show {110} faces and therefore pseudohexagonal outline.

On suitable specimens, the crystallographic orientation of a mica flake can be determined by the percussion figure test. A blow with a dull point on a cleavage plate produces a six-rayed percussion figure, the most prominent line of which is parallel to (010), the others being at 60° intervals. Thus for 1M micas the optic axial plane is parallel to one of the percussion rays, while for the $2M_1$ micas it bisects the angle between two rays.

PARAGENESIS

The paragenesis of each variety of mica is discussed in the appropriate section; the following list, however, outlines the principal occurrences in igneous, metamorphic and sedimentary rocks.

Igneous
　　Muscovite: granites, granitic pegmatites and aplites.
　　Phlogopite: peridotites.
　　Biotite: gabbros, norites, diorites, granites, pegmatites.
　　Lepidolite and zinnwaldite: pegmatites and high-temperature veins.

Metamorphic
　　Muscovite, paragonite and biotite: phyllites, schists and gneisses.
　　Phlogopite: metamorphosed limestones and dolomites.

Sedimentary
　　Muscovite and paragonite: detrital and authigenic sediments.
　　Glauconite: greensands.

REFERENCE

SMITH, J. V. and YODER, H. S..(1956) 'Experimental and theoretical studies of the mica polymorphs', *Min. Mag.*, vol. 31, p. 209.

Muscovite $\qquad$ $K_2Al_4[Si_6Al_2O_{20}](OH,F)_4$

MONOCLINIC (−)

α 1·552–1·574
β 1·582–1·610
γ 1·587–1·616
δ 0·036–0·049
$2V_\alpha$ 30°–47°
$\alpha : z$ 0°–5°, $\beta : x$ 1°–3°, $\gamma = y$, O.A.P. $\perp$(010)
Dispersion: $r > v$. D 2·77–2·88. H 2½–3.
Cleavage: {001} perfect.
Twinning: Composition plane {001}, twin axis [310].
Colour: Colourless, or light shades of green, red or brown; colourless in thin section.
Pleochroism: Weak: absorption greater for vibration directions in the plane of cleavage.

Muscovite is one of the most common of the micas and occurs in a wide variety of geological environments. Its well known properties of electrical and thermal insulation have made it a mineral of industrial importance, and in technical applications the perfect lamellar cleavage of mica and the mechanical strength of its cleavage sheets are additional assets. Muscovite and phlogopite are the most transparent of the micas and having a comparatively low content of iron they have the best electrical insulating properties. They often occur in large blocks (books) in which the area of cleavage sheet is a prime factor in their economic value, but the absence of structural defects and inclusions (mostly iron oxides) is also important.

STRUCTURE

The general features of the structures of all micas have already been described (p. 193). Muscovite shows very little polymorphic variation and the most common unit cell has a 5·19, b 9·04, c 20·08 Å, β 95° 30′, and contains two formula units. In muscovite one quarter of the tetrahedral sites are occupied by Al and three quarters by Si. The twelve-fold coordinated positions between composite layers are fully occupied by potassium ions, and the stacking of successive layers gives rise in this case to the $2M_1$ polymorph (see p. 195). Some fine-grained specimens from sediments and low grade metamorphic rocks have the 1M or 1Md (disordered) structure.

7*

CHEMISTRY

The principal isomorphous replacements which occur in muscovite are as follows:

> For K: Na, Rb, Cs, Ca, Ba.
> For octahedral Al: Mg, Fe^{+2}, Fe^{+3}, Mn, Li, Cr, Ti, V.
> For (OH): F.
> (Si_6Al_2) can vary to (Si_7Al).

The rose-col oured muscovites (rose-muscovites) have very nearly the idea composition, with low manganese and lithium content, and total iron usually lower than manganese (Table 18, anal. 1). The varieties of muscovite which result from various substitutions are discussed below, but certain replacements and combinations of replacements result in compositions and structures which can no longer be regarded as appropriate to muscovite; these are dealt with more fully in sections on other micas.

Muscovites with between 2 and 4 per cent Fe_2O_3 have often been reported, and some with equally high FeO content (usually associated with high SiO_2) are also known. Most muscovites contain less than 1 per cent MnO but purple and blue specimens containing about 2 per cent MnO have been described. Chromium is normally present in muscovites only in trace amounts, but chromian muscovites (fuchsites) with as much as 6 per cent Cr_2O_3 are known. Micas with high lithium contents are known as lepidolites and are discussed as a separate mineral species, p. 217: up to about 3·5 per cent Li_2O may enter, however, without changing the $2M_1$ muscovite structure. It may be that rather than replacing aluminium, lithium enters vacant octahedral sites, as in the lepidolites. The average fluorine content of natural muscovites is about 0·6 per cent, and fluor-muscovite in which (OH) is completely replaced by fluorine has been synthesized.

Sericite is a term which is used to describe fine-grained white mica (muscovite or paragonite). Such micas are not necessarily chemically different from muscovite although they often have high SiO_2, MgO and H_2O, and low K_2O.

The name phengite is used to describe muscovites in which the Si : Al ratio is greater than 3 : 1 and in which increase of Si is accompanied by substitution of Mg or Fe^{+2} for Al in octahedral sites.

Hydromuscovites have high H_2O and low K_2O content; K^+ ions are perhaps replaced by $(H_3O)^+$ ions. Illite is perhaps the least well defined term commonly applied to mica minerals (see under Clay Minerals, p. 260); chemical analyses show some substitution of silicon for aluminium giving a high Si : Al ratio, accompanied by a deficit of potassium.

Hydrothermal studies in the system $K_2O–Al_2O_3–SiO_2–H_2O$ show that the upper stability limit of muscovite is represented by the curve (Fig. 73, p. 204) above which sanidine, corundum and water are stable phases. The equilibrium curve for the reaction muscovite + quartz ⇌ potassium feldspar + sillimanite + vapour has also been determined; it lies only 15°C below the muscovite breakdown curve. This reaction has some bearing on the breakdown of muscovite in nature, but other reactions involving muscovite and the formation of feldspar may occur, and furthermore, the presence of chemical substitutions in natural muscovites may give rise to considerably different breakdown conditions.

The weathering of muscovite may proceed through illite and hydromuscovite to montmorillonite and eventually kaolinite, by loss of potassium and increase of water and silica.

OPTICAL AND PHYSICAL PROPERTIES

The refractive indices of rose muscovites are lower than the averages for all muscovites, and their 2V is higher. This is in accordance with a trend throughout the muscovites for refractive indices (and birefringence) to increase with increase in iron (particularly Fe^{+3}) and Mn content, and for those with least Mg and Fe to have the largest 2V. Refractive indices increase also with decreasing Al content.

Although the colour of rose muscovite is similar to that of lepidolite there is no correlation between colour and Li content. It seems that the pink colour of rose muscovite and of lepidolite is due to the small amount of Mn present perhaps as Mn^{+3}, its preponderance over Fe^{+3}, and the absence of Fe^{+2}. The colour of pale green muscovites is probably due to Fe^{+2}, and the buff or brown specimens have more Fe^{+3}. Fuchsite is pleochroic with α colourless to light green, β green, and γ dark green; its refractive indices increase with chromium content. Lithian muscovites have lower refractive indices, but their optical properties are influenced more by the content of iron and manganese than by the percentage of Li_2O. The refractive indices of phengites, illites and hydrous muscovites are higher than those of normal muscovites because of the replacement of $[Al]^4$ by Si and of $[Al]^6$ by Fe^{+2} or Mg.

Parallel intergrowths of muscovite with biotite are not uncommon and in most cases their respective optic axial planes are mutually inclined at 60°. The hardness of muscovite on the Moh's scale is usually given as $2\frac{1}{2}$–3, but as would be expected from the sheet-like structure, hardness varies with direction, from $2\frac{1}{2}$ parallel to (001) to about 4 perpendicular to (001)

DISTINGUISHING FEATURES

Muscovite differs from phlogopite and biotite in having its optic axial plane perpendicular to (010). It may be possible to determine the [010] direction by a percussion figure (see p. 200); if not, X-ray methods may be used. Biotite specimens are generally much darker. Muscovite usually has a higher 2V than phlogopite, biotite and talc, and this serves to distinguish it from the latter mineral for which the optic axial plane is also perpendicular to (010). The high birefringence of muscovites distinguishes them from kaolinites, chlorites and other platy silicates with the exception of pyrophyllite which, however, has a higher 2V. X-ray powder patterns may be used to distinguish di-octahedral from tri-octahedral micas, and they can also be used to distinguish between the different polymorphs of muscovite.

PARAGENESIS

Muscovite occurs in a wide range of regionally metamorphosed sediments and is found in rocks belonging to each of the zones of progressive regional metamorphism. In low grade environments it is found for example in albite–chlorite–sericite schists, or in sericite phyllites; where the original sediments were rich in aluminium, muscovite is often associated with chlorite and chloritoid. At the highest grades of metamorphism muscovite is commonly dissociated to form potassium feldspar and sillimanite. Muscovite is also formed during the metamorphism of intermediate and acid rocks, those of intermediate composition giving rise to calcite–albite–sericite–chlorite schists, and those of acid composition to muscovite–quartz schists.

Muscovite is less common than biotite in acid igneous rocks, but occurs in the muscovite and muscovite–biotite granites. It is the most common

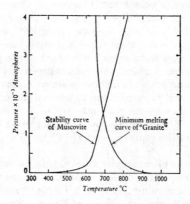

Fig. 73. *Stability curve of muscovite (after Yoder, H. S. & Eugster, H. P., 1955, Geochim. et Cosmochim. Acta, vol. 8, p. 225).*

mica in aplites and has been reported as a constituent of some rhyolite porphyries. Most muscovite-bearing granites contain both potassium feldspar and plagioclase and are also often rich in quartz. In such granites, muscovite occurs in interstitial crystals as well as in small dispersed flakes within feldspar. A similar relationship is also common in the quartz- and mica-rich rock, greisen, which is generally considered to have been derived from a granite modified by autometasomatic changes that occurred during the last phase of its crystallization.

The PT stability curve of muscovite intersects the PT minimum melting curve of granite at approximately 1500 atmospheres pressure and 700°C (Fig. 73). Thus muscovite can crystallize from a liquid of granite composition at pressures above 1500 atmospheres, but below this pressure muscovite can form only in the solid state. The larger interstitial muscovite crystals in granites could thus have formed in equilibrium with the liquid, or have crystallized in the solid state at any pressure or temperature, below the stability curve of muscovite. The smaller flakes of muscovite commonly dispersed within the feldspar probably crystallized by the leaching of $K_2O \cdot 6SiO_2$ from the feldspar at temperatures below the granite liquidus.

Some muscovite-bearing granites contain cordierite, e.g. the Dartmoor granite, and in such granites the muscovite may, in part or whole, have been derived from the alteration of xenocrystal cordierite.

Muscovite is the characterisitc product of fluorine metasomatism (greisenization) at granite–slate contacts, and the production of the white mica at the expense of such minerals as feldspar, andalusite and cordierite is a reversal of the processes by which these minerals are formed in thermal metamorphism. Greisenization is especially typical in the inner aureoles of muscovite-bearing granites, e.g. Dartmoor, Skiddaw and Leinster granites. It is a common constituent of pegmatites associated with granite and granodiorite. In this paragenesis muscovite occurs both as large crystalline 'books' and as fine-grained sericite; the latter often replaces feldspar, tourmaline, spodumene, beryl, topaz or kyanite, and is usually located in the wall rock at the pegmatite margins; dendritic intergrowths with quartz are not uncommon.

Muscovite is less common in sediments than was originally believed, and much of the fine-grained micaceous material of these rocks has been shown to consist of mixed-layer structures of muscovite and montmorillonite, mixtures of 2M muscovite, pyrophyllite and kaolinite, and illite.

REFERENCES

LAMBERT, R. ST J. (1959) 'The mineralogy and metamorphism of the Moine Schists of the Morar and Knoydart districts of Inverness-shire', *Trans. Roy. Soc. Edin.*, vol. 63, p. 553.

YODER, H. S. and EUGSTER, H. P. (1955) 'Synthetic and natural muscovites', *Geochim. et Cosmochim. Acta*, vol. 8, p. 225.

Paragonite

$Na_2Al_4[Si_6Al_2O_{20}](OH)_4$

MONOCLINIC (−)

α 1·564–1·580
β 1·594–1·609
γ 1·600–1·609
δ 0·028–0·038
$2V_\alpha$ 0°–40°
β nearly parallel to x, $\gamma = y$
O.A.P. $\perp$(010)
Dispersion: $r > v$. D 2·85. H 2½.
Cleavage: {001} perfect.
Colour: Colourless, pale yellow; colourless in thin section.

The chemical composition of paragonite differs from that of muscovite in that sodium replaces potassium. The substitution of potassium by the smaller sodium ion results in a smaller unit cell, particularly in the z direction, but in other respects the structure of paragonite is similar to that of muscovite (polymorph $2M_1$). Brammallite is a clay mineral which bears a similar relation to paragonite as illite does to muscovite.

At room temperature there is only very little solid solution of paragonite in muscovite and of muscovite in paragonite; at temperatures just below the solidus, about 20 per cent of each end-member is soluble in the other.

The optical properties of paragonite and muscovite are very similar, and the two minerals can be distinguished by chemical analysis for alkalis, or by X-ray diffraction. Paragonite usually occurs in massive scaly aggregates. It has been reported in schists and phyllites, in muscovite–biotite gneisses, in quartz veins and in fine-grained sediments.

Glauconite

$$(K,Na,Ca)_{1\cdot2-2\cdot0}(Fe^{+3},Al,Fe^{+2},Mg)_{4\cdot0}[Si_{7-7\cdot6}Al_{1-0\cdot4}O_{20}](OH)_4\cdot n(H_2O)$$

MONOCLINIC $(-)$

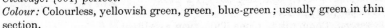

α $1\cdot592-1\cdot610$
$\beta = \gamma$ $1\cdot614-1\cdot641$
δ $0\cdot014-0\cdot030$
$2V_\alpha$ $0°-20°$
α approximately $\perp(001)$
$\beta = y$, O.A.P. (010)
Dispersion: $r < v$. D $2\cdot4-2\cdot95$. H 2.
Cleavage: {001} perfect.
Colour: Colourless, yellowish green, green, blue-green; usually green in thin section.
Pleochroism: α yellowish green or green, $\beta = \gamma$ deeper yellow or bluish green.

Glauconite is a mica mineral which occurs almost exclusively in marine sediments, particularly in greensands. It is generally found in rounded fine-grained aggregates of ill-formed platelets, but better formed crystals do occur and these allow a fairly complete characterization of the mineral. Thus although in many respects glauconite can validly be considered as a clay mineral (cf. illite), it is here included among the micas. Although glauconite is a di-octahedral mica, it differs from muscovite in having a considerable proportion of divalent ions in Y sites. Its crystal structure is similar to that of biotite (1M polymorph), but its composition is best discussed in relation to muscovite. The total of Y site ions is usually very close to four and the number of inter-layer cations (X sites) is always less than two but greater than the number of Al ions in tetrahedral positions (Z sites). The excess X ions are compensated in glauconite by the presence of divalent instead of trivalent ions in Y. Of the trivalent ions in Y sites, Fe^{+3} predominates over Al.

In optical properties glauconite resembles biotite rather than muscovite, and its refractive indices and depth of colour increase with Fe^{+3} content. Other green minerals which might be mistaken for glauconite include the chlorites, which generally have a lower birefringence.

It is generally accepted that glauconites are formed from a variety of starting materials by marine diagenesis in shallow water during periods of slow or negative sedimentation. They are found in impure limestones, sandstones (e.g. Table 18, anal. 3) and siltstones; greensands are so called because of the high proportion of glauconite which they contain. From their content of both ferric and ferrous iron it may be deduced that glauconites are formed under moderately reducing conditions of the type which may, in some cases at least, occur through the action of sulphate-reducing bacteria on decaying organisms. Some glauconites, however, may form by the coagulation of suspended colloidal particles.

Phlogopite $K_2(Mg,Fe^{+2})_6[Si_6Al_2O_{20}](OH,F)_4$

MONOCLINIC $(-)$

α 1·530–1·590
β 1·557–1·637
γ 1·558–1·637
δ 0·028–0·049
$2V_\alpha$ 0–15°
$\beta = y, \gamma : x = 0°$–5°, O.A.P. (010)
Dispersion: $r < v$. D 2·76–2·90. H 2–2$\frac{1}{2}$.
Cleavage: {001} perfect.

Twinning: Composition plane {001}, twin axis [310].
Colour: Colourless, yellowish brown, green, reddish brown, dark brown; colourless, pale yellow or pale green in thin section.
Pleochroism: α yellow, $\beta = \gamma$ brownish red, green, or yellow.

Phlogopite is an important member of the mica group and, as the above formula shows, it belongs to the tri-octahedral class of minerals with layered structures. The nomenclature adopted here is : phlogopite, Mg : Fe $> 2 : 1$; biotite, Mg : Fe $< 2 : 1$. Biotites, however, often have some further substitution of Al in octahedral and tetrahedral sites, tending towards compositions in the range between eastonite $K_2Mg_5Al(Si_5Al_3)$-$O_{20}(OH)_4$ and the iron-rich siderophyllite $K_2Fe_5Al(Si_5Al_3)O_{20}(OH)_4$ (see Fig. 74, p. 212). Since there appears to be no break in these solid solution series the terminology is somewhat arbitrary and is adopted solely for the convenience of subdividing a very large range of compositions and properties. There have been other suggestions for defining phlogopite and biotite, as, for example, by their colour, since generally the more iron-rich members of the series are darker.

STRUCTURE

In phlogopite the octahedral sites of the mica structure are completely filled. The most common polymorph is 1M, but 2M, 3T and disordered structures sometimes occur. The pure magnesium end-member phlogopite has a 5·314, b 9·204, c 10·314 Å, β 99° 54', Z = 1, but the cell parameters are affected by substitutions; d_{001}, for example, is reduced as F substitutes for (OH) and increased by the substitution of Al for Si. The c parameter of phlogopites decreases as iron content increases although the ionic radius of Fe^{+2} is greater than that of Mg^{+2}. It is assumed that this apparent anomaly is due to the greater polarizing power of the Fe^{+2} ion. The iron : magnesium ratio of a member of the phlogopite–biotite series can be determined approximately by measuring the ratios of intensities of appropriate X-ray powder reflections.

CHEMISTRY

A greater amount of sodium can be incorporated in the phlogopite structure than in muscovite, and minor amounts of Rb, Cs and Ba also occur. Phlogopites often contain small amounts of manganese; those in which the manganese content is appreciable are called manganophyllites. Common replacements in octahedral sites include Fe^{+3}, Ti, Al and more rarely, Li. There is, in general, evidence of only very limited solid solution between muscovite and the phlogopite–biotite series.

Hydrothermal synthesis of phlogopite has been achieved using a variety of starting materials, and its stability curve is reproduced in Fig. 76, p. 215. Above the stability curve breakdown is very slow, yielding forsterite, leucite, orthorhombic $KAlSiO_4$ and vapour. No method has been found to produce a substitute for natural mica in the form of large blocks from which undistorted sheets may be split, but synthetic fluorphlogopite is well suited for the manufacture of glass-bonded ceramics and reconstituted synthetic mica sheet.

Weathering of minerals in the phlogopite–biotite series generally produces a 'clay mica' analogous to the illites produced from muscovite, and further weathering of 'clay biotites' converts them to vermiculites.

OPTICAL AND PHYSICAL PROPERTIES

Increase of iron content is generally associated with an increase in refractive indices, but for natural specimens no precise correlation is observed since refractive indices are also increased considerably by constituents such as manganese and titanium, and are decreased by fluorine. The effects of Fe^{+3} and Ti are greater than those of Fe^{+2} and Mn.

The colours of phlogopites are influenced mainly by iron and titanium content. Those rich in titanium are usually reddish brown regardless of their Mg : Fe ratio: those poor in titanium and rich in ferrous iron tend to be blue-green or shades of brown according to the ferric iron content. As with refractive indices, no strict correlation between colour and composition is discernible.

Acicular inclusions of rutile, and sometimes of tourmaline, aligned in specific directions (perpendicular to (010) and at 60° intervals) occur in some phlogopites. These are responsible for the phenomenon of 'asterism' observed when a small light source is viewed through a thin sheet of mica. Inclusions and colours are sometimes arranged in zones, with inclusion-free zones showing no asterism. Colour zoning may be either alternating (e.g. light and dark green) or of the core–margin type (e.g. medium brown core, pale yellow margin).

DISTINGUISHING FEATURES

Phlogopite can usually be distinguished from muscovite which has a greater 2V, and from the more iron-rich biotites which have higher refractive indices. Lepidolite can be similar to phlogopite in appearance and optical properties, and is best distinguished from it by a lithium flame test, or by an X-ray powder photograph.

PARAGENESIS

The relation between paragenesis and composition in the phlogopite–biotite series as a whole is illustrated in Fig. 75, p. 215; the two main occurrences of phlogopite are in metamorphosed limestones (e.g. Table 18, anal. 4) and in ultrabasic rocks. Phlogopite is also a characteristic product of the regional metamorphism of impure magnesium limestone, and there it is generally considered to have been derived by reaction between dolomite and earlier formed potassium feldspar or muscovite:

$$3CaMg(CO_3)_2 + KAlSi_3O_8 + H_2O \rightarrow (OH)_2KMg_3AlSi_3O_{10} + 3CaCO_3 + 3CO_2$$
dolomite   potassium feldspar   phlogopite

$$3CaMg(CO_3)_2 + (OH)_2KAl_3Si_3O_{10} \rightarrow (OH)_2KMg_3AlSi_3O_{10}$$
dolomite   muscovite   phlogopite
$$+ 3CaCO_3 + 3CO_2 + Al_2O_3$$

The excess alumina in the second reaction may be used to form spinel. Phlogopite is a particularly characteristic constituent of kimberlite in which it is commonly present in amounts of 6 to 8 per cent. In some kimberlites phlogopite displays reaction rims of iron ore, chlorite and calcite, and occurs also as rims attached to corroded grains of chromium-rich diopside. Inclusions of phlogopite rock and other less phlogopite-rich inclusions are known from some kimberlite pipes.

Phlogopite is a primary mineral in some leucite-rich rocks. In the West Kimberley area of Western Australia, for example, it occurs in massive, vesicular and fragmental rocks consisting of varying proportions of leucite, katophoritic amphibole and diopside. Other phlogopite and leucite-bearing rocks are wyomingite (leucite, phlogopite, pyroxene) and jumillite (leucite, phlogopite, pyroxene, olivine, sanidine). Of the few well authenticated occurrences of manganophyllite most are associated, as at Långban, Sweden, with manganese deposits of metasomatic origin.

The relation between the experimentally determined stability curve of phlogopite and the melting curves of granites and basalts is discussed in the section on biotite.

REFERENCES

HOLMES, A. (1936) 'A contribution to the petrology of kimberlite and its inclusions', *Trans. Geol. Soc. S. Africa*, vol. 39, p. 379.

KOHN, J. A. and HATCH, R. A. (1955) 'Synthetic mica investigations, VI: X-ray and optical data on synthetic fluorphlogopite', *Amer. Min.*, vol. 40, p. 10.

YODER, H. S. and EUGSTER, H. P. (1954) 'Phlogopite synthesis and stability range' *Geochim. et Cosmochim. Acta*, vol. 6, p. 157.

Biotite $K_2(Mg,Fe^{+2})_{6-4}(Fe^{+3},Al,Ti)_{0-2}[Si_{6-5}Al_{2-3}O_{20}](OH,F)_4$

MONOCLINIC (−)

α 1·565–1·625
β 1·605–1·696
γ 1·605–1·696
δ 0·04–0·08
$2V_\alpha$ 0°–25°
$\gamma : x$ 0°–9°, $\beta = y$, O.A.P. (010)
Dispersion: weak.
  Fe-rich biotites $r < v$.
  Mg-rich biotites $r \lesseqgtr v$.
D 2·7–3·3. H $2\frac{1}{2}$–3.
Cleavage: {001} perfect.

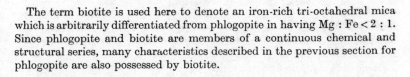

Twinning: Composition plane {001}, twin axis [310].
Colour: Black, deep shades of brown, reddish brown or green; yellow, brown or green in thin section.
Pleochroism: Strong: α greyish yellow, brownish green or brown; $\beta = \gamma$ dark brown, dark green or dark reddish brown.

The term biotite is used here to denote an iron-rich tri-octahedral mica which is arbitrarily differentiated from phlogopite in having Mg : Fe < 2 : 1. Since phlogopite and biotite are members of a continuous chemical and structural series, many characteristics described in the previous section for phlogopite are also possessed by biotite.

STRUCTURE

In biotite, as in phlogopite, the octahedral cation sites of the mica structure ideally are completely filled. The most common polymorph has the 1M structure with a 5·3, b 9·2, c 10·2 Å, β 100°, Z = 1, but other polymorphs and disordered structures sometimes occur. The effect of the iron content on cell parameters has been discussed in the section on phlogopite. Variation in cell size may accompany several types of chemical substitution involving Mn, Al and F as well as Fe, so that it does not provide a reliable method for estimating the ratio Mg : Fe in a biotite.

CHEMISTRY

The compositions of most biotites fall within the field outlined by four end-members, phlogopite, annite, eastonite and siderophyllite (Fig. 74). Thus in biotite as compared with phlogopite, magnesium is replaced by ferrous iron and also by trivalent ions (Fe^{+3},Al), and aluminium replaces silicon in tetrahedral sites usually beyond the ratio Al : Si $= 2 : 6$. Biotite which is rich in both ferrous and ferric iron is called lepidomelane.

Other common substitutions are:

For K : Na, Ca, Ba, Rb, Cs. Of these, sodium is usually present in higher concentration than the others but rarely exceeds 0·5 atoms per formula unit.

For Fe^{+2} : Mn, rarely exceeding 0·2 atoms.

For Al : Li.

Fluorine can replace hydroxyl ions and this substitution is most common when there is a rather large titanium content (e.g. Table 18, anal. 5). The role of Ti in the biotite structure is uncertain since it may be replacing Si in tetrahedral, or (Fe,Mg) in octahedral sites; the latter appears more likely

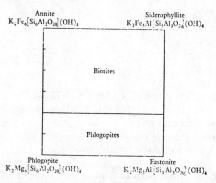

Fig. 74. *Phlogopite–biotite compositional fields. Most phlogopites and biotites fall within these fields; the division between them is arbitrarily chosen to be where Mg : Fe = 2 : 1.*

in view of the size of the Ti ion. With regard to the dual role of Al ions, it is thought that minerals formed at higher temperatures tend to have more Al in fourfold coordination. The total number of ions in octahedral sites often falls short of the possible six per formula unit, but very rarely falls below five. To this extent, therefore, minerals exist which are intermediate between tri-octahedral and di-octahedral micas since these have six and four atoms in octahedral sites respectively.

Micas with various Fe : Mg ratios on the join phlogopite–annite have been synthesized, using hydrothermal techniques in which the partial pressure of oxygen is controlled as well as temperature and total pressure.

Among the alteration products from biotite are chlorite, muscovite and sericite; illite, kaolinite and other clay minerals; calcite, epidote–zoisite, leucoxene and rutile; pyrite and other sulphides. Mineralizing solutions commonly leach iron and magnesium, and substitute potassium, yielding secondary muscovite and sericite pseudomorphous after biotite. The alteration of biotite by weathering produces either montmorillonite or vermiculite.

OPTICAL AND PHYSICAL PROPERTIES

The discussion of the relation between optical properties and chemical composition in the section on phlogopite is applicable to the whole of the phlogopite–biotite series. Refractive indices generally show an increase with increasing iron content but are also affected appreciably by other substitutions (e.g. increase with Mn, Ti, decrease with F), so that an optical method of determining the Fe/Mg ratio is not reliable. Most biotites (those with the 1M structure) have the optic axial plane parallel to (010), but for those with the $2M_1$ structure it is perpendicular to (010).

The colours of biotites are generally deeper than those of phlogopite and are related in a general way to composition; colour zoning is uncommon. High Ti content gives a reddish brown colour while high ferric iron gives green: the relative amounts of these two elements, however, rather than their absolute values, determine the colour, and intermediate proportions of Ti and Fe^{+3} result in yellowish or greenish brown colorations. Biotite often exhibits pleochroic haloes which are attributed to the presence of inclusions of zircon or other minerals containing elements belonging to the radioactive series U–Ra and Th–Ac.

Biotite often occurs in large well formed crystals with tabular {001} habit and pseudo-hexagonal outline. The percussion figure test may be applied to determine crystallographic orientation, but as with other micas it is not always easy to perform or interpret (see p. 2OO).

DISTINGUISHING FEATURES

Biotite is generally darker in colour and more highly pleochroic than the other micas, and has higher refractive indices. It can be distinguished from muscovite by its low 2V. Vermiculite has lower refractive indices and birefringence, and chlorites have a much lower birefringence. Lepidolites can be distinguished by their paler colour and by the lithium flame test. X-ray powder patterns are distinctive from those of di-octahedral micas.

PARAGENESIS

Biotite occurs in a greater variety of geological environments than any of the other micas. In metamorphic rocks it is formed under a wide range of temperature and pressure conditions, and it occurs abundantly in many contact and regionally metamorphosed sediments. Among the intrusive igneous rocks it occurs commonly in granites and granite pegmatites, granodiorites, tonalites, diorites, norites, quartz and nepheline-syenites and quartz monzonites. Biotite is particularly characteristic of the intermediate rocks of calc-alkali affinities and occurs in a wide range of rocks of hybrid origin. It is found less frequently in extrusive igneous rocks, but occurs in rhyolites, trachytes, dacites, latites, andesites and some basalts.

Thermal metamorphism. During the thermal metamorphism of many argillaceous rocks biotite, as small flakes interspersed in the chlorite–sericite groundmass, is generally the first new product of the recrystallization; it is only rarely absent from the succeeding higher grade hornfelses.

The formation of biotite occurs at the expense of the chlorite, white mica, iron ore and rutile of the original sediment. Biotite is often associated with andalusite and cordierite in the low grade hornfelses but both minerals normally do not crystallize until after the initial formation of biotite. At higher grades of thermal metamorphism the amount of biotite diminishes, and it is ultimately replaced by potassium feldspar, orthopyroxene and sillimanite, or by potassium feldspar and cordierite.

Regional metamorphism. The crystallization of biotite in rocks of argillaceous composition marks the onset of the PT conditions of the biotite zone, typical rocks of which include biotite schist, biotite–sericite schist, biotite–chlorite schist and albite–biotite schist. The textural relations in many pelitic and semi-pelitic sediments do not suggest that the biotite forms at the expense of any specific pre-existing material, but the increase in biotite in the biotite zone is coincident with a decrease in chlorite and especially in muscovite. Biotite is a stable mineral of the garnet zone of regional metamorphism, and is an important constituent of many garnet–mica schists (e.g. Table 18, anal. 7). Biotite is common also in many rocks of the succeeding zones of regional metamorphism, and its presence in the staurolite, kyanite and sillimanite zones (e.g. anal. 8) is related in part to the limited substitution of Fe^{+2} by Mg in staurolite, and in the two highest zones to the common absence of other ferromagnesian minerals.

Variation in the composition (and colour) of biotites with different grade of metamorphism occurs and in many cases decrease in Fe^{+2}, Mn and Fe^{+3} and increase in Ti and Mg can be correlated with increasing grade of metamorphism.

Opposite trends are sometimes observed, however, and the variation of biotite composition is clearly influenced by the nature of the other ferromagnesian minerals present, as well as by metamorphic grade.

Igneous rocks. The relation between paragenesis and composition in the phlogopite–biotite series as a whole is illustrated in Fig. 75. In general, with increasing acidity of the host rock, the biotites show an increase in Fe^{+2} and a decrease in Mg content. Within a particular intrusion this trend is followed in passing from early to later formed biotites, and in addition there may be enrichment in Al and Fe^{+3}, decrease in Si and Ti, and similar variation in trace element concentrations, e.g. increase of Ga:Al, Li:Mg, Mn:Fe^{+2} and Rb:K, and decrease in Ni:Mg, Co:Fe^{+2} and Ba:K ratios.

Although biotite occurs more commonly in the intermediate and acid plutonic rocks it is also an important constituent of some basic rocks. Thus biotite is an abundant constituent in the quartz–biotite norites and cordierite norites of the Haddo House district, where its crystallization may be due to the assimilation of andalusite–cordierite schists and cordierite–biotite gneisses in gabbroic magma.

Biotite occurs much less frequently in extrusive than in plutonic rocks, and when present it is commonly partially altered to other minerals. An explanation of the different behaviour of biotite in plutonic and volcanic rocks, in terms of the experimentally determined stability curve of phlogopite and its relation to the minimum melting curves of granite and

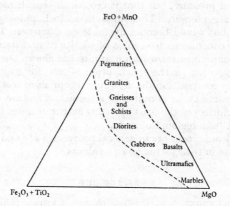

Fig. 75. *Variation of chemical composition of phlogopites and biotites with rock type (after Engel, A. E. J. & Engel, C. G., 1960, Bull. Geol. Soc. Amer., vol. 71, p. 1).*

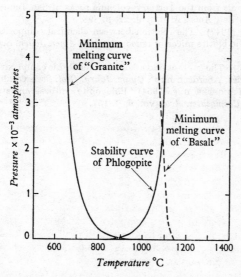

Fig. 76. *Relation of upper stability curve of phlogopite to the determined minimum melting curve of granite and the estimated minimum melting curve of basalt (after Yoder, H. S. & Eugster, H. P., 1954, Geochim. et Cosmochim. Acta, vol. 6, p. 157).*

of basalt, has been given by Yoder and Eugster (1954). In Fig. 76 it is seen that the phlogopite stability curve lies above the granite melting curve for all but the lowest pressure, but that it crosses the basalt melting curve at some intermediate pressure. Thus in a basic rock phlogopite would be stable at depth but would become unstable on extrusion. The validity of extending these conclusions to a mica of biotite composition is somewhat doubtful, since experimental work on annite has shown that the stability curve is much affected by the substitution of iron for magnesium. Micas having a biotitic composition do, however, occur in extrusive rocks, and commonly are partially or completely resorbed, a feature which is most marked in the biotites of the least siliceous extrusives, e.g. in the volcanic rocks of the San Juan region, Colorado.

Biotites of volcanic rocks are in general poorer in Fe^{+2} and richer in Fe^{+3} and Ti than those in their intrusive equivalents.

REFERENCES

ENGEL, A. E. J. and ENGEL, C. G. (1960) 'Progressive metamorphism and granitization of the Major paragneiss, northwest Adirondack Mountains, New York. Part II, Mineralogy', *Bull. Geol. Soc. Amer.*, vol. 71, p. 1.

LAMBERT, R. ST J. (1959) 'The mineralogy and metamorphism of the Moine schists of the Morar and Knoydart districts of Inverness-shire', *Trans. Roy. Soc. Edin.*, vol. 63, p. 553.

LARSEN, E. S., JR., GONYER, F. A. and IRVING, J. (1937) 'Petrologic results of a study of the minerals from the Tertiary volcanic rocks of San Juan Region, Colorado. 6. Biotite', *Amer. Min.*, vol. 22, p. 898.

NOCKOLDS, S. R. (1947) 'The relation between chemical composition and paragenesis in the biotite micas of igneous rocks', *Amer. Journ. Sci.*, vol. 245, p. 401.

READ, H. H. (1935) 'The gabbros and associated xenolithic complexes of the Haddo House district, Aberdeenshire', *Quart. Journ. Geol. Soc.*, vol. 91, p. 591.

YODER, H. S. and EUGSTER, H. P. (1954) 'Phlogopite synthesis and stability range', *Geochim. et Cosmochim. Acta*, vol. 6, p. 157.

Lepidolite

$K_2(Li,Al)_{5-6}[Si_{6-7}Al_{2-1}O_{20}](OH,F)_4$

MONOCLINIC (OR TRIGONAL) $(-)$

α 1·525–1·548
β 1·551–1·585
γ 1·554–1·587
δ 0·018–0·038
$2V_\alpha$ 0°–58°
$\gamma : x$ 0°–7°, $\beta = y$, O.A.P. (010)
Dispersion: $r > v$. D 2·80–2·90. H $2\frac{1}{2}$–4.

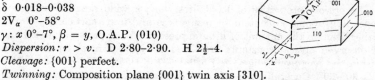

Cleavage: {001} perfect.
Twinning: Composition plane {001} twin axis [310].
Colour: Colourless, shades of pink, purple; colourless in thin section.
Pleochroism: Absorption greater for vibration directions in the plane of cleavage.

STRUCTURE

The essential features of the lepidolite structure are those already described as typical of a mica. The polymorphic structures exhibited are 1M (a 5·3, b 9·2, c 10·2 Å, β 100°, Z = 1), 2M$_2$ (a 9·2, b 5·3, c 20 Å, β 98°, Z = 2), and more rarely 3T (a 5·3, c 30·0 Å, Z = 3†, trigonal); lepidolites do not crystallize with the 2M$_1$ structure adopted by muscovites and by muscovites with relatively small lithium substitution.

CHEMISTRY

In addition to the substitutions indicated in the general formula for lepidolite, considerable amounts of sodium, rubidium and caesium may substitute for potassium; iron, manganese and magnesium may enter octahedral sites. Other ions often present in small quantities are: Ca, Ba, Sr, Ga, Nb and Ti. Lepidolite is one of the few minerals with appreciable Rb content and it has found considerable use in the radioactive method of age determination in which the ^{87}Rb : ^{87}Sr ratio is determined.

In muscovite up to about 3·3 per cent Li$_2$O may enter without essentially changing its structure and such materials may be referred to as lithian muscovites. Analyses of lepidolites show that there is a continuous range of Li$_2$O content between 3·3 and 7 per cent, and since Si : Al is usually less than 7 : 1 it can be shown that between 5 and 6 Y sites are occupied out of a total of 6. Thus there appears to be a continuous chemical series between di-octahedral muscovite and tri-octahedral lepidolite, with a structural

† $3K(Li,Al)_{2\frac{1}{2}-3}(Si_{3-3\frac{1}{2}}Al_{1-\frac{1}{2}})O_{10}(OH,F)_2$.

transition at about 3·3 per cent Li_2O, from the $2M_1$ polymorph common for muscovite and lithian muscovites, to the 1M, $2M_2$ and 3T of lepidolites. Some specimens of lepidolite, however, may contain physical mixtures of micas with high and low lithium content.

Lepidolites often have a considerable amount of F substituting for (OH). The substitution of appreciable Fe^{+2} in octahedral sites gives compositions in the range for zinnwaldite, which itself could be regarded as an iron-lepidolite or as a lithian biotite.

OPTICAL AND PHYSICAL PROPERTIES

The optical properties of lepidolites show a wide range of variation depending upon the content of manganese and iron (particularly ferric) rather than on the amount of lithium present. The upper and lower limits of observed optical constants are listed above, but most lepidolites lie within the narrower ranges: α 1·529–1·537, β 1·552–1·565, γ 1·555–1·568, $2V_\alpha$ 30°–50°. Generally the effect of increasing iron or manganese is to increase the refractive indices and to decrease 2V, so that the higher values for iron- and manganese-rich lepidolites approach the lower limits for muscovites. Lithian muscovites have lower refractive indices than true muscovites and fall in the lepidolite range. The polymorphs of lepidolite are not distinguishable by their optical properties although there is a tendency for 1M specimens to have a higher 2V.

As with rose muscovites the colour of lepidolites is related, not to their lithium content, but to the dominance of Mn over Fe^{+3} ions in the absence of Fe^{+2}. Thus with higher Mn/Fe ratios, colours deepen from colourless or grey through shades of pink and lilac to purple. If Fe is high enough to mask the effect of Mn the resulting colour is brown.

DISTINGUISHING FEATURES

Lepidolite can usually be distinguished from muscovite by its lower refractive indices, its colour, and by the lithium flame test. It is easily confused, however, with rose muscovite and although it usually has a more purplish tinge, an X-ray powder photograph or an Li_2O determination may be necessary to distinguish these micas. These methods are also necessary for distinguishing between lepidolite and lithian muscovite.

PARAGENESIS

Lepidolite is the most common lithium-bearing mineral, and occurs almost exclusively in granite pegmatites (e.g. Table 18, anal. 9) associated with other lithium minerals (amblygonite $LiAl(F,OH)PO_4$, spodumene, zinnwaldite), tourmaline, topaz, cassiterite, beryl and quartz. It has also been reported in granites and aplites and from high temperature hydrothermal veins. In pegmatites, lepidolite is mainly derived by metasomatic replacement of biotite, or more commonly muscovite.

Zinnwaldite

$K_2(Fe^{+2}{}_{2-1},Li_{2-3}Al_2)[Si_{6-7}Al_{2-1}O_{20}](F,OH)_4$

MONOCLINIC $(-)$

α 1·535–1·558
β 1·570–1·589
γ 1·572–1·590
$\delta \simeq 0·035$
$2V_\alpha$ 0°–40°
$\beta = y$, $\gamma : x = 0°$–$2°$, O.A.P. (010)
Dispersion: weak $r > v$. D 2·90–3·02. H $2\frac{1}{2}$–4.
Cleavage: {001} perfect.
Twinning: Composition plane {001}, twin axis [310].
Colour: Grey brown, yellowish brown, pale violet; colourless or light brown in thin section.
Pleochroism: $\alpha < \beta < \gamma$; α colourless to yellow brown, β colourless to grey brown, γ colourless to grey brown.

Zinnwaldite is one of the less common tri-octahedral micas; its properties are similar to those of the biotites and like them it can occur in any of three polymorphic forms (1M, 3T, 2M) of which 1M is the most common (a 5·27, b 9·09, c 10·07 Å, $\beta \simeq 100°$; $Z=1$). Very few specimens have been chemically analysed but it appears that a large number of chemical substitutions can occur, e.g. Ti, Fe^{+2}, Fe^{+3}, Mn and Mg for Al in Y sites, and partial replacement of K by Na, Ba, Rb, Sr and small amounts of Ca. As with lepidolites, there is usually considerable replacement of (OH) by F, and the number of ions in Y sites is often considerably less than the theoretical value of six. Zinnwaldites resemble lepidolites also in their high Si : Al ratio as well as in their lithium content; they contain little or no magnesium. Zinnwaldite occurs mainly in granite pegmatites and in cassiterite-bearing veins. It is usually associated with other lithium-bearing minerals (lepidolite, spodumene), and often with topaz, cleavelandite, beryl, tourmaline, monazite and fluorite.

Margarite

$Ca_2Al_4[Si_4Al_4O_{20}](OH)_4$

MONOCLINIC $(-)$

α 1·630–1·638
β 1·642–1·648
γ 1·644–1·650
δ 0·012–0·014
$2V_\alpha$ 40°–67°
$\beta : x$ 6°–8°, $\gamma = y$, O.A.P. $\perp$(010)
Dispersion: $r < v$.   D 3–3·1.   H $3\frac{1}{2}$–$4\frac{1}{2}$.
Cleavage: {001} perfect.
Twinning: Composition plane {001}, twin axis [310].
Colour: Greyish pink, pale yellow, pale green; colourless in thin section.
Pleochroism: Very weak or absent.

The common micas have potassium as the inter-layer cation and this is often replaced to a small degree by calcium and to a greater extent by sodium; in the distinct mineral species paragonite, nearly all of the X positions are occupied by sodium. More rarely, as in margarite and clintonite, calcium is the main inter-layer cation and this substitution is compensated by an increased $[Al]^4$: Si ratio. These minerals have the typical appearances of a mica but are harder and their cleavage sheets are less elastic, so that they are often called the 'brittle micas'.

Margarite is a di-octahedral mica, analogous to muscovite, with unit cell a 5·13, b 8·92, c 19·50 Å, β 95°, Z = 2. Calcium may be replaced by small amounts of Ba, Sr, K, etc, and to a greater extent by Na; in the latter case charge balance is restored, at least in part, either by replacement of O^{-2} by $(OH)^-$ or by an increase in Si. Y sites are occupied almost entirely by Al, but small substitutions of Fe^{+3}, Fe^{+2}, Mn and Mg are evident. Refractive indices and 2V are decreased by the substitution of Na for Ca.

Margarite may be distinguished from muscovite and talc by higher refractive indices and lower birefringence, and from chlorite and chloritoid by the green colour of the latter minerals.

The most common occurrence of margarite is in emery deposits, along with diaspore and corundum from which it is probably derived. It also occurs in association with tourmaline and staurolite in chlorite and mica schists.

Clintonite
Xanthophyllite

$Ca_2(Mg,Fe)_{4.6}Al_{1.4}[Si_{2.5}Al_{5.5}O_{20}](OH)_4$

MONOCLINIC (−)

α 1·643–1·648
β 1·655–1·662
γ 1·655–1·663
$\delta \simeq 0·012$

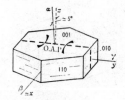

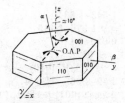

Clintonite	Xanthophyllite
$2V_\alpha \simeq 32°, \beta \simeq x, \gamma = y,$	$2V_\alpha = 0°–23°, \gamma \simeq x, \beta = y,$
$\alpha:z \simeq 5°$, O.A.P. $\perp$(010)	$\alpha:z \simeq 10°$, O.A.P. (010)

Dispersion: weak $r < v$. D 3–3·1. H $3\frac{1}{2}$ on (001), 6 $\perp$(001).
Cleavage: {001} perfect.
Twinning: composition plane {001}, twin axis [310].
Colour: Colourless, yellow, green, reddish brown; colourless in thin section.
Pleochroism: α colourless, yellow, orange or reddish brown; $\beta = \gamma$ green or brown.

In the same way that margarite is related to muscovite by the substitution of Ca for K, so the brittle micas clintonite and xanthophyllite may be regarded as calcium analogues of phlogopite. The difference between clintonite and xanthophyllite lies probably in polymorphism of the layer stacking, clintonite having a two-layer and xanthophyllite a one-layer cell. As in the case of biotites, the two polymorphs give rise to different optical orientations.

In both clintonite and xanthophyllite small substitutions of Na and K for Ca can occur but the totals in both X and Y sites vary very little from their ideal values, 2 and 6. Substitution of Na for Ca and reduction of Fe content are both associated with a fall in refractive indices.

Clintonite and xanthophyllite can be distinguished from other micas of similar colour since the latter have higher birefringence, lower hardness and are not brittle. Chlorites are also less hard and less brittle but most have lower birefringence than the brittle micas. Chloritoid may be distinguished by its larger 2V, and in most cases by being optically positive.

The most common occurrences of clintonites and xanthophyllites are with talc in chlorite schist, and with spinel, grossular, calcite, vesuvianite, clinopyroxene (fassaite) and phlogopite in metasomatically altered limestones.

Stilpnomelane

$(K,Na,Ca)_{0-1.4}(Fe^{+3},Fe^{+2},Mg,Al,Mn)_{5.9-8.2}[Si_8O_{20}](OH)_4(O,OH,H_2O)_{3.6-8.5}$

MONOCLINIC ($-$)

α 1·543–1·634
$\beta = \gamma$ 1·576–1·745
δ 0·030–0·110
$2V_\alpha \simeq 0°$
$\beta = y$, O.A.P. (010)
D 2·59–2·96. H 3–4.

Cleavage: {001} perfect, {010} imperfect.

Colour: Stilpnomelane—golden brown, deep reddish brown or black; ferrostilpnomelane—dark green: pale yellow, dark brown or green in thin section.

Pleochroism:	Stilpnomelane	Ferrostilpnomelane
	α bright golden yellow.	pale yellow.
	$\beta = \gamma$ deep reddish brown to nearly black.	deep green.

STRUCTURE

The structure of stilpnomelane has not been fully determined, but its physical and chemical characteristics, and cell parameters, are all consistent with a layered structure related closely to that of talc. Its talc-like sheets are based on an orthogonal (pseudohexagonal) cell with $a \simeq 5.4$ Å, $b \simeq 9.4$ Å, the parameters of which are large because of the considerable content of Fe^{+2} and Fe^{+3} in the central octahedral layer. The d_{001} spacing (12·1 Å) suggests that the 'talc' units are separated by a composite layer in which a sheet of (OH) and (O) ions and water molecules is sandwiched between two sheets containing iron, magnesium and aluminium ions (Fig. 77). Some exchangeable K ions occur in 'zeolitic' sites in the (O,OH,H_2O) sheet. Repeating units of the structure are stacked above one another with a β angle of about 93°.

CHEMISTRY

Stilpnomelanes exhibit a large range of compositions, the principal variations being in Fe^{+2}, Fe^{+3} and to a lesser extent Mg. It seems probable that when Fe^{+3} is replaced by Fe^{+2}, (OH)$^-$ replaces O^{-2} as in the Fe^{+3}-rich amphiboles. The reddish brown to black ferric iron-rich varieties are called stilpnomelanes, and the term ferrostilpnomelane is used to describe the dark green minerals rich in ferrous iron. Mn-rich varieties are known as parsettensite.

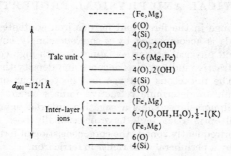

Fig. 77. *Successive planes of atoms in the structure of stilpnomelane (after Gruner, J. W., 1944, Amer. Min., vol. 29, p. 291).*

Table 19. STILPNOMELANE ANALYSES

	1.	2.		NUMBERS OF IONS ON THE BASIS OF 8 Si			
				1.		2.	
SiO_2	48·03	45·29	Si	8·00		8·00	
TiO_2	0·23	0·02	Al	1·272⎫		1·158⎫	
Al_2O_3	6·48	5·57	Ti	0·029		0·002	
Fe_2O_3	4·12	23·95	Fe^{+3}	0·516		3·182	
FeO	22·88	8·99	Mg	1·226		0·868	
MnO	2·67	1·14	Fe^{+2}	3·188	6·93	1·327	7·52
MgO	4·94	3·30	Mn	0·376		0·170	
CaO	0·83	4·28	Na	—		—	
Na_2O	0·00	—	Ca	0·148		0·809	
K_2O	0·83	—	K	0·176⎭		—⎭	
H_2O^+	6·90	6·12	(OH)	4·00		4·00	
H_2O^-	2·64	1·79	(O,OH,H_2O)	23·67		23·21	
Total	100·55	100·45					
α	1·551	1·626					
γ	1·594	1·715					
$2V_\alpha$	0°	—					
D	2·62	—					

1. Ferrostilpnomelane, garnet–calcite–chlorite–ferrostilpnomelane schist, western Otago, New Zealand (Hutton, C. O., 1938, *Min. Mag.*, vol. 25, p. 172).
2. Stilpnomelane, spherical vesicles in granophyre inclusion in olivine gabbro, Kangerdlugssuaq, east Greenland (Wager, L. R. & Deer, W. A., 1939, *Meddel. om Grønland*, Bd 105, Nr. 4).

OPTICAL AND PHYSICAL PROPERTIES

The great range in the ferric and ferrous iron contents of the stilpnomelane minerals is accompanied by a correspondingly large variation in their optical and physical properties. Minerals with high contents of Fe^{+3} have higher refractive indices, birefringence and density than those rich in ferrous iron. The micaceous cleavage and deep colour of stilpnomelane make it difficult to determine refractive indices accurately. The great majority of stilpnomelanes show a negative uniaxial figure but minerals having a small optic axial angle have occasionally been noted. Stilpnomelane is not infrequently zoned; the core, consisting of ferrostilpnomelane is surrounded by a peripheral zone richer in ferric iron.

DISTINGUISHING FEATURES

Stilpnomelane may be mistaken for biotite; both minerals occur in green and brown pleochroic varieties, and have a very small optic axial angle (most stilpnomelanes are sensibly uniaxial) and similar pleochroism. The basal cleavage of stilpnomelane, however, is less perfect than that of biotite, and the former has a second cleavage perpendicular to {001}. In the extinction position stilpnomelane does not show the characteristic mottling effect of biotite. Ferrostilpnomelanes are distinguished by their greater birefringence from chlorite, chloritoid and clintonite. In hand specimen stilpnomelane can be distinguished by its brittle character from both biotite and chlorite.

PARAGENESIS

Stilpnomelane occurs in iron- and manganese-rich low grade regionally metamorphosed sediments and associated veins. Thus it is found, together with minnesotaite and greenalite, as a major constituent of the silicate–iron formations of the Lake Superior region, as a widespread and often abundant constituent of the schists of western Otago, New Zealand (anal. 1), and as a common mineral in the glaucophane-bearing metamorphic rocks of the Kanto Mountains, central Japan. Stilpnomelane also occurs in reconstituted acid gneiss xenoliths in the gabbros and also in granophyres (anal. 2) of the Skaergaard complex, east Greenland.

REFERENCES

HUTTON, C. O. (1938) 'The stilpnomelane group of minerals', *Min. Mag.*, vol. 25, p. 172.
——— (1956) 'Further data on the stilpnomelane mineral group', *Amer. Min.*, vol. 41, p. 608.

Pyrophyllite

$Al_4[Si_8O_{20}](OH)_4$

MONOCLINIC $(-)$

α 1·534–1·556
β 1·586–1·589
γ 1·596–1·601
$\delta \simeq$ 0·050
$2V_\alpha$ 53°–62°
$\gamma = y$, β approx. $\parallel x$, O.A.P. $\perp$(010)
Dispersion: weak, $r > v$. D 2·65–2·90. H 1–2.
Cleavage: {001} perfect
Colour: White, yellow, pale blue, greyish or brownish green; pearly lustre; colourless in thin section.
Pleochroism: Absorption greater for vibration directions in (001) plane.

Pyrophyllite, like the micas, has a layered structure in which a sheet of octahedrally coordinated Al ions is sandwiched between two sheets of linked SiO_4 tetrahedra (Fig. 78). Two-thirds of the available octahedral sites are occupied by Al and the remainder are empty. The layers thus formed are electrically neutral so that no additional cations are accommodated between them. The commonest polymorph is $2M_1$ (see p. 195) with a 5·16, b 8·90, c 18·64 Å, β 99° 55′, Z = 2.

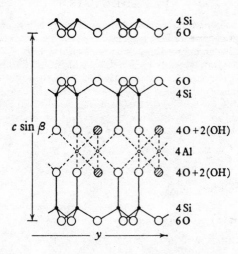

Fig. 78. *Illustration of structure of pyrophyllite as viewed along x axis (after Pauling, L., 1930, Proc. Nat. Acad. Sci. U.S.A., vol. 16, p. 123)*

Pyrophyllites show little deviation from the ideal chemical formula; small replacements of Si by Al, and of $[Al]^6$ by Mg, Fe^{+2}, Fe^{+3}, may occur, and minor amounts of Ca, Na and K may be present. Pyrophyllite can be readily synthesized from its constituent oxides, and it is a stable phase within the range 420° to 575°C under varying water pressures in alumina-silica mixtures high in silica.

Pyrophyllite is found mainly in three forms, fine-grained foliated lamellae with platy cleavage, radiating granular larger crystals and needles, and massive compact spherulitic aggregates of smaller crystals. It can be distinguished from talc and muscovite by its higher 2V, and from kaolinite which has lower birefringence. Distinction from talc may also be made by the chemical test for aluminium in which a deep blue coloration is produced by heating a specimen after moistening with a cobalt solution.

Pyrophyllite is a comparatively uncommon mineral which occurs largely through the hydrothermal alteration of feldspars and is often accompanied by quartz.

Talc

$Mg_6[Si_8O_{20}](OH)_4$

MONOCLINIC $(-)$

α 1·539–1·550
β 1·589–1·594
γ 1·589–1·600
$\delta \simeq 0.05$
$2V_\alpha$ 0°–30°
$\gamma = y$, β nearly parallel to x, O.A.P. $\perp$(010)
Dispersion: $r > v$. D 2·58–2·83. H 1.
Cleavage: {001} perfect.
Colour: Colourless, white, pale green, dark green, brown; colourless in thin section.

Talc is the major constituent of rocks known as soapstone or steatite, blocks of which can be used for thermal and electrical insulating purposes.

STRUCTURE

The structure of talc is like that of pyrophyllite except that octahedral sites in the composite layers are occupied by magnesium instead of aluminium, and none are vacant; talc is thus a tri-octahedral layered mineral. In both talc and pyrophyllite the stacking of successive layers is not regular, but it approximates to the $2M_1$ sequence with a 5·28, b 9·15, c 18·9 Å, β 100° 15′, $Z = 2$. The X-ray powder patterns of talc and pyrophyllite are similar but the d values of talc are larger and in particular d_{060} is 1·52 Å as compared with 1·495 Å for pyrophyllite. Basal spacings are not affected by organic liquids nor by heating to 700°C since there are no interchangeable cations and no water molecules between the structural layers.

CHEMISTRY

There appears to be little variation in the chemical composition of talc; sometimes small amounts of Al or Ti substitute for Si, and small amounts of iron, manganese or aluminium may substitute for magnesium. The relatively minor contents of Ca and alkalis also may substitute for magnesium, but are more likely to be present as interlayer ions or in impurities. Minnesotaite is an unusual talc with almost complete substitution of Fe for Mg. Some analyses show an unusually high water content, but some of this is probably tightly held adsorbed water. The thermal decomposition of talc results in the formation of clinoenstatite and cristobalite.

The stability curve of talc is illustrated in Fig. 79, a *PT* diagram for the system MgO–SiO_2–H_2O. Talc can be prepared at all temperatures below 800°C from mixtures of $3MgO$ and $3SiO_2$ at water vapour pressures between 6000 and 30,000 lb/in².

Table 20. TALC ANALYSIS

		NUMBERS OF IONS ON BASIS OF 24 (O,OH)	
SiO_2	62·61		
Al_2O_3	tr.	Si	7·989
FeO	2·46	Fe^{+2}	0·261⎫
MnO	0·01	Mn	0·007 ⎬6·01
MgO	30·22	Mg	5·743⎭
H_2O^+	4·72	(OH)	4·018
Total	100·02		
α	1·550		
γ	1·596		
D	2·791		

1. Talc, altered peridotite, northern Sweden (Du Rietz, T., 1935, *Geol. För. Förh.*, vol. 57, p. 133).

OPTICAL AND PHYSICAL PROPERTIES

Talc usually occurs in massive foliated or fibrous aggregates or in globular stellar groups, but the rarer tabular crystals exhibit perfect {001} cleavage, yielding flexible slightly elastic lamellae. Talc in nearly all its forms has a greasy feel and pearly lustre, and it is taken as one of the standards of hardness, having the value 1 on the Mohs scale. The variations in optical properties shown by talc specimens may result from small amounts of substituent ions (Ti, Mn, etc.) or from adsorbed water.

DISTINGUISHING FEATURES

Pyrophyllite and muscovite have a larger 2V than talc, and the 'high silica' mica, phengite, has higher refractive indices. Brucite has refractive indices similar to β and γ for talc, but it is uniaxial positive.

PARAGENESIS

The two common parageneses of talc are in association with the hydrothermal alteration of ultrabasic rocks and the low grade thermal metamorphism of siliceous dolomites. In ultrabasic rocks talc commonly occurs as lenticular veins and along faults and shear planes. The hydrothermal solutions may in some cases be derived from the original ultrabasic

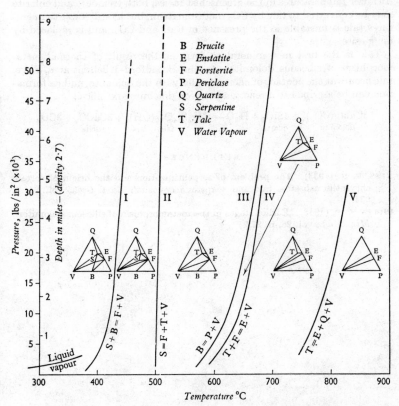

Fig. 79. *Pressure–temperatures curves (I–V) of univariant equilibrium in the system MgO–SiO₂–H₂O. Equation on each curve indicates the reaction to which the curve refers. Triangular diagram on each divariant region between curves indicates, for all compositions, the stable assemblages under the range of P,T conditions represented by the region. Lower left—vapour pressure curve of water ending at the critical temperature and pressure (after Bowen, N. L. & Tuttle, O. F., 1949, Bull. Geol. Soc. Amer., vol. 60, p. 439, and Roy, D. M. & Roy, R., 1957, Amer. Journ. Sci., vol. 255, p. 574).*

body, but in others an external source is indicated. Steatization is commonly but not always associated with serpentinization; the conversion of serpentine to talc may occur by the addition of silica and removal of magnesia, or by the addition of CO_2:

$$2Mg_3Si_2O_5(OH)_4 + 3CO_2 \rightarrow Mg_3Si_4O_{10}(OH)_2 + 3MgCO_3 + 3HO_2$$
serpentine · talc · magnesite

At lower temperatures in the greenschist facies, both tremolite and chlorite may be converted to talc by CO_2 metasomatism, but at still lower temperatures talc is unstable in the presence of CaO and CO_2, and is replaced by magnesite.

Talc is the first new mineral to form as the result of thermal metamorphism of siliceous dolomites. In the Broadford–Kilchrist area, Skye, talc occurs at the contact of chert nodules with the dolomite, and its formation can be ascribed to a reaction between dolomite and silica:

$$3CaMg(CO_3)_2 + 4SiO_2 + H_2O \rightarrow Mg_3Si_4O_{10}(OH)_2 + 3CaCO_3 + 3CO_2$$
$$\text{dolomite} \quad\quad \text{quartz} \quad\quad\quad\quad\quad \text{talc} \quad\quad\quad \text{calcite}$$

REFERENCES

HESS, H. H. (1933) 'The problem of serpentinization and the origin of certain chrysotile asbestos, talc and soapstone deposits', *Econ. Geol.*, vol. 28, p. 634.

TILLEY, C. E. (1948) 'Earlier stages in the metamorphism of siliceous dolomites', *Min. Mag.*, vol. 28, p. 272.

Chlorite

$(Mg,Al,Fe)_{12}[(Si,Al)_8O_{20}](OH)_{16}$

MONOCLINIC $(+)$ or $(-)$

Unoxidized	Oxidized
α 1·57–1·66	1·60–1·67
β 1·57–1·67	1·61–1·69
γ 1·57–1·67	1·61–1·69
δ 0–0·01	0–0·02
2V 20°$(-)$–60°$(+)$	0°–20°$(-)$

Acute bisectrix approx. $\perp$(001), O.A.P. (010)

Dispersion: Strong $r < v$. D 2·6–3·3. H 2–3.

Cleavage: {001} perfect.

Twinning: (a) Twin plane {001}; (b) Twin axis [310], composition plane {001}.

Colour: Green, white, yellow, pink, red, brown; mostly colourless or green in thin section. Anomalous interference colours common.

Pleochroism: Weak to moderate with either $\alpha < \beta = \gamma$ or $\alpha = \beta > \gamma$; stronger absorption colours are usually dark or olive green.

The chlorites are a group of minerals with layered structure, which in many respects resemble the micas. Their principal occurrences are as products of hydrothermal alteration in igneous rocks, in chlorite schists and together with clay minerals, in argillaceous sediments. They often occur in large crystalline blocks with perfect cleavage yielding flexible but inelastic (cf. micas) basal laminae, but are also widespread as fine-grained scaly or massive aggregates.

STRUCTURE

The structure of chlorite is one of regularly alternating talc-like $Y_6Z_8O_{20}(OH)_4$ and brucite-like $Y_6(OH)_{12}$ sheets. The pseudo-hexagonal networks of these components have an a parameter of approximately 5·3 Å, and the cell which results from their superposition has a 5·3, b 9·2, c 14·3 Å, β 97°, Z = 1. The height of the cell ($c \sin \beta$) is the thickness of one chlorite layer, and the β angle results from a layer displacement of $a/3$ in successive cells (see Fig. 80). Other polymorphic forms occur, and the layer stacking is often disordered. (Mg,Al,Fe) replacements may occur in either the 'brucite' or the 'talc' component or in both, and particular sites within these components may in some cases be preferentially occupied by one kind of atom.

The cell parameters of chlorites vary with chemical composition. Thus the substitution of Al for Si together with Al for (Mg,Fe) reduces the basal spacing d_{001}: the value of b is relatively unaffected by Al substitution, but both *a* and *b* increase with substitution of Fe or Mn for Mg. The relative intensities of basal X-ray reflections may also be used as a guide to composition.

Some layered minerals (the septechlorites, see p. 241) which are chemically similar to chlorites and which have been described as 'chamosite' (Brindley, 1951) are structurally more closely related to the kandites or serpentines, and therefore give powder patterns characteristic of the latter minerals. They have a strong basal reflection at about 7 Å, none at 14 Å, and are decomposed on heating to 500°–600°C.

Both vermiculites and montmorillonites have basal reflections at $\simeq 14$ Å but can be distinguished from chlorites by heating to about 600°C when for chlorites the 001 reflection·is enhanced, and also by the swelling characteristics of the former minerals, not generally possessed by chlorites.

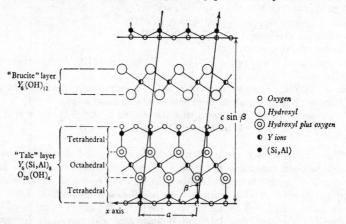

Fig. 80. *Projection of the chlorite structure on* (010) *(after McMurchy, R. C., 1934, Zeit. Krist., vol. 88, p. 420).*

CHEMISTRY

The chemistry of the chlorite minerals, as well as their structure, can be described in relation to a chlorite with hypothetical composition $Mg_6Si_8O_{20}$ $(OH)_4 + Mg_6(OH)_{12}$ which has equal numbers of talc and brucite layers. In chlorites a wide range of substitutions occurs in both layers; silicon is replaced by aluminium within the range $Si_7[Al]^4$–$Si_4[Al_4]^4$, and magnesium in both the talc and brucite components is replaceable principally by aluminium within the range $Mg_{11}[Al]^6$ to $Mg_8[Al_4]^6$. Replacement of Si by Al causes charge unbalance in the 'talc' sheet and it has not been established to what extent this is compensated by substitution of Al for Mg within the same component, or in the brucite layer, or in both. While the range of these replacements is restricted, any degree of substitution of Fe^{+2} for Mg may occur also, so that the ratio $Fe^{+2} : (Fe^{+2} + Mg)$ can lie between zero and unity. One other important aspect of chlorite composition is the role of ferric iron. The variations in chlorite chemistry can be classified in a number of ways employing boundaries which are to a great extent arbitrary. The method adopted here is that recommended by Hey (1954) which in many respects is consistent with earlier attempts at classification and with accepted nomenclature. A first subdivision is made between chlorites with more than 4 per cent Fe_2O_3 and those with less, and these are termed oxidized and unoxidized respectively. The unoxidized chlorites are the most common,

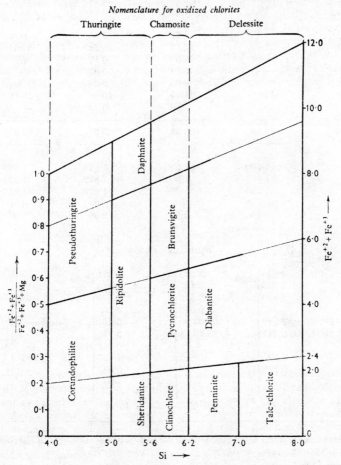

Fig. 81. *Nomenclature of chlorites and oxidized chlorites (after Hey, M. H., 1954, Min. Mag., vol. 30, p. 277).*

and for these, divisions are drawn according to Si content, where the numbers of silicon atoms per formula unit are 5, 5·6, 6·2 and 7 out of a maximum of 8. At these compositions there will thus be 3, 2·4, 1·8 and 1·0 atoms of Al in tetrahedral sites, and an equal number of Al (or $Al + Fe^{+3}$)

Table 21. CHLORITE ANALYSES

	1.	2.	3.	4.
SiO_2	23·20	27·64	25·62	31·44
TiO_2	—	0·22	0·88	—
Al_2O_3	24·42	22·48	21·19	17·62
Fe_2O_3	3·48	0·06	3·88	—
FeO	13·40	12·06	21·55	tr.
MnO	—	0·02	0·35	tr.
MgO	22·76	24·32	15·28	37·64
CaO	1·04	0·00	0·16	tr.
Na_2O	—	0·17	0·00	—
K_2O	—	0·06	0·00	—
H_2O^+	12·00	11·45	10·87	13·19
H_2O^-	—	1·80	0·19	—
Total	100·30	100·34	99·97	99·89
α	1·600	1·600	1·622	1·572
β	1·603	1·600	1·622	1·572
γ	1·610	1·606	1·626	1·575
2V	$(+)60°$	$(+)0°-8°$	$0°$	$(+)6°-14°$
D	2·85	2·80	2·96	3·02

NUMBERS OF IONS†

	1.	2.	3.	4.
Si	4·645 ⎱8·00	5·523 ⎱8·00	5·364 ⎱8·00	5·830 ⎱8·00
Al	3·355 ⎰	2·477 ⎰	2·636 ⎰	2·170 ⎰
Al	2·410	2·819	2·595	1·682
Ti	—	0·032	0·138	—
Fe^{+3}	0·522	—	0·611	—
Fe^{+2}	2·245	2·015	3·775	—
Mn	— ⎰12·19	— ⎰12·11	0·062 ⎰11·98	— ⎰12·09
Mg	6·793	7·243	4·767	10·403
Ca	0·223	—	0·035	—
Na	—	—	—	—
K	—	—	—	—
(OH)	16·03	15·27	15·18	16·32

1. Dark green corundophilite, emery deposit, Chester County, Massachusetts (Shannon, E. V. & Wherry, E. T., 1922, *Journ. Wash. Acad. Sci.*, vol. 12, p. 239).
2. Sheridanite, dravite–chlorite rock, Nelson, New Zealand (Hutton, C. O. & Seelye, F. T., 1945, *Trans. Roy. Soc. New Zealand*, vol. 75, p. 160; includes V 0·06, Ni tr.).
3. Ripidolite, chlorite–epidote–albite schist, south Devon (Tilley, C. E., 1938, *Geol. Mag.*, vol. 75, p. 497).
4. Clinochlore, metamorphosed limestone, Philipsburg, Montana (McMurchy, R. C., 1934, *Zeit. Krist.*, vol. 88, p. 420).

Table 21. CHLORITE ANALYSES—*continued*

5.	6.	7.	8.	
28·32	27·11	20·82	26·40	SiO_2
0·09	0·35	—	—	TiO_2
19·03	17·42	17·64	18·23	Al_2O_3
1·19	2·91	8·70	5·70	Fe_2O_3
14·85	30·98	37·96	25·87	FeO
0·09	—	—	0·04	MnO
23·72	9·75	4·15	11·35	MgO
0·62	0·21	—	0·42	CaO
0·01	—	—	0·17	Na_2O
0·00	—	—	0·17	K_2O
11·95	11·07	10·31	10·60	H_2O^+
0·06	0·51	—	1·05	H_2O^-
99·93	100·31	99·58	100·00‡	Total
1·620	—	—	—	α
1·621	1·638	1·662	—	β
1·625	—	1·662	1·620	γ
(+)14°	—	(−)0°	—	2V
2·82	2·988	3·31	3·034	D

NUMBERS OF IONS†

5.		6.		7.		8.		
5·654	8·00	5·864	8·00	4·834	8·00	5·747	8·00	Si
2·346		2·136		3·166		2·253		Al
2·130		2·307		1·662		2·425		Al
0·012		0·057		—		—		Ti
0·180		0·473		1·518		—		Fe^{+3}
2·480		5·605		7·374		5·645		Fe^{+2}
0·014	12·01	—	11·63	—	11·99	0·007	11·97	Mn
7·058		3·143		1·436		3·681		Mg
0·132		0·048		—		0·097		Ca
—		—		—		0·071		Na
—		—		—		0·047		K
15·94		15·98		16·00		16·00		(OH)

5. Pycnochlorite, rodingite, Hindubagh, Pakistan (Bilgrami, S. A. & Howie, R. A., 1960, *Amer. Min.*, vol. 45, p. 791).
6. Brunsvigite, spilite, Great Island, New Zealand (Battey, M. H., 1956, *Geol. Mag.*, vol. 93, p. 89).
7. Dark olive-green thuringite, Schmiedefeld, Thuringia (Engelhardt, W. von, 1942, *Zeit. Krist.*, vol. 104, p. 142).
8. Green oolitic chamosite, siltstone, Wickwar, Gloucestershire (Bannister, F. A. & Whittard, W. F., 1945, *Min. Mag.*, vol. 27, p. 99).

‡ Recalculated to 100 per cent. after deducting impurities.
† Where (OH) is given as 16·00, formula has been calculated on basis of 28 oxygen equivalents, ignoring H_2O^+; in other cases 36 (O, OH) has been assumed.

in octahedral sites. The oxidized chlorites are divided only at silicon contents 5·6 and 6·2. Both main groups are further subdivided according to their content of total iron and the resulting 'areas' of composition, with their associated names, are shown in Fig. 81. In this way chlorites are described by three parameters: ferric iron, silicon, and total iron.

Chlorites with the compositions of the end-members of Fig. 81, $Mg_{12}Si_8O_{20}(OH)_{16}$ and $(Mg_8Al_4)(Si_4Al_4)O_{20}(OH)_{16}$, have not been reported, but these are the ideal formulae of the minerals serpentine and amesite respectively, both of which are structurally related to the kaolinite group. In fact very few specimens with the chlorite structure have compositions outside the range Si 4·5 to 7·0. In addition to the major substitutions described above, many chlorites contain small amounts of Mn, Cr, Ni, Ti, etc.; no special names are required for these, but the names gonyerite and pennantite have been used for Mn-rich chlorites, and kochubeite and kämmererite for certain Cr-rich specimens.

The compositions of oxidized chlorites are capable of two different interpretations. In many of them a high content of Fe_2O_3 is associated with a low figure for H_2O^+, and when a formula is calculated on the basis of 28 oxygen equivalents the total of octahedral ions falls somewhat short of the ideal twelve. It has been suggested that these 'oxidized chlorites' are indeed chlorites which have been oxidized, effecting the reaction $Fe^{+2} \rightarrow Fe^{+3}$ with loss of hydrogen. In these cases a better fit to the ideal chlorite formula is obtained if Fe_2O_3 is first expressed as its equivalent of FeO. Some chlorites, however, which have a high content of Fe_2O_3, nevertheless have normal water content and give a normal chlorite formula when ferric iron is treated as such. Thus when ferric iron is primary, its occurrence in the structure is compensated by the replacement of Al for Si, but when it is the product of oxidation the associated substitution is $(O)^{-2}$ for $(OH)^-$.

Most chlorites have approximately the ideal number of octahedral ions (twelve) and so are members of the serpentine, $Mg_{12}Si_8O_{20}(OH)_{16}$–amesite, $(Mg_8Al_4)(Si_4Al_4)O_{20}(OH)_{12}$, series. Many others, however, have Y less than twelve even after expressing Fe_2O_3 as FeO equivalent (in some of them Fe_2O_3 content is in any case negligible), and these may be regarded as chlorites in which the constituent talc and brucite components are partially replaced by their well known di-octahedral analogues pyrophyllite and gibbsite respectively.

D.t.a. curves of chlorites generally have endothermic peaks at about 600° and 850°C which probably correspond to dehydration of first the 'brucite' and then the 'talc' layers of the structure, but the positions of these as well as the exothermic peak at about 900°C may vary considerably according to chemical composition. The most common decomposition products from chlorites are olivine and spinel.

In the system $MgO–Al_2O_3–SiO_2–H_2O$ the range of compositions yielding solid solutions in the chlorite structure is from penninite $(Mg_{11}Al)(Si_7Al)O_{20}$ $(OH)_{16}$ to amesite $(Mg_8Al_4)(Si_4Al_4)O_{20}(OH)_{16}$. In the same compositional range (and beyond it in one direction to the serpentine composition $Mg_{12}Si_8O_{20}(OH)_{16}$) a second isomorphous series can be synthesized the members of which have a 'tri-octahedral kaolinite' structure. These have a

7 Å instead of a 14 Å inter-layer spacing and are the septechlorites (see p. 241): the precise stability relationships between the two polymorphic forms have not been established, but higher pressures and temperatures yield the normal chlorite. The iron-rich analogue of amesite is the mineral chamosite, and this can also exist in either the septechlorite or normal chlorite form. Since the type locality material from Chamoson has the normal chlorite structure the name has been retained for a subdivision of the oxidized chlorites (Fig. 81).

OPTICAL AND PHYSICAL PROPERTIES

The two variables, Si and total Fe, chosen to represent the chemical compositions of unoxidized chlorites, are also the principal factors influencing optical properties. Refractive indices increase with increasing iron and with decreasing silicon content. Chlorites are monoclinic or triclinic and are therefore biaxial, but often refractive indices for the two vibration directions in the (001) plane are so close that 2V is too small to measure. In Fig. 82 the chlorites are regarded as uniaxial and it is seen that the birefringence (ϵ–ω) decreases from positive through zero to negative values as iron or silicon increase. Division of the main types of chlorite according to optic sign puts penninite, clinochlore, ripidolite, sheridanite, corundophilite and klementite as positive, and diabantite, brunsvigite, thuringite, chamosite and delessite as negative. Chromium chlorites are generally optically positive, but those with more than about 6 per cent Cr_2O_3 are negative. In addition to ω and (ϵ–ω), Fig. 82 shows how density increases with iron and decreases with silicon content. The effects of manganese and chromium on the optical properties are similar to those of ferrous and ferric iron respectively. Pleochroism is generally exhibited more strongly by chlorites with higher iron content. Pleochroic haloes similar to those found in micas sometimes occur in chlorites and in some cases at least are associated with inclusions of zircon at their centres. Chromium chlorites are strongly pleochroic and are often pink or violet, while the manganese chlorite pennantite is orange-red.

DISTINGUISHING FEATURES

Chlorites are usually green and pleochroic, and some show anomalous interference colours. Birefringence is much lower than that of the micas, illites, montmorillonites and vermiculite, and refractive indices are higher than those of kaolinite. Some serpentines have a similar flaky morphology but have lower refractive indices than chlorites and show little or no pleochroism. Those 'chamosite' specimens which do not have the structure of a chlorite may yet have similar optical properties, and distinction is best made by X-ray powder patterns of heated and unheated samples.

PARAGENESIS

Chlorite is widely distributed in low grade metamorphic rocks, and is the most characteristic mineral of the greenschist facies. Chlorites are common constituents of igneous rock in which they have generally been derived by the hydrothermal alteration of primary ferromagnesian minerals. They are also a common product of weathering and occur in many argillaceous rocks as well as in some iron-rich sediments.

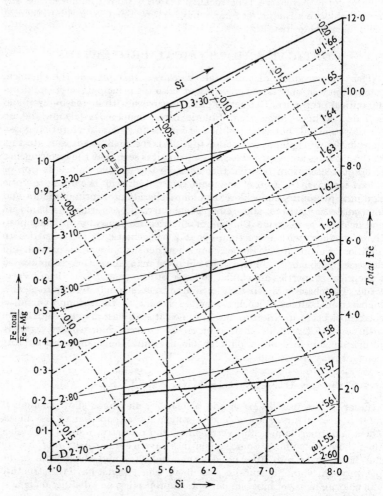

Fig. 82. *Refractive index (ω) (see above), birefringence ($\epsilon-\omega$), and specific gravity (D) of chlorites in relation to composition. For oxidized chlorites ω and D are higher and ($\epsilon-\omega$) is lower in proportion to percentage of Fe_2O_3. The boundaries of the chlorite species and varieties are shown (cf. Fig. 81) (after Hey, M. H., 1954, Min. Mag., vol. 30, p. 277).*

Metamorphic rocks. The chlorites in regionally metamorphosed basic igneous rocks are usually rich in aluminium, having in many cases been derived by a reaction involving Al-rich hornblende and/or epidote.

In pelitic sediments chlorite is generally stable until the onset of the PT conditions of the biotite zone. The transformation of chlorite to biotite however, is possible only by reaction with a potassium-rich mineral. The formation of biotite from an aluminium-poor chlorite and muscovite is not a simple reaction, and probably involves the production of an aluminium-rich chlorite in addition to biotite.

Greenschists in western Otago, New Zealand, have been derived by the low grade regional metamorphism not only of basic igneous rocks but also of tuffs containing argillaceous and arenaceous impurities. In some low grade regionally metamorphosed basic rocks the common assemblage is actinolite–epidote–chlorite–albite but in some rocks local concentration of H_2O and/or CO_2 pressure has promoted the breakdown of actinolite to chlorite and calcite with the development of calcite–chlorite–epidote–albite rocks. At higher grades of metamorphism chlorite decreases in amount and, together with epidote and/or actinolite, is involved in the formation of an aluminium-rich amphibole and plagioclase.

Igneous rocks. Chlorite is a common product of the hydrothermal alteration of pyroxenes, amphiboles and biotite in igneous rocks. The composition of the chlorite is often related to that of the original igneous mineral, and the more iron-rich chlorites, thuringite, delessite and daphnite, are commonly found as replacements of the iron-rich ferromagnesian minerals. Partial and complete chloritization of biotite is particularly common in granites and in most cases the transformation is markedly pseudomorphous.

Chlorite is commonly found filling amygdales in lavas, and together with epidote, alkali feldspar, quartz, sericite, zeolites, carbonates and pyrite, it is an important product of the intense hydrothermal alteration (propylitization) of andesites and to a lesser extent of basalts. Chlorite also occurs as dense slickensided lamellar coatings along joint planes and fissures particularly in basalts. Chlorite (Table 21 anal. 6) is an abundant constituent of the spilites of northern New Zealand, and here occurs in angular interstitial areas, in small rounded pools, in fine veinlets and in amygdales.

The association of chlorite with albite and quartz is an essential characteristic of adinoles, and chlorite–quartz pseudomorphs after andalusite in the adinoles are developed in Devonian slates metasomatized by albite dolerite at Dinas Head, Cornwall. The corundophilite (Table 21, anal. 1) in the chlorite-bearing schists of the emery deposits of Chester County, Massachusetts, is also of metasomatic origin and at this locality is associated with margarite and white mica.

Chlorite also occurs in fissure veins in some massive igneous rocks, and many low temperature hydrothermal veins of alpine-type in low grade metamorphosed sediments carry chlorite in addition to adularia and quartz. Manganese chlorites are generally associated with manganese ore deposits.

Sedimentary rocks. Chlorite group minerals are common constituents of argillaceous sediments, in which they occur both as detrital and as authigenic crystals. Due to their usual fine-grained nature their characterization is often difficult, and in many sediments the chlorite is present in mixed-layer structures, e.g. in regular interstratification with vermiculite. The chlorites are derived by the aggradation of less organized sheet minerals, by the degradation of pre-existing ferromagnesian minerals, and by crystallization from dilute solutions of their components.

REFERENCES

AGRELL, S. O. (1939) 'The adinoles of Dinas Head, Cornwall', *Min. Mag.*, vol. 25, p. 305.

ALBEE, A. L. (1962) 'Relationships between the mineral association, chemical composition and physical properties of the chlorite series', *Amer. Min.*, vol. 47, p. 851.

CHAYES, F. (1955) 'Potash feldspar as a by-product of the biotite-chlorite transformation', *Journ. Geol.*, vol. 63, p. 75.

HEY, M. H. (1954) 'A new review of the chlorites', *Min. Mag.*, vol. 30, p. 277.

Septechlorites $Y_6[Z_4O_{10}](OH)_8$

The four minerals amesite, chamosite, greenalite and cronstedtite are closely related chemically to the chlorites but the name septechlorite has been proposed for them as they are structurally characterized by serpentine-like layers with $d_{001} \simeq 7$ Å. All septechlorites possess a layered structure, each layer having a tetrahedral $(Si, Al)_2O_5$ component, and linked to it a tri-octahedral ('brucite-type') component. As with serpentines and kandites, various arrangements of layer stacking are possible, leading to different unit cells. Compositional relationships between chlorites, septechlorites and serpentines are illustrated in Fig. 83.

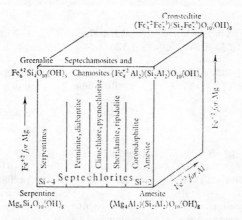

Fig. 83. *Compositional relationships between chlorites, septechlorites and serpentines (after Nelson, B. W. & Roy, R., 1958, Amer. Min., vol. 43, p. 707). The septechlorites can occur as the low-temperature polymorph at any composition which forms a chlorite. Chlorite nomenclature is that used in Fig. 81.*

Chamosites often occur in fine-grained yellow, greenish grey or greenish brown aggregates, associated with other clay minerals and iron oxides, in lateritic clay deposits. They are also found as ooliths and in the groundmass, together with siderite and kaolinite, in sedimentary ironstones. Amesite occurs as pale green crystals at Chester, Massachusetts, U.S.A., associated with diaspore, magnetite and corundophilite. The known occurrence of greenalite is restricted to the iron formation of the Mesabi Range, Minnesota, but cronstedtite, in the form of brown or black plates of varying size and perfection, is more common.

Serpentine

$Mg_3[Si_2O_5](OH)_4$

MONOCLINIC (−)

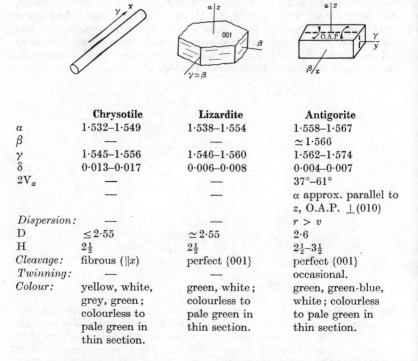

	Chrysotile	**Lizardite**	**Antigorite**
α	1·532–1·549	1·538–1·554	1·558–1·567
β	—	—	$\simeq 1·566$
γ	1·545–1·556	1·546–1·560	1·562–1·574
δ	0·013–0·017	0·006–0·008	0·004–0·007
$2V_\alpha$	—	—	37°–61°
	—	—	α approx. parallel to z, O.A.P. $\perp$(010)
Dispersion:	—	—	$r > v$
D	$\leq 2·55$	$\simeq 2·55$	2·6
H	$2\frac{1}{2}$	$2\frac{1}{2}$	$2\frac{1}{2}$–$3\frac{1}{2}$
Cleavage:	fibrous ($\Vert x$)	perfect {001}	perfect {001}
Twinning:	—	—	occasional.
Colour:	yellow, white, grey, green; colourless to pale green in thin section.	green, white; colourless to pale green in thin section.	green, green-blue, white; colourless to pale green in thin section.

The principal minerals of the serpentine group all have the approximate composition $H_4Mg_3Si_2O_9$, and comparatively little substitution of other ions is found to occur in natural specimens. The most well-known serpentine mineral, chrysotile, often occurs in veins of silky fibres and is the most important source of commercial asbestos. The tensile strength of chrysotile asbestos may be greater than that of amphibole fibres, but where acid as well as heat resistant properties are required the fibres of the latter mineral are generally more suitable. Chrysotile fibres are usually aligned approximately across the veins (although slip fibres also occur) and their length, though generally less than half an inch, can reach as much as six inches. The structure of all serpentines is essentially a tri-octahedral analogue of the kaolinite structure, but there are three principal polymorphic forms: chrysotile, antigorite and lizardite.

STRUCTURE

Although some of the serpentine minerals are fibrous, the structures of all of them are nevertheless of a layered type similar to that found in the kaolinite group. Serpentines differ from the latter minerals, however, in being tri-octahedral, and in the mode of stacking of their fundamental

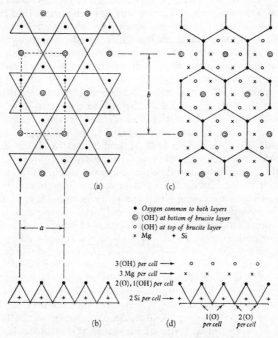

Fig. 84. *Structure of serpentine layer: (a) Tetrahedral Si_2O_5 network in plan. (b) Tetrahedral network as viewed along y axis. (c) Tri-octahedral component of serpentine layer (plan). (d) Serpentine layer as viewed along y axis (after Zussman, J., 1954, Min. Mag., vol. 30, p. 498).*

layers. One part of the serpentine layer is a pseudo-hexagonal network of linked SiO_4 tetrahedra, with approximate parameters a 5·3, b 9·2 Å. All tetrahedra in the sheet point one way, and joined to it is a brucite layer in which, on one side only, two out of every three hydroxyls are replaced by apical oxygens of the SiO_4 tetrahedra (Fig. 84). The perpendicular repeat distance between composite sheets of this type is approximately 7·3 Å.

Consideration of the dimensions of a brucite layer and of a tridymite layer shows that the joining of the two components will probably involve appreciable mis-matching. (When referred to an ortho-hexagonal cell, corresponding parameters are approximately $5\cdot4 \times 9\cdot3$ Å for brucite and $5\cdot0 \times 8\cdot7$ Å for tridymite.) The several ways in which the two components can nevertheless accommodate one another are probably responsible for many of the unusual crystallographic and morphological features of the serpentine minerals. Moreover, as with other layered minerals, various regular and disordered stacking arrangements may occur, giving rise to additional polymorphs. There are three ways in which better matching of the layer components can be achieved, (a) by substitution of larger ions for Si in the tetrahedral layer and/or smaller ions for Mg in the octahedral layer; (b) by distortion of the ideal octahedral and/or tetrahedral networks, probably resulting in a strained configuration which could perhaps be stabilized by strong inter-layer bonding; (c) by curvature of the composite sheet with its tetrahedral component on the inside of the curve. Combinations of the above methods may occur.

Many experimental results point to the existence of serpentine minerals with curved sheet structures. Most chrysotiles appear to have their fundamental layers curved about the x axis only, forming either concentric hollow cylinders or rolls elongated parallel to x. The chrysotile unit cell is two-layered ($Z = 4$) with $c \simeq 14\cdot7$ Å, and $\beta \simeq 93°$ and $90°$ for the two polymorphs clino- and ortho-chrysotile respectively.

Much of the matrix material containing veins of chrysotile is the variety of serpentine called lizardite. This is extremely fine-grained but it is seen under the electron microscope to have platy morphology. In lizardite the unit cell is effectively single-layered and ortho-hexagonal (i.e. $\beta = 90°$), although specimens may consist of a mixture of layers in different orientations. A synthetic serpentine in which all silicon is replaced by germanium has platy morphology and a 6-layered ortho-hexagonal cell: this is an extreme example of the reduction of mis-match by ionic substitution.

Antigorite is another serpentine mineral which is structurally distinct. Antigorite specimens have b dimensions and (001) spacings similar to those of chrysotile and lizardite, but the a dimension of the unit cell is large and in most cases is in the region of 40 Å. An explanation of the large a parameter has been sought in terms of curvature of serpentine layers about y in such a way as to form corrugations parallel to y, the periodicity of corrugation being a (Fig. 85). The fibrous antigorites are sometimes called picrolite, and in these y is consistently parallel to the fibre axis as compared with x in most chrysotiles.

Detailed information about the nature of chrysotile fibres has been deduced from X-ray and electron diffraction patterns, and from numerous electron micrographs. The fundamental fibrils have various diameters but the average outer diameter is of the order of 250 Å and the inner diameter about 100 Å.

X-ray diffraction methods have shown that there is an orientational relationship between serpentine and the product of its thermal decomposition, olivine.

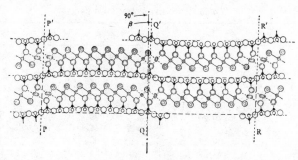

Fig. 85. *Structure of antigorite as viewed along y axis. The curved layers (radius of curvature 75 Å) reverse polarity at PP′, RR′ and near QQ′ (after Kunze, G., 1956, Zeit. Krist., vol. 108, p. 82).*

CHEMISTRY

The chemistry of the serpentine group as a whole is relatively simple in that most natural specimens deviate little from the ideal composition $H_4Mg_3Si_2O_9$. The principal replacements which do occur are of silicon by aluminium, and of magnesium by aluminium, ferrous iron and ferric iron. That nickel may adopt the role of magnesium is shown by the synthesis of a pure nickel serpentine and by the existence of garnierite, a naturally occurring nickel serpentine, but most magnesium serpentines contain little nickel (on average about 0·25 per cent). Minerals with a tri-octahedral kaolinite-type sheet structure which have a very high iron content are known to occur (e.g. greenalite and the non-chloritic variety chamosite, see p. 241), yet little substitution of iron for magnesium occurs in serpentines. Where serpentines are formed in peridotitic rocks, most of the iron present in the original olivine or pyroxene is incorporated in magnetite or haematite impurity and does not enter the serpentine structure.

On heating serpentine in air, olivine is formed at about 600°C:

$$2Mg_3Si_2O_5(OH)_4 \rightarrow 3Mg_2SiO_4 + SiO_2 + 4H_2O$$

The d.t.a. curves for serpentines show an endothermic peak at about 700°–800°C corresponding to the expulsion of 'structural' water, and this is followed usually at about 800°–820°C by an exothermic peak related to the formation of olivine. A weak, broad, low temperature endothermic peak is shown by some serpentines, corresponding to the expulsion of water which is held on the surface of fine-grained material. In chemical analyses of chrysotile some water of this kind may be registered erroneously as H_2O^+ since prolonged heating at 110°C is required to dislodge it completely.

Experimental studies of the system $MgO–SiO_2–H_2O$ (Bowen and Tuttle, 1949) have shown that serpentine can be prepared at temperatures below 500°C and at pressures from 2000 to 40,000 lb/in². Under hydrothermal

Table 22. SERPENTINE ANALYSES

	1.	2.	3.
SiO_2	41·83	41·25	43·60
TiO_2	0·02	0·02	0·01
Al_2O_3	0·30	0·54	1·03
Fe_2O_3	1·29	1·32	0·90
Cr_2O_3	—	—	0·02
FeO	0·08	0·09	0·81
NiO	—	—	0·16
MnO	0·04	0·07	0·04
MgO	41·39	41·84	41·00
CaO	tr.	0·02	0·05
Na_2O	—	—	0·01
K_2O	—	—	0·03
H_2O^+	13·66	13·68	12·18
H_2O^-	1·57	0·97	0·08
Total	100·18	99·80	99·92
α	—	—	1·5615
β	—	—	1·5660
γ	—	—	1·5670
$2V_\alpha$	—	—	$47\frac{1}{2}°$
D	—	—	2·607

NUMBERS OF IONS ON THE BASIS OF 9 (O, OH)

	1.	2.	3.
Si	1·950 $\rbrace$1·95	1·924 $\rbrace$1·95	2·028 $\rbrace$2·03
Al	—	0·030	
Al	0·016	—	0·057
Fe^{+3}	0·045	0·046	0·032
Cr	—	—	—
Fe^{+2}	0·003	0·004	0·032
Mn	0·001 $\rbrace$2·94	0·002 $\rbrace$2·96	0·002 $\rbrace$3·00†
Mg	2·877	2·904	2·863
Ca	—	0·001	0·003
Na	—	—	0·001
K	—	—	0·001
(OH)	4·248	4·250	3·807

1. Chrysotile, cross-fibre vein (metamorphosed limestone occurrence), Transvaal (Brindley, G. W. & Zussman, J., 1957, *Amer. Min.*, vol. 42, p. 461).
2. Lizardite, matrix containing chrysotile vein of analysis no. 1, Transvaal (Deer, W. A., Howie, R. A. & Zussman, J., 1962, *Rock-Forming Minerals*, vol. 3, Longmans).
3. Antigorite, vicinity of Caracas, Venezuela (Hess, H. H., Smith, R. J. & Dengo, G., 1952, *Amer. Min.*, vol. 37, p. 68).

† Includes 0·006 Ni.

conditions above 500°C serpentine breaks down and reacts with forsterite to give talc (see Fig. 79, p. 229). Without the introduction of reagents other than water, serpentinization of olivine has been achieved only at temperatures below 400°C (serpentine + brucite $\rightleftharpoons$ forsterite + vapour), and for iron-bearing olivines serpentinization requires still lower temperatures, and is accompanied by the formation of either magnetite or haematite.

OPTICAL AND PHYSICAL PROPERTIES

The fine-grained nature of most serpentine specimens usually makes a complete optical description impossible. Lizardites have a mean refractive index of between 1·54 and 1·55 while the plate-like grains of antigorite in general have higher refractive indices, but the ranges of refractive index

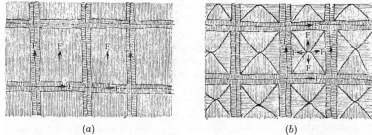

(a)   (b)

Fig. 86. (a) *Illustration of serpentine 'mesh' structure.* (b) *Illustration of serpentine 'hour-glass' structure. F denotes fast vibration direction.*

for antigorites and lizardites are barely separated, so that distinction between them cannot reliably be made by this method. Chrysotile fibres yield different values of refractive index for the directions parallel and perpendicular to their length, and most have positive elongation. A true interpretation of the optical properties of chrysotile may be complicated by the rolling (or at least curvature) of the fundamental serpentine layers, by the random orientation of fibrils about the fibre axis, and also by the phenomenon of form birefringence consequent upon the extremely small particle size.

An exceptional phenomenon is that of 'mesh', 'window' or 'hour glass' structures displayed by many massive serpentine specimens when viewed in thin section between crossed polarizers; examples of these are sketched in Fig. 86. Some features of these structures are no doubt inherited from the morphology of the olivine or pyroxene which has subsequently been serpentinized.

Lizardite occurs mostly in extremely fine-grained aggregates; the massive green serpentine often contains both lizardite and chrysotile, and other mixtures of varieties can also occur.

DISTINGUISHING FEATURES

Antigorites may be distinguished from micas since the latter have higher birefringence. The chlorite delessite has higher refractive indices, and ripidolite is noticeably pleochroic. Serpentine asbestos fibres have γ less than 1·58, while fibres of amphibole asbestos have γ greater than 1·58. When ground in a mortar, amphibole fibres rub to a powder, but chrysotile fibres form a matted aggregate which can only be powdered with great difficulty. Amphibole fibres do not stain with a solution of iodine in glycerol.

PARAGENESIS

The principal occurrences of serpentine minerals are in altered ultrabasic rocks, e.g. dunites, pyroxenites and peridotites. Experimental studies on the system $MgO–SiO_2–H_2O$ have indicated that serpentines cannot form at temperatures above 500°C, and that formation of serpentine by the action of water on forsterite can occur only below 400°C.

The problem of serpentine paragenesis also concerns the conditions favourable for the formation of each of the structural varieties, in particular antigorite. In most cases it appears that antigorite is derived from chrysotile, but shearing stress, in addition to thermal metamorphism may be necessary in order to effect the transformation.

The sequence of events which leads to the formation of chrysotile asbestos fibre veins is not known with certainty although various possibilities have been discussed. The fibre may form at the same time as the matrix serpentine rock from the same parent material, or it may form later. In the latter case the fibres may replace existing matrix material, perhaps starting at a fissure and growing inwards, or they may grow in pre-existing fissures from solutions which permeate the rock.

Large economic deposits of chrysotile asbestos derived from peridotite occur in the Thetford area of Quebec and with a similar paragenesis in South Africa, Russia and elsewhere. Certain serpentines of the Transvaal are examples, however, of a different paragenesis and are found in metamorphosed limestones or dolomites (e.g. Table 22, anals. 1, 2). In the Transvaal, serpentinized dolomitic rocks are associated with diabase sills, and in these circumstances veins of chrysotile, parallel to the contact, are free from magnetite and other impurities except for small amounts of talc. The siliceous dolomite is transformed to forsterite which is subsequently serpentinized.

REFERENCES

BOWEN, N. L. and TUTTLE, O. F. (1949) 'The system $MgO–SiO_2–H_2O$', *Bull. Geol. Soc. Amer.*, vol. 60, p. 439.

HESS, H. H., SMITH, R. J. and DENGO, G. (1952) 'Antigorite from the vicinity of Caracas, Venezuela', *Amer. Min.*, vol. 37, p. 68.

RIODON, P. H. (1955) 'The genesis of asbestos in ultrabasic rocks', *Econ. Geol.*, vol. 50, p. 67.

ROY, D. M. and ROY, R. (1954) 'An experimental study of the formation and properties of synthetic serpentines and related layer silicate minerals', *Amer. Min.*, vol. 39, p. 957.

WILKINSON, J. F. G. (1953) 'Some aspects of the alpine-type serpentinites of Queensland', *Geol. Mag.*, vol. 90, p. 305.

CLAY MINERALS

The constituents of clays may be assigned to one of two groups, those called clay minerals, which by their nature give to the clay its plastic properties, and the others which are accessory 'non-clay minerals'. The clay minerals have a number of characteristics in common. Their structures are, with a few minor exceptions, based on composite layers built from components with tetrahedrally and octahedrally coordinated cations. Most of them occur as platy particles in fine-grained aggregates which when mixed with water yield materials which have varying degrees of plasticity. Chemically, all are hydrous silicates (principally of aluminium or magnesium) which, on heating, lose adsorbed and constitutional water, and at high temperatures yield refractory materials. Important differences among the clay minerals, however, lead to their subdivision into several main groups. The four important layered clay mineral groups are: kandites, illites, smectites and vermiculites. These have characteristic basal spacings of approximately 7 Å, 10 Å, 15 Å and 14·5 Å respectively, but for some categories (the kandite mineral halloysite, smectites and vermiculites) the layer separation is variable since swelling may occur through the intercalation of water or organic liquids, and shrinkage may result from dehydration. The clay minerals attapulgite and sepiolite have chain-like crystal structures and are less common than the layered clay minerals. The particles of clay minerals may be crystalline or amorphous, platy or fibrous, and, though nearly always small, may vary from colloid dimensions to those above the limit of resolution of an ordinary microscope.

Chemical composition may vary according to the extent of replacement of Si, Al and Mg by other cations, the nature and quantity of inter-layer cations, and the water content (see Table 23). The clay minerals vary in their dehydration and breakdown characteristics and in their decomposition products, and they also differ in their cation exchange properties according to the nature of their inter-layer cations and residual surface charges. Their uses are many, some, for example, being particularly suitable as components of drilling muds, some for catalysts in petroleum processing, some for fillers in paper manufacture, and some for ceramic and refractory ware. The clay minerals are the main constituents of one class of sediments (consequently called argillaceous) which on accumulation and compaction yield shales or mudstones. Whether in sedimentary deposits or not the clays are usually products of either weathering or hydrothermal alteration, different clays resulting according to physico-chemical conditions and the nature of parent materials, e.g. feldspars, micas, volcanic glasses, or ferromagnesian minerals.

The principal clay mineral groups are:

1. Kandite group, including kaolinite, dickite and nacrite, halloysite and meta-halloysite.

Table 23. ANALYSES OF CLAY MINERALS

	1.	2.	3.	4.
SiO_2	45·80	44·46	56·91	46·54
TiO_2	—	0·15	0·81	0·17
Al_2O_3	39·55	36·58	18·50	36·37
Fe_2O_3	0·57	0·36	4·99	0·72
FeO	0·18	0·07	0·26	0·36
MnO	—	—	—	0·00
MgO	0·14	0·18	2·07	0·50
CaO	0·41	0·19	1·59	0·22
Na_2O	—	0·01	0·43	0·46
K_2O	0·03	0·51	5·10	8·06
H_2O^+	13·92	13·38	5·98	6·31
H_2O^-	0·17	4·05	2·86	0·52
P_2O_5	—	0·18	—	0·06
Total	100·77	100·12	99·50	100·31
α	1·562	—	—	—
β	1·566	—	—	1·575
γ	1·568	—	—	1·580
D	—	—	--	2·65±0·02

NUMBERS OF IONS

(ON THE BASIS OF 18 (O,OH) FOR 1 AND 2; 24 (O,OH) FOR 3 AND 4)

	1.	2.	3.	4.
Si	3·94	4·01	7·50 ⎫ 8·00	6·00 ⎫ 8·00
Al	—	—	0·50 ⎭	2·00 ⎭
Al	4·01 ⎫	3·89 ⎫	2·38 ⎫	3·53 ⎫
Ti	— ⎪	0·01 ⎪	0·08 ⎪	— ⎪
Fe^{+3}	0·04 ⎪ 4·08	0·02 ⎪ 3·95	0·50 ⎪ 3·62	0·07 ⎪ 3·76
Fe^{+2}	0·01 ⎬	0·01 ⎬	0·03 ⎬	0·04 ⎬
Mn	— ⎪	— ⎪	— ⎪	— ⎪
Mg	0·02 ⎭	0·02 ⎭	0·41 ⎪	0·10 ⎪
Ca	0·04	0·02	0·22 ⎭	0·02 ⎭
Na	—	0·00	0·11 ⎫ 0·97	0·11 ⎫ 1·44
K	0·00	0·06	0·86 ⎭	1·33 ⎭
OH	7·98	8·04	5·26	5·45†

1. Kaolinite, hydrothermal veins of Cu–Pb–Zn ore, Niigata, Japan (Nagasawa, K.. 1953, *Journ. Earth Sci.*, *Nagoya Univ.*, vol. 1, p. 9).
2. White halloysite, Bedford, Indiana (Kerr, P. F., Hamilton, P. K. & Pill, R. J., 1950, *Reference clay minerals. Amer. Petroleum Inst.*, *Res. Proj.* 49, Columbia Univ., New York).
3. Illite, Fithian, Illinois (Kerr, P. F., Hamilton, P. K. & Pill, R. J., 1950, ibid.).
4. Hydromuscovite, Ogofau, Carmarthenshire, South Wales (Brammall, F., Leech, J. G. C. & Bannister, F. A., 1937, *Min. Mag.*, vol. 24, p. 507; includes F 0·02, Li_2O tr.).

† Includes 0·02 F.

Table 23. ANALYSES OF CLAY MINERALS—*continued*

	5.	6.	7.	8.
SiO_2	51·14	45·32	43·62	34·04
TiO_2	—	—	0·00	—
Al_2O_3	19·76	27·84	5·50	15·37
Fe_2O_3	0·83	0·70	0·66	8·01
FeO	—	—	—	—
MnO	—	—	0·06	—
MgO	3·22	0·16	24·32	22·58
CaO	1·62	2·76	2·85	0·00
Na_2O	0·11	0·10	0·08	0·00
K_2O	0·04	0·12	0·04	0·00
H_2O^+	7·99	14·48	5·48	19·93
H_2O^-	14·81	8·16	17·42†	—
P_2O_5	—	—	—	—
Total	99·52	99·64	100·03	99·93
α	—	—	1·490	—
β	—	—	1·531	—
γ	—	1·540	1·534	—
D	—	—	—	—

NUMBERS OF IONS ON THE BASIS OF 20 (O) AND 4 (OH)

	5.		6.		7.		8.		
Si	7·81	}8·00	6·92	}8·00	7·00	}8·00	Si	5·44	}8·00
Al	0·19		1·08		1·00		Al	2·56	
Al	3·37		3·92		0·04		Al	0·32	
Ti	—		—		—		Ti	—	
Fe^{+3}	0·09	}4·19	0·08	}4·04	0·08	}5·94	Fe^{+3}	0·96	}6·00
Fe^{+2}	—						Fe^{+2}	—	
Mn	—		—		0·01		Mn	—	
Mg	0·73		0·04		5·81		Mg	4·72	
Ca	0·27		0·46		0·49		Mg	0·64	
Na	0·03	}0·31	0·04	}0·52	0·02	}0·52	Ca	—	}0·64
K	0·01		0·02		0·01		K	—	
OH	4·00		4·00		4·00		Na	—	
H_2O	2·05		—		0·93		M^{+2}§	0·64	
M‡	0·58		0·98		1·01		H_2O	8·64	
							OH	4·00	

5. Pink montmorillonite from shale, Montmorillon, France (Ross, C. S. & Hendricks, S. B., 1945, *U.S. Geol. Surv.*, *Prof. Paper* 205B).

6. Beidellite, Black Jack Mine, Owyhee Co., Idaho, U.S.A. (Shannon, E. V., 1922, *Proc. U.S. Nat. Mus.*, vol. 62, art. 15, p. 4).

7. Pale blue saponite, lava vesicles, Allt Ribhein, Skye, Scotland (Mackenzie, R. C., 1957, *Min. Mag.*, vol. 31, p. 672).

8. Vermiculite, Kenya (Mathieson, A. McL. & Walker, G. F., 1954, *Amer. Min.*, vol. 39, p. 231).

† At 300°C.
‡ M = total charge on inter-layer cations.
§ M^{+2} = No of inter-layer cations (or equivalents).

	Kandites	Illites	Smectites	Vermiculites
Structure type:	1:1 tetrahedral and octahedral components (diphormic)	2:1 (triphormic)	2:1 (triphormic)	2:1 (triphormic)
Octahedral component:	di-octahedral	mostly di-octahedral	di- or tri-octahedral	mostly tri-octahedral
Principal inter-layer cations:	nil	K	Ca, Na	Mg
Inter-layer water:	only in halloysite (one layer water mols.)	some in hydromuscovite	Ca, two layers; Na, one layer water mols.	two layers
Basal spacing:	7·1 Å (10 Å in halloysite)	10 Å	variable; most $\simeq 15$ Å (for Ca)	variable; 14·4 Å when fully hydrated
Glycol:	taken up by halloysite only	no effect	takes two layers glycol, 17 Å	takes one layer glycol, 14 Å
Chemical formula:	$Al_4Si_4O_{10}(OH)_8$, little variation	$K_{1·0-1·5}Al_4(Si,Al)O_{20}(OH)_4$	$M^+_{0·66}(Y^{+3}, Y^{+2})_{4-6}(Si,Al)_8O_{20}(OH)_4 \cdot nH_2O$	$M^{+2}_{0·66}(Y^{+3}, Y^{+3})_6(Si,Al)_8O_{20}(OH)_4 \cdot 8H_2O$
Acids:	kaolinite scarcely soluble in dil. acids	readily attacked	attacked	readily attacked
Heating 200°C:	halloysite collapsed to 7·4 Å, others unchanged	no marked change	collapse to approx. 10 Å	exfoliation; shrinkage of layer spacing
Heating 650°C:	kaolinite → metakaolinite 7 Å. dickite → metadickite strong 14 Å	10 Å	9·6–10 Å	collapse to 9 Å
Optics α	1·55–1·56	1·54–1·57	1·48–1·51	1·52–1·57
γ	1·56–1·57	1·57–1·61	1·50–1·53	1·54–1·58
δ	$\simeq 0·006$	$\simeq 0·03$	0·01–0·02	0·02–0·03
2V	24°–50°	<10°	variable	<10°
Paragenesis:	alteration of acid rocks, feldspars, etc. Acidic conditions	alteration of micas, feldspars, etc. Alkaline conditions. High Al and K concentrations favourable	alteration of basic rocks, volcanic material. Alkaline conditions. Availability of Mg and Ca, deficiency of K	alteration of biotite flakes or of volcanic material, chlorites, hornblende, etc.

2. Illite group, including illite, hydro-micas, phengite, brammallite, glauconite and celadonite.
3. Smectite group, including montmorillonite, nontronite, hectorite, saponite and sauconite.
4. Vermiculite.
5. Palygorskite group, including palygorskite, attapulgite and sepiolite.

All except the fifth group are discussed in the following pages. Table 24 lists very briefly some of the important characteristics of the various clay mineral groups.

Kaolinite group (Kandites) $\qquad$ $Al_4[Si_4O_{10}](OH)_8$

TRICLINIC OR MONOCLINIC (−)

α 1·553–1·565†
β 1·559–1·569
γ 1·560–1·570
$\delta \simeq 0·006$
$2V_\alpha$ 24°–50°
$\beta : x = 1°–3\frac{1}{2}°, \gamma = y$, O.A.P. $\perp$(010)
Dispersion: weak, $r > v$. D 2·61–2·68.
H $2–2\frac{1}{2}$.

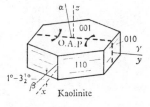

Kaolinite

Cleavage: {001} perfect.
Twinning: Rare.
Colour: White, sometimes with reddish, brownish or bluish tints; colourless in thin section.
Pleochroism: Very slight. Least absorption for vibration direction perpendicular to cleavage.

Kaolinite is the most important member of the kandite group; dickite and nacrite are rarer polymorphs, and halloysite is a hydrated form.

STRUCTURE

The fundamental unit of the kaolinite structure is an extended sheet which can be regarded as having two constituents. A layer of composition $(Si_4O_{10})^{-4}$ is formed by the linkage of SiO_4 tetrahedra in a hexagonal array, the bases of tetrahedra being approximately coplanar and their vertices all pointing in one direction. The apical oxygens, together with some additional $(OH)^-$ ions located over the centres of hexagons, form the base of a gibbsite-type layer of composition $(OH)_6–Al_4–(OH)_2O_4$. Plan and elevation views of this composite $Al_4Si_4O_{10}(OH)_8$ layer are shown in Figs. 87 and 88. Only two out of each set of three available sites are occupied by Al ions.

The three alternative sets of two $[Al]^6$ sites which may be occupied are equivalent if only one ideal layer is considered, but when a second layer is superimposed, different structures are produced according to the direction of its displacement with respect to the first. Successive layers of kaolinite are superimposed so that oxygens at the base of one are paired by close approach to hydroxyl ions at the top of its neighbour. This results in a single-layered triclinic unit cell with a 5·15, b 8·95, c 7·39 Å, α 91·8°, β 104·8°, γ 90°, Z = 1. In an ideal structure α and β would be 90° and 103·5° respectively as a result of layer displacements of zero along y and $a/3$ along x, the

† These values all refer to kaolinite *sensu stricto*.

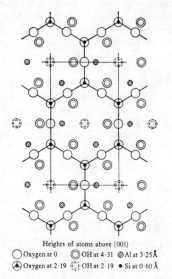

Heights of atoms above (001)

◯ Oxygen at 0   ◎ OH at 4·31   ⊘ Al at 3·25Å

✦ Oxygen at 2·19   ⬚ OH at 2·19   ● Si at 0·60 Å

Fig. 87. *Projection of idealized kaolinite layer on (001) (after Brindley, G. W. & Robinson, K., 1946, Min. Mag., vol. 27, p. 242).*

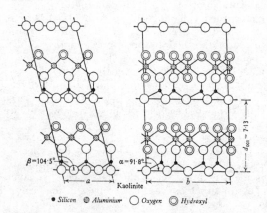

$\beta = 104\cdot5°$ $\alpha = 91\cdot8°$

a Kaolinite b $d_{001} = 7\cdot13$

● *Silicon*   ⊘ *Aluminium*   ◯ *Oxygen*   ◎ *Hydroxyl*

Fig. 88. *The structure of kaolinite as viewed along y and x axes, showing the stacking of successive layers in the x and y directions respectively (after Brindley, G. W., 1951, X-ray identification and crystal structures of clay minerals. Min. Soc., London).*

deviations from these values are a result of distortions in the kaolinite layer.

The minerals dickite and nacrite are chemically identical to kaolinite but have their layers stacked in different regular sequences. Thus dickite has a 2-layered and nacrite a 6-layered monoclinic cell. Halloysite, with formula $Al_4Si_4(OH)_8O_{10} \cdot 8H_2O$, has a single layer of water molecules between its structural sheets; consequently stacking is disordered and the inter-layer distance (d_{001}) is increased from approximately 7·2 Å to 10 Å. In halloysite it is probable that the sandwiched water molecules have a specific arrangement with respect to the sheets of oxygens or hydroxyl ions on either side, forming hydrogen bonds with them. The inter-layer water of halloysite may be replaced by glycol which causes an increase in the d_{001} spacing from 10 Å to about 11 Å; other kandites show no swelling property.

CHEMISTRY

The chemical composition of kaolinite itself is subject to little variation. Analyses show that small amounts of various ions may substitute in the structure, but because of the fine-grained nature of clays it is difficult to be certain that all impurities have been eliminated, so that the limits of substitution cannot easily be defined. While the formula of kaolinite can be written in terms of oxides as $Al_2O_3 \cdot 2SiO_2 \cdot 2H_2O$, that of halloysite is ideally $Al_2O_3 \cdot 2SiO_2 \cdot 4H_2O$. In this fully hydrated form of halloysite, $2H_2O$ corresponds to structural (OH) ions and the remainder occurs as inter-layer water. Most, if not all, of the inter-layer water is not recorded in the H_2O^+ values presented in chemical analyses but appears as H_2O^-. Although minerals which structurally are tri-octahedral analogues of kaolinite (e.g. serpentine, amesite, chamosite, cronstedtite) are well known, substitution in kaolinite of (Mg,Fe) for Al, with or without Al for Si, leading towards tri-octahedral composition, is negligible.

Kaolinite has a low cation exchange capacity (about 10 m.eq/100 gm) compared with other clays (e.g. illite 20 and montmorillonite 100 m.eq/100 gm): for halloysite the value is about 40 m.eq/100 gm. While kaolinite shows a lower cation exchange capacity than most clay minerals, its anion exchange capacity is higher and may be attributed to the presence of replaceable $(OH)^-$ ions on the outside of the structural sheets. The ability of kaolinite to fix phosphate ions is of great importance in soil science.

Differential thermal analysis and dehydration experiments are widely used for the characterization and identification of clays. The dehydration of halloysite proceeds in a number of stages. Some of its adsorbed water (surface and interlayer) is lost on heating to 110°C as with any other mineral, but the remainder comes off gradually and is not completely expelled until about 400°C. For kaolinite, little or no surface adsorbed water is present and most of the dehydration (loss of constitutional OH) takes place between 400° and 525°C, and this is responsible for an endothermic peak in its d.t.a. pattern. For dickite and nacrite this peak occurs at about 100°C higher and this may be largely a result of greater particle size, rather than an indication of higher stability.

When the kaolinite minerals are heated so that all water molecules and (OH) ions are driven off (a stage which is almost reached by about 650°C for the majority of specimens and is complete by 800°C for all), the products are called meta-kaolinite, meta-dickite, etc. When kaolinite minerals are heated beyond 800°C their layered structures are further disrupted and cannot be reconstituted by rehydration. The final products of decomposition are mullite and cristobalite, with a defect spinel phase occurring at an intermediate stage.

The hydrothermal synthesis of kaolinite, and in some cases dickite and nacrite, has been achieved commencing with gels of suitable Al_2O_3–SiO_2 or $Al(OH)_3$–SiO_2 composition at temperatures between 250° and 400°C. All kaolinite minerals decompose at approximately 400°C, throughout the range of pressures 2500 to 25,000 lb/in². The main product of the hydrothermal decomposition of kaolinite is hydralsite, approximate formula $2Al_2O_3 \cdot 2SiO_2 \cdot H_2O$, which has not been found in nature. In hydrothermal equilibrium conditions above 575°C kaolinite is completely converted to mullite and cristobalite.

OPTICAL AND PHYSICAL PROPERTIES

The kaolinite minerals may occur in compact massive blocks, in vermiform or granular aggregates, as radiating platelets, or as piles of platelets (or 'books'), the latter form being particularly common for dickite. The perfect {001} cleavage yields flexible but inelastic plates which are sometimes large enough for determination of optical properties. Such measurements must, however, be interpreted with care since they may be considerably affected by the presence of impurities and/or adsorbed water. Penetration of the crystals by organic liquid immersion media changes the refractive indices of some clay minerals but does not affect kaolinite or meta-halloysite. Birefringence measurements, moreover, may vary according to the immersion liquid used, indicating that the particles are small enough for form birefringence to be superimposed upon true birefringence. For the fine-grained specimens only an average refractive index can be measured, which for halloysite (approx. 1·530) is lower than for kaolinite. In all of the crystalline varieties γ is parallel to y and the optic plane perpendicular to (010). Electron micrographs of kaolinite show a high proportion of particles with well defined straight edges and sometimes thin elongated plates with prominent 60° angles. Halloysite has a fibrous rather than platy morphology and moreover the fibres, unlike those of amphibole asbestos, appear in electron micrographs to be tubular or scroll-like.

The density of a clay mineral cannot easily be determined with precision since it varies considerably with state of hydration. For kaolinite, values of about 2·63 gm/cm³ are usually obtained and are reproducible, but halloysites may vary from 2·55 gm/cm³ for dehydrated material to 2·0 gm/cm³, according to water content. The density of dickite and of nacrite is approximately 2·60 gm/cm³ which is close to the theoretical value. The plastic properties of kaolinite and other clay minerals when mixed with water are well known, but are not fully understood. There is an optimum amount of water required to produce maximum plasticity and various views are held as to the number of layers of water molecules which are adsorbed on clay particles. There is evidence that the water molecules are arranged in a definite pattern rather than in a disordered liquid state, and that they are probably linked by hydrogen bonds to each other and to the oxygen and hydroxyl ions on the outsides of kaolinite layers : the adsorbed water is said to be more dense and more viscous than ordinary water.

DISTINGUISHING FEATURES

Optical properties, if available, can be used to distinguish kaolinite from dickite and nacrite. Dickite is optically positive, and has a lower refractive index with $\beta : x = 14°–20°$; nacrite is negative but also has a greater extinction angle $\beta : x$. Sericite and montmorillonite have greater birefringence and the latter has a lower refractive index. X-ray powder patterns of untreated and of heated and glycollated specimens may, however, be necessary, in conjunction with d.t.a., staining, and other tests, in order to distinguish fine-grained kaolinite minerals from each other and from other clay and non-clay layered minerals (Grim, 1953; Mackenzie, 1957; Brown, 1961).

PARAGENESIS

Probably the most common of the clay minerals are those of the kaolinite group and they are formed (often accompanied by quartz, iron oxides, pyrite, siderite and muscovite and by other clay minerals) principally by the hydrothermal alteration or weathering of feldspars, feldspathoids and other silicates.

Experimental work indicates that at low temperatures and pressures, acid conditions favour kaolinite formation, and alkaline conditions promote the formation of smectites or, if sufficient potassium is present, mica (above about 400°C at moderate pressures pyrophyllite is formed). Field occurrences indicate that the rocks which alter to kaolinite are usually the more acid types (granites, quartz diorites, etc.) while calcium- or sodium-rich rocks generally yield montmorillonite. The kaolinite produced by alteration sometimes occurs in situ (e.g. the hydrothermal deposits of Cornish kaolin), but more often is a product of weathering and transportation. Again non-alkaline conditions are required for kaolinite formation, and weathering by alkaline rather than acid (or pure) water generally yields montmorillonite.

REFERENCES

BROWN, G. (Editor) (1961) *The X-ray identification and crystal structures of clay minerals*, Min. Soc., London.
GRIM, R. E. (1953) *Clay Mineralogy*, McGraw Hill, New York.
MACKENZIE, R. C. (Editor) (1957) *The differential thermal investigation of clays*, Min. Soc., London.

Illite

$$K_{1-1\cdot5}Al_4[Si_{7-6\cdot5}Al_{1-1\cdot5}O_{20}](OH)_4$$

MONOCLINIC $(-)$

α $1\cdot54-1\cdot57$
β $1\cdot57-1\cdot61$
γ $1\cdot57-1\cdot61$
$\delta \simeq 0\cdot03$

$2V_\alpha$ generally less than $10°$ α approximately $\perp(001)$.
D $2\cdot6-2\cdot9$.   H $1-2$.
Cleavage: {001} perfect.
Colour: White and various pale colours; colourless in thin section.

Illites, smectites and vermiculites are all clay minerals which are structurally related to the micas, but closest similarity to the micas is shown by the illite group of minerals. Most illites are di-octahedral, like muscovite, but some are tri-octahedral like biotite. The chemical formula most commonly assigned to illite is of the form $K_yAl_4(Si_{8-y},Al_y)O_{20}(OH)_4$ where y is less than 2 and is usually between 1 and $1\cdot5$. Thus illite differs from muscovite in having more silica and less potassium; clay minerals which are similar to illite, but which differ from muscovite in other ways, are conveniently regarded as members of the illite group.

STRUCTURE

The structure of illite is essentially that of a mica in that it contains layers with a plane of octahedrally coordinated cations sandwiched between two inward pointing sheets of linked $(Si,Al)O_4$ tetrahedra. The mica structure (which consists of composite sheets of this type alternating with layers of potassium ions) has been more fully described on page 193. A single layer of a di-octahedral illite differs from muscovite only in the chemical substituents occupying the well defined atomic sites, but these differences lead to important structural variations when the superposition of layers is considered. Most of the illite minerals have fewer inter-layer cations than muscovite so that forces between layers are weaker and there is consequently less regularity of stacking. The most common polymorph for illites therefore has a disordered one-layered monoclinic cell (1Md, see p. 195), and its X-ray powder pattern is similar to that of a mica but has a few broad hk diffraction bands replacing the sharp hkl reflections given by a well-ordered crystal). The unit cell of illite has a $5\cdot2$, b $9\cdot0$ Å, Z = 1, and the interlayer repeat distance is about 10 Å.

Basal reflections are unaffected by stacking irregularities, so that illites may be recognized by their strong 10 Å reflection and successive higher orders of varying intensity. Since illites generally contain little or no inter-layer water and are not penetrated by organic liquids the basal reflections are unaffected by heating to 500°C, and an illite which is uncontaminated by a smectite, vermiculite, or halloysite, should show no swelling charac-teristics when treated with glycol.

Brammallite is a less common illite in which sodium is the inter-layer cation.

CHEMISTRY

Table 25 illustrates some of the chemical variations which could occur in specimens loosely described as di-octahedral illitic clay material. It seems reasonable to include all of these categories (except muscovite) in the 'illite group' and the name illite (e.g. Table 23, anal. 3) may itself be reserved for the specimens in which the principal substitutions are of type 3, i.e. substitution of Si for Al and a deficit of potassium as compared with muscovite.

Table 25. PRINCIPAL VARIATIONS IN ILLITE COMPOSITION
WITH REFERENCE TO MUSCOVITE

	X	$[Y]^6$	$[Z]^4$	$(OH)^-$	$(O)^{-2}$
1. Muscovite	K_2	Al_4	Si_6Al_2	4	20
2. (a)⎫ Hydro-	$[K, (H_3O)^+]_2$	Al_4	Si_6Al_2	4	20
(b)⎭ muscovite	K_{2-x}	Al_4	Si_6Al_2	$4+x$	$20-x$
3. Illite	K_{2-x}	Al_4	$Si_{6+x}Al_{2-x}$	4	20
4. Phengite	K_2	$Al_{4-x}(Mg, Fe^{+2})_x$	$Si_{6+x}Al_{2-x}$	4	20

An important member of the illite group is phengite, in which potassium is not deficient and excess silica is compensated by replacement of $[Al]^6$ by $[Mg, Fe^{+2}]^6$. For this variety the name phengite (see p. 202) is preferred to sericite which has a less specific significance. Thus the term sericite, generally used to describe a fine-grained white mica which may be musco-vite or paragonite, is also used for specimens which deviate from the muscovite composition in any or all of the ways shown in Table 25, and often refers to mixed-layered aggregates.

The presence of a considerable number of inter-layer potassium ions in illites prevents the entry into the structure not only of water and organic liquids but also other cations, so that illites have a low cation exchange capacity. The exchange that does take place is thought to do so largely at crystal edges (as for kaolinite) where there are unsatisfied valencies. The cation exchange capacity of illites is generally between 10 and 40 m.eq/100 gm and thus is greater than that for most kaolinites but less than those for halloysite, montmorillonite and vermiculite. The illites in soils, however, are often degraded forms deficient in potassium, and these have a high capacity to take up and fix potassium from fertilizing salts.

The dehydration of illites, whether di- or tri-octahedral, proceeds in a number of stages. Most of the water adsorbed on the surface of particles and the small amount which may be inter-layered with illite sheets comes off rapidly below 110°C, and the remainder more slowly between 110° and 350°C. Water formed by expulsion of (OH)⁻ ions comes off rapidly at first between 350° and 600°C, but a small amount remains and is given off on further heating. By contrast, micas lose little or no water at the lower temperatures and their constitutional water from (OH)⁻ ions is driven off at somewhat higher temperatures than that of illite, probably because of larger particle size.

Differential thermal analysis curves of illite show three endothermic peaks, one between 100°–200°C representing loss of loosely held water, one at 550°–650°C corresponding to loss of (OH)⁻, and one at 850°–950°C corresponding to disruption of the remaining structure. This is followed by an exothermic peak at 900°–1000°C when spinel is formed.

Syntheses of illites have rarely been reported, though it is likely that in experiments to form muscovite some of the products may have been of the illite type. Illite has been produced from montmorillonite in the laboratory by treatment with a $1N$ KCl solution and then boiling in a $1N$ KOH solution, and by other methods; this reaction may have considerable relevance to the process of potassium fixation in soils.

OPTICAL AND PHYSICAL PROPERTIES

Illite specimens show a rather wide variation of refractive indices owing to the various substitutions possible (refractive indices increase with iron content), the degree of hydration, and interlayering with other minerals. The refractive indices exhibited are a little below those of the corresponding micas muscovite and biotite. Measurement of optical properties generally cannot be made with great accuracy because of the extremely small size of illite particles.

Pure illites are colourless, but impurities such as fine-grained iron oxides or hydroxides may colour them yellow, green, or brown, etc., and they may show slight pleochroism. Electron micrographs of illites exhibit very few well-formed particles, the irregularity of shapes being similar to that shown by montmorillonites. Densities, like refractive indices, cannot be precisely defined since they are affected by degree of hydration, and by the presence of fine-grained impurities, but generally they are a little lower than those of corresponding micas.

DISTINGUISHING FEATURES

The extremely fine-grained nature of most illite specimens makes identification by optical methods difficult. Average refractive indices are similar to those for corresponding micas, but 2V is generally smaller than that of muscovite. Reliable identification can only be achieved by a combination of chemical analysis, d.t.a., and X-ray diffraction applied to samples before and after treatment by heat and with organic liquids.

PARAGENESIS

Illites are the dominant clay minerals in shales and mudstones, and they also occur in other sediments such as limestones. The illites of sediments may have been deposited as such after their formation by weathering of silicates, principally feldspars, but in some occurrences they are derived by alteration of other clay minerals during diagenesis. Illites may also occur through the degradation of muscovite, or in appropriate conditions by recrystallization of colloidal sediments. Illites may also have a hydrothermal origin and they are often found in alteration zones around hot springs or metalliferous veins. Laboratory experiments suggest that for both hydrothermal and sedimentary occurrences the formation of illite is generally favoured by alkaline conditions and by high concentrations of aluminium and potassium.

REFERENCES

BROWN, G. (Editor) (1961) *The X-ray identification and crystal structures of clay minerals*, Min. Soc., London.

MACKENZIE, R. C. (1957) 'The illite in some Old Red Sandstone soils and sediments', *Min. Mag.*, vol. 31, p. 681.

YODER, H. S. and EUGSTER, H. P. (1955) 'Synthetic and natural muscovites', *Geochim. et Cosmochim. Acta*, vol. 8, p. 225.

Montmorillonite Group (Smectites)

$$(\tfrac{1}{2}Ca,Na)_{0.7}(Al,Mg,Fe)_4[(Si,Al)_8O_{20}](OH)_4 \cdot nH_2O$$

MONOCLINIC (−)

α 1·48–1·61
β 1·50–1·64
γ 1·50–1·64
δ 0·01–0·04
$2V_\alpha$ mostly small
α approximately $\perp$(001), $\beta = y$, O.A.P. (010)
D variable, 2–3. H 1–2.
Cleavage: {001} perfect.

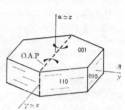

Montmorillonite, Beidellite, Nontronite

Colour: Commonly white, yellow or green; colourless, yellow, green in thin section.

The name montmorillonite (after Montmorillon, Vienne, France) was originally applied to a clay mineral with composition similar to that of pyrophyllite except for the presence of excess water, $Al_4Si_8O_{20}(OH)_4 \cdot nH_2O$. Chemical variation of this basic formula yields a group of clay minerals which are related by a common structure and by similarity of chemical and physical properties, and are therefore classed as the 'montmorillonite group'. According to present usage one member of this group is itself called montmorillonite and has the formula $(Na)_{0.7}(Al_{3.3}Mg_{0.7})Si_8O_{20}(OH)_4 \cdot nH_2O$. An alternative term once used for this type of clay is 'smectite', and this has now been revived to describe the group as a whole (Mackenzie, 1957a), which contains the following principal members: montmorillonite, beidellite, nontronite, saponite, hectorite and sauconite. The latter three are tri-octahedral smectites which are based on the formula and structure of talc rather than pyrophyllite. All are 'swelling' clay minerals in that they can take up water or organic liquids between their structural layers, and all show marked cation exchange properties. They are useful, as are most other clay minerals, in the preparation of ceramics, drilling muds, paper, rubber, paints and moulding sands.

STRUCTURE

The structure is based upon that of pyrophyllite (Fig. 78, p. 225). The latter mineral consists of superimposed layers each of which contains a plane of Al ions sandwiched between two inward pointing sheets of linked SiO_4 tetrahedra. The central section may be regarded as a layer of gibbsite, $Al_2(OH)_6$, in which two out of every three (OH) ions are replaced by apical oxygens of an Si_4O_{10} pseudo-hexagonal network. In pyrophyllite itself there is no replacement of either Si or Al ions, so that the composite sheets are electrically neutral and there are no cations between them. In smectites the charge balance is upset by substitutions in both octahedral and tetra-hedral sites and is redressed by the presence of a small number of interlayer cations, usually Na or Ca. The repeat distances along orthogonal axes within the structural layers are $a \simeq 5 \cdot 2$, $b \simeq 9 \cdot 1$ Å $(b \simeq a\sqrt{3})$.

For pyrophyllite the inter-layer spacing d_{001} is approximately 8·9 Å and for the micas and illites it is about 10 Å. In smectites the basal spacing can vary over a wide range with a minimum, corresponding to the fully collapsed state, at about 9·6 Å. Water is readily adsorbed between the structural layers; it enters as integral numbers of complete layers of water molecules arranged in a specific manner with relation to their neighbouring tetrahedral networks. The number of layers of water molecules is influenced to some extent by the nature of the inter-layer cation, calcium mont-morillonites (the most common in nature) usually having two layers per cell and $d_{001} \simeq 15 \cdot 5$ Å, and the sodium varieties having one $(d_{001} \simeq 12 \cdot 5$ Å$)$, two (15·5 Å), three (19 Å) or more layers per cell. Since specimens may contain randomly mixed cells with various water contents the range of effective basal spacings that may be recorded is continuous between 10 and about 21 Å, and can vary with humidity and the nature of the cation. The X-ray powder patterns of dehydrated montmorillonite and saponite are similar to those of pyrophyllite and talc respectively.

The inter-layer spaces in smectites can be penetrated not only by water and exchange cations but also by certain organic cations and by various organic liquids. Polar organic liquids such as glycol are adsorbed in integral numbers of layers and yield regular layer sequences with characteristic basal spacings. The only other common swelling clay constituents are halloysite, which expands with glycerol to about 11 Å, and vermiculite to 14 Å.

On heating at between 100° and 200°C smectites lose their interlamellar water reversibly, and the basal spacing shifts from between 12 and 15 Å to about 10 Å. With heating at 500°C, d_{001} is reduced further to between 9·6 and 10 Å depending upon the nature of the inter-layer cation.

Many clay samples (e.g. bentonites) prove to be mixtures of more than one clay mineral which may be either regularly or randomly interstratified, and the two cases can be distinguished by the X-ray powder pattern.

CHEMISTRY

The chemical formulae of all smectites are similar to those of either pyrophyllite or talc in which substitutions in octahedral or tetrahedral sites by ions of lower valency are accompanied by the addition of an equivalent number of inter-layer cations. The average extent of such substitution requires about 0·66 additional monovalent cations (or their equivalent) per formula unit, and these ions are in general exchangeable. The smectites are subdivided according to the substitutions involved and these are illustrated in an idealized manner in Table 26. Thus in mont-morillonite and hectorite substitution is almost entirely in the Y sites, while in beidellite and saponite it takes place principally in the Z sites.

Substitutions other than those shown in Table 26 commonly occur. Tetrahedral positions may be occupied by small numbers of titanium ions (but small amounts of rutile impurities are often present) and possibly also by ferric ions; in addition to the constituents already mentioned, octahedral sites may contain minor amounts of Fe^{+2}, Mn and Ni. Furthermore, intermediates may exist possessing features of two or more of the groups of Table 26. Thus, montmorillonite often has some replacement of Si by Al,

Table 26. SMECTITES, PYROPHYLLITE AND TALC

	Z	Y	X (exchange cations)
Di-octahedral			
Pyrophyllite	Si_8	Al_4	—
Montmorillonite	Si_8	$Al_{3.34}Mg_{0.66}$	$(\frac{1}{2}Ca,Na)_{0.66}$
Beidellite	$Si_{7.34}Al_{0.66}$	Al_4	$(\frac{1}{2}Ca,Na)_{0.66}$
Nontronite	$Si_{7.34}Al_{0.66}$	Fe_4^{+3}	$(\frac{1}{2}Ca,Na)_{0.66}$
Tri-octahedral			
Talc	Si_8	Mg_6	—
Saponite	$Si_{7.34}Al_{0.66}$	Mg_6	$(\frac{1}{2}Ca,Na)_{0.66}$
Hectorite	Si_8	$Mg_{5.34}Li_{0.66}$	$(\frac{1}{2}Ca,Na)_{0.66}$
Sauconite	$Si_{6.7}Al_{1.3}$	$Zn_{4-5}(Mg, Al, Fe^{+3})_{2-1}$	$(\frac{1}{2}Ca,Na)_{0.66}$

and there is usually some Mg in octahedral coordination in beidellite and in nontronite, so that montmorillonite–beidellite–nontronite appear to form a continuous series. The total number of Y ions lies within the ranges 4·00–4·44 and 5·76–6·00 and it is unlikely that there is complete solid solution between the di- and tri-octahedral members. Saponite (Table 23, anal. 7) usually contains some trivalent ions in Y sites and has correspondingly more Al replacing Si; hectorite usually has some replacement of (OH) by F.

Cation exchange. The most commonly occurring exchangeable cations are sodium and calcium, but smectites can be prepared containing potassium, caesium, strontium, magnesium, hydrogen and other inter-layer cations which are to varying degrees exchangeable. In several analyses of di-octahedral smectites the total of Y ions exceeds four and it is likely that some of the Mg ions occupy inter-layer sites and contribute to the cation exchange capacity. The inter-layer cations of smectites may be already in the specimen when it is formed, or may be the result of subsequent exchange, since some cations are more readily substituted than others. The cation exchange capacity is usually in the range 80–150 m.eq./100 gm but varies with particle size and the nature of the cation, usually being greater for Ca than for Na. Generally the replacing power of ions with higher valency is greater and their replaceability is less, so that calcium is more firmly held. The principal cause of cation exchange in smectites is the unbalance of charge in the fundamental layers, and not the presence of unsatisfied surface valencies.

Inter-layer molecules. The amount of inter-layer water adsorbed varies according to the type of smectite, the nature of the inter-layer cations and the physical conditions. Calcium smectites usually take up two layers of water molecules in each space, while the amount taken by sodium compounds appears to be continuously variable, and in general they show a greater swelling capacity. Some of the inter-layer water may be regarded as molecules of water of hydration surrounding the replaceable cations Various organic molecules can also be accommodated in inter-layer spaces, and because of this smectites (the principal constituent of fuller's earths) are extensively used as decolorizing agents, for purifying fats and oils, and in the refinement of petroleum.

Thermal effects. On heating, the inter-layer water of smectites is lost mostly between 100° and 250°C but some remains to about 300°C at which temperature slow loss of constitutional (OH) water begins. Rapid loss of (OH) water takes place at about 500°C and is complete at about 750°C. The dehydration of montmorillonite is at least partly reversible as long as it is not taken to completion, and even after heating to 600°C some inter-layer water can be regained slowly.

Differential thermal analysis curves of smectites show considerable variations, but in general they display at least one endothermic peak at low temperatures corresponding to the loss of inter-layer water, and another one (or two) corresponding to loss of (OH) water with a maximum at about 700°C.

Experimental. Smectites have been synthesized in many different ways, e.g. from mixtures of oxides and water heated under pressure, by leaching sodium silicate and sodium aluminate with $MgCl_2$, and by boiling $MgCl_2$ and hydrated silica with $Ca(OH)_2$ or NaOH. In general the formation of montmorillonite may be said to be favoured by alkaline conditions and the presence of magnesium.

OPTICAL AND PHYSICAL PROPERTIES

Smectites occur most commonly in fine-grained aggregates which may be vermiform, lamellar or spherulitic. Sometimes the constituents of such aggregates are well oriented and give the appearance of well-formed crystals, but examination under the electron microscope reveals that the fundamental particles are extremely thin platelets, which for montmorillonite and saponite are mostly irregular in outline. The most common colours of montmorillonites are pink, buff, grey or light brown, and many are white, while nontronites are usually bright green. Those which are coloured show distinct pleochroism, the colours for nontronite being green parallel to (001), and yellow perpendicular to (001). Because of their fine-grained nature, and because their optical properties are affected by hydration and sometimes by the immersion liquid as well as by compositional changes, only approximate ranges of optical constants are given for smectites in Table 27.

Table 27. OPTICAL PROPERTIES OF SMECTITES

	α	$\beta=\gamma$	δ	$2V_\alpha$
Montmorillonite-beidellite series	1·48–1·57	1·50–1·60	0·02–0·03	0°–30°
Nontronite	1·56–1·61	1·57–1·64	0·03–0·045	25°–70°
Saponite	1·48–1·53	1·50–1·59	0·01–0·036	moderate
Hectorite	$\simeq 1·49$	$\simeq 1·52$	$\simeq 0·03$	small
Sauconite	1·55–1·58	1·59–1·62	0·03–0·04	small

Refractive indices are only slightly influenced by the substitutions Si–Al and Al–Mg, but are considerably dependent upon iron content. All smectites are optically negative, but $2V_\alpha$ is variable over a wide range. Refractive indices increase with loss of inter-layer water, and specific gravities are also affected considerably by degree of hydration.

DISTINGUISHING FEATURES

The average refractive indices for smectites are similar to those for illites and kaolinites, but minerals of the kaolinite group have lower birefringence than most smectites, and illites generally have higher birefringence. Dehydrated montmorillonites and saponites which have low iron content have refractive indices similar to those of pyrophyllite and talc respectively but birefringences are lower. Optical methods alone are in general not reliable for the identification of smectites and it is usually necessary to observe several other properties, such as d.t.a. curves, dehydration curves and X-ray powder patterns before and after treatment by heating and by organic liquids.

PARAGENESIS

Montmorillonite and beidellite are the principal constituents of bentonite clay deposits. These have been formed by the alteration of eruptive igneous rocks, usually tuffs and volcanic ash, and contain in addition varying amounts of cristobalite, zeolites, biotite, quartz, feldspar, zircon, etc. Except for the Wyoming bentonites, calcium rather than sodium is the naturally occurring exchange cation. 'Fuller's earth' is a name given to a clay which has a high absorptive capacity (see p. 267); its principal clay mineral constituent is usually montmorillonite. Most of the fuller's earth in Europe has been produced by weathering of basic igneous rocks, or occurs in a sedimentary product derived from them. The name is also used in England to denote a particular stratigraphical formation. Smectites also occur as hydrothermal alteration products around metalliferous veins or deposits, and near hot springs and geysers.

Smectites are widely found (often mixed with illites) in soils and in shales which have resulted from the weathering of basic rocks. Probably the most important single factor in determining that montmorillonite shall form in any of the environments mentioned above is the availability of sufficient magnesium. Thus montmorillonite results from the weathering of basic rocks mainly in conditions of poor drainage when magnesium is not removed. In good drainage conditions magnesium is leached and kaolinite results. Other factors which favour the formation of smectites are an alkaline environment, availability of calcium, and paucity of potassium. Alteration of basic igneous rocks yields mostly montmorillonite, and acid rocks tend to yield illites unless Mg and Ca are high and K low in concentration.

Saponite occurs mainly associated with mineral veins, but also in amygdaloidal cavities in basalt (e.g. Table 23, anal. 7). Nontronite is found both in mineral veins (often with opal and quartz) and as an alteration product of volcanic glasses.

REFERENCES

BROWN, G. (Editor) (1961) *The X-ray identification and crystal structures of clay minerals*, Min. Soc., London.

MACEWAN, D. M. C. (1948) 'Complexes of clays with organic compounds, I', *Trans. Faraday Soc.*, vol. 44, p. 349.

MACKENZIE, R. C. (Editor) (1957a) *The differential thermal investigation of clays*. Min. Soc., London.

—— (1957b) 'Saponite from Allt Ribhein, Fiskavaig Bay, Skye', *Min. Mag.*, vol. 31, p. 672.

WEAVER, C. E. (1958) 'The effects and geologic significance of potassium "fixation" by expandable clay minerals derived from muscovite, biotite, chlorite and volcanic material', *Amer. Min.*, vol. 43, p. 839.

Vermiculite $(Mg,Ca)_{0\cdot7}(Mg,Fe^{+3},Al)_{6\cdot0}[(Al,Si)_8O_{20}](OH)_4\cdot 8H_2O$

MONOCLINIC $(-)$

α $1\cdot525-1\cdot564$
β $1\cdot545-1\cdot583$
γ $1\cdot545-1\cdot583$
δ $0\cdot02-0\cdot03$
$2V_\alpha$ $0°-8°$
α approx. $\perp(001)$; O.A.P. (010)
Dispersion: $r \leq v$. D $\simeq 2\cdot3$. H $\simeq 1\frac{1}{2}$.
Cleavage: {001} perfect.

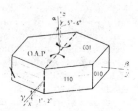

Colour: Colourless, yellow, green, brown; colourless in thin section.
Pleochroism: α paler shades than β and γ.

Vermiculite could well be regarded as a tri-octahedral member of the smectite group but its special characteristics warrant its description as a separate mineral. The name, which is derived from the Latin *vermiculare*, to breed worms, alludes to the peculiar exfoliation phenomenon exhibited when specimens are rapidly heated. In its natural state the mineral has little useful application, but when exfoliated it provides a low density material with excellent thermal and acoustic insulation properties.

STRUCTURE

The structure of vermiculite (Fig. 89) is basically that of talc since it contains a central octahedrally coordinated layer of (Mg,Fe) ions which lies between two inward pointing sheets of linked SiO_4 tetrahedra. As in talc and phlogopite, the central part of this composite layer may be regarded as one of brucite in which two out of three (OH) ions on each side are replaced by the apical oxygen of an SiO_4 tetrahedron. In talc the layers as a whole are electrically neutral, no inter-layer cations occur, and cohesion between successive sheets is very slight. In vermiculite the principal changes from the talc composition, $Mg_6Si_8O_{20}(OH)_4$, are a replacement of Si by Al, compensated by the presence of inter-layer cations, mainly magnesium. A further difference from talc is the occurrence of water molecules between the structural layers. The inter-layer water molecules and cations occupy definite positions with respect to the oxygens of neighbouring talc-like layers. The water molecule sites form a distorted hexagonal pattern such that each molecule is linked by a hydrogen bond to an oxygen on the silicate layer surface, and in a naturally occurring Mg–vermiculite two of these hexagonal networks occur in each interlayer space. Weak hydrogen bonding links together water molecules in the same plane, and the pairs of water planes are held together by the exchangeable cations which lie midway between them: the cations thus have a hydration shell of water molecules around them. Not all available sites are in fact occupied by water molecules in normal atmospheric conditions and many of the water molecules do not enclose a cation. Those which do not surround a cation may be referred to as unbound water, and this water is readily expelled below 110°C. The basal spacing (d_{002}) at ordinary temperatures and humidity is approximately 14·4 Å, but on dehydration successive changes occur (accompanied by endothermic peaks on a d.t.a. curve) which result in basal spacings of 13·8 Å, 11·6 Å and 9 Å. The unit cell of the structure has $a \simeq 5·3$, $b \simeq 9·2$, $c \simeq 29$ Å, β 97°, Z = 2.

The structure of Mg–vermiculite resembles that of a chlorite in many respects but differs mainly in the reduced occupation of the interlamellar

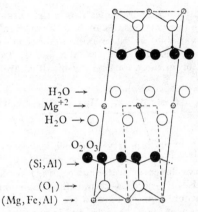

Fig. 89. *The crystal structure of Mg-vermiculite projected on* (010) (*after Mathieson, A. McL., & Walker, G. F.*, 1954, Amer. Min., *vol.* 39, *p.* 231).

atomic sites; the 'brucite' sheet of chlorite is replaced by a partially filled H_2O–Mg^{+2}–H_2O double sheet in vermiculite. It is clear from the above structural concepts that the nature of the exchange cation will influence the degree of hydration and consequently the observed basal spacings.

CHEMISTRY

Vermiculites are chemically very similar to tri-octahedral smectites, since both consist of talc-like layers in which a deficiency of positive charge is compensated by the presence of some inter-layer cations. In mont-morillonite and hectorite this deficiency is caused principally by substitution in the octahedral part of the composite layers and is compensated on the average by 0·66 monovalent ions or their equivalent. The most common inter-layer ions in smectites are sodium and calcium, though magnesium sometimes occurs in this role. In vermiculites a larger charge deficiency is caused principally by tetrahedral substitution as in beidellites and saponite (Al or Fe^{+3} for Si) and is compensated generally by about 0·7 divalent cations, or their equivalent, between the layers. In natural specimens (e.g. Table 23, anal. 8) these are most commonly magnesium ions, though calcium and very rarely sodium also occur. Accordingly the cation exchange capacity of vermiculites (between 100 and 260 m.eq/100 gm) is greater than that of smectites, and indeed is the highest of all the clay minerals.

The naturally occurring inter-layer cations can be exchanged for others, so that vermiculites with Mg, Ca, Na, K, Rb, Cs, Ba, Li, H and $(NH_4)^+$ as inter-layer cations can be prepared. The octahedral sites in vermiculites are occupied mainly by Mg and Fe^{+2}, but appreciable substitution by Al and Fe^{+3} occurs, and in minor amounts Ti, Li, Cr, Ni and other ions are often present.

Vermiculites and tri-octahedral smectites both contain water molecules between their talc-like layers but the amount of water taken up by natural vermiculites is less variable, and the maximum for them corresponds to two layers of water molecules in each available space. The ranges of substitution which occur in most natural vermiculites are indicated by the formula:

$$(Mg,Ca)_{0\cdot7-1\cdot0}\underbrace{Mg_{3\cdot5-5\cdot0}(Fe^{+3},Al)_{2\cdot5-1\cdot0}}_{6\cdot0}\underbrace{Al_{2\cdot0-2\cdot5}Si_{6-5\cdot5}}_{8\cdot0}O_{20}(OH)_4 \cdot (H_2O)_{7\cdot0-9\cdot0}$$

Vermiculites also show the property of absorbing organic liquids between their layers, but take up less than do the smectites. Ca–, Mg– and H–vermiculites have two layers of water molecules, Ba–, Li– and Na– have one, and $(NH_4)^+$–, K–, Rb– and Cs–vermiculites have none.

The unusual phenomenon of exfoliation occurs when vermiculite is heated suddenly to about 300°C or more, and is due to the rapid generation of steam which cannot escape without buckling and separating the structural layers. Exfoliation, which may cause as much as a thirty-fold expansion in the direction perpendicular to the cleavage planes, can also be brought about by treatment with H_2O_2 and it is thought that in this case oxygen is liberated by chemical action with inter-layer magnesium ions. Vermiculite does not exfoliate if the water is driven off slowly, even at 250°C. Differential thermal analysis curves of vermiculites generally show three principal endothermic peaks corresponding to the expulsion of inter-layer water, and a further two due to the disruption of the structure by loss of (OH) ions. Exothermic peaks occur at various temperatures according to the chemistry of the initial material.

The results of hydrothermal studies of vermiculite under equilibrium conditions suggest that vermiculite is unlikely to have formed at a temperature higher than 300°C. Since vermiculites are rich in iron it is argued also that they are derived from biotite rather than phlogopite and that the leaching of potassium, for example by weathering, is compensated in the first place by low temperature oxidation of ferrous to ferric iron.

OPTICAL AND PHYSICAL PROPERTIES

Although vermiculite occurs with minute particle size as a constituent of soil clays, it is also found in large crystalline plates, principally when it is an alteration product of biotite. Optical properties may therefore be measured more easily than for other clay minerals, but again variable hydration and cation content lead to a range of optical parameters. Some vermiculites contain considerable amounts of iron and these have higher refractive indices.

DISTINGUISHING FEATURES

Vermiculites generally have lower refractive indices than biotite or hydrobiotite and higher refringence than chlorites. Their birefringence is lower than that of either biotite or talc. X-ray powder patterns of vermiculites which have been treated with an ammonium salt and glycerol serve to distinguish vermiculite from montmorillonite and chlorite. The principal differences between vermiculites and smectites may be summarized as follows : 1. Vermiculites generally have a larger grain size. 2. Vermiculites have higher cation exchange capacity and greater substitution of $[Al]^4$ for Si. 3. In vermiculite the deficiency of positive charge in the 'talc' layers lies mainly in the tetrahedral component. 4. Vermiculites take up at most one layer of glycol molecules, giving a basal spacing of about 14 Å, whereas smectites take double layers, the basal spacing swelling to 17 Å. 5. Smectites dehydrate more readily, and vermiculites re-hydrate more readily. 6. Vermiculites are formed mainly by the weathering of large flakes of biotite.

The distinction between the two groups, however, is not precise, and some smectites (e.g. saponites) possess several of the above characteristics.

PARAGENESIS

One of the two main types of occurrence of vermiculite is as an alteration product of biotite either by weathering or by hydrothermal action. Derived in this way it is found sometimes as large crystal pseudomorphs after the mica, but it is also widespread as a clay constituent of certain soils. The second major occurrence of vermiculite is in the region of contact between acid intrusives and basic or ultrabasic rocks, in which circumstances it may be associated with corundum, apatite, serpentine, chlorite or talc.

Vermiculites derived from mica type minerals are comparatively rare in marine sediments since the potassium of sea water readily contracts them ; those which occur in marine sediments are derived from non-micaceous sources such as volcanic material, chlorite, and hornblende. Vermiculites are also found associated with carbonatites, and in metamorphosed limestones.

REFERENCES

MATHIESON, A. MCL. and WALKER, G. F. (1954) 'Crystal structure of magnesium vermiculite', *Amer. Min.*, vol. 39, p. 231.

WALKER, G. F. (1957) 'On the differentiation of vermiculites and smectites in clays', *Clay Min. Bull.*, vol. 3, p. 154.

WEAVER, C. E. (1958) 'The effects and geological significance of potassium "fixation" by expandable clay minerals derived from muscovite, biotite, chlorite and volcanic material', *Amer. Min.*, vol. 43, p. 839.

Apophyllite

$KFCa_4[Si_8O_{20}]8H_2O$

TETRAGONAL (+)

ω 1·534–1·535
ε 1·535–1·537
δ 0·002

Dispersion: High, sometimes anomalous. D 2·33–2·37. H 4½–5.
Cleavage: {001} perfect, {110} poor.
Colour: Colourless, white, pink, pale yellow or green; colourless in thin section.

Apophyllite is an uncommon mineral which is of interest largely because of its unusual atomic structure (Fig. 90): this bears some relationship to that of the micas since a basic part of it is a sheet of composition Si_8O_{20}.

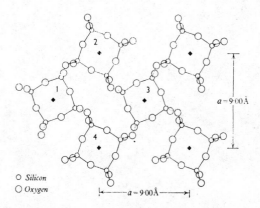

O Silicon
O Oxygen

Fig. 90. (001) *Projection of silicon–oxygen sheets of apophyllite; tetrad axes pass through the corners and centre of the unit cell. In rings numbered 1 and 3, tetrahedra point upwards, and in those numbered 2 and 4, tetrahedra point downwards (after Taylor, W. H. & Náray-Szabó, St., 1931, Zeit. Krist., vol. 77, p. 146).*

Instead of forming an approximately hexagonal network, however, the (Si–O) tetrahedra are arranged in four-fold and eight-fold rings, and alternate rings of four tetrahedra point in opposite directions. Between the sheets of tetrahedra lie the K, F, Ca ions and water molecules. The water molecules are hydrogen bonded to oxygens of the silicate network. The principal chemical replacements which may occur in apophyllite are of Na for K, Al for Si and (OH) for F.

Apophyllite has perfect {001} cleavage giving surfaces with a pearly iridescent lustre. It is characterized by its tetragonal habit and anomalous interference colours. The main occurrence is as a secondary mineral in amygdales or druses in basalts, where it is often accompanied by zeolites, datolite, pectolite and calcite.

REFERENCE

SAHAMA, TH. G. (1965) 'Yellow apophyllite from Korsnäs, Finland'. *Min. Mag.*, vol. 34 (Tilley vol.), p. 406.

Prehnite

$Ca_2Al[AlSi_3O_{10}](OH)_2$

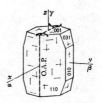

ORTHORHOMBIC (+)

α 1·611–1·632
β 1·615–1·642
γ 1·632–1·665
δ 0·022–0·035
$2V_\gamma$ 65°–69°
O.A.P. (010); $\alpha = x$, $\gamma = z$.
Dispersion: Usually $r > v$. D 2·90–2·95. H 6–6½.
Cleavage: {001} good, {110} weak.
Twinning: Fine lamellar twinning may occur.
Colour: Pale green, yellow, grey or white; colourless in thin section.

STRUCTURE

Prehnite (a 4·61, b 5·47, c 18·48 Å; $Z = 2$) was previously included in the brittle mica family because of its good platy cleavage and its Ca content, and more recently it has been confirmed that it has essentially a layered structure.

CHEMISTRY

Prehnite does not show any marked variation in composition (Table 28); the alkalis, manganese and magnesium are usually low, and the only appreciable substitution is of iron for aluminium. Most of the structural water is lost only on heating to between 600° and 750°C: prehnite cannot therefore be classed with the zeolites with which it is often associated. Prehnite can be synthesized rapidly at relatively low temperatures from a glass of appropriate composition at pressures above 3000 bars: at 4000 bars and temperatures above 450°C it is converted to anorthite and wollastonite.

OPTICAL AND PHYSICAL PROPERTIES

The refractive indices and birefringence increase with the amount of iron. Distinct individual crystals are relatively rare; tabular groups, barrel-shaped aggregates and reniform globular masses are common, often giving a characteristic imperfect columnar 'bow-tie' or 'hour-glass' appearance. Optical anomalies are often found, many specimens having incomplete extinction and abnormal interference colours, due possibly to the super-imposition of two systems of thin layers.

Table 28. PREHNITE ANALYSES

	1.	2.	NUMBERS OF IONS ON THE BASIS OF 24 (O,OH)	1.	2.
SiO_2	42·86	43·7	Si	5·930 ⎱ 6·00	5·989 ⎱ 6·00
TiO_2	0·01	tr.	Al	0·070 ⎰	0·011 ⎰
Al_2O_3	24·41	24·05	Al	3·900	3·874
Fe_2O_3	0·52	0·93	Fe^{+3}	0·050	0·096
FeO	0·28	0·03	Mg	0·003	0·022
MnO	0·06	0·00	Ti	0·001 ⎱ 4·00	— ⎱ 4·00
MgO	0·03	0·11	Fe^{+2}	0·033	0·003
CaO	26·89	26·85	Mn	0·008	—
Na_2O	0·32	0·04	Na	0·081	0·010
K_2O	0·01	0·00	Ca	3·973 ⎰ 4·06	3·943 ⎰ 3·95
H_2O^+	4·45	4·54	K	0·001 ⎰	— ⎰
H_2O^-	0·08	0·03	OH	4·096	4·150
Total	99·92	100·36			
α	1·613	1·615			
β	1·624	1·624			
γ	1·638	1·643			
$2V_\gamma$	68°	69°			
D	2·936	—			

1. White fibrous prehnite, rodingite, Hindubagh, Pakistan (Bilgrami, S. A. & Howie, R. A., 1960, *Amer. Min.*, vol. 45, p. 791).
2. Translucent, very pale green, botryoidal prehnite, cavities in dolerite, Prospect Quarry, New South Wales (Coombs, D. S., Ellis, A. J., Fyfe, W. S. & Taylor, A. M., 1959, *Geochim. Cosmochim. Acta*, vol. 17, p. 53; includes P_2O_5 0·02, Ag 0·01, Pb 0·04, SnO 0·01).

DISTINGUISHING FEATURES

Prehnite differs from many hydrothermal minerals in its relatively high relief and its strong birefringence. Wollastonite, topaz and lawsonite have lower birefringence, while datolite, with which prehnite is often associated, has a stronger birefringence and a poorer cleavage.

PARAGENESIS

Prehnite occurs chiefly in basic volcanic rocks as a secondary or hydrothermal mineral in veins, cavities and amygdales and is frequently associated with zeolites. It is also found in veins in plutonic rocks and as pseudomorphs after such minerals as clinozoisite and laumontite. It is found in contact metamorphosed impure limestones and marls and in rocks such as rodingite or garnetized gabbros which have suffered calcium meta-somatism. In New Zealand prehnite-bearing rocks occur on a regional scale, where they are found in a zone of low grade incipient metamorphism; here the prehnite is commonly associated with pumpellyite.

REFERENCE

COOMBS, D. S., ELLIS, A. J., FYFE, W. S. and TAYLOR, A. M. (1959) 'The zeolite facies; with comments on the interpretation of hydrothermal syntheses', *Geochim. et Cosmochim. Acta*, vol. 17, p. 53.

PART 4
FRAMEWORK SILICATES

FELDSPAR GROUP

Alkali Feldspars	$(K,Na)[AlSi_3O_8]$
Plagioclase	$Na[AlSi_3O_8]–Ca[Al_2Si_2O_8]$
Celsian	$Ba[Al_2Si_2O_8]$

INTRODUCTION

The members of the feldspar group of minerals are the most abundant constituents of the igneous rocks. The ubiquity of the feldspars together with their wide range in composition has led inevitably to their use as the primary tool in the classification of the igneous rocks. In the great majority of these rocks, whether acid, alkaline, intermediate or basic, the feldspars are the major constituents, and they are absent only from some ultrabasic and rare alkaline rocks. Feldspars are the most important constituents of the simple pegmatites and are common in mineral veins. They are major constituents of most gneisses and schists, and occur also in many thermally as well as regionally metamorphosed rocks. Although the feldspars are susceptible to alteration and weathering they are second in abundance to quartz in the arenaceous sediments, in which they occur as detrital grains and as authigenic crystals. It is only in the argillaceous, and to a greater degree in the carbonate rocks, that the feldspars are of relatively minor importance.

To achieve a proper understanding of feldspar relationships it has proved necessary to characterize them not only according to chemical composition, but also according to structural state, which depends upon the temperature of crystallization and upon subsequent thermal history. A feldspar which has been quenched so that it retains the structure appropriate to its high-temperature formation is called a high-temperature feldspar. Most feldspars of volcanic rocks are of this type. Low-temperature feldspars are those with structures appropriate either to crystallization at low temperature, or to slow cooling from elevated temperatures; these are found for example in plutonic rocks. Feldspars may occur also in intermediate-temperature structural states.

The majority of feldspars may be classified chemically as members of the ternary system $NaAlSi_3O_8–KAlSi_3O_8–CaAl_2Si_2O_8$. These compositions are referred to respectively as sodium, potassium and calcium feldspar (rather than soda, potash and lime feldspar). Members of the series between $NaAlSi_3O_8$ and $KAlSi_3O_8$ are called alkali feldspars, and those between $NaAlSi_3O_8$ and $CaAl_2Si_2O_8$ plagioclase feldspars. The alkali feldspars generally contain less than 5 to 10 per cent of the calcium 'molecule' in solid solution, but the sodium-rich members can contain a little more. Similarly the plagioclase feldspars generally contain less than 5 to 10 per cent of the potassium 'molecule'. The distinction between alkali and plagioclase feldspar at compositions with approximately equal calcium and potassium content is somewhat arbitrary (see Fig. 91).

The pure calcium end-member, anorthite, is triclinic, and no essentially different names are used to describe structural states at different temperatures. The potassium end-member can exist in a number of different

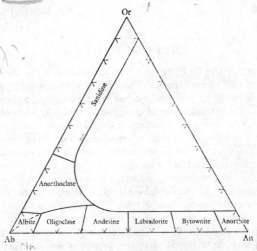

Fig. 91. *Illustrating solid solution in the feldspars. The nomenclature of the plagioclase series and the high-temperature alkali feldspars is also shown.*

structural states. Those with structures corresponding to the highest temperatures of crystallization are monoclinic and are called sanidines, while a lower temperature monoclinic potassium feldspar is called orthoclase. The lowest temperature potassium feldspars are microclines. These are triclinic, but different specimens of microcline have crystal lattices with different obliquities. Those with maximum obliquity are called maximum microclines while others are termed intermediate microclines. A variety of potassium feldspar, adularia, is one which is recognized principally by its habit and paragenesis, and which is thought to be structurally inhomogeneous. The pure sodium end-member is called low-albite or high-albite (or intermediate-albite) according to structural state. The albites are normally triclinic but on strong heating a transition to monoclinic symmetry occurs. Pericline is the sodium feldspar counterpart of adularia, and has a similarly restricted paragenesis and a characteristic habit.

The alkali feldspars have been classified, on the basis of their optical properties, into four series. These are:

1. high-albite–high-sanidine
2. high-albite–low-sanidine (sanidine)
3. low-albite–orthoclase
4. low-albite–microcline

The high-albite–high-sanidine series is one of complete solid solution, but within it there is a change of symmetry from triclinic (Ab_{100} to Ab_{63}) to monoclinic (Ab_{63} to Ab_0). The triclinic members of this series are called anorthoclase and the remainder range from sodium-rich to potassium-rich sanidine. In the second high-temperature series, high-albite–low-sanidine, solid solution is limited at each end, and specimens with intermediate composition consist of two phases separated on a sub-microscopic scale. These are called cryptoperthites, and this series also is divided at Ab_{63}, so that it contains anorthoclases, anorthoclase–cryptoperthites, sanidine–cryptoperthites and sanidines (see Fig. 91).

In the lower temperature series, low-albite–orthoclase and low-albite–microcline, solid solution is more limited in extent and phase separation occurs on a scale which can be seen with the aid of a microscope. These intergrowths are called orthoclase- or microcline microperthites. If the presence of two phases can be seen without the aid of a microscope, the term perthite is used. Some alkali feldspars, called moonstones, display on particular surfaces a sheen or iridescence, attributed to lamellar micro- or cryptoperthitic intergrowth. The term 'moonstone' however, is sometimes applied also to plagioclase feldspars showing similar phenomena.

For the plagioclase series, as for the alkali feldspars, the terms high-temperature, low-temperature (and intermediate-temperature) are again relevant. A purely chemical definition of a plagioclase can be given in terms of Ab–An 'molecular' percentages, but specific names are used to denote the six compositional ranges into which the series has been divided. Thus albite, oligoclase, andesine, labradorite, bytownite and anorthite refer to An percentages 0–10, 10–30, 30–50, 50–70, 70–90 and 90–100 respectively. These divisions were chosen merely for convenience and have no structural significance. Position within a chemical range may be further indicated by such phrases as sodium-rich (or sodic) oligoclase, calcic bytownite, etc. The high-temperature series from albite to anorthite is one of almost complete solid solution, but X-ray investigation has shown that the low-temperature series is structurally complex. The various structural types designated are: low-albite, peristerite, intermediate and anorthite: it should be noted that 'intermediate' in this sense means intermediate between two low-temperature states. Plagioclases with peristerite structure are known to consist of a fine intergrowth of two phases, and some specimens show iridescence. The exhibition of a similar sheen by some labradorites may be called 'labradorescence'.

Most perthites are intergrowths of sodium-rich feldspar in a potassium-rich feldspar host; an intergrowth of potassium-rich feldspar in a plagioclase host is called antiperthite.

The barium ion is present in small quantities in the great majority of feldspars but only rarely occurs as a major constituent. In general, feldspars are considered here as barium varieties when their BaO content is in excess of approximately 2 per cent. Barium feldspar with more than 90 per cent of the $BaAl_2Si_2O_8$ molecule is described as celsian: Ba-bearing feldspars with less than 30 per cent of the $BaAl_2Si_2O_8$ molecule are termed hyalophane.

The name as originally given was *feldtspat* and it is believed that this had reference to the presence of the spar (spath) in tilled fields (Swedish; *feldt* or *fält*) overlying granite, rather than to the German *Fels*, meaning rock.

Alkali Feldspars

(K, Na) [AlSi$_3$O$_8$]

MONOCLINIC ($-$), TRICLINIC ($+$) or ($-$)

	Microcline, Microcline-microperthite, Low-albite series	Orthoclase, Orthoclase-microperthite, Low-albite series	Sanidine, Anorthoclase, High-albite series	High-sanidine, High-albite series
α	1·514–1·529	1·518–1·529	1·518–1·527	1·518–1·527
β	1·518–1·533	1·522–1·533	1·522–1·532	1·523–1·532
γ	1·521–1·539	1·522–1·539	1·522–1·534	1·524–1·534
δ	0·007–0·010	0·006–0·010	0·006–0·007	0·006–0·007
$2V_\alpha$	66°–103°	33°–103°	18°–54°†	63°–54°†
$\alpha : (001)$	15°–20°	5°–19°	5°–9°	9°

For optic orientation see Figs. 107–110, pp. 306, 307.

Dispersion:	$r > v, r < v$	$r > v, r < v$	$r > v, r > v$	$r < v, r > v$
D	2·56–2·63	2·55–2·63	2·56–2·62	2·56–2·62
H	6–6½	6–6½	6	—

Cleavage: {001}, {010} perfect; {100}, {110}, {$\bar{1}$10}, {$\bar{2}$01} partings.

Twinning: Simple, multiple and repeated twinning. Principal twin laws: Carlsbad, Baveno, Manebach; albite, pericline and 'tartan' twinning shown by triclinic feldspars only. For details see pp. 292–297.

Colour: Normally colourless or white, but sometimes pink, yellow, red or green; colourless in thin section.

STRUCTURE

The following discussion of the structures of alkali feldspars is divided into three parts: (1) Potassium feldspars with little or no sodium; (2) Sodium feldspars with little or no potassium; (3) Alkali feldspars in general.

1. Potassium feldspars

Sanidine. The essential features of the crystal structure of the feldspar minerals were first determined by Taylor (1933) in his study of a sanidine. Its unit cell was determined as monoclinic, space group $C2/m$, with a 8·6 Å, b 13·0 Å, c 7·2 Å, β 116° and 4KAlSi$_3$O$_8$ per cell. The structure is typical of a 'framework' silicate in which tetrahedra of (Si,Al)O$_4$ are linked to one another (by shared oxygens) in all directions rather than in chains or in sheets. Although discrete chains of tetrahedra do not exist in the structure, its nature may be more easily understood by considering the atomic arrangement as the linking of chains in two directions perpendicular to their length. The chains themselves are formed by the linking of horizontal

† A value of 45° has also been given for high-albite.

rings of four tetrahedra as shown in Fig. 92. The repeat distance in the chain direction is approximately four times the height of a tetrahedron. When viewed in the direction of the chain axis a horizontal ring appears approximately as in Fig. 92b and this can be further simplified in its representation as in Fig. 92c. In the actual structure the rings are considerably distorted; they are tilted out of the horizontal plane, and are twisted about the chain axis direction. Successive horizontal rings of a chain are, however, related by vertical glide planes (reflection in (010) and translation of $a/2$) passing through their cer.tres, and the view down the chain axis may be idealized as in Fig. 92d; the first, third, fifth, etc., rings are represented by thick and the even number rings by thin lines. The linkage of rings in directions at right angles to their length is as follows. At the level of the first ring a network of oxygen linkages is formed as shown in black

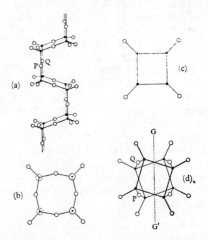

Fig. 92. *Idealized illustrations of the feldspar 'chain' (see text) (after Taylor, W. H., 1933, Zeit. Krist., vol. 85, p. 425).*

in Plate 1, producing a plane of four-membered and eight-membered rings of tetrahedra. Vertical symmetry planes and glide planes are marked MM′ and GG′. A similar network is formed by the rings of second tetrahedra below the first network and this is shown in red in Plate 1; the two arrays are linked by the oxygen atoms (such as P, Q, Fig. 92) forming vertical four-membered rings. The resultant framework of tetrahedra has large interstices which are occupied by potassium ions, and these too are shown in Plate 1, lying on reflection planes and approximately midway between horizontal diad axes. They are rather irregularly coordinated by nine oxygens, the K–O distances being about 3 Å. Although the projection along x is suitable for visualizing the structure as a whole, other projections yield simpler views of a single formula unit. A projection of the sanidine structure on (010) is shown in Fig. 93, in which atoms are labelled only within the

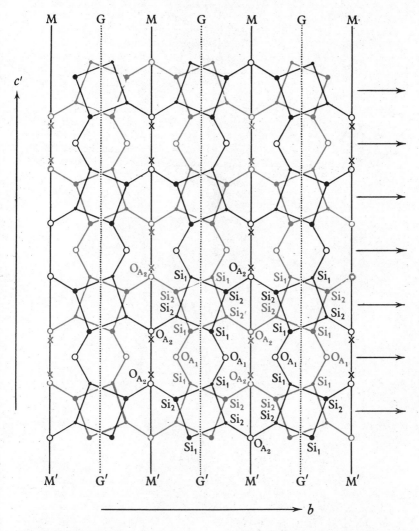

Plate 1. *In black: Schematic illustration of the cross linkage of the feldspar 'chains' to form a sheet.*

In red: Similar sheet to that shown in black but a/2 below it and related to it by a vertical glide plane. Oxygens linking tetrahedra within the 'chains' are not shown in this diagram.

unique area, and Fig. 94a shows part of the structure as viewed along the normal to (001). Consideration of y coordinates shows that atoms K and O_{A2} are in special positions on symmetry planes, O_{A1} is in a special position on a diad axis, and the remaining atoms are in general positions.

An accurate three-dimensional structure determination of a high-temperature sanidine has yielded information about the distribution of Si and Al ions among the tetrahedral sites. Since all (Si,Al)–O distances were found to be equal (1·64 Å) it is inferred that the Al atoms (one to every three silicons) are distributed randomly between the two distinct tetrahedral sites labelled Si_1 and Si_2.

Orthoclase. The essential features of the structures of sanidine and orthoclase are very similar. In orthoclase, however, there is partial ordering of the (Si,Al) atoms, with approximately (0·30 Al + 0·70 Si) at site Si_1 and

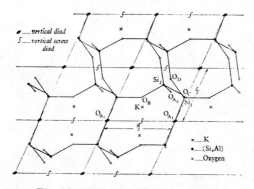

Fig. 93. (010) *projection of sanidine.*

(0·19 Al + 0·81 Si) at site Si_2. The environment of the potassium atom is essentially the same in both structures. Orthoclase is monoclinic $C2/m$ with a 8·56, b 13·0, c 7·19 Å, $\beta \simeq 116°$, and has 4 $KAlSi_3O_8$ per unit cell.

Microcline. The lowest temperature form of potassium feldspar, microcline, is triclinic. The cell parameters of microcline (space group $C\bar{1}$) vary in different specimens, but those of one for which an accurate structure determination has been carried out are a 8·5784, b 12·9600, c 7·2112, α 90° 18′, β 115° 58′, γ 89° 7½′.

Since the microcline cell is triclinic it does not possess the symmetry planes and axes of the monoclinic feldspars, and because of this loss of symmetry there are four distinct silicon atom sites $Si_1(o)$ and $Si_1(m)$, $Si_2(o)$ and $Si_2(m)$ instead of only two, Si_1 and Si_2, as in the monoclinic feldspars. The essential features of triclinic feldspars are best illustrated by a projection on (001) in which the atoms of only one formula unit are inserted. This is done for the albite structure in Fig. 94b, and although structural detail differs, the labelling and approximate location of atom sites are valid for microcline too (with replacement of Na by K). The triclinic structure may be contrasted

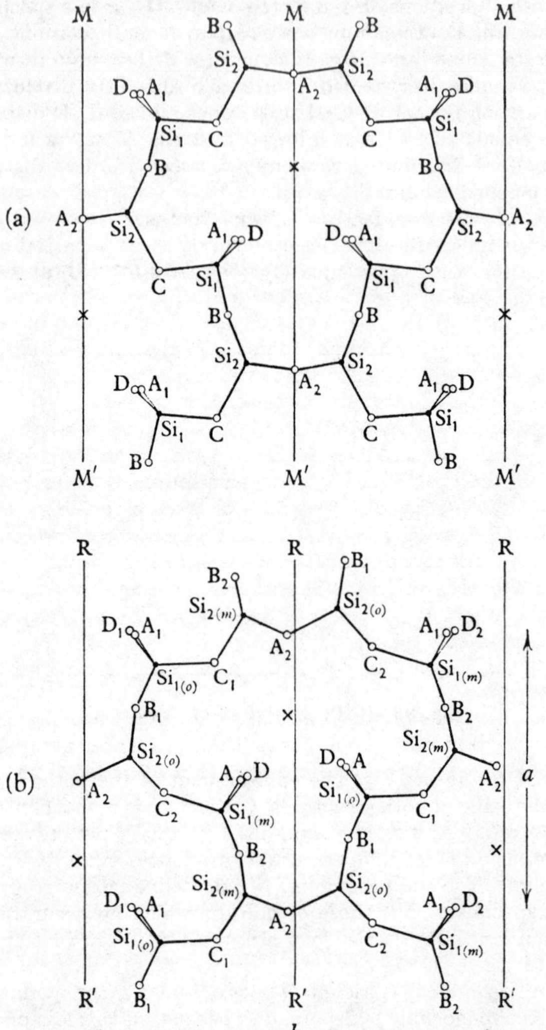

Fig. 94. (a) *Part of sanidine structure viewed along normal to* (001). *MM'
are mirror planes (after Taylor, W. H., 1933, Zeit. Krist., vol. 85,
p. 425). (b) Part of albite structure viewed along normal to* (001). *RR' are
not mirror planes (after Taylor, W. H., Darbyshire, J. A. and Strunz, H.,
1934, Zeit. Krist., vol. 87, p. 464).* × .... potassium.

with that of sanidine in Fig. 94a. The atoms K and O_{A2} are no longer exactly on the plane $y = 0$, and other atoms also have slightly changed coordinates. The average bond lengths Si–O in the four different tetrahedra in this case are not equal, and thus it is inferred that partial ordering of the Al atoms occurs. The fraction of each site occupied by Al has been determined as 0·56, 0·25, 0·07, 0·08 for sites $Si_1(o)$, $Si_1(m)$, $Si_2(o)$, $Si_2(m)$ respectively.

Variations in the microcline cell can occur, ranging from those which are barely distinguishable from monoclinic, to microcline which has $\alpha = 90° 41'$, $\gamma = 87° 30'$ and which is termed 'maximum microcline': others are known as 'intermediate microclines'. The degree of departure from monoclinic symmetry may be called 'obliquity' and a measure of this can be obtained from an X-ray powder pattern.

The concept of order–disorder relationships for the (Al,Si) distribution, which was suggested to explain the grosser differences between microcline and sanidine, may be invoked again to explain the continuous series of microcline obliquities. In support of this it has been shown that on heating a microcline at 1050°C its obliquity diminishes with longer duration of heating and eventually a sanidine is produced.

Microcline rarely occurs untwinned, sometimes shows either albite or pericline twinning, but most often shows both, in the well-known cross-hatched or 'tartan' pattern. The peculiar relations between pericline and albite twinning in a microcline crystal are taken as evidence that it first crystallized with monoclinic symmetry and subsequently became triclinic.

Adularia. The potassium feldspar adularia shows variations in optical and structural parameters in different areas of single grains. Adularia is regarded as a distinctive variety by virtue of its morphology and its restricted paragenesis.

2. Sodium feldspars

Albite. The structure of albite, $Na(Si_3Al)O_8$, is in general similar to that of the potassium feldspars. Albite is triclinic, with space group $C\bar{1}$, and its cell parameters are (for low-albite) a 8·14, b 12·8, c 7·16, α 94° 20′, β 116° 34′, γ 87° 39′. Comparison of cell edges with those of the potassium feldspars shows a marked contraction in a, the direction of the 'chain' axis, and little change in b and c. The positions of atoms in one formula unit, viewed in the direction normal to (001), are depicted in Fig. 94b. Compared with sanidine, shifts of atoms of up to 0·3 Å are involved and the loss of symmetry planes is apparent. The full structural detail shows also the absence of diad axes. As in the case of microcline there are four distinct positions for occupation by (Si,Al).

Two modifications of albite are known to occur in nature, a low-temperature form which occurs mainly in plutonic rocks, and a high-temperature albite which occurs in lavas and can be produced artificially by prolonged heating of low-temperature albite. The principal structural difference between low- and high-temperature albite lies in the distribution of Al atoms among the four non-equivalent tetrahedral sites. In low-albite their approximate content is given as $Al_{0·8}$, $Al_{0·0}$, $Al_{0·2}$, $Al_{0·1}$ in sites $Si_1(o)$, $Si_1(m)$, $Si_2(o)$, $Si_2(m)$ respectively.

In the case of high-temperature albite the (Si,Al)–O bond length is the same for all tetrahedral sites, corresponding to occupation of each by ($\frac{3}{4}$Si + $\frac{1}{4}$Al), and it is inferred that the Si,Al distribution is completely disordered. In both low- and high-temperature albites the sodium atom is coordinated by six or seven nearest oxygen neighbours, by contrast with the ninefold coordination of K in potassium feldspar. It is clear that the order–disorder characteristics of low- and high-temperature albites are in some respects similar to those of the potassium feldspars, microcline and high-sanidine. High-albite and high-sanidine have highly disordered (Si,Al) distributions, whereas low-albite and microcline represent arrangements with a considerable degree of order. In the latter two cases Al is concentrated principally in corresponding tetrahedral sites.

The cell parameters of high-albite differ slightly from those of low-albite. The a and b parameters are larger, and the α and γ angles are less oblique. A comparatively rare sodium feldspar, with characteristic habit, called pericline, bears a similar relation to low-albite as does adularia to microcline. It too shows variation in optical properties and evidence of variation in structural parameters in different regions of a single specimen. Specimens of albite with intermediate lattice parameters and presumably with structural states intermediate between low- and high-albite have been synthesized, but are very rare in nature.

3. Alkali feldspars

Most natural alkali feldspars are not homogeneous but contain separate potassium-rich and sodium-rich phases. The highest temperature forms of alkali feldspar, however, form a complete solid solution series.

High-albite–high-sanidine. All synthetic alkali feldspars belong to this series but only the potassium-rich end ($> Or_{67}$) is represented in natural specimens. The series is one of complete solid solution although at the composition $Or_{37}Ab_{63}$ there is a change in symmetry: specimens more potassium-rich than this are monoclinic at room temperature while those which are more sodium-rich are triclinic. The composition at which this change in symmetry occurs is temperature dependent, and above 1000°C compositions up to nearly pure albite are monoclinic. Prolonged heat treatment of natural alkali feldspars alters their properties so that they conform to the high-albite–high-sanidine series, and their compositions can then be estimated by measurement of the $\bar{2}01$ spacing (Fig. 95) in an X-ray powder pattern.

High-albite–sanidine. In natural specimens belonging to this series, unmixing of sodium-rich and potassium-rich phases appears to occur within the range of composition Or_{25}–Or_{60}. The change in symmetry from triclinic at the sodium-rich end to monoclinic at the potassium-rich end divides the series into anorthoclase ($< Or_{37}$) and sanidine ($> Or_{37}$). The unmixing in the range Or_{25}–Or_{60} occurs on a very fine scale (detectable by X-rays but not with the microscope) yielding anorthoclase and sanidine cryptoperthites. Although part of the series is triclinic, nevertheless the angle of the $\bar{2}01$ reflection (which does not depend upon b, α or γ) again can be used to determine the composition of anorthoclases and sanidines and, when measured for a homogenized cryptoperthite, gives its bulk composition. Whether or not an alkali feldspar is unmixed can often be determined from a powder pattern; if the phases have sufficiently different composition two $\bar{2}01$ peaks will appear instead of only one for a homogeneous specimen.

The cross-hatched twinning generally exhibited by anorthoclase suggests (as in the case of microcline) that it originally crystallized with monoclinic symmetry, i.e. above the inversion temperature, and subsequently became triclinic on cooling. Although microclines and anorthoclases both show cross-hatched twinning they should not be confused; microclines are potassium-rich low-temperature forms, and anorthoclases are sodium-rich high-temperature forms, and the two are readily distinguishable by their optical properties and pericline twin planes (see p. 297).

Low-albite–orthoclase. At temperatures on the equilibrium diagram lower than those pertaining to cryptoperthites, a greater proportion of the range from pure sodium to pure potassium feldspar corresponds to a region

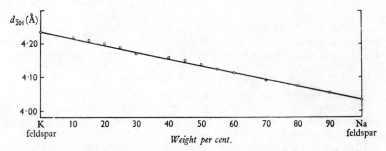

Fig. 95. *Spacing of $\bar{2}01$ planes in a series of alkali feldspars crystallized at 900°C. and 300 bars pressure of H_2O (after Bowen, N. L. & Tuttle, O. F., 1950, Journ. Geol., vol. 58, p. 489).*

of unmixing, and the unmixing occurs on a coarser scale. The separate phases are visible under the microscope, and the specimens, which appear to be restricted to Or_{20}–Or_{85} are called microperthites. In the range Or_{85}–Or_{100} the specimens are not unmixed, and in the range Or_0–Or_{20}, apart from those very close to pure albite, most specimens have appreciable calcium in solid solution and are more conveniently regarded as plagioclases.

The sodium phase in microperthites can show either pericline or albite twinning or both.

Low-albite–microcline. There is very little solid solution in this series and the distinction between it and the orthoclase series becomes meaningful only at the potassium-rich end. Microcline itself, although discussed previously as a single phase, is usually perthitic or microperthitic, so that in effect the low-albite–microcline series, such as it is, has been dealt with in the section on microcline.

MORPHOLOGY AND TWINNING

Since triclinic feldspars do not deviate greatly from monoclinic symmetry several characteristic habits are common to both monoclinic and triclinic members of the feldspar group of minerals. Some of the habits which occur most frequently have well developed {001} and {010} forms, and the presence of {110} in addition often yields a prominent prism zone parallel to the z axis (Fig. 96a). Sometimes, as in feldspar microlites, crystals are elongated parallel to the x axis and the prism zone formed by {010} and {001} predominates (Fig. 96b). While orthoclases and microclines can have either of these typical habits, sanidines generally have the flattened appearance shown in Fig. 96c. Albite crystals are also often tabular parallel to (010) but they are sometimes elongated parallel to y as in the 'pericline'

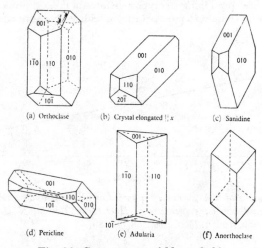

(a) Orthoclase (b) Crystal elongated ∥ x (c) Sanidine

(d) Pericline (e) Adularia (f) Anorthoclase

Fig. 96. *Some common feldspar habits.*

habit. Adularia crystals have an orthorhombic appearance as (001) and (10Ī) make nearly equal angles with the z axis. The high-temperature sodium-rich feldspar anorthoclase is often found in rhomb-shaped crystals.

Feldspars have perfect {001} and good {010} cleavages which in the monoclinic varieties intersect at right angles; in the triclinic feldspars these cleavages are only approximately perpendicular to one another.

Perthites. Micro- and cryptoperthitic intergrowths are thought to be responsible for the schiller effects seen in those alkali feldspar specimens which are generally referred to as moonstones. The segregation of potassium- and sodium-rich feldspar sometimes occurs in irregular blebs but more often takes place at definite planes in the crystal. These planes, which can be seen best on (010) sections of microperthites, are approximately parallel to the y axis and generally make an angle of about 73° with (001).

Twin laws. Many different kinds of pseudo-symmetry are exhibited by the feldspar structures and accordingly twinning is very common and may follow a number of different laws. In Table 29 the more common twin

Table 29. FELDSPAR TWIN LAWS

Name	Twin axis	Composition plane	Remarks
Normal twins			
Albite	$\perp$ (010)	(010)	Repeated; triclinic only.
Manebach	$\perp$ (001)	(001)	Simple.
Baveno (right)	$\perp$ (021)	(021)	⎱ Simple, rare in
Baveno (left)	$\perp$ (0$\bar{2}$1)	(0$\bar{2}$1)	⎰ plagioclases.
X	$\perp$ (100)	(100)	
Prism (right)	$\perp$ (110)	(110) ·.	
Prism (left)	$\perp$ (1$\bar{1}$0)	(1$\bar{1}$0)	
Parallel twins			
Carlsbad	[001] (z axis)	(hk0), usually (010)	Simple.
Pericline	[010] (y axis)	(h0l), 'rhombic section' parallel to y.	⎫ Repeated; triclinic only.
Acline A	[010] (y axis)	(001)	
Acline B	[010] (y axis)	(100)	⎭
Estérel	[100] (x axis)	(0kl) 'rhombic section' parallel to x.	⎫ Repeated.
Ala A	[100] (x axis)	(001)	
Ala B	[100] (x axis)	(010)	⎭
Complex twins			
Albite–Carlsbad (Roc Tourné)	$\perp z$	(010)	⎫
Albite–Ala B	$\perp x$	(010)	
Manebach–Acline A (Scopie)	$\perp y$	(001)	⎬ Repeated
Manebach–Ala A	$\perp x$	(001)	
X–Carlsbad	$\perp z$	(100)	
X–Acline B	$\perp y$	(100)	⎭

laws which are found in feldspars are divided into three groups; normal, parallel and complex. Normal twins have their twin axis normal to a possible crystal face and this face is parallel to the composition plane. For a centrosymmetric crystal this twinning process is equivalent to reflection in the composition plane. Parallel twins have as twin axis a possible crystal edge (i.e. a zone axis); the composition plane is parallel to the twin axis and need not define a possible crystal face. Sometimes an individual B is related to one A by a normal twin law, and an individual C is related to B by a parallel twin law with the same composition plane as the normal twin. C and A are then related by a 'complex' twin law. The twin axis of the resultant complex twin lies in the composition plane and is normal to a possible crystal edge (i.e. at 90° to the twin axis of the parallel twin). The intermediate individual B, which is related to A and C by simple twin laws, may or may not be present. The relationships in a complex twin are illustrated in the stereogram of Fig. 97.

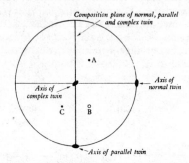

Fig. 97. *Stereographic illustration of relationships in a complex twin.*

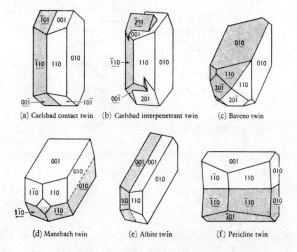

(a) Carlsbad contact twin   (b) Carlsbad interpenetrant twin   (c) Baveno twin

(d) Manebach twin   (e) Albite twin   (f) Pericline twin

Fig. 98. *Some common feldspar twins.*

Illustrations of some common feldspar twins are presented in Fig. 98. Carlsbad, Baveno and Manebach twins are found in both monoclinic and triclinic feldspars, mainly with only two individuals but sometimes with three, four or even six.

Albite and pericline twins occur very frequently in triclinic alkali feldspars and of the two the albite law is the more common. The structures of triclinic feldspars do not deviate very much from monoclinic symmetry; (010) is a pseudo-mirror plane and y is a pseudo-diad axis. In albite twinning [normal twin; axis $\perp$(010); composition plane (010)], at the junction of the twin individuals, (010) is a real mirror plane relating the triclinic structures on either side. In pericline twinning [parallel twin; axis y; composition plane $(h0l)$], at the twin junction, y is a true diad axis relating the two triclinic structures. The monoclinic feldspars cannot show albite or pericline twinning since for them the twin axes ($\perp$(010), and y) coincide with the true diad possessed by the untwinned structure.

Rhombic section. In pericline twinning the composition plane lies in the zone of faces parallel to y ($h0l$ faces); it contains the y axis, but its precise location is determined by the geometry of the triclinic cell. The com-

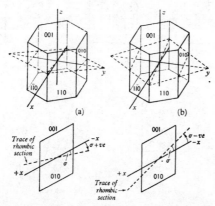

Fig. 99. *Rhombic section (indicated by broken lines) in two different orientations (after Chudoba, K., 1933. The determination of the feldspars in thin section (Translated by W. Q. Kennedy). London (Murby)).*

position plane is known as the 'rhombic section' since its intersections with (110) and (1$\bar{1}$0) (or these faces produced) form the sides of a rhombus. The position of the rhombic section is specified by the angle σ which its trace makes with the trace of (001), measured on (010). Two examples are illustrated in Fig. 99, the first (a) with a small positive value of σ and the second (b) with a numerically larger negative value of σ.

The location of the rhombic section can be alternatively described by the use of the property of the rhombus that its diagonals intersect at right angles. One diagonal is the y axis itself and the other is the intersection of the rhombic section with the plane (010). Thus the pericline twin plane can be defined as that which contains the y axis and which cuts (010) twinned in a line 90° from y.

In the following paragraphs each of the alkali feldspar species is discussed in turn with reference to the twin laws which it exhibits.

Orthoclase. Carlsbad twins are most common and other twins are rarely found. Carlsbad twins may be either of the interpenetrant or contact type, and in the latter the re-entrant angle between the (001) and ($\bar{1}01$) normals is very small. Under the microscope the twins are best seen in sections cut parallel to the *y* crystallographic axis (i.e. normal to the composition plane). Since orthoclase is monoclinic both individuals show straight extinction, but except in sections parallel or normal to the *z* axis they show different birefringence (Fig. 100a). If the crystal is rotated about *y* both halves remain in extinction.

Baveno twins form nearly square prisms since the angle (001) : (021) is approximately 45°. Multiple twins with three or four individuals are not

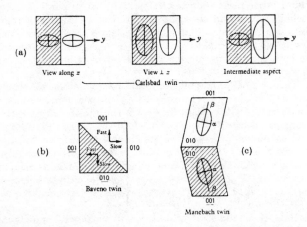

Fig. 100. *Illustration of optical relationships in (a) Carlsbad, (b) Baveno and (c) Manebach twinning in orthoclase.*

uncommon. Under the microscope Baveno twinning is easily recognized, particularly on a (100) section, by the orientation of the composition plane with respect to the {001} or {010} cleavage. In a (100) section there is straight extinction in each individual, and because the twin plane is approximately at 45° to (010) the two parts extinguish simultaneously. Their optical orientations, however, will be opposed (Fig. 100b).

Manebach twinning is in general more difficult to identify since re-entrant angles are extremely small and the composition plane is parallel to the principal cleavage. Sections cut parallel to *y* show straight extinction in each individual and, except for those accurately parallel or normal to (001), the birefringences differ. In (010) sections extinction directions make an angle of about 10° on either side of the composition plane (001) (Fig. 100c).

Sanidine. For sanidine, as for orthoclase, Carlsbad twinning occurs most frequently, but Baveno and Manebach twins are also found.

Albite. Sodium feldspars may show simple twinning on the Carlsbad, Baveno or Manebach laws but more often they twin on the albite, pericline, acline, Estérel or Ala laws. In all of these, twinning is usually repeated and the albite and pericline laws are by far the most common. Sometimes albite and pericline twinning may be shown simultaneously.

Microcline. Microcline is characterized by a combination of albite and pericline twinning which is different from that found in albite. Most microclines are microperthitic and retain the morphology of the monoclinic feldspar from which they have unmixed. The peculiar relationship between the two twin laws in microcline may be taken as evidence that microclines originally crystallized in the monoclinic system. Parts of the crystal have become triclinic with y parallel to the monoclinic y axis and these twin on the pericline law; other parts become triclinic with (010) parallel to (010) of the monoclinic lattice and these twin on the albite law. The regions in which albite and pericline twinning take place are closely interwoven and when viewed between crossed polarizers in a direction approximately parallel to both composition planes, the typical cross-hatched, or 'tartan' pattern is seen.

The orientation of the rhombic section in microclines as determined by the lattice parameters is given by $\sigma \simeq -83°$. Their pericline twinning is best seen on (001) rather than (100), and since the albite composition plane makes an angle of nearly 90° with all planes of the type $(h0l)$, the twinning is well defined on (001), and the cross-hatch intersections are approximately at right angles. On (100) only albite twinning is seen, roughly at 90° to the (001) cleavage, while on (010) only pericline twinning is seen, making an angle of about 83° with the (001) cleavage. Sometimes microperthitic lamellae are also seen on (010), lying in the direction [106], making an angle of about 73° with (001).

Anorthoclase. A combination of pericline and albite twinning similar to that found in microcline also occurs in anorthoclases, showing that these too were probably once monoclinic. The twinning of anorthoclase and microcline can be distinguished, however, since their pericline twin composition planes (rhombic sections) are in very different orientations. The value of σ for anorthoclase lies between $-2°$ and $-5°$ as compared with $-83°$ for microcline (and $+35°$ for low-albite). The two cases are illustrated in Fig. 101 which shows the twinning visible on principal sections. In both microcline and anorthoclase, and indeed in any example of pericline twinning, if a section is viewed strictly along the y axis direction (i.e. along the twin axis) adjacent pericline lamellae will show similar birefringence and optical orientation so that the twin boundaries may not be visible.

CHEMISTRY

The alkali feldspars are essentially a series varying from $KAlSi_3O_8$ to $NaAlSi_3O_8$ but normally also containing a certain amount of $CaAl_2Si_2O_8$ in solid solution. The amount of anorthite present is fairly small, generally less than 5 per cent for $Or_{100}Ab_0$ to $Or_{50}Ab_{50}$, and then tends to increase slightly in the more sodium-rich members of the series. Other ions which may be present in limited amounts include Ba, Ti, Fe^{+3}, Fe^{+2}, Mg, Sr and rarely Mn. Analyses of alkali feldspars are shown in Table 30, where each analysis has been recalculated on the basis of 32 oxygen atoms in the unit cell. The barium-rich feldspars (those with more than about 2 per cent BaO) are treated in a separate section; for the remaining feldspars the Ba is considered to substitute for K. Ferric iron is considered to replace Al, as also is the small amount of Ti sometimes found. Mg, the minor amounts of Fe^{+2}, Sr, and occasional Mn, are all taken to be replacing Ca and recalculated into the anorthite molecule, though it is doubtful whether appreciable Fe^{+2} does in fact occur in the structure, rather than in impurities.

In orthoclase and microcline TiO_2 is generally low, but Fe_2O_3 may be present in appreciable amounts: it is probable, however, that for normal alkali feldspars Fe_2O_3 in excess of about 0·5 per cent represents either impurities, or material which has exsolved on cooling. The latter is present either as discrete particles of iron-bearing mineral, or as iron staining on the grain boundaries and cleavage planes: aventurine feldspar is a variety

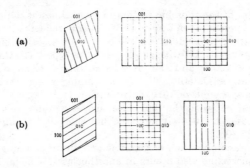

(a)

(b)

Fig. 101. (a) *Albite and pericline twinning in microcline.* (b) *Albite and pericline twinning in anorthoclase.*

with inclusions of haematite. MgO is low in alkali feldspars, but BaO may sometimes become important and amount to 1 per cent or greater. In some pegmatite microclines the rare alkalies may reach major element amounts, as in the Varuträsk rubidium-microcline which contains 0·53–3·30 per cent Rb_2O: this microcline is also notably rich in caesium, and contains in addition up to 0·34 per cent Li_2O. A certain amount of the Na_2O together with some of the CaO reported in analyses of microperthite or perthite is probably due to the presence of a plagioclase phase which is almost invariably present to a greater or lesser degree; it is usually so dominantly sodic as to be albite, though more calcic perthitic blebs are known.

Analyses of sanidine and anorthoclase often show slightly greater amounts of alien ions in solid solution because of their higher temperature of formation, thus TiO_2 may amount to around 0·1 per cent while Fe_2O_3 varies from 0·04 to 0·40 per cent and is sometimes present in still greater quantity even in glass-clear crystals. The rare alkalies are considerably less common in these feldspars than in the microclines although Li_2O and Rb_2O are occasionally reported in small amounts. The anorthite molecule is generally fairly low in sanidine, which typically has less than 1 per cent CaO; in anorthoclase, however, the amount of CaO tends to rise as the Na/K ratio increases towards the composition of albite, and may be as much as 3–4 per cent.

Adularia is confined to the Alpine vein type of paragenesis and as such its compositional range is relatively small, a typical composition being

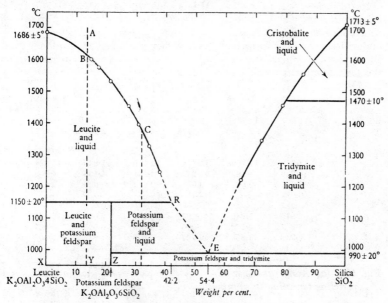

Fig. 102. *Equilibrium diagram of the binary system $KAlSi_2O_6$ (leucite)–SiO_2 (after Schairer, J. F. & Bowen, N. L., 1955, Amer. Journ. Sci., vol. 253, p. 681).*

around $Or_{90}Ab_9An_1$. Iron and magnesium are usually fairly low while barium is noticeably rather high and may approach 1 per cent BaO.

Iron-rich potassium feldspars occur as clear yellow crystals in a miarolitic pegmatite at Itrongay, Madagascar, and show a range of up to 10 per cent of the iron-orthoclase molecule, $KFeSi_3O_8$, the Fe^{+3} ion replacing Al in the structure (e.g. Table 30, anal. 14).

Experimental work. Orthoclase has an incongruent melting point at $1150 \pm 20°C$ (Fig. 102) and the composition of the liquid formed is leucite 57·8, silica 42·2 per cent. The eutectic temperature between potassium feldspar and tridymite is $990 \pm 20°C$ at a composition leucite 45·6, silica

Table 30. ALKALI FELDSPA·

	1.	2.	3.	4.	5.	6.	7.
SiO$_2$	65·76	64·76	64·66	63·66	65·58	64·20	63·68
TiO$_2$	0·08	—	—	—	—	—	0·01
Al$_2$O$_3$	20·23	19·96	19·72	19·54	19·58	19·10	19·57
Fe$_2$O$_3$	0·18	0·08	0·08	0·10	0·21	0·40	0·29
FeO	—	tr.	—	—	—	—	0·24
MgO	0·10	tr.	tr.	—	0·12	—	0·05
BaO	0·63	—	—	—	—	—	0·34
CaO	1·19	0·84	0·34	0·50	0·49	0·34	0·40
Na$_2$O	8·44	5·54	3·42	0·80	5·90	2·60	1·56
K$_2$O	3·29	8·12	11·72	15·60	7·88	12·76	14·21
H$_2$O$^+$	0·37	0·54	0·18	—	0·23	0·72	0·04
H$_2$O$^-$	0·08	—	—	—	0·14	—	0·07
Total	100·35	99·84	100·12	100·20	100·13	100·12	100·46
α	1·528	1·5256	1·5217	1·5188	—	1·5204	—
β	1·533	1·5296	1·5259	1·5230	—	1·5240	—
γ	1·537	1·5326	1·5279	1·5236	—	1·5265	—
2V	78°	82·8°	69·1°	43·6°	—	79·9°	83°–86°
Ext. on (010)	14°	11·7°	9·5°	5·3°	—	7·5°	—
D	—	2·5950	2·5778	2·5632	2·587	2·5771	—

NUMBERS OF IONS ON

	1.	2.	3.	4.	5.	6.	7.
Si	11·719	11·750	11·794	11·759	11·825	11·831	11·730
Al	4·249	4·269	4·240	4·254	4·126	4·148	4·249
Fe^{+3}	0·024	0·011	0·011	0·014	0·029	0·055	0·040
Ti	0·011	—	—	—	—	—	0·001
Mg	0·027	—	—	—	0·032	—	0·014
Na	2·916	1·949	1·209	0·286	2·063	0·929	0·557
Ca	0·227	0·163	0·006	0·099	0·095	0·067	0·078
K	0·748	1·880	2·727	3·676	1·813	3·000	3·340
Ba	0·044	—	—	—	—	—	0·024
Z	16·00	16·03	16·04	16·03	16·02	16·03	16·02
X	3·96	3·99	4·00	4·06	4·00	4·00	4·05†
Mol. % ⎰Or	20·0	47·1	68·1	90·5	45·3	75·1	83·1
⎱Ab	73·6	48·8	30·2	7·1	51·5	23·2	13·7
An	6·4	4·1	1·7	2·4	3·2	1·7	3·2

1. Sodium-rich orthoclase cryptoperthite, ijolite–nepheline-syenite, Mogok, Burma (Tilley, C. E 1954, *Amer. Journ. Sci.*, vol. 252, p. 65).
2. Orthoclase microperthite with white schiller, Burma (Spencer, E., 1930, *Min. Mag.*, vol. 2: p. 291).
3. Orthoclase microperthite (moonstone), Ceylon (Spencer, E., 1937, *Min. Mag.*, vol. 24, p. 453).
4. Orthoclase, Mogok, Burma (Spencer, E., 1930, *Min. Mag.*, vol. 22, p. 291).
5. Microcline perthite, nepheline-syenite, Korea (Yoshizawa, H., 1933, *Chikyu*, vol. 19, p. 432).
6. Microcline microperthite, quartz–feldspar–tourmaline pegmatite, Orissa, India (Spencer, E 1937, *Min. Mag.*, vol. 24, p. 453).
7. Microcline microperthite, charnockite, St. Thomas' Mt., Madras (Howie, R. A., 1955, *Trans. Ro*, *Soc. Edinburgh*, vol. 62, p. 725).

† Includes Fe^{+2} 0·037.

8.	9.	10.	11.	12.	13.	14.	
64·46	67·27	63·62	63·70	66·97	64·28	64·94	SiO_2
—	—	0·08	—	0·04	—	0·00	TiO_2
18·55	18·35	19·12	21·83	18·75	19·19	16·74	Al_2O_3
0·14	}0·92	}0·47	0·18	}0·88	0·09	2·56	Fe_2O_3
—			—		—	0·00	FeO
0·00	0·00	0·05	0·14	0·00	0·10	0·04	MgO
—	—	1·56	—	—	0·11	—	BaO
0·17	0·15	0·05	2·75	0·36	0·11	0·03	CaO
0·49	6·45	2·66	7·55	7·88	0·92	0·79	Na_2O
16·07	7·05	12·09	3·75	5·39	15·30	15·33	K_2O
—	0·08	0·11	0·19	0·01	0·36	—	H_2O^+
0·06	0·08	0·00		0·03		0·00	H_2O^-
99·94	100·35	99·81	100·09	100·31	100·46	100·43	Total
—	1·5232	—	1·5290	1·5239	1·5192	1·5265	α
—	1·5289	—	1·5350	1·5299	1·5228	1·531	β
—	1·5296	—	1·5365	1·5308	1·5245	1·5315	γ
—	33°	—	51°–52°	46°	68·4°	32°–33½°	$2V_\alpha$
—	—	—	6°–8°	—	5·25°	5°	Ext. on (010)
—	—	—	2·589	—	2·5661	—	D

THE BASIS OF 32(O)

11·938	12·030	11·770	11·383	11·932	11·852	12·011	Si
4·050	3·868	4·169	4·598	3·938	4·170	3·650	Al
0·019	0·124	0·096	0·024	0·118	0·012	0·356	Fe^{+3}
—	—	0·011	—	0·005	—	—	Ti
—	—	0·013	0·038	—	0·028	0·011	Mg
0·176	2·236	0·954	2·616	2·722	0·329	0·283	Na
0·033	0·029	0·010	0·526	0·069	0·022	0·006	Ca
3·797	1·609	2·855	0·855	1·226	3·599	3·618	K
—	—	0·113	—	—	0·008	—	Ba
16·01	16·02	16·05	16·00	15·99	16·03	16·02	Z
4·01	3·87	3·95	4·03	4·02	3·99	3·92	X
94·8	41·5	75·5	21·2	30·5	90·5	92·4‡	Or⎫
4·4	57·7	23·9	64·8	67·8	8·3	7·2	Ab⎬ Mol. %
0·8	0·8	0·6	14·0	1·7	1·2	0·4	An⎭

8. Maximum microcline, pegmatite in grennaite, Norra Kärr, Sweden (MacKenzie, W. S., 1954, *Min. Mag.*, vol. 30, p. 354).

9. Sanidine, rhyolite, Mitchell Mesa, Texas (Tuttle, O. F., 1952, *Amer. Journ. Sci.*, Bowen vol., p. 553).

10. Sanidine, leucite–nepheline dolerite, Vogelsberg, Germany (Tilley, C. E., 1958, *Amer. Min.*, vol. 43, p. 758).

11. Anorthoclase, inclusions in augite, Euganean Hills, Italy (Schiavinato, G., 1951, *Periodico Min. Roma*, vol. 20, p. 193).

12. Anorthoclase, Grande Caldeira, Azores (Tuttle, O. F., 1952, *Amer. Journ. Sci.*, Bowen vol., p. 553).

13. Adularia, St. Gotthard, Switzerland (Spencer, E., 1937, *Min. Mag.*, vol. 24, p. 453).

14. Amber-yellow ferriferous orthoclase, Itrongay, Madagascar (Coombs, D. S., 1954, *Min. Mag.*, vol. 30, p. 409).

‡ Includes 9·0 mol. per cent. Fe-Orthoclase.

54·4 per cent (or potassium feldspar 58·2, silica 41·8 per cent). Thus a melt of composition A, undersaturated with respect to silica, would cool to B, when leucite would begin to crystallize. With continued falling temperature and crystallization of leucite the composition of the melt would move along the liquidus curve from B to R: at this reaction point R the liquid reacts with the leucite transforming it into orthoclase; the orthoclase forms roughly twice as rapidly as leucite goes into solution, the reaction being approximately represented by:

$$5KAlSi_2O_6 + \underbrace{3KAlSi_3O_8 + 5SiO_2}_{} \rightarrow 8KAlSi_3O_8$$

leucite   melt   orthoclase

With the original composition of the melt at A, crystallization is completed while some leucite remains, the final product being leucite and orthoclase in the ratio YZ : XY. For a melt with a slight excess of silica, e.g. of composition C, some liquid will remain after the conversion at the reaction point R of all the leucite to orthoclase. The temperature would then continue to fall and the composition of the melt would move along the curve RE with orthoclase continuing to crystallize: at the eutectic E crystallization would be completed and the whole mass would solidify as a mixture of orthoclase and tridymite. If, however, perfect equilibrium is not obtained, the leucite being mantled by orthoclase so that it fails to react completely with the liquid at R, melts of composition A may also give a final product including both orthoclase and free silica.

Studies of the relevant hydrous systems show that with increasing water vapour pressure and with an increasing percentage of water dissolved in the melt, the melting point of orthoclase is appreciably lowered. Orthoclase no longer melts incongruently at a water pressure of about 2500 bars (see Fig. 141, p. 369).

The melting point of albite is 1118°C. Bowen and Tuttle (1950) crystallized albite hydrothermally from a glass and found that under a pressure of water vapour of 1000 bars albite crystals melt at about 900°C to a hydrous albite liquid. Tuttle and Bowen (1950) showed that such material synthesized in the laboratory had X-ray and optical properties different from those of natural albites from pegmatites, but that the natural albites could in some cases be converted, by prolonged heating at a temperature near the melting point, to a form essentially the same as the synthetic material. The synthetic material is referred to as high-temperature albite whereas most naturally occurring albite is low-temperature albite. The synthetic crystals were all of the high-temperature form even when crystallized at temperatures as low as 250°C.

Along the alkali feldspar join, $KAlSi_3O_8$–$NaAlSi_3O_8$, in the system $NaAlSiO_4$–$KAlSiO_4$–SiO_2, there is an unbroken series of solid solutions between the alkali feldspars, with a minimum on the melting and freezing curves at 1063° ± 3°C at 35 wt per cent potassium feldspar. Furthermore, all alkali feldspar compositions with greater than 49 wt per cent potassium feldspar react on heating to give rise to leucite which disappears only at higher temperatures. The composition–temperature projections of the equilibrium diagrams for the system at 2000 bars, 1000 bars and, effectively, zero water vapour pressure are shown in Fig. 103, from which it will be seen that the first 1000 bars of water pressure lowers the minimum of the liquidus by about 220°C, but an additional 1000 bars gives a further lowering of only 73°C, indicating that the lowering effect rapidly decreases at higher pressure. The leucite field is almost eliminated at 2000 bars pressure of water, and it is suppressed entirely at 2500 bars pressure. When alkali feldspar glasses are crystallized at low temperatures with water vapour under pressure to facilitate crystallization, two feldspars and not a single homogeneous feldspar are obtained. The position of the solvus, or unmixing curve, is indicated in each of the three diagrams of Fig. 103, and it is seen that, unlike the solidus and liquidus curves, the position of the

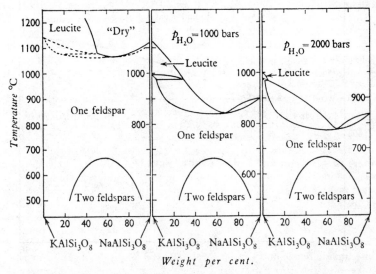

Fig. 103. *Isobaric equilibrium diagrams for the alkali feldspars in dry melts and at 1000 bars and 2000 bars pressure of H_2O (after Bowen, N. L. & Tuttle, O. F., 1950, Journ. Geol., vol. 58, p. 489).*

solvus is only slightly raised (6°/1000 bars) by the change of water pressure (as water does not take part in the equilibria involved at the solvus). At 1000 bars water pressure the solvus is at 660° ± 10°C at a composition close to 55 per cent $NaAlSi_3O_8$: the asymmetry of this solvus indicates that at temperatures below about 500°C albite can have only small amounts of potassium feldspar in solid solution. The projection for the ternary system $KAlSi_3O_8$–$NaAlSi_3O_8$–H_2O at 5000 bars water pressure is given in Fig. 104; the maximum for the solvus is at 715° ± 5°C. For the quaternary system $KAlSi_3O_8$–$NaAlSi_3O_8$–$CaAl_2Si_2O_8$–H_2O at 5000 bars water pressure, the projection of the determined liquidus diagram when gas is present is given in Fig. 105. This diagram differs from that deduced for the system at 2000 bars and it has been suggested that, assuming equilibrium was maintained and an estimate of pressure based on the depth of crystallization is available, the compositions of the coexisting feldspars can yield a measure of the temperature of formation. This problem has been approached from a theoretical viewpoint by Barth (1956), who devised a diagram relating the coexisting feldspar compositions to the temperature (Fig 106).

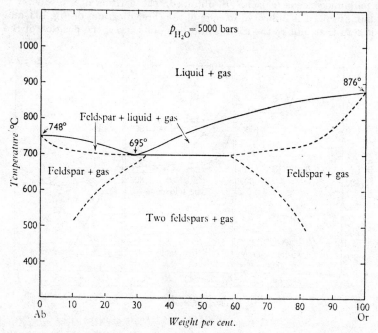

Fig. 104. *Projection of the ternary system $NaAlSi_3O_8$–$KAlSi_3O_8$–H_2O at 5000 bars pressure of H_2O (after Yoder, H. S., Stewart, D. B. & Smith, J. R.,* 1957, Carnegie Inst. Washington, Ann. Rep. Dir. Geophys. Lab., p. 206).

Further experimental work on the alkali feldspars includes various attempts to substitute other ions in $KAlSi_3O_8$. Iron-sanidine, $KFeSi_3O_8$, with Fe^{+3} substituting for Al, has been synthesized: it melts incongruently to iron-leucite and a liquid, the iron-leucite subsequently melting incongruently to haematite and a liquid. The monoclinic polymorph iron sanidine typically results, but under different experimental conditions a triclinic polymorph can be synthesized.

The alkali feldspars are very susceptible to alteration from the action of hydrothermal solutions and from the normal processes of weathering.

Decomposition products commonly include kaolinite, halloysite, sericite, quartz or gibbsite. Although the turbid, brownish appearance of many feldspars, particularly orthoclase, has often been ascribed to the presence of a kaolin-like mineral or incipient sericite, it has been shown that in many cases when the 'turbid' objects are examined under a high magnification they are seen to consist of liquid-filled vacuoles with a fairly strong negative relief. These are thought to be primary or deuteric, trapped during magmatic crystallization, or by related hydrothermal activity: some of the

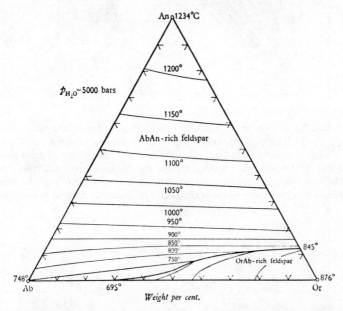

Fig. 105. *Projection of the quaternary system* $NaAlSi_3O_8$–$KAlSi_3O_8$–$CaAl_2Si_2O_8$–H_2O *at 5000 bars pressure of* H_2O *(after Yoder, H. S., Stewart, D. B. & Smith, J. R.,* 1957, Carnegie Inst. Washington, Ann. Rep. Dir. Geophys. Lab., *p.* 206).

vacuoles, however, appear to form on weathering. In most conditions of hydrothermal alteration of feldspars associated with ore deposits, sericite is formed because most metalliferous solutions are alkaline: kaolin, however, is formed near the surface by acid waters and may replace sericite because of leaching by carbonate and sulphate waters.

OPTICAL AND PHYSICAL PROPERTIES

In orthoclase (Fig. 107) and adularia which occur in rocks formed at low temperatures, or in those which have slowly cooled from higher temperatures, the optic axial plane is normal to (010). The same orientation is

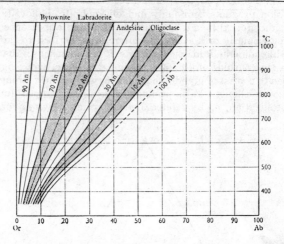

Fig. 106. *The co-existence of alkali feldspar and plagioclase (after Barth, T. F. W., 1956, 3rd Réunion Internat. de la Reactivité à l'état solide, Madrid, p. 363). Abscissa gives the composition of alkali feldspars in terms of Or and Ab; ordinate gives the temperature (°C). The curves indicate the equilibrium relation between the composition of the plagioclases and the composition of the alkali feldspars at various temperatures.*

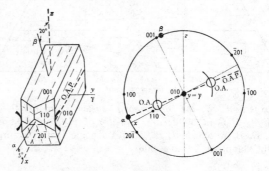

Fig. 107. (a) *Optical orientation of orthoclase.* (b) *Stereogram of the optical orientation of orthoclase.*

shown by microcline (Fig. 108) and by many alkali feldspars, sanidines and anorthoclases (Fig. 109) in volcanic rocks, but in a small number of sanidines (high-sanidine) in rocks formed at high temperatures and cooled rapidly the optic axial plane (Fig. 110) is parallel to (010).

The optic axial angles and orientation of the optic axial plane are the most important and easily measured diagnostic properties by which the alkali feldspars can be divided into the four series: microcline–low-albite,

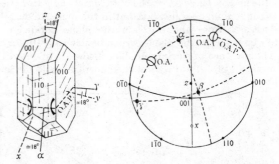

Fig. 108. (a) *Optical orientation of microcline.* (b) *Stereogram of the optical orientation of microcline.*

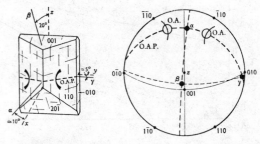

Fig. 109. (a) *Optical orientation of anorthoclase.* (b) *Stereogram of the optical orientation of anorthoclase.*

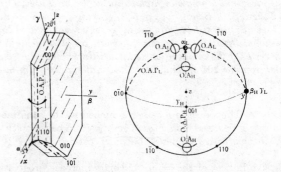

Fig. 110. (a) *Optical orientation of high-sanidine.* (b) *Stereogram showing the optical orientation of high- and low-sanidine.* $O.A.P._H$, *optic axial plane of high-sanidine;* $O.A.P._L$, *optic axial plane of low-sanidine.*

orthoclase–low-albite, sanidine–anorthoclase–high-albite and high-sanidine–
high-albite. In the first three series the optic axial angle increases from the
potassium to the sodium end-member, but in the high-sanidine–high-albite
series 2V decreases from about 62° in the plane parallel to (010) for
$KAlSi_3O_8$ to about 55° in the plane perpendicular to (010) for high-albite
(Fig. 111). The presence of calcium in alkali feldspars in quantities greater
than the equivalent of 3–4 per cent of the anorthite molecule increases the

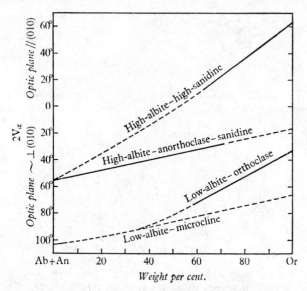

Fig. 111. *Variation of the optic axial angles and composition of the alkali
feldspars, low-albite–microcline, low-albite–orthoclase, high-albite–anorthoclase–sanidine, high-albite–high-sanidine (after Tuttle, O. F., 1952,
Amer. Journ. Sci., Bowen vol., p. 553). Because of the wide range in the
$2V_\alpha$ values of natural feldspars the diagram cannot be used to determine
compositions. It will serve, however, to place an alkali feldspar in one of
the four series if the composition is known approximately from chemical
analysis, from the $\bar{2}01$ spacing on heated material, or from measurement
of the refractive indices.*

optic axial angle. This effect is most pronounced in the sanidine–anorthoclase–high-albite series, and estimates of composition based on the measurement of 2V in this series may not be more precise than ± 10 per cent
$KAlSi_3O_8$.

The refractive indices of the alkali feldspars increase progressively with
increasing amounts of the albite molecule. The rate of increase for the α and
γ values in the orthoclase–low-albite series is greater than for the sanidine–
anorthoclase–high-albite series; the β index is less affected by the thermal

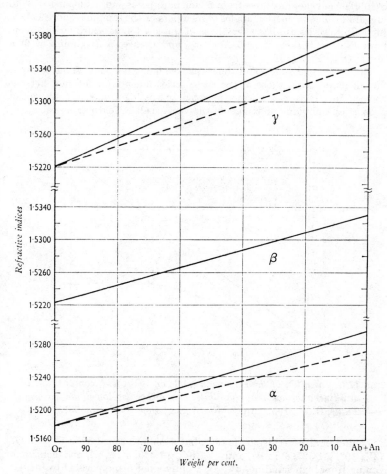

Fig. 112. *Variation of refractive indices with composition of the alkali feldspars (after Tuttle, O. F., 1952, Amer. Journ. Sci., Bowen vol., p. 553). α and γ for the sanidine–anorthoclase–high-albite series are shown as dashed lines, α and γ for the orthoclase–low-albite series as full lines. The β index is essentially the same in both series.*

state of the feldspar and is thus a more reliable guide to the composition of an alkali feldspar (Fig. 112). Because of the relatively large effects of small quantities of anorthite in solid solution, estimates of composition from refractive index measurements can, however, only be used as approximations.

In the orthoclase–low-albite series the extinction angle on (010), i.e.

α' : (001) cleavage, increases from 5° for pure potassium feldspar to 19° for low-albite. The extinction angles of members of the sanidine–anorthoclase–high-albite series are less than those of the low-temperature series of comparable composition; it is 5° for Or_{80} and rises to a maximum of 9° at about Or_{30} (Fig. 113).

The optic axial angles and the refractive indices of some alkali feldspars do not fit precisely those of the three series but are gradational between them. Thus it is not always possible to distinguish, solely on optical properties, individual members of the various alkali feldspar series.

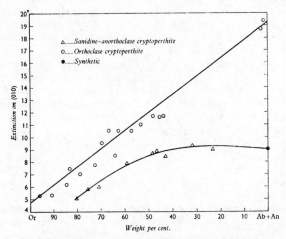

Fig. 113. *Variation of the extinction angle on* (010) *with composition in the sanidine–anorthoclase–high-albite, and orthoclase–low-albite series* (*after Tuttle, O. F.*, 1952, Amer. Journ. Sci., *Bowen vol., p. 553*).

Zoning in alkali feldspars is rare, but sanidines zoned from Or_{77} to Or_{60} ($2V_\alpha$ 15°, γ 1·527, α' : x 4°, and $2V_\alpha$ 30°, γ 1·529, α' : x 8°), and continuous zoning from high sanidine, $2V_\alpha$ 7·8°, optic axial plane parallel to (010), to low-sanidine, $2V_\alpha$ 17·5°, optic axial plane perpendicular to (010), have been reported.

DISTINGUISHING FEATURES

The alkali feldspars are distinguished from the members of the plagioclase series by the absence (except in microcline and anorthoclase) of lamellar twinning, by lower refractive indices, lower specific gravity and the presence of cryptoperthitic or perthitic textures: from quartz by twinning, lower refractive indices and biaxial character.

Orthoclase may be distinguished from sanidine and anorthoclase by its higher optic axial angle, and the presence of microperthitic textures, and from high-sanidine by the orientation of the optic axial plane. Orthoclase is distinguished from microcline by the straight extinction in the zone [010] and the absence of multiple twinning. The cleavage angle (001):(010) in orthoclase is 90° and serves to distinguish it from plagioclase, in which the angle is $\simeq 94°$. It is not possible to distinguish orthoclase or sanidine from either of the triclinic alkali feldspars, anorthoclase or microcline, by cleavage angle.

Microcline is distinguished from other feldspars, except in rare examples, by the 'tartan' twinning in which the two sets of twin lamellae are approximately at right angles to each other, and in which the twinning corresponding to the pericline twins of plagioclase is approximately perpendicular to (001). For most plagioclase compositions the albite and pericline twin lamellae are not at right angles, the trace of the pericline twins makes a small angle with the (001) plane and it is not seen in sections parallel to the basal plane. In the tartan twinning of microcline, the spindle-shaped albite and pericline lamellae wedge out in proximity to each other.

The dispersion of the orthoclase microperthites and microcline microperthites is $r > v$; for sanidine in which the optic axial plane is (010) the dispersion is $r < v$, and for those in which the optic axial plane is perpendicular to (010) the dispersion is $r > v$; for low-albite the dispersion is $r < v$, for high-albite it is $r > v$.

Anorthoclase may be distinguished from sanidine and orthoclase by its tartan twinning, and from orthoclase by lower optic axial angle. The twinning is on a much finer scale than that in microcline and its pericline twin lamellae are almost parallel to (001). It is also distinguished from microcline by a smaller optic axial angle and extinction angle on (001).

There are a number of techniques for staining potassium feldspar in thin sections so that it may easily be distinguished from quartz or untwinned plagioclase feldspar. A rapid method which can be used at room temperature involves uncovering the thin section and etching it with HF by placing it face downwards over an HF bath for 15–30 seconds to prepare the minerals for staining. The stain is applied by immersing the section in a solution of sodium cobaltinitrite (60 g per 100 ml water) for 15–20 seconds, after which the section is rinsed immediately in water. Potassium feldspar takes a pale yellow stain and although white mica and the clay minerals may sometimes absorb the stain they may be distinguished, where potassium feldspar is also present for comparison, by their different relief and intensity of stain. Quartz and plagioclase feldspar are unaffected, though in antiperthite the alkali feldspar blebs may take the stain.

PARAGENESIS

The potassium–sodium feldspars are essential constituents of alkali and acid igneous rocks and are particularly abundant in syenites, granites, granodiorites and their volcanic equivalents; the alkali feldspars are also major constituents of pegmatites and many acid and intermediate gneisses. In the plutonic rocks the alkali feldspar is usually orthoclase,

orthoclase microperthite, microcline, microcline microperthite or microcline perthite, and in volcanic rocks sanidine, sanidine cryptoperthite, anorthoclase cryptoperthite, or anorthoclase. In plutonic rocks the range of the potassium component of the alkali feldspars is Or_{20} to Or_{97} but in the acid plutonic rocks the variation in composition is more restricted and many of the alkali feldspars of these rocks have a composition about Or_{70}. In many syenites and their pegmatites the alkali feldspar is an orthoclase cryptoperthite (Table 30, anal. 1), microcline microperthite or microcline perthite (Table 30, anal. 5) containing between 20 and 50 per cent of the potassium end-member. In the alkali feldspar adularia, of 'alpine' vein paragenesis, the content of the potassium component varies between 80 and 93 per cent.

There is a considerable overlap in the compositions of the alkali feldspars of plutonic and volcanic rocks, but in the latter the potassium component is rarely greater than 75 per cent. The alkali feldspars of the more acid volcanic rocks are generally richer in potassium than the feldspars of alkaline rocks; i.e. the composition of the alkali feldspar of rhyolites varies between Or_{40} and Or_{65}, while in trachytes the common range is Or_{20}–Or_{30}. The alkali feldspars are uncommon in basic rocks but occur in association with olivine in some lamprophyres, and in small amounts, in teschenite, theralite, shonkinite and monchiquite.

Except for those feldspars close to albite in composition and a few sanidines, the alkali feldspars consist of two phases, one potassium- and the other sodium-rich. The texture and appearance of the alkali feldspars show considerable variations and depend partly on their composition, and partly on their post-crystallization history; some of the common types of perthite are illustrated in Fig. 114. A genetic classification of perthites, based on the size of the exsolved phase, in which the various types of perthite are correlated with decreasing temperature of formation and increasing time subsequent to the crystallization of a homogeneous feldspar, is shown below:

1. Sanidine or anorthoclase   Homogeneous crystals
2. X-ray perthite $< 1\,\mu$
3. Cryptoperthite 1–$5\,\mu$
4. Microperthite 5–$100\,\mu$
5. Perthite 100–$1000\,\mu$ (1 mm)
6. Orthoclase (or microcline)
   and albite

Sanidine, anorthoclase, as well as X-ray perthite normally occur in volcanic rocks, cryptoperthite in small hypabyssal intrusions, microperthite and perthite in small plutons, and the individual phases orthoclase or microcline and albite in large plutons. In addition to the relationship between alkali feldspar type and geological environment of their formation, the distribution of the sodium component in co-existing alkali and plagioclase feldspars is closely related to the temperature at which they crystallized. Thus the coefficient of distribution K_T (i.e. the ratio of the mol. fraction of Ab in alkali feldspar to the mol. fraction of Ab in plagioclase) varies from 0·10 to 0·20 in the feldspars of 'alpine'-type veins, from 0·20 to 0·35 in pegmatites, from 0·35 to 0·40 in granites and is approximately 0·60 in trachytes.

Some acid and alkali plutonic rocks contain a single perthitic feldspar, in others two feldspars are present, namely a nearly sodium-free microcline or orthoclase, and a sodium-rich plagioclase. The rocks of the first group, in which the sodium feldspar is present in perthite, are classified as hyper-solvus granites, syenites and nepheline-syenites, as the original feldspar crystallized at a temperature above that of the solvus in the binary system

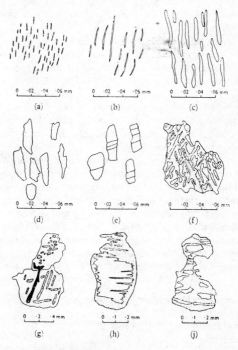

Fig. 114. *Perthite types, (a) stringlets, (b) strings, (c) rods, (d) beads, (e) fractured beads, (f) interlocking, (g) interpenetrating, (h) and (j) replacement (after Alling, H. L., 1938, Journ. Geol., vol. 46, p. 142).*

$NaAlSi_3O_8$–$KAlSi_3O_8$. The acid and alkaline rocks which contain a sodium-rich plagioclase in addition to the potassium feldspar are classified as subsolvus granites, syenites and nepheline-syenites.

The crystallization of feldspars in rhyolites, trachytes and phonolites has been discussed by Tuttle and Bowen (1958) who have indicated the general trend of crystallization and the position of the solidus (LK_SP in Fig. 115) in the ternary system $NaAlSi_3O_8$–$KAlSi_3O_8$–$CaAl_2Si_2O_8$. The figure shows a single field boundary K_LD which divides the fields of alkali feldspar and plagioclase feldspar and corresponds to liquid compositions which are in equilibrium with two feldspars, alkali feldspar from P to K_S, and plagioclase feldspar from K_S to L.

For compositions to the right of the solidus curve LK_SP, equilibrium crystallization occurs with the formation of a single feldspar until the composition of the liquid reaches the field boundary, when the second feldspar begins to crystallize. The plagioclase feldspar changes from an

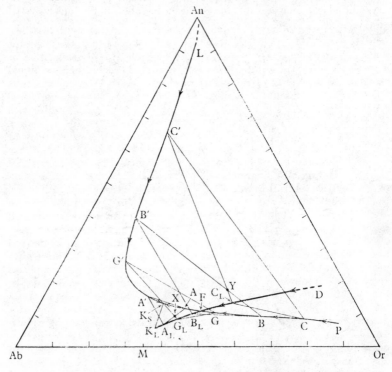

Fig. 115. *Ternary diagram of the system* $NaAlSi_3O_8$–$KAlSi_3O_8$–$CaAl_2Si_2O_8$ *showing the approximate composition of liquids co-existing in equilibrium with two feldspars (after Tuttle, O. F. & Bowen, N. L., 1958, Mem. Geol. Soc. Amer., No. 74).*

anorthite-rich to a more albite-rich composition along the solidus LB′, and the alkali feldspar from potassium-rich to more sodium-rich feldspars, the compositions of which are represented along the solidus from P to B, until no liquid remains. Crystallization in the compositional field K_SK_LF may be illustrated by considering a liquid of composition X. A plagioclase having a calcium content initially greater than G′ crystallizes first, and the composition of the liquid changes to G_L. At this temperature the composition of the plagioclase is G', and a potassium-rich feldspar of composition G begins to crystallize. The composition of the liquid changes along the field boundary curve to A_L, the plagioclase reacts with the liquid, changing in composition from G' to A', and the alkali feldspar changes in composition from G to A. At the temperature of A_L the mixture consists of an alkali feldspar A, liquid A_L and a small amount of plagioclase of composition A'. Just below the temperature of A_L all the plagioclase has reacted with the liquid and the mixture consists of roughly equal amounts of liquid close to A_L in composition, and an alkali feldspar approximately A in composition. With further crystallization the composition of the liquid leaves the field boundary curve and moves towards the albite–orthoclase join, and the alkali feldspar changes in composition towards X. Crystallization is completed when the crystal attains the composition X and no liquid remains. Thus for compositions within the field K_sK_LF crystallization is characterized by the initial formation of a plagioclase, followed later by an alkali feldspar. With equilibrium crystallization the plagioclase reacts with the liquid and is resorbed completely leaving an alkali feldspar and liquid, crystallization being completed when the composition of the alkali feldspar reaches the composition of the original mixture. The probability that the late crystallization of rhyolite, trachyte and phonolite liquids will give rise to the formation of a single alkali feldspar is increased by fractionation during crystallization. In the quickly chilled volcanic rocks such fractionation is effected by the zoning of plagioclase, and the later crystallization of a single feldspar phase is indicated by the formation of sodium-rich sanidine rims around plagioclase.

Fractionation may also affect the mineral composition of rocks derived from liquids which lie to the right of the solidus curve LK_sP. Thus equilibrium crystallization of a liquid of composition Y (Fig. 115) is completed at B_L with the formation of a plagioclase and a potassium-rich feldspar. Fractionation by zoning of the plagioclase would cause the liquid composition to change beyond B_L towards K_L, to leave the field boundary at a point between G_L and A_L, and change in composition along a curved path to M, the $NaAlSi_3O_8$–$KAlSi_3O_8$ binary system minimum. Thus from compositions above the solidus curve $G'K_sP$ a single alkali feldspar may form during the later stages of crystallization and such a crystallization course may account for the feldspar relationships in those granites, syenites and shonkinites in which plagioclase occurs as cores in alkali feldspars.

Origin of perthite. Three processes, unmixing of an originally homogeneous alkali feldspar, simultaneous crystallization of a potassium-rich and a sodium-rich feldspar, and replacement of potassium by sodium feldspar, have each been considered either as the sole process in the formation of perthite, or individually for one or other specific occurrence. Perthites homogenized in the laboratory, on subsequent slow cooling may re-develop the perthitic texture and there is no doubt, particularly in the case of fine regular perthitic intergrowths, that unmixing operates in many instances. Simultaneous crystallization of a potassium- and a sodium-rich feldspar is much less likely and this process is not supported by the crystallization relationships in synthetic feldspar systems. In many pegmatites, vein perthite, patch perthite, chessboard albite and albite occur together. Such associations cannot be satisfactorily explained except on the basis of sodium metasomatism.

Many pegmatites also contain intergrowths of alkali feldspar and quartz, so-called graphic granite. The feldspar is usually a microcline microperthite but some albite or sodic oligoclase may be included in the intergrowths. They resemble the products of synthetic eutectic crystallization and the intergrowths have been considered to result from the simultaneous crystallization of alkali feldspar and quartz. This interpretation has been based on the relatively small range of feldspar : quartz ratios in the intergrowths. The quartz, however, does not in general display a constant orientation with respect to the feldspar, and in some examples the textural relationships are more in accord with the formation of the intergrowths by the partial replacement of alkali feldspar by quartz. A replacement process is most probably also responsible for the formation of the wart-like associations of plagioclase and vermicular quartz, usually described as myrmekite. Such intergrowths, which are especially common in granites, are usually located between adjacent crystals of potassium feldspar and plagioclase and commonly project from the plagioclase into the orthoclase or microcline.

In the rapakivi granites large crystals of potassium feldspar are mantled by plagioclase (albite or oligoclase). Although such mantling can be explained with reference to the system $NaAlSi_3O_8$–$KAlSi_3O_8$–SiO_2–H_2O, other explanations have been postulated to account for the development of the rapakivi texture, e.g. the local migration of sodium derived from the unmixing of perthite. Potassium feldspar is also commonly developed in country rocks around granites, within xenoliths enclosed in granites, and as porphyroblasts in schists and gneisses especially where these rocks are in proximity to acid and intermediate plutonic rocks. Such alkali feldspar porphyroblasts are particularly characteristic of pelitic xenoliths, the composition of which renders it unlikely that the feldspar crystallized as a result of a simple molecular reconstruction of the shale. Their formation is most probably due to the local concentration of potassium and sodium derived either from migrating solutions or by solid diffusion.

Potassium feldspar is a stable product of both high grade thermal and regional metamorphism. It is a typical mineral of the sillimanite zone of metamorphism, and in argillaceous rocks does not occur in rocks of lower metamorphic grade. The formation of potassium feldspar in high grade metamorphic rocks is due largely to the instability of the micas in this P,T environment, and the following reactions may operate:

1. $K(Mg,Fe)_3AlSi_3O_{10}(OH)_2 + 3SiO_2 \rightarrow KAlSi_3O_8 + 3(Mg,Fe)SiO_3 + H_2O$
   biotite   orthoclase   orthopyroxene

2. $2K(Mg,Fe)_{1.5}Al_2Si_3O_{10}(OH)_2 + 3SiO_2 \rightarrow 2KAlSi_3O_8$
   siderophyllite   orthoclase
   $+ (Mg,Fe)_3Al_2Si_3O_{12} + 2H_2O$
   pyrope-almandine

3. $KAl_3Si_3O_{10}(OH)_2 + SiO_2 \rightarrow KAlSi_3O_8 + Al_2SiO_5 + H_2O$
   muscovite   orthoclase   sillimanite

The alkali feldspar of the granulite facies is often dark greenish to brown, or greenish black in hand specimen and has a fine microperthitic structure. The potassium feldspars of the rocks of the charnockite series are predominantly microcline perthites and microcline microperthites (e.g. Table 30, anal. 7).

REFERENCES

BARTH, T. F. W. (1956) 'Zonal structure in feldspars of crystalline schists', 3rd *Réunion International de la Réactivité à l'état solide, Madrid*, sect. 3, p. 363.

—— (1962) 'The feldspar geologic thermometers', *Norsk. Geol. Tidssk.*, vol. 42, p. 330.

BOWEN, N. L. and TUTTLE, O. F. (1950) 'The system $NaAlSi_3O_8-KAlSi_3O_8-H_2O$', *Journ. Geol.*, vol. 58, p. 489.

CARMICHAEL, I. S. E. (1960) 'The feldspar phenocrysts of some Tertiary acid glasses', *Min. Mag.*, vol. 32, p. 587.

—— (1963) 'The crystallization of feldspar in volcanic acid liquids', *Quart. Journ. Geol. Soc.*, vol. 119, p. 95.

CARR, D. R. and KULP, J. L. (1957) 'Potassium-argon method of geochronometry', *Bull. Geol. Soc. Amer.*, vol. 68, p. 763.

JONES, J. B. and TAYLOR, W. H. (1961) 'The structure of orthoclase', *Acta Cryst.*, vol. 14, p. 443.

MACKENZIE, W. S. (1954) 'The orthoclase–microcline inversion', *Min. Mag.*, vol. 30, p. 354.

—— (1957) 'The crystalline modifications of $NaAlSi_3O_8$', *Amer. Journ. Sci.*, vol. 255, p. 481.

SCHAIRER, J. F. (1950) 'The alkali-feldspar join in the system $NaAlSiO_4-KAlSiO_4-SiO_2$', *Journ. Geol.*, vol. 58, p. 512.

—— and BOWEN, N. L. (1947) 'Melting relations in the systems $Na_2O-Al_2O_3-SiO_2$ and $K_2O-Al_2O_3-SiO_2$', *Amer. Journ. Sci.*, vol. 245, p. 193.

TAYLOR, W. H. (1933) 'The structure of sanidine and other feldspars', *Zeit. Krist.*, vol. 85, p. 425.

—— DARBYSHIRE, J. A. and STRUNZ, H. (1934) 'An X-ray investigation of the feldspars', *Zeit. Krist.*, vol. 87, p. 464.

TUTTLE, O. F. and BOWEN, N. L. (1950) 'High-temperature albite and contiguous feldspars', *Journ. Geol.*, vol. 58, p. 572.

—— —— (1958) 'Origin of granite in the light of experimental studies in the system $NaAlSi_3O_8-KAlSi_3O_8-SiO_2-H_2O$', *Mem. Geol. Soc. Amer.*, No. 74.

Plagioclase

Na[AlSi$_3$O$_8$]–Ca[Al$_2$Si$_2$O$_8$]

TRICLINIC (+) or (−)

	High-temperature Albite	Albite	Anorthite
	NaAlSi$_3$O$_8$	NaAlSi$_3$O$_8$	CaAl$_2$Si$_2$O$_8$
α	1·527	1·527	1·577
β	1·532	1·531	1·585
γ	1·534	1·538	1·590
δ	0·007	0·010$_5$	0·013$_5$
2V	45°(−)	77°(+)	78°(−)

For optic orientation see Fig. 121, p. 331

Dispersion:	$r > v$	$r < v$	$r < v$
D	2·62	2·63	2·76
H	—	6–6½	6–6½

Cleavage: {001} perfect, {010} good, {110} poor.

Twinning: (a) Multiple lamellar albite twins [Composition plane (010), twin axis ⊥(010)]. (b) Simple Carlsbad twins [Composition plane (010), twin axis z]. (c) Many other normal, parallel and complex twins (see Table 29, p. 293).

Colour: Normally colourless or white, but sometimes yellow, pink, green or black; colourless in thin section.

Insoluble in HCl, except anorthite.

The plagioclase feldspars are ubiquitous and represent the commonest rock-forming mineral series. High-temperature plagioclases occur in some volcanic rocks while the low-temperature albite–anorthite series are found in most igneous rocks, are common in metamorphic rocks, and occur in sediments both as primary and as authigenic minerals.

It should be noted that although the variation in refractive indices of the low-temperature series is essentially continuous from albite to anorthite, many of the other optical and physical properties vary in a more complex manner between the end-member values quoted above, and for more detailed information reference must be made to the appropriate section below.

The plagioclase feldspar series includes the six minerals albite, oligoclase, andesine, labradorite, bytownite and anorthite: the divisions are taken at anorthite mol. percentages 0–10, 10–30, 30–50, 50–70, 70–90 and 90–100 respectively. The intergrowth of potassium and plagioclase feldspars with plagioclase as the dominant phase or host is termed antiperthite.

STRUCTURE

The structures of the plagioclase feldspars have triclinic symmetry and are similar to those already described for albite (p. 289), involving a framework of linked (Si,Al)–O tetrahedra, the large interstices of this framework being filled by (Ca,Na) ions. In matters of detail the structures of plagioclases are complex, and vary according to chemical composition, conditions of crystallization and thermal history. As in the case of albite, so also for the whole plagioclase series, there are high-, low- and intermediate-temperature structural states. In the high-temperature series there is solid solution over the entire range. 'High' plagioclases from An_0 to An_{90} possess the high-albite structure which has a C face centred cell with $a \simeq 8{\cdot}17$, $b \simeq 12{\cdot}88$, $c \simeq 7{\cdot}10$ Å, $Z = 4$. (The structures of both low- and high-temperature albite are discussed under alkali feldspars.) Specimens with composition An_{90}–An_{100}, when quenched from high temperatures, do not show the high-albite structure perhaps because inversion from it towards the low-temperature form is extremely rapid. The difference between high- and low-temperature states is again a matter of the degree of order in the distribution of Si and Al atoms among the tetrahedral sites.

The low-temperature series is not continuous but contains four structural divisions, the compositional ranges of which are approximately as shown below:

The *low-albite* structure can take only very little calcium into solid solution (to about An_3).

Peristerites. In the range An_3 to An_{22}, plagioclases are generally submicroscopic intergrowths of sodium-rich and calcium-rich regions. The two phases probably have the structures and compositions of the limiting members of the range, i.e. low-albite and intermediate structure respectively, and they are related in orientation by having their (010) planes nearly parallel. Some of these unmixed specimens show a characteristic schiller effect and consequently they have been named peristerites, but this name is sometimes applied to the whole range whether or not schiller can be seen. Peristerites can be homogenized by heating to yield a member of the high-temperature plagioclase series with high-albite structure.

Low-temperature anorthite has a fully ordered structure in which the equal numbers of Si and Al atoms alternate with strict regularity. The unit cell is primitive rather than face centred and the c dimension is double that in albite (anorthite has a 8·18, b 12·88, c 14·17 Å, α 93° 10′, β 115° 51′, γ 91° 13′, $Z = 8$). The unit cell can be regarded as made up of four albite-like sub-cells, all differing slightly in the structural arrangement of their contents.

When some sodium replaces calcium in the anorthite structure there must be an equivalent replacement of Si for Al and so the regular alternation of Si and Al can no longer occur. Instead of a continuous regular arrangement of the four sub-cells a domain structure occurs with faults occurring at the domain boundaries. The effect of these faults is to cause diffuseness of the reflections which have $(h+k+l)$ odd, and with increasing sodium the frequency of faults and the diffuseness increase until at about Ab_{20} these reflections are no longer observable. At this composition therefore the structure appears to be body-centred although it is really a faulted primitive structure.

When plagioclases in the range An_{77}–An_{100} are heated, the effect on the $(h+k+l)$ odd reflections is similar to that of increasing the Na content. The change from primitive through a transitional to an apparently body-

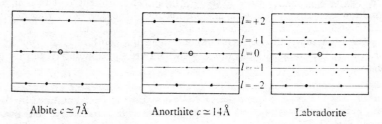

Albite $c \simeq 7$Å   Anorthite $c \simeq 14$Å   Labradorite

Fig. 116. *Diagram showing schematically the additional reflections from anorthite through doubling of c, and the pairs of subsidiary reflections which replace them in labradorite.*

centred structure is a reversible function of temperature. For natural Ca-rich plagioclases the diffuseness of the $(h+k+l)$ odd reflections is an indication of temperature of crystallization.

Increase of Na beyond about Ab_{27} gives rise to further changes in the plagioclase structure. A more complicated system of faults occurs and the effect on X-ray diffraction photographs is to replace the reflections with $(h+k)$ odd, l odd, by pairs of subsidiary reflections (Fig. 116), the separation of which varies linearly with composition.

Plagioclases which give diffraction effects of this sort have been referred to as 'intermediate'. When 'intermediate' plagioclases are heated the extra reflections become diffuse, and for natural specimens, their diffuseness may give an indication of temperature of crystallization while their positions indicate chemical composition.

The boundary between 'intermediate' plagioclases and peristerites is not clearly defined, neither is that between the 'intermediate' and the anorthite structures.

The lattice parameters of plagioclase feldspars vary systematically with

An content, so that it is possible to estimate their compositions by measuring the separations of suitable pairs of reflections on X-ray powder patterns. In the range An_0–An_{20}, for example, the separation 131–1$\bar{3}$1 is a useful indication of composition for low-temperature plagioclases. Except for plagioclases more calcium-rich than An_{90}, however, the thermal state of the feldspar also influences peak positions so that in general either thermal state or composition must be known in order to determine the other.

MORPHOLOGY AND TWINNING

The principal forms exhibited by plagioclase crystals are similar to those of the alkali feldspars, and because of the slight obliquity of the triclinic cell plagioclase habits differ but little from those of some monoclinic feldspars. Crystals are often tabular with {010} prominent but are sometimes elongated parallel to the x axis, and more rarely parallel to z. The unusual pericline habit of albite which is elongated parallel to y is illustrated in Fig. 96, p. 292. The cleavelandite habit of albite is platy parallel to (010). Perfect cleavage on {001} and good {010} cleavage intersect at an angle of about 94°, and poor {110} and {1$\bar{1}$0} cleavages are sometimes observable.

The plagioclases with composition An_3–An_{22}, which are divided on a very fine scale into sodium-rich and calcium-rich regions, often yield crystals which are iridescent, particularly when viewed on the (010) face. These are known as peristerites, an allusion to the play of colours seen on a pigeon's neck. The iridescence (or 'chatoyance') is similar to that exhibited by the perthitic intergrowths of alkali feldspars; the term 'moonstone' has been applied to both but is perhaps better restricted to alkali feldspars. These effects are said to result from reflection (or diffraction) occurring at the boundaries between perthite or peristerite lamellae, but an alternative explanation in terms of the diffusion of light by neighbouring small domains of differing optical properties has been suggested. Feldspars with composition in the labradorite range often show a somewhat different type of iridescence, also seen best on (010). Aventurine feldspar has plate-like inclusions of an iron mineral which give the specimen a spangled appearance.

Plagioclase feldspars usually show repeated twinning on a microscopic scale, but occasionally simple Manebach, and very rarely, simple Baveno twins occur. Carlsbad twinning is quite common and may be either repeated or simple. Repeated twins on the albite and/or pericline laws are most frequent of all, albite twinning rarely being absent, and twins on other laws (e.g. acline, ala, albite–Carlsbad, albite–Ala B) are not uncommon, see Table 29, p. 293. Pericline and albite twinning often occur in the one crystal, and other combinations of two or more laws have been observed.

The position of the rhombic section (see p. 295) depends upon the angles of the crystal lattice and these are influenced in the plagioclase series both by chemical composition and by structural state. In low temperature specimens σ ranges from about $+35°$ for An_0 to about $-20°$ for An_{100}, while for high-temperature plagioclases σ changes little with composition from the value ($4°-6°$) for high-albite.

CHEMISTRY

Although essentially aluminosilicates of Na and Ca varying from pure $NaAlSi_3O_8$ to pure $CaAl_2Si_2O_8$, the plagioclase series normally contains a certain amount of the orthoclase molecule, $KAlSi_3O_8$, varying up to 5 mol. per cent. Or from anorthite to labradorite and then tending to increase gradually towards the sodic end of the series (Fig. 91). Other ions which may be present in very limited amounts include Ti, Fe^{+3}, Fe^{+2}, Mn, Mg, Ba and Sr. Analyses of plagioclases are shown in Table 31, where each analysis has been recalculated on the basis of the 32(O) contained in the unit cell. In such recalculations it has been considered that Fe^{+3} is replacing Al in the structure. Most of the iron reported in feldspar analyses is shown to be Fe^{+3}; the small amounts of Fe^{+2} sometimes recorded must be considered either as an impurity or as replacing Ca. In the absence of any evidence as to possible impurity in the sample, these ions have all therefore been considered to be replacing Ca and contributing to the anorthite molecule.

In Table 31 the analyses are re-stated in terms of the molecular percentage of the albite, anorthite and orthoclase end-members. These values vary slightly from the weight percentage figures sometimes quoted, being coincident at the albite and anorthite end-members, but having a divergence of approximately 1–1½ per cent near An_{50}, where the molecular percentage gives a lower value for the anorthite component than does the weight percentage.

The development of antiperthite is usually found in plagioclases of the oligoclase and andesine range (e.g. anal. 4): it is less common in albite and almost unknown in labradorite and more calcic feldspars.

Experimental work. The equilibrium diagram for the plagioclase feldspars (Fig. 117) shows a solid solution without maximum or minimum, the melting point of anorthite being at 1550°C, and that of albite at 1100°C. From this equilibrium diagram it can be seen that a liquid of composition $An_{50}Ab_{50}$ (A) begins to crystallize at about 1450°C, the first crystals having the composition of approximately $An_{82}Ab_{18}$ (B). With further cooling and attainment of perfect equilibrium both liquid and crystals change their composition along the liquidus and solidus respectively until at 1285°C the crystals reach a composition of $An_{50}Ab_{50}$ (D) as the last of the liquid, of composition (C), is used up. This continuous change in composition of the plagioclase crystals with falling temperature is only possible given sufficient time for the earlier crystals to react with the liquid: if there is insufficient time for this interchange of material the crystals will be zoned. The resultant product will then have an average composition of $An_{50}Ab_{50}$ but the inner core will be more calcic and the outer zones more sodic. Thus as a result of fractionation by zoning a continuous offsetting of the composition of the liquid towards albite is brought about together with a great increase in the range of consolidation temperatures. Such zoning, from more calcic cores to sodic rims, is common in plagioclases, but examples are also fairly common with oscillatory zoning where the composition is alternately less and more calcic: simple reverse zoning where the crystals become more calcic outwards is not rare.

The shape of the region where liquid and crystals are stable in the ternary system $NaAlSi_3O_8$–$CaAl_2Si_2O_8$–H_2O is essentially that of Fig. 117 but with the liquidus temperatures depressed over 300°C by the addition of water at 5000 bars.

Among other experimentally investigated systems containing a plagioclase field perhaps the most important is the ternary system $CaMgSi_2O_6$ (diopside)–$CaAl_2Si_2O_8$ (anorthite)–$NaAlSi_3O_8$ (albite). Diopside with albite

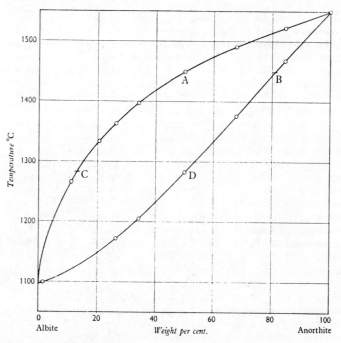

Fig. 117. *Equilibrium diagram of the plagioclase feldspars (after Bowen, N. L., 1913, Amer. Journ. Sci., 4th Ser., vol. 35, p. 577).*

or anorthite was believed originally to form a binary eutectic, but a re-investigation of the diopside–anorthite system has indicated that the diopside–anorthite relationship may not be completely binary, probably because the diopside present contained a small amount of Al occupying Mg and Si positions in the structure. In the ternary system there is only one boundary curve separating the plagioclase and diopside fields. Plagioclase of a given composition crystallizes at an appreciably lower temperature from a melt containing diopside, and the temperature at which the melt becomes completely crystalline also is lowered. The liquidus diagram for the $CaMgSi_2O_6$(diopside)–$CaAl_2Si_2O_8$(anorthite)–water system shows that,

Table 31. PLAGIOCLASE FELDSPAR

	1.	2.	3.	4.
SiO_2	67·84	67·41	64·10	58·10
TiO_2	0·00	—	0·00	tr.
Al_2O_3	19·65	20·50	22·66	26·44
Fe_2O_3	0·03	0·07	0·14	0·04
FeO	0·02	—	0·17	0·15
MgO	0·04	0·10	0·25	0·03
CaO	0·00	0·81	3·26	7·84
Na_2O	11·07	10·97	9·89	6·48
K_2O	0·29	0·36	0·05	1·10
H_2O^+	0·56	0·15	0·17	0·03
H_2O^-	0·30		0·06	0·06
Total	99·80	100·37	100·75	100·27
α	1·529	1·5283	1·5351	—
β	1·533	1·5327	1·5393	—
γ	1·539	1·5392	1·5437	—
2V	79°(+)	79½°(+)	89°(+)	88°(+)
α' :(010)	—	18½°–19°	11½°	—
D	—	2·619	2·646	—

NUMBERS OF IONS ON

Si	11·964	11·785	11·267	10·413
Al	4·085	4·225	4·695	5·586
Fe^{+3}	0·004	0·009	0·018	0·005
Mg	0·011	0·026	0·065	0·008
Fe^{+2}	0·003	—	0·025	0·023
Na	3·785	3·718	3·370	2·252
Ca	—	0·152	0·614	1·505
K	0·066	0·080	0·011	0·252
Z	16·05	16·02	15·98	16·00
X	3·87	3·98	4·08	4·04
Mol.% ⎧Ab	98·0	93·5	82·5	56·0
⎨An	0·3	4·5	17·2	37·7
⎩Or	1·7	2·0	0·3	6·3

1. Albite, pegmatite, near Court House, Amelia Co., Virginia (Kracek, F. C. & Neuvonen, K. J., 1952, *Amer. Journ. Sci.*, Bowen vol., p. 293).
2. Albite, with quartz and sphene in crevice in amphibolite, Val Devero, Italy (Azzini, F., 1933, *Atti Accad. Sci. Veneto-Trentino-Istriana*, vol. 23, p. 45).
3. Glassy oligoclase, pegmatite, Kioo Hill, Kenya (Game, P. M., 1949, *Min. Mag.* vol. 28, p. 682).
4. Andesine antiperthite, two-pyroxene granulite, charnockite series, Madras (Howie, R.A., 1955, *Trans. Roy. Soc. Edinburgh*, vol. 62, p. 725).

ANALYSES

5.	6.	7.	8.	
52·96	49·06	44·17	43·88	SiO_2
tr.	—	tr.	—	TiO_2
29·72	32·14	34·95	36·18	Al_2O_3
0·84	0·27	0·56	0·08	Fe_2O_3
—	—	0·08	0·00	FeO
—	0·20	0·00	—	MgO
12·28	15·38	18·63	19·37	CaO
4·21	2·57	0·79	0·22	Na_2O
0·13	0·17	0·05	0·00	K_2O
0·08	0·13	0·84	0·28	H_2O^+
	0·03	0·17	0·08	H_2O^-
100·22	99·95	100·24	100·10	Total
1·560	1·5657	1·574	1·5754	α
1·565	1·5701	1·582	1·5833	β
1·570	1·5754	1·586	1·5885	γ
—	89°(−)	78°(−)	76·8°–77·7°(−)	2V
23½°	—	—	—	$\alpha':(010)$
2·705	—	—	2·749	D

THE BASIS OF 32(O)

9·589	8·990	8·237	8·126	Si
6·343	6·942	7·683	7·898	Al
0·114	0·037	0·078	0·011	Fe^{+3}
—	0·055	—	—	Mg
—	—	0·012	—	Fe^{+2}
1·477	0·913	0·285	0·079	Na
2·383	3·202	3·723	3·844	Ca
0·030	0·040	0·012	—	K
16·05	15·97	16·00	16·03	Z
3·89	4·03	4·03	3·92	X
38·0	22·7	7·1	2·0	Mol.% ⎧ Ab
61·2	76·3	92·6	98·0	⎨ An
0·8	1·0	0·3	—	⎩ Or

5. Labradorite, Millard Co., Utah (Meen, V. B., 1933, *Univ. Toronto Studs.*, *Geol. Ser.*, no. 35, p. 37).
6. Bytownite, norite, Rustenburg platinum mines, Transvaal (Kracek, F. C. & Neuvonen, K. J., 1952, *loc. cit.*).
7. Anorthite, olivine norite, Grass Valley, California (Kracek, F. C. & Neuvonen, K. J., 1952, *loc. cit.*).
8. Anorthite, calc-silicate rock, Sittampundi complex, India (Subramaniam, A. P., 1956, *Bull. Geol. Soc. Amer.*, vol. 67, p. 317; includes SrO 0·01).

at 5000 bars water vapour pressure, the composition of the eutectic is shifted from 42 weight per cent to about 73 per cent. An, and the eutectic temperature is lowered from 1274° to 1095°C.

An experimental illustration of the spilite reaction was obtained by heating either synthetic anorthite, or natural basic plagioclase, with SiO_2 and water in a bomb, together with Na_2CO_3 and $NaHCO_3$, the plagioclase being thereby albitized. Pure albite was obtained at 264°–331°C and oligoclase and andesine at 360°–550°C.

Some plagioclases appear clouded due to the presence of numerous minute dark particles distributed throughout the crystals. This clouding is distinct from the turbidity due to alteration caused by the development of kaolinite or sericite and is due to the presence of iron-bearing minerals, typically magnetite, ilmenite, or haematite, but also spinel, garnet, biotite, rutile or hornblende. Such clouding has been attributed to the exsolution of iron ore, originally contained in the plagioclase in solid solution, due to thermal metamorphism. It has also been suggested that the iron-bearing material has been introduced into the crystal after its formation (see p. 337).

Alteration. The plagioclase feldspars are susceptible to changes by the action of hydrothermal solutions, the more sodic varieties being more stable than those richer in the anorthite molecule. Among alteration products recorded are montmorillonite, scapolite, prehnite and various zeolites. The albitization of more basic plagioclase is a well-known phenomenon, particularly in spilites.

The alteration of plagioclase has been investigated experimentally. Crystals of albite suspended in an autoclave with pure water at 200°–350°C and 300 bars pressure break down to particles having colloidal dimensions which constitute an alumina–silica gel, and which subsequently form crystals of a zeolite (probably analcite). Hydrolysis equilibria involving albite and its decomposition products in an aqueous chloride environment at elevated temperatures and pressures show that at high temperatures (> 400°C, 15,000 lb/in² total pressure) albite is altered to paragonite plus quartz, which may become converted to pyrophyllite: at lower temperatures corresponding reactions are the decomposition of albite to montmorillonite and the alteration of montmorillonite to kaolinite.

OPTICAL AND PHYSICAL PROPERTIES

The optical properties of the plagioclases are directly related to their anorthite content. The relief and birefringence are both low and similar to those of quartz, but although the birefringence is rather irregularly variable the refractive indices increase steadily with increasing anorthite content and can be used to determine the composition of the plagioclase. The perfect {001} and good {010} cleavages, together with a systematic variation in the optic orientation within the series, allow the extinction angles to be used to determine the albite–anorthite ratio, and particular use is made of these in conjunction with the multiple albite twinning with composition plane (010). The optic axial angle for natural low-temperature plagioclase varies from approximately $2V_\alpha$ 75°, through 90°, to $2V_\gamma$ 75° but changes sign three times in the series, and is of less diagnostic value. Other properties varying with the composition and used for determining the plagioclases include the specific gravity, and the birefringence in sections of known orientation.

The refractive indices of the plagioclase feldspars are closely related to the chemical composition. A determinative chart is given in Fig. 118: it is important to note that the measurement of the refractive indices must be accurate to $\pm 0 \cdot 001$ to obtain an accuracy of ± 2 per cent An. The refractive indices of high-temperature plagioclases vary slightly from those of the normal low-temperature series: the difference in the α indices is very small

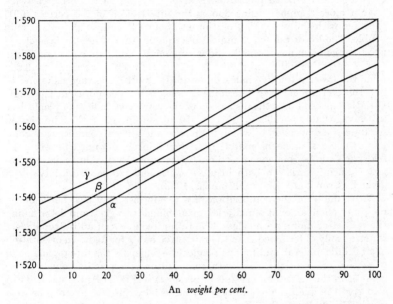

Fig. 118. *Determinative chart for the plagioclase series (after Chayes, F., 1952, Amer. Journ. Sci., Bowen, vol., p. 85).*

but that for γ is more noticeable, e.g. natural low-temperature albite has α 1·5274, γ 1.5379, whereas synthetic high-temperature albite has α 1·527, γ 1·534. Thus measurements of α will give a reliable estimate of the composition of a plagioclase regardless of its structural state: if the composition is so determined, the structural state may be indicated by X-ray methods or by the optic axial angle.

An approximation for the refractive indices of the more sodic plagioclases may be made in thin section by observing the Becke line on boundaries with quartz (ω 1·544, ϵ 1·553), or with the mounting medium where its refractive index is reliably known (that of Canada Balsam may vary from 1·532 to 1·542 depending on age and method of preparation). In this way it may be possible to place a plagioclase more sodic than about An_{48} into one of five compositional subdivisions.

The normal immersion method using sodium light is relatively rapid and is capable of giving sufficient accuracy of refractive indices of the plagioclase series for normal purposes. When working with cleavage fragments two varieties may be recognized: the perfect basal cleavage {001} and the slightly less perfect cleavage parallel to {010} give fragments lying on a cleavage plane displaying the two orientations illustrated in Fig. 122. The somewhat rectangular fragments lying on the {001} cleavage have the {010} cleavage almost vertical and show the multiple albite twin lamellae parallel to {010} under crossed polarizers. Fragments lying on the {010} cleavage have a more angular outline due to the intersection of the perfect {001} cleavage with the poor {100} parting at about 64° and no albite twins are visible. The lower refractive indices obtainable from either of these cleavage fragments do not normally differ appreciably, and are also close to the true α refractive index, so that it is usually sufficiently accurate to determine the lower refractive index on an {001} or {010} cleavage flake and to plot this on the α curve to determine the plagioclase composition. The single variation method uses the dispersion of the refractive indices of plagioclase in cleavage flakes parallel to {001} or {010} in conjunction with an immersion medium the dispersion of which is known: the refractive indices are compared, using a monochromator, until matching is obtained between the feldspar and the immersion medium. Details of the double variation procedure, using variation both in wavelength and temperature, have been given by Crump and Ketner (Emmons, 1953).

An estimate of the composition of a plagioclase may also be made by melting a small amount of material, quenching it to a glass and determining the refractive index of the glass. The refractive index of an isotropic glass is more easily determined than the refractive index for a known orientation in a triclinic mineral, and for the plagioclase feldspars the rate of change in refractive index of the glass with composition is approximately twice as great as in the indices for crystals of plagioclase (Fig. 119); the method can also give the average composition for material with strong zoning or with exsolution intergrowths. The refractive indices of orthoclase and albite glasses are rather similar (1·487 and 1·489 respectively), thus the presence of even substantial amounts of the orthoclase molecule has little effect on the determination of the anorthite content: the original structural state of the plagioclase is of no consequence.

The optic axial angle of plagioclases for the normal low-temperature series is always large (> 75°), the optic sign being (+) for albite, changing to (−) in the more calcic oligoclase range, becoming (+) again for most andesines and reverting to (−) in bytownite and anorthite. High-temperature plagioclases have different optics: for albite the change of 2V and sign from $2V_\gamma$ 83° for natural low-temperature crystals to $2V_\alpha$ 45° can be induced by heating at 1080°C for three weeks. Data for both low- and high-temperature plagioclases are shown in Fig. 120.

The optic orientation varies considerably with the composition. In low-temperature albite the optic axial plane is approximately perpendicular to z, but in the more calcic plagioclases it tilts over (Fig. 121) until in anorthite it is almost parallel to z.

The variation in the optic orientation causes the extinction angles on {001} and {010} cleavage fragments to vary systematically with composition. Determinative curves for use with cleavage fragments are given in Fig. 122. The extinction angles are measured from the fast vibration

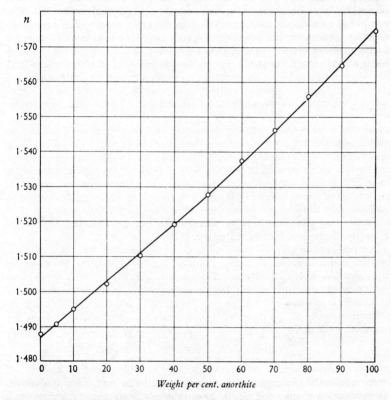

Fig. 119. *Refractive indices of glasses of plagioclase compositions (after Schairer, J. F., Smith, J. R. & Chayes, F., 1956, Carnegie Inst. Washington, Ann. Rep. Dir. Geophys. Lab., p. 195).*

direction (α') to the cleavage trace, the sign convention being shown in Fig. 122.

The maximum extinction angles of albite twins in sections normal to {010} or in the so-called symmetrical zone are diagnostic (Fig. 123). In thin section the alternate twin lamellae give symmetrical extinction angles on either side of the twin plane. Such sections may be recognized by the sharpness of the composition plane between albite twin lamellae, which should show no lateral movement when the microscope focus is raised or lowered, by the equal interference colours of the twin lamellae when the twin plane is parallel to the vibration directions of the polarizers, and by adjacent lamellae giving equal extinction angles on either side of the twin plane. Values which show more than a 5 per cent divergence in the extinction angles for the adjacent twin lamellae should be discarded, lesser variations may be averaged: it is essential to take measurements from several (6–12) suitable grains, and the *highest* symmetrical extinction angle must then be used. In all plagioclase determinative methods using extinction observations, the position of extinction may sometimes be more easily recognized with the aid of a 'sensitive tint plate'. The composition obtained from Fig. 123 using this method is ambiguous in that albite and

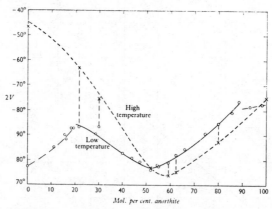

Fig. 120. *Optic axial angles of low-temperature natural plagioclases* (*circles*) *and of some of the same samples after they had been heated near the solidus* (*crosses*). *The cross at* An_{100} *represents the* $2V$ *of anorthite synthesized in the dry way* (*after Smith, J. R., 1958, Amer. Min., vol. 43, p. 1188*).

sodic oligoclase can give similar values to andesine and calcic oligoclase: the refractive indices will generally eliminate this ambiguity, otherwise a combined twin method may be used. The latter method makes use of the difference in the extinction of the albite and Carlsbad twins for two individuals related by the Carlsbad law, this difference being given by the dotted curve (A) of Fig. 123: for Ab_{100} to Ab_{24} the maximum difference does not exceed 5°, while from Ab_{25} to Ab_{50} it rises from 6° to 16°. It is, however, important to be sure that the additional twinning is according to the Carlsbad law and not, for example, Ala B twinning which also has its composition plane parallel to (010): this may be ensured by the precautions outlined in the section below on a further use of combined albite–Carlsbad twins.

The extinction angle in sections normal to x is also diagnostic, and varies approximately 1° for each 1 per cent An from An_0 to An_{70} and then by about

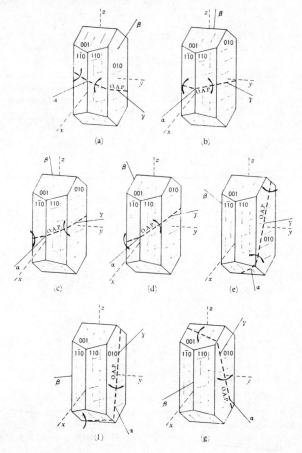

Fig. 121. *Optic orientation of the plagioclase feldspars:* (a) *high-albite*, (b) *low-albite*, (c) *oligoclase*, (d) *andesine*, (e) *labradorite*, (f) *bytownite*, (g) *anorthite*.

$\frac{1}{2}°$ for each 1 per cent An to An_{100}. The composition of the plagioclase can thus be obtained from only one suitable section, i.e. it is not necessary to measure the maximum extinction angle for a large number of sections. Such a section is normal to both the {001} and {010} cleavages, shows the albite twin lamellae on {010}, the {001} cleavage forms an angle of 86° with the {010} cleavage and albite twin lamellae, and the cross-section tends to show an almost square outline (Fig. 123).

Extinction angles of combined Carlsbad and albite twins in the symmetrical zone normal to {010} also have a relationship which enables their measurement on a single section to be sufficient to determine the plagioclase composition (Fig. 124); such sections, however, are sometimes rare. The mean of the two extinction angles on the portions related by the albite law, measured from α' to $\{010\}$, is plotted in conjunction with the extinction

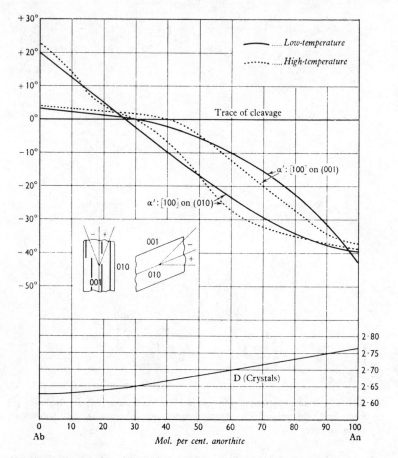

Fig. 122. *Extinction angles (to α') on plagioclase cleavage flakes parallel to (001) and (010); specific gravity of plagioclase grains.*

angle from α' to $\{010\}$ for the second half of the Carlsbad twin (if the second portion also shows albite twinning the mean extinction angle is again used). Suitable sections may be recognized by the fact that when the trace of the twin plane is oriented at 45° to the vibration directions of the polarizers, the albite twinning disappears and the crystal appears to be a simple Carlsbad

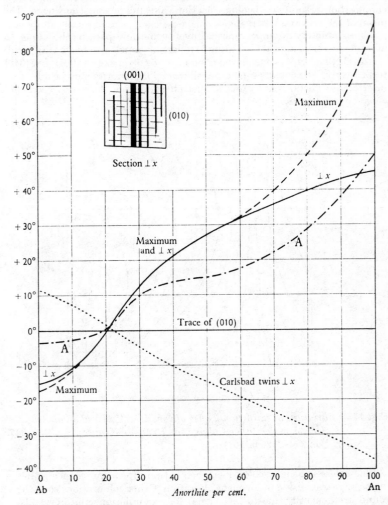

Fig. 123. *Extinction angles (with respect to α') in the 'symmetrical zone' and in sections normal to x.*

twin; when the trace of the twin plane is parallel to the vibration directions of the polarizers both albite and Carlsbad twins disappear, or are almost invisible.

A description of methods for determining plagioclase compositions and twin laws by means of the universal microscope stage is beyond the scope of this text. However, the most comprehensive accounts written in English are those of Chudoba (1933), Emmons (1943), Turner (1947) and Slemmons (1962), that of Emmons dealing with the 5-axis universal stage whereas the others deal with the 4-axis stage.

The characteristic appearance of aventurine feldspars in the albite to labradorite range appears to be due to reflecting lamellae of haematite parallel to {112} and {150} causing the phenomenon to appear on {001} and {010} respectively. The colours sometimes shown by labradorite may be due to an interference phenomenon; this schiller effect has not, however, been conclusively explained.

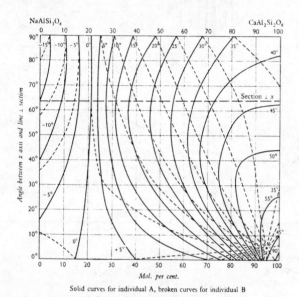

Solid curves for individual A, broken curves for individual B

Fig. 124. *Variation of extinction angles of combined Carlsbad–albite twins in the plagioclase series (after Calkins & Hess, in Kennedy, G. C., 1947, Amer. Min., vol. 32, p. 561).*

Plagioclase is usually colourless when entirely fresh but typically has a white appearance due to incipient alteration. Other colourations sometimes found are generally due to inclusions: for example, anorthite crystals in xenoliths may be pink or blue from enclosed sillimanite or corundum (sapphire), while the bytownite of a contaminated eucrite from Carlingford, Eire, is so full of iron ore as to be almost black in hand specimen.

DISTINGUISHING FEATURES

In thin section the plagioclase feldspars may be distinguished by their low relief, lack of colour, low birefringence, and the biaxial character of their interference figures. The albite twinning on {010} giving rise to lamellae of different birefringence is characteristic: in its absence, or in a section approaching parallelism to {010}, the presence of a good cleavage may distinguish plagioclase from quartz and the refractive indices may distinguish the more calcic varieties from the potassium feldspars. In thin section, if the presence of untwinned plagioclase is suspected, it may be advantageous to stain the potassium feldspars, using sodium colbaltinitrite solution (p. 311). Although cordierite sometimes shows twinning and occurs in transparent grains with similar optical characters, its tendency to form yellowish alteration products may distinguish it. The distinction of untwinned plagioclase from quartz relies on the lack of cleavage in the latter, together with its uniaxial character and generally fresher and clearer appearance.

The determination of individual plagioclases within the series is covered mainly by the previous section dealing with optical properties: in general the determination of a refractive index is recommended, or the determination of the refractive index of the plagioclase glass. In thin section, in the absence of universal stage techniques, an extinction angle method giving a unique solution is to be preferred, such as the methods using combined albite–Carlsbad twinning. For zoned crystals the measurement of the refractive index of the glass is a convenient method to obtain the bulk composition while the composition of individual zones may be estimated by a study of their extinction angles. The measurement of 2V on slightly zoned crystals will tend to give too high an An content as the 2V is usually measured at the centre of a grain. An indication of the thermal history of the material may be obtained from the 2V curves of Fig. 120 if the composition of the plagioclase is also determined by other techniques.

PARAGENESIS

Igneous rocks. Plagioclase is the most abundant mineral in the great majority of basic and intermediate lavas, in which it occurs both as phenocrysts and as a groundmass constituent. In almost all of these rocks the plagioclase shows some degree of zoning. In many lavas and particularly those of intermediate composition the zoning of the plagioclase extends over a wide range and may be oscillatory in character. In basalts the plagioclase phenocrysts usually have a wide homogeneous core of bytownite composition which is surrounded by narrower zones of more sodium-rich plagioclase. The broad cores of uniform composition indicate slow crystallization and it is obvious that the growth of these crystals occurred before extrusion and final consolidation of the magma.

Albite is the most characteristic mineral of the spilites. In some of these lavas relict labradorite or andesine is enclosed within the albite, a relationship considered to indicate that the composition of the plagioclase is the result of a late magmatic metasomatic process by which normal basalts are albitized to spilites. In other spilites, however, the sodium-rich plagioclase appears to be a product of crystallization from magma containing unusually large amounts of volatiles, notably water.

Under plutonic conditions the first plagioclase to crystallize from most basic magmas, like that of basalts, has a bytownite composition. In layered basic intrusions plagioclase sometimes occurs in feldspar-rich bands formed by the accumulation of the primary precipitate plagioclase; the crystals of these bands are usually idiomorphic and free from conspicuous zoning. In contrast, primary precipitate plagioclase may be entirely absent from the ferromagnesian-rich bands in which the feldspar occurs as a product of the late crystallization of interprecipitate liquids; these plagioclases are poikilitic in texture and commonly show conspicuous zoning. In the differentiated basic rocks of such intrusions the compositional range of the plagioclase may extend from An_{85} to An_{30}.

Anorthite is a comparatively rare mineral but occurs in some orogenic calc-alkali suites where it is found in basic plutonic rocks and as phenocrysts in basic lavas, e.g. it occurs in almost unzoned phenocrysts, An_{94-96}, and as crystal ejecta in the tholeiitic volcanic zone of north-east Japan.

In addition to the plagioclase-rich bands of layered intrusions, plagioclase also occurs as the only essential constituent of large masses of anorthosite. In these rocks the plagioclase may be bytownite, labradorite or andesine in composition, e.g. the anorthosites of the Adirondacks consist essentially of plagioclase the composition range of which is An_{38} to An_{50}.

Plagioclase feldspars are the main constituents of dolerites and many other hypabyssal rocks.

Metamorphic rocks. The composition of plagioclase in metamorphic rocks is generally related to the grade of the host rock. Thus albite is the stable plagioclase in the chlorite and biotite zones of regional metamorphism, occurring in such rocks as chlorite–biotite–epidote–albite amphibolites and chlorite–albite schists, and the anorthite component is not present in notable quantity until the garnet zone. Plagioclase between An_7 and An_{15} in composition is absent in low to medium grade schists; this compositional break corresponds with the change in grade between the greenschist and almandine amphibolite facies. The sharp break can be correlated with the unmixed constitution of plagioclases in the compositional range An_3 to An_{22} as shown by the presence of discrete submicroscopic lamellae of An_3 and An_{22} in plagioclase of peristerite composition. The lower limit of the amphibolite facies in rocks of basic, semipelitic and quartzo-feldspathic composition can thus be delineated by the transition from assemblages containing low-temperature albite to assemblages containing low-temperature plagioclase with the intermediate structure.

Where rocks of the amphibolite facies are subjected to a further increase in confining pressure and to a moderate increase in temperature, conditions of the granulite facies are reached; a characteristic reaction of the boundary conditions may be represented by the reaction:

$$Ca_2Mg_3Al_4Si_6O_{22}(OH)_2 + SiO_2 \rightarrow 2CaAl_2Si_2O_8 + 3MgSiO_3 + H_2O$$
$$\text{amphibole} \qquad\qquad\qquad \text{anorthite} \quad \text{orthopyroxene}$$

The plagioclase feldspars of the intermediate and acid rocks of the granulite facies commonly are sodic andesine, thus in the rocks of the charnockite series the majority of the plagioclase is between An_{30} and An_{35} in composition, although labradorite is present in some of the more basic charnockitic rocks. Rocks of the amphibolite facies affected by increasing temperature and decreasing pressure develop typical associations of thermal metamorphism, and the characteristic association biotite–hornblende–plagioclase is converted to the biotite–pyroxene–plagioclase assemblage of the pyroxene hornfels facies in which part of the plagioclase is derived from the breakdown of hornblende. This reaction may be expressed by the equation:

$$NaCa_2Mg_3Fe^{+2}Al_3Si_6O_{22}(OH)_2 + 4SiO_2 \rightarrow \underbrace{NaAlSi_3O_8 + CaAl_2Si_2O_8}$$

amphibole   plagioclase

$$+ CaMgSi_2O_6 + Mg_2FeSi_3O_9 + H_2O$$

diopside   orthopyroxene

Plagioclase feldspar is not stable in the *PT* environment of the eclogite facies; under these conditions the albite and anorthite components of the plagioclase enter respectively into the composition of omphacitic pyroxene and garnet as shown below:

$$NaAlSi_3O_8 + (Mg,Fe)_2SiO_4 \rightarrow \underbrace{NaAlSi_2O_6 + 2(Mg,Fe)SiO_3}$$

albite   olivine   omphacite

$$CaAl_2Si_2O_8 + (Mg,Fe)_2SiO_4 \rightarrow Ca(Mg,Fe)_2Al_2Si_3O_{12}$$

anorthite   olivine   garnet

Calcium-rich plagioclase is an important product of thermally metamorphosed calcareous rocks: anorthite also occurs in this paragenesis.

In some rocks the plagioclase feldspars have a clouded appearance which is distinct from the turbidity shown by feldspars affected by weathering or hydrothermal alteration. The clouding of plagioclase has commonly been attributed to thermal metamorphism, and clouded feldspars are frequently observed in rocks within metamorphic aureoles. The clouding is due to the presence of minute dark particles probably of iron oxide, either derived from the exsolution of Fe^{+3} originally substituting for Al in the feldspar structure, or due to the introduction of iron into the crystal subsequent to its crystallization. In the first process, exsolution is doubtless accelerated during the annealing conditions of the metamorphism. In many cases of more intense clouding the process is probably due to diffusion of iron into the crystal after its formation.

Sedimentary rocks. Albite is a common authigenic mineral and forms contemporaneously with sedimentation as well as by replacement of detrital material. In accordance with the chemical relationships of the alkali feldspars at low temperature, authigenic albite rarely contains more than 3 mol. per cent potassium feldspar. The calcium content is generally even lower and the usual upper limit is about 0·3 per cent, equivalent to 1 mol. per cent $CaAl_2Si_2O_8$. In some sediments the replacement origin of authigenic albite is demonstrated by the development of idiomorphic crystals in cavities, and by the replacement of fossils. In other sediments the interlocking fabric indicates that the sodium feldspar may be of indigenous origin, formed by the partial solution of detrital grains under pressure at points of contact and precipitated at places of lower pressure. Much of the authigenic albite shows simple growth twins, and is free of multiple twin lamellae.

REFERENCES

BARTH, T. F. W. (1962) 'The feldspar geologic thermometers', *Norsk. Geol. Tidssk.*, vol. 42, p. 330.

BROWN, W. L. (1960) 'The crystallographic and petrologic significance of peristerite unmixing in the acid plagioclases', *Zeit. Krist.*, vol. 113, p. 330.

CARMICHAEL, I. S. E. (1960) 'The feldspar phenocrysts of some Tertiary acid glasses', *Min. Mag.*, vol. 32, p. 587.

—— (1963) 'The crystallization of feldspar in volcanic acid liquids', *Quart. Journ. Geol. Soc.*, vol. 119, p. 95.

CHUDOBA, K. (1933) *The determination of the feldspars in thin section* (Translated by W. Q. Kennedy). Murby, London.

EMMONS, R. C. (1943) 'The universal stage (with five axes of rotation)', *Mem. Geol. Soc. Amer.*, no. 8.

———— (1953) 'Selected petrogenic relationships of plagioclase', *Mem. Geol. Soc. Amer.*, no. 52.

ESKOLA, P., VUORISTO, U. AND RANKAMA, K. (1935) 'An experimental illustration of the spilite reaction', *Compt. Rend. Soc. géol. Finlande*, no. 9.

MACGREGOR, A. G. (1931) 'Clouded felspars and thermal metamorphism', *Min. Mag.*, vol. 22, p. 524.

POLDERVAART, A. and GILKEY, A. K. (1954) 'On clouded plagioclase', *Amer. Min.*, vol. 39, p. 75.

ROSENBLUM, S. (1956) 'Improved technique for staining potash feldspars', *Amer. Min.*, vol. 41, p. 662.

SLEMMONS, D. B. (1962) 'Determination of volcanic and plutonic plagioclases using a three- or four-axis universal stage', *Geol. Soc. Amer., Special Paper* no. 69.

TURNER, F. J. (1947) 'Determination of plagioclase with the four-axis universal stage', *Amer. Min.*, vol. 32, p. 389.

TUTTLE, O. F. and BOWEN, N. L. (1950) 'High-temperature albite and contiguous feldspars', *Journ. Geol.*, vol. 58, p. 572.

—— —— (1958) 'Origin of granite in the light of experimental studies in the system $NaAlSi_3O_8$–$KAlSi_3O_8$–SiO_2–H_2O', *Mem. Geol. Soc. Amer.*, No. 74.

BARIUM FELDSPARS

Celsian		Hyalophane	

Celsian $\qquad$ Ba[Al$_2$Si$_2$O$_8$]
Hyalophane $\qquad$ (K,Na,Ba)[(Al,Si)$_4$O$_8$]

MONOCLINIC (+) OR (−)

	Celsian	Hyalophane
α	1·579–1·587	1·520–1·542
β	1·583–1·593	1·524–1·545
γ	1·588–1·600	1·526–1·547
δ	0·009–0·013	0·005–0·010
2V$_\gamma$	83–92°	101–132°
α:z	3–5°	0–20° (α:x)
O.A.P.	(010), $\beta = y$	$\perp$(010), $\gamma = y$
Dispersion:	—	$r > v$
D	3·10–3·39	2·58–2·82
H	6–6½	6–6½
Cleavage:	{001} perfect, {010} good, {110} poor.	{001} perfect, {010} good.

Twinning: Carlsbad, Manebach, Baveno laws.
Colour: Colourless, white, or yellow; colourless in thin section.

Barium feldspars are structurally very similar to potassium feldspars and there is probably an isomorphous series from orthoclase to celsian with hyalophane as an intermediate member. Hyalophane generally has 5–30 per cent of the celsian molecule present. Another crystalline form of BaAl$_2$Si$_2$O$_8$, the mineral paracelsian, is monoclinic (pseudo-orthorhombic): it can be changed readily to celsian by heating.

The barium ion is present in small quantities in the great majority of feldspars, but only rarely occurs as a major constituent: in general, feldspars are considered here as barium varieties when their barium content is in excess of approximately 2 per cent BaO. In addition to replacing potassium, barium also may replace calcium and sodium. Celsian has a composition BaAl$_2$Si$_2$O$_8$: calciocelsian is a variety with 25 per cent of the anorthite molecule. Barium-bearing plagioclase feldspars are rather more rare, but barium-oligoclase and barium-bytownite are known. The high-temperature synthetic celsian is hexagonal.

The increasing contents of barium are associated with higher refractive indices and higher specific gravities.

The barium feldspars have a very restricted paragenesis and most of them occur in association with manganese deposits. They are known from the Kaso mine, Japan, from Broken Hill, New South Wales, from the Benallt manganese mine, North Wales, and from Otjosundu, South-West Africa.

SILICA MINERALS

Quartz
Tridymite, Cristobalite

SiO_2

	Quartz	Tridymite	Cristobalite
	TRIGONAL (+)	ORTHORHOMBIC (+)	TETRAGONAL (−)
	ω 1·544	α 1·469–1·479	ϵ 1·484
	ϵ 1·553	β 1·470–1·480	ω 1·487
		γ 1·473–1·483	
	δ 0·009	0·002₅–0·004	0·003
		2V, 40°–90°	
Orientation:		O.A.P.(100), $\alpha = y$	
D	2·65	2·26	2·33
H	7	7	6–7
Cleavage:	none	poor prismatic cleavage	none
Twinning:	(1) Twin axis z (2) Twin plane {11$\bar{2}$0}. (3) Twin plane {11$\bar{2}$2}.	Common on {110}.	Spinel-type twins on {111}.
Colour:	Colourless, white or variable; black, purple, green, etc.	Colourless or white.	Colourless, white or yellowish.

Colourless in thin section

Insoluble in acids except HF. Soluble in molten Na_2CO_3.

Quartz is one of the most abundant minerals and occurs as an essential constituent of many igneous, sedimentary and metamorphic rocks. It is also found as an accessory mineral, and as a secondary mineral in veins and metasomatic deposits. Quartz appears to have replaced the name crystal or rock crystal for this mineral towards the end of the 18th Century. It may have been derived from the Saxon word 'Querkluftertz', or cross-vein-ore, which could easily have become condensed to Querertz and then to quartz: this hypothesis is supported by the old Cornish name for crystalline silica, 'cross-course-spar'.

The more important SiO_2 polymorphs and their temperature ranges of stability are as follows:

α-Quartz: stable at atmospheric temperatures and up to 573°C.

β-Quartz: stable from 573°C to 870°C. Can exist metastably above 870°C.

α-Tridymite : can exist at atmospheric temperatures and up to 117°C but is not the stable form in this range.

β_1-Tridymite : can exist between 117°C and 163°C but is not the stable form in this range.

β_2-Tridymite : can exist above 163°C and is the stable form from 870° to 1470°C ; above 1470°C it can exist but is unstable : melts at 1670°C.

α-Cristobalite : can exist at atmospheric temperatures and up to 200°–275°C but is not the stable form in this range.

β-Cristobalite : can exist above 200°–275°C and is stable from 1470° to its melting point, 1713°C.

Coesite : a high-pressure phase, produced at 450°–800°C and 38,000 atmos. pressure. Found in rocks subjected to the impact of large meteorites.

Keatite : a high-pressure synthetic phase, not yet found in nature, produced at 380°–585°C and 330–1200 atmos. pressure. Stability range unknown.

Stishovite : a high density form of silica, D 4·3, synthesized at 130,000 atmospheres and > 1200°C ; recognized in Meteor Crater, Arizona.

Silica glass (vitreous silica ; lechatelierite) ; can exist at room temperatures and up to 1000°C when its rate of crystallization rapidly increases. It is an unstable glass at all temperatures below 1713°C.

Cryptocrystalline silica (chalcedony): compact varieties containing minute crystals of quartz with submicroscopic pores.

It should be noted that the nomenclature here used is that of α for a lower temperature phase and β for a higher temperature phase. Four different notations for polymorphic modifications exist and to avoid confusion the lengthier though more precise method of using the prefixes high- and low- is sometimes preferable.

STRUCTURE

The three principal crystalline forms of SiO_2 (quartz, tridymite and cristobalite) have quite distinct crystal structures, each with a well defined field of stability under equilibrium conditions. The transformations from one to another are, however, somewhat sluggish, so that the higher temperature forms, cristobalite and tridymite, can exist metastably below their inversion temperatures. Each of the three, quartz, metastable tridymite and metastable cristobalite, has furthermore a low- and high-temperature modification designated α- and β- respectively. The six structures are described below, the form with highest symmetry for each pair being dealt with first : cell parameters are listed in Table 32. In each case the structure is built from SiO_4 tetrahedra which are linked by sharing each of their corners with another tetrahedron. In the three-dimensional framework thus formed every silicon has four oxygens and every oxygen has two silicons as nearest neighbours.

β-Quartz has hexagonal symmetry and belongs to the enantiomorphous crystal class 622. A projection of the ideal structure on the basal plane

Table 32. SYMMETRY AND CELL PARAMETERS OF FORMS OF SILICA

Form of SiO$_2$	System	a Å	b Å	c Å
α-Quartz	Trigonal	4·913	—	5·405
β-Quartz	Hexagonal	5·01	—	5·47
α-Tridymite	Orthorhombic (pseudo-hexagonal)	9·88	17·1	16·3
β-Tridymite	Hexagonal	5·03	—	8·22
α-Cristobalite	Tetragonal (pseudo-cubic)	4·97	—	6·92
β-Cristobalite	Cubic	7·13	—	—

(0001) is shown in Fig. 125. SiO$_4$ tetrahedra may be regarded as based on a cube of side p with silicon at its centre and oxygens at four of its eight corners (Fig. 126). When viewed along diad axes they appear as squares which are shaded in Fig. 125; lower edges of tetrahedra are shown by a broken line while upper edges are solid. Tetrahedra are grouped to form regular hexagonal and trigonal helices, and their heights (referred to their Si atoms) are expressed as fractions of the c repeat distance. In the ideal structure built from regular tetrahedra the height of the cell $= 3p$ and the side $a = p(1 + \sqrt{3})$ so that c/a should be 1·098. The structure contains helices of Si–O–Si–O . . . atoms which are either all right-handed or all left-handed in each of the enantiomorphous forms of quartz.

α-Quartz has trigonal symmetry and belongs to the enantiomorphous crystal class 32. Its structure is similar to that of β-quartz but the SiO$_4$ tetrahedra are less regular and are rotated from their ideal positions, thus the α–β transformation is one of relatively minor atomic movements

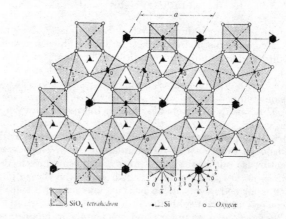

Fig. 125. *Structure of β-quartz projected on* (0001).

involving no breakage of Si–O bonds or interchange of atoms. By contrast with tridymite and cristobalite, quartz has a very densely packed arrangement of tetrahedra, and the disposition of its oxygen ions is not related to either hexagonal or cubic close packing.

The cell parameters of α-quartz have been measured for many specimens and by many workers, and for some time the constancy of values obtained

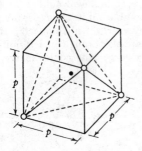

Fig. 126. *Regular tetrahedron inscribed in cube.*

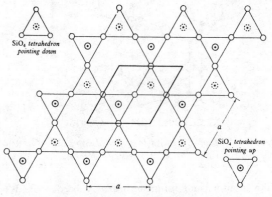

Fig. 127. *A single sheet of the β-tridymite structure viewed along the z axis. Unit cell outlined.*

for quartz from different localities led to its use as a standard for the calibration of X-ray powder cameras. Accurate methods of measurement, however, reveal significant differences which are probably associated with solid solution of impurity ions.

β-Tridymite is hexagonal, and its structure is best regarded as formed by the linkage of sheets parallel to (0001), one of which is illustrated in Fig. 127. The sheet is formed by an open network of SiO_4 tetrahedra, sharing oxygens to form six-membered rings. The triangular bases of all tetrahedra lie in the

(0001) plane but their apices point alternately in opposite directions. Successive parallel sheets of tetrahedra share apical oxygens and are related by mirror planes passing through them so that the silicons and basal oxygens of a downward pointing tetrahedron in one sheet lie directly above those of an upward pointing tetrahedron in the sheet below. A perspective view of the structure is shown in Fig. 128. In the ideal structure the c axis will be four times the height of a tetrahedron standing on its base, and the a axis twice the tetrahedral edge, so that c/a would be $2\sqrt{\frac{2}{3}}$ ($= 1\cdot633$).

α-Tridymite is orthorhombic but its structure involves only slight changes from the high-temperature form. Unlike quartz, tridymite has a very open structure containing channels through which quite large ions could pass, and in which even very large ions could be trapped in the process of crystallization.

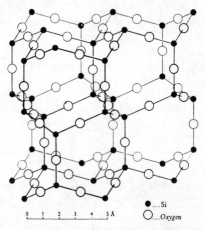

Fig. 128. *The structure of β-tridymite (after Bragg, W. L.*, 1937, Atomic Structure of Minerals. *Cornell University Press*).

β-Cristobalite is cubic and its structure may be described by analogy with that of β-tridymite since it is based upon similar sheets of six-membered rings of SiO_4 tetrahedra. Tetrahedra in successive sheets are again linked by Si–O–Si bonds which are normal to (0001) but the basal oxygens of a tetrahedron, instead of being directly superimposed, are rotated by 60° with respect to those of the tetrahedron below it. With reference to the apical oxygens which join successive sheets, the basal oxygens are disposed as illustrated in the stereograms of Fig. 129. Thus as far as the oxygen layers are concerned, although these are not densely packed, their relationship in tridymite and cristobalite is similar to hexagonal and cubic close packing respectively. The two structures are also similar to those of wurtzite and sphalerite respectively. The repeat distance perpendicular to (0001) in cristobalite is the height of six tetrahedra instead of four as in tridymite. The idealized structure of β-cristobalite has in fact cubic symmetry and can alternatively be described with a cubic cell containing $8\,SiO_2$. From this point of view the structure may be likened to that of diamond, with silicon atoms occupying the positions of carbons, and an oxygen at the mid-point of each Si–Si join (Fig. 130). Variations in the size

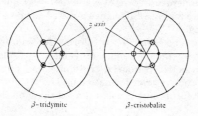

β–tridymite   β–cristobalite

Fig. 129. *Poles represent locations of six basal oxygens with reference to the oxygen bridging two tetrahedra.*

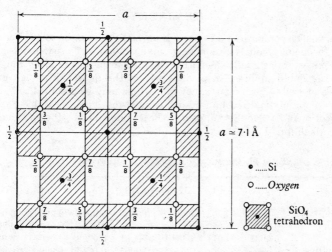

Fig. 130. *Idealized structure of β-cristobalite projected on to (001).*

of the unit cell of cristobalite may be attributed to impurities in natural specimens, since cristobalite, like tridymite, has a very open structure which can easily accommodate foreign ions. α-Cristobalite is tetragonal but its structure is very closely related to that of β-cristobalite.

The open structures of tridymite and cristobalite may be kept open by thermal agitation at high temperatures, and their persistence at lower temperatures probably owes much to the supporting influence of foreign ions.

The introduction of foreign cations into structural cavities is probably accompanied by the charge balancing substitution of Al for Si. The extreme case of regular substitution of half of the Si atoms by Al, and introduction of an equal number of Na atoms, results in the structure of nepheline, $NaAlSiO_4$, which closely resembles that of tridymite with half of its voids filled by Na ions. Similarly, the regular filling of half the voids of cristobalite gives the higher temperature form of $NaAlSiO_4$, carnegieite. There can be no 'quartz' structure for $NaAlSiO_4$ since quartz has no voids for the accommodation of Na ions.

While transformations from α- to β-forms for each of the three SiO_2 minerals involve only minor atomic movements (displacive transformations), the changes between quartz, tridymite and cristobalite are more disruptive (reconstructive transformations). The change from quartz to a higher temperature form must involve the breaking of Si–O bonds and the migration of both Si and O atoms in several directions. The change from tridymite to cristobalite similarly involves the breaking of bonds and changing the disposition of nearest neighbours, but since both have similar layer units (parallel to (0001) in tridymite and (111) in cristobalite), this could be achieved with more restricted atomic movements.

CHEMISTRY

Quartz. The composition of quartz is normally very close to 100 per cent SiO_2. In chemical analyses showing small amounts of other oxides, etc. these oxides are generally due either to small inclusions of other minerals or to the liquid infillings in cavities within the quartz. For high grade crystals of visibly pure quartz, however, these may be assumed to be at a minimum: analytical results for such samples are given in Table 33. The substitution of Al^{+3} for Si^{+4} appears to be accompanied by the introduction of the alkali ions Li^+ or Na^+.

Table 33. CHEMICAL ANALYSES OF QUARTZ SAMPLES

	Li_2O	Na_2O	K_2O	Al_2O_3	Fe_2O_3	MnO_2	TiO_2
Colourless	0·0005	0·0004	0·0002	0·0008	0·0000	0·00002	0·0001
Smoky	0·0004	0·0000	0·0000	0·0008	0·0005	0·00002	0·0002
Rose	0·0038	0·0011	0·0001	0·0001	0·0003	0·00005	0·0015
Amethyst	—	—	—	0·0004	0·0216	0·00000	0·0004

The relations between the several forms of silica together with their stability fields are indicated in Fig. 131, in which temperature is plotted against vapour pressure. The latter has not been measured for these minerals but illustrates their relative stabilities.

Relatively large crystals of synthetic quartz were first produced in 1900 using a technique based on the greater solubility of quartz in a solution of sodium metasilicate at temperatures above 300°C than below it. Modern

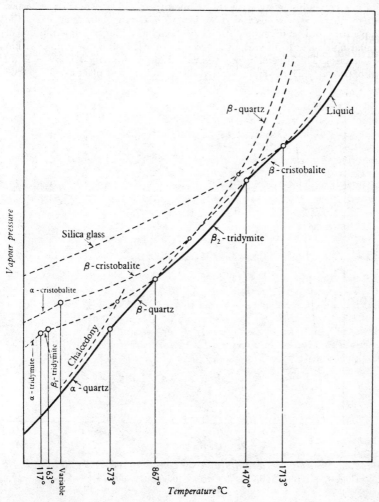

Fig. 131. *The stability relations of the silica minerals (after Fenner, C. N., 1913, Amer. Journ. Sci., 4th ser., vol. 36, p. 331).*

requirements of high-grade quartz for piezoelectric uses has led to an intensive study of its synthetic production, and crystals up to 300 g can be grown in one month. Experimental work on the effect of pressure and temperature on the rate of formation of quartz from silicic acid shows that quartz does not appear in significant quantities until the two other phases, cristobalite and keatite, have formed.

The α–β quartz inversion takes place at about 573°C but the exact temperature varies inversely with the temperature of formation : over 95 per cent of quartz specimens invert within a 2·5°C range. In most cases the temperature of this inversion can be used only as a 'finger-print' method of comparing quartz from various sources and for the study of zoning within rock masses. The inversion point is raised approximately 1°C by each 40 bars of pressure. The β-quartz–tridymite inversion takes place at 867° ± 3°C :

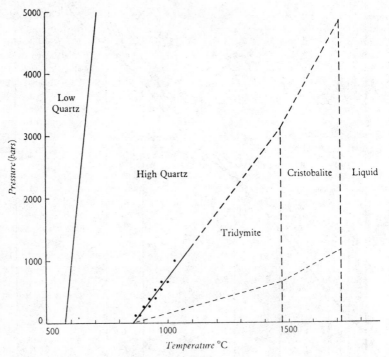

Fig. 132. *Pressure–temperature diagram for* SiO_2 *(after Tuttle, O. F. & Bowen, N. L.,* 1958, Mem. Geol. Soc. Amer., *no.* 74).

at 1000 bars pressure the temperature of this inversion is raised by approximately 180°C (Fig. 132).

The solubility of quartz, measured in a continuous flow apparatus, is 1 g per million g of water at 400°C and 500 lb/in² and about 2600 g per million g of water at 500°C and 1500 lb/in². Both solution and crystallization are accelerated several orders of magnitude by NaOH or NaCl solutions.

Quartz is one of the most stable minerals and, in addition to being resistant chemically to most attacking solutions, its hardness and lack of cleavage help it to resist many of the other agencies of weathering. The replacement of quartz by orthoclase has been recorded in which the crystal structure of the quartz has governed the position of the feldspar replacement. The micro-etching or 'frosting' of quartz grains by carbonate replacement has also been described.

Tridymite. Natural tridymites depart from pure SiO_2 and contain appreciable aluminium and alkalies. This can be related to the more open structure of tridymite which can accommodate the relatively large ions of the alkali group, the Si^{+4} ion being replaced by Al^{+3} in tetrahedral coordination.

The inversion points and fields of stability of tridymite are shown in Fig. 131: its melting point is $1670° \pm 10°C$. It has been crystallized from silica gel in the presence of fluorides and carbonates of sodium and potassium, but attempts to produce tridymite by crystallizing pure amorphous silica at various temperatures and pressures have rarely been successful. At water vapour pressures above approximately 400 bars, tridymite melts directly to a hydrous liquid: at pressures above about 1400 bars it is not formed as a stable phase. The tridymite–cristobalite inversion takes place at 1470°C at atmospheric pressure. Because cristobalite is more dense than tridymite, this inversion temperature is lowered by an increase in pressure.

Cristobalite. Like tridymite, cristobalite has a very open structure compared with that of quartz, permitting replacement of Si^{+4} by Al^{+3} together with the introduction of alkali or alkali earth ions to balance the charge deficiency.

Using powdered silicic acid with water at pressures of 15,000 to 59,000 lb/in^2 and temperatures of 330° to 440°C, cristobalite is always found to be the first phase to form, later becoming converted to keatite and then quartz. The melting point of cristobalite is $1713° \pm 5°C$. The inversion of β-quartz to β-cristobalite takes place at 1027°C but this reaction is metastable below 650 atmospheres.

Coesite. The dense high-pressure phase coesite was first synthesized at 35,000 atmospheres (Coes, 1953). It is almost insoluble in HF, but is dissolved and volatilized in fused $(NH_4)HF_2$. A less dense high pressure phase, silica K or keatite, has been produced from silica gel, with water and a very small amount of alkali in an autoclave at 5000–18,000 lb/in^2 and 380°–585°C: it is soluble in cold HF, and unlike coesite it has not been recognized in nature.

The very high density polymorph of SiO_2, *stishovite*, has been synthesized at 1200°–1400°C and at pressures of around 130,000 atmospheres. It is even more insoluble than coesite in HF.

OPTICAL AND PHYSICAL PROPERTIES

Quartz. The refractive indices show little variation from ω 1·544, ϵ 1·553. Accurate measurements using optical quartz of known purity, for λ 589·29 mμ, gave values of ω 1·544258, ϵ 1·553380, referred to 18°C. The enantiomorphism of quartz causes it to be 'optically active'; the plane of polarization of light passing along the optic axis is rotated either clockwise or anticlockwise depending on the 'hand' of the crystal. This rotary polarization may affect the interference figure seen in convergent light, so that for sections appreciably thicker than normal the central part of the black cross is faint or absent and the space within the inner ring may be brightly coloured.

In some metamorphic rocks quartz develops undulatory extinction due to strain, and in such quartz fine lamellae may occur which have been attributed to translation gliding. Undulatory extinction has been produced experimentally at pressures of about 138,000 atmospheres, the optic axis being displaced by $2°$–$7°$. In some instances quartz may show a distinctly biaxial character, with 2V as high as $8°$ or $10°$. These strain phenomena are generally eliminated if later recrystallization occurs.

Twinning, although rarely seen in thin sections, is fairly common and may be observed in some hand specimens of well-developed crystals of quartz. The commonest twin laws are:

    (a) Twin axis z, twin plane $\{10\bar{1}0\}$, Dauphiné law.
    (b) Twin plane $\{11\bar{2}0\}$, Brazil law.
    (c) Twin plane $\{11\bar{2}2\}$, Japanese law.
    (d) Twin plane $\{10\bar{1}1\}$, Estérel law.
    (e) Twin plane $\{10\bar{1}2\}$, Sardinian law.
    (f) Twin plane $\{11\bar{2}1\}$, Breithaupt law.
    (g) Combined Dauphiné-Brazil law.

By far the commonest twins are those on the Dauphiné, Brazil and Dauphiné-Brazil laws: none of these types of twinning can be detected optically in thin sections of the normal thickness.

The piezoelectric property of quartz is shown in the development of electric charge on the surface of a quartz crystal when subjected to mechanical stress, or the converse effect of mechanical deformation produced when a crystal is subjected to an electrical field: this latter property has been applied to controlling and stabilizing the frequency of electronic oscillator circuits.

The enantiomorphism of quartz gives rise to right- or left-handed crystals. The convention used is that in a right-handed crystal the face $(11\bar{2}1)$ of the trigonal bipyramid, if present, lies to the right of the $(10\bar{1}0)$ face lying below the predominant positive rhombohedron $(10\bar{1}1)$: the trigonal trapezohedron $\{51\bar{6}1\}$ may also be present. In a left-handed crystal the equivalent forms are $(2\bar{1}\bar{1}1)$ and $\{6\bar{1}\bar{5}1\}$. There appears to be an equal numerical distribution of right- and left-handed crystals.

The colour of quartz ranges through colourless, yellow, grey-brown to black, pink and violet, the coloured varieties being called citrine, smoky quartz, rose quartz and amethyst respectively. Citrine appears to owe its colour to a submicroscopic distribution of colloidal ferric hydroxide, whereas the colour of rose quartz has been ascribed to manganese and it can be imitated by the addition of 0·01 per cent MnO to amorphous silicon hydroxide, though there is also some evidence for the rose colour being associated with titanium and lithium. The colour in amethyst is related to the presence of iron, possibly in conjunction with exposure to natural radioactivity. The colour of smoky quartz may be linked with the presence of Al in the lattice. Asterism in rose quartz is due to rutile needles: the latter may also be responsible for the greyish blue and blue quartz typical of granulite facies rocks, though in some such blue quartz the TiO_2 is in a colloidal state. Pegmatitic blue quartz owing its colour to tiny needles of tourmaline is also known.

Liquid inclusions in quartz sometimes contain either a gas phase or small crystals of such minerals as sylvine or halite. Attempts made to determine the temperature of formation of individual quartz specimens by measuring the temperature at which the bubbles disappear from liquid inclusions indicate temperatures for pegmatitic quartz of 120° to 300°C, though large variations are sometimes found between adjacent inclusions.

A feeble cleavage may occur in quartz on $\{10\bar{1}1\}$ or $\{01\bar{1}1\}$. Experimental deformation of quartz at 450°C and 4000 atmospheres gives rise to cleavage fragments with rhombohedral or prismatic bounding planes.

Chalcedony is a group name for the compact varieties of silica composed of minute crystals of quartz with submicroscopic pores. The colour and texture vary considerably according to the impurities present but in general such materials may be sub-divided into chalcedony, in which the colour is fairly uniform, and agate, in which the colour is arranged in bands or concentric zones. The terms chert and flint are used for opaque dull-coloured or black chalcedony, and in common usage chert is taken as the name for this material when it occurs in stratified or massive form in rocks, while the term flint is normally restricted to dark chalcedony occurring in nodular form in a rock matrix, particularly in the Chalk. Flint commonly has about 1 per cent water and has a lower specific gravity (2·57–2·64) than quartz (2·65). The red opaque massive form of chalcedony is sometimes called jasper.

Tridymite. The refractive indices of tridymite vary slightly due to the presence of varying amounts of Al and Na; synthetic material has α 1·469, γ 1·473, D 2·26. Twinning is fairly common and gives rise to wedge-shaped crystals of two or more individuals, including the trillings from which tridymite derives its name.

Cristobalite. Synthetic material has refractive indices close to ϵ 1·484, ω 1·487, but for natural material slightly higher values have sometimes been reported. The birefringence is generally low but some fine-grained cristobalite is apparently almost isotropic, possibly due to overlapping crystallites. Interpenetrant spinel-type twins on $\{111\}$ are fairly common.

Opal is a hydrous cryptocrystalline form of cristobalite with sub-microscopic pores containing water: it may be colourless, milky white, yellow, red, green, blue or black. In precious opal a play of delicate colours is seen, and the commoner varieties also show a rather pearly reflection or opalescence. Opal has a composition of $SiO_2 \cdot nH_2O$, with the water content around 6 to 10 per cent in precious opal. The structure of precious opal has been shown to consist of a close-packed array of regular silica spheres: these form a three-dimensional diffraction grating, which is responsible for the play of colours. The specific gravity is 2·01–2·16 and the refractive index varies from 1·441 to 1·459.

Coesite. Synthetic coesite has α 1·590–1·594, γ 1·597–1·604, 2V, 54°–64°, specific gravity 2·92.

Stishovite. Synthetic material has ω 1·800, ϵ 1·845, whereas fine-grained natural stishovite appears to have refractive indices in the 1·77–1·78 range: specific gravity 4·28.

DISTINGUISHING FEATURES

Quartz is most readily distinguished by its lack of colour, cleavage and visible twinning, and by its low relief and weak birefringence. Typically it is fresh and unaltered and is unattacked by acids other than HF, and in hand specimen often has a distinctive crystal habit and vitreous lustre: its hardness and lack of cleavage easily distinguish it from calcite. In thin section its uniaxial figure distinguishes it from cordierite or the feldspars, and in addition the alkali feldspars normally have lower refractive indices and often lower birefringence. Beryl and scapolite differ in being length-fast and optically negative: nepheline is also negative, gelatinizes with acids and is rarely completely clear. Criteria for distinguishing natural α-quartz from that formed originally above 573°C include the presence of threefold symmetry either in the distribution of Dauphiné or Brazil twinning as revealed by etching, or in colour and inclusions.

Tridymite and cristobalite may be identified by their moderate relief, their refractive indices of 1·47–1·49 being considerably less than that of Canada Balsam. The twinning of tridymite and the wedge-shaped crystals are characteristic. The refractive indices of tridymite are lower than those of cristobalite and these two minerals differ in optic sign.

PARAGENESIS

Quartz. Next to the feldspars, quartz is the most abundant mineral in the Earth's crust. It is a common constituent in many igneous, sedimentary and metamorphic rocks, and also occurs as secondary material often forming a cementing medium in sediments. Quartz is also a common constituent of hydrothermal veins.

In granites, microgranites, adamellites, etc., quartz typically forms shapeless grains but it may show euhedral outlines in the fine-grained rapidly cooled rhyolites, pitchstones and quartz porphyries, although in some of these rocks the quartz phenocrysts may later suffer magmatic corrosion. Inversion temperatures of natural quartzes which crystallized in chemically similar environments are considered to be inversely related to growth temperatures: on a chart of the inversion-break on heating against that on cooling, rhyolitic quartz and granitic quartz show a statistical grouping into separate areas (Fig. 133). The most probable explanation is that the quartz of many granites crystallized during the low temperature late stages of magmatic activity: quartz from granites of metasomatic origin might also be expected to exhibit similar differences from that of rhyolite. A study of 25 specimens of quartz from the Beinn an Dubhaich, Skye, granite has shown that they have inversion characteristics resembling those from rhyolites, and that the quartz from this particular Tertiary granite has undergone little recrystallization and has retained the inversion characteristics of primary crystallization from a magma.

In the igneous rocks of intermediate acidity the amount of quartz is less than in those of granitic composition, and in basic rocks, it usually amounts to less than 5 per cent though it is more abundant in some quartz dolerites and similar rock types. Quartz is chemically incompatible with nepheline and the other feldspathoids and is thus absent from the under-saturated igneous rocks.

Because of its chemical and physical resistance to corrosion quartz is an abundant detrital mineral and becomes concentrated during sedimentary processes to give rise to sands and sandstones of various types. Secondary

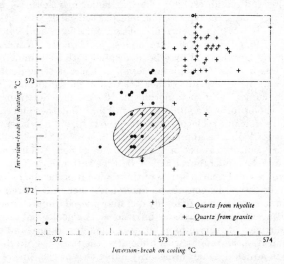

Fig. 133. *The α–β inversion of quartz from granites and rhyolites (after Keith, M. L. & Tuttle, O. F., 1952, Amer. Journ. Sci., Bowen vol., p. 203). The 25 specimens of quartz from the Beinn an Dubhaich granite, Skye, have inversion temperatures which all fall in the shaded area.*

quartz is often deposited around pre-existing grains (of quartz or other minerals) and is a common cementing material in sediments. In some relatively porous sandstones the secondary quartz may be deposited in crystallographic continuity with the detrital quartz, the boundary between the two generations of silica being visible only by the occasional presence of a rim of iron-staining on the detrital grain. Authigenic quartz sometimes occurs in limestones, where it may form well-developed crystals, and small doubly terminated crystals of quartz have been found embedded in limonite in a ferruginous sandstone replacing dolomite. In some oolites, quartz fragments occur as nuclei, and examples are known where the quartz grains have become enlarged by secondary silica and transgress across the calcareous boundaries.

Quartz is a common mineral in many metamorphic rocks, occurring in the metamorphosed equivalents of quartz-bearing sediments and igneous rocks. Although in the low grades of metamorphism quartz may survive unchanged, in the higher grades it undergoes recrystallization with concomitant increase in grain size. In addition much quartz is developed by the release of SiO_2 in reactions taking place during metamorphism.

Intergrowths of quartz and other minerals are fairly common, particularly those of quartz and potassium feldspar as in graphic or micrographic granite, and quartz and plagioclase (myrmekite, see p. 316) in association with potassium feldspar. Such intergrowths are common in many types of acid igneous and metamorphic rocks: particular mention may be made of the intimately intergrown quartz and feldspar typical of many granophyres.

Tridymite. The typical occurrence of tridymite is in acid volcanic rocks such as rhyolite, obsidian, trachyte, andesite and dacite. In such rocks it is often found in cavities and may be associated with such minerals as sanidine, and less frequently, augite or fayalite. There is some doubt whether it ever occurs magmatically rather than as a 'metamorphic' mineral in terms of pneumatolytic metamorphism. Rocks collected from Mt. Pelée soon after the eruptions contained no tridymite but the mineral began to appear in the volcanic rocks of this centre about six months later. Tridymite has been recorded as an abundant mineral in some of the rhyolitic tuffs of the Tertiary volcanic rocks of the San Juan region, Colorado, where in part it acts as the binder for the tuffs and formed after the tuff was deposited. In the rhyolites and quartz latites of this region it is the chief silica mineral and many of the rocks contain as much as 25 per cent tridymite. It is a fairly common constituent of highly metamorphosed impure limestones and arkoses adjacent to basic igneous intrusions. The geological interpretation of the occurrence of tridymite in terms of the temperature and pressure of its crystallization is fraught with difficulty: the presence of cristobalite or tridymite in a rock does not necessarily imply that at the time of formation of these minerals the temperature was above the respective inversion-points (1470° and 870°C).

Cristobalite. Like tridymite, cristobalite is typically a mineral of volcanic rocks, where it may occur in cavities, often in association (metastable) with tridymite. It has been found in hollow spherulites (lithophysae) in obsidian and in rhyolite, trachyte, andesite, dacite and olivine basalt. It is often a late product of crystallization, sometimes replacing tridymite, and may also be associated with anorthoclase, chlorite and even calcite. Cristobalite is also known from thermally metamorphosed sandstones and from sandstone xenoliths in basaltic or other basic rocks, where the sandstone has been converted into buchite. As noted above for tridymite, the ability of cristobalite to occur as an unstable form, outside its equilibrium field, means that no definite conclusions normally can be drawn as to conditions at the time of its crystallization.

Coesite. This recently discovered SiO_2 polymorph occurs with quartz and fused silica glass in sheared porous sandstones at Meteor Crater, Arizona.

and in granite and pumaceous tuff near the rim of the Rieskessel crater, Bavaria, developed by the shock wave generated by the meteoritic impact. Fine-grained *stishovite* also occurs in the Meteor Crater impact-metamorphosed sandstone.

REFERENCES

BUERGER, M. J. (1935) 'The silica framework crystals and their stability fields', *Zeit. Krist.*, vol. 90, p. 186.

COES, L., JR. (1953) 'A new dense crystalline silica', *Science*, vol. 118, p. 131.

FENNER, C. N. (1913) 'Stability relations of the silica minerals', *Amer. Journ. Sci.*, 4th ser., vol. 36, p. 331.

FRONDEL, C. (1945) 'History of the quartz oscillator-plate industry, 1941–1944', *Amer. Min.*, vol. 30, p. 205.

—— and HURLBUT, C. S., JR. (1955) 'Determination of the atomic weight of silicon by physical measurements on quartz', *Journ. Chem. Phys.*, vol. 23, p. 1215.

TUTTLE, O. F. and ENGLAND, J. L. (1955) 'Preliminary report on the system SiO_2–H_2O', *Bull. Geol. Soc. Amer.*, vol. 66, p. 149.

NEPHELINE GROUP

Nepheline $Na_3(Na,K)[Al_4Si_4O_{16}]$
Kalsilite $K[AlSiO_4]$

HEXAGONAL $(-)$

	Nepheline	Kalsilite
ϵ	1·526–1·542	1·532–1·537
ω	1·529–1·546	1·538–1·543
δ	0·003–0·005	0·005–0·006
Dispersion:	weak	weak
D	2·56–2·665	2·59–2·625
H	5½–6	6
Cleavage:	{10$\bar{1}$0}, {0001}, poor.	{10$\bar{1}$0}, {0001}, poor.
Twinning:	{10$\bar{1}$0}, {33$\bar{6}$5}, {11$\bar{2}$2}.	
Colour:	Colourless: white, grey; colourless in thin section.	
	Gelatinizes in strong HCl.	

Nepheline and kalsilite are not isostructural, but both structures have a tridymite-type framework in which approximately half of the silicon atoms are replaced by aluminium; the electrical neutrality is maintained by the presence of alkali atoms in the structural cavities. In addition to structural differences for different compositions, polymorphism is present over the greater part of the chemical range of the series. At the pure sodium end of the series low-temperature nepheline is the stable phase up to about 900°C, at which temperature it inverts to high-temperature nepheline; the latter inverts at 1245°C to the high-temperature polymorph, carnegieite. The temperature of both inversions is raised by the substitution of sodium by potassium; that of low- to high-temperature nepheline rises rapidly and reaches a maximum of 1248°C at a composition Ne_{95} while in more potassium-rich nephelines the low-temperature phase inverts directly to carnegieite, the limiting composition of which is about Ne_{73}.

At the potassium end of the series, kalsilite inverts at approximately 850°C to orthorhombic $KAlSiO_4(O_1)$. The relationships for compositions between Ne_{30} and Ne_{10} are more complex than shown in Fig. 137, p. 362, and include a second orthorhombic phase and trikalsilite in addition to tetra-kalsilite (H_4 in Fig. 137). The rare mineral kaliophilite which has a similar compositional range to kalsilite is probably metastable at atmospheric pressure, but its relationship to kalsilite and to the other potassium-rich phases is not fully understood.

Solid solution of potassium in the nepheline structure is limited to about 25 mol. per cent at ordinary temperatures, but the amount of solid solution increases with increasing temperature and reaches about 70 per cent at 1070°C. At the potassium-rich end of the series the amount of sodium that can enter the kalsilite structure rises from zero to about 25 per cent at 1070°C. Both nepheline and kalsilite solid solutions may be quenched to room temperature without unmixing.

The prefixes subpotassic, mediopotassic and perpotassic are used to describe nepheline solid solutions in which the numbers of potassium atoms replacing sodium (on the basis of 32 oxygens) are between 0 and 0·25, between 0·25 and 2·0 and between 2·0 and 4·73 respectively.

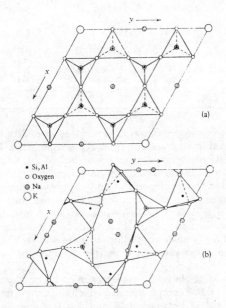

Fig. 134. (a) *Idealized structure of nepheline,* $Na_3KAl_4Si_4O_{16}$*, projected on the* (0001) *plane, based on the high-tridymite arrangement of tetrahedra.* (b) *Structure of nepheline, projected on the* (0001) *plane (after Hahn, T. & Buerger, M. J., 1955, Zeit. Krist., vol. 106, p. 308). Both figures show the linkage of* SiO_4 *and* AlO_4 *tetrahedra and the positions of K and Na ions.*

STRUCTURE

The symmetry and lattice parameters of minerals in the nepheline group are given in Table 34. In the nepheline structure the tetrahedra with the apices pointing in one direction along the z-axis are occupied by silicon, while those which point in the opposite direction are occupied by aluminium; the resulting negative charge is balanced by alkali atoms occupying cavities in the framework (Fig. 134). In nepheline of ideal composition,

$Na_6K_2Al_8Si_8O_{32}$, the tridymite-type framework is distorted, and the alkali sites are of two different sizes. Two of the eight intraframework sites

Table 34. SYMMETRY AND LATTICE PARAMETERS OF SOME OF THE PHASES IN THE $NaAlSiO_4$–$KAlSiO_4$ SYSTEM

	$NaAlSiO_4$ weight %	Symmetry	Lattice parameters (Å)		
			a	b	c
Nepheline	100–30	Hexagonal	10·0	—	8·4
High-temperature carnegieite	100–90	Cubic	7·3	—	—
Kalsilite	0–20	Hexagonal	5·2	—	8·7
Orthorhombic $KAlSiO_4(O_1)$	0–10	Orthorhombic	9·1	15·7	8·6
Trikalsilite	≃ 30	Hexagonal	15·4	—	8·6
Tetrakalsilite	≃ 25	Hexagonal	20·5	—	8·5

have nine-fold oxygen coordination (cation–oxygen distance 2·9 Å), and they are occupied by potassium. The six smaller sites have eight-fold oxygen coordination (cation–oxygen distance 2·65 Å), and these sites are occupied by sodium. Some nephelines have less potassium than the ideal composition and in these some of the larger voids are occupied by sodium; in other nephelines more than 1 in 4 of the cavities may be occupied by potassium, and it is thus possible for both sites to admit either sodium or potassium atoms. Occupation of all the voids by potassium does not occur, and the range of replacement of sodium by potassium in the nepheline solid solutions does not exceed approximately 25 mol. per cent at normal temperatures.

The substitution of Na by K is accompanied by an increase in both the a and c parameters. For compositions in which the value of x (in the formula $Na_{8-x}K_xAl_8Si_8O_{32}$) is between 0·25 and 2·0 the linear increase in cell volume is 5·82 Å³ per K ion, and between 2·0 and 4·7 it is 11·8 Å³ per K ion. It is not known whether there is a discontinuity in the cell volumes for compositions from x 0 to 0·25, i.e. the compositional range in which nepheline occurs in both low- and high-temperature forms (see Fig. 137). A similar change in lattice parameters occurs in those nephelines the compositions of which can be described precisely only with reference to the ternary system $NaAlSiO_4$–$KAlSiO_4$–SiO_2, i.e. in those nephelines in which there is replacement of Al by Si and of Na by vacant sites (see p. 360). The experimentally determined composition at which the change occurs may be expressed as:

$$Na_{5·97}K_{1·64} \square_{0·39}Al_{7·61}Si_{8·39}O_{32}$$

It would thus appear that the change in lattice parameters occurs in omission solid solution nephelines when the six smaller voids are occupied by sodium atoms and when there are no sodium atoms in the larger voids suitable for potassium, i.e. omission substitution perhaps occurs only in relation to the large potassium sites (Fig. 135).

The high-temperature polymorph, carnegieite, is cubic, a $7\cdot325$ Å at $750°C$, and has a cristobalite-type framework structure (see p. 344). Low-temperature carnegieite is intimately twinned and its symmetry is probably low; the lattice parameters and symmetry, however, have not been determined.

The composition at which the change from the nepheline to the kalsilite structure takes place is not known precisely, but it occurs in the composi-

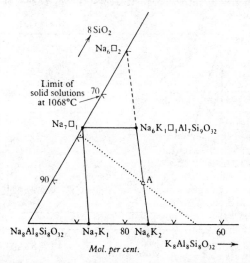

Fig. 135. *Diagram showing part of the system $NaAlSiO_4$–$KAlSiO_4$–SiO_2; compositions are plotted on a molecular per cent basis. Dotted line represents approximately the limit of nepheline solid solutions at $700°C$. The position of the break in lattice parameters, marked by the point A, lies very close to the line representing six of the eight alkali sites filled by Na atoms (after Hamilton, D. L. & MacKenzie, W. S., 1960, Journ. Petr., vol. 1, p. 56).*

tional range Ne_{30} to Ne_{20}. The cell dimensions of kalsilite, $a \simeq 5\cdot2$, $c \simeq 8\cdot7$ Å, differ from those of nepheline, $a \simeq 10\cdot0$, $c \simeq 8\cdot4$ Å, and the unit cell contains $K_2Al_2Si_2O_8$.

CHEMISTRY

Almost all nephelines contain more silicon and less aluminium than is represented by the formula $NaAlSiO_4$; the sum of the Si and Al atoms, however, is usually close to the ideal cell content of 16 atoms in tetrahedral coordination. The excess of SiO_2 compared with the compositions of solid solutions between $NaAlSiO_4$ and $KAlSiO_4$ is shown in the normative percentages of the sodium molecule (Ne), the potassium molecule (Ks) and

SiO_2 (Q) in Table 35. Although in the synthetic system $Na_2Al_2Si_2O_8$–$CaAl_2Si_2O_8$, nepheline can take 35 mol. per cent anorthite into solid solution, most natural nephelines contain only relatively small amounts of calcium. In many specimens the paucity of calcium can be correlated with the small calcium content in the magmas from which the nepheline crystallized, but nephelines formed in a calcium-rich environment also do not in general contain appreciably greater amounts. This may be related either to the lesser solubility of calcium in the nepheline structure at the lower temperature of crystallization of natural minerals, or to the entry of calcium preferentially into other phases crystallizing earlier or together with the nepheline.

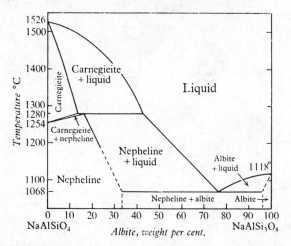

Fig. 136. *Phase diagram of the system* $NaAlSiO_4$ *(nepheline, carnegieite)–* $NaAlSi_3O_8$ *(albite) (after Greig, J. W. & Barth, T. F. W., 1938, Amer. Journ. Sci., 5th ser., vol. 35A, p. 93).*

The nepheline unit cell contains 16 (Si + Al) but, as noted above, there are usually more than 8 silicon and less than 8 aluminium atoms per cell. The negative charge on the framework is thus less than 8; in consequence the cell contains less than 8 alkali atoms, and thus in most nephelines the intraframework cavities are not fully occupied. In order to indicate vacancies in cation sites the general nepheline formula can be expressed:

$$Na_xK_yCa_z \square_{8-(x+y+z)}Al_{(x+y+2z)}Si_{16-(x+y+2z)}O_{32}$$

where $\square$ are the vacant sites.

Sodium nepheline inverts at 1254°C to the cubic polymorph carnegieite, but although the latter can exist metastably at lower temperatures and undergoes a rapid reversible metastable transformation, at 692°C on heating, and at 687°C on cooling, to a twinned low-temperature, low symmetry form, neither of the two forms of carnegieite has been found in nature.

In the synthetic system $NaAlSiO_4$–$NaAlSi_3O_8$ (Fig. 136) about 33 wt per

Table 35. NEPHELINE AND KALSILITE ANALYSES

	1.	2.	3.	4.	5.
SiO_2	44·65	41·88	40·20	38·47	38·48
TiO_2	0·00	0·03	0·05	0·00	0·05
Al_2O_3	32·03	32·99	32·51	30·81	31·01
Fe_2O_3	0·59	0·74	1·82	1·63	1·12
MgO	0·00	0·00	0·10	0·63	0·00
CaO	0·71	0·78	1·44	0·20	0·03
Na_2O	17·25	16·11	10·86	2·09	0·30
K_2O	3·66	6·82	12·22	25·65	28·33
H_2O^+	0·96	0·71	0·00	0·20	0·67
H_2O^-	0·21	0·03	0·00	0·00	—
Total	100·06	100·16	99·77	99·94	100·00
ϵ	1·531	—	1·539	1·537	1·533
ω	1·535	—	1·543	1·543	1·539

NUMBERS OF IONS ON THE BASIS OF 32 OXYGENS

	1.	2.	3.	4.	5.
Si	8·585	8·179	8·014	8·044	8·125
Al	7·361	7·595	7·641	7·596	7·720
Ti	—	0·005	0·007	—	0·008
Fe^{+3}	0·085	0·109	0·369‡	0·301§	0·180||
Mg	—	0·102†	0·030	0·196	—
Na	6·428	6·098	4·198	0·847	0·123
Ca	0·147	0·163	0·308	0·045	0·006
K	0·897	1·699	3·018	6·846	7·635
$\sum R$¶	7·61	8·12	7·92	7·78	7·77
Ne	81·9	76·1	54·7	9·9	96·8
Ks	12·9	23·6	45·3	88·9	1·4
Q	5·2	0·3	—	1·2	1·8

1. Nepheline, phonolite, New Zealand (Tilley, C. E., 1954, *Amer. Journ. Sci.*, vol. 252, p. 65).
2. Nepheline, foyaite, Transvaal (Tilley, C. E., 1956, *Kon. Ned. Geol. Mijnb., Geol. Ser.*, Brouwer vol., p. 403; includes MnO 0·07).
3. Nepheline, potash ankaratrite, Congo (Sahama, Th. G., 1952. *Amer. Journ. Sci.*, Bowen vol., p. 460; includes FeO 0·57).
4. Kalsilite, venanzite, Italy (Bannister, F. A., Sahama, Th. G. & Wiik, H. B., 1952. *Min. Mag.*, vol. 30, p. 46; includes FeO 0·26).
5. Kalsilite, complex phenocryst of kalsilite and nepheline, Congo (Sahama, Th. G., Neuvonen, K. J. & Hytönen, K., 1956, *Min. Mag.*, vol. 31, p. 200. Analysis recalculated after correcting for 10 per cent nepheline, 31·1 atomic per cent K:(K+Na+Ca) in sample; total iron as Fe_2O_3: analysis includes MnO 0·01).

† Includes Mn 0·012.
‡ Includes Fe^{+2} 0·096.
§ Includes Fe^{+2} 0·045.
\|\| Includes Mn 0·002.

¶ $\sum R = (Na + K + 2Ca)$

cent albite (equivalent to $Ne_{85}Q_{15}$) can be accommodated in solid solution
in nepheline. In the system $NaAlSiO_4$–$NaAlSi_3O_8$–H_2O the limit of nepheline–albite solid solution at 750°C and a water pressure of 1000 bars is
$Ne_{75}Ab_{25}$.

The phase relations in the system nepheline–kalsilite are shown in Fig.
137. Compositions between Ne_{100} and $Ne_{37.5}$ at temperatures above
1070°C consist of a single-phase solid solution: in this compositional range
the phase relations at temperatures below those of the solidus and above

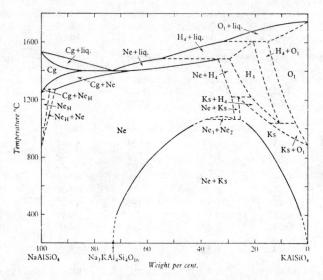

Fig. 137. *Phase diagram of the system* $NaAlSiO_4$–$KAlSiO_4$. *Inferred phase*
boundaries are shown by broken lines. Cg carnegieite, Ne_H high-tempera-
ture nepheline, Ne low-temperature nepheline, Ks kalsilite, H_4 tetrakal-
silite, O_1 orthorhombic kalsilite (after Tuttle, O. F. & Smith, J. V., 1958,
Amer. Journ. Sci., *vol.* 256, *p.* 571).

those of the solvus are complex due to the presence of orthorhombic kalsilite (O_4) and tetrakalsilite (H_4). An additional polymorph, with composition $\simeq Ne_{30}$, trikalsilite, has been found in potassium-rich lavas of North
Kivu, Congo.

The maximum temperature of the solvus is 1070°C at a composition of
approximately Ne_{30}. The form of the solvus is eccentric and at room temperature it intersects the $NaAlSiO_4$–$KAlSiO_4$ join at Ne_{73} ($\simeq Na_3KAl_4Si_4O_{16}$)
and Ne_0. Compositions between Ne_{73} and Ne_0 have a different minimum
temperature of stable existence as given by the solvus, and under equilibrium conditions intergrowths of nepheline and kalsilite will form at the
appropriate temperature on cooling. The unmixing of nepheline solid

solution is thus comparable with the formation of alkali feldspar inter-growths, and in the same manner that the feldspar intergrowths can be homogenized by heating, so also can nepheline–kalsilite solid solutions.

It has been suggested that in the $NaAlSiO_4$–$KAlSiO_4$ solid solution series the composition $Na_3KAl_4Si_4O_{16}$ is unique, and that at subsolidus tempera-tures $Na_3KAl_4Si_4O_{16}$ is a compound. The reasons for regarding this com-position as a compound are based on the assumption that some sites in the structure are more suitable for potassium and some more suitable for sodium. The uniqueness of this composition is also manifest by the dis-continuous variation in the lattice parameters of the series (see p. 358), the common approximation to this composition of nephelines from plu-tonic rocks, and the observation that the sodium-rich limb of the solvus approaches this composition but does not cross it. Thus the solid solution of $NaAlSiO_4$ in $Na_3KAl_4Si_4O_{16}$ is considered to be different from the solid solution of $KAlSiO_4$ in $Na_3KAl_4Si_4O_{16}$ because different atomic sites are involved; i.e. these are two binary systems at low temperatures. The persistence of the change in shape of the curve of lattice parameters plotted against composition in the ternary system $NaAlSiO_4$–$KAlSiO_4$–SiO_2 gives additional support to these arguments, since the uniqueness of the compo-sition at which all sites suitable for Na atoms are filled is retained in the omission solid solution series from $Na_6K_2Al_8Si_8O_{32}$ to $Na_6 \square _2Al_6Si_{10}O_{32}$.

Nepheline is frequently altered and the common alteration products include analcite, cancrinite, sodalite and the fibrous zeolites, natrolite and thomsonite. Nepheline also alters to a colourless mica, possibly paragonite, the basal plane of which is frequently oriented parallel to the (0001) cleavage of the nepheline.

OPTICAL AND PHYSICAL PROPERTIES

The effect of the substitution of Na by K on the refractive indices of the nepheline minerals is small. The relatively minor increase in refractive indices with increasing substitution of potassium is commonly masked by the effects of omission solid solution and by the presence of Ca in alkali cation sites. In consequence refractive indices cannot be used to estimate chemical composition. The replacement of sodium by potassium increases the density of nepheline solid solutions, but due to variation in the number of Si and Al atoms and in the value of $\sum R$ ($=Na+K+2Ca$) the measure-ment of density is not a useful method for estimating compositions. The refractive indices of kalsilite overlap those of the more potassium-rich nepheline solid solutions, and kalsilite cannot be distinguished from them by optical measurements.

DISTINGUISHING FEATURES

The main diagnostic features of nepheline are its low birefringence and poor cleavage, which together with its uniaxial character, distinguish it from the alkali feldspars; nepheline is readily soluble in HCl. Apatite and melilite have a similar range of birefringence, but both have higher refringence. Scapolites have higher refractive indices and those which have a high meionitic content have higher birefringence. Analcite and sodalite are isotropic, and leucite characteristically displays complex twinning. The difference in refringence and birefringence between nepheline and kalsilite is too small to distinguish in thin section between individual grains of the two minerals.

PARAGENESIS

Nepheline is the most characteristic mineral of the alkaline rocks and occurs as a primary phase in many plutonic, hypabyssal and volcanic rocks of extremely varied mineralogical and chemical composition. It has three common parageneses and forms as a primary phase of magmatic crystallization, as a product of metasomatism and as a result of reaction (contamination) of both basic and acid magmas with calcium-rich sediments.

The nephelines of nepheline-syenites and nepheline gneisses do not vary greatly in composition, the range of which is approximately between $Ne_{73}Ks_{27}$ and $Ne_{75}Ks_{21}Q_4$. In such rocks the nepheline is associated with low-temperature feldspars of the albite–microcline series. In volcanic rocks the composition of nepheline varies more widely and is more closely related to the composition of the host rock. Thus, compared with nephelines of plutonic paragenesis they include more sodium- and more potassium-rich varieties, and in terms of the $NaAlSiO_4$ and $KAlSiO_4$ components the compositional range is $Ne_{86}Ks_{14}$ to $Ne_{55}Ks_{45}$. Furthermore many volcanic nephelines contain more than 4 Si per formula unit and the excess, calculated as SiO_2, may be as much as 6 per cent.

In volcanic rocks, nepheline is associated with feldspars of the high-temperature anorthoclase–sanidine series. This contrast in the compositions of nephelines which have crystallized in chemically similar but physically different environments is related to the nepheline structure, thus nephelines close to the ideal composition of $Na_3KAl_4Si_4O_{16}$ are characteristically associated with lower temperatures of crystallization; at higher temperatures the tolerance of both alkali sites of the structure is increased and permits a greater departure from the $Na_3KAl_4Si_4O_{16}$ composition.

In addition to changes in the composition of nepheline by adjustment of the Na : K ratio, and by the replacement of Si by Al at lower crystallization temperatures, ionic exchange between nepheline and feldspar occurs at sub-solidus temperatures. In contrast, however, to the chemical exchanges between nepheline and silicate liquid, those between nepheline and feldspar most probably involve only the intra-framework ions, and the Al : Si ratios in both phases remain constant at sub-solidus temperatures. This conclusion is based on the absence of exsolved feldspar in nephelines of plutonic and metamorphic rocks, and on the absence of feldspar developed from nepheline in the experimental system $NaAlSiO_4$–$KAlSiO_4$–SiO_2–H_2O.

Some nepheline-bearing rocks are metasomatic in origin and have arisen by the so-called process of nephelinization. In most examples of such rocks, e.g. in the Haliburton–Bancroft area, Ontario; Alnö, Sweden; and Fen, Norway, the nephelinization is due to the action of fluids derived from nepheline-bearing magmas on country rocks of varying compositions, i.e. limestones, amphibolites and granitic gneisses. Textural evidence of the nephelinization includes the presence of nepheline enclosing rounded and embayed grains of feldspar, and of vermicular nepheline–albite intergrowths.

Localized occurrences of nepheline-bearing basic rocks formed by the reaction of basic magmas with carbonate-rich sediments occur at the olivine gabbro–limestone contact, Camas Mòr, Muck, and the dolerite–Chalk junction, Scawt Hill, Northern Ireland. At these localities the syntectic assemblages include nepheline dolerite, melilite–nepheline dolerite and theralite, rocks comparable mineralogically with nephelinite, melilite nephelinite and nepheline tephrite lavas.

Kalsilite is an important constituent of the groundmass of some potassium-rich lavas, but also occurs in complex nepheline–kalsilite phenocrysts of some less potassium-rich lavas; kalsilite is unknown in plutonic rocks.

REFERENCES

BARTH, T. F. W. (1963) 'The composition of nepheline', *Schweiz. Min. Petr. Mitt.*, vol. 43, p. 153.

HAMILTON, D. L. (1961) 'Nephelines as crystallization temperature indicators', *Journ. Geol.*, vol. 69, p. 321.

—— and MACKENZIE, W. S. (1960) 'Nepheline solid solution in the system NaAlSiO$_4$–KAlSiO$_4$–SiO$_2$', *Journ. Petr.*, vol. 1, p. 56.

SAHAMA, TH. G. (1962) 'Order–disorder in natural nepheline solid solutions', *Journ. Petr.*, vol. 3, p. 65.

TILLEY, C. E. (1958) 'The leucite nepheline dolerite of Meiches, Vogelsberg, Hessen', *Amer. Min.*, vol. 43, p. 759.

TUTTLE, O. F. and SMITH, J. V. (1958) 'The nepheline–kalsilite system II: Phase relations', *Amer. Journ. Sci.*, vol. 256, p. 571.

Petalite

$Li[AlSi_4O_{10}]$

MONOCLINIC (+)

α 1·504–1·507
β 1·510–1·513
γ 1·516–1·523
δ 0·011–0·017
$2V_\gamma$ 82°–84°
$\alpha : x$ 2°–8°, $\beta : z$ 24°–30°, $\gamma = y$, O.A.P. $\perp$ (010).
Dispersion: $r > v$. D 2·412–2·422. H 6$\frac{1}{2}$.
Cleavage: {001} perfect; {201} good.
Twinning: Lamellar, twin plane (001), common.
Colour: Greyish white to white, more rarely pink or green; colourless in thin section.

The structure of petalite (a 11·76, b 5·14, c 7·62 Å, β 112·4°, Z = 2) consists of a framework of SiO_4 and AlO_4 tetrahedra linked by sharing apices. Alternatively the SiO_4 tetrahedra can be regarded as being arranged in sheets parallel to (001) which are joined to one another through AlO_4 tetrahedra.

The composition is normally fairly close to $LiAlSi_4O_{10}$, with Li_2O at around 4·1 per cent and only minor replacement of Li by Na or K: the element lithium was first discovered in this mineral. Iron is sometimes present to a limited extent, replacing Al. Petalite can be synthesized from its component oxides or from LiOH, $Al(OH)_3$ and silicic acid: it is formed at 330° to 680°C. It commonly alters to montmorillonite, which may form a pinkish coating.

The optical properties show little variation. Petalite has lower refractive indices than quartz or the feldspars: the cleavage, large positive 2V and small extinction angle ($\alpha : x = 2°$–8°) on to the best cleavage are characteristic. It gives a red Li coloration to a flame.

Petalite occurs chiefly in granitic pegmatites and related rocks, where it is found typically associated with tourmaline, spodumene, lepidolite, topaz, amblygonite, apatite, pollucite, etc. In the Varuträsk pegmatite, Sweden, it is relatively abundant and occurs in the lithium replacement unit of the pneumatogenic stage which is considered to have crystallized in the 600°–400°C temperature range.

Leucite

$K[AlSi_2O_6]$

TETRAGONAL (PSEUDOCUBIC) (+)

n 1·508–1·511 δ 0·001
Dispersion: Moderate.   D 2·47–2·50.   H $5\frac{1}{2}$–6.
Cleavage: {110} very poor.
Twinning: {110} repeated.
Colour: White or grey, colourless in thin section.
Decomposed by HCl.

STRUCTURE

At ordinary temperatures leucite is tetragonal (pseudocubic) with $a \simeq 13·0$, $c \simeq 13·7$ Å, but it gradually changes on heating until at about 625°C it is cubic with a 13·4 Å. Both cubic and tetragonal leucite have

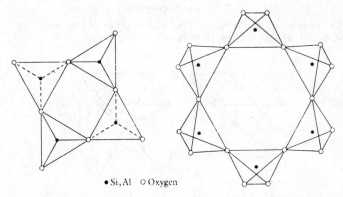

● Si, Al   ○ Oxygen

Fig. 138. *Rings of four and six tetrahedra of the type which occur in the leucite structure.*

16($KAlSi_2O_6$) in the unit cell but, whereas in the cubic cell oxygens occupy a set of 96-fold equivalent positions, in the tetragonal cell they are distributed among six sets of 16-fold positions. The structure is based on an (Si,Al)–O framework similar to that of analcite $NaAlSi_2O_6 \cdot H_2O$ and pollucite $CsAlSi_2O_6 \cdot xH_2O$. In all three minerals $(Si,Al)O_4$ tetrahedra are linked by sharing corners to form rings of six tetrahedra and rings of four tetrahedra as illustrated in Fig. 138. In cubic leucite the six- and four-membered rings are respectively normal to triad and tetrad axes. The content of the lower half of the cubic cell is illustrated in Fig. 139, where large circles show the positions of K ions in leucite but also represent the positions of Cs in pollucite and of water molecules in analcite. These 16 positions are in line with the centres of channels (formed by six-membered

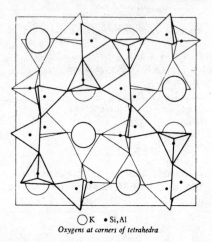

○ K　● Si, Al
Oxygens at corners of tetrahedra

Fig. 139. *Lower half of the unit cell of leucite (after Náray-Szabó, St. N., 1938, Zeit. Krist., vol. 99, p. 277).*

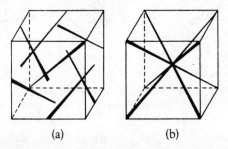

(a)　　　　　　(b)

Fig. 140. *Arrangement of channels parallel to triad axes, (a) non-intersecting as in leucite and analcite, (b) intersecting as in sodalite (after Barrer, R. M. & Falconer, J. D., 1956, Proc. Roy. Soc., A, vol. 236, p. 227).*

rings of tetrahedra) which run along four non-intersecting triad directions (Fig. 140). At ordinary temperatures the potassium ions in leucite are probably too small to fill the large cavities in the cubic structure, and the resultant collapse of the (Si,Al)–O framework about them can be correlated with the change to lower symmetry. The distortion of the structure involves the movement of potassium ions away from their normal positions, but the deviation decreases with increasing temperature and disappears at about 625°C. Differential thermal analysis studies of the low ⇌ high-temperature leucite inversion show that the transformation is not a simple process but involves either the formation of a transient intermediate phase, or an Al–Si order–disorder relationship.

CHEMISTRY

The compositions of natural leucite do not depart significantly from the ideal formula, $KAlSi_2O_6$; the Si:Al ratio approximates closely to 2:1 (Table 36) and the replacement of K by Na rarely exceeds 10 per cent. Pure

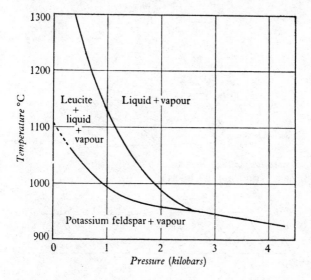

Fig. 141. *Projection on the PT plane of the system* $KAlSi_3O_8$–H_2O *(after Goranson, R. W., 1938, Amer. Journ. Sci., 5th ser., vol. 35A, p. 71).*

leucite melts congruently at 1686°C. Potassium feldspar melts incongruently at 1150°C to leucite and liquid, the composition of which is leucite 57·8, silica 42·2 per cent. In the system $KAlSi_3O_8$–H_2O, leucite is not stable above approximately 2500 bars water pressure when the temperature is 950°C; above 2500 bars potassium feldspar melts to a liquid of hydrated feldspar composition (Fig. 141). In the system $NaAlSi_3O_8$–$KAlSi_3O_8$–H_2O the leucite field diminishes in size with increasing water pressure. Thus in the dry system the leucite field extends to 51 per cent $NaAlSi_3O_8$, at a P_{H_2O} of 1000 bars to 29 per cent, and at 2000 bars to 5 per cent $NaAlSi_3O_8$ (see Fig. 103, p. 303). The range of crystallization temperatures at 1000 and 2000 bars water pressure is from 1135° to 1000°C and 1000°C to 960°C respectively. In the system $NaAlSiO_4$–$KAlSiO_4$–SiO_2 leucite is the first phase to crystallize from a wide range of potassium-rich liquids (Fig. 142). From such liquids leucite continues to crystallize down to a temperature of 1020°C either alone or together with nepheline or potassium feldspar. At the reaction point, at 1020°C, leucite reacts with the liquid to give nepheline and orthoclase.

The relationships in the system $NaAlSiO_4$–$KAlSiO_4$–SiO_2–H_2O at a P_{H_2O} of 1000 bars are shown in Fig. 143. Compared with the anhydrous system the liquidus temperatures are substantially lower and the stability field of leucite is considerably reduced. There is a well marked minimum

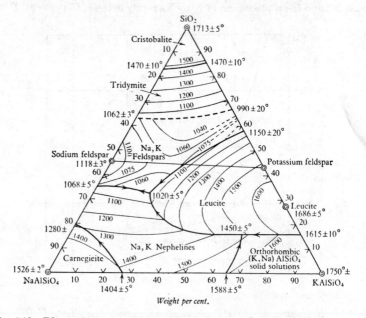

Fig. 142. *Phase diagram for the system NaAlSiO₄–KAlSiO₄–SiO₂ (after Schairer, J. F., 1950, Journ. Geol., vol. 58, p. 512).*

(M) on the nepheline–feldspar boundary curve at about 750°C, and the reaction point, or peritectic, R, at a temperature of approximately 800°C is more clearly defined than the corresponding reaction point ($\simeq 1020$°C) in the anhydrous system. Extensive solid solution exists along the join $KAlSi_2O_6$–$NaAlSi_2O_6$, amounting to 28 weight per cent $NaAlSi_2O_6$ at 1000 bars P_{H_2O}. The solid solution increases as the water vapour pressure decreases and is about 40 per cent in the dry system. Some leucites crystallized from hydrous melts display a lamellar texture. The lamellae are not the result of inversion twinning but probably represent an exsolved 'analcitic' or 'sodic leucite' phase.

Leucite has been prepared from analcite by heating the latter in a con-

Table 36. LEUCITE AND PSEUDOLEUCITE ANALYSES

	1.	2.	3.		Numbers of ions on the basis of 6 oxygens		
					1.	2.	3.
SiO_2	54·62	54·66	57·42	Si	1·992	1·992	2·034
TiO_2	0·00	0·17	0·24	Al	0·986⎫	0·995⎫	0·912⎫
Al_2O_3	22·93	23·15	21·85	Ti	—⎪	0·005⎪	0·006⎪
Fe_2O_3	0·26	0·36	1·70	Fe^{+3}	0·007⎪	0·010⎪	0·045⎪
FeO	0·26	0·11	0·00	Mg	—⎬1·00	0·002⎬1·02	0·004⎬0·98†
MnO	—	0·01	0·03	Fe^{+2}	0·008⎪	0·003⎪	—⎪
MgO	0·00	0·04	0·07	Ca	0·002⎭	0·004⎭	0·007⎭
CaO	0·08	0·11	0·19	Na	0·047⎫	0·045⎫	0·328⎫
Na_2O	0·66	0·63	4·78	K	0·978⎬1·03	0·932⎬0·98	0·606⎬0·93
K_2O	21·02	20·04	13·40				
H_2O^+	0·12	0·36	0·27				
H_2O^-	0·00	0·05	0·03				
Total	99·95	99·77	100·26				
n	1·509	—	—				

1. Leucite, leucitite, Congo (Sahama, Th. G., 1952, *Amer. Journ. Sci.*, Bowen vol., p. 457).
2. Leucite, giant leucite aggregate, Congo (Sahama, Th. G., 1960, *Journ. Petr.*, vol. 1, p. 146; includes P_2O_5 0·08).
3. Pseudoleucite, tinguaite, Montana (Zies, E. G. & Chayes, F., 1960, *Journ. Petr.*, vol. 1, p. 86; includes BaO 0·28).

† Includes Mn 0·001, Ba 0·004.

centrated solution of potassium chloride at 200°C, and the two minerals are readily interconvertible by ion exchange:

$$NaAlSi_2O_6 \cdot H_2O + K^+aq. \rightleftharpoons KAlSi_2O_6 + Na^+aq. + H_2O$$

analcite   leucite

The extent to which the exchange of Na by K has occurred can be measured by determining the loss of water: hydrothermally synthesized analcite contains 8·46 per cent H_2O and the derived leucite has 0·75 per cent.

OPTICAL AND PHYSICAL PROPERTIES

The small range of ionic replacements shown by leucite is accompanied by correspondingly minor variation in the optical and physical properties; the refractive index is generally $1·510 \pm 0·001$ and the density $2·485 \pm 0·015$ gm/cm³. Though normally uniaxial, leucite may show a very small optic axial angle and weak anisotropy; except in very small crystals, it shows complex repeated twinning on {110} which in hand specimen shows as striations on the crystal faces. The striated faces are not co-planar but form re-entrant angles; these disappear on heating the crystal to the low- ⇌ high-temperature inversion temperature. Leucite is usually developed in equant and often euhedral crystals with icositetrahedral {211}, or more rarely the dodecahedral {110}, habit, and exhibits octagonal outlines in thin section. Skeletal growths and inclusions, the latter arranged in regular, either radial or concentric patterns, are not uncommon. On heating low-temperature leucite the c parameter changes from 13·65 Å at 20°C to 13·40 Å at 625°C; the a parameter over the same temperature range expands from 12·95 to 13·40 Å.

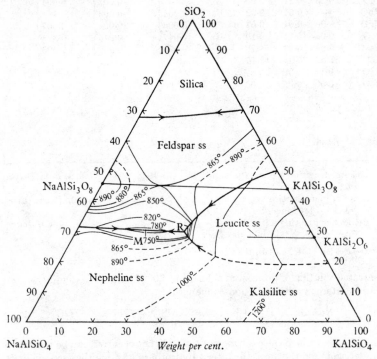

Fig. 143. *Liquidus relationships in part of the system $NaAlSiO_4$–$KAlSiO_4$–SiO_2–H_2O at a P_{H_2O} of 1000 bars projected onto the anhydrous base of the tetrahedron. M, minimum on liquidus surface along the nepheline–feldspar boundary curve; R, reaction point (after Fudali, R. F., 1963, Bull. Geol. Soc. Amer., vol. 74, p. 1101).*

DISTINGUISHING FEATURES

Leucite is distinguished from analcite by the common presence of complex twinning, and by having a higher refractive index. These characteristics also serve to distinguish leucite from the sodalite group of minerals which in addition are sometimes pale blue in thin section. Microcline has a higher birefringence and higher refringence.

PARAGENESIS

Leucite is a characteristic mineral of potassium-rich basic lavas such as leucite basanite, leucite tephrite, leucite–melilite basalt and leucite ankaramite; it is also an essential constituent of the potassium-rich ultrabasic volcanic rocks, ugandite (olivine + augite + leucite) and katungite (melilite + leucite glass with or without leucite). In some rocks leucite is completely replaced by an intergrowth of potassium-rich alkali feldspar and nepheline, or is surrounded by a rim consisting mainly of potassium feldspar and nepheline. These intergrowths, some of which show a zonal arrangement, are described as *pseudoleucite*. Pseudoleucite occurs mainly in volcanic rocks, and pseudoleucites with well defined crystal boundaries are confined to quickly chilled rocks. Pseudoleucite is found also in some plutonic rocks, e.g. the borolanite of Assynt, Scotland, but here the intergrowths are less defined and have rounded margins which merge into the other rock constituents.

The genesis of pseudoleucite has been ascribed to a number of different processes, e.g. to the breakdown of sodium-rich leucite to an intergrowth of potassium feldspar and nepheline, to the reaction of early formed leucite with magmatic liquids, the so-called pseudoleucite reaction, and to the decomposition of potassium-rich analcite. It is evident from the data of the synthetic system $NaAlSiO_4$–$KAlSiO_4$–SiO_2–H_2O that extensive solid solution of $NaAlSi_2O_6$ in leucite can occur at the temperature of crystallization, and that the amount of solid solution varies with the pressure of water vapour. At subsolidus temperature such sodium-rich leucites are unstable and they break down to nepheline and feldspar. Furthermore it has been shown that small amounts of nepheline and sanidine develop in natural leucites containing approximately 10 per cent $NaAlSi_2O_6$ ($\simeq 1.4$ weight per cent Na_2O) when held at 650°C and P_{H_2O} of 1000 bars for several days, while mixtures of leucite, nepheline and sanidine have been obtained by heating natural pseudoleucites at 850°C and P_{H_2O} of 285 bars. The subsolidus reaction leucite $\rightarrow$ nepheline + feldspar accounts satisfactorily for the characteristics of most pseudoleucites, and is, no doubt, the explanation of nepheline–feldspar assemblages in plutonic alkali rocks whose compositions lie in the primary field of leucite.

The existence of a reaction point in both the anhydrous and hydrous systems $NaAlSiO_4$–$KAlSiO_4$–SiO_2 and $NaAlSiO_4$–$KAlSiO_4$–SiO_2–H_2O has already been noted, and it is thus possible for pseudoleucite to form by a solid–liquid reaction. This mode of formation may well account for those examples in which the leucite is surrounded by a reaction rim of pseudoleucite, e.g. the leucite phenocrysts (Na_2O 1–1.5 per cent), rimmed by pseudoleucite (Na_2O 6–7 per cent) in the leucite theralite of the Nyamlagira volcano, Congo, described by Bowen and Ellestad (1937). With regard to the possible formation of pseudoleucite from the decomposition of potassium-rich analcite there is no experimental evidence that any extensive solid solution of $KAlSi_2O_6$ in analcite occurs under normal magmatic conditions. Nevertheless an analcite containing 4·48 per cent K_2O, equivalent to 21 per cent leucite, as phenocrysts in basalt has been described, and the possibility that some pseudoleucites may have arisen from the breakdown of an analcite solid solution cannot entirely be discounted.

REFERENCES

BOWEN, N. L. and ELLESTAD, R. B. (1937) 'Leucite and pseudoleucite', *Amer. Min.*, vol. 22, p. 409.

FAUST, G. T. (1963) 'Phase transitions in synthetic and natural leucite', *Schweiz. Min. Petr. Mitt.*, vol. 43, p. 165.

FUDALI, R. F. (1963) 'Experimental studies bearing on the origin of pseudoleucite and associated problems of alkali rock systems', *Bull. Geol. Soc. Amer.*, vol. 74, p. 1101.

SODALITE GROUP

Sodalite		$Na_6[Al_6Si_6O_{24}]Cl_2$
Nosean		$Na_8[Al_6Si_6O_{24}]SO_4$
Haüyne		$(Na,Ca)_{4-8}[Al_6Si_6O_{24}](SO_4,S)_{1-2}$

CUBIC

	Sodalite	Nosean	Haüyne
n	1·483–1·487	1·495	1·496–1·505
D	2·27–2·33	2·30–2·40	2·44–2·50
H	5½–6	5½	5½–6
Cleavage:	{110} poor.	{110} poor.	{110}
Twinning:	{111}	{111}	{111}
Colour:	Pale pink, grey, yellow, blue, green; colourless or very pale pink or blue in thin section.	Grey, brown, or blue; colourless or blue in thin section.	White, grey, green or blue; colourless or pale blue in thin section.

STRUCTURE

The aluminosilicate framework is formed by the linkage of SiO_4 and AlO_4 tetrahedra in approximately equal numbers, each corner oxygen being shared by two tetrahedra. In sodalite (a 8·91 Å, Z = 1), cage-like cubo-octohedral units are formed (Fig. 144) bounded by six rings of four tetrahedra parallel to {100} and eight rings of six tetrahedra parallel to {111}: the six-membered rings define a set of channels which intersect to form large cavities. The cavities are occupied by chlorine ions and these are tetrahedrally coordinated by sodium ions.

In nosean (a 9·05 Å, Z = 1) single $(SO_4)^{-2}$ ions replace randomly the two Cl^- per cell of sodalite. Haüyne (a 9·13 Å, Z = 1) contains a greater number of $(SO_4)^{-2}$ ions and also has some Ca replacing Na.

CHEMISTRY

Sodalite is the most sodium-rich member of the sodalite group and differs from the other minerals of the group in containing chlorine as an essential constituent. There is little variation in the Na content beyond a slight substitution of Na by both K and Ca. Some analyses report appreciable amounts of sulphur.

Sodalite may be synthesized easily by hydrothermal treatment of the component oxides together with NaCl, or by heating muscovite or kaolinite with NaCl at about 500°C. So-called 'basic' sodalite, in which the Cl is replaced by OH, can be produced from Na–Al silicate gels or from analcite. It is believed that for the synthesis of the hackmanite variety trace amounts of sulphur are necessary. Sodalite may be altered to thomsonite, natrolite, gismondine, kaolinite or cancrinite.

Nosean has the composition $Na_8Al_6Si_6O_{24} \cdot SO_4$ with a limited amount of substitution of Ca for Na permitting an increase in the sulphate ions over the ideal value of one per unit cell: the upper limit will be two sulphate ions, for varieties grading towards haüyne in composition. Small amounts of Fe^{+3} sometimes occur, presumably substituting for Al though in some samples it may represent iron ore impurities. Ca varies, and may amount to over 4 per cent CaO. Sulphate is the dominant anion but it may be partially replaced by chlorine. Nosean has been synthesized by hydrothermal treatment of a gel of composition $Na_2O \cdot Al_2O_3 \cdot 2SiO_2 + Na_2SO_4$, nosean being produced in the presence of an excess of alkali.

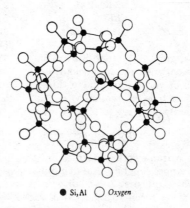

● Si,Al ○ *Oxygen*

Fig. 144. *Part of the aluminosilicate framework in the structure of sodalite (after Bragg, W. L., 1937, Atomic Structure of Minerals, Cornell Univ. Press).*

Haüyne differs chemically from nosean in having a much higher proportion of Ca and in being richer in the sulphate radicle. Its formula is intermediate between that of nosean $(Na_8Al_6Si_6O_{24} \cdot SO_4)$ and a hypothetical end-member $Ca_4Al_6Si_6O_{24} \cdot SO_4$, but the addition of extra SO_4^{-2} groups is possible to a limit of two per unit cell, the charge balance being maintained by the addition of Na or Ca. Some haüynes have minor replacement of Al by Fe^{+3}, and the substitution of K for Na is more important in haüyne (e.g. anal. 5) than in other members of the sodalite group, probably due to its relatively open structure. Chlorine may partially replace the sulphate ion.

Lazurite is the sodalite group mineral dominant in lapis-lazuli, ultramarine being a synonym generally applied specifically to synthetic materials. Natural lazurite contains both sulphide and sulphate sulphur in addition to

Table 37. SODALITE, NOSEAN AND HAÜYNE ANALYSES

	1.	2.	3.	4.	5.	6.
SiO_2	36·69	36·70	36·36	36·69	34·04	32·52
Al_2O_3	31·40	32·01	32·09	28·45	28·27	27·61
Fe_2O_3	0·85	0·07	0·07	0·47	—	—
CaO	0·19	—	—	0·63	9·51	6·47
Na_2O	25·96	24·79	24·73	23·90	10·39	19·45
K_2O	0·23	0·17	0·12	—	5·44	0·28
SO_3	—	—	—	7·30	10·02	10·46
S	0·38	tr.	0·00	—	—	2·71
Cl	5·64	7·00	6·79	1·05	0·76	0·47
H_2O^+	0·30	0·36	0·86	}2·15	}0·34	—
H_2O^-	0·04	0·00	0·12			—
	101·71	101·39	101·70	100·64	100·34	99·97
$O \equiv Cl, S$	1·39	1·58	1·53	0·23	0·17	0·55
Total	100·32	99·81	100·17	100·41	100·17	99·42
n	1·487	1·487	1·483	—	—	—
D	2·285	2·286	2·278	2·299	—	—

NUMBERS OF IONS ON THE BASIS OF THE 21(O) IN THE $3Al_2O_3 \cdot 6SiO_2$ FRAMEWORK

	1.	2.	3.	4.	5.	6.
Si	5·933 ⎫	5·925 ⎫	5·894 ⎫	6·203 ⎫	6·055 ⎫	5·998 ⎫
Al	5·986 ⎬12·02	6·091 ⎬12·02	6·132 ⎬12·03	5·670 ⎬11·93	5·927 ⎬11·98	6·000 ⎬12·00
Fe^{+3}	0·102 ⎭	0·008 ⎭	0·008 ⎭	0·060 ⎭	—	—
Na	8·138 ⎫	7·760 ⎫	7·772 ⎫	7·834 ⎫	3·583 ⎫	6·954 ⎫
Ca	0·033 ⎬9·225†	— ⎬7·80	— ⎬7·81‡	0·114 ⎬7·95	1·813 ⎬6·86§	1·279 ⎬8·30
K	0·047 ⎭	0·035 ⎭	0·025 ⎭	— ⎭	1·233 ⎭	0·066 ⎭
Cl	1·546 ⎫	1·915	1·866	0·301 ⎫	0·229 ⎫	0·146 ⎫
S	0·115 ⎬	—	—	— ⎬1·23	— ⎬1·57	0·936 ⎬2·53
SO_4	—	—	—	0·926 ⎭	1·336 ⎭	1·448 ⎭
OH	0·324	0·380	0·928	2·415	0·403	

1. Light grey sodalite, pegmatite cutting nepheline-syenite, Kola peninsula (Fersman, A. E. & Bonshtedt, E. M., 1937, *Minerals of the Khibina and Lovozero tundras*; includes MgO 0·03).
2. White or colourless hackmanite, tinguaite, Magnet Cove, Arkansas (Miser, H. D. & Glass, J. J., 1941, *Amer. Min.*, vol. 26, p. 437; includes $CaCO_3$ 0·29).
3. Blue sodalite, associated with colourless hackmanite (anal. 2), Magnet Cove, Arkansas (Miser, H. D. & Glass, J. J., *loc. cit. supra*; includes MnO 0·06, $CaCO_3$ 0·50).
4. Light blue-grey nosean, ejected block, Laacher See, Lower Rhine (Rath, G. vom, 1864, *Zeits. deutsch. geol. Ges.*, vol. 16, p. 82).
5. Haüyne, haüyne riedenite, Monte Vulture, Italy (Rittmann A., 1931, *Schweiz. Min. Petr. Mitt.*, vol. 11, p. 250; includes FeO 0·69, MgO 0·48, CO_2 0·4).
6. 'Lazurite', lapis lazuli, central Asia (Brögger, W. C. & Backström, H., 1891, *Zeit. Kryst.*, vol. 18, p. 209).

† Includes Mg 0·007.
‡ Includes Mn 0·008.
§ Includes Fe^{+2} 0·103 Mg 0·127.

calcium and sodium and may be considered as a sulphide-bearing haüyne. For synthetic ultramarines the general formula is $M_8Al_6Si_6O_{24}S_x$, where M = alkalies or alkali earths and $x = 1$–2.

OPTICAL AND PHYSICAL PROPERTIES

The minerals of the sodalite group are isotropic or, rarely, weakly anisotropic: nosean and haüyne may show weak birefringence in samples containing inclusions. The refractive index is lowest for sodalite and increases with the introduction of sulphate in nosean and rises slightly higher for haüyne, but for all the minerals of the group the refractive index is comparatively low and considerably less than that of Canada Balsam. The specific gravities of minerals of the group rise from sodalite (2·27 to 2·33) to haüyne (2·44 to 2·50); for nosean the lighter varieties (2·30) are those poor in Ca while those with around 4 per cent CaO have a higher specific gravity.

The colour of the minerals of the sodalite group is extremely variable, ranging from colourless or white, to grey, yellow, green, brown, pink or most typically blue. Blue, green, red and violet ultramarines have been synthesized, and for these the depth of colour is considered to be related mainly to the sulphur content. In sodalite itself, however, the blue colour does not appear to be directly related to the chemistry of its major constituents: thus in Table 37, anal. 3 of blue sodalite does not show any marked variation from anal. 1 of a light grey sodalite or from anal. 2 of a white or colourless hackmanite. Hackmanite is a variety of sodalite which has a distinct pink tinge when freshly fractured, but whose colour fades on exposure to light and returns when the mineral is kept in the dark for a few weeks, or is bombarded by X-rays. This phenomenon of tenebresence is probably related to trace amounts of both sodium mono- and poly-sulphide.

DISTINGUISHING FEATURES

The minerals of the sodalite group may be distinguished by their isotropic character and by their refractive index being considerably less than that of Canada Balsam. Fluorite has an even lower refractive index and a much better cleavage and leucite generally has weakly birefringent twins. Within the sodalite group chemical tests may differentiate the minerals: when the mineral on a glass slide is treated with nitric acid and the solution is allowed to evaporate slowly, the formation of cubic crystals of NaCl indicates sodalite, while monoclinic needles of gypsum indicate haüyne. If neither product is formed before the addition of $CaCl_2$, and both appear after it is added, nosean is indicated.

PARAGENESIS

Sodalite commonly occurs in nepheline-syenites and associated rock types (Table 37, anal. 1). It is typically associated with nepheline, cancrinite, melanite and fluorite. Sodalite may also occur in metasomatized calcareous rocks at alkaline igneous contacts. The hackmanite variety is also found in nepheline-syenites and related rocks: at Magnet Cove, Arkansas (anal. 2), it occurs surrounded by a mottled zone of blue sodalite (anal. 3) in irregular lenses in a tinguaite dyke. It is well-known also from the Kola peninsula and from the nepheline-syenites of the Bancroft area, Ontario.

Nosean occurs chiefly in phonolites and related under-saturated volcanic rocks and in volcanic bombs and ejected blocks. The nosean phonolite of the Wolf Rock, Cornwall, is well-known for its abundant phenocrysts of nosean, which have a clear rim and a centre turbid with iron ore. It is not common in other than volcanic rocks, though a series of nosean-bearing aegirine-augite syenites and porphyries have been reported.

Haüyne is found in phonolites and related rock types: the ejected blocks in the 'peperino' of the Alban Hills provide fine examples of white haüyne, with leucite and melilite. Haüyne also occurs in some monticellite alnöites and nepheline alnöites.

Lazurite occurs in lapis lazuli in metamorphosed limestone or at the contacts of pegmatites with limestone.

REFERENCES

BARTH, T. F. W. (1932) 'The chemical composition of noselite and haüyne', *Amer. Min.*, vol. 17, p. 466.

KIRK, R. D. (1955) 'The luminescence and tenebrescence of natural and synthetic sodalite', *Amer. Min.*, vol. 40, p. 22.

Helvite $Mn_4[Be_3Si_3O_{12}]S$
Danalite $Fe_4[Be_3Si_3O_{12}]S$
Genthelvite $Zn_4[Be_3Si_3O_{12}]S$

CUBIC

	Helvite	Danalite	Genthelvite
n	1·728–1·749	1·749–1·770	1·740–1·746
D	3·20–3·44	3·28–3·44	3·44–3·70
H	6	6	$6\frac{1}{2}$
Cleavage:	{111}, poor.	{111}, poor.	{111}, poor.
Twinning:	{111}	—	—
Colour:	Honey-yellow, brown, reddish brown; pale yellow or pale brown to colourless in thin section.	Yellow, pink, reddish brown, red; pink to colourless in thin section.	Purplish pink, reddish brown; pale pink or colourless in thin section.

The structure of the helvite group of minerals (a 8·12–8·29 Å; Z = 2) is similar to that of sodalite. The Al atoms of the sodalite structure may be considered to be replaced by Be, the Na by Mn, Fe^{+2} or Zn, and the Cl by S.

The three minerals of the group form an isomorphous series whose composition may be expressed as $R_4Be_3Si_3O_{12}S$, with R representing Mn, Fe or Zn. Specimens with pure end-member composition are not known: all contain both Mn and Fe and the majority also contain Zn. Helvite may alter to an earthy ochre-yellow material considerably poorer in beryllium: a black surface oxidation product of manganese oxides and hydroxides may also occur.

The minerals of this group resemble garnet in their properties and appearance: they are isotropic and have relatively high refractive indices but generally have specific gravities lower than those of garnet. Helvite group minerals may be detected by covering a small amount of mineral powder with dilute H_2SO_4, adding a pinch of As_2O_4, boiling the solution for one or two minutes, decanting the acid, washing the powder and examining it under a binocular microscope: any helvite present will be stained a bright canary yellow.

Helvite occurs both in granites and granite pegmatites and in contact metasomatic rocks and skarns. In granite pegmatites it is typically associated with lithium minerals such as petalite and spodumene: it is probably formed in rocks relatively poor in·aluminium whereas beryl is formed in aluminium-rich rocks. Danalite and genthelvite are also found in granites and granite pegmatites and in contact metamorphosed rocks.

Cancrinite–Vishnevite

$$(Na,Ca,K)_{6-8}[Al_6Si_6O_{24}](CO_3,SO_4,Cl)_{1-2} \cdot 1-5H_2O$$

HEXAGONAL $(-)$

ϵ 1·503–1·488
ω 1·528–1·490
δ 0·025–0·002

Dispersion: very weak. D 2·51–2·32. H 5–6.

Cleavage: {10$\bar{1}$0} perfect, {0001} poor.

Twinning: Lamellar, rare.

Colour: Colourless, white, light blue to light greyish blue, honey-yellow, reddish ; colourless in thin section.

Gelatinizes in acids ; carbonate-rich varieties effervesce in HCl.

STRUCTURE

The structure of cancrinite (a 12·58–12·76, c 5·11–5·20 Å, Z = 1) is not known in detail; it is thought, however, to consist of a framework (composition $Al_6Si_6O_{24}$) in which (Si,Al)–O tetrahedra are linked to form four-, six- and twelve-membered rings. These rings define cavities and channels within which the Na and Ca ions, and also the larger CO_3^{-2} and SO_4^{-2} ions, and water molecules, are accommodated.

CHEMISTRY

The cancrinite–vishnevite minerals form a solid solution series in which the main substitution is $CO_3 \rightleftharpoons SO_4$; other substitutions include the replacement of Na by Ca and K. The carbonate-rich members of the series (cancrinites) contain appreciably more calcium ions per formula unit than the sulphatic varieties (vishnevites). There is, however, no corresponding increase in the numbers of sodium ions in the sulphatic varieties which in consequence contain a smaller number of $(CO_3 + SO_4)$ anions per formula unit than the carbonate-rich members of the series (Table 38, anals. 1 and 2). Thus more of the intra-framework positions are vacant in vishnevite, and it is mainly on this account that the density of the members of the series varies from approximately 2·5 for cancrinite to about 2·3 for vishnevite. Chlorine is the dominant intra-framework anion in some cancrinites, and in such minerals (Table 38, anal. 3) $\sum C + S + Cl$ (2·5–3·0) is higher than in either cancrinite or vishnevite in which $\sum C + S + Cl$ varies between 1·0 and 2·0.

Cancrinite of composition $Na_8[Al_6Si_6O_{24}](CO_3)$ can be synthesized from a mixture of α-cristobalite, γ-alumina and Na_2SiO_3 in correct stoichiometric proportions for the formation of nepheline, together with the required

Table 38. CANCRINITE–VISHNEVITE ANALYSES

	1.	2.	3.		NUMBERS OF IONS ON THE BASIS OF 12 (Si+Al) 1.	2.	3.
SiO_2	33·98	35·29	32·23				
Al_2O_3	29·11	28·79	28·98				
CaO	4·80	1·49	10·36	Si	5·971	6·118	5·824
Na_2O	18·69	15·65	11·01	Al	6·032	5·886	6·174
K_2O	0·64	4·15	7·11	Na	6·368⎫	5·260⎫	3·858⎫
H_2O^+	4·34	7·62	—	Ca	0·904 ⎬7·42	0·277 ⎬6·51†	2·006 ⎬7·50
H_2O^-	0·23	—	—	K	0·144⎭	0·919⎭	1·640⎭
CO_2	7·00	1·01	1·26	H_2O	2·544	4·408	—
SO_3	1·37	5·76	4·11	C	1·679⎫	0·239⎫	0·310⎫
Cl	0·42	—	6·25	S	0·180 ⎬1·98	0·749 ⎬0·99	0·557 ⎬2·78
				Cl	0·125⎭	—⎭	1·913⎭
Total	100·58	100·05	101·31				
$O \equiv Cl$	0·10	—	1·56				
					$100C:(C+S)$		
	100·48	100·05	99·75		90·7	24·2	—
D	2·422	2·35	2·444				

1. Cancrinite, Ontario, Canada (Phoenix, R. & Nuffield, E. W., 1949, *Amer. Min.*, vol. 34, p. 452).
2. Vishnevite, Ilmen mountains, U.S.S.R. (Zavaritsky, A. N., 1929, *Mém. Soc. Russe Min.*, vol. 38, p. 201; includes Fe_2O_3 0·19, MgO 0·10).
3. Microsommite, Monte Somma, Vesuvius (Rauff, H., 1878, *Zeit. Krist.*, vol. 2, p. 445).

† Includes Fe^{+3} 0·025, Mg 0·026.

amount of anhydrous Na_2CO_3. The synthesis has been effected in the temperature and P_{H_2O} ranges of 500° to 750°C and 10,000 to 30,000 lb/in² respectively. At temperatures below 600°C the product is hexagonal with cell parameters $a \simeq 12·7$, $c \simeq 5·2$ Å, comparable with natural cancrinites; at higher temperatures the product has cubic symmetry, a 9·02 Å, and is similar in structure to nosean, a 9·05 Å. The transition from the low- to the high-temperature polymorph is insensitive to water vapour pressures between 10,000 and 30,000 lb/in².

OPTICAL AND PHYSICAL PROPERTIES

The optical properties of the cancrinite–vishnevite series show a fair correlation with the varying contents of CO_3 and SO_4, both the ϵ and ω indices being lower in the more sulphatic varieties. The rate of decrease of the ω index with increasing content of the vishnevite component is greater than that of the ϵ index, and the birefringence varies from about 0·025 for cancrinite to between 0·002 to 0·004 for vishnevite. Anomalous biaxial optical characters are shown by some cancrinites; the chlorine-rich cancrinite, microsommite, is optically positive.

DISTINGUISHING FEATURES

The carbonate-rich varieties of the cancrinite–vishnevite series are distinguished from nepheline by their stronger birefringence, from scapolite by their different cleavage and lower refractive indices, and from calcite by their much weaker birefringence. Cancrinite may be confused with basal and near basal sections of muscovite, but is normally distinguished by its uniaxial optical character, as it is also from biaxial zeolites. Vishnevite has lower refractive indices and better cleavage than nepheline.

PARAGENESIS

Members of the cancrinite–vishnevite series are common constituents of many nepheline-syenites and nepheline-syenite pegmatites. The cancrinite may occur as individual grains formed during the late stages of crystallization, or as reaction rims between nepheline and calcite. The sequence nepheline → cancrinite → calcite is probably correctly interpreted as a normal magmatic reaction series in which cancrinite has formed by reaction between the early nepheline with the CO_2-rich residual liquids. This interpretation is consistent with the phase relations in the synthetic system nepheline–calcite in which cancrinite occurs as a binary compound and melts incongruently, under a P_{CO_2} of 110 bars, to nepheline and liquid. Cancrinite occurs commonly as a secondary mineral particularly replacing nepheline.

REFERENCES

EDGAR, A. D. and BURLEY, B. J. (1963) 'Studies on cancrinites. I.—polymorphism in sodium carbonate rich cancrinite – natrodavyne', *Canadian Min.*, vol. 7, p. 631.

PHOENIX, R. and NUFFIELD, E. W. (1949) 'Cancrinite from Blue Mountain, Ontario', *Amer. Min.*, vol. 34, p. 452.

Scapolite

$(Na,Ca,K)_4[Al_3(Al,Si)_3Si_6O_{24}](Cl,CO_3,SO_4,OH)$

TETRAGONAL $(-)$

	Marialite†	Meionite†
	$Na_4[Al_3Si_9O_{24}]Cl$	$Ca_4[Al_6Si_6O_{24}]CO_3$
ϵ	1·540–1·541	1·556–1·564
ω	1·546–1·550	1·590–1·600
δ	0·005–0·009	0·034–0·038
Dispersion:	Moderate	Moderate
D	2·50–2·62	2·74–2·78
H	5–6	5–6

Cleavage: {100}, {110} good.

Colour: Colourless, white, bluish grey, pale greenish yellow, yellow, pink, violet, brown or orange-brown; colourless in thin section.

Sodium-rich scapolites are almost insoluble, calcium-rich scapolites decompose in HCl.

STRUCTURE

The scapolite structure (Fig. 145) consists of ring-like groups of four (Si,Al)–O tetrahedra which are arranged to form chains parallel to the z-axis; linkage between the individual chains is effected by other rings of four (Si,Al)–O tetrahedra. Within this relatively open framework are cavities of smaller and larger dimensions; the former are occupied by Na and Ca ions and the latter by Cl, CO_3 and SO_4 ions. The cell dimensions of synthetic marialite and meionite are a 12·075, c 7·516 Å and a 12·13, c 7·69 Å respectively.

CHEMISTRY

Scapolites form a solid solution series, the principal end-members of which can be expressed empirically as $3NaAlSi_3O_8 \cdot NaCl$, chloride marialite, and $3CaAl_2Si_2O_8 \cdot CaCO_3$, carbonate meionite. Pure end-member compositions, however, are not found in natural minerals, the compositional limits of which are between 17·4 to 87·3 per cent of the meionitic component, calculated as $(Ca + Mg + Fe + Mn + Ti):(Ca + Na + K + Mg + Fe + Mn + Ti)$. In many scapolites substantial replacement of Na by K occurs, and SO_4 is often present in appreciable amounts (Table 39).

† Values of ϵ, ω, δ and D of intermediate members of the series lie between those quoted for the end-members. Marialite and meionite refer to compositions Me_{0-20} and Me_{80-100} respectively; compositions Me_{20-50} and Me_{50-80} are known as dipyre and mizzonite respectively.

Table 39. SCAPOLITE ANALYSES

| | | | | NUMBERS OF IONS ON THE BASIS OF 12 (Si,Al) | | |
	1.	2.	3.	1.	2.	3.
SiO_2	57·89	47·52	41·32	Si 8·331	7·382	6·459
TiO_2	0·01	—	—	Al 3·668	4·618	5·542
Al_2O_3	21·62	25·21	30·07	Fe^{+3} 0·007⎫	—⎫	—⎫
Fe_2O_3	0·07	—	—	Mg 0·006⎪	0·033⎪	0·069⎪
FeO	—	0·30	0·23	Fe^{+2} —⎪	0·039⎪	0·030⎪
MnO	0·01	0·02	—	Mn 0·001⎬3·90	0·003⎬4·03	—⎬4·08
MgO	0·03	0·14	0·30	Na 2·930⎪	1·360⎪	0·152⎪
CaO	4·81	15·48	20·09	Ca 0·742⎪	2·577⎪	3·364⎪
Na_2O	10·50	4·52	0·50	K 0·212⎭	0·020⎭	0·464⎭
K_2O	1·16	0·10	2·33	H 0·422	0·228	0·636
H_2O^+	0·44	0·22	0·61	C 0·218⎫	0·458⎫	0·874⎫
H_2O^-	0·06	0·08	—	S 0·003⎬0·94	0·486⎬0·96	0·070⎬0·94
CO_2	1·11	2·16	4·10	Cl 0·722⎭	0·016⎭	—⎭
SO_3	0·03	4·17•	0·60			
Cl	2·96	0·06	—			
	100·70	100·01	100·15	Me%† 19·3	65·7	84·8
$O \equiv Cl$	0·67	0·01	—			
Total	100·03	100·00	100·15			
ϵ	1·541	1·564	1·556			
ω	1·549	1·587	1·590			
D	2·619	2·72	—			

1. Marialite, syenite pegmatite, Ontario (Shaw, D. M., 1960, *Journ. Petr.*, vol. 1, p. 218).
2. Mizzonite, garnet–hornblende–pyroxene–scapolite gneiss, Ghana (Knorring, O. von & Kennedy, W. Q., 1958, *Min. Mag.*, vol. 31, p. 846; includes P_2O_5 0·03).
3. Meionite, limestone xenolith in granodiorite, U.S.S.R. (Bobrovnik, D. P., 1948, *Doklady Acad. Sci. U.S.S.R.*, vol. 59, p. 311).

† Me = 100 (Ca + Mg + Fe + Mn + Ti) : (Na + K + Ca + Mg + Fe + Mn + Ti).

The main substitution is $NaSi \rightleftharpoons CaAl$ as in the plagioclase feldspars ; the charge on the (Si,Al)–O framework for the ideal marialite and meionite compositions varies between 3 and 6 and the valency balance is maintained as shown below :

$$(Na,Ca)_4[Al_3(Al,Si)_3Si_6O_{24}](Cl,CO_3,OH,SO_4)$$

$$4 \rightarrow 8 \qquad 3 \rightarrow 6 \qquad 1 \rightarrow 2$$
$$(+) \qquad (-) \qquad (-)$$
$$\underbrace{}$$
$$4 \rightarrow 8$$
$$(-)$$

The precise role of H_2O, reported in varying quantity in all scapolite analyses, is not known, but in calculating the numbers of ions on the basis of 12 (Si,Al) per formula unit (Table 39) it is considered to be an integral part of the scapolite composition.

OPTICAL AND PHYSICAL PROPERTIES

The mean refractive index $(\epsilon + \omega)/2$ and the birefringence show an approximately linear variation with composition; both values increase with increasing content of the meionite component (Fig. 146). The equation

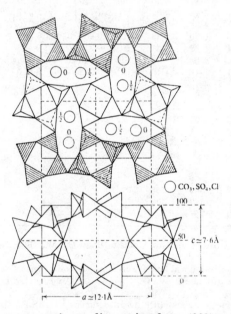

Fig. 145. *The structure of scapolite projected on* (001) *and* (100) (*after* Schiebold, E. & Seumel, G., 1932, Zeit. Krist., vol. 81, p. 110).

relating the mean refractive index to the proportion of the meionite end-member is:

$$(\epsilon + \omega)/2 = 1.5346 + 0.000507 \text{ (Me per cent)}.$$

For most scapolites the uncertainty in estimating the meionite content from the value of the mean refractive index is ± 6.5 per cent, but the uncertainty may be greater for specimens containing relatively large amounts of K, S or Cl. Compositions estimated from birefringence values do not involve an appreciably greater uncertainty.

DISTINGUISHING FEATURES

Scapolites are distinguished from the feldspars by cleavage angle, uniaxial character, straight extinction and absence of twinning; in addition calcium-rich scapolites have considerably greater birefringence. The optically negative character, cleavage and, except for the sodium-rich varieties, the higher birefringence of scapolites distinguish them from quartz. Scapolites are distinguished from cancrinite by their stronger refringence, different cleavage and greater resistance to decomposition in HCl.

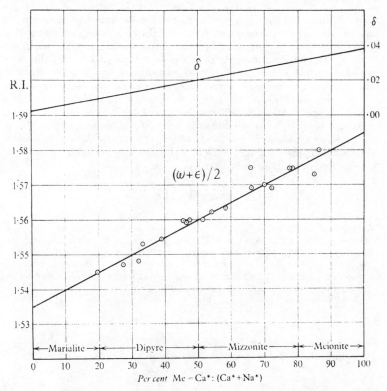

Fig. 146. *Relationship between chemical composition of scapolites expressed as mol. per cent meionite* $[=Ca^*: (Ca^*+Na^*) = (Ca+Mg+Fe+Mn+Ti): (Na+K+Ca+Mg+Fe+Mn+Ti)]$ *and mean refractive index,* $(\epsilon+\omega)/2$, *and birefringence.*

PARAGENESIS

The parageneses of scapolites are essentially confined to metamorphic and metasomatic environments; except for some pegmatite occurrences scapolite does not occur as a primary constituent of igneous rocks. Scapolite occurs in a wide range of regionally metamorphosed rocks, and the more calcium-rich varieties in particular are found in medium and high grade rocks such as amphibolites and gneisses (Table 39, anal. 2). In these rocks it is evident that the crystallization of scapolite, rather than plagioclase, was controlled in the main by the presence of a high CO_2 pressure:

$$3CaAl_2Si_2O_8 + CaCO_3 \rightarrow Ca_4Al_6Si_6O_{24}CO_3$$
$$\text{anorthite} \quad \text{calcite} \quad \text{meionite}$$

In many metamorphic rocks scapolite is metasomatic in origin, and it is a common constituent in skarns developed at the contacts of calcareous sediments and adjacent plutonic intrusions. The formation of metasomatic scapolite may also occur on a regional scale; thus for example chlorine-rich dipyre is widely developed in the Precambrian granulites and marbles of the Cloncurry district, Queensland. Here the formation of the scapolite was associated with the albitization of calcareous shales, and with the metasomatic introduction of sodium and chlorine contemporaneously with the regional metamorphism of the original sediments. Scapolite is also found in pneumatolytically and hydrothermally altered basic igneous rocks, as in the Kragerø region, southern Norway, where the widespread formation of scapolite–hornblende rocks occurred during a post-consolidation pneumatolytic metamorphism of the original basic igneous rocks by gases and solutions rich in Cl, CO_2 and water.

REFERENCES

BURLEY, B. J., FREEMAN, E. B., and SHAW, D. M. (1961) 'Studies on scapolite', *Canadian Min.*, vol. 6, p. 670.
EDWARDS, A. B. and BAKER, G. (1953) 'Scapolitization in the Cloncurry district, Queensland', *Journ. Geol. Soc. Australia*, vol. 1, p. 1.
SHAW, D. M. (1960) 'The geochemistry of scapolite. Part I. Previous work and general mineralogy. Part II. Trace elements, petrology and general geochemistry', *Journ. Petr.*, vol. 1, pp. 218 and 261.

Analcite

$Na[AlSi_2O_6] \cdot H_2O$

CUBIC

n 1·479–1·493

D 2·24–2·29   H $5\frac{1}{2}$

Cleavage: {001} very poor.

Twinning: {001}, {110} lamellar.

Colour: White, pink or grey; colourless in thin section.

STRUCTURE

Analcite is cubic with $a \simeq 13\cdot7$ Å and $16(NaAlSi_2O_6 \cdot H_2O)$ per unit cell. Its aluminosilicate framework is built of $(SiAl)O_4$ tetrahedra linked in such a way that each corner oxygen is shared by two tetrahedra, the framework containing rings of six tetrahedra and of four tetrahedra respectively normal to triad and tetrad axes. A set of sixteen large cavities forming continuous channels (see Fig. 140) are occupied by water molecules, whereas of an adjacent set of twenty-four smaller cavities sixteen are occupied by sodium and the remainder are vacant. The structure is similar to that of leucite (see p. 368).

CHEMISTRY

The only appreciable chemical variation in natural analcites is the partial replacement of sodium by potassium or calcium and the substitution of Al for Si which necessitates an increase in the (Na + K + Ca) ions to maintain the charge balance. Clear analcite phenocrysts associated with pseudoleucite in the Highwood Mountains area of Montana are rich in potassium (4·48 per cent K_2O; Table 40, anal. 3). In a series of analcites from an igneous differentiation series it has been shown that with decreasing temperature the main substitution is NaAl → Si; the $SiO_2 : H_2O$ molecular ratio remains at 4 : 2. Wairakite is the calcium analogue of analcite, in which the sodium is replaced by calcium on a valency basis, i.e. Ca for 2Na, giving $CaAl_2Si_4O_{12} \cdot 2H_2O$.

Analcite can be synthesized from aluminosilicate gels or from glasses of appropriate composition. Analcites have been produced hydrothermally varying from $Na_4Al_4Si_6O_{20} \cdot 3H_2O$ (partially dehydrated natrolite composition) to $Na_2Al_2Si_6O_{16} \cdot 3H_2O$ (hydrous albite composition): the water contents of these synthetic analcites vary linearly with Si, but the range of NaAl : Si ratios is much greater than that found in natural material.

Table 40. ANALCITE ANALYSES

| | 1. | 2. | 3. | | NUMBERS OF IONS ON THE BASIS OF 7(O) | | |
					1.	2.	3.
SiO$_2$	52·89	56·05	51·41				
Al$_2$O$_3$	24·63	22·36	23·03	Si	1·964	2·004	1·904
MgO	—	0·02	0·43	Al	1·078	0·962	1·006
CaO	0·19	tr.	1·19	Mg	—	0·001	0·024
Na$_2$O	13·31	13·44	8·48	Na	0·958	0·950	0·609
K$_2$O	0·73	0·10	4·48	Ca	0·008	—	0·047
H$_2$O$^+$	7·66	8·13	9·32	K	0·035	0·005	0·212
H$_2$O$^-$	0·29	0·01	0·28	OH	1·898	1·978	2·303
Total	99·70	100·15	99·97				
n	1·487	1·485	1·493				
δ	0·002	—	—				
D	2·268	2·252	—				

1. Analcite, pegmatitic patch in borolanite, Loch Borolan, Assynt, Scotland (Stewart, F. H., 1941, *Min. Mag.*, vol. 26, p. 1).
2. Analcite, cavity in basalt, Table Mountain, Golden, Colorado (Yoder, H. S. & Weir, C. E., 1960, *Amer. Journ. Sci.*, vol. 258–A, p. 420; includes TiO$_2$ 0·01, Fe$_2$O$_3$ 0·03).
3. Potassium-bearing analcite, phenocrysts in basalt, Highwood Mts., Montana (Larsen, E. S. & Buie, B. F., 1938, *Amer. Min.*, vol. 23, p. 837; includes Fe$_2$O$_3$ + FeO 1·35).

OPTICAL AND PHYSICAL PROPERTIES

Analcite occurs in clear or opaque well-formed crystals (often icositetrahedra), in radiating aggregates, or in irregular granular masses. The structure of analcite ideally is cubic and although some specimens are isotropic many show slight birefringence (usually $\leqslant 0.001$): some of these analcites are anomalously biaxial and show repeated lamellar twinning on {001} or {110}.

Wairakite is colourless to white and has D 2·26, H 5½–6. It is biaxial with α 1·498, γ 1·502, 2V$_\gamma$ 70°–105°, and is commonly twinned on {110}: the orientiation is $\alpha \simeq y$, $\beta \simeq x$, $\gamma \simeq z$.

DISTINGUISHING FEATURES

Analcite is very similar to leucite, but the latter mineral has a slightly higher refractive index, a different paragenesis, is anhydrous and usually shows complex twinning. Sodalite resembles analcite but can be distinguished by a chemical test for chlorine. When analcite is treated with conc. HCl it gelatinizes and takes a stain from a solution of *malachite green*.

PARAGENESIS

Analcite occurs as a primary mineral of late formation in some inter-mediate and basic igneous rocks; at a later stage it crystallizes from hydro-thermal solutions and occurs in vesicles in association with such minerals as prehnite and the zeolites. The distinction between magmatic and hydrothermal analcite, however, is not easily made when the analcite occurs as interstitial grains; in many reports of so-called primary analcite there is insufficient evidence to indicate the precise mode of origin of the mineral.

In plutonic igneous rocks analcite is found as a primary mineral in teschenites, where the analcite may amount to about 20 per cent: in some teschenites the analcite, however, is secondary after nepheline. In glen-muirites (analcite essexites) the analcite may amount to 17 per cent; analcite is also abundant in the so-called analcite syenites.

In hypabyssal igneous rocks primary analcite is found in certain olivine dolerites: in the doleritic sills of western Scotland analcite is often abundant, particularly in analcite dolerite or crinanite.

In volcanic rocks analcite is known as a primary constituent in some basalts, where typically it is restricted to the groundmass; it is known also from trachybasalts, where it may be associated with pseudoleucite. The hydrothermal crystallization of analcite in igneous rocks typically occurs in vesicles, where analcite may be found in association with prehnite, chaba-zite, thomsonite, stilbite, etc. Water-clear analcite has been found in asso-ciation with chabazite in cavities and seams in the amygdaloidal basalts of Antrim. Boreholes drilled in alkaline parts of a geyser basin in Yellowstone Park showed that the Na and Ca of the feldspars in rhyolitic and dacitic lavas are replaced by K, while at higher levels the Na gives rise to the for-mation of considerable analcite.

In sedimentary rocks analcite may occur as an authigenic mineral in sandstones; analcite-rich rocks interbedded with phosphatic siltstones and sandstones, and consisting of 35 per cent analcite set in a cryptocrystalline groundmass of laumontite, fluorite, calcite and quartz, are known. A thick series of greywackes with beds of volcanic tuff in New Zealand Triassic sediments show an alteration of glassy fragments to analcite and heulan-dite: with increasing depth the analcite is replaced by a laumontite-bearing assemblage. In the Eocene lacustrine beds of the Green River Formation of Wyoming, Utah and Colorado, analcite is by far the most widespread and abundant of the silicate minerals. A formation in the central Sahara some 20 metres thick, extending over 10,000 to 15,000 square kilometres, consists essentially of analcite: this analcite is considered to be either a primary precipitate or to have been derived from the alteration of pyroclastics or clays, though no traces of these are seen.

Analcite pseudomorphs after leucite are also known, and it has been suggested that the analcite of some igneous rocks is an alteration product of leucite.

Wairakite, the calcium analogue of analcite, was originally recorded in tuffaceous sandstones and breccias, vitric tuffs, and ignimbrite which had been altered by alkaline hydrothermal fluids associated with geothermal steam in New Zealand.

REFERENCES

CAMPBELL, A. S. and FYFE, W. S. (1965) 'Analcime–albite equilibria'. *Amer. Journ. Sci.*, vol. 263, p. 807.

COOMBS, D. S. (1965) 'Sedimentary analcime rocks and sodium-rich gneisses', *Min. Mag.*, vol. 34 (Tilley vol.), p. 144.

FENNER, C. N. (1936) 'Bore-hole investigations in Yellowstone Park', *Journ. Geol.*, vol. 44, p. 225.

SAHA, P. (1959) 'Geochemical and X-ray investigation of natural and synthetic analcites', *Amer. Min.*, vol. 44, p. 300.

STEINER, A. (1955) 'Wairakite, the calcium analogue of analcime, a new zeolite mineral', *Min. Mag.*, vol. 30, p. 691.

WILKINSON, J. F. G. (1963) 'Some natural analcime solid solutions', *Min. Mag.*, vol. 33, p. 498.

ZEOLITE GROUP

Zeolite group (Na_2,K_2,Ca,Ba) $[(Al,Si)O_2]_n \cdot xH_2O$

Name	Formula	System	n_{min}	n_{max}	2V	D
Natrolite	$Na_2[Al_2Si_3O_{10}] \cdot 2H_2O$	Orth.	1·473	1·496	58°–64° (+)	2·20–2·26
Mesolite	$Na_2Ca_2[Al_2Si_3O_{10}]_3 \cdot 8H_2O$	Mon.	1·504	1·512	80° (+)	2·26
Scolecite	$Ca[Al_2Si_3O_{10}] \cdot 3H_2O$	Mon.	1·507	1·521	36°–56° (−)	2·25–2·29
Thomsonite	$NaCa_2[(Al,Si)_5O_{10}]_2 \cdot 6H_2O$	Orth.	1·497	1·544	42°–75° (+)	2·10–2·39
Gonnardite	$Na_2Ca[(Al,Si)_5O_{10}]_2 \cdot 6H_2O$	Orth.	1·497	1·508	50° (−)	2·3
Edingtonite	$Ba[Al_2Si_3O_{10}] \cdot 4H_2O$	Orth.	1·541	1·557	54° (−)	2·7–2·8
Phillipsite	$(\tfrac{1}{2}Ca,Na,K)_3[Al_3Si_5O_{16}] \cdot 6H_2O$	Mon.	1·483	1·514	60°–80° (+)	2·2
Harmotome	$Ba[Al_2Si_6O_{16}] \cdot 6H_2O$	Mon.	1·503	1·514	80° (+)	2·41–2·47
Gismondine	$Ca[Al_2Si_2O_8] \cdot 4H_2O$	Mon.	1·515	1·546	15°–90° (−)	2·2
Garronite	$NaCa_{2·5}[Al_6Si_{10}O_{32}] \cdot 13·5H_2O$	Tetr.?	1·500	1·512	—	2·15
Chabazite	$Ca[Al_2Si_4O_{12}] \cdot 6H_2O$	Trig.	1·470	1·494	—	2·05–2·10
Gmelinite	$(Na_2,Ca)[Al_2Si_4O_{12}] \cdot 6H_2O$	Trig.	1·474	1·494	—	2·1
Levyne	$Ca[Al_2Si_4O_{12}] \cdot 6H_2O$	Trig.	1·491	1·505	—	2·1
Erionite	$(Na_2,K_2,Ca,Mg)_{4·5}[Al_9Si_{27}O_{72}] \cdot 27H_2O$	Hex.	1·468	1·476	—	2·02
Faujasite	$(Na_2,Ca)[Al_2Si_4O_{12}] \cdot 8H_2O$	Cubic	1·48		—	1·92
Heulandite	$(Ca,Na_2)[Al_2Si_7O_{18}] \cdot 6H_2O$	Mon.	1·476	1·512	var.	2·1–2·2
Stilbite	$(Ca,Na_2,K_2)[Al_2Si_7O_{18}] \cdot 7H_2O$	Mon.	1·484	1·513	30°–49° (−)	2·1–2·2
Epistilbite	$Ca[Al_2Si_6O_{16}] \cdot 5H_2O$	Mon.	1·485	1·519	44° (−)	2·2
Ferrierite	$(Na,K)_4Mg_2[Al_6Si_{30}O_{72}](OH)_2 \cdot 18H_2O$	Orth.	1·48		50° (+)	2·15
Brewsterite	$(Sr,Ba,Ca)[Al_2Si_6O_{16}] \cdot 5H_2O$	Mon.	1·510	1·523	47° (+)	2·45
Mordenite	$(Na_2,K_2,Ca)[Al_2Si_{10}O_{24}] \cdot 7H_2O$	Orth.	1·472	1·487	76°–90° (±)	2·12–2·15
Dachiardite	$(\tfrac{1}{2}Ca,Na,K)_5[Al_5Si_{19}O_{48}] \cdot 12H_2O$	Mon.	1·491	1·499	65°–73° (+)	2·16
Laumontite	$Ca[Al_2Si_4O_{12}] \cdot 4H_2O$	Mon.	1·502	1·525	26°–47° (−)	2·2–2·3
Ashcroftine	$KNaCa[Al_4Si_5O_{18}] \cdot 8H_2O$	Tetr.	1·536	1·545	—	2·61
Yugawaralite	$Ca[Al_2Si_5O_{14}] \cdot 4H_2O$	Mon.	1·495	1·504	70° (+)	2·2

The zeolites may be defined as hydrated aluminosilicates of the alkali and alkaline earth metals, with an infinitely extended three-dimensional anion network, and thus they have the atomic ratio $O:(Al+Si)=2$. They are remarkable for their continuous and in part reversible dehydration and for their base-exchange properties. They typically occur in amygdales and cavities in basic volcanic rocks and in other late-stage hydrothermal environments.

Analcite is commonly included as a member of the zeolite group. It has

13*

close affinities with the feldspathoids, however, and has a somewhat higher temperature paragenesis than the other zeolites, and it is therefore treated separately, p. 389.

STRUCTURE

The basic feature of all zeolite structures is an aluminosilicate framework composed of $(Si,Al)O_4$ tetrahedra, each oxygen of which is shared between two tetrahedra. The net negative charge on the framework is balanced by the presence of cations, in most cases Ca, Na, or K, which are situated in cavities within it. This feature is embodied also in the structures of the feldspar and feldspathoid minerals. The feldspars have compact structures in which the (Na,Ca,K) ions are in relatively small cavities and are completely surrounded by oxygens of the framework: the cations and framework are strongly interdependent so that cations cannot easily move unless framework bonds are broken, and replacement of Na or K by Ca necessarily involves a change in the Si:Al ratio. The feldspathoids have somewhat more open aluminosilicate frameworks and their (Na,Ca,K) ions (and in some cases certain anions), occupy, but do not always fill, larger cavities which are intercommunicating. Thus in the feldspathoids there are channels through which ions can be either extracted or introduced, and some through which small molecules may pass, without disruption of the framework. The zeolite aluminosilicate frameworks are similar but some are still more open, containing larger cavities and larger channels (specific gravity of zeolites 2–2·3, feldspathoids 2·3–2·5, feldspars 2·6–2·7); zeolites may therefore exhibit to a greater extent the properties of ion exchange and molecular absorption. An additional feature which differentiates the zeolites still further from minerals of the other two groups is the presence of water molecules within the structural channels. These are relatively loosely bound to the framework and cations, and like the cations can be removed and replaced without disrupting framework bonds. Since the zeolite framework is structurally almost independent of the (Na,Ca,K) cations, and since the latter do not fill all the cavities, replacements of the type $Ca \rightleftharpoons 2(Na,K)$ can occur as well as the more usual $CaAl \rightleftharpoons (Na,K)Si$.

The channel systems in the various zeolites are formed by different combinations of linked rings of tetrahedra; the wider the channels at their narrowest parts, the larger the cation that can be introduced into the structure. Those with 8- and 12-membered rings have channels large enough for the admission of organic molecules as well as cations; thus zeolites can act as ion or molecular sieves, each having its characteristic upper limit for the size of ion or molecule to which it is permeable. A grading of some zeolites according to the open-ness of structure is shown in Table 41. Channel width, however, is not the only criterion for permeability, since the presence of many cations may block the channels, and ionic or molecular diffusion is also affected by water content. Cation exchange capacity in general diminishes with loss of water; cations are most mobile in zeolites with low cation content. Na is more mobile than Ca since it is monovalent and is thus held by a weaker electrostatic bond.

Table 41. NUMBERS OF TETRAHEDRA IN RINGS, AND APPROXIMATE DIAMETERS
OF CHANNELS IN VARIOUS FELDSPATHOIDS AND ZEOLITES

Minerals	Nos. of tetrahedra in rings	Minimum diameter of widest channel
Sodalite, Nosean	4 and 6	2·2 Å
Analcite	4 and 6	2·2 Å
Harmotome, Phillipsite	4 and 8	3·2 Å
Levyne	4, 6 and 8	3·2 Å
Erionite	4, 6 and 8	3·6 Å
Chabazite	4, 6 and 8	3·9 Å
Heulandite	5, 6 and 8	—
Gmelinite	4, 6, 8 and 12	6·4 Å
Faujasite	4, 6 and 12	9 Å

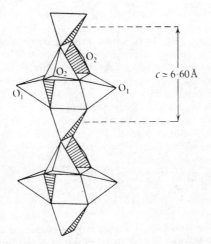

$c \simeq 6·60$ Å

Fig. 147. *The aluminosilicate chain of tetrahedra common to the structure of the natrolite group of zeolites. Chains are linked to one another laterally via oxygen atoms O_1 and O_2.*

In most zeolites the water molecules are probably distributed among a number of possible sites and can jump from one to another. In general the Ca zeolites absorb more water, and in chabazite, heulandite and stilbite, water retentivity is greater with Ca than with K in the framework.

The zeolites can be subdivided, on the basis of their structures, into a number of sub-groups.

1. Natrolite group; including natrolite, mesolite, scolecite, thomsonite, gonnardite and edingtonite. A fundamental chain-like unit (Fig. 147) figures prominently in the structures of this group and its members all

have fibrous morphology. Other zeolites, however, also may be fibrous (e.g. erionite).

2. Harmotome group; including harmotome, phillipsite, gismondine and garronite. In these minerals tetrahedra form 'chains' similar to those in the feldspars, but the chains are linked laterally in a different manner. The network contains mainly fourfold and eightfold rings, the latter constituting the channel openings.

3. Chabazite group; including chabazite, gmelinite, levyne and erionite. In these structures there exist single or double six-fold rings of tetrahedra perpendicular to a hexad or triad axis (Fig. 148). In addition eight-fold (and in gmelinite 12-fold) rings occur, forming wide channel systems.

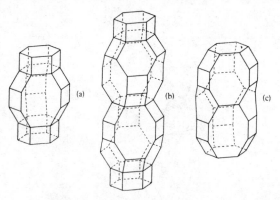

Fig. 148. *Cage-like units of the structures of* (a) *gmelinite,* (b) *levyne,* (c) *erionite. The corners of each polygon represent the centres of* $(Si,Al)O_4$ *tetrahedra but oxygen atoms are not represented (after Barrer, R. M. &* *Kerr, I. S.,* 1959, Trans. Faraday Soc., *vol. 55, p.* 1915).

4. Faujasite group; including faujasite and some synthetic zeolites. In this group tetrahedra are linked to form cubo-octahedral cage-like units which themselves are so joined as to give the structure cubic or pseudo-cubic symmetry.

5. Mordenite group; including mordenite and dachiardite. The characteristic feature of these structures is a chain containing five-fold rings of tetrahedra; such chains can be linked laterally in various ways. Wide channels are formed by twelve-fold rings in mordenite and by ten-fold rings in dachiardite.

6. Heulandite group; including heulandite, stilbite, epistilbite, ferrierite and brewsterite. Although the crystal structure of brewsterite is the only one known with certainty, they all appear to be structurally related.

Among those zeolites the structures of which are not yet known, are laumontite (and its partially dehydrated variant leonhardite) and ashcroftine.

CHEMISTRY

The zeolites form a well-defined group of hydrated silicates of aluminium and the alkalies or alkaline earths, and are characterized chemically also by having the molecular ratio $Al_2O_3 : (Ca,Sr,Ba,Na_2,K_2)O$ equal to unity, and the ratio $O : (Al + Si) = 2$. Analyses of 9 minerals in the zeolite group are given in Table 42. When zeolites are heated, water is given off continuously rather than in separate stages at definite temperatures, and the dehydrated or partially dehydrated mineral can re-absorb water usually to its original amount when again exposed to water vapour.

The fields of synthesis and stability of the zeolites have been investigated by Coombs *et al* (1959). These authors consider that in quartz-bearing systems sodium and calcium zeolites are not stable at temperatures above about 320°C although they may be synthesized readily at temperatures as high as 450°C.

OPTICAL AND PHYSICAL PROPERTIES

The zeolites, when pure, are colourless or white, but many specimens are coloured because of the presence of finely divided oxides of iron or other

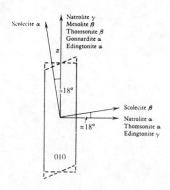

Fig. 149. *The optical orientations of some fibrous zeolites.*

impurities. Their densities range between 2·0 and 2·3 gm/cm³ except for the barium-rich zeolites, for which D is between 2·4 and 2·8. Refractive indices range between 1·47 and 1·52 and birefringence between zero and 0·015. The optical orientations of several zeolites are illustrated in Fig. 149.

PARAGENESIS

Zeolites typically occur in amygdales and fissures, chiefly in basic volcanic rocks, and are also found in veins and other late-stage hydrothermal environments. In some igneous rocks they occur as alteration products of

Table 42. ZEOLITE

	1.	2.	3.	4.	5.
SiO_2	47·60	37·17	46·10	46·98	57·28
Al_2O_3	27·40	31·93	25·05	26·43	17·76
Fe_2O_3	—	—	0·55	—	—
MgO	—	—	0·32	—	—
BaO	—	—	—	—	—
CaO	0·13	13·98	14·17	10·06	7·18
Na_2O	15·36	4·00	tr.	4·57	2·95
K_2O	0·23	tr.	0·03	0·05	—
H_2O^+	}9·47	}13·35	13·78	}11·94	}15·42
H_2O^-			0·13		
Total	100·19	100·43	100·13	100·03	100·59
α	1·4799	1·529	—	1·5065	1·501
β	—	1·531	—	1·5074	1·504
γ	1·4918	1·542	—	—	1·509
2V	59° 37′(+)	51° 39′(+)	—	90°	—
$\alpha:z$	—	—	—	8°	—
D	2·245	2·373	2·285	2·258	—

NUMBERS OF IONS ON THE BASIS OF 80 (natrolite, thomsonite,
48 (laumontite) AND

Si	23·98	19·87	24·14	9·04	26·35
Al	16·27	20·12	15·46	5·99	9·63
Fe^{+3}	—	—	0·22	—	—
Mg	—	—	0·05	—	—
Na	15·00	4·14	—	1·70	2·63
Ca	0·07	8·01	7·95	2·07	3·54
K	0·15	—	0·02	0·01	—
H_2O	15·91	23·80	24·07	7·66	23·66
Z	40·25	39·99	39·82	15·03	35·98
R†	15·22	12·55	8·47	3·78	6·17

1. Clear natrolite prisms, Puy de Marmant, Puy-de-Dôme, France (Hey, M. H., 1932, *Min. Mag.*, vol. 23, p. 243).
2. Radiating glassy prisms of thomsonite, Old Kilpatrick, Dunbartonshire (Hey, M. H., 1932, *Min. Mag.*, vol. 23, p. 51).
3. Scolecite, amygdales in Tertiary basalt, Ben More, Mull (M'Lintock, W. F. P., 1915, *Trans. Roy. Soc. Edinburgh*, vol. 51, p. 1).
4. Clear crystals of mesolite, Syhadree Mts., Bombay (Hey, M. H., 1933, *Min. Mag.*, vol. 23, p. 421).
5. Heulandite, amygdaloidal basalt, Lanakai Hills. Hawaii (Dunham, K. C., 1933, *Amer. Min.*, vol. 18, p. 369).

ANALYSES

6.	7.	8.	9.	
56·24	48·78	50·70	45·60	SiO_2
17·16	18·04	22·53	22·54	Al_2O_3
—	tr.	0·04	0·02	Fe_2O_3
0·40	—	—	—	MgO
—	—	—	0·22	BaO
8·56	9·77	11·54	7·72	CaO
tr.	0·98	0·40	1·50	Na_2O
0·32	0·60	0·30	5·63	K_2O
16·80	}22·04	12·00	}16·58	H_2O^+
0·96		2·41		H_2O^-
100·44	100·21	99·92	99·81	Total
1·488	1·4848	1·505–1·513	1·498	α
1·498	1·4852	—	—	β
1·500	1·4858	1·516–1·521	1·503	γ
—	—	(+)	—	2V
—	—	38°	—	$\alpha:z$
—	—	2·26–2·29	2·13	D

colecite), 30 (mesolite), 72 (heulandite, stilbite, chabazite), 2 (phillipsite) oxygens.

26·50	24·86	15·78	10·10	Si
9·53	10·84	8·27	5·89	Al
—	—	0·01	—	Fe^{+3}
0·28	—	—	—	Mg
—	0·97	0·24	0·64	Na
4·32	5·34	3·85	1·84	Ca
0·19	0·39	0·12	1·59	K
27·92	37·47	14·96	12·25	H_2O
36·03	35·70	24·06	15·99	Z
4·79	6·70	4·21	4·07	R†

6. Stilbite, vesicular Tertiary basalt, Ritter hot spring, Oregon (Hewett, D. F., Shannon, E. V. & Gonyer, F. A., 1928, *Proc. U.S. Nat. Mus.*, vol. 73, art. 16).
7. Pseudo-rhombohedral chabazite, vein in andesite, Bor, Yugoslavia (Majer, V., 1953, *Jugoslav. Akad. Znan. Umjet.*, p. 175 and p. 191).
8. Laumontite, drusy cavities in quartz porphyry, Saale, Germany (Koch, R. A., 1958, *Neues Jahrb. Min., Monat.*, p. 58).
9. Phillipsite, amygdale in Tertiary basalt, Glenariff, Co. Antrim, Northern Ireland (Walker, G. P. L., 1963, *Min. Mag.*, vol. 33, p. 173).

† $R = (Mg + Na + Ca + K + Ba)$.

aluminosilicates such as the feldspars or nepheline. They are also known as authigenic minerals in sandstones and other sedimentary rocks. The occurrence of the individual minerals of the zeolite group are detailed below.

The so-called 'rule' of Cornu states that in a series of zeolites crystallizing with falling temperature the zeolites will appear in the order of increasing hydration. The reverse sequence of events may occur as a result of metamorphism, though on the whole it is only rarely that a clear and consistent trend of this type can be recognized.

The sequence of deposition of the amygdaloidal minerals in the Watchung basalt of New Jersey was determined to be laumontite, stilbite, thomsonite, calcite, stilbite, chabazite, thomsonite, analcite, apophyllite, calcite and mesolite. In the zeolites of the Tertiary lavas of Northern Ireland the most abundant species, in order of frequency, are chabazite, thomsonite, levyne, natrolite, mesolite, stilbite, gmelinite, heulandite and phillipsite. Chabazite and thomsonite characterize the upper parts of the lava succession: below

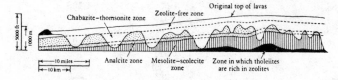

Fig. 150. *Diagrammatic section across the Tertiary lavas of eastern Iceland showing the zonal distribution of amygdale minerals (after Walker, G. P. L., 1960, Journ. Geol., vol. 68, p. 515).*

they are joined by natrolite (and analcite) and in some areas, where zeolitization has been most intense, by stilbite and heulandite as well. These zeolite zones may reflect the temperature distribution in the lavas during zeolitization, the zones being discordant and clearly superimposed on the lavas. A somewhat thicker series of zones is apparent in the Tertiary basalts of eastern Iceland where the lowest zone is rich in mesolite and scolecite (together with many other zeolites); this is succeeded by an analcite zone, and then by a restricted assemblage mostly of chabazite and thomsonite (Fig. 150). These zeolites are mainly those tending to be low in silica, consistent with their occurrence in undersaturated basic rocks.

A general grouping of the calcic zeolites has been proposed illustrating the tendency of specific zeolites to occur in environments (A) supersaturated with respect to SiO_2, (B) saturated, and (C) undersaturated (Fig. 151).

The mineral assemblages in which zeolites are characteristic are of such widespread occurrence that a new mineral and metamorphic facies, the zeolite facies, has been proposed. Originally the facies was to cover only regionally developed zeolitic assemblages which largely replace the pre-existing rocks and conform to the mineralogical and chemical requirements of a metamorphic facies: subsequently, however, it has been extended to include the zones of diagenesis and low grade metasomatism.

Zeolite facies rocks occur in the South Island of New Zealand, where Triassic volcanic greywackes show an extensive development of heulandite or laumontite. The zeolite facies is taken to include all those assemblages produced under physical conditions in which the assemblages quartz–heulandite, quartz–laumontite and quartz–analcite are formed.

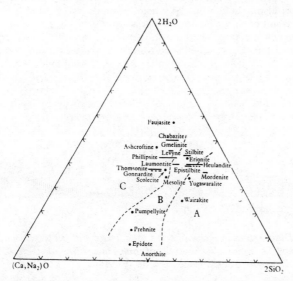

Fig. 151. *Compositions, in molecular proportions, of the calcium zeolites and other Ca–Al silicates. For the zeolites and anorthite, $(Ca, Na_2)O$ is numerically equal to Al_2O_3, $A = field$ of phases favoured by super-saturation with respect to silica; $B = field$ of phases commonly coexisting with silica minerals; $C = field$ of phases favoured by a silica-poor environment (after Coombs, D. S., Ellis, A. D., Fyfe, W. S. & Taylor, A. M., 1959, Geochim. et Cosmochim. Acta, vol. 17, p. 53).*

REFERENCES

AMES, L. L. (1960) 'The cation sieve properties of clinoptilolite', *Amer. Min.*, vol. 45, p. 689.

COOMBS, D. S., ELLIS, A. D., FYFE, W. S. and TAYLOR, A. M. (1959) 'The zeolite facies, with comments on the interpretation of hydrothermal syntheses', *Geochim. et Cosmochim. Acta*, vol. 17, p. 53.

FENNER, C. N. (1936) 'Bore-hole investigations in Yellowstone Park', *Journ. Geol.*, vol. 44, p. 225.

HEY, M. H. (1932) 'Studies on the zeolites. Part III. Natrolite', *Min. Mag.*, vol. 23, p. 243.

M'LINTOCK, W. F. P. (1915) 'On the zeolites and associated minerals from the Tertiary lavas around Ben More, Mull', *Trans. Roy. Soc. Edinburgh*, vol. 51, p. 1.

MEIER, W. M. (1960) 'The crystal structure of natrolite', *Zeit. Krist.*, vol. 113, p. 430.

WALKER, G. P. L. (1951) 'The amygdale minerals in the Tertiary lavas of Ireland. I. The distribution of chabazite habits and zeolites in the Garron plateau area, County Antrim', *Min. Mag.*, vol. 29, p. 773.

PART 5

NON-SILICATES

OXIDES

Periclase   MgO

n 1·736

Dispersion: Moderate.   D 3·56–3·68.   H 2½.
Cleavage: {001} perfect.
Twinning: Spinel-type twins on {111} in synthetic crystals.
Colour: Greyish white to yellow or brown; colourless in thin section.
Soluble in dilute HCl.

Periclase has a structure similar to that of halite, NaCl, with magnesium and oxygen ions occupying the sites of sodium and chlorine respectively; the cell edge is 4·212 Å, with Z = 4.

Iron, zinc, and possibly manganese, may substitute partly for magnesium in the natural mineral: the iron-bearing variety, ferropericlase, may contain 5–10 per cent FeO. Periclase can be synthesized readily from $MgCl_2$ or $Mg(OH)_2$ or by heating natural magnesite: a complete series of synthetic crystals from MgO to FeO can be obtained and the name magnesio-wüstite has been used for synthetic ferroan periclase. A common alteration product is brucite, $Mg(OH)_2$, which may in turn alter to hydromagnesite. Ferropericlase alters to brucite with separation of iron oxide.

In the synthetic series MgO–FeO the refractive index rises from 1·736 to 2·32. The colour varies from white to yellow or brown with the entry of iron.

The cubic cleavage, isotropic character and high relief are distinctive, and the alteration to fibrous brucite is characteristic. With $AgNO_3$ solution periclase gives a brown stain of Ag_2O.

Periclase is a relatively high temperature mineral resulting from the metamorphism of dolomites and magnesian limestones. It is found typically in contact aureoles, having been formed by the dissociation of dolomite $(CaMg(CO_3)_2 \rightarrow CaCO_3 + MgO + CO_2)$, surrounded by a rim of brucite developed by the hydration of the periclase. In the sequence of minerals in the progressive metamorphism of siliceous dolomites it forms after wollastonite but at a lower temperature than monticellite.

Cassiterite

SnO_2

TETRAGONAL $(+)$

ω 1·990–2·010
ϵ 2·093–2·100
δ 0·096–0·098

Dispersion: Strong. D 6·98–7·02. H 6–7.

Cleavage: {100} and {110} poor, {111} parting.

Twinning: Common on {011}, may be repeated.

Colour: Commonly reddish brown to almost black; in thin section almost colourless, yellow, brown or red.

Pleochroism: Variable–very weak to strong; yellow, brown, or red; absorption $\epsilon > \omega$.

Adamantine lustre. Attacked slowly by acids: fusible in alkalis.

The structure (a 4·73, c 3·18 Å; Z = 2) resembles that of rutile, each tin ion being surrounded by six oxygen ions approximately at the corners of a regular octahedron, and each oxygen having three tin ions around it forming a nearly equilateral triangle.

Cassiterite typically contains tantalum and niobium and generally appreciable amounts of ferrous or ferric iron, and smaller amounts of MnO, TiO_2 and Sc_2O_3. It can be synthesized by the action of steam on $SnCl_4$ at red heat or by passing HCl gas over amorphous tin oxide.

It has extremely high refractive indices and birefringence, and although normally uniaxial positive some material shows anomalous optics with a $2V_\gamma$ of 0° to 38°. The strongly coloured varieties may show moderate to intense pleochroism, a typical example having ω pale greenish yellow, ϵ deep reddish brown. Twinning is common on {011} giving the familiar 'knee' twin: this may be repeated cyclically. In reflected light it is light grey and strongly anisotropic. Cassiterite is normally lighter in colour in thin section than rutile and has less extreme birefringence and refractive indices: allanite has a very much lower birefringence and melanite garnet is only weakly birefringent.

Cassiterite is usually found in acid igneous rocks such as granites and microgranites, and occurs frequently in granite pegmatites, greisen and high-temperature hydrothermal veins. It is often found associated with wolframite, tourmaline, topaz, lepidolite and fluorite. It may sometimes result from the weathering of stannite (Cu_2FeSnS_4) and teallite ($PbSnS_2$) and has been found pseudomorphing haematite and orthoclase. Wood-tin is a colloform variety formed by secondary processes in the zone of oxidation. Cassiterite is a common detrital mineral in sediments derived from tin-bearing acid rocks: the important Malayan tin deposits are alluvial in origin.

Corundum

α-Al$_2$O$_3$

TRIGONAL (−)

ϵ 1·760–1·763
ω 1·768–1·772
δ 0·008–0·009

Dispersion: Moderate.   D 3·98–4·02.   H 9.

Cleavage†: None; parting on {0001} and on {10$\bar{1}$1}.

Twinning†: Lamellar on {10$\bar{1}$1}, common; simple twinning on {0001} or {10$\bar{1}$1}, less common.

Colour: White, grey, blue, red, yellow, green; only weakly coloured in thin section.

Pleochroism: Absorption $\omega > \epsilon$, e.g. in thick sections ω dark blue, ϵ light blue, or ω blue, ϵ yellow-green.

Insoluble in all acids.

STRUCTURE

The unit cell has a_{hex} 4·760, c_{hex} 12·98 Å; a_{rh} 5·130 Å, α 55° 17′, Z_{rh} = 2. The oxygen ions are arranged in approximately hexagonal closest packing. Between the oxygen layers there are sites for cations octahedrally coordinated by six oxygen ions, but in corundum only two-thirds of the available positions are filled. Groups of three oxygen ions form a common face of two neighbouring octahedra and thus the groups are linked to a pair of Al ions. The cell dimensions of synthetic corundum or ruby show a linear increase with increasing Cr content.

Although only α-Al$_2$O$_3$ is found in nature, other modifications are known from synthetic and experimental work, including β-Al$_2$O$_3$ which is hexagonal and may contain alkalis and Ca, and γ-Al$_2$O$_3$ which may be cubic: on heating, these forms are both converted to corundum.

CHEMISTRY

Although corundum consists essentially of pure Al$_2$O$_3$, minor amounts of other ions may be found, notably Fe^{+3} (see Table 43). Ruby contains a moderate amount of chromium (e.g. anals. 3, 4) while the colour of the blue sapphire variety is related to the presence of iron and titanium. Yellow and green corundum contain varying amounts of ferric and ferrous iron, e.g. the green corundum of anal. 2 contains 0·18 per cent FeO and no ferric iron. The melting point of pure corundum is in the range 2000° to 2050°C.

† Indices for cleavage and twin planes are based upon the morphological cell with c 6·49 Å.

Table 43. CORUNDUM ANALYSES

	1.	2.	3.	4.	5.
SiO_2	0·20	0·68	0·137	0·542	0·94
TiO_2	0·32	tr.	0·00	0·00	0·37
Al_2O_3	98·84	96·72	98·8	97·5	89·40
Cr_2O_3	tr.	0·00	0·945	1·81	—
Fe_2O_3	0·14	0·00	0·0147	0·0252	9·17
FeO	0·06	0·18	—	—	—
V_2O_5	0·00	tr.	0·0320	0·0582	—
NiO	tr.	0·09	0·00	0·00	—
MnO	tr.	tr.	0·00	0·00	—
MgO	0·04	0·96	0·02265	0·0328	—
CaO	0·34	1·16	—	—	—
CuO	—	—	0·00237	0·0016	—
CdO	—	—	0·0168	0·0351	—
MoO_3	—	—	0·00448	0·0117	—
Total	99·94	99·79	99·97	100·02	99·88

1. Dark blue corundum, contact altered marble, Urals (Gavrusevich, B. A., 1941, *Doklady Acad. Sci. USSR*, vol. 31, p. 686).
2. Green corundum, syenite pegmatite, Urals (Gavrusevich, B.A., ibid).
3. Natural gem ruby, light in colour (Alexander, A. E., 1948, *Journ. Gemm.*, vol. 1, no. 8, p. 4).
4. Natural gem ruby, dark in colour (Alexander, A. E., ibid).
5. Yellow iron-corundum, metamorphosed lithomarge (porcellanite) in dolerite plug, Tievebulliagh, Northern Ireland (Agrell, S. O. & Langley, J. M., 1958, *Proc. Roy. Irish Acad.*, vol. 59, B, p. 93) : ϵ 1·785, ω 1·794.

Corundum can be produced artificially by heating Al_2O_3 gel, or by heating gibbsite, boehmite or diaspore, corundum being the stable phase above about 450°C : commercially, large amounts are manufactured for abrasives by heating bauxite.

In synthetic gem production the Verneuil process is used, small amounts of chromium or ferric iron being added to give the appropriate colour. For synthetic star-sapphires a small amount of TiO_2 is also added; this crystallizes as rutile needles in three directions at 120° and perpendicular to the z axis. The addition of vanadium to synthetic corundum gives it the appearance of alexandrite : in daylight the crystal appears green whereas in artificial light it has a reddish colour. Synthetic ruby can also be produced hydrothermally, generally on a seed of natural ruby.

OPTICAL AND PHYSICAL PROPERTIES

In thin section corundum has a high relief, and although its double refraction is low it may show rather high birefringence in some sections as, because of its extreme hardness, the thin sections may be thicker than normal. Although usually uniaxial negative, some specimens have an anomalous biaxial character with an optic angle of 30° or more: this feature may be related to twinning. Twinning on {10$\bar{1}$1} is common, often in lamellar seams or as glide-twins: twinning also occurs on {0001}, and this plane is sometimes visible as a basal parting. As described above the colours of the various varieties of corundum are related to the amount of other ions replacing aluminium.

The entry of Cr or Fe raises the refractive indices slightly: e.g. whereas the normal values are ϵ 1·760, ω 1·768, a dark red ruby with 7·57 per cent Cr_2O_3 has ϵ 1·762, ω 1·770, and the iron-corundum of anal. 5 (Table 43) has ϵ 1·785, ω 1·794.

DISTINGUISHING FEATURES

The combination of very high relief, low to moderate birefringence and the occurrence of twin lamellae, is diagnostic. Sapphirine, although much rarer in occurrence than sapphire, may occur in similar environments but is always biaxial and does not have the twin lamellae. The hardness, form, high specific gravity, insolubility and high melting point are also characteristic.

PARAGENESIS

Corundum may occur on a fairly large scale in pegmatites and other rocks associated with nepheline-syenites: in the Haliburton and Bancroft areas in Ontario corundum is erratically distributed through a banded complex of rocks rich in scapolite, nepheline and andesine, and is abundantly developed in contact zones between this complex and a younger hybrid alkaline syenite. Experimental evidence indicates that a 2 per cent increase of Al_2O_3 from the eutectic composition in the system $K_2O–Al_2O_3–SiO_2$ raises the liquidus temperature by 180°C: thus it is likely that a small increase in normative corundum in a magma produces a large rise in the liquidus temperature. This means that even the hottest magmas of granitic composition are not likely to contain much alumina in excess of that required for the feldspars and hence that they are restricted in potential corundum. Dyke rocks containing corundum, such as the plumasites and corundum plagioclasites, may be derived by the desilication of an acid igneous rock in contact with more basic material, or may be of hydrothermal origin. It also occurs in some aluminium-rich xenoliths in igneous rocks, e.g. in corundum–spinel xenoliths in norite as at Haddo House, Aberdeenshire, and in the aluminous xenoliths in the tholeiitic sills of Mull where the corundum forms deep blue crystals 1 mm to 1½ cm across.

In metamorphic rocks corundum is found in silica-poor hornfelses: it also occurs in thermally or regionally metamorphosed bauxitic deposits as in the emery deposits of Samos and Naxos in the Aegean Sea. Most of the gem quality corundum is obtained from placer deposits. Corundum is also found as a normal detrital mineral in sediments of all ages, having been derived from pre-existing igneous or metamorphic rocks; the colourless or yellow varieties are of commonest occurrence.

REFERENCES

MOYD, L. (1949) 'Petrology of the nepheline and corundum rocks of south-eastern Ontario', *Amer. Min.*, vol. 34, p. 736.

READ, H. H. (1931) 'On corundum–spinel xenoliths in the gabbro of Haddo House, Aberdeenshire', *Geol. Mag.*, vol. 68, p. 446.

SCHAIRER, J. F. (1955) 'The ternary systems leucite–corundum–spinel and leucite-forsterite–spinel', *Journ. Amer. Ceram. Soc.*, vol. 38, p. 153.

Haematite

$\alpha\text{-}Fe_2O_3$

TRIGONAL $(-)$

$$\epsilon \quad 2\cdot87\text{--}2\cdot94$$
$$\omega \quad 3\cdot15\text{--}3\cdot22$$
$$\delta \quad 0\cdot28$$

Dispersion: Very strong. D 5·256 (usually less). H 5–6.

Cleavage†: None, but may show parting on {0001} and {10$\bar{1}$1}.

Twinning†: On {0001}, and on {10$\bar{1}$1} usually lamellar.

Colour: Black, steel-grey, and bright to dull red (some crystals may be iridescent); opaque in thin section, blood-red in thin splinters.

Pleochroism: In reflected light may show reflection pleochroism from white to grey-blue.

Distinctive cherry-red streak. Soluble in HCl. Becomes magnetic in a reducing flame.

The common massive ore is red haematite; this may be botryoidal with a radial fibrous structure giving 'kidney ore', or when broken up into compact splinters 'pencil ore'. The crystalline material with metallic lustre is known as specular haematite, specularite or iron-glance, or as micaceous haematite when the structure is platy. The red earthy haematite is sometimes called reddle or red ochre. Martite is a name given to haematite occurring in dodecahedral or octahedral crystals pseudomorphous after magnetite or pyrite: $\gamma\text{-}Fe_2O_3$ is the mineral maghemite, which has a spinel-type structure.

STRUCTURE

The structure of haematite consists of layers of oxygen ions and layers of iron ions perpendicular to the triad axis. The oxygen ions are arranged in a slightly distorted hexagonal packing, while successive cation layers contain equal numbers of ions all in six-fold coordination, thus differing from the spinel structure where two-thirds of the cations in alternate layers are in four-fold coordination. The unit cell has a_{rh} 5·427 Å, α 55° 18′, $Z_{rh} = 2$; a_{hex} 5·0345, c_{hex} 13·749 Å, $Z_{hex} = 6$.

Haematite is weakly ferro-magnetic with a Curie point of 675°C. The ferro-magnetism has been attributed to the interleaving of a small amount of deformed $\gamma\text{-}Fe_2O_3$ (maghemite) or to an order–disorder relationship.

CHEMISTRY

The ideal composition of haematite is Fe_2O_3, but a small amount of MnO and FeO may be found, while any appreciable SiO_2 and Al_2O_3 probably

† Indices for cleavage and twin planes are based upon the morphological cell with *c* 6·87 Å.

represent impurities. TiO_2 may occur in minor quantity but when present in any large amount it is probably due to the intergrowth of ilmenite.

Experimentally it has been shown that at 800°C not more than 5 per cent TiO_2 can enter $\alpha\text{-}Fe_2O_3$: at temperatures of more than 1050°C, however, there is complete solid solution between haematite and ilmenite. Only very small (< 1 per cent) amounts of Fe_3O_4 (magnetite) can be taken into solid solution. In the system $Fe_2O_3\text{-}Al_2O_3$, haematite can take approximately 10 weight per cent Al_2O_3 into solid solution at 1000°C. On heating in air, haematite dissociates to Fe_3O_4 at about 1390°C: its true melting point under sufficient pressure of oxygen to prevent dissociation is probably between 1700° and 1800°C. As little as 10 weight per cent TiO_2 raises the temperature of the haematite → magnetite transformation in air from 1390° to 1524°C.

OPTICAL AND PHYSICAL PROPERTIES

In thin section haematite is dark blood-red in transmitted light, and may show dichroism from brownish red (ω) to yellowish red (ϵ): the dispersion is very strong. In reflected light it is a bright white with a grey undertone; it is anisotropic and shows weak reflection pleochroism from white (ω) to pale grey-blue (ϵ), this becoming more marked in oil. Haematite has a moderate reflective power of about 21–28 per cent in air, and may show deep red inner reflections.

DISTINGUISHING FEATURES

When present as a powder or in thin scales haematite is easily distinguished from magnetite or ilmenite by its blood-red colour. In massive material the red streak is a useful distinction (cinnabar also with a red streak is much heavier and may show a perfect prismatic cleavage), while the opaque metallic material is lighter in colour in reflected light than magnetite or ilmenite. The hydrated iron oxides are usually softer and may have a brown streak. Haematite is only weakly magnetic, but on heating under reducing conditions a magnetic product is obtained.

PARAGENESIS

Haematite is rare in igneous rocks but is a very important ore of iron occurring chiefly in sediments and their metamorphosed equivalents; it is also found in soils and as a weathering product of iron-bearing minerals.

In igneous rocks it occurs when the magma is poor in ferrous iron, i.e. in granites, syenites, rhyolites, trachytes, etc., and as a late-stage product of volcanic activities as thin crystals sublimated on to earlier material. It is also found as an intergrowth representing exsolved material in other iron ore minerals and in such material as aventurine. Intimately mixed and oriented aggregates of haematite and chlorite may result from the pseudomorphous replacement of olivine in basalt.

In metamorphic rocks haematite typically results from the metamorphism of magnetite, siderite and the hydrated iron oxides. It is common in the Pre-Cambrian rocks throughout the world, occurring in metamorphosed banded iron ores, e.g. jasper beds or jaspilites.

In sediments, haematite and its alteration products are the commonest cause of a red coloration in rocks; it may occur as a cementing medium in sandstones, and as oolitic haematite often associated with limestone as in the Clinton ores of eastern U.S.A. Many of the commercially important haematite ores associated with sediments are related to the metasomatic introduction of the haematite by solutions, the iron often having been derived from the weathering of overlying sediments.

REFERENCES

CONGRÈS GÉOLOGIQUE INTERNATIONAL (XIX) (1952). *Symposium sur les gisements de fer du monde*, Edited by Blondel & Marvier. Algiers.

TURNOCK, A. C. and EUGSTER, H. P. (1963) 'Fe–Al oxides: phase relationships below 1000°C.', *Journ. Petr.*, vol. 3, p. 533.

Ilmenite

$FeTiO_3$

TRIGONAL ($-$)

Refractive indices $\simeq 2\cdot7$
(opaque)
δ very strong

Dispersion: Strong.   D $4\cdot70$–$4\cdot78$.   H 5–6.
Cleavage†: None; parting on $\{0001\}$ and $\{10\bar{1}1\}$.
Twinning†: $\{0001\}$ simple, $\{10\bar{1}1\}$ lamellar.
Colour: Black (opaque); in reflected light greyish white with a brown tinge, weak reflection pleochroism.
Very slowly soluble in HCl, variable solubility in HF.

STRUCTURE

Ilmenite is a titanate of ferrous iron ($Fe^{+2}Ti^{+4}O_3$) rather than a double oxide of ferric iron and titanium ($Fe^{+3}Ti^{+3}O_3$). Its structure is somewhat similar to that of haematite but with some distortion in the oxygen layers. Along the direction of the triad axis, pairs of Ti ions alternate with pairs of Fe^{+2} ions; thus each cation layer is a mixture of Fe^{+2} and Ti. The unit cell has a_{rh} $5\cdot534$ Å, α $54°$ $51'$, $Z_{rh} = 2$; a_{hex} $5\cdot089$, c_{hex} $14\cdot163$ Å.

In the series $FeTiO_3$–Fe_2O_3 there is a steady decrease in the rhombohedral cell edge from ilmenite to haematite. With the introduction of considerable Mn as in pyrophanite the cell dimensions increase appreciably.

CHEMISTRY

The formula of ilmenite may be more fully expressed as $(Fe,Mg,Mn)TiO_3$ with only a limited amount of Mg and Mn. Crichtonite is a distinct species containing both Fe^{+3} and Fe^{+2}, as well as more Ti than ilmenite. Analyses of two ilmenites are given in Table 44: the Fe_2O_3 content shown by these analyses is most probably present in the form of haematite. Although natural ilmenites can take up to about 6 per cent Fe_2O_3 into solid solution, exsolution lamellae of haematite or of titanohaematite may also be present.

Experimentally it has been found that at 1050°C complete solubility exists between ilmenite and haematite but at lower temperatures there is an increasingly large miscibility gap, extending from approximately 33 to 67 mol. per cent at 950°C.

The alteration of ilmenite may take place in three successive stages to patchy ilmenite, amorphous iron-titanium oxide, and leucoxene. The latter

† Indices for cleavage and twin planes are based upon the morphological cell with $c \simeq 7\cdot08$ Å.

Table 44. Ilmenite analyses

	1.	2.		Numbers of ions on the basis of 6 (O) 1.	2.
SiO_2	0·51	0·11	Al	—	0·032
TiO_2	50·02	48·90	Fe^{+3}	0·161	0·216
Al_2O_3	—	0·54	Ti	1·941	1·852
Fe_2O_3	4·19	5·70	Mg	0·034 ⎫	0·042 ⎫
FeO	42·18	43·32	Fe^{+2}	1·820 ⎪	1·824 ⎪
MnO	1·44	0·35	Mn	0·062 ⎬ 1·96	0·015 ⎬ 1·92
MgO	0·46	0·56	Ca	0·040 ⎭	0·035 ⎭
CaO	0·71	0·65			
H_2O	0·13	—			
Total	99·64	100·13			

1. Ilmenite, fayalite ferrogabbro, Skaergaard intrusion, east Greenland (Vincent, E. A. & Phillips, R., 1954, *Geochim. Cosmochim Acta*, vol. 6, p. 1).
2. Ilmenite, two-pyroxene granulite of the charnockite series, Madras, India (Howie, R. A., 1955, *Trans. Roy. Soc. Edinburgh*, vol. 62, p. 725).

is normally finely crystalline rutile, but leucoxene composed of finely divided brookite is also known. The reported breakdown product arizonite is probably a mixture of minerals including haematite, pseudobrookite and rutile, and sometimes also containing anatase.

OPTICAL AND PHYSICAL PROPERTIES

The specific gravity is slightly increased by the partial replacement of Fe^{+2} by Mn and decreased by the replacement of Fe^{+2} by Mg. The reflectivity of ilmenite in air, relative to a pyrite standard of 54·5, is in the range 18–21.

DISTINGUISHING FEATURES

Ilmenite may give rise to a greyish white alteration product, leucoxene, which may serve to distinguish it from magnetite. It also has a tendency to form skeletal crystals. In reflected light it may be distinguished from magnetite by its reflection pleochroism (more marked in oil), and from haematite by its grey-white colour with light brownish tinge. A test for titania may be made by dissolving a small amount in HCl and adding a drop of the solution to an H_2SO_4 solution of phenol, which gives a brick-red colour. Ilmenite is only weakly magnetic; its response to a hand magnet is noticeable but feeble.

PARAGENESIS

Ilmenite is common as an accessory mineral in many igneous and metamorphic rocks and may also occur as veins and disseminated deposits, sometimes of large extent, in association with gabbros, norites, anorthosites, etc. It is one of the earlier constituents of a magma to crystallize, but the important magmatic ilmenite ore deposits are, as a rule, in rocks rich in pyroxene rather than olivine, and often the associated pyroxene is an orthopyroxene. In metamorphic rocks it is found in many orthogneisses, and particularly in rocks of the granulite facies. Ilmenite is a ubiquitous mineral in detrital sediments and may become concentrated in beach sands as in Florida and India, and on a minor scale at Menaccan, Cornwall (menaccanite). The west coast of the South Island of New Zealand has millions of tons of sand deposits estimated to contain an average of 5·5 per cent ilmenite.

REFERENCES

BUDDINGTON, A. F. and LINDSLEY, D. H. (1964) 'Iron-titanium oxide minerals and synthetic equivalents', *Journ. Petr.*, vol. 5, p. 310.

GJELSVIK, T. (1957) 'Geochemical and mineralogical investigations of titaniferous iron ores, west coast of Norway', *Econ. Geol.*, vol. 52, p. 482.

TAYLOR, R. W. (1964) 'Phase equilibria in the system $FeO-Fe_2O_3-TiO_2$ at 1300°C.', *Amer. Min.*, vol. 49, p. 1016.

Rutile

TiO$_2$

TETRAGONAL (+)

ω   2·605–2·613
ε   2·899–2·901
δ   0·286–0·296

Dispersion: Very strong.   D 4·23–5·5.   H 6–6½.

Cleavage: {110} good, {100} moderate; parting on {092} and {011}.

Twinning: Common on {011}, often geniculate or cyclic. Also glide twins on {011} and {092} and rare contact twins on {031}.

Colour: Characteristically reddish brown, may be black, violet, yellow or green (synthetic–white); typically yellowish to reddish brown in thin section.

Pleochroism: Weak to distinct, ε > ω in brownish red, yellow and green.

    Insoluble in acids; decomposed by alkali carbonate fusion.

STRUCTURE

    The unit cell has $a \simeq 4\cdot59$, $c \simeq 2\cdot96$ Å; Z = 2. Each Ti ion is surrounded by six O ions at the corners of a slightly distorted regular octahedron, while each O is surrounded by three Ti ions lying in a plane at the corners of an approximately equilateral triangle (Fig. 152).

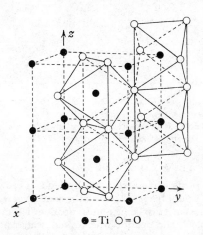

           ● = Ti   ○ = O

Fig. 152. *The structure of rutile showing bands of octahedra parallel to z (after Evans, R. C., 1964, An Introduction to Crystal Chemistry, Cambridge).*

CHEMISTRY

Although essentially TiO_2 (Table 45, anal. 1), some rutiles contain considerable amounts of both ferrous and ferric iron and major amounts of Nb and Ta. The close similarity in ionic radius between Ti^{+4} and both Nb^{+5} and Ta^{+5} enables the latter ions to enter titanium minerals, the structure being electrostatically balanced either by vacancies in some lattice positions or by the complementary substitution of divalent ions such as Fe^{+2} (e.g. anal. 2); the niobian variety of rutile has been termed ilmenorutile. In the varieties rich in tantalum, tin is often found in moderate amounts, and chromium and vanadium may also be present.

Rutile can be produced artificially by heating a solution of $TiCl_4$ to 950°C. Single crystals of pure rutile are produced by flame-fusion methods. The melting point of pure TiO_2 is 1825°C. Rutile is also produced by heating anatase to above 730°C.

Table 45. RUTILE ANALYSES

	1.	2.		1.	2.
				NUMBERS OF IONS ON THE BASIS OF 2 (O)	
TiO_2	98·77	66·28	Si	0·003 ⎫	0·005 ⎫
SnO_2	—	1·24	Al	0·002 ⎪	—
SiO_2	0·23	0·32	Cr	0·002 ⎪	—
Cr_2O_3	0·16	—	Ti	0·991 ⎬ 1·00	0·777 ⎬ 1·02
Al_2O_3	0·14	—	Ta	— ⎪	0·065 ⎪
Nb_2O_5	—	8·64	Nb	— ⎪	0·061 ⎪
Ta_2O_5	—	15·44	Sn	— ⎪	0·008 ⎪
FeO	0·55	8·00	Fe^{+2}	0·006 ⎭	0·104 ⎭
MnO	—	tr.			
H_2O	—	0·18			
Total	99·85	100·10			

1. Rutile, Queensland, Australia (Johnstone, S. J., 1954, *Minerals for the chemical and allied industries.* Chapman and Hall).
2. Tantalo-rutile, Globe Hill, Western Australia (Edwards, A. B., 1940, *Proc. Austral. Inst. Mining & Metall.*, No. 120, p. 731).

OPTICAL AND PHYSICAL PROPERTIES

In thin section rutile is characteristically reddish brown by transmitted light, the depth of colour being related to the content of ferric iron, niobium, and tantalum, some varieties being almost opaque. The synthetic rutile now in production is black and opaque when taken from the furnace but when heated in oxygen changes through dark blue, light blue and green to a pale milky yellow or colourless final stage : it has a dispersion much higher than diamond (B–G $\simeq$ 0·3) and is used as a gem stone.

DISTINGUISHING FEATURES

In thin section rutile usually has a characteristic deep red-brown colour which together with the very high relief and extreme birefringence is diagnostic: baddeleyite (ZrO_2) is normally less strongly coloured and has much lower birefringence. Compared with cassiterite, rutile has a good prismatic cleavage, a much higher birefringence and a considerably lower specific gravity.

PARAGENESIS

Rutile is the commonest form of TiO_2 in nature, being the high-temperature polymorph: since it has the smallest molecular volume of the TiO_2 polymorphs it tends to occur in high $P–T$ assemblages. It is very widely distributed as minute grains in many igneous rocks, chiefy in plutonic rocks, and is also an accessory mineral in metamorphic rocks, being particularly common in some amphibolites, eclogites and similar rocks, and in metamorphosed limestones.

Its occurrence in larger crystals is limited to some granite pegmatites and apatite and quartz veins. It is also of fairly common occurrence as inclusions in other minerals, notably quartz, where it may take the form of long hair-like needles: intergrowths of rutile with ilmenite and occasionally with biotite are also found. In sediments it may be formed as fine needle-like crystals during the reconstitution processes in clays and shales, and is also found in their contact metamorphosed equivalents: rutile is also a common detrital mineral.

Anatase

TiO_2

TETRAGONAL (−)

$$\epsilon \quad 2\cdot488$$
$$\omega \quad 2\cdot561$$
$$\delta \quad 0\cdot073$$

Dispersion: Strong. D 3·82–3·97. H 5½–6.

Cleavage: {001} and {011} perfect.

Twinning: Rare, on {112}.

Colour: Brown, yellow, greenish blue, blue, black; showing lighter shades of the same colours in grains or thin sections.

Pleochroism: Usually weak, $\omega < \epsilon$ or $\omega > \epsilon$.

Insoluble in acids.

Anatase is polymorphous with rutile, and, as in the latter, each Ti ion is surrounded by six O ions and every O ion lies between three Ti ions (Fig. 153). The structural difference lies in the mutual arrangement of the O octahedra: in anatase the shared edges at top and bottom of the octahedra are at right angles to each other, while in rutile two opposite parallel edges are shared. Anatase has a 3·78, c 9·51 Å, c/a 2·515, Z = 4.

Although essentially TiO_2, minor amounts of Fe and Sn may occur; niobian and tantalian varieties are known. Anatase can be synthesized

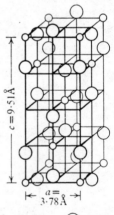

O Titanium   ◯ Oxygen

Fig. 153. *The structure of anatase (after Bragg, W. L.,* **1937**, Atomic Structure of Minerals, *Cornell Univ. Press*).

by hydrolysing sulphuric acid solutions of titania or $TiCl_4$ at about 200°C. The rate of transformation of anatase to rutile depends on the fineness of the material, and also on temperature, pressure and time: it is slow below about 600°C.

Anatase is typically found in shades of yellow or blue, ranging to orange, reddish brown and bluish green. Although normally uniaxial, biaxial crystals with a small 2V are also known: some crystals show zoning.

It is distinguished from rutile and brookite by its uniaxial optically negative character: compared with other minerals it has a very high relief, and its colour and tetragonal form are often diagnostic.

Anatase is the low-temperature polymorph of TiO_2 and is found as a minor constituent of igneous and metamorphic rocks and in veins and druses in granite pegmatites: it also occurs as an alteration product of other Ti-bearing minerals such as sphene and ilmenite. It is a fairly common detrital mineral in sediments, where it is often of authigenic origin.

Brookite

TiO_2

ORTHORHOMBIC (+)

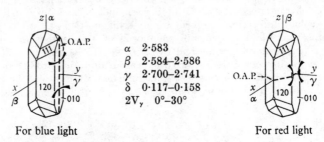

α	2·583
β	2·584–2·586
γ	2·700–2·741
δ	0·117–0·158
$2V_\gamma$	0°–30°

For blue light   For red light

O.A.P. (001) for red light, (100) for blue light; Bx_a always $\perp$ (010).
Dispersion: Strong, variable.   D 4·08–4·18.   H 5½–6.
Cleavage: {120} poor, {001} very poor.
Twinning: Possibly on {120}?
Colour: Yellowish to brown, red-brown or black; yellow or brown in thin section.
Pleochroism: Very weak, in yellow and brown.
   Insoluble in acids.

Each Ti ion in the structure is surrounded by an octahedral group of O ions and each O is surrounded by three Ti ions. The structure differs from that of rutile and anatase in the mutual arrangement of the oxygen octahedra: in brookite these lie in zig-zag lines rather than in straight rows ($a \simeq 5·45$, $b \simeq 9·18$, $c \simeq 5·15$ Å; Z = 8).

The composition is essentially TiO_2, but brookite usually contains a small amount of Fe^{+3}: a niobian-bearing variety is known. Attempts to synthesize brookite yield anatase at low temperatures, which inverts to rutile on heating.

Brookite is yellowish brown to dark brown in transmitted light. The dispersion is very strong, with the optic axial plane (001) for red and yellow light with 2V decreasing and reaching 0° for yellowish green (at about 555 mμ at 25°C) when it is uniaxial. In green and blue light 2V increases with decreasing wavelength, with the optic axial plane (100): γ is parallel to y in all cases. This phenomenon of crossed axial plane dispersion is best observed under monochromatic light of various wavelengths: in white light the interference figure is symmetrical but anomalous and without true isogyres.

The high refractive indices and birefringence and the abnormally strong dispersion are fairly characteristic. Rutile has a better cleavage while pseudobrookite (an entirely different mineral, Fe_2TiO_5, though resembling brookite) has a larger 2V and no marked dispersion.

Brookite occurs as an accessory mineral in some igneous and metamorphic rocks and in hydrothermal veins. It is often of secondary origin and associated with sphene, chlorite, etc., and is not uncommon as a detrital mineral.

Perovskite
(Ca,Na,Fe⁺²,Ce)(Ti,Nb)O₃

$(Ca,Na,Fe^{+2},Ce)(Ti,Nb)O_3$

MONOCLINIC? (PSEUDO-CUBIC) (+)

$$n \ 2 \cdot 30 – 2 \cdot 38$$
$$(2V_\gamma \simeq 90°)$$
$$\beta = y, \gamma : z \simeq 45°$$

Dispersion: $r > v$ (over γ). D $3 \cdot 98 – 4 \cdot 26$. H $5\frac{1}{2}$.

Cleavage: {001} poor.

Twinning: (a) Interpenetrant twinning on {111}.

(b) Complex lamellar twinning.

Colour: Black, brown, or yellow; dark brown to colourless in thin section.

Pleochroism: Weak, with absorption $\gamma > \alpha$.

Decomposed by concentrated H_2SO_4 and by HF.

The ideal perovskite structure is cubic ($a \simeq 3 \cdot 8$ Å, Z = 1) and, taking the composition as ABO_3, the atomic coordinates are $A \ \frac{1}{2}\frac{1}{2}\frac{1}{2}$; $B \ 000$; $O \ \frac{1}{2}00$,

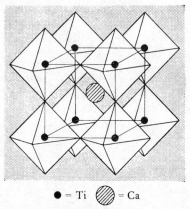

● = Ti ◯ = Ca

Fig. 154. *The ideal structure of perovskite* (*after Náray-Szabó, St. V.,* 1943, Naturwiss., vol. 31, p. 202).

$0\frac{1}{2}0$, $00\frac{1}{2}$. The B ions are surrounded by regular octahedra of oxygens which share corners to form a three dimensional framework (Fig. 154). The A ions occupy large holes between the octahedra and each is surrounded by twelve oxygens. The actual structure is related to the ideal cube by shear on (010) leaving $a \simeq b \simeq c \simeq 7 \cdot 65$ Å and a rhombus-shaped $a : c$ face with β 90°40'.

Although the composition is essentially $CaTiO_3$, most analyses show considerable substitution of rare earths or alkalis for Ca and often of Nb or Ta for Ti. *Knopite* is a variety rich in rare earths, chiefly Ce but also La and minor Y. The niobian variety, *dysanalyte*, has Nb (and lesser Ta) replacing Ti, with at the same time a substitution of Na for Ca to retain electrostatic balance. *Loparite* is a type of dysanalyte particularly rich in rare earths: minor Zr may also occur in niobian varieties. Ferrous iron, replacing calcium, may also be important.

Perovskite is colourless to dark brown in thin section and has a very high relief: small crystals may appear completely isotropic, but larger grains generally appear to have weak birefringence usually in conjunction with complex lamellar twinning. The refractive index increases slightly in the cerium-bearing varieties but data are insufficient to allow a correlation between optical properties and chemical composition.

In igneous rocks perovskite occurs as an accessory mineral in basic and alkaline types, in which it is often found as a deuteric mineral, commonly in association with melilite, leucite or nepheline. The rare earth variety, knopite, is found in alkaline plutonic rocks such as those of the Kola peninsula. Perovskite also occurs in some contact metamorphosed impure limestones.

SPINEL GROUP

CUBIC

	n	D	$a(\text{Å})$	
Spinel	1·719	3·55	8·103	$MgAl_2O_4$
Hercynite	1·835	4·40	8·135	$Fe^{+2}Al_2O_4$
Gahnite	1·805	4·62	8·08	$ZnAl_2O_4$
Galaxite	1·92	4·04	8·28	$MnAl_2O_4$
Magnesioferrite	2·38	4·52	8·383	$MgFe^{+3}_2O_4$
Magnetite	2·42	5·20	8·396	$Fe^{+2}Fe^{+3}_2O_4$
Maghemite	2·52–2·74	4·88	8·34	$\gamma\text{-}Fe^{+3}_2O_3$
Ulvöspinel	—	4·78	8·53	$Fe^{+2}_2TiO_4$
Franklinite	2·36	5·34	8·420	$ZnFe^{+3}_2O_4$
Jacobsite	2·3	4·87	8·51	$MnFe^{+3}_2O_4$
Trevorite	2·3	5·26	8·43	$NiFe^{+3}_2O_4$
Magnesio- chromite	2·00	4·43	8·334	$MgCr_2O_4$
Chromite	2·16	5·09	8·378	$Fe^{+2}Cr_2O_4$

Dispersion: Moderate. H $7\frac{1}{2}$–8.
Cleavage: None; octahedral {111} parting may be developed.
Twinning: Common on {111}, the spinel law.
Colour: Variable; red, brown, blue, black, green, yellow, grey or almost colourless; the darker varieties are almost opaque in thin section.
    Insoluble or soluble with difficulty in acids.
    Decomposed by fusion with $KHSO_4$.

This group may be subdivided into three series, according to whether the trivalent ion is Al, Fe, or Cr:

	Spinel series (Al)	Magnetite series (Fe^{+3})	Chromite series (Cr)
Mg	Spinel	Magnesioferrite	Magnesiochromite
Fe^{+2}	Hercynite	Magnetite	Chromite
Zn	Gahnite	Franklinite	
Mn	Galaxite	Jacobsite	
Ni		Trevorite	

In addition, the minerals maghemite ($\gamma\text{-}Fe_2O_3$) and ulvöspinel (Fe_2TiO_4) have the spinel structure, the former having a cation deficiency while in the latter the replacement $2Fe^{+3} \rightleftharpoons Fe^{+2} + Ti^{+4}$ occurs.

STRUCTURE

In the minerals of the spinel group there are 32 oxygen ions and 24 cations in the unit cell (a 8·08–8·53 Å, $Z=8$); 8 of the cations are in 4-fold coordination (the A positions), and 16 in 6-fold coordination (the B positions), see Fig. 155. Perpendicular to a triad axis, layers of oxygen ions alternate with layers of cations: the cation layers in which all the cations are in 6-fold coordination alternate with others in which the cations are distributed among A and B positions in the proportions of two A to one B. Two structural types occur, differing in their distribution of cations among the A and B positions, and known as normal and inverse spinels. With the general formula $R_8{}^{+2}R_{16}{}^{+3}O_{32}$ the two distributions are:

Normal $8R^{+2}$ in A, $16R^{+3}$ in B
Inverse $8R^{+3}$ in A, $8R^{+2}+8R^{+3}$ in B

$FeAl_2O_4$ (hercynite), $ZnAl_2O_4$ (gahnite) and $MnAl_2O_4$ (galaxite) are normal spinels while $MgFe_2O_4$ (magnesioferrite) and $Fe \cdot Fe_2O_4$ (magnetite)

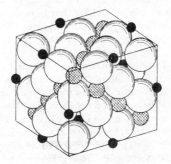

Fig. 155. *Perspective view of the structure of spinel. Large spheres represent oxygen, small black spheres represent four-fold coordination positions (A) and cross-hatched spheres six-fold positions (B) (after Verwey, E. J. W. & Heilmann, E. L., 1947, Journ. Chem. Physics, vol. 15, p. 174).*

have the inverse structure: thus magnetite may be written $Fe^{+3}(Fe^{+2}Fe^{+3})$ O_4.

A further structural variety within the spinel group is demonstrated by the ability of the spinels to take up in solid solution the oxides Al_2O_3 and Fe_2O_3, the end-members being represented by γ-Al_2O_3 and γ-Fe_2O_3 (maghemite): the latter has the inverse spinel structure with a cation deficiency.

The general formula giving the cell edge a of members of the spinel group as a function of the ionic radii of the divalent ions R^{+2} and of the trivalent ions R^{+3} is: $a(\text{Å}) = 5 \cdot 790 + 0 \cdot 95R^{+2} + 2 \cdot 79R^{+3}$.

CHEMISTRY

In the spinel group the pure end-members are rare as natural minerals, but the species may be subdivided on the basis of the dominant R^{+2} and R^{+3} ions, the varieties being designated by the next most dominant constituent.

Spinel series

Spinel, $MgAl_2O_4$. Spinel *sensu stricto*, followed by hercynite, is the commonest mineral in the spinel series. There is a continuous replacement series from spinel to hercynite, $Fe^{+2}Al_2O_4$: spinels with a considerable amount of Fe^{+2} replacing Mg, with the $Mg:Fe^{+2}$ ratio from 3 to 1, are termed *pleonaste* or ceylonite. Zinc may substitute for magnesium, giving an isomorphous series from spinel to gahnite, $ZnAl_2O_4$; these Zn-bearing spinels are termed gahnospinel or zincian spinel. The Al ion may be replaced by Cr, grading into magnesiochromite in the chromite series: the varietal name picotite is restricted to hercynite with appreciable Cr replacing Al, much of the so-called picotite being pleonaste or ferroan chromian spinel.

Spinel may readily be synthesized by sintering or fusing MgO and Al_2O_3 with or without a mineralizer such as boric oxide or water vapour. It is produced commercially by the Verneuil process, often being coloured red by the addition of Cr_2O_3. The melting point of normal spinel, $MgAl_2O_4$, is $2135° \pm 20°C$.

The colour of spinel varies from almost colourless through a great range of colours including red (Cr), blue (Fe^{+2}), brown (Fe^{+3}), yellow, pink, etc. Most of the gem spinels are spinel *sensu stricto*, including the so-called ruby spinel, one of the best examples of which is the 'Black Prince's Ruby' in the Imperial State Crown: the name balas ruby is used for paler varieties.

Hercynite, $Fe^{+2}Al_2O_4$. In addition to the substitution $Fe^{+2} \rightleftharpoons Mg$ considerable $Al \rightleftharpoons Fe^{+3}$ substitution may occur (Table 46, anal. 2) though there does not appear to be a complete natural series to magnetite. The substitution $Al \rightleftharpoons Cr$ is continuous, there being complete solid solution between hercynite and chromite: the term *picotite* is used for a variety of hercynite with appreciable chromium, with $Al > Cr$ and with $Fe:Mg$ between 3 and 1. The system $FeAl_2O_4$ (hercynite)–Fe_3O_4 (magnetite) has been investigated experimentally: above $858°C$ there is complete solid solution, but below this temperature the two phase region of exsolution widens with decreasing temperature. Hercynite is dark green to black in colour.

Gahnite, $ZnAl_2O_4$. There is normally considerable substitution of Fe and Mg for Zn (anal. 3), and there is probably complete solid solution between $ZnAl_2O_4$ and $MgAl_2O_4$. Gahnite is usually a dark bluish green.

Galaxite, $MnAl_2O_4$. This is the rarest member of the spinel series and is mahogany-red to black in colour: replacements include $Mn \rightleftharpoons Fe^{+2}$ and $Al \rightleftharpoons Fe^{+3}$.

Magnetite series

Magnesioferrite, $MgFe_2^{+3}O_4$. In natural minerals considerable replacement of Mg by Fe^{+2} takes place. Analyses are rare, as the mineral is usually intergrown or intimately associated with haematite: it is magnetic and brownish black to black in colour.

Magnetite, $Fe^{+2}Fe_2^{+3}O_4$. Anal. 4 (Table 46) is of material close to the theoretical end-member composition. Small amounts of Al substitute for

Table 46. SPINEL ANALYSES

	1.	2.	3.	4.	5.	6.	7.
SiO_2	—	—	0·12	0·27	0·10	1·15	0·12
TiO_2	0·13	0·64	0·00	tr.	19·42	1·37	0·14
Al_2O_3	65·40	53·02	55·91	0·21	1·39	0·04	10·28
Cr_2O_3	—	—	—	—	0·07	—	59·40
Fe_2O_3	4·32	7·12	—	68·85	28·37	89·15	3·30
FeO	8·03	36·83	7·90	30·78	46·06	8·67	14·09
MnO	0·10	0·02	0·42	—	0·33	—	0·14
MgO	22·23	2·37	0·12	tr.	2·29	tr.	12·62
ZnO	0·24	—	35·85	---	—	—	—
CaO	—	—	tr.	tr.	0·06	tr.	0·14
Total	100·45	100·00	100·32	100·11	100·06	100·38	100·23
n	1·742	>1·80	1·795	—	—	—	—
D	3·720	4·21	4·55	—	—	—	—
a(Å)	—	—	8·10	8·395	8·450†	8·343	8·311

NUMBERS OF IONS ON THE BASIS OF 32 (O)

	1.	2.	3.	4.	5.	6.	7.
Si	—	—	0·029	0·083	0·030	0·334	—
Al	15·344	14·590	15·891	0·077	0·483	0·014	3·142
Cr	—	—	—	—	0·016	—	12·178
Fe⁺³	0·647	1·252	—	15·886	6·289	19·104	0·645
Ti	0·020	0·111	—	—	4·303	0·294	0·028
Mg	6·592	0·824	0·043	—	1·005	—	4·852
Fe⁺²	1·336	7·190	1·594	7·896	11·348	2·065	3·057
Zn	0·025	—	6·382	—	—	—	—
Mn	0·017	0·004	0·085	—	0·081	—	0·031
Ca	—	—	—	—	0·019	—	0·039

Group totals:
- 1: 16·01, 7·97
- 2: 15·95, 8·02
- 3: 15·92, 8·10
- 4: 15·92, 8·10
- 5: 24·04‡
- 6: 21·81
- 7: 15·99, 7·98

1. Greenish black spinel, granite–marble contact zone, Kuronakh river, S. Yakutia, Siberia (Serdyuchenko, D. P. & Moleva, V. A., 1953, *Doklady Acad. Sci. U.S.S.R.*, vol. 88, p. 547).
2. Hercynite, silica-poor hornfels, Belhelvie, Aberdeenshire (Stewart, F. H., 1942, *Min. Mag.*, vol. 26, p. 260). Recalc. after subtraction of garnet impurity of known composition.
3. Gahnite, pegmatite, Chiapaval, S. Harris, Scotland (Knorring, O. von & Dearnley, R., 1960, *Min. Mag.*, vol. 32, p. 366).
4. Magnetite, Lover's Pit, Mineville, New York (Newhouse, W. H. & Glass, J. J., 1936, *Econ. Geol.*, vol. 31, p. 699).
5. Titaniferous magnetite+ulvöspinel, hypersthene–olivine gabbro, Skaergaard intrusion, east Greenland (Vincent, E. A., Wright, J. B., Chevallier, R. & Mathieu, S., 1957, *Min. Mag.*, vol. 31, p. 624; includes V_2O_3 1·97).
6. Maghemite, Alameda Co., California (Newhouse, W. H. & Glass, J. J., 1936, *Econ. Geol.*, vol. 31, p. 699).
7. Chromite, dunite, Twin Sisters Mountains, Washington (Stevens, R. E., 1944, *Amer. Min.*, vol. 29, p. 1.).

† This value is for homogenized material: the cell dimensions for the individual phases are magnetite 8·404, ulvöspinel 8·491 Å
‡ Includes V 0·465.

Fe^{+3} and generally similar small proportions of Ca, Mn and Mg replace Fe^{+2}, though continuous replacement between Mg and Fe^{+2} to magnesioferrite can occur. A considerable amount of Ti can enter the magnetite structure and there is a continuous relationship between magnetite and the ulvöspinel molecule Fe_2TiO_4. Anal. 5 is of a titaniferous magnetite: for such minerals the structural balance of $R^{+3} : R^{+2}$ of 2 : 1 is not possible, the metal ions, however, still total 24 per unit cell. The term titanomagnetite is best restricted to those specimens where the presence of an ulvöspinel phase can be demonstrated by X-ray or similar techniques. Other replacements occurring in magnetite include the partial substitution of Cr and V for Fe^{+3}, whereas Fe^{+2} may be partially replaced by Ni, Co and Zn in addition to Mg, Mn and some Ca.

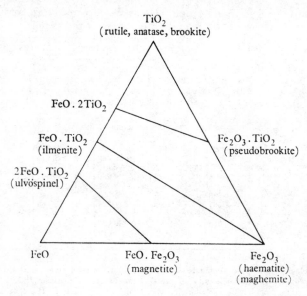

Fig. 156. *The system $FeO–Fe_2O_3–TiO_2$, showing the major high temperature solid solution series magnetite–ulvöspinel, haematite–ilmenite, pseudobrookite–$FeTi_2O_5$. Phases are plotted on mol. per cent basis.*

Magnetite may be synthesized by the oxidation of iron at high temperatures in air or steam, by heating Fe_2O_3 in a reducing atmosphere, or by heating $FeCO_3$ in steam or nitrogen at dull red heat. It is the stable form in air above 1388°C, haematite (α-Fe_2O_3) being the stable form beneath that temperature. The melting point of pure magnetite is 1594°C. At 1452°C magnetite can contain 30 per cent Fe_2O_3 which on cooling separates out as haematite along the {111} planes of the magnetite. Phase equilibrium studies in the ternary system $FeO–Fe_2O_3–TiO_2$ show that magnetite (solid solution) is the primary crystalline phase in the composition range 0 to 12 wt per cent TiO_2, with liquidus temperatures decreasing from 1594° to a minimum of 1524°C. Three solid solution series exist in the system: the pseudobrookite series (orthorhombic), the haematite–ilmenite series (trigonal) and the magnetite–ulvöspinel series (Fig. 156); in the latter series a continuous solid solution exists at high temperatures, with exsolution taking place below 600°C. Magnetite is black with a black streak and is opaque in thin section. Many varieties are soluble in HCl but some magnetites require fusion with a flux before decomposition.

Maghemite, γ-Fe_2O_3. Some natural magnetites contain an excess of Fe_2O_3 grading towards the end-member maghemite (Table 46, anal. 6). For such a series of mixed crystals in the range Fe_3O_4–Fe_2O_3, the number of metal ions per 32 oxygens falls below the theoretical 24 for pure Fe_3O_4, and for end-member maghemite would be 21·33. Maghemite is metastable and inverts to haematite (α-Fe_2O_3) on heating: the inversion temperature varies from 200° to 700°C depending on the previous history of the sample.

Ulvöspinel, $Fe_2^{+2}TiO_4$. No chemical analysis of completely pure natural material is available, though the occurrence of ulvöspinel as exsolution blebs within magnetite and other ores is being increasingly recognized. Anal. 5 (Table 46) on recalculation into possible spinel molecules and ilmenite gives 49·82 wt. per cent of the ulvöspinel molecule: the type mineral in the dolerite of Södra Ulvön, Sweden, has 51·8 per cent Fe_2TiO_4. The melting point of synthetic Fe_2TiO_4 is 1470°C.

Franklinite, $ZnFe_2^{+3}O_4$. Although essentially an oxide of zinc and ferric iron, franklinite normally contains a considerable proportion of Mn^{+2} substituting for Zn.

Jacobsite, $MnFe_2^{+3}O_4$. This is a relatively rare ore: appreciable Mn^{+3} may replace Fe^{+3} and some replacement of Mn^{+2} by Mg may occur.

Trevorite, $NiFe^{+3}O_4$. Minor amounts of Mg and Fe^{+2} may replace Ni.

Chromite series

Magnesiochromite, $MgCr_2O_4$. All natural magnesiochromites contain a considerable amount of Fe^{+2} replacing Mg, and there is a continuous variation through to chromite itself which has $Fe^{+2} > Mg$. There is also appreciable replacement of Cr by Al and by Fe^{+3}.

Chromite, $FeCr_2O_4$. The majority of natural chromites show a considerable amount of Mg replacing Fe^{+2} (anal. 7) and generally have appreciable aluminium and lesser ferric iron. Zinc-bearing chromites are also known.

OPTICAL AND PHYSICAL PROPERTIES

In the spinel group the lowest refractive indices and specific gravities occur in the members of the aluminous spinel series. The chromite series have intermediate values for these properties, and the highest refractive indices and specific gravities occur in the magnetite series though there is a considerable overlap in the specific gravities of the magnesian magnetites and chromites. The minerals of the magnetite series are normally opaque except in the very thinnest flakes, and their refractive indices (> 2·3) are not usually determined. The spinel series are the most transparent, even hercynite generally appearing transparent dark green in thin section, and they are also the most refractory members of the group, the melting point of pure spinel ($MgAl_2O_4$) being $2135° \pm 20°C$.

Assuming that the physical properties of spinels are additive functions of the molecular proportions of the end-members and that components other than those plotted are not present in significant amounts, it is possible to construct diagrams relating n, a and D with composition in various portions of the spinel group (Fig. 157).

Twinning is common on {111}, the spinel law. The twinning is usually simple, but multiple or lamellar twins are known. There is no well developed cleavage but in spinel and magnetite an octahedral parting may occur.

Magnetite is a typical ferrimagnetic material and has a Curie point (i.e. the temperature at which, on heating, the ferrimagnetism is lost and the substance becomes paramagnetic) of $578°C$. It is black with a black streak and is opaque in thin section: in reflected light it appears grey and has moderate reflectivity. Chromite is black in hand specimen but gives a chocolate brown streak; in thin section it may appear yellowish brown to brown or black.

DISTINGUISHING FEATURES

The isotropic nature, high relief and lack of cleavage are characteristic. Spinel differs from garnet in often having a well developed octahedral form, and occasional {111} twins. In the absence of these features the pink, red or brown spinels may be distinguished from members of the garnet series by their slightly lower refractive indices and specific gravities. Periclase differs from spinel in having perfect {001} cleavage.

PARAGENESIS

The spinel series

Spinel *sensu stricto* is a common high-temperature mineral in metamorphic rocks and in alumina-rich xenoliths. It occurs, often with forsterite and diopside, in contact metamorphosed limestones (e.g. Table 46, anal. 1), and it is found in a similar association in regionally metamorphosed limestones, where it may occur with chondrodite, phlogopite, calcite, etc. In thermally metamorphosed argillaceous rocks poor in SiO_2, spinel or pleonaste may form, often with cordierite or orthopyroxene.

Hercynite, the ferroan aluminium spinel, is found commonly in metamorphosed argillaceous sediments somewhat richer in iron than those yielding pleonaste (anal. 2). It occurs also in some basic and ultrabasic igneous rocks and in metamorphic pyroxenites, and is also found in some acid granulitic assemblages, the iron spinel, unlike spinel itself, being stable in the presence of free silica.

Gahnite, the zinc spinel, occurs chiefly in granitic pegmatites (e.g. anal. 3) but is also found in metasomatic replacement veins. The rare manganese aluminium spinel, galaxite, is known mainly from manganese-rich vein deposits.

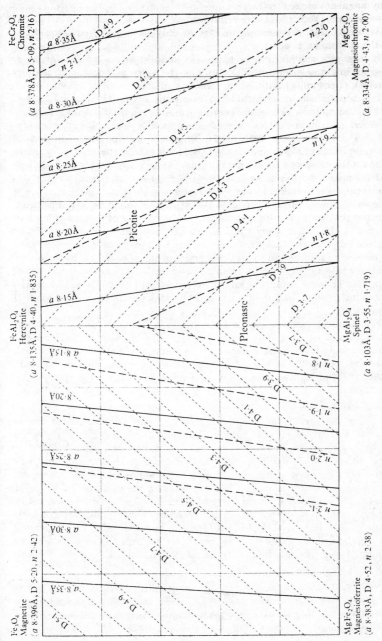

Fig. 157 *Refractive indices, specific gravities and cell edges for some members of the spinel group.*

The magnetite series

Pure magnesioferrite is a rare mineral usually found in volcanic regions: the more common ferroan magnesioferrite may occur in similar associations to those of magnetite.

Magnetite is one of the most abundant and ubiquitous oxide minerals in igneous and metamorphic rocks and is the principal magnetic ore (e.g anal. 4). It occurs typically as an accessory mineral in many igneous rocks, but is occasionally concentrated in magmatic segregations or by crystal settling, sometimes forming magnetite bands, e.g. in the Bushveld complex. In many igneous rocks the magnetite is appreciably titaniferous, particularly in the more basic rock types. Magnetite also occurs in important amounts in many skarn deposits, where it has been metasomatically introduced into calcareous rocks: here it may be associated with an andradite–hedenbergite assemblage and often with sulphides and oxides of Zn, Pb and Cu. It is also found in varying amounts in thermally metamorphosed sediments, any hydrated ferric oxide cement or limonitic staining being reduced first to haematite and then at higher grades of metamorphism to magnetite. In sedimentary rocks magnetite frequently occurs as a heavy detrital mineral, and under suitable conditions it may become concentrated by stream or tidal action to give magnetite sands of economic importance.

Maghemite usually results from the supergene alteration of magnetite deposits. The few examples known of spinel ores with ulvöspinel as the dominant molecule occur in basic igneous rocks or their metamorphosed equivalents.

Franklinite occurs in the zinc ore deposits in Pre-Cambrian limestone at Franklin and Sterling Hill, New Jersey, as the result of complex metamorphic and metasomatic processes. The manganese and ferric iron spinel, jacobsite, occurs in metasomatic manganese deposits, whereas the rare nickel iron spinel, trevorite, is known from a green talcose phyllite in the Transvaal.

The chromite series

In general terms the magnesiochromites and the chromites (*sensu stricto*) have the same paragenesis, the commonest member of the series probably being ferroan magnesiochromite. Chromite in igneous rocks may form distinct bands due to crystal sorting and accumulation and in these and other magmatic segregations it may form important economic deposits as a source of chromium. The Masinloc mine in the Philippine Islands, at present the world's largest producer of refractory-grade chrome ore, works ore occurring in a layered ultramafic complex. Chromium-bearing spinels occur in the olivine-rich inclusions found in basaltic rocks, but in general are members of the spinel series rather than the chromite series. As a heavy mineral, it is sometimes found in detrital stream and beach sands: it is also known from meteorites.

REFERENCES

BARTH, T. F. W. and POSNJAK, E. (1932) 'Spinel structures: with and without variate atom equipoints', *Zeit. Krist.*, vol. 82, p. 325.

BASTA, E. Z. (1959) 'Some mineralogical relationships in the system Fe_2O_3–Fe_3O_4 and the composition of titanomagnetite', *Econ. Geol.*, vol. 54, p. 698.

JACKSON, E. D. (1963) 'Stratigraphic and lateral variation of chromite composition in the Stillwater complex', *Min. Soc. Amer.*, *Special Paper 1, I.M.A., Papers, Third Gen. Meeting*, p. 46.

NICHOLLS, G. D. (1955) 'The mineralogy of rock magnetism', *Adv. in Phys.* (*Phil. Mag. Supp.*), vol. 4, p. 113.

STEVENS, R. E. (1944) 'Composition of some chromites of the Western Hemisphere', *Amer. Min.*, vol. 29, p. 1.

VINCENT, E. A. and PHILLIPS, R. (1954) 'Iron–titanium oxide minerals in layered gabbros of the Skaergaard intrustion, east Greenland,' *Geochim. et Cosmochim. Acta*, vol. 6, p. 1.

434

HYDROXIDES

Brucite Mg(OH)$_2$

TRIGONAL $(+)$

ω 1·560–1·590
ϵ 1·580–1·600
δ 0·012–0·020

Dispersion: Strong. D 2·39. H 2½.
Cleavage: Basal {0001} perfect; may be fibrous.
Colour: White, greenish or brownish; colourless in thin section.
  May show anomalous birefringence. Soluble in HCl.

Brucite has a layered structure (a 3·14 Å, c 4·76 Å ; Z = 1), with two sheets
of OH parallel to the basal plane and with a sheet of Mg ions between them,

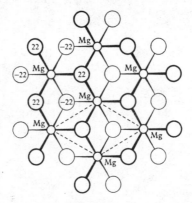

Fig. 158. *The structure of brucite, showing two sheets of hydroxyls with Mg atoms between them forming one layer of the structure (after Bragg, W. L., 1937, Atomic Structure of Minerals. Cornell Univ. Press).*

each Mg lying between six OH (Fig. 158). The OH groups are in hexagonal
close packing, with each OH linked to 3 Mg on one side and fitted into 3 OH
of the next layer.

  Fe^{+2} and Mn may replace Mg to a limited extent. A fibrous variety,
nemalite, often appears to be rich in iron but this is generally due to the
presence of magnetite among the fibres. Ferrobrucite, the iron-bearing
variety, may turn brown on exposure. Although brucite commonly arises

due to the alteration of periclase, it is itself readily altered to hydromagnesite, $3MgCO_3 \cdot Mg(OH)_2 \cdot 3H_2O$.

Brucite may exhibit optical anomalies due to deformation or to fibre aggregates; in nemalite, the fibrous variety, the z axes are perpendicular to the length of the fibre. The birefringence varies with wavelength from 0·020 to 0·015, giving anomalous interference colours. The softness and perfect cleavage are notable: muscovite and talc differ in being optically negative, and colourless chlorite has a lower birefringence.

The most common occurrence of brucite is as an alteration product of periclase in contact metamorphosed dolomites. It is also found as a low-temperature hydrothermal vein mineral in serpentinites and chlorite schists.

Gibbsite

$Al(OH)_3$

MONOCLINIC (+)

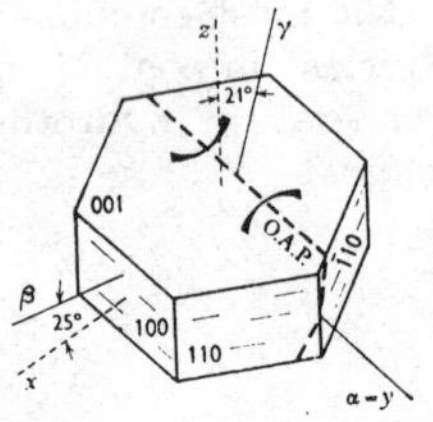

α 1·56–1·58
β 1·56–1·58
γ 1·58–1·60
δ ≃ 0·02
$2V_\gamma$ 0° to 40°
α = y, γ:z ≃ −21°, O.A.P. ⊥(010)
Dispersion: strong, r > v. D ≃ 2·4. H 2½–3½.
Cleavage: {001} perfect.
Twinning: Common on {001}; parallel twins [130], {001}; less commonly on {100} and {110}.
Colour: White, pale pink, pale green, grey, light brown; colourless to pale brown in thin section.

The fundamental unit of the structure is a layer of Al ions sandwiched between two sheets of close packed hydroxyl ions. In the brucite, $Mg(OH)_2$, structure all of the octahedrally coordinated sites between the oxygen layers are occupied by cations; in gibbsite only two out of three are occupied. In both gibbsite and brucite the layers may be regarded as built of octahedra linked laterally by sharing edges; the network so formed may be described by an orthogonal (pseudo-hexagonal) cell with parameters (for gibbsite) $a \simeq 8{\cdot}6$, $b \simeq 5$ Å ($\simeq a/\sqrt{3}$). In brucite the oxygen layers are in the sequence of hexagonal close packing ABABA..., whereas in gibbsite the sequence is ABBAABB.... Thus in the ideal structure of gibbsite, oxygens at the bottom of one layer lie directly above oxygens at the top of the layer below (Fig. 159). The structure of gibbsite is in fact somewhat distorted from the ideal, resulting in a monoclinic cell: there are two layers in each cell which has a 8·64, b 5·07, c 9·72 Å, β 94° 34′; Z = 8.

Analyses of gibbsite usually show the presence of Fe_2O_3 and minor amounts of other oxides. It seems likely that some Fe^{+3} and perhaps small amounts of other ions could substitute for Al in the structure, but some oxides are no doubt present as impurities. Heating gibbsite produces γ-alumina, usually with boehmite formation as an intermediate stage. In the system Al_2O_3–H_2O, gibbsite is the stable form at lower temperatures; at higher temperatures diaspore is the stable phase, but boehmite can exist metastably, and above about 450°C corundum is the stable phase.

Gibbsite often occurs in small tabular {001} crystals with pseudo-hexagonal outline conferred by the forms {100} and {110}: it may also occur in prismatic crystals and in lamellar or stalactitic aggregates. Gibbsite may be distinguished from muscovite by its positive optical sign, and from kaolinite which has lower birefringence. It has lower refractive indices and lower 2V than boehmite and diaspore.

Gibbsite, diaspore, and boehmite are the three hydrates of alumina which are the main constituents of bauxites and laterites, and gibbsite is often the predominant mineral. Bauxites (mainly aluminium hydrates) result from the weathering, under tropical conditions, of aluminium silicate rocks yielding clays which are subsequently desilicated. Among the minerals associated with the alumina hydrates in bauxites and in laterites (ferruginous bauxites), are the analogous iron compounds (goethite and lepidocrocite),and also haematite and the clay minerals kaolinite and halloysite

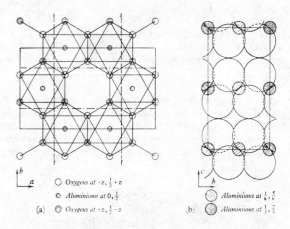

b
a
c
b

○ Oxygens at $-z, \frac{1}{2}+z$

◎ Aluminiums at $0, \frac{1}{2}$

(a) ◎ Oxygens at $+z, \frac{1}{2}-z$

(b) Aluminiums at $\frac{1}{6}, \frac{5}{6}$

Aluminiums at $\frac{1}{3}, \frac{2}{3}$

Fig. 159. *Ideal structure of gibbsite:* (a) *projection on xy plane assuming* $\beta = 90°$ *(true $\beta = 94°$ 34'),* (b) *projection along x axis (after Megaw, H. D.,* 1934, Zeit. Krist., *vol.* 87, *p.* 185).

Some gibbsite may be found in emery deposits which are formed by the metamorphism of bauxites; it can occur as an alteration crust on corundum. Gibbsite also occurs as a low temperature hydrothermal mineral in veins or cavities in aluminium-rich igneous rocks.

Diaspore

α-AlO(OH)

ORTHORHOMBIC (+)

α 1·682–1·706
β 1·705–1·725
γ 1·730–1·752
δ 0·04–0·05
$2V_\gamma$ 84°–86°
α = z, β = y, γ = x, O.A.P. (010).
Dispersion: Weak, r < v. D 3·2–3·5. H 6½–7.
Cleavage: {010} perfect; {110}, {210}, {100} less common.
Colour: White, grey-white or colourless; colourless in thin section. Iron or manganese varieties green, grey, brown, yellow, pink in hand specimen.
Pleochroism: Strongly coloured specimens may have absorption α < β < γ.

The structure of diaspore is based upon layers of oxygen atoms the sequence of which is that of hexagonal close packing. Aluminium ions occupy octahedrally coordinated sites between layers in such a way as to form strips of octahedra, the direction of which defines the c parameter of the unit cell (Fig. 160). The strips have the width of two octahedra and

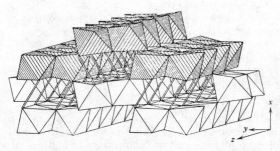

Fig. 160. *A pictorial representation of the structure of diaspore, with hydrogen-bonded oxygens connected by rods (after Ewing, F. J., 1935, Journ. Chem. Phys., vol. 3, p. 203).*

yield an orthorhombic cell in which a is twice the distance between oxygen layers, and $b/2 \simeq c\sqrt{3}$. The cell parameters are a 4·40, b 9·42, c 2·84 Å; Z = 4.

When diaspore is heated corundum is produced, while the outward form of the diaspore crystal is retained; there is a close orientational relationship between diaspore and its decomposition products. The structural relationships between aluminium and analogous iron compounds are illustrated in Table 47.

Table 47

	Oxygens in hexagonal array	Oxygens in cubic array
AlO(OH)	diaspore	boehmite
Al_2O_3	corundum	γ–alumina
FeO(OH)	goethite	lepidocrocite
Fe_2O_3	haematite	γ–Fe_2O_3 (maghemite)

The principal substitutions which may be found in diaspore are of relatively small amounts of iron and, to a lesser extent, of manganese. On heating, diaspore decrepitates strongly, separating into white scales, and on stronger heating, water is given off. Diaspore is sometimes called α-alumina hydrate and its formula written as α-$Al_2O_3\cdot H_2O$ although there are no water molecules in its structure. The compounds within the system Al_2O_3–H_2O are gibbsite, bayerite, boehmite, diaspore, corundum, and γ-alumina, the first five of which are known definitely to occur as minerals. With increasing temperature, first gibbsite, then diaspore, then corundum, is the stable phase, and boehmite exists probably metastably at intermediate temperatures.

Diaspore crystals commonly occur in the form of thin plates on {010} elongated parallel to z; they are sometimes acicular, and rarely tabular parallel to {100}. Diaspore also occurs in thin scales and as massive aggregates and it is sometimes stalactitic. While normally colourless, diaspore may be coloured by the presence of iron and manganese.

Diaspore may be distinguished from corundum in grains or thin section by the higher refractive indices and lower birefringence of the latter, and from sillimanite which has lower refringence and birefringence.

The principal occurrences of diaspore are in bauxite and in emery deposits, but diaspore and boehmite occur also in fireclays. Hydrolysis of silicates in a tropical climate produces an alumina silica gel; after subsidence and burial, diaspore crystallizes from the gel and is followed by kaolinite formation. In emery deposits (e.g. at Chester, Massachusetts) diaspore occurs as an intermediate stage in the formation of corundum by the metamorphism of gibbsite in bauxite deposits. Diaspore is frequently found as one of the products of hydrothermal alteration of aluminous minerals, e.g. sillimanite, kyanite, andalusite, pyrophyllite, corundum.

Boehmite

γ-AlO(OH)

ORTHORHOMBIC (+)

α 1·64–1·65
β 1·65–1·66
γ 1·65–1·67
δ ≃ 0·015
$2V_γ$ ≃ 80°(?)
α = y or z, β = z or y, γ = x. O.A.P. (001) or (010).
D ≃ 3·0. H 3½–4.
Cleavage: {010} very good.
Colour: White when pure; colourless in thin section.

The structure of boehmite is similar to that of lepidocrocite and it is illustrated in Fig. 161. It contains double sheets of octahedra with Al ions at their centres, and the sheets themselves are composed of chains of

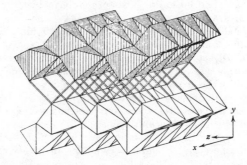

Fig. 161. *A pictorial representation of the structure of boehmite, with hydrogen-bonded oxygens connected by rods (after Ewing, F. J., 1935, Journ. Chem. Phys., vol. 3, p. 420).*

octahedra the repeat distance of which defines the *a* parameter of the unit cell (*a* 3·69, *b* 12·24, *c* 2·86 Å). In diaspore the oxygens are in a hexagonal close packed layer; those within the double octahedral layers in boehmite are in a cubic packing relationship. These differences in oxygen packing are consistent with the behaviour of the two polymorphs of AlO(OH) on dehydration in that diaspore yields α-alumina (trigonal) and boehmite yields γ-alumina which has the cubic structure of a spinel (see Table 47, p. 439). Boehmite has a good cleavage on {010}, the plane defining structural layers of AlO(OH) octahedra.

Most specimens of boehmite, whether naturally occurring or synthetic, are submicroscopic in texture, so that there is some uncertainty as to its optical properties: X-ray methods are usually necessary for its positive identification. Boehmite is a principal constituent of some bauxite deposits in which it is sometimes found together with its dimorph, diaspore. The bauxite clay deposits are the main source of aluminium metal; alumina is produced by calcination and the metal is recovered by an electrolytic process.

Goethite

α-FeO·OH

ORTHORHOMBIC (−)

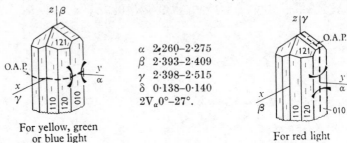

$$\alpha \quad 2\!\cdot\!260\text{--}2\!\cdot\!275$$
$$\beta \quad 2\!\cdot\!393\text{--}2\!\cdot\!409$$
$$\gamma \quad 2\!\cdot\!398\text{--}2\!\cdot\!515$$
$$\delta \quad 0\!\cdot\!138\text{--}0\!\cdot\!140$$
$$2V_\alpha 0°\text{--}27°.$$

For yellow, green or blue light

For red light

O.A.P. (100) for red light, (001) for green light; Bxa always ⊥ (010).
Dispersion: Extreme. D ≃ 4·3. H 5–5½.
Cleavage: {010} perfect, {100} moderate.
Colour: Yellowish brown to red; yellow to orange-red in thin section. In reflected light, grey with moderate anisotropism.
Pleochroism: Variable, in yellow and orange, absorption α > γ > β.
Soluble in HCl. Yellow streak. Dehydrates to α-Fe_2O_3.

The structure of goethite is similar to that of diaspore (AlO·OH), the unit cell containing 4(FeO·OH). It consists essentially of hexagonally close-packed oxygen ions with the iron ions in the octahedral interstices.

Most analyses of goethite show a certain amount of SiO_2 in addition to Fe_2O_3 and H_2O, this SiO_2 being due to admixture and impurity in the sample: Mn^{+3} may be present substituting for Fe^{+3}. Goethite can be prepared artificially by oxidizing solutions of ferrous compounds and by slow hydrolysis of ferric salts.

The optic axial angle varies both with the wavelength and with the temperature, goethite being uniaxial negative at normal temperatures for wavelengths between 610 and 620 mμ. It often occurs in fibrous varieties which may show anomalous optical effects.

Goethite differs from haematite in having a yellow streak, and in general it is more nearly yellowish in colour than lepidocrocite which is brownish. On dehydration it gives haematite (α-Fe_2O_3), whereas lepidocrocite gives magnetic spinel-type maghemite (γ-Fe_2O_3).

Goethite commonly occurs as a weathering product of iron-bearing minerals such as siderite, magnetite, pyrite, etc. It is normally formed under oxidizing conditions, and includes much material hitherto classed as limonite: it is the pigment in yellow ochre. It accumulates as a direct precipitate from both marine and meteoric waters and occurs in bogs and springs. In some sedimentary iron ores of economic importance it may be the principal constituent, as in the Lorraine basin of France.

Lepidocrocite

γ-FeO·OH

ORTHORHOMBIC $(-)$

α 1·94
β 2·20
γ 2·51
δ 0·57
$2V_\alpha$ 83°
O.A.P. (001); $\alpha = y, \beta = z, \gamma = x$.
Dispersion: Slight.   D 4·09.   H 5.
Cleavage: {010} perfect, {100} and {001} moderate.
Colour: Brownish to red; yellow to orange and red in thin section. In reflected light, greyish white with strong anisotropism.
Pleochroism: Strong, absorption $\alpha < \beta < \gamma$, light yellow to orange-red.
   Soluble in HCl. Orange streak. Dehydrates to γ-Fe$_2$O$_3$.

   The structure of lepidocrocite consists of iron-centred oxygen octahedra linked together in chains parallel to x by sharing diagonally opposite edges: it is thus similar to that of boehmite.

   Lepidocrocite is dimorphous with goethite and, as for the latter, the traces of SiO$_2$ reported in analyses are due to impurities: some Mn^{+3} may replace Fe^{+3}. It can be prepared artificially by the slow oxidation of dilute solutions of ferrous salts.

   It is strongly pleochroic from yellow to orange-red and differs from goethite in having a larger 2V, smaller dispersion, and maximum absorption parallel to the length of the fibres. Dehydration gives γ-Fe$_2$O$_3$, maghemite, which is ferromagnetic, whereas goethite yields paramagnetic α-Fe$_2$O$_3$, haematite.

   Like goethite, lepidocrocite occurs typically under oxidizing conditions as a weathering product of iron-bearing minerals. It is the pigment in brown ochre, and may occur intermingled with goethite.

Limonite

$$FeO \cdot OH \cdot nH_2O$$

n 2·0–2·1

D 2·7–4·3   H 4–5½

Colour: Yellow, brown, orange-brown and brownish black. Some botryoidal forms may have a green or red iridescent tarnish.

Streak: Yellow to brownish red.

Massive, earthy or occasionally vitreous. Soluble in HCl.

Although considered originally to have a definite formula ($2Fe_2O_3 \cdot 3H_2O$), limonite has been shown to consist mainly of cryptocrystalline goethite or lepidocrocite along with adsorbed water: some haematite may also be present. The name limonite is now retained as a field term or to describe hydrated oxides of iron with poorly crystalline characters whose real identity is not known.

Analyses of limonite, in addition to showing a variable water content, frequently report other elements due to the intimate mixture of the hydrous iron oxides with colloidal silica, phosphates, clay minerals and organic decomposition products as well as small amounts of hydrous aluminium oxides.

It is normally isotropic, but may also show anomalous birefringence. In transmitted light it is yellow, through shades of brown, to red, appearing brownish red by reflected light.

Limonite is common as an alteration product of iron-bearing minerals, but is found in all kinds of rock. It is common as a biogenic precipitate in swamps, etc., forming a large part of bog iron ore, and is also typically found in the gossan or weathered outcrop of many metalliferous veins and occurs as microscopic particles staining other minerals. It is often associated with haematite and with manganese ores: its chief mineralogical component is goethite.

SULPHIDES

Pyrite

FeS_2

CUBIC

D 4·95–5·03. H 6–6½.

Cleavage: {001} poor.
Twinning: Interpenetrant on {011} with twin axis [001].
Colour: Brassy yellow; black when fine-grained; greenish or brownish black streak. Metallic lustre; iridescent tarnish; opaque even in thinnest sections.

STRUCTURE

Pyrite is cubic with cell edge $a \simeq 5\cdot42$ Å; Fe atoms are at the corners and face centres of the cube, and S atoms are arranged in 'dumb-bell' pairs

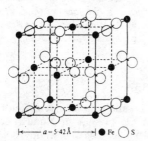

Fig. 162. *The structure of pyrite (after Strunz, H., 1957, Mineralogische Tabellen. Akad. verlag., Leipzig).*

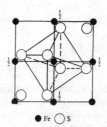

Fig. 163. *Projection of pyrite structure on (001) showing octahedral coordination of Fe by S.*

centred at the mid-points of the cube edges and at the cube's body centre (Fig. 162). The four S–S joins are respectively parallel to four non-intersecting body diagonal directions. Each iron atom is surrounded by six sulphur atoms at the corners of an octahedron (Fig. 163), and each sulphur atom is equidistant from three iron atoms which form a triangular planar group to one side of it. If the mid-points of sulphur pairs are considered, these are in the arrangement of cubic close packing, and an Fe atom lies in each of the octahedral holes. Compared with many other sulphides the structure of pyrite is very densely packed. Both NiS_2 (vaesite, a 5·679 Å) and CoS_2 (cattierite, a 5·535 Å) possess the pyrite structure, and the substitution of Fe by Ni or Co in pyrite increases the cell edge.

The mineral *marcasite* is a dimorph of pyrite and although its unit cell does not bear any obvious relation to that of pyrite, a similar environment of atoms occurs in its structure. It is orthorhombic with a 4·44, b 5·41, c 3·38 Å and two formula units in the unit cell. Part of the structure is shown in Fig. 164, where octahedral coordination of Fe by S, similar to that in pyrite, may be seen.

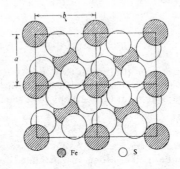

Fig. 164. *Illustration of structure of marcasite, showing pairs of S atoms with their mid-points at the centres of four edges and two faces of the unit cell, and showing the coordination octahedron of S atoms about Fe at the body centre (after Buerger, M. J., 1937, Zeit. Krist., vol. 97, p. 504).*

CHEMISTRY

Minor contents of elements other than iron and sulphur have often been reported for pyrite, but very often these are present in impurities, for example, copper in chalcopyrite, lead in galena, arsenic in arsenopyrite, and zinc in sphalerite. It is possible, however, that very small amounts of the above mentioned elements may be present in pyrite in solid solution. Hauerite, MnS_2, is isostructural with pyrite, but there is only very limited replacement of Fe by Mn in pyrite. Pyrite with small amounts of Ni and Co substituting for Fe are not uncommon; specimens with larger contents of these two elements are comparatively rare and are known as bravoite.

Pyrite can be prepared artificially in a variety of ways, for example, by heating pyrrhotite in air or H_2S, or by heating sulphur and ferric oxide at 230°C using glycerol as a solvent medium. In most of the wet chemical methods of preparation (e.g. from sulphur and ferrous sulphide, H_2S on ferric sulphate or ferric chloride), weakly acid, neutral or alkaline conditions favour the formation of pyrite, whereas in strongly acid conditions (and generally at lower temperatures) marcasite is formed. In the Fe–S system the equilibrium relation

$$FeS_2 \rightleftharpoons Fe_{1-x}S + liquid$$
$$\text{pyrite} \qquad \text{pyrrhotite}$$

is of particular interest. The pyrrhotite in equilibrium with pyrite shows increasing iron deficit with increasing temperature, while the pyrite composition remains constant. This relationship is illustrated in Fig. 165 and has been used as a geological thermometer for natural pyrite–pyrrhotite equilibrium assemblages. The Fe:S ratio of a pyrrhotite may be estimated by an X-ray powder method (see p. 451).

Other systems involving pyrite which have been investigated include, Fe–S–O, Cu–Fe–S, Fe–Zn–S (see sphalerite), and Fe–As–S. Alteration of pyrite usually proceeds by oxidation to sulphates and eventually to iron hydroxides and their hydrates. Among the common minerals which form as pseudomorphs after pyrite are haematite, chalcocite and graphite.

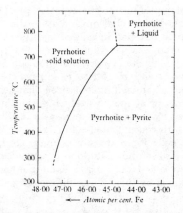

Fig. 165. *A part of the FeS–S equilibrium diagram at a pressure of about* 10 *bars (after Arnold, R. G.*, 1958, Carnegie Inst. Washington, Ann. Rep. Dir. Geophys. Lab., *vol.* 57, *p.* 218).

OPTICAL AND PHYSICAL PROPERTIES

The reflectivity of pyrite for white light is 54·5 per cent; it is sometimes used as a standard for reflectivity measurements on other minerals. Although pyrite is cubic it almost invariably exhibits some anisotropy; among the possible reasons for this are, arsenic or nickel impurity, a surface film of marcasite, variation in Fe:S ratio, and, internal strain, but it has also been suggested that the anisotropy of pyrite is related to the low symmetry (class 23) of its crystal structure.

One crystal habit adopted by pyrite is the pentagonal dodecahedron (pyritohedron), but cubes and octahedra also commonly occur. Crystal faces are sometimes striated due to the alternate development of two forms in one crystal, e.g. {100} and {210}, with one predominating. The directions of striations on different faces betray the hemihedral symmetry of the crystal class even in the cube. Interpenetration twins sometimes occur with the shape of a cross, the 'iron cross' twin. Although well formed crystals are not uncommon, much pyrite occurs in massive aggregates, in radiating clusters and in reniform, globular, granular and stalactitic formations. A fine-grained black amorphous, or cryptocrystalline, material of colloidal origin and with the composition of pyrite has been called *melnikovite* (melnikovite pyrite).

Marcasite, in appearance, can be very much like pyrite; it sometimes shows tabular or pyramidal habit but it is more usually found in radiating fibrous masses. Its density is $4·89$ gm/cm^3, hardness $6-6\frac{1}{2}$, and it is optically strongly anisotropic.

DISTINGUISHING FEATURES

Pyrite is similar in appearance to chalcopyrite, pyrrhotite and marcasite. It can be distinguished from chalcopyrite since the latter mineral has a deeper yellow colour in reflected light, and is softer, being scratched by a knife. Pyrrhotite is bronze rather than brass-coloured, is also scratched by a knife and is usually magnetic. Pyrite is insoluble in HCl whereas pyrrho-ite is attacked. Pyrite and marcasite can usually be distinguished if polished surfaces are examined in polarized light since pyrite crystals appear to be isotropic or at most weakly birefringent. The two minerals may be distinguished by a simple chemical test in which finely powdered material is treated with concentrated cold nitric acid. When action ceases, a little heat is applied: for marcasite sulphur precipitates whereas for pyrite sulphur goes into solution as sulphuric acid. The result of this test is not always conclusive, and the most reliable method for distinguishing pyrite from marcasite is by their X-ray diffraction patterns.

PARAGENESIS

Pyrite is the most abundant of the sulphide minerals and its occurrence is widespread. It occurs in large masses or veins of hydrothermal origin, both as a primary and as a secondary mineral in igneous and in sedimentary (principally argillaceous and carbonaceous) rocks. Many metamorphosed sediments (e.g. black graphitic slates) contain pyrite. Large masses of pyrite are found in contact metamorphic ore deposits; in these and in other occurrences it is often associated with sulphides of copper and of other metals, some of which have been formed by replacement of pyrite. Pyrite is also formed as a skarn mineral, as a volcanic sublimate, and as a minor constituent of some salt deposits. Some examples of typical pyrite para-geneses are given below.

The sulphides of the Skaergaard intrusion are of magmatic origin, having crystallized from a sulphide liquid immiscible with a silicate liquid of gabbroic composition.

The pyrite ore bodies at Rio Tinto, Spain, which occur at slate–porphyry contacts, are regarded as the most extensive in the world. Conflicting views are held as to the mode of formation of the Rio Tinto ores, but a hydro-thermal origin seems most likely.

The occurrence of pyrite is sometimes associated with volcanic activity. The Samreid Lake, Ontario, deposits for example, consist mainly of pyrite and pyrrhotite, with intergrown magnetite. It is thought that iron hydroxide gels and perhaps magnetite were converted to pyrite by H_2S, and that pyrrhotite was formed later at the expense of pyrite at higher temperatures.

In sediments, pyrite and glauconite are often found together. They form diagenetically in muds on the sea floor, usually in shallow water and under reducing conditions. Poorly crystallized forms of pyrite are more generally found in sedimentary and in low temperature hydrothermal deposits. Raspberry-like aggregates of tiny spherical particles of pyrite are referred to as 'framboidal' and their presence in sediments has been attributed to the action of micro-organisms, or sometimes to colloidal deposition.

Among the minerals after which pseudomorphs of pyrite have been found are pyrrhotite, haematite, chalcopyrite, arsenopyrite, marcasite, fluorite, calcite and barytes. Marcasite does not occur as a magmatic mineral: it is formed only in sediments or in metalliferous veins, usually in conditions of low temperature.

REFERENCES

FRIEDMAN, G. M. (1959) 'The Samreid lake sulphide deposit, Ontario; an example of a pyrrhotite–pyrite iron formation', *Econ. Geol.*, vol. 54, p. 268.

KULLERUD, G. and YODER, H. S. (1959) 'Pyrite stability relations in the Fe–S system', *Econ. Geol.*, vol. 54, p. 533.

Pyrrhotite

Fe₇S₈–FeS

MONOCLINIC (PSEUDO-HEXAGONAL)

D 4·6 (for Fe₇S₈). H 3½–4½.

Cleavage: None; {0001} parting. Twinning {10Ī2}.
Colour: Bronze-yellow, brownish or reddish; metallic lustre; opaque even in thinnest sections: dark greyish black streak.

Pyrrhotite has the approximate composition FeS but always contains less iron than is indicated by this formula. Stoichiometric FeS is known as *troilite*, is non-magnetic, and occurs mainly in meteorites.

STRUCTURE

The detailed structure of pyrrhotite is complex but it is based upon a simple scheme in which the sulphur atoms are arranged in approximately

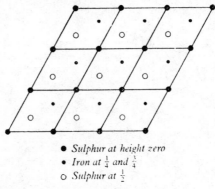

● *Sulphur at height zero*
● *Iron at ¼ and ¾*
○ *Sulphur at ½*

Fig. 166. *Idealized structure of pyrrhotite (NiAs type) projected on (0001).*

hexagonal close packing with its sequence ABABAB.... Those positions which in cubic close packing would be labelled 'C', are occupied, in this case between every pair of sulphur layers, by iron atoms. Thus each iron has three sulphurs above it and a set of three below which are rotated through 60° with respect to the first set. Each sulphur lies at the centre of a triangular prism of iron atoms. A projection of several cells of this structure on (0001) is shown in Fig. 166. The complete layer sequence is ACBCACBCACBC...(A and B are sulphur, C is iron), so that each cell has two layers of sulphur and two of iron. This structure, the NiAs (niccolite) type, has hexagonal holosymmetry (class 6/*mmm*) and its smallest unit cell has dimensions $a \simeq 3\cdot45$ Å, $c \simeq 5\cdot8$ Å, with $Z = 2$ ($Fe_{1-x}S$). Minor deviations from this ideal structure occur for most compositions within the range Fe_7S_8–FeS, leading to larger hexagonal or monoclinic (pseudohexagonal) unit cells. Troilite, for example, is hexagonal with a 5·958, c 11·74 Å.

It is clear from density measurements, and from the decrease in cell dimensions as the Fe:S ratio decreases, that the non-stoichiometric formula of ferrous sulphide is a consequence of missing iron atoms rather than replacement of some iron atoms by sulphur. The extent and pattern of ordering of these vacant sites can account for the superstructures exhibited, higher temperatures and greater disorder producing the simpler cell. The structure of Fe_7S_8 is like that of NiAs but with a regular arrangement of vacant metal sites giving rise to lower symmetry and specific magnetic properties. The decrease in the cell parameters of pyrrhotite as iron deficiency increases can be used for the determination of the compositions of homogeneous pyrrhotites.

CHEMISTRY

Small amounts of Ni, Co, Mn and Cu can substitute for Fe in pyrrhotite, but in many specimens these elements are probably present in impurities, e.g. Ni and Co in pentlandite $(Fe,Ni)_9S_8$, and Cu in chalcopyrite.

Most analyses of natural pyrrhotites show a deficiency of iron below that required for the stoichiometric formula FeS. If the formula is written $Fe_{1-x}S$, the range of pyrrhotite compositions is such that x varies from zero to about 0·125. Pyrrhotite has been synthesized by the direct combination of iron and sulphur, and by heating pyrite in an atmosphere of H_2S at 550°C. Laboratory studies of systems involving pyrrhotite include Fe–S, Fe–S–O, Fe–S–Se, Cu–Fe–S, Fe–Zn–S (see sphalerite), Fe–Ni–S and Fe–As–S. In the Fe–S system the pyrrhotite in equilibrium with pyrite shows increasing iron deficit with increasing temperature. This relationship is illustrated in Fig. 165 and has been used as a geological thermometer for natural pyrite–pyrrhotite equilibrium assemblages. Temperatures of formation deduced in this way agree fairly well with those determined by the sphalerite–pyrrhotite method mentioned on p. 458. Phase relations in the system Fe–Zn–S show that although there can be considerable replacement of Fe for Zn in sphalerite, there is little or no solid solution of Zn in pyrrhotite.

Natural alteration products of pyrrhotite include pyrite, marcasite and other sulphides, but alteration may also take place by oxidation to iron sulphates, carbonates and oxides. Among the minerals which have been found pseudomorphous after pyrrhotite are: pyrite, marcasite, chalcopyrite, arsenopyrite, magnetite and quartz.

OPTICAL AND PHYSICAL PROPERTIES

Pyrrhotite usually occurs in massive or granular aggregates, but tabular {0001} and pyramidal habits, and sometimes rosette formations, are not uncommon. The bronze-coloured surface of pyrrhotite tarnishes very easily and often shows iridescent colours, but polished sections may be examined by reflected light, and the mineral can then be seen to be strongly anisotropic. Density varies with Fe:S ratio, and values between 4·55 and 4·87 g/cm^3 have been recorded. Many specimens of pyrrhotite are capable of acting as a magnet; those which are furthest from the stoichiometric formula show the effect most strongly, and troilite, with composition FeS, is ideally antiferromagnetic.

DISTINGUISHING FEATURES

Pyrrhotite is decomposed by HCl with evolution of H$_2$S whereas pyrite is not. Other distinguishing features are its bronze rather than brass colour and its lower hardness. Troilite is attacked more readily by dilute nitric acid than is pyrrhotite.

PARAGENESIS

Pyrrhotite occurs mainly in basic igneous rocks but is also found in pegmatites, in contact metamorphic deposits, in high temperature hydrothermal veins and in sediments. Sometimes pyrrhotite is found alone but more often it occurs in association with other sulphides, e.g. pyrite, marcasite, chalcopyrite, pentlandite and sphalerite. Troilite is usually found in meteorites, but terrestrial pyrrhotites with stoichiometric composition have been reported, though these are rare.

REFERENCES

KULLERUD, G. and YODER, H. S. (1959) 'Pyrite stability relations in the Fe–S system', *Econ. Geol.*, vol. 54, p. 533.

WAGER, L. R., VINCENT, E. A. and SMALES, A. A. (1957) 'Sulphides in the Skaergaard intrusion, east Greenland', *Econ. Geol.*, vol. 52, p. 855.

Chalcopyrite

$CuFeS_2$

TETRAGONAL

D 4·1–4·3.   H 3½–4.

Cleavage: {011}, {111}, generally poor.
Twinning: Lamellar on {112}, {012}, {110}; deformation twins on {110} and {012}; interpenetrant twins.
Colour: Brass-yellow; often tarnished and iridescent. Opaque even in thinnest sections. Greenish black streak.

STRUCTURE

Chalcopyrite is tetragonal with a 5·25, c 10·32 Å and 4($CuFeS_2$) in the unit cell. The structure, illustrated in Fig. 167, is similar to that of sphalerite

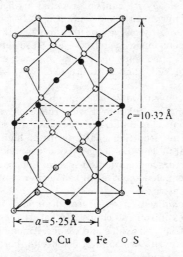

$c = 10·32$ Å

$a = 5·25$ Å

○ Cu   ● Fe   ○ S

Fig. 167. *The structure of chalcopyrite (after Pauling, L. & Brockway, L. O., 1932, Zeit. Krist., vol. 82, p. 188).*

with c chalcopyrite $\simeq 2a$ sphalerite. In each half of the chalcopyrite cell, 4 Zn of sphalerite are replaced by 2 Cu and 2 Fe, the sulphur positions remaining unchanged. In successive half-cells in the z direction, Cu and Fe positions are interchanged so that, along any line of metal atoms parallel to z, Cu and Fe alternate, thus giving rise to the doubled c parameter. As in sphalerite, the sulphur atoms are arranged in layers stacked in cubic close packing; these layers are parallel to {112} planes of the chalcopyrite tetragonal cell. In chalcopyrite each metal atom is coordinated by a tetrahedron of sulphurs and each sulphur by a tetrahedron of metal atoms (2Fe and 2Cu). A high-temperature form of chalcopyrite, prepared by prolonged heating of pure $CuFeS_2$ and then quenching, is cubic with a 5·26 Å, and the Zn sites of sphalerite are, in this form, probably randomly occupied by equal numbers of Cu and Fe atoms.

CHEMISTRY

Since chalcopyrite is often intergrown with other copper and iron sulphides many analyses yield atomic proportions which do not accord closely with the ideal formula. Minor and trace amounts of many elements have been reported present in chalcopyrite, e.g. Ag, Au, Pt, Pb, Co, Ni, Mn, Sn, Zn replacing Cu or Fe, and As or Se replacing S. For some specimens, however, these elements may be present in admixed impurities, for example As in arsenopyrite, Sn in stannite, Zn in sphalerite and Pt in sperrylite. Although the high-temperature form of chalcopyrite is isostructural with sphalerite, there is only limited solid solution of ZnS in $CuFeS_2$ and of $CuFeS_2$ in ZnS. Chalcopyrite can be prepared artificially in a variety of ways, e.g. fusion of pyrite with chalcocite (Cu_2S), heating mixed powders of pyrite and copper, and by the action of ammoniacal cuprous chloride on $KFeS_2$. Phase relations in the system Cu–Fe–S are complex, and involve a wide range of Cu–Fe solid solutions embracing such sulphides as digenite (Cu_9S_5), bornite (Cu_5FeS_4) and cubanite ($CuFe_2S_3$) as well as pyrite and pyrrhotite.

In general, chalcopyrite and other sulphides which originate at high temperatures can at first tolerate a wide range of solid solution, but on cooling under favourable conditions exsolution of separate phases may occur. Thus, when an iron-rich chalcopyrite of high temperature origin cools, the excess iron can no longer be accommodated, and cubanite ($CuFe_2S_3$) then appears as an oriented separate phase: similarly sphalerite may be exsolved from chalcopyrite, and chalcopyrite may be exsolved from bornite or from sphalerite.

Chalcopyrite is oxidized on exposure to air and water, or with slight heating, to sulphates of iron and copper. In nature these are usually altered further to carbonates, hydroxides and oxides. Among the common pseudomorphs after chalcopyrite are copper, chalcocite, bornite, pyrite, tetrahedrite, calcite and iron oxides.

OPTICAL AND PHYSICAL PROPERTIES

Chalcopyrite usually occurs in massive aggregates which are sometimes botryoidal or reniform. Oriented intergrowths occur with tetrahedrite, cubanite, galena and sphalerite. Chalcopyrite is optically anisotropic and the reflection coefficient for a polished surface varies with direction from 42·0 to 46·1 per cent.

DISTINGUISHING FEATURES

Chalcopyrite is distinguished from pyrite by the greater hardness of the latter. It is distinguished from pyrrhotite by its colour and lack of ferromagnetism, and from bornite by its colour. In small grains it can resemble gold but chalcopyrite is brittle, and gold forms an amalgam with mercury.

PARAGENESIS

Chalcopyrite is the most widely occurring copper-bearing mineral and is an important ore of the metal. It is formed together with other sulphides among ores of primary magmatic origin and in metalliferous veins in igneous rocks, and it is also formed by metasomatic and contact metamorphic replacements due to magmatic sulphide solutions. At Rio Tinto, Huelva, Spain, the lenticular ore bodies associated with slate–porphyry contacts are mainly pyrite and chalcocite but they also contain appreciable disseminated chalcopyrite.

Chalcopyrite is not uncommon in sediments, and indeed such occurrences are among the important sources of copper ore. In some cases, as in the copper shales (Kupferschiefer) of the Mansfeld district of Germany for example, the ores are believed to have formed during sedimentation. The copper compounds were probably leached out of surrounding rocks and eventually precipitated and concentrated on lake or sea bottom. In other sediments, however, e.g. in sandstone and silicified dolomite at Katanga, in the Congo, the copper ores are believed to have formed by infiltration of solutions subsequent to sedimentation. The alteration products malachite, azurite and chrysocolla are often found near the surface of copper ore deposits. Chalcopyrite is a common mineral in the secondary enrichment zones of many ore deposits, as for example in the low grade porphyry copper ores at Bingham, Utah.

REFERENCE

FLEISCHER, M. (1955) 'Minor elements in some sulphide minerals', *Econ. Geol.*, 50th anniv. vol., pt. II, p. 970.

Sphalerite

ZnS

n 2·37.   D 4·1.   H $3\frac{1}{2}$–4.

Cleavage: {011} perfect.

Twinning: {111} and {211}; multiple contact twins and lamellar inter-growths.

Colour: Black, brown, yellow, red, green, white or colourless; light yellowish, brownish or colourless in thin section.

Resinous or adamantine lustre.

STRUCTURE

The cubic unit cell has $a \simeq 5\cdot41$ Å and contains four formula units. Zinc atoms are located at the corners and face centres of the unit cube and sulphur atoms have coordinates $(\frac{1}{4},\frac{1}{4},\frac{1}{4})$, $(\frac{3}{4},\frac{3}{4},\frac{1}{4})$, $(\frac{1}{4},\frac{3}{4},\frac{3}{4})$ and $(\frac{3}{4},\frac{1}{4},\frac{3}{4})$ (Fig. 168). The latter positions are the centres of four out of the eight smaller

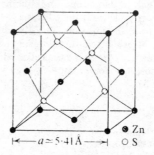

Fig. 168. *The structure of sphalerite.*

cubes into which the large cube can be divided, and they too lie at the points of a face-centred lattice. Each sulphur is coordinated by four zinc atoms at the corners of a regular tetrahedron and the zinc atoms are surrounded by sulphurs in a similar fashion. Although purely covalent tetrahedral bonds could be formed between zinc and sulphur atoms in the structure, there is evidence that the bonding is partially ionic in character. Since all tetrahedra of Zn are similarly oriented, the structure has tetrahedral symmetry rather than that of the cube, and opposite senses of the direction [111] are not equivalent. Substitution of Fe for Zn in the sphalerite structure results in a linear increase in the cell edge.

The high-temperature polymorph of ZnS is *wurtzite*, the structure of which is hexagonal with *a* 3·81, *c* 6·26 Å, and two ZnS per unit cell. The relation between the structures of wurtzite and sphalerite is that between hexagonal and cubic types of packing. This may best be seen by viewing the structures along [0001] and [111] respectively, for layers of Zn atoms occupy positions ABAB... in wurtzite and ABCABC... in sphalerite, and the same is true for layers of sulphur atoms. The structure of wurtzite is illustrated in Fig. 169. Again the coordinations of Zn by S and of S by Zn are tetrahedral and all tetrahedra of Zn point one way, making the symmetry hemimorphic and [0001] a polar axis. Layer sequences other than the two described also occur, giving rise to polytypes with multi-layered cells, and also to disordered structures. Most natural specimens of ZnS are mixtures of cubic and hexagonal polytypes, with cubic predominating.

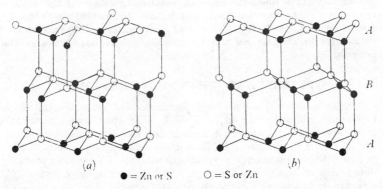

● = Zn or S   ○ = S or Zn

Fig. 169. *The structures of (a) sphalerite and (b) wurtzite showing sequence of layers (after Evans, R. C., 1964, An Introduction to Crystal Chemistry, Cambridge).*

CHEMISTRY

The principal substituent for zinc in the sphalerite structure is iron, the highest iron content reported being 26 weight per cent Fe, which corresponds to 45 mol. per cent FeS. Experimental studies give as an upper limit about 40 mol. per cent FeS in (Zn,Fe)S at 900°C and 1 atmosphere pressure. Some of the iron reported in natural specimens may be present as pyrrhotite. In natural sphalerites as much as 4 to 5 per cent of Cd and Mn have been reported. Minor and trace concentrations of other elements, e.g. Ga, Ge, In, Co and Hg may occur as well as Fe, Mn and Cd, substituting for Zn in sphalerite. Copper, silver and tin are also often recorded in sphalerite analyses but some of these elements may be present in small inclusions of other minerals. Blebs of chalcopyrite, for example, are often found in sphalerite, and are attributed to exsolution on cooling from a higher temperature ZnS–CuFeS$_2$ solid solution. Antimony and bismuth as well as lead, when reported, are probably present in galena.

Pure sphalerite transforms to the wurtzite polymorph at 1020°C if oxidation is prevented, but the inversion temperature is lowered by the presence of iron or manganese. Wurtzite can exist metastably below the inversion temperature, but grinding is sufficient to convert it to sphalerite. The amount of iron that can be accommodated in the sphalerite structure increases with increasing temperature, so that, subject to careful consideration of equilibrium conditions, the iron content of a sphalerite (readily determined from its cell parameter) can be used as a geological thermometer.

Both sphalerite and wurtzite have been prepared artificially. On heating in air, sphalerite is oxidized to zinc sulphate, but if much iron is present ferric and ferrous sulphates are also formed and at higher temperatures (above 1000°C) zinc ferrites result. ZnS may also be converted to ZnO by heating, and sometimes the oxide is pseudomorphous after the sulphide. Goslarite (ZnSO$_4 \cdot$2H$_2$O) and smithsonite (ZnCO$_3$) are sometimes found as alteration products after sphalerite, and other replacement minerals include hemimorphite, iron oxides and hydroxides, galena, stannite and chalcopyrite.

OPTICAL AND PHYSICAL PROPERTIES

Sphalerite crystals often adopt tetrahedral or dodecahedral habits, frequently exhibiting curved faces. Multiple contact twins, penetration twins, and lamellar intergrowths are common, twinning principally on {111} and {211}; the twinning on {111} is sometimes caused by pressure. Wurtzite generally shows hemimorphic pyramidal habit; it is sometimes tabular or fibrous and is usually untwinned. Although sphalerite has a perfect {011} cleavage its brittleness leads to conchoidal fracture.

Pure Zn sphalerites can be colourless and transparent but translucency decreases and the colour deepens as iron content increases. Spectroscopic analyses of sphalerites suggest that the colours of different specimens may be associated with the presence of certain elements, green with Co and Fe, red with Sn, In, Ag and Mo, and yellow often with Ge, Ca, Cu, Hg and Cd. Although crystallographically cubic, sphalerite is not often optically isotropic. The positive uniaxial anisotropy exhibited may be due to intergrowth of sphalerite with wurtzite polytypes: sometimes sphalerite shows strain birefringence. Sphalerite shows high dispersion; the refractive index is 2·47 for violet, about 2·37 for yellow light and about 2·30 for infra-red. Wurtzite is uniaxial positive, with ω 2·356 and ϵ 2·378, and its specific gravity is similar to that of sphalerite, i.e. approximately 4·1.

DISTINGUISHING FEATURES

Although extremely variable in colour, sphalerite can usually be recognized by its resinous lustre, high refractive index, weak or zero birefringence, cleavage, and lamellar twinning.

PARAGENESIS

Except for the zinc oxide and silicate deposits at Franklin Furnace, New Jersey, the primary ore mineral of zinc is the sulphide, the occurrence of which, usually together with galena, is extremely widespread. At Broken Hill, New South Wales, lead and zinc sulphides have replaced metamorphic rocks, usually along zones of folding, shearing and crushing. The sphalerite and galena are accompanied by other sulphides and by silver minerals. Sulphide ore minerals are sometimes found, e.g. at Bingham, Utah, as replacements of limestone and are there associated with quartz, calcite, wollastonite, diopside and garnet.

Sphalerite and galena may occur in deep-seated veins in unmetamorphosed sediments and lavas, e.g. at Bawdwin, Burma, where mineralization may have occurred through the penetration of fault zones in rhyolite and rhyolite tuff by intrusive granitic magma. Sphalerite and galena probably of lower temperature hydrothermal origin are found commonly in veins and replacements in dolomitic limestone, and as disseminations in limestone and sandstone. Pseudomorphs of sphalerite after galena, tetrahedrite and calcite have been reported. Wurtzite, though less common, is often found together with sphalerite.

REFERENCE

KULLERUD, G. (1953) 'The FeS–ZnS system. A geological thermometer', *Norsk. Geol. Tids.*, vol. 32, p. 61.

Galena

PbS

CUBIC

n 3·91.   D 7·5–7·6.   H 2½.

Cleavage: {001} perfect, {111} parting.

Twinning: Penetration and contact twinning on {111}; lamellar and deformation twins on other planes.

Colour: Lead grey; metallic lustre and lead grey streak; opaque in thin section.

STRUCTURE

The structure of galena is similar to that of rock salt, lead and sulphur atoms occupying the positions of sodium and chlorine respectively. Thus each lead atom is octahedrally coordinated by six sulphurs and each sulphur by six leads. There are 4 formula units in the unit cell, the edge of which is 5·94 Å.

CHEMISTRY

Substitution of other atoms for lead in galena is not very extensive. Among the elements which do occur in small amounts are: Sb, As, Bi, Ag, Tl, Zn, Cd, Fe, Mn and Cu. In many cases these may be present in impurity minerals (acanthite Ag_2S, sphalerite, chalcopyrite, etc.) rather than in the galena structure. There is a complete range of solid solution between galena and clausthalite (PbSe).

Galena is decomposed by dilute nitric acid with the separation of sulphur and formation of $PbSO_4$; some specimens effervesce, giving off H_2S. Galena melts at 1115°C. It can be prepared by heating pyrite with a solution of $PbCl_2$. Galena and pyrrhotite form a eutectic intergrowth at about 750° with composition 71 per cent PbS, 29 per cent FeS. Among the alteration products of galena are cerussite, anglesite and pyromorphite, and pseudomorphs after galena include chalcocite and covellite.

OPTICAL AND PHYSICAL PROPERTIES

Galena is isotropic, and has a reflection coefficient of 32·2 per cent in white light. Common forms developed are the cube and octahedron, although the latter is rarely present alone, and the habit is often tabular on (001). Massive specimens can be coarse- or fine-grained, and fibrous aggregates sometimes occur: specimens often exhibit a lineage structure. Galena has a perfect cubic cleavage and specimens often show abundant triangular pits. There appears to be a close relationship between the nature of crystal parting and the presence and location of impurities and trace elements.

Galena deforms readily along cube planes and slip occurs in the [110] direction. Oriented overgrowths of galena on other minerals and of these on galena often occur, e.g. galena on pyrite, chalcopyrite or pyrrhotite, and anglesite on galena.

DISTINGUISHING FEATURES

Galena is easily recognizable, except perhaps when fine-grained, by its colour, metallic lustre, lead-grey streak, perfect {100} cleavage and low hardness. It can be distinguished from stibnite by its cubic cleavage, high density and darker colour. Galena is also characterized by its isotropy in reflected light.

PARAGENESIS

Galena is the principal ore of lead; it occurs most frequently together with sphalerite, and the lead–zinc ores often contain recoverable amounts of copper, silver, antimony and bismuth. Occurrences of lead and zinc sulphides may be of low, intermediate or high temperature origin. Thus galena of high temperature origin is found in veins and replacements in pegmatites, calc-silicate rocks, limestones and other sediments, and in lavas; in some limestones and sandstones the galena is believed to be of lower temperature hydrothermal origin. In addition to various sulphides, commonly associated minerals include barytes, fluorite, quartz and calcite; pseudomorphs after cerussite, anglesite and pyromorphite are known.

The abundances of the various isotopes of lead (^{206}Pb, ^{207}Pb, ^{208}Pb) in galena specimens have been used to estimate their ages.

REFERENCE

RUSSELL, R. D. and FARQUHAR, R. M. (1960) *Lead isotopes in Geology.* Interscience Publishers, New York.

SULPHATES

Barytes

$BaSO_4$

ORTHORHOMBIC $(+)$

α 1·636–1·637
β 1·637–1·639
γ 1·647–1·649
$\delta \simeq 0·012$
$2V_\gamma$ 37°
$\alpha = z, \beta = y, \gamma = x$; O.A.P. (010)

Dispersion: $r < v$ weak.   D $\simeq$ 4·5.   H $2\frac{1}{2}$–$3\frac{1}{2}$.
Cleavage: {001} perfect, {210} very good, {010} good.
Twinning: Glide twinning on {110} frequent in massive material.
Colour: White, yellowish, grey, pale green, pale blue, red, brown; colourless in thin section.
Pleochroism: Slight in coloured varieties; absorption $\gamma > \beta > \alpha$.

STRUCTURE

The structure of barytes is illustrated in Fig. 170. The SO_4 ions are approximately regular tetrahedra lying with S and two oxygens on mirror planes at $y = 0$ and $\frac{1}{2}$; the other two oxygens of each tetrahedron are equidistant from, and on opposite sides of, these planes. Ba ions also lie on the mirror planes and link the sulphate ions in such a way that each Ba is coordinated by twelve oxygens. Other minerals with structures similar to that of barytes are anglesite ($PbSO_4$) and celestine ($SrSO_4$); cell parameters of all three are given below:

	aÅ	bÅ	cÅ
Barytes	8·878	5·450	7·152
Anglesite	8·480	5·398	6·958
Celestine	8·359	5·352	6·866

CHEMISTRY

Although specimens of barytes are generally nearly pure $BaSO_4$, barium can be replaced by strontium in a continuous solid solution series from barytes to celestine. Members of this series with a preponderance of the Ba 'molecule' are called strontiobarytes, and those near the Sr end, barytocelestine. Appreciable replacement of Ba by Pb or by Ca is uncommon, and it has been shown that at room temperature only about 6 per cent $CaSO_4$ can enter into solid solution in the barytes structure. The solubility of barytes in water is very slight but it is increased by heating and by the presence of chlorides. When gently heated, some crystals of barytes decrepitate, giving off H_2S; the variety hepatite does this to a marked extent and consequently it is also known as stinkstein.

$BaSO_4$ crystals have been prepared by double decomposition using $BaCl_2$ and sulphate solutions. A common alteration product is witherite $BaCO_3$, and barytes is often pseudomorphously replaced by carbonates, sulphates and sulphides.

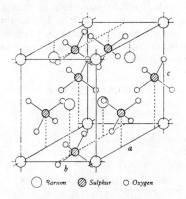

$\bigcirc$ *Barium* $\oslash$ *Sulphur* $\circ$ *Oxygen*

Fig. 170. *Perspective view of the structure of barytes (after Jong, W. F. de, 1959, Kompendium der Kristallkunde. Springer-Verlag, Wien).*

OPTICAL AND PHYSICAL PROPERTIES

Barytes commonly occurs in well formed crystals but it also occurs as globular concretions and as fibrous, lamellar, granular, and earthy aggregates. Clusters of platy crystals are found, usually containing sand grains and coloured pink, which assume rosette shapes and are called 'desert roses'. Crystals of barytes have a vitreous to resinous (and sometimes pearly) lustre, and are colourless or white when pure. Yellow, red and brown varieties result from the presence of impurities, principally iron oxides and hydroxides, sulphides, and organic matter. Many specimens are blue, probably as a result of exposure to radiation from radium: it is known that exposure of barytes to radium radiation turns it blue, and the presence of Ra in natural specimens is quite likely in view of the similarities between the Ba and Ra atoms. Some specimens of barytes are fluorescent (white, yellow or orange) in ultra-violet light and are subsequently phosphorescent; thermoluminescence also occurs. Barytes is brittle, shows perfect {001} cleavage, and less perfect cleavage on {210} and {010}: the {210} cleavages intersect at an angle of approximately 78°. The average hardness of barytes is about 3 on the Mohs scale but it varies with direction in the crystal. The density of natural barytes varies somewhat because of chemical substitutions; Sr decreases and Pb increases the density. Refractive indices and birefringence are lowered slightly by the substitution of Sr and Ba and increased by substitution of Pb, while the optic axial angle is increased by either of these replacements.

DISTINGUISHING FEATURES

Barytes is not easily distinguished from celestine except by its greater density, which also helps to distinguish it from other minerals, e.g. aragonite, albite, calcite and gypsum. In addition, albite is harder than barytes, gypsum is softer, and calcite effervesces while barytes is insoluble in dilute HCl: barytes gives a green flame coloration. The cleavages of minerals in the barytes group are characteristic, and are distinct from the three orthogonal cleavages of anhydrite. Barytes and celestine have lower refringence and birefringence than anglesite.

PARAGENESIS

Barytes is the most common barium mineral, occurring mainly as a gangue mineral in metalliferous hydrothermal veins, and as veins or cavity filling concretions in limestones, sandstones, shales and clays. In addition to vein deposits, barytes occurs as surface deposits as a residual product of limestone weathering, and it may also occur in association with hot springs. Among the minerals commonly associated with barytes are lead and zinc minerals, pyrite, quartz, carbonates and fluorite. Barytes and fluorite often show regional zonal relationships.

REFERENCE

DUNHAM, K. C. (1948) 'Geology of the Northern Pennine orefield', *Mem. Geol. Surv. Gt. Britain.*

Celestine

$SrSO_4$

ORTHORHOMBIC ($+$)

α $1\cdot621$–$1\cdot622$
β $1\cdot623$–$1\cdot624$
γ $1\cdot630$–$1\cdot631$
$\delta \simeq 0\cdot009$
$2V_\gamma$ $50°$
$\alpha = z, \beta = y, \gamma = x$; O.A.P. (010)

Dispersion: $r < v$, moderate. D $\simeq 3\cdot96$. H 3–$3\frac{1}{2}$.
Cleavage: {001} perfect, {210} good, {010} poor.
Twinning: Very rare.
Colour: Colourless, white, pale blue, reddish, greenish, brownish; colourless in thin section.
Pleochroism: Blue crystals weakly pleochroic; indigo, lavender-blue, blue-green, violet; absorption $\gamma > \beta > \alpha$.

The structure of celestine is similar to that of barytes, with Sr taking the place of Ba; its cell parameters are given on p. 462. There is a complete solid solution series between $BaSO_4$ and $SrSO_4$, but solid solution of $CaSO_4$ in $SrSO_4$ is limited. Natural specimens, however, rarely contain more than two or three per cent of the Ba or Ca component. Alteration products from celestine, some of which may be pseudomorphous, include strontianite, calcite, witherite, quartz, chalcedony, barytes and sulphur.

Celestine occurs in fibrous or rounded aggregates and also as well-formed crystals with tabular {001} habit. The colours of celestine specimens are mostly caused by impurities, but the blue of some is probably produced by irradiation. Celestine is similar to barytes in many respects but its density is lower. Gypsum is softer and calcite effervesces with dilute HCl; celestine gives a crimson flame coloration. The cleavages of minerals in the barytes group are characteristic, and are distinct from the three ortho-gonal cleavages of anhydrite.

Celestine is the principal mineral source of strontium (much used in pyrotechnics) and it occurs mostly in fissures and cavities in dolomites and dolomitic limestones. It is also found in evaporite deposits and in hydro-thermal veins. Large nodules of celestine are found in Trias marl at Yate, Gloucestershire.

Gypsum

CaSO$_4$·2H$_2$O

MONOCLINIC (+)

α 1·519–1·521
β 1·523–1·526
γ 1·529–1·531
δ ≃ 0·01
2V$_γ$ ≃ 58°
γ:z ≃ 52°; O.A.P. (010).
Dispersion: r > v, strong.
Inclined dispersion of bisectrix.
D 2·30–2·37. H 2.
Cleavage: {010} perfect, {100} and {011} distinct.
Twinning: Very common on {100}; less common {Ī01}.
Colour: Usually white or colourless, sometimes grey, red, yellow, brown, blue; colourless in thin section.

Morphological setting

STRUCTURE

Euhedral crystals of gypsum often occur in the habit depicted above, and in most morphological studies the clinodome was taken as the form {111} and prism as {110}; this description yields axial ratios 0·6910 : 1 : 0·4145, and β 98° 58′. The Bravais lattice of gypsum is illustrated in Fig. 171 which shows also six different ways in which two out of the four shortest vectors in the (010) plane may be chosen for the parameters *a* and *c*. The repeat distance perpendicular to (010) is 15·18 Å (=b), and this coincides in direction with the diad axis. The cell containing the smallest vectors is *A*-centred and has *a* 5·68, *b* 15·18, *c* 6·29 Å, β 113° 50′, and this is the cell to which indexing in the present text refers. The morphological sketch and axial ratios, however, correspond to the *F*-cell.

In the structure of gypsum (Fig. 172) there are pairs of adjacent layers parallel to (010) which contain Ca ions and tetrahedral SO$_4$ ions. Between successive pairs of layers the water molecules are located in such a way that they are hydrogen bonded to oxygens of sulphate groups. Each Ca ion is coordinated by six oxygens of SO$_4$ groups and by two water molecules. The perfect (010) cleavage is consistent with the layered nature of the structure, and furthermore the direction of strongest linkages [001] corresponds to the fibre axis in the satin spar variety of gypsum.

CHEMISTRY

Gypsum shows very little variation in chemical composition, and the main point of interest in its chemistry concerns the products of its dehydration. Three principal phases occur in the system calcium sulphate–water:

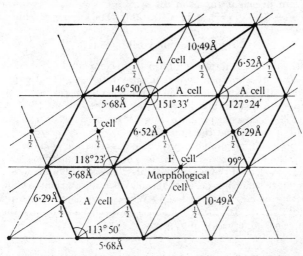

Fig. 171. *The Bravais lattice of gypsum projected on* (010), *showing the six ways of choosing unit cells defined by two out of the four shortest vectors.*

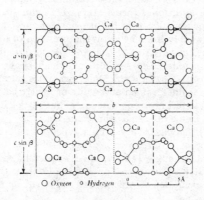

Fig. 172. *The structure of gypsum projected on to the planes perpendicular to the z and x axes of the I unit cell (after Atoji, M. & Rundle, R. E., 1958, Journ. Chem. Phys., vol. 29, p. 1306).*

$CaSO_4 \cdot 2H_2O$ (gypsum), $CaSO_4 \cdot \frac{1}{2}H_2O$ (hemi-hydrate or bassanite), and $CaSO_4$ (anhydrite). There is also another form of $CaSO_4$ which may be regarded as dehydrated hemihydrate. When heated in air, gypsum is converted slowly to the hemi-hydrate at about 70°C or below, and rapidly at 90°C and above; heating gypsum at higher temperatures produces anhydrite, and this change is monotropic.

Of the four principal phases in the system $CaSO_4$–H_2O, two, the hemi-hydrate and γ-$CaSO_4$, exist only metastably. Thus under equilibrium conditions the reaction

$$\text{gypsum} \rightleftharpoons \text{anhydrite} + \text{water}$$

occurs without the formation of intermediate compounds. The temperature of transition of gypsum to anhydrite in pure water is 42°C but gypsum may persist metastably above this temperature. The temperature of the transition is lowered considerably, however, by the presence of NaCl, and it is also reduced by increasing pressure; it is also affected by the presence of Na, Mg, and K sulphates and their hydrates.

D.t.a. curves of gypsum show a double endothermic peak between 100° and 200°C, the first representing the loss of $1\frac{1}{2}$ molecules of water and the second peak the loss of the remaining water. Plaster of Paris consists largely of hemi-hydrate which has been produced by heating gypsum to about 170°C over a period of one to three hours. When water is added to plaster of Paris, the dihydrate is re-formed, and the mass sets hard through the formation of interlocking crystals of gypsum.

OPTICAL AND PHYSICAL PROPERTIES

Gypsum often occurs as euhedral transparent crystals, in which form it is known as selenite. Crystals of selenite commonly adopt a tabular habit {010}, showing the additional forms {120} {$\bar{1}$11} and {011}; sometimes a lenticular appearance results from the presence of curved faces the formation of which is probably influenced by the presence of impurities such as NaCl. Another distinctive habit is that of translucent fibrous aggregates (fibres parallel to z axis), the surfaces of which show a pearly sheen; this variety is known as satin spar. Most gypsum occurs as massive rock gypsum; when this is fine-grained and white or lightly coloured it finds use as an ornamental stone known as alabaster, but it is often darkened by impurities of clays, iron oxides and other minerals.

The perfect {010} cleavage of crystalline gypsum results in platy cleavage fragments which, because of further cleavages {100} and {011}, often show a lozenge-shaped outline (angle 114°) with edges parallel to those of the two smallest a and c lattice parameters (Fig. 171). Contact twins on (100) are often found, the appearance of which gives rise to the names 'swallow tail' or 'arrow-head'.

Dispersion of 2V with temperature is large for gypsum, 2V decreasing with temperature; at constant temperature and varying wavelength, dispersion of 2V $(r > v)$ and inclined dispersion of the bisectrix are also strong.

DISTINGUISHING FEATURES

Gypsum is easily distinguished from anhydrite since the latter mineral has higher refringence and birefringence: in addition anhydrite has characteristic pinacoidal cleavages and a higher density.

PARAGENESIS

Gypsum is the most common of the sulphate minerals. Its main occurrences are as sedimentary deposits associated with limestones, shales, marls and clays, and in evaporite deposits. Sea water contains about $3\frac{1}{2}$ per cent by weight of dissolved materials, about 80 per cent of which is sodium chloride and about 4 per cent calcium sulphate. The usual sequence of deposition of salts from sea water has been shown experimentally to be: calcium carbonate – calcium sulphate – sodium chloride – sulphates and chlorides of magnesium–sodium bromide and potassium chloride. If all the salt of a 1000 ft column of water were precipitated it would make only 15 ft of salt deposits of which about 0·4 ft would be calcium sulphate, 11·6 ft would be halite and the remainder potassium and magnesium-bearing salts. In evaporites the calcium sulphate sometimes occurs as gypsum, sometimes as anhydrite, and very often both minerals occur together. It appears that in general anhydrite is a secondary mineral produced by the dehydration of gypsum, a reaction which involves a decrease in volume of the solid phase; sometimes halite fills the resultant voids and a halite–anhydrite assemblage results. The water released by the dehydration of gypsum may result in the local solution, redistribution and deposition of the soluble salts of the surrounding evaporites. In many areas gypsum has been dissolved in percolating waters (the solubility is increased by the presence of NaCl or $CaCO_3$), which in the dry season are drawn to the surface by capillary action, are evaporated, and leave gypsum deposited as crystals, sometimes in aggregates described as 'desert roses'. Large gypsum deposits are also found in saline lakes and salt pans.

Whereas anhydrite is usually secondary, gypsum can be either primary or secondary. Gypsification of anhydrite occurs frequently along contacts of evaporites with carbonate rocks, and it proceeds along anhydrite cleavages, the textures showing that the gypsum is secondary. Where large volumes of anhydrite have been altered to gypsum by hydration, masses of gypsum are found with relict nodules of anhydrite.

Gypsum is sometimes produced by the action of sulphuric acid solution on the calcium in the rocks through which it is moving. In clays and marls the acid solution may be produced by the weathering of sulphides, and in metalliferous veins by the oxidation of sulphides. Gypsum is also found in deposits of native sulphur and it is produced in volcanic regions by the action of sulphurous vapours on calcium-bearing minerals. Among the minerals which may be found in association with gypsum are halite, celestine, calcite, aragonite, dolomite, pyrite, sulphur and quartz.

REFERENCES

CONLEY, R. F. and BUNDY, W. M. (1958) 'Mechanism of gypsification', *Geochim. et Cosmochim. Acta*, vol. 15, p. 57.

MACDONALD, G. J. F. (1953) 'Anhydrite-gypsum equilibrium relations', *Amer. Journ. Sci.*, vol. 251, p. 884.

STEWART, F. H. (1963) 'Marine evaporites', *U.S. Geol. Surv., Prof. Paper* 440–Y.

470

Anhydrite

CaSO$_4$

ORTHORHOMBIC (+)

α 1·569–1·574
β 1·574–1·579
γ 1·609–1·618
δ ≃ 0·04
2V$_γ$ 42°–44°
α = y, β = x, γ = z; O.A.P. (100).
Dispersion: r < v. D 2·9–3·0. H 3–3½.
Cleavage: {010} perfect, {100} very good, {001} good.
Twinning: Simple or repeated {011}.
Colour: White or colourless when pure; often grey and more rarely bluish mauve, red or brown; colourless in thin section.

STRUCTURE

The unit cell of anhydrite (a 6·991, b 6·996, c 6·238 Å) has two edges approximately equal, but the structure (Fig. 173) is not pseudotetragonal. Sulphur atoms (which are at the centres of tetrahedra of oxygens) and calcium atoms lie on the lines of intersection of mirror planes (100) and (010).

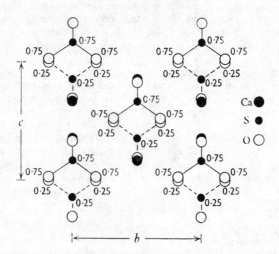

Fig. 173. *The structure of anhydrite (after Cheng, G. C. & Zussman, J.,* 1963, Acta Cryst., vol. 16, p. 767).

These two planes contain approximately evenly spaced Ca and SO₄ ions, whereas layering is not so well defined parallel to (001), thus the (001) cleavage is not as perfect as those on (100) and (010).

CHEMISTRY

Chemical analyses of anhydrite show only minor variations. Small amounts of Sr and Ba sometimes occur replacing Ca; other oxides recorded are probably present as impurities, and H_2O when present is mainly due to the presence of gypsum. Anhydrite is soluble in acids but in water its solubility is slight and decreases with increasing temperature. Crystals of anhydrite may be prepared by slowly cooling fusions of $CaSO_4$ with $CaCl_2$, $BaCl_2$, or $NaCl$, or of $CaCl_2$ with K_2SO_4, and also by heating gypsum with $NaCl$ or $CaCl_2$ solution in a closed tube. Fine-grained anhydrite may be prepared by precipitating $CaSO_4$ from a solution containing a high concentration of $MgCl_2$ or $CaCl_2$ at ordinary temperatures; gypsum is obtained at lower concentrations and at lower temperatures.

The alteration of anhydrite to gypsum by hydration is accompanied by an increase in volume and by mechanical deformation. Among the minerals which may be found as pseudomorphs after anhydrite are: quartz, siderite, calcite, dolomite, gypsum and marcasite.

OPTICAL AND PHYSICAL PROPERTIES

Anhydrite usually occurs in massive aggregates of varying grain size, sometimes as groups of parallel or radiating fibres. Crystals, when they occur, usually have a thick tabular habit on pinacoidal faces, and may be elongated parallel to x or z: the crystals show three pinacoidal cleavages of which {010} is the best. Perfect crystals of pure anhydrite are transparent but specimens are often white, or coloured red, grey or brown by impurities of iron oxides, etc. Some anhydrite is coloured blue or violet, and this colour disappears on heating and reappears on exposure to radium radiation: thus the colour is thought to be a natural radiation colour, the source of radiation being either external, or present as an impurity within the anhydrite.

DISTINGUISHING FEATURES

Anhydrite may be distinguished from barytes by its lower density, and in thin section by its pinacoidal cleavages. It is harder and more dense than gypsum and has higher relief and birefringence, and it is more dense than calcite.

PARAGENESIS

The principal occurrences of anhydrite are as a constituent of evaporites and as a product of hydrothermal alteration of limestone and dolomite rocks. In evaporite deposits, anhydrite or gypsum may occur, and sometimes both are found together. According to the results of experiments on the solubility of anhydrite and gypsum, anhydrite should be deposited directly by the evaporation of sea water above 42°C, or at a lower tempera-ture from a more saline solution: at lower temperatures and lower salinities gypsum should be deposited. Other experimental results, however, indicate that the primary precipitation of anhydrite from sea water is improbable, and that anhydrite is nearly always a secondary mineral produced by the dehydration of gypsum. Anhydrite also occurs in salt plugs and domes. In metalliferous veins it is sometimes produced through the oxidation of sulphides.

REFERENCE

STEWART, F. H. (1951) 'The petrology of the evaporites of the Eskdale no. 2 boring, east Yorkshire. Part II. The Middle Evaporite bed. Part III. The Upper Evaporite bed', *Min. Mag.*, vol. 29, pp. 445 and 557.

CARBONATES

The carbonates are a group of minerals in which the essential structural unit is the $(CO_3)^{-2}$ ion. Although there are approximately 60 known carbonate minerals many of them are comparatively rare, and some of the less common species are hydrated, contain hydroxyl or halogen ions, or are compounds with sulphate or phosphate radicals. The more common rock-forming carbonate minerals, and the properties of the pure end-members, are listed below:

Name	Formula	System	ϵ	ω		
			α	β	γ	$2V_a$
Calcite	$CaCO_3$	Trigonal	1·486	—	1·658	—
Magnesite	$MgCO_3$	,,	1·509	—	1·700	—
Rhodochrosite	$MnCO_3$	,,	1·597	—	1·816	—
Siderite	$FeCO_3$	,,	1·635	—	1·875	—
Dolomite	$CaMg(CO_3)_2$	,,	1·500	—	1·679	—
Aragonite	$CaCO_3$	Ortho-rhombic	1·530	1·680	1·685	18°
Strontianite	$SrCO_3$	,,	1·518	1·665	1·667	8°
Witherite	$BaCO_3$	,,	1·529	1·676	1·677	16°

Name	D	a(Å)	b(Å)	c(Å)	a_{rh}(Å)	α	Z
Calcite	2·72	4·990	—	17·061	6·37	46°05′	2
Magnesite	2·98	4·633	—	15·016	5·675	48°10′	2
Rhodochrosite	3·70	4·777	—	15·66	5·91	47°43′	2
Siderite	3·96	4·69	—	15·30	5·77	47°45′	2
Dolomite	2·86	4·807	—	16·01	6·015	47°07′	2
Aragonite	2·94	4·95	7·95	5·73	—	—	4
Strontianite	3·72	5·13	8·42	6·09	—	—	4
Witherite	4·30	5·26	8·84	6·56	—	—	4

The minerals of the carbonate group here considered include the above species together with ankerite, $Ca(Mg,Fe^{+2},Mn)(CO_3)_2$, which is related to dolomite, and huntite, $Mg_3Ca(CO_3)_4$, a mineral first described as late as 1953 but which is being increasingly recognized as an alteration product of dolomite- or magnesite-bearing rocks.

Calcium carbonate is polymorphous and exists in at least five modifications. The two polymorphs commonly found in nature are calcite and aragonite. In addition two synthetic forms known only at high pressures are calcite II and calcite III. Vaterite (μ-CaCO$_3$) is a metastable hexagonal form which crystallizes at ordinary temperatures and pressures. It is optically positive, as distinct from the negative optical character of most carbonates; refractive indices have been quoted as ω 1·550, ϵ 1·660; specific gravity 2·54. Vaterite has been recorded from the shells of certain young gasteropods and, in a geological environment, from a calc-silicate rock at Ballycraigy, Northern Ireland. Various calcium carbonate hydrates have been reported, many of which occur as natural minerals: their properties and synthetic preparation have been discussed by Brooks *et al* (1950).

Table 48. CARBONATE ANALYSES

	1.	2.	3.	4.	5.	6.	7.
FeO	0·00	0·56	0·77	58·81	0·22	12·06	—
MnO	tr.	0·12	60·87	2·86	0·00	0·77	—
MgO	0·04	46·62	tr.	0·20	21·12	12·85	0·03
CaO	55·92	0·43	0·51	0·08	31·27	29·23	55·96
CO$_2$	43·95	51·93	38·26	38·08	47·22	44·70	43·95
Total	99·91	99·66	100·41	100·03	99·97	100·23	100·07
ϵ	1·488	1·5145	1·5904	1·633	—	1·515	1·5296(α)
ω	1·661	1·7044	—	1·873	1·6801	1·710	1·6849(γ)
D	2·720	3·015	3·570	3·927	2·86	2·97	2·936

NUMBERS OF IONS ON THE BASIS OF 6(O)

	1.	2.	3.	4.	5.	6.	7.
Mg	0·002 ⎤	1·963 ⎤	— ⎤	0·011 ⎤	0·973 ⎤	0·626 ⎤	0·001 ⎤
Fe^{+2}	— ⎪ 2·00	0·013 ⎪ 1·99	0·025 ⎪ 2·01	1·892 ⎪ 2·00	0·006 ⎪ 2·02	0·330 ⎪ 2·00†	— ⎪ 2·00
Mn	— ⎪	0·003 ⎪	1·968 ⎪	0·093 ⎪	— ⎪	0·022 ⎪	— ⎪
Ca	1·997 ⎦	0·013 ⎦	0·021 ⎦	0·003 ⎦	1·036 ⎦	1·024 ⎦	1·999 ⎦
C	2·00	2·004	1·993	2·000	1·993	1·995	2·000

1. Calcite, Mariatrost, Austria (Schoklitsch, K., 1935, *Zeit. Krist.* vol. 90, p. 433).
2. Magnesite, Serra das Eguas, Bahia, Brazil (Fornaseri, M., 1941, *Rend. Soc. Min. Ital.*, vol. 1 p. 60).
3. Rhodochrosite, Ljubija district, Bosnia (Barić, L. & Tućan, F., 1925, *Ann. Géol. Pénins. Balkan. Beograd*, vol. 8, p. 129).
4. Siderite, Ivigtut, Greenland (Sundius, N., 1925, *Geol. För. Förh. Stockholm*, vol. 47, p. 269).
5. Dolomite, Haley, Ontario (Harker, R. I. & Tuttle, O. F., 1955, *Amer. Journ. Sci.*, vol. 253, p. 209; includes SiO$_2$ 0·12, H$_2$O$^-$ 0·02).
6. Ankerite, Oak Colliery, Oldham, Lancashire (Broadhurst, F. M. & Howie, R. A., 1958. *Geol. Mag.*, vol. 95, p. 397; includes SiO$_2$ 0·15, Al$_2$O$_3$ 0·28, Fe$_2$O$_3$ 0·10, Na$_2$O 0·06, K$_2$O 0·01, H$_2$O$^-$ 0·02).
7. Aragonite, Matsushiro, prov. of Iwami, Japan (Yamaguchi, K., 1927. *Journ. Geol. Soc. Japan*, vol. 34, p. 159; β 1·6804, 2V$_a$ 18° 15′; includes insol. 0·13).
† Includes Fe^{+3} 0·002.

A very full account of the properties of the calcium and magnesium carbonates is given by Graf and Lamar (1955) and by Graf (1960). Other carbonates of fairly common occurrence in hydrothermal veins or in association with ore deposits, and which are not further considered here, include:

	Formula	System	α	β	γ	2V	D	Colour
Cerussite	$PbCO_3$	Ortho-rhombic	1·803	2·074	2·076	$8\frac{1}{2}°(-)$	6·57	White
Malachite	$Cu_2(OH)_2CO_3$	Monoclinic	1·655	1·875	1·909	43°(−)	4·05	Green
Azurite	$Cu_3(OH)_2(CO_3)_2$	Monoclinic	1·730	1·758	1·838	68°(+)	3·80	Blue
Smithsonite	$ZnCO_3$	Trigonal	1·625(ε)	—	1·850(ω)	—	4·4	White

REFERENCES

BROOKS, R., CLARK, L. M. and THURSTON, E. F. (1950) 'Calcium carbonate and its hydrates', *Phil. Trans. Roy. Soc. London*, vol. 243, A, p. 145.

GRAF, D. L. (1960) 'Geochemistry of carbonate sediments and sedimentary carbonate rocks. Part I. Carbonate mineralogy—carbonate sediments', *Illinois Geol. Surv., Circ.*, 297.

———— and LAMAR, J. E. (1955) 'Properties of calcium and magnesium carbonates and their bearing on some uses of carbonate rocks', *Econ. Geol.*, 50th Anniv. vol., p. 639.

Calcite

CaCO$_3$

TRIGONAL $(-)$

$$\epsilon \quad 1\cdot486\dagger{-}(1\cdot550)$$
$$\omega \quad 1\cdot658{-}(1\cdot740)$$
$$\delta \quad 0\cdot172{-}(0\cdot190)$$

Dispersion: Very strong. D 2·715–(2·94). H 3.

Cleavage‡: {10Ī1} perfect.

Twinning: {01Ī2} lamellar, very common; {0001} common; {10Ī1} not common.

Colour: Colourless or white, but sometimes grey, yellow, or light shades of pink, green or blue; colourless in thin section.

Easily soluble with brisk effervescence in cold dilute HCl.

STRUCTURE

The structure of calcite can be described by analogy with that of halite: Na and Cl ions are replaced by Ca and $(CO_3)^{-2}$ ions respectively and the unit cell is distorted by compression along a triad axis to give a face-centred rhombohedral cell with a_{rh} 6·42 Å, α 101° 55'. The distortion of the cube is necessary to accommodate the large planar CO_3 groups which contain a carbon ion at the centre of an equilateral triangle of oxygens. This cell thus contains 4 $CaCO_3$ corresponding to the 4 NaCl in the cubic unit cell of halite; it is not, however, a true cell of the rhombohedral Bravais lattice since successive CO_3 triangles along the rhomb edge point in opposite directions. A true face-centred rhombohedral cell thus has a_{rh} 2 × 6·42 Å, α 101° 55' and contains 32 $CaCO_3$. The rhombohedron with α 101° 55' corresponds to the common cleavage rhomb of calcite which is usually indexed as {100} using Miller indices (Miller-Bravais {10Ī1}).

A smaller rhombohedral cell can be chosen to describe the lattice, however, with parameters a_{rh} 6·37, α 46° 05'; this is a primitive cell containing 2 $CaCO_3$ and if the faces of this cell are taken as {100} those of the cleavage rhomb become {211} (Miller-Bravais {10Ī4}). The relationship between the morphological (cleavage rhomb) pseudo-cell and the true unit cell is shown in Fig. 174, and data for the various cells are listed in Table 49. The $d_{10Ī4}$ spacing of calcite has been used as a means of defining the unit of X-ray wavelength.

† Value for pure calcite: higher values are due to the substitution of other ions for Ca.

‡ Indices for cleavage, twinning, etc., refer to the hexagonal cell with $a \simeq 20$ Å (see Table 49).

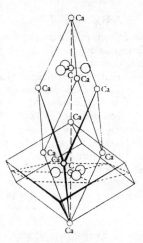

Fig. 174. *The structure of calcite. The elongated cell is the true rhombohedral unit cell (Z = 2): the cleavage rhombohedron cell corresponding to a face-centred rhombohedron is also shown (after Ewald, P. P. & Hermann, C.,* 1931, Strukturbericht 1913–1928).

Table 49. CALCITE UNIT CELLS

		X-ray smallest cell	Cleavage rhomb pseudo-cell	Cleavage rhomb true-cell
Rhombohedral axes	a_{rh}(Å)	6·37	6·42	12·85
	α_{rh}	46° 05′	101° 55′	101° 55′
	Z_{rh}	2	4	32
	Cleavage rhomb indices	{211}	{100}	{100}
Hexagonal axes	a_{hex}(Å)	≃ 5	≃ 10	≃ 20
	c_{hex}(Å)	≃ 17	≃ 8·5	≃ 17
	Z_{hex}	6	12	96
	Cleavage rhomb indices	{10$\bar{1}$4}	{10$\bar{1}$1}	{10$\bar{1}$1}

The percentage of calcite in a calcite–dolomite rock or in a calcite–aragonite rock can be determined by measuring the relative intensities of suitable X-ray powder diffraction lines in a series of mixtures of known proportions and applying these results to samples of unknown composition.

CHEMISTRY

Although many divalent cations may partially replace Ca in calcite, most calcite is relatively free from other ions and is fairly close in composition to pure $CaCO_3$ (e.g. Table 48, anal. 1).

Substitutions which commonly occur include that of Mg, and up to 9 mol. per cent Mg can be found in calcite associated with dolomite. Experimental work shows that at 500°C the solubility of $MgCO_3$ is about 5 mol. per cent, rising to about 27 mol. per cent at 900°C. The exsolution of dolomite in natural calcite is sometimes observed.

Manganese-bearing calcites are known with up to 42 mol. per cent $MnCO_3$, and experimental work indicates that calcite with up to 50 mol. per cent $MnCO_3$ can exist. The substitution of Fe^{+2} for some Ca is also fairly common, though iron-bearing calcites are perhaps less frequent than iron-bearing dolomites and members of the ankerite series. In natural samples up to 5 to 10 mol. per cent $FeCO_3$ has been reported.

Small amounts of Sr commonly substitute for Ca, though Sr is less abundant in calcites than in aragonites, the larger Sr ion being more acceptable in the aragonite structure. The recrystallization of aragonite to calcite probably only takes place when much of the Sr has been removed. Barium, cobalt and zinc may also occur partially replacing Ca.

The calcite–aragonite polymorphism is brought about by the fact that the radius of the calcium ion is very close to the limiting value for the transition from the rhombohedral carbonate structure type to that of the orthorhombic carbonates. Calcite is the low-pressure polymorph (see aragonite, p. 498 and Fig. 181); it can be transformed to aragonite by grinding at room temperature for a few hours. Experimental work shows that calcite melts incongruently to liquid and vapour at $1310°C \pm 10°C$ at 1000 bars pressure. In the presence of water vapour at 1000 bars, calcite begins to melt at 740°C. In the system $CaO-CO_2-H_2O$ at this pressure, univariant equilibria $CaO + calcite + Ca(OH)_2 + liquid$ and $calcite + Ca(OH)_2 + liquid + vapour$ occur at 683° and 675°C respectively (Fig. 175): the development of liquid at moderate temperatures and pressures has mportant petrological implications.

The solubility of calcite in water increases with increasing CO_2 pressure and decreasing temperature. The precipitation of $CaCO_3$ from $CaCl_2$ and Na_2CO_3 in solution produces calcite at below 35°C, but mixtures of calcite and aragonite, and also vaterite (μ-$CaCO_3$), are precipitated at higher temperatures.

The dissociation temperature of calcite at 1 atmosphere is 894·4°C; at 100 and 500 lb/in² CO_2 pressure it is 985° and 1100°C respectively.

The alteration of calcite is accomplished mainly by solution and replacement, due to its ease of solubility in slightly acid waters.

OPTICAL AND PHYSICAL PROPERTIES

Calcite is uniaxial and optically negative with extreme birefringence. The substitution of other ions for Ca raises the refractive indices: a chart correlating ω with composition for the common rhombohedral carbonates is given in Fig. 176. The strong birefringence ($\omega - \epsilon = 0 \cdot 172$) is ascribed to the particular configuration of the CO_3 groups in the crystal structure. The three oxygen atoms lying in a plane and surrounding a carbon atom are more strongly polarized by an electric field parallel to the plane than by a field perpendicular to it: thus light travels more slowly, i.e. the refractive index is greater, when the electric vector is perpendicular to the z axis.

Although most calcite is colourless or white, natural varieties in yellow, pale blue, violet, red or green are known. The entry of appreciable manganese into the structure usually introduces a pale pink to rose-red colour.

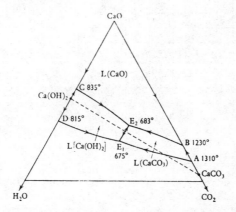

Fig. 175. *Enlarged and distorted view of the liquidus field boundaries in the system* CaO–CO_2–H_2O *at 1000 bars.* $L(CaO)$, $L(CaCO_3)$ *and* $L[Ca(OH)_2]$ *are liquidus surfaces with* CaO, $CaCO_3$ *and* $Ca(OH)_2$ *respectively as primary crystalline phases (after Wyllie, P. J. & Tuttle, O. F., 1960, Journ. Petr., vol. 1, p. 1).*

Many specimens of calcite show luminescence or thermoluminescence, and in ultra-violet radiation many calcites show a weak to strong fluorescence at various wavelengths. These phenomena differ for specimens from different localities and have been ascribed to various trace elements: the danger of indiscriminate use of fluorescence in mineral identification must be emphasized.

The specific gravity of calcite, like the refractive indices, is raised by any of the usual substituent ions entering the structure. The hardness is 3 on Mohs' scale, but varies from $2\frac{1}{2}$ on {0001} to about $3\frac{1}{4}$ on a surface parallel to the z axis.

The main lamellar twinning in calcite is that on {01$\bar{1}$2}, which gives rise to striae parallel to the edges and to the long diagonal of the cleavage rhomb. This type of twinning can be produced artificially by subjecting calcite to deformation, when in addition to twin gliding on {01$\bar{1}$2}, there is often translation gliding on $\{10\bar{1}1\}$; translation gliding on $\{02\bar{2}1\}$ is also known. The mechanical twinning of calcite can be demonstrated by pressing a knife-blade into one edge of a cleavage rhombohedron: a wedge-shaped opening of constant angle develops and part of the rhombohedron is displaced, the contact or twin plane being $\{01\bar{1}2\}$.

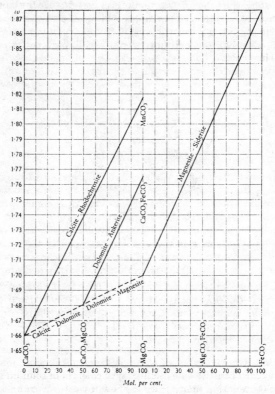

Fig. 176. *Variation of ω with composition in the rhombohedral carbonates (after Kennedy, G. C., 1947, Amer. Min., vol. 32, p. 561).*

DISTINGUISHING FEATURES

Calcite may be recognized as a rhombohedral carbonate by its effervescence with dilute HCl, its perfect $\{10\bar{1}1\}$ cleavage, and its extremely high birefringence. It may be distinguished from the other rhombohedral carbonates by various chemical and physical properties. The refractive indices of calcite are lower than for the other carbonates, with the ϵ index considerably beneath that for Canada Balsam. The glide twins, which may be particularly evident in calcite of metamorphic rocks, are on $\{10\bar{1}2\}$ rather

than on {02$\bar{2}$1} as in dolomite, thus in a cleavage rhombohedron of calcite
the twin lamellae lie parallel to the long diagonal of the rhomb (but not to
the short diagonal as in dolomite), and other sets are parallel to the rhombohedral edges. The specific gravity of calcite is considerably less than that
for dolomite and the other rhombohedral carbonates.

Staining techniques, as applied to hand specimens or thin sections, may
be of considerable use in the distinction of calcite from other carbonates. In
general, organic dyes stain calcite in acid solutions, and dolomite and magnesite in basic solutions: Friedman (1959) recommends the use of two different stains, alizarin red S and Feigl's solution, for differentiating calcite,
high-magnesium calcite, dolomite, aragonite, gypsum and anhydrite. Other
stains specific for calcite are Harris' haematoxylin or copper nitrate, and a
newer method for hand specimens or thin sections makes use of the strong
fluorescence acquired by calcite when attacked by a saturated solution of
uranyl acetate followed by treatment with a 10 per cent solution of ammo
nium acetate: dolomite is unaffected (see also pp. 491–2).

PARAGENESIS

Calcite is one of the most ubiquitous minerals, and in addition to being
an important rock-forming mineral in sedimentary environments, it also
occurs in metamorphic and igneous rocks and is a common mineral of
hydrothermal and secondary mineralization.

In sedimentary rocks calcite is the principal constituent of most limestones. It occurs both as a primary precipitate and in the form of fossil
shells. Calcite is the stable form of $CaCO_3$ and although approximately
equal numbers of organisms make their shells of calcite and aragonite (or,
as for some of the mollusca, of both), the aragonite eventually undergoes
recrystallization to calcite. The Chalk of Western Europe although earlier
considered to be chemically precipitated $CaCO_3$ has now been shown to
consist of up to 80 per cent organic debris, though on a much finer scale than
in other fossiliferous limestones.

Precipitated calcite in sediments occurs in the calcrete of surface limestones, and in travertine deposits where, in limestone regions, underground
streams may carry considerable quantities of calcium in solution as calcium
bicarbonate. On reaching the open air the rise in temperature brings about a
release of CO_2, and the growth of mosses and reeds at the exit may extract
further CO_2 from the solution, leading to the precipitation of $CaCO_3$ as
calcite. The precipitation of $CaCO_3$ in fresh-water lake marls and in marine
conditions is generally in the form of aragonite, giving rise to aragonite
muds or to aragonite ooliths: in time, however, many of these recrystallize
giving rise to calcite mudstones and to an oolitic rock composed of calcite
ooliths. Calcite also occurs in sedimentary rocks as a secondary deposit
acting as a cementing medium, as in some oolites and other calcareous
rocks, and also in sandstones. A particular form of the latter may occur in
which large crystals of calcite contain many thousands of sand grains, a
famous example being the sand-calcite of the Fontainebleau district in the
Paris basin: in other cases the calcite may be in crystals of up to 1 cm across,

which cause the rock to break preferentially along the calcite cleavage planes giving rise to a phenomenon known as lustre mottling, as each crystal unit gives a more or less brilliant reflection when viewed from an appropriate angle. Veins of fibrous calcite, sometimes known as 'beef', occur in some shales, and have the fibres parallel to z: the veins may show cone-in-cone structure due to the sensitivity of the rhombohedral cleavage of the fibres to shear.

When sedimentary calcite in limestone undergoes metamorphism a relatively small amount of overburden is sufficient to prevent its breakdown and the escape of CO_2, and in the normal course of events the calcite merely recrystallizes to form a marble. Calcite is thus a relatively common mineral in calcareous sediments which have been thermally or regionally metamorphosed. When the original sediments contained other material in addition

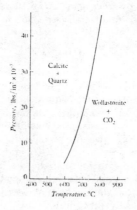

Fig. 177. *The experimentally determined univariant P_{CO_2}–T curve for the reaction $CaCO_3 + SiO_2 \rightleftharpoons CaSiO_3 + CO_2$ (after Harker, R. I. & Tuttle, O. F., 1956, Amer. Journ. Sci., vol. 254, p. 239).*

to $CaCO_3$, or when metasomatic introduction of further elements occurs during the metamorphism, the calcite may react and give rise to various mineral assemblages. Where, in addition to $CaCO_3$, SiO_2 is present, the reaction $CaCO_3 + SiO_2 \rightleftharpoons CaSiO_3 + CO_2$ may take place, with the formation of wollastonite. The disappearance of the calcite–quartz assemblage to give rise to wollastonite is thus of considerable interest as a geological thermometer (Fig. 177). In certain circumstances the CO_2 pressure may be effectively reduced, however, either by a dilution by some other volatile component or by the escape of CO_2 through fissures, and the calcite may then react at somewhat lower temperatures: thus it is probable that a decarbonation reaction will proceed more readily in an impure wet limestone than in a pure dry one. In both thermally and regionally metamorphosed impure limestones calcite may be found in association with such other calc-silicate minerals as diopside, tremolite, vesuvianite, or grossular garnet, and also with forsterite.

Calcite frequently crystallizes in the later stages of hydrothermal deposition, occurring in veins and cavities. Well-formed crystals may be found in amygdales in basic igneous rocks, where it is often associated with zeolites or with quartz. One of the best known localities in Iceland for the Iceland spar variety of calcite is at Helgustadir where crystals of optical quality occur associated with quartz, heulandite and stilbite. In many hydrothermal veins calcite is associated with fluorite, barytes, dolomite, quartz or sulphides.

Calcite also occurs in certain alkaline igneous rocks, notably the carbonatites and some nepheline-syenites. It has been suggested that the frequent association of carbonates with alkaline rocks is due to the syntexis of a magma with carbonate rock. The experimental work on the system $CaO-CO_2-H_2O$, however, offers supporting evidence in favour of a true magmatic origin for carbonatites. The low-temperature liquids in this system can be regarded as simplified carbonatite magmas in which CaO represents the basic oxides with CO_2 and H_2O representing the volatile constituents, and in this system it has been shown that the high melting temperature of calcite is lowered markedly by the addition of CO_2 and H_2O under pressure.

REFERENCES

FRIEDMAN, G. M. (1959) 'Identification of carbonate minerals by staining methods', *Journ. Sed. Petr.*, vol. 29, p. 87.

GOLDSMITH, J. R. (1959) 'Some aspects of the geochemistry of carbonates' in *Researches in geochemistry*. Wiley, New York.

GRAF, D. L. (1960) 'Geochemistry of carbonate sediments and sedimentary carbonate rocks. Part I. Carbonate mineralogy—carbonate sediments', *Illinois Geol. Surv.*, *Circ.* 297.

—— and LAMAR, J. E. (1955) 'Properties of calcium and magnesium carbonates and their bearing on some uses of carbonate rocks', *Econ. Geol.*, 50th Anniv. vol., p. 639.

TURNER, F. J., GRIGGS, D. T. and HEARD, H. (1954) 'Experimental deformation of calcite crystals', *Bull. Geol. Soc. Amer.*, vol. 65, p. 883.

WYLLIE, P. J. and TUTTLE, O. F. (1960) 'The system $CaO-CO_2-H_2O$ and the origin of carbonatites', *Journ. Petr.*, vol. 1, p. 1.

Magnesite

$MgCO_3$

TRIGONAL $(-)$

$$\epsilon \quad 1.509\dagger-(1.563)$$
$$\omega \quad 1.700-(1.782)$$
$$\delta \quad 0.190-(0.218)$$

Dispersion: Very strong. D $2.98-(3.48)$. H $3\frac{1}{2}-4\frac{1}{2}$.

Cleavage‡: $\{10\bar{1}1\}$ perfect.

Twinning: Translation gliding may occur on $\{0001\}$ in the direction $[10\bar{1}1]$.

Colour: White or colourless, but the iron-bearing varieties may be yellow or brown; colourless in thin section.

Pleochroism: Rare; in coloured varieties the absorption may be $\epsilon < \omega$.

Slightly soluble in cold dilute HCl, soluble with effervescence in warm HCl.

The structure of magnesite is similar to that of calcite but with a slightly smaller cell due to the smaller size of the magnesium ion. Pure synthetic magnesite has a 4.6330, c 15.016 Å; a_{rh} 5.6752 Å, α $48°$ $10.9'$, $Z_{rh} = 2$.

Although pure end-member magnesite has the composition $MgCO_3$, there appears to be a complete solid solution series between magnesite and siderite, $FeCO_3$. The ferroan variety, breunnerite, extends from 5 to 50 mol. per cent $FeCO_3$. The substitutions of Mn for Mg and of Ca for Mg are both limited in amount. Experimental work shows evidence of slight solid solution of calcite in magnesite (Fig. 178, p. 490). Magnesite is an important raw material for basic refractories: after heating and sintering, the product known as 'dead-burned magnesite' is produced which has the composition MgO (periclase).

The refractive indices and birefringence of magnesite increase linearly with the substitution of Fe^{+2} or Mn for Mg (see Fig. 176, p. 480).

Magnesite resembles dolomite in being only slightly soluble in cold dilute HCl, but it dissolves with effervescence in warm acid. It differs from dolomite and calcite in usually showing no twin lamellae, and in having higher refractive indices.

The most common occurrence of magnesite is as an alteration product of various magnesium-rich igneous and metamorphic rocks. Peridotites commonly become transformed to serpentinites and if such rocks undergo low or medium grade metamorphism under conditions in which CO_2 is available magnesite may be formed. The presence of monomineralic deposits of magnesite associated with talc and chlorite in Shetland has been ascribed to localized shearing movements, assisted by the penetration of hydrothermal fluids. It also occurs in evaporite deposits and as the result of Mg metasomatism of pre-existing sediments.

† Pure magnesite: higher values are due to the substitution of Mg by other ions.

‡ Indices for cleavage, twinning, etc., refer to the hexagonal cell with $a \simeq 19$ Å (see Table 49).

Rhodochrosite $MnCO_3$

TRIGONAL (−)

$$\epsilon \quad (1\cdot540)-1\cdot597\dagger-(1\cdot617)$$
$$\omega \quad (1\cdot750)-1\cdot816-(1\cdot850)$$
$$\delta \quad (0\cdot19)-0\cdot219-(0\cdot23)$$

Dispersion: Strong. D $(3\cdot20)-3\cdot70-(4\cdot05)$. H $3\frac{1}{2}$–4.
Cleavage‡: $\{10\bar{1}1\}$ perfect.
Twinning: Rare lamellar twins on $\{01\bar{1}2\}$.
Colour: Rose-pink, pink, red, brown or brownish yellow; colourless or pale pink in thin section.
Pleochroism: Red varieties may show pleochroism with absorption $\omega > \epsilon$.

Dissolves with effervescence in warm dilute acids. On exposure to air it may develop a brown or black surface alteration product.

STRUCTURE

The structure of rhodochrosite is similar to that of calcite, with smaller cell parameters due to the lesser size of the manganese ion compared with that of calcium. Pure synthetic rhodochrosite has a 4·777, c 15·66 Å, c/a 3·28; a_{rh} 5·91 Å, α 47° 43′, $Z_{rh} = 2$.

CHEMISTRY

Both Ca and Fe^{+2} may substitute for Mn and most analyses of rhodochrosite show small amounts of these ions (e.g. Table 48, p. 474, anal. 3). There appears to be a complete solid solution series between rhodochrosite and siderite, and a variety of rhodochrosite containing up to 20 per cent $FeCO_3$ has been called ponite, the term manganosiderite being used when $Mn \simeq Fe$. The occurrence of natural kutnohorite, $CaMn(CO_3)_2$, and the experimentally determined subsolidus relations for the $CaCO_3$–$MnCO_3$ system indicate that in the Mn–Ca isomorphous series natural material probably does not exist between 50 and approximately 80 mol. per cent $MnCO_3$. Small amounts of Mg may also substitute for Mn and a ferroan zincian rhodochrosite with 24 mol. per cent $ZnCO_3$ has been called capillitite.

Rhodochrosite breaks down at about 610° to 635°C and the resultant MnO becomes oxidized to hausmannite (Mn_3O_4) at around 700°C. The natural alteration of rhodochrosite involves the production of a superficial

---

† Value for pure rhodochrosite: other values are due to the substitution of Mn by other ions.

‡ Indices for cleavage, twinning, etc., refer to the hexagonal cell with $a \simeq 19$ Å (see Table 49).

brown or black layer of complex manganese oxides: it may eventually alter to manganite ($MnO \cdot OH$) or to pyrolusite (MnO_2).

OPTICAL AND PHYSICAL PROPERTIES

The refractive indices for pure end-member $MnCO_3$ are ϵ 1·597, ω 1·816. These values vary linearly towards the other carbonate end-members when Mn is substituted by Ca, Fe^{+2} or Mg (see Fig. 176, p. 480), Ca reducing the refractive indices considerably, Fe^{+2} increasing them: Mg reduces the values to a slight extent. The birefringence and specific gravity vary similarly. The colour is variable, ranging from almost colourless to yellow, pink or red; the presence of appreciable Fe^{+2} replacing Mn has the effect of increasing the depth of the yellowish tint. Manganese oxide alteration products may cause the mineral to become brown along the cleavages or to develop a superficial brown or black colour.

DISTINGUISHING FEATURES

Rhodochrosite differs from the other trigonal carbonates in its typical pink colour (though this may not always be present and some manganoan calcites show a pinkish tinge), and its common alteration to brown or black oxides of manganese is characteristic. It may be distinguished from minerals of other groups by its well developed rhombohedral cleavage and effervescence with warm HCl. The presence of manganese may be confirmed by addition of a small amount of potassium periodate to a solution of the material in sulphuric or nitric acids when, after boiling, the permanganate colour will be obtained.

PARAGENESIS

Rhodocrosite is found in high temperature metasomatic deposits, associated with other manganese minerals such as rhodonite, spessartine, braunite, tephroite, etc. It also occurs as a primary mineral in hydrothermal veins as at Butte, Montana, one of the few localities where rhodochrosite is of economic importance. It has also been found in pegmatites, and may occur in association with the other manganese minerals in metamorphosed sediments as in the Lower Cambrian manganese ore of Wales.

REFERENCES

GOLDSMITH, J. R. (1959) 'Some aspects of the geochemistry of carbonates', *Researches in Geochemistry*. Wiley, New York.

WAYLAND, R. G. (1942) 'Composition, specific gravity and refractive indices of rhodochrosite; rhodochrosite from Butte, Montana', *Amer. Min.*, vol. 27, p. 614.

Siderite

$FeCO_3$

TRIGONAL $(-)$

ϵ $(1\cdot575)$–$1\cdot635$†
ω $(1\cdot782)$–$1\cdot875$
δ $(0\cdot207)$–$0\cdot242$

Dispersion: Strong. D $(3\cdot50)$–$3\cdot96$. H 4–$4\frac{1}{2}$.
Cleavage‡: $\{10\bar{1}1\}$ perfect.
Twinning: Occasional lamellar twinning on $\{01\bar{1}2\}$, rare twins on $\{0001\}$.
Colour: Yellowish brown, brown or dark brown; colourless to yellowish brown in thin section.

Slowly soluble in cold dilute HCl: dissolves with effervescence in hot acid. On heating, CO_2 is driven off leaving an iron oxide.

The name siderite has also been applied to meteoritic irons: for this reason some authorities prefer the name chalybite. The term sphaerosiderite is used for the spherulites of siderite sometimes found in clay ironstones.

STRUCTURE

The structure of siderite is similar to that of calcite, but with smaller cell parameters due to the smaller ionic radius of Fe^{+2} as compared with Ca. The unit cell has a $4\cdot69$–$4\cdot73$, c $15\cdot37$–$15\cdot46$ Å, c/a $3\cdot27$; a_{rh} $5\cdot77$–$5\cdot84$ Å, α $47°$ $45'$, $Z_{rh} = 2$.

CHEMISTRY

Substitution of Fe^{+2} by other metallic ions is common in siderite and the mineral is rarely found as pure $FeCO_3$. Both Mn and Mg commonly substitute for Fe^{+2} (e.g. Table 48, p. 474, anal. 4), and there is complete solid solution between siderite and rhodochrosite and between siderite and magnesite. The manganese-rich variety has been called oligonite or oligon spar; magnesian siderite is sometimes known as sideroplesite (5 to 30 mol. per cent $MgCO_3$) or pistomesite (30 to 50 mol. per cent $MgCO_3$). The substitution of Ca for Fe^{+2} appears to be limited to 10 to 15 per cent $CaCO_3$, probably due to the appreciable difference in size of these ions.

Siderite may be produced artificially by heating $(NH_4)_2CO_3$ with $FeCl_2$. It decomposes at about 580°C and the resultant FeO becomes oxidized at about 600°C.

† Value for pure siderite: lower values are due to the substitution of Fe by other ions.

‡ Indices for cleavage, twinning, etc., refer to the hexagonal cell with $a \simeq 19$ Å (see Table 49).

The commonest alteration product of siderite is a hydrous ferric oxide, generally goethite, often known loosely as limonite. It may also alter to haematite and magnetite.

OPTICAL AND PHYSICAL PROPERTIES

For the pure end-member, $FeCO_3$, the extrapolated refractive indices are ϵ 1·635, ω 1·875, with D 3·96. With the substitution of Mn for Fe^{+2} the refractive indices, birefringence, and specific gravity are reduced, and the substitution of Mg for Fe^{+2} reduces the values of these properties to an even greater extent (Fig. 176, p. 480).

DISTINGUISHING FEATURES

Within the group of trigonal carbonates, siderite differs from calcite in its relative insolubility in cold dilute HCl, and from magnesite in its fairly common lamellar twinning. Its refractive indices are always greater than that of Canada Balsam while for calcite, dolomite and magnesite $\epsilon < 1·54$. Its specific gravity is considerably higher than for any other common rhombohedral carbonate, though smithsonite ($ZnCO_3$) has D 4·0–4·4: on heating, siderite forms a black iron oxide which may be magnetic. It may be distinguished from minerals of other groups by its well developed rhombohedral cleavage and high birefringence.

PARAGENESIS

Siderite most commonly occurs in bedded sedimentary rocks, where it is the chief iron-bearing mineral in clay ironstones. In the oolitic Jurassic ironstones of the English Midlands it is one of the principal ore minerals, together with chamosite and hydrated iron oxides. The origin of these deposits is not entirely certain but it is generally assumed that the iron was derived from continental sources by the normal processes of weathering, being transported as the bicarbonate and precipitated when CO_2 was not present in sufficient amount to maintain all the iron as the soluble bicarbonate. Much siderite results from carbonation of chamosite, and it may also be formed by the penecontemporaneous replacement of calcite by $FeCO_3$.

Siderite also occurs as a hydrothermal mineral in metallic veins, where it may often be a manganoan variety: the iron-rich carbonates of the Coeur d'Alene district of Idaho are associated with Pb, Ag and Zn sulphide ore bodies. Its occurrence in the Ivigtut cryolite deposit is well known (anal. 4), where it is considered to be of pegmatitic-pneumatolytic origin. Siderite may also be found in metamorphosed iron carbonate sediments approaching eulysites in composition.

REFERENCE

SMYTHE, J. A. and DUNHAM, K. C. (1947) 'Ankerites and chalybites from the northern Pennine orefield and the north-east coalfield', *Min. Mag.*, vol. 28, p. 53.

Dolomite

$CaMg(CO_3)_2$

TRIGONAL $(-)$

ϵ 1·500†–(1·520)
ω 1·679–(1·703)
δ 0·179–(0·185)

Dispersion: Strong. D 2·86–(2·93). H $3\frac{1}{2}$–4.

Cleavage‡: {$10\bar{1}1$} perfect.

Twinning: Common on {0001}, {$10\bar{1}0$}, {$11\bar{2}0$}; rare on {$10\bar{1}1$}. Glide twinning {$02\bar{2}1$}.

Colour: Colourless or white, often tinged with yellow or brown; colourless in thin section.

Poorly soluble in cold dilute HCl, unless freshly powdered. Rhombohedral faces are often curved.

STRUCTURE

The unit cell has a 4·807, c 16·01 Å; c/a 3·330; a_{rh} 6·015 Å, α 47° 07′, $Z_{rh} = 2$. The structure of dolomite resembles that of calcite but has a slightly lower symmetry. The diads in calcite which intersect in the carbon atom and on which the oxygens lie are not present in dolomite, and neither are the glide planes {$11\bar{2}0$}; the symmetry of dolomite thus consists of only a triad axis and a centre of symmetry. It is best considered as combining one layer of $CaCO_3$ from calcite and one layer of $MgCO_3$ from magnesite. The replacement of some Mg by Fe^{+2} has the effect of increasing the size of the unit cell.

CHEMISTRY

Although the composition is normally fairly close to pure $CaMg(CO_3)_2$, many dolomites contain small amounts of Fe^{+2} replacing Mg, giving the mineral a brownish tinge in hand specimen: among the purest dolomites are that of Table 48, anal. 5 (p. 474), and the water-clear dolomite from Gabbs, Nevada. There is a continuous replacement of Mg by Fe^{+2}, through ankerite towards $CaFe(CO_3)_2$: the term dolomite is here restricted to material with Mg:Fe > 4. Mn also may replace Mg and although dolomite with more than about 3 per cent MnO is rare a continuous series to kutnohorite, $CaMn(CO_3)_2$, may exist. Zn- and Pb-bearing dolomites are also known. There is also some evidence for the existence of natural dolomite with up to 5 mol. per cent excess structural $CaCO_3$.

†Value for pure dolomite.

‡ Indices for cleavage, twinning, etc., refer to the hexagonal cell with $a \simeq 19$ Å (see Table 49, p. 477).

Artificial dolomite has never been directly precipitated in the laboratory from solutions at ordinary temperatures and pressures. Its field of stability for moderate temperatures and high CO_2 pressures has been determined (Fig. 178): this confirms the small deviation from the ideal 1:1 Ca:Mg ratio of dolomite, in the direction of excess Ca, for material in equilibrium with magnesian calcite at high temperature. In experimental runs at low temperatures rather calcium-rich dolomite-like materials or protodolomites, are produced, and it may be that the necessity for obtaining an ordered arrangement of Ca and Mg at relatively rapid rates of crystallization is responsible for the difficulty of producing dolomite at ordinary temperatures. Ions other than Ca, Mg and CO_3 may be important in the precipitation of dolomite; for example, synthetic dolomite can be precipitated from a solution of $MgCl_2$, $CaCl_2$ and urea at slightly elevated pressures

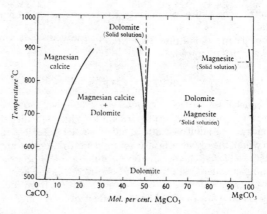

Fig. 178. *The $CaCO_3$–$MgCO_3$ system at CO_2 pressures sufficient to prevent decomposition of the carbonates (after Goldsmith, J. R., 1959, in* Researches in Geochemistry, *John Wiley, New York*).

(above 2 or 3 atmospheres) and at 220°C, but the presence of 6 to 7 per cent NaCl in the solution extends the temperature range over which dolomite can be precipitated down to as low as 150°C. The presence of sulphates has also been suggested as an essential condition for the low temperature precipitation of dolomitic carbonates.

The thermal dissociation of dolomite takes place in two steps, firstly $CaMg(CO_3)_2 \rightarrow CaCO_3 + MgO + CO_2$, at around 800° C, followed by the breakdown of the calcite component, $CaCO_3 \rightarrow CaO + CO_2$, at just over 900°C. Commercially, dolomite is of considerable importance as a refractory, for which purpose it is calcined at about 1500°C resulting in a sintered mixture of MgO (periclase) and CaO. It is also used in the extraction of magnesia from sea water.

OPTICAL AND PHYSICAL PROPERTIES

In transmitted light pure dolomite is colourless with ϵ 1·500, ω 1·679: the substitution of Fe^{+2} for Mg, however, increases the refractive indices (see Fig. 176, p. 480) and also the birefringence. The substitution of Mn for Mg has a similar though lesser effect. Glide twinning occurs on $\{02\bar{2}1\}$ giving lamellar twins. The experimental deformation of dolomite rock has shown that after being subjected to 3000 atmospheres pressure at 380°C a cylinder of dolomite was shortened by 9·4 per cent and had twin gliding on $\{02\bar{2}1\}$ and translation gliding on $\{0001\}$.

Dolomite when pure is colourless or pearly white but the small amount of Fe^{+2} which often substitutes for Mg commonly gives it a yellow or brown colour. The more iron-rich dolomites often weather to a darker brown. The presence of appreciable Mn gives rise to a rose-pink colour.

DISTINGUISHING FEATURES

Dolomite may be distinguished as a rhombohedral carbonate by its extremely high birefringence in conjunction with its perfect $\{10\bar{1}1\}$ cleavage. It often shows a rhombohedral form, the rhombohedral faces commonly being slightly curved. The distinction of dolomite from the other rhombohedral carbonates may be made by various physical and chemical tests. Dolomite is considerably denser than calcite (D 2·86 compared with 2·72), and has higher refractive indices. Glide twinning occurs on $\{02\bar{2}1\}$ rather than on $\{01\bar{1}2\}$ as in calcite, thus in a cleavage rhombohedron of dolomite the glide twin lamellae lie parallel to the short diagonal of the rhomb as well as parallel to the long diagonal as in calcite (in which other sets of twin lamellae lie parallel also to the rhombohedral edge). Twinned grains may be distinguished from calcite by their extinction angle measured between the fast direction ϵ' and the trace of the twin lamellae. Suitable sections cut the twin lamellae at high angles, showing them sharply defined; these sections are inclined at low angles to the optic axis, and show a pronounced change in relief on rotation in plane polarized light. The angle between ϵ' and the trace of the twin lamellae is greater than 55° in calcite and usually between 20° and 40° in dolomite. Also, when one grain shows two sharply defined sets of twin lamellae, ϵ' (the direction of lower refractive index) lies in the acute angle for dolomite, while for calcite it lies in the obtuse angle of intersection.

Dolomite, unlike calcite, is only slowly soluble in cold dilute acids, and does not effervesce: freshly powdered dolomite will, however, react, and dissolves readily with effervescence in warm acids. Treatment with copper nitrate solution and fixing with ammonia gives a deep blue colour on calcite but not on dolomite. When carbonate chips are boiled with copper nitrate alone, aragonite or calcite develops a pale (Cambridge) blue colour after boiling for up to five minutes: dolomite is unaffected in this period. With a 0·1 per cent solution of sodium alizarinsulphonate in $N/15$ HCl calcite forms a transparent reddish violet lake while dolomite is unaffected. A test which may be useful for uncovered thin sections as well as on grains, as no heating is involved, is due to Lemberg: if a few grains or the thin section are immersed for 10 minutes in cold Lemberg's solution ($AlCl_3$ and logwood dye) and then washed, calcite will be found to have reacted and become coated with gelatinous aluminium hydroxide which takes up the red dye. A direct test for Mg may be made by covering the section except for the sample grain, adding a drop of dilute H_2SO_4 and warming slightly; after effervescence has ceased moisten with $(NH_4)_2CO_3$ solution, place a drop of microcosmic salt solution near by, warm the slide and gently unite the two drops: orthorhombic crystals of magnesium ammonium phosphate indicate the presence of Mg. Dolomite may be distinguished from magnesite by heating to about 550°C for one hour, when magnesite changes to periclase which can be readily distinguished microscopically from the unaltered dolomite.

PARAGENESIS

Dolomite typically is a mineral of sedimentary environments, though there are important occurrences in metamorphic and hydrothermal metasomatic deposits. A few sedimentary deposits are known to have contained dolomite initially, such dolomite being termed primary. Secondary dolomite is formed where the primary aragonite and calcite of limestones have reacted with magnesium compounds to form dolomite. Primary dolomite may thus include dolomite associated with evaporite deposits, as in the Permian evaporites of north-east England. A thin bed of nearly pure unconsolidated dolomite occurs about a foot below the surface of the Great Salt Lake Desert, west of Knolls, Utah, and is believed to have been precipitated from a saline lake left isolated from Great Salt Lake. Dolomite derived from pre-existing dolomitic rocks and later deposited as a clastic sediment may also be considered primary in this sense.

Secondary dolomite formed from limestone by metasomatic alteration can be divided into two classes. One occurs over relatively wide areas at one horizon and was formed very soon after deposition of the limestone, the dolomitization having probably occurred while the sediment was in an unconsolidated condition on the sea floor, this being referred to as penecontemporaneous dolomitization. In the other type of occurrence the dolomite formed much later than the lithification of the limestone, the magnesian solutions having entered through faults and joints in the rock; this is known as subsequent dolomitization. Secondary dolomitization is a very selective process, sometimes replacing only the matrix and sometimes only shell fragments, depending partly on whether recrystallization has taken place and whether the $CaCO_3$ is present as calcite or aragonite. The magnesium for dolomitization must have been derived from sea water but the mechanism involved is not clear: the necessity for obtaining an ordered arrangement of Ca and Mg in the structure of dolomite may imply that at normal temperatures the time factor may be of considerable importance. The present-day formation of dolomitic sediments in a number of saline lakes and in a shallow inlet of the sea has been ascribed to elevated pH caused by plant growth in shallow saline water. The thermal dissociation of dolomite, in which the $MgCO_3$ component breaks down first, has been suggested as a possible source of hydrothermal solutions rich in Mg and CO_2 which may invade the country rock and under certain conditions give rise to the dolomitization of limestone. It is possible that the formation of primary and secondary dolomites are part of a cycle, beginning with a dry climate and relatively deep normal sea water in which limestones are forming, followed by shallowing and consequent supersalinity; primary dolomite is precipitated in the upper layer while underlying unconsolidated limestones are concurrently dolomitized from the top down.

Well crystallized dolomite also occurs in hydrothermal veins, often associated with ores of lead, zinc and copper, or with fluorite, barytes, calcite, siderite and quartz. A dolomite-rich alkaline intrusive dyke has been recorded cutting the Permian evaporite deposits of New Mexico, and consists of sodic plagioclase phenocrysts, dolomite rhombs, and small amygdales of dolomite and natrolite set in a groundmass of orthoclase, biotite and ilmenite. Dolomitic or dolomitic-sideritic carbonatites (beforsites) are known from many carbonatite complexes. Dolomite is also typically associated with altered ultrabasic igneous rocks where it may occur with magnesite in serpentinites and talc-bearing rocks.

In metamorphic rocks dolomite occurs chiefly in thermally or regionally metamorphosed magnesian or dolomitic limestones where it may recrystallize to form a dolomitic marble. At a higher grade of metamorphism the dolomite may break down in two stages (1) $CaMg(CO_3)_2 \rightarrow CaCO_3 + MgO + CO_2$, (2) $MgO + H_2O \rightarrow Mg(OH)_2$, thus leading to the formation of periclase and later brucite, giving the rock types pencatite, or with more abundant calcite, predazzite. In the progressive metamorphism of siliceous dolomite-bearing limestones the dolomite enters into the formation of talc, tremolite, forsterite and periclase, and may itself be temporarily re-formed by the reaction 2 talc + 3 calcite $\rightarrow$ 1 tremolite + 1 dolomite + CO_2 + H_2O. The exsolution of dolomite in calcite has been recorded in marbles associated with granulite facies metamorphism and from carbonate rocks almost completely engulfed in a quartz-bearing pyroxene diorite: from the subsolidus relations between $CaCO_3$ and $CaMg(CO_3)_2$ a calcite host is to be expected for such exsolution intergrowths.

REFERENCES

ALDERMAN, A. R. and SKINNER, H. C. W. (1957) 'Dolomite sedimentation in the south-east of South Australia', *Amer. Journ. Sci.*, vol. 255, p. 561.

BOWEN, N. L. (1940) 'Progressive metamorphism of siliceous limestone and dolomite', *Journ. Geol.*, vol. 48, p. 225.

GRAF, D. L. and GOLDSMITH, J. R. (1956) 'Some hydrothermal syntheses of dolomite and protodolomite', *Journ. Geol.*, vol. 64, p. 173.

——— and LAMAR, J. E. (1955) 'Properties of calcium and magnesium carbonates and their bearing on some uses of carbonate rocks', *Econ. Geol.*, 50th anniv. vol., p. 639.

TILLEY, C. E. (1948) 'Earlier stages in the metamorphism of siliceous dolomites', *Min. Mag.*, vol. 28, p. 272.

TURNER, F. J.; GRIGGS, D. T., HEARD, H. and WEISS, L. W. (1954) 'Plastic deformation of dolomite rock at 380°C', *Amer. Journ. Sci.*, vol. 252, p. 477.

Ankerite

$Ca(Mg,Fe^{+2},Mn)(CO_3)_2$

TRIGONAL $(-)$

ϵ 1·510–1·548
ω 1·690–1·750
δ 0·182–0·202

Dispersion: Strong.   D 2·93–3·10.   H $3\frac{1}{2}$–4.
Cleavage†: $\{10\bar{1}1\}$ perfect.
Twinning: Common on $\{0001\}$, $\{10\bar{1}0\}$, $\{11\bar{2}0\}$.
Colour: White, yellow, yellowish brown or brown, more rarely grey or blue; colourless in thin section.

Soluble with difficulty in cold dilute HCl, unless freshly powdered. Darkens in colour on heating and may become magnetic.

STRUCTURE

The crystal structure of ankerite is similar to that of dolomite but with slightly larger cell parameters due to the replacement of Mg by the larger Fe^{+2} ion. The unit cell has $a \simeq 4·82$, $c \simeq 16·10$ Å, $c/a \simeq 3·34$; $a_{rh} \simeq 6·05$, $\alpha \simeq 47°\ 00'$; $Z_{rh} = 2$.

CHEMISTRY

The chief substitution which takes place is that of Fe^{+2} for Mg, with generally an appreciable amount of Mn also in the Fe–Mg position. The term ankerite is used here for material with Mg:Fe ⩽ 4:1, i.e. the mineral is termed ferroan dolomite if it has up to 20 per cent of the Mg positions filled by Fe^{+2} or Mn, and ankerite if it is richer than this in ferrous iron and manganese. No natural occurrence of ferrodolomite, $CaFe(CO_3)_2$, has been recorded, but ferroan ankerites with 20 to 37 per cent $FeCO_3$ are known. Ferroan ankerites often occur in association with siderites and it has been suggested that the isomorphous series from dolomite may end at near 75 per cent $(Fe,Mn)CO_3 \cdot CaCO_3$. this is substantiated by experimental work on the subsolidus relations on the join $CaMg(CO_3)_2$–$CaFe(CO_3)_2$. It is possible that the composition of the ankerite in equilibrium with calcite and siderite is temperature dependent, and may be of value in geothermometry.

OPTICAL AND PHYSICAL PROPERTIES

Increasing replacement of Mg by Fe^{+2} increases the refractive indices (Fig. 176), birefringence and specific gravity. The effect of the introduction of Mn into the (Mg,Fe) position is less than that of Fe. The colour is variable

† Indices for cleavage, twinning, etc., refer to the hexagonal cell with $a \simeq 19$ Å (see Table 49, p. 477).

but ankerite is typically white or yellowish white in hand specimen; it turns yellowish brown or brown, however, when oxidation of the iron has taken place.

DISTINGUISHING FEATURES

Ankerite may be recognized as a trigonal carbonate by its perfect rhombohedral cleavage, extreme birefringence, and solubility with effervescence in warm acid. Its frequent occurrence in rhombohedra and its poor solubility in cold dilute acid distinguish it from the calcite group. It may differ from dolomite in having a darker brown appearance due to weathering or oxidation, otherwise the distinction must be made chemically, by the higher refractive indices, or by the greater specific gravity. On heating ankerite, in addition to becoming darker in colour due to oxidation, it may become magnetic.

PARAGENESIS

In sedimentary rocks ankerite occurs as a result of both hydrothermal and low-temperature metasomatism. Large concentrations of ankerite often accompany galena–sphalerite–fluorite–barytes veins, as in the northern Pennine orefield where it has replaced limestone or quartz dolerite: the more iron-rich varieties occur in the inner fluorite–galena zone, while the more magnesian ankerites are found in the outer zones. In association with the lead–silver–zinc sulphide assemblage of the Coeur d'Alene district of Idaho, ankerite occurs farther away from the ore bodies than siderite but nearer than calcite, and has a typical composition of

$$Ca_{1.00-1.12}(Fe_{0.50-0.70}Mg_{0.20-0.26}Mn_{0.06-0.12})(CO_3)_2.$$

The lower temperature metasomatic ankerites occur chiefly in veins in shales, in clay ironstones, and along cleats or joints in coal: this material has often been mis-identified as dolomite, subsequent analyses showing it to be highly ferroan in character. Manganese also is usually found in considerable amounts in this type of ankerite, the Mn:Fe ratio being considerably higher than the average for sediments. Ankerite has been found associated with celestine and pyrite inside ammonite chambers in limestone, and forming the shell-substance of non-marine lamellibranchs in clay ironstone, where it is considered to be later than the clay ironstone (Table 48, anal. 6).

It occurs in certain high grade metamorphic rocks derived from iron-rich sediments, such as the cummingtonite–garnet–sideroplesite–ankerite schists from the Lewisian. Ankerite has also been found as globular masses in adinoles.

REFERENCES

HAWKES, L. and SMYTHE, J. A. (1935) 'Ankerites from the Northumberland coalfield', *Min. Mag.*, vol. 24, p. 65.

SMYTHE, F. S. and DUNHAM, K. C. (1947) 'Ankerites and chalybites from the northern Pennine orefield and the north-east coalfield', *Min. Mag.*, vol. 28, p. 53.

Huntite

$Mg_3Ca(CO_3)_4$

δ very strong. D 2·696.

Colour: White; colourless in thin section.

Occurs in soft compact porous masses which crumble in water. Soluble with effervescence in cold HCl (1:1).

The structure of huntite is similar to that of calcite, but the Mg and Ca ions are ordered: the unit cell has a_{rh} 6·075 Å, α 102° 56'; a_{hex} 9·505, c_{hex} 7·821 Å.

Analyses give fairly close agreement with the formula $Mg_3Ca(CO_3)_4$. The typical grain size of less than two microns does not allow the optical properties to be determined satisfactorily, the ω refractive index, however, is probably around 1·615–1·620. Huntite occurs in compact chalk-like masses which are relatively brittle when cut with a knife but which are easily scored by a fingernail. It is porous, and crumbles when placed in water. The easy solubility and brisk effervescence in cold acids establish it as a carbonate: further distinction may require X-ray or d.t.a. evidence.

Huntite occurs typically as an alteration or weathering product of dolomite- or magnesite-bearing rocks. In Currant Creek, Nevada, it is found in vugs in a magnesite–deweylite rock, and is believed to have been precipitated as a very fine powder from cool ground waters which became Mg-rich in traversing the magnesite deposit. Elsewhere it is known from fault zones and in caves.

Aragonite

CaCO$_3$

ORTHORHOMBIC (−)

α 1·530–1·531
β 1·680–1·681
γ 1·685–1·686
δ 0·155–0·156
$2V_\alpha$ 18°–18½°
$\alpha = z, \beta = x, \gamma = y$; O.A.P. (100).
Dispersion: $r < v$, weak.   D 2·94–2·95.   H 3½–4.
Cleavage: {010} imperfect, {110} poor.
Twinning: Common, twin plane {110}, giving lamellar twins parallel to z, or repeated twins leading to pseudohexagonal groups.
Colour: Typically colourless or white; colourless in thin section.

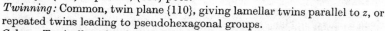

Effervesces with dilute HCl. When immersed in hot Co(NO$_3$)$_2$ solution aragonite chips or grains become lilac-coloured.

STRUCTURE

The calcium ions lie approximately in the positions of a hexagonal close-packed structure which has been deformed by compression along the hexad axis; layers of Ca ions are parallel to (001). This is in contrast to the deformed cubic close-packed arrangement of Ca in calcite and explains the pseudohexagonal symmetry of aragonite. In calcite the triangular CO$_3$ groups occur half-way between Ca layers, and each oxygen has two Ca as nearest neighbours, whereas in aragonite the CO$_3$ groups do not lie midway between Ca layers and are rotated 30° to right or left so that each oxygen

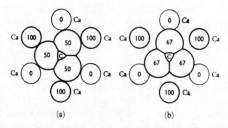

Fig. 179. *The arrangement of the CO$_3$ groups (a) in calcite, and (b) in aragonite. Each oxygen atom is linked to two Ca atoms in calcite, and to three Ca atoms in aragonite (after* Bragg, W. L., 1937, Atomic Structure of Minerals, *Cornell Univ. Press).*

atom has three neighbouring Ca atoms (Fig. 179). As a consequence successive CO_3 groups along z point alternately in the $+y$ and $-y$ directions (Fig. 180): thus although the Ca ions are in a hexagonal array, the arrangement of the CO_3 groups lowers the symmetry to orthorhombic. The unit cell has a 4·96, b 7·98, c 5·74 Å; $Z = 4$.

In general terms the structures of the carbonate group of minerals are governed by the radius of the metallic ion: if this exceeds about 1·0 Å the aragonite-type structure is preferred to that of calcite. Since the calcium ion is close to this critical value, $CaCO_3$ is dimorphous, appearing with both structures.

CHEMISTRY

Most aragonites are relatively pure and conform to the ideal formula (e.g. Table 48, p. 474, anal. 7). Many aragonites contain small but appreciable amounts of strontium, the ionic radii of Sr and Ca being fairly similar. Pb also substitutes for Ca, and the name tarnowitzite has been given to this plumbian aragonite.

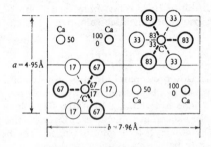

Fig. 180. *The structure of aragonite projected on* (001) (*after Bragg, W. L.*, 1937, Atomic Structure of Minerals, *Cornell Univ. Press*).

Aragonite can be readily synthesized by mixing carbonate solutions with solutions containing calcium ions under conditions of controlled temperature and ageing. With the addition of sodium polyphosphate, $CaCO_3$ precipitated from sodium chloride and carbonate solutions is largely or wholly aragonite. In general the crystallization of aragonite is favoured by temperatures of 50° to 80°C, and by the presence of salts of Sr, Pb, Ba or $CaSO_4$ in solution. The P–T curve defining the stability fields of calcite and aragonite has been determined experimentally (Fig. 181), confirming that aragonite is metastable at room temperature and one atmosphere pressure.

Aragonite commonly alters to calcite. It has been found that in some corals the aragonite portion contains about twice as much Sr as does the calcite portion, and it has been suggested that Sr inhibits the alteration of aragonite to calcite under natural conditions and that only when much of the Sr is removed may the alteration take place.

OPTICAL AND PHYSICAL PROPERTIES

Except for varieties rich in Sr or Pb, the range of optical properties of aragonite is small; the substitution of Sr for Ca lowers the refractive indices and optic axial angle while the entry of Pb has the opposite effect. The strong birefringence, as for calcite, has been ascribed to the orientation of the CO_3 group in the structure. Repeated twinning on the twin plane {110}, with composition plane also {110}, gives pseudohexagonal aggregates; in basal sections these show a distribution of twinned individuals in sectors, with the optic axial plane of each of the six sectors arranged at approximately 60° to that of the neighbouring sectors.

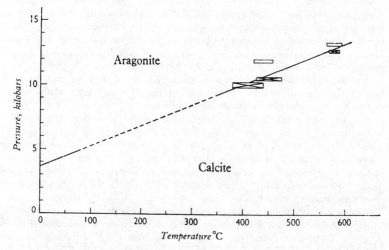

Fig. 181. *The equilibrium curve for* $CaCO_3$. *The open rectangles represent runs which gave aragonite and those with crosses represent runs which gave calcite (after Clark, S. R., Jr., 1957, Amer. Min., vol. 42, p. 564).*

DISTINGUISHING FEATURES

Aragonite may be distinguished from calcite by its greater specific gravity (2·94 compared with 2·71 for calcite and 2·86 for dolomite): it sinks in bromoform whereas calcite and dolomite float. Aragonite lacks the perfect rhombohedral cleavage of calcite and dolomite, and has higher refractive indices than calcite. Meigen's reaction is commonly used as a chemical test for aragonite: when grains or a powder of the mineral are boiled for a few minutes with a solution of $Co(NO_3)_2$ a lilac or violet colour rapidly appears, staining the mineral. Calcite remains colourless or becomes slightly blue only after prolonged boiling. A neutral solution of a mixture of manganese and silver sulphates when used in the cold on calcite or aragonite gives a far more rapid reaction with the latter, with deposition of black MnO_2 and Ag: the reaction is sufficiently localized to reveal intimate intergrowths of calcite and aragonite. It differs from the zeolites and other white or colourless minerals, other than the carbonates, by effervescing in acid. The other members of the aragonite group may be distinguished by their higher specific gravities and by the distinctive flame tests for Ba, Sr or Pb.

PARAGENESIS

Aragonite is less common than calcite: at normal temperatures and pressures it is metastable and fairly readily inverts to calcite. Many organisms with calcareous skeletons build their shells of aragonite: in certain molluscs (e.g. in many lamellibranchs) calcite and aragonite may occur in separate layers in the same shell, while in the cephalopods, aragonite and calcite are segregated in different parts of the skeleton, e.g. the ammonite shell consists of aragonite while the aptychus is made of calcite. The aragonite of fossil shells is gradually converted into calcite, although at a much slower rate than for synthetic material: under suitable conditions of burial, shells as old as the latter half of the Mesozoic may still contain aragonite. It is the normal material of pearls.

Primary precipitation of $CaCO_3$ from sea water also occurs as aragonite, giving rise to aragonite muds, and under suitable conditions to aragonite ooliths. It is also found associated with gypsum or celestine in marls or clays, and in pisolites or sinter deposits from geysers and hot springs: it may form stalactites in caves in limestone districts, and some 'cave-pearls' occurring in pools in such caves have been shown to have layers of very fine-grained aragonite.

Aragonite occurs as a secondary mineral in cavities in volcanic rocks, chiefly andesites and basalts, and may sometimes be associated with zeolites. It is also found pseudomorphous after other minerals such as gypsum, and as a secondary mineral in altered dolomite. In the oxidized zone of ore deposits aragonite may occur together with limonite, malachite, calcite, etc.

Aragonite is a widespread metamorphic mineral in Californian glaucophane schists. In the greenschist facies calcite is stable, but deep burial in regions of low temperature gradient, as in rapidly subsiding geosynclines, brings about the crystallization of aragonite as the stable carbonate at temperatures and pressures of the order of 200° to 300°C and 6000 to 10,000 bars (see Fig. 181). Partial inversion to calcite is frequently observed.

REFERENCES

BRAGG, W. L. (1924) 'The refractive indices of calcite and aragonite', *Proc. Roy. Soc. London.*, vol. 105, A, p. 370.

BROWN, W. H., FYFE, W. S. and TURNER, F. J. (1962) 'Aragonite in California glaucophane schists, and the kinetics of the aragonite–calcite transformation', *Journ. Petr.*, vol. 3, p. 566.

CLARK, S. P., JR. (1957) 'A note on calcite–aragonite equilibrium', *Amer. Min.*, vol. 42, p. 564.

GRAF, D. L. and LAMAR, J. E. (1955) 'Properties of calcium and magnesium carbonates and their bearing on some uses of carbonate rocks', *Econ. Geol.*, 50th anniv. vol., p. 639.

SUBBA RAO, M. and YOGANARAIMHAN, S. R. (1965) 'Preparation of pure aragonite and its transformation to calcite', *Amer. Min.*, vol. 50, p. 1489.

WRAY, J. L. and DANIELS, F. (1957) 'Precipitation of calcite and aragonite', *Journ. Amer. Chem. Soc.*, vol. 79, p. 2031.

Strontianite

$SrCO_3$

ORTHORHOMBIC (−)

α 1·516–1·520
β 1·664–1·667
γ 1·666–1·669
δ 0·149–0·150
$2V_\alpha$ 7°–10°
$\alpha = z, \beta = y, \gamma = x$; O.A.P. (010).
Dispersion: $r < v$, weak. D ≃ 3·72. H 3½.
Cleavage: {110} good, {021} and {010} poor.
Twinning: Common on {110}, single, repeated and lamellar twins.
Colour: Colourless, white, yellow, greenish or brownish; colourless in thin section.

Soluble in dilute HCl. When moistened with HCl gives an intense red colour to a flame.

The structure of strontianite is similar to that of aragonite, but with slightly larger cell parameters (a 5·128, b 8·421, c 6·094 Å ; Z = 4) due to the strontium ion being larger than that of calcium. Some calcium is generally present substituting for strontium and in natural material the Ca:Sr ratio may reach approximately 1:4. The intermediate composition $CaSr(CO_3)_2$ has been synthesized and has cell dimensions intermediate between those of strontianite and aragonite. Barium may also substitute for strontium in the natural mineral, and a complete synthetic series $SrCO_3$–$BaCO_3$ has been prepared.

Substitution of Ca for Sr causes an increase in refractive indices and a decrease in the specific gravity. The solubility in HCl, and the intense red colour imparted to a flame are diagnostic.

Strontianite most commonly occurs as fibrous masses in veins in limestones and marls but is also known from igneous rocks, possibly as an alteration of celestine. Strontianite-rich rocks have been recorded in association with Nyasaland carbonatites. It is often associated with witherite, barytes, celestine, fluorite and lead-bearing minerals, and is named after the Strontian, Argyllshire, locality, where it occurs in association with lead mineralization.

Witherite

$BaCO_3$

ORTHORHOMBIC $(-)$

α 1·529
β 1·676
γ 1·677
δ 0·148
$2V_\alpha$ 16°
$\alpha = z,\ \beta = y,\ \gamma = x$; O.A.P. (010).

Dispersion: $r > v$, very weak. D 4·29–4·30. H 3½.
Cleavage: {010} distinct, {110} and {012} poor.
Twinning: Always present; repeated twins on {110} giving pseudohexagonal forms.
Colour: Colourless, white, greyish or light yellowish brown; colourless in thin section.

The structure of witherite is similar to that of aragonite, but with larger cell parameters (a 5·26, b 8·84, c 6·56 Å; Z = 4). It is normally fairly close in composition to $BaCO_3$, though Ca, Sr and Mg may replace Ba to a small extent: Pb does not appear to substitute for Ba despite the common occurrence of witherite with galena. The mineral alstonite, $CaBa(CO_3)_2$, is a distinct species and is not isomorphous with either aragonite or witherite. The dissociation temperature of witherite at atmospheric pressure is about 1380° to 1400°C.

Witherite typically has a pyramidal habit and the constant presence of repeated twinning on {110} is noteworthy. It is soluble with effervescence in dilute HCl and may be distinguished from most other carbonates by causing the precipitation of white $BaSO_4$ on the addition of sulphuric acid to such a solution. The high specific gravity of witherite is characteristic: the green barium coloration given to a flame is also diagnostic.

It occurs chiefly in low temperature hydrothermal veins, nearly always in sedimentary rocks, associated with galena, anglesite ($PbSO_4$), barytocalcite and barytes, and may sometimes result from alteration of the latter mineral. It is, after barytes, the most common barium mineral and is of economic importance.

PHOSPHATES

Apatite

$Ca_5(PO_4)_3(OH,F,Cl)$

HEXAGONAL $(-)$

ϵ $1\cdot624$–$1\cdot666$
ω $1\cdot629$–$1\cdot667$
δ $0\cdot001$–$0\cdot007$

Dispersion: Moderate.   D $3\cdot1$–$3\cdot35$.   H 5.
Cleavage: {0001} and {10$\bar{1}$0}, poor.
Twinning: Twin plane {11$\bar{2}$1} or {10$\bar{1}$3}, rare.
Colour: Green, white, yellow, blue, brown, etc.; generally colourless in thin section.
Pleochroism: Coloured varieties may show weak to moderate pleochroism, with absorption $\epsilon > \omega$.
     Soluble in HNO_3 or in HCl.

Members of the apatite group are common accessory minerals in almost all igneous rocks and are also found in sedimentary and metamorphic rocks. They are the most abundant phosphorus-bearing minerals; the commonest varieties are represented by the isomorphous series with end-members:

Fluor-apatite	$Ca_5(PO_4)_3F$
Chlorapatite	$Ca_5(PO_4)_3Cl$
Hydroxyapatite	$Ca_5(PO_4)_3OH$
Carbonate-apatite	$Ca_5(PO_4,CO_3,OH)_3(F,OH)$?

Of these, fluor-apatite is by far the commonest, and the term apatite is sometimes used synonymously with fluor-apatite.

STRUCTURE

Each F atom is surrounded by three Ca atoms at one level, and in addition Ca–O columns are linked with PO_4 groups forming a hexagonal network (Fig. 182). The differing sizes of the monovalent anions lead to a variation in the cell parameters: the values for the end-member compositions are:

	a(Å)	c(Å)	c/a
Fluor-apatite	$9\cdot35$	$6\cdot87$	$0\cdot735$
Chlorapatite	$9\cdot61$	$6\cdot76$	$0\cdot704$
Hydroxyapatite	$9\cdot41$	$6\cdot87$	$0\cdot731$
Carbonate-apatite	$9\cdot34$	$6\cdot88$	$0\cdot736$

CHEMISTRY

In the formula $Ca_5(PO_4)_3(OH,F,Cl)$, fluorine, chlorine, and the hydroxyl ion can mutually replace each other to form the almost pure end-members. Complete solid solution is obtained in synthetic preparations and it appears probable that there is a complete isomorphous series in natural apatites. Analyses of several apatites are given in Table 50, where they have been recalculated on the basis of $26(O,OH,F,Cl)$. Ca may be partially replaced by Mn (anal. 4), and an Mn:Ca ratio of 1:8 is not uncommon. Sr or the rare-earths, predominantly Ce, may also replace Ca to a considerable extent and fluor-apatites with over 11 per cent SrO are known.

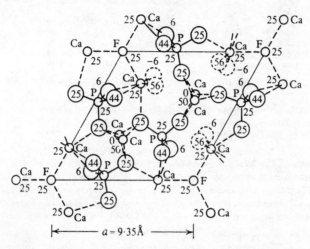

Fig. 182. *The structure of fluor-apatite*, $Ca_5(PO_4)_3F$, *showing the lower half only of the unit cell (after* Bragg, W. L., 1937, Atomic Structure of Minerals, *Cornell Univ. Press).*

The analyses of some apatites show appreciable CO_2 (up to 5 or 6 per cent): *francolite* is a name used for an apatite containing both appreciable CO_2 and more than 1 per cent of fluorine, whereas the name *dahllite* is applied to apatite with abundant CO_2 but with a small content of fluorine, i.e. a carbonate-hydroxyapatite. After earlier uncertainty it now seems likely that the CO_2 is not present as calcite or aragonite impurities, but is part of the apatite structure. Its exact role in the structure remains somewhat problematical: it has been variously considered as entering the (OH,F,Cl) group, or partially replacing Ca or PO_4 or both.

Fluor-apatite may be synthesized by the fusion of $Ca_3(PO_4)_2$ with CaF_2, whereas hydroxyapatite is most readily obtained by precipitation from solutions of calcium salts with the addition of ammoniacal phosphate solutions. Chlorapatite has been prepared by passing phosphorus tri-chloride vapour over red-hot lime. Various other elements and radicals have

Table 50. APATITE ANALYSES

	1.	2.	3.	4.	5.	6.
Fe_2O_3	—	—	0·03	—	—	0·25
FeO	0·21	—	—	0·26	0·32	—
MnO	1·52	0·07	0·01	5·32	0·02	—
MgO	0·54	0·10	0·02	0·04	0·05	0·53
CaO	52·40	55·84	55·88	50·31	55·08	54·84
SrO	—	—	—	—	0·03	—
Na_2O	—	—	—	0·00	0·04	0·20
K_2O	—	—	—	—	0·01	—
P_2O_5	40·98	42·05	42·00	41·50	42·40	35·01
F	1·15	0·16	3·73	3·41	1·63	5·60
Cl	3·74	—	0·00	—	0·2	0·03
H_2O^+	0·06	1·86	0·05	0·25	0·98	1·51
H_2O^-	—	—	0·00	0·03	0·08	0·16
CO_2	—	—	—	—	—	4·43
	100·60	100·23	101·80	101·47	100·84	102·66
$O \equiv F, Cl$	1·33	0·07	1·57	1·44	0·72	2·36
Total	99·27	100·16	100·23	100·03	100·12	100·30
ϵ	1·653	1·644	1·630	1·6411	—	†
ω	1·658	1·651	1·633	1·6459	1·642	
D	—	3·21	—	3·22	3·14	3·116

NUMBERS OF IONS ON THE BASIS OF 26 (O, OH, F, Cl)‡

	1.	2.	3.	4.	5.	6.
P	6·000	5·953	5·962	5·980	6·014	4·930 } 5·94
C	—	—	—	—	—	1·006
Fe^{+3}	—	—	0·004	—	—	0·031
Mg	0·139	0·025	0·005	0·010	0·012	0·131
Fe^{+2}	0·030	—	—	0·037	0·045	—
Mn	0·223 } 10·10	0·010 } 10·04	0·001 } 10·07§	0·767 } 9·99	0·003 } 9·96‖	— } 10·00
Na	—	—	—	—	0·012	0·064
Ca	9·710	10·004	10·040	9·175	9·837	9·774
Sr	—	—	—	—	0·003	—
F	0·630 } 1·80	0·084 } 2·16	1·979 } 2·03	1·835 } 2·12	0·868 } 2·02	2·946 } 4·63
OH	0·068	2·074	0·056	0·284	1·098	1·671
Cl	1·097	—	—	—	0·056	0·008

1. Greenish yellow chlorapatite, in cavities in quartz diorite, Kurokura, Japan (Harada, Z., 1938, *Journ. Fac. Sci. Hokkaido Univ.*, ser. 4, vol. 4, p. 11).
2. Yellow hydroxyapatite, Holly Springs, Georgia, U.S.A. (Mitchell, L., Faust, G. T., Hendricks, S. B. & Reynolds, D. S., 1943, *Amer. Min.*, vol. 28, p. 356; includes insol. 0·15).
3. Fluor-apatite, stilpnomelane–calcite vein, near Dolgelly, North Wales (Matthews, D. W. & Scoon, J. H., *Min. Mag.*, 1964, vol. 33, p. 1032; includes Al_2O_3 0·08%; Sr 430, Y 140 p.p.m.).
4. Bluish green manganapatite, pegmatite, Varuträsk, Sweden (Quensel, P., 1937, *Geol. För. Förh.*, vol. 59, p. 257; includes insol. 0·35).
5. Yellowish white hydroxy-fluor-apatite, two pyroxene granulite, Hitterö, Norway (Howie, R. A., 1964, *Indian Geophys. Union*, Krishnan vol., p. 297).
6. Francolite, altered lava, Namaqualand, South Africa (Villiers, J. E. de, 1942, *Amer. Journ. Sci.*, vol. 240, p. 443; includes insol. 0·10).

† α 1·614–1·617, β 1·627, γ1·627–1·630, $2V_\alpha$ 0–36°.
‡ Numbers of ions for the carbonate-apatite (anal. 6) calculated on the basis of 10 (Ca, Mg, etc.).
§ Includes Al 0·016.
‖ Includes K 0·002.

been substituted in synthetic apatites, including Sr, Pb, Ba, Y, Si, and SO_4. Carbonate-apatites have only been prepared by the treatment of $CaCO_3$ by alkaline phosphate solutions, the carbonate-apatite thus formed being due to incomplete replacement of CO_3^{-2} by PO_4^{-3}.

OPTICAL AND PHYSICAL PROPERTIES

Apatite is optically negative and is normally uniaxial, though biaxial varieties with an optic axial angle of up to 20° are known: the carbonate-bearing apatites in particular may have anomalous optics, e.g. the francolite of Table 50, anal. 6.

The large variations in composition within the apatite group make the accurate correlation of optical data difficult. In general, however, the refractive indices are highest for chlorapatite and are reduced by the substitution of OH and still more by the substitution of F (Fig. 183). The partial replacement of P by C also brings about a general reduction of refractive

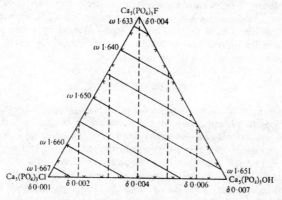

Fig. 183. *Optical properties of the fluor-, chlor- and hydroxyapatite series.*

indices: the entry of Mn increases the refractive indices and also increases the specific gravity. The substitution of Sr for Ca does not appreciably alter the refractive indices though the specific gravity is considerably increased. The birefringence also varies with the substitution in the (OH,F,Cl) group, being lowest for chlorapatite (0·001), intermediate for fluor-apatite (around 0·004) and highest for hydroxyapatite (0·007). The birefringence of some carbonate-apatites may be even stronger, e.g. that of anal. 6 (Table 50) is 0·013. The cryptocrystalline variety of apatite, collophane, may appear isotropic or show only weak birefringence: this is due to the aggregate polarization effect produced by a mass of superimposed submicroscopic crystallites.

The colour of apatite is extremely variable. The intensity of the colour increases with an increase in Mn-content of the apatite, but the colour itself depends on the state of oxidation of the manganese: thus Mn^{+2} produces pale pink and blue tones, Mn^{+3} blue, and Mn^{+7} violet. Ferric and ferrous iron together produce a green colour in both synthetic and natural apatites: some other colours may be due to rare-earths. Some apatites show a yellow or a pale violet fluorescence. The coloured varieties of apatite may, in thick sections, show moderate pleochroism with absorption $\epsilon > \omega$; blue apatite, for example, may have ϵ greenish blue, ω light blue. Zonal distribution of the colour is also known, particularly for the blue pegmatitic manganapatites.

DISTINGUISHING FEATURES

The high relief and low birefringence of apatite serve to distinguish it from most light-coloured minerals. Its straight extinction and the absence of a good cleavage help to distinguish it from sillimanite and melilite. Topaz is optically positive as well as being biaxial, while eudialyte has a more distinct cleavage and, in general, lower refractive indices. Vesuvianite and zoisite have considerably higher relief and may show anomalous inter- ference colours. The coloured slightly pleochroic varieties may be distin- guished from tourmaline by having absorption $\epsilon > \omega$, tourmaline having $\omega \gg \epsilon$. The addition of a drop of nitric acid followed by some ammonium molybdate will confirm the presence of a phosphate by giving a yellow precipitate of ammonium phosphomolybdate.

PARAGENESIS

Apatite is a common accessory mineral in many types of rock and is the most abundant phosphorus-bearing mineral. It occurs as an accessory mineral in almost all igneous rocks from basic to acid, and in some may amount to as much as 5 per cent by volume, though 0·1 to 1 per cent is the more normal range. In most igneous apatites, the fluor-apatite molecule is generally dominant, often with appreciable OH in addition, giving a hydroxy-fluor-apatite. Apatite is a fairly common mineral of granitic pegmatites where the bluish manganese-bearing varieties often occur, e.g. anal. 4: they may be associated with lithium minerals such as lepidolite and spodumene, and with beryl. Apatite also occurs in hydrothermal veins and cavities (e.g. anal. 1) and is found in Alpine-type veins, with quartz, adu- laria, etc.

Carbonatites generally contain appreciable apatite. There are several apatite-rich areas in the Khibina tundra, Kola peninsula, where apatite- nepheline rocks occur, including a strontian apatite ('saamite'). Apatite forms about 3 per cent of the Palabora shonkinite, in the Transvaal, and locally apatite–diopside rock and apatite rock have up to 96 per cent phos- phate. Carbonate-apatite also occurs in the calcitic carbonatites (alvikites) of the Alnö alkaline complex, and may amount to 13 per cent in the sövites.

Apatite occurs in both thermally and regionally metamorphosed rocks. Fluor-apatite is a frequent associate of chondrodite and phlogopite in metasomatized calc-silicate rocks and impure limestones, whereas chlorapa- tite may occur associated with scapolite in such rocks which have undergone chlorine metasomatism: carbonate-apatite is also known from contact metamorphosed rocks as at Magnet Cove, Arkansas. The intrusion of igneous sills and dykes into the Permian phosphate-bearing beds of Montana has converted collophane and francolite to colourless fine-grained apatite, sometimes giving quartz–apatite veins. The hydroxyapatite (Table 50, anal. 2) in talc schist and the fluor-hydroxyapatite in chlorite schist, both from a serpentinite near Holly Springs, Georgia, are considered to be metamorphic in origin, the hydrous environment being essential for their formation.

Apatite is not uncommon in sedimentary rocks where it occurs both as a detrital mineral and as a primary deposit. Deposits containing appreciable vertebrate remains are often highly phosphatic, and fish scales or bones may act as nuclei for the secondary concentration of calcium phosphate to form nodules. In some areas phosphatic deposits are developed on a vast scale, constituting independent formations covering a wide area; e.g. the Permian Phosphoria Formation of western North America in which beds containing up to 80 per cent phosphate are interbedded with phosphatic shales and impure limestones: such phosphate-rich strata are termed phosphorites. The mineralogy of such phosphorites is complex, the phosphate occurring as a cryptocrystalline, often concretionary, virtually isotropic material. The name *collophane* has been applied to the cryptocrystalline mineral component, and is a term analogous to 'limonite': it is of use only when the apatite-like phase cannot be definitely identified. It may well be that the principal mineral of some phosphorites is francolite or possibly, in some cases, dahllite. True coprolites are a relatively uncommon constituent of sediments but may include cryptocrystalline collophane.

REFERENCES

AMES, L. L., JR. (1959) 'The genesis of carbonate apatites', *Econ. Geol.*, vol. 54, p. 829.

BEEVERS, C. A. and MCINTYRE, D. B. (1946) 'The atomic structure of fluor-apatite and its relation to that of tooth and bone material', *Min. Mag.*, vol. 27, p. 254.

MCCONNELL, D. (1952) 'The problem of the carbonate apatites. IV. Structural substitutions involving CO_3 and OH', *Bull. Soc. franç. Min. Crist.*, vol. 75, p. 428.

Monazite

$(Ce,La,Th)PO_4$

MONOCLINIC $(+)$

α 1·774–1·800
β 1·777–1·801
γ 1·828–1·851
δ 0·045–0·075
$2V_\gamma$ 6°–19°
$\gamma:z = 2°–7°$; O.A.P. $\perp$ (010).
Dispersion: Usually $r < v$, weak.
  D 5·0–5·3. H 5.
Cleavage: {100} moderate, {001} variable.
Twinning: Twin plane {100}, common : also rare lamellar twinning on {001}.
Colour: Yellow or reddish brown; yellow or colourless in thin section.
Pleochroism: Very weak, light yellow to very light yellow.
  Slowly decomposed by acids.

The structure ($a \simeq 6\cdot78$, $b \simeq 7\cdot00$, $c \simeq 6\cdot45$ Å, $\beta \simeq 104°$; $Z = 4$) consists of distorted PO_4 tetrahedra with each metal atom roughly equidistant from nine oxygen atoms. There is a systematic decrease in cell dimensions with the increasing substitution of the smaller Ca and Th ions for Ce and La.

The commonest varieties of monazite have 4 to 12 per cent ThO_2, though Th-free monazite is known; the variety cheralite has around 30 per cent ThO_2. Minor amounts of the other rare-earths, and of U, Al and and Fe^{+3} may also occur. The isotope ratios $^{238}U/^{206}Pb$, $^{235}U/^{207}Pb$, $^{207}Pb/^{206}Pb$ and $^{232}Th/^{208}Pb$ in monazite have been extensively used for determining the absolute ages of monazite-bearing pegmatites. Huttonite, $ThSiO_4$, is isostructural with monazite, and there may be a continuous series between the two minerals, with the coupled substitution $Th^{+4}Si^{+4} \rightleftharpoons Ce^{+3}P^{+5}$.

Monazite is typically light yellow or yellowish brown in thin section or in grains, but rarely shows any appreciable pleochroism. The refractive indices are high and are increased by the entry of Th. Partly metamict monazite has been reported, however, with a low birefringence and n 1·79. Zircon is uniaxial and has higher refractive indices, sphene has higher birefringence, staurolite is more strongly pleochroic, and both olivine and epidote have a larger 2V.

It occurs as a rather rare accessory mineral in granitic rocks and in syenitic and granitic pegmatites. Monazite of metasomatic origin in dolomitic marble is also known. It is moderately resistant to weathering and is frequently concentrated as a detrital mineral in stream and beach sands : such concentrates may be worked as a source of cerium and other rare-earths.

HALIDES

Fluorite CaF₂

Fluorite $\qquad\qquad\qquad\qquad\qquad\qquad\qquad\qquad\qquad\qquad$ CaF_2

CUBIC

n 1·433–1·435

Dispersion: Weak. D 3·18. H 4.

Cleavage: {111} perfect.

Twinning: {111}, commonly as interpenetrant cubes.

Colour: Extremely variable; colourless, white, yellow, green, blue and purple varieties are the most common. Colourless, pale green or pale violet in thin section.

Soluble in H_2SO_4 with evolution of HF: slightly soluble in HCl.

STRUCTURE

The unit cell has a 5·463 Å; Z = 4. The calcium ions are arranged on a cubic face-centred lattice, while each fluorine ion is at the centre of one of the smaller cubes obtained by dividing the unit cube into eight parts. Each Ca is thus coordinated by 8 F ions and each F is surrounded by 4 Ca ions arranged at the corners of a regular tetrahedron. This is the simplest of the structures commonly assumed by AX_2 compounds and represents the highest possible coordination (8:4), the radius ratio condition being that radius A : radius $X > 0.732$.

CHEMISTRY

Most fluorite is at least 99 per cent CaF_2, and the small amounts of Si, Al and Mg sometimes reported are probably due to impurities or inclusions. The chief substitutions which can occur are the replacement of part of the Ca by Sr or by Y and Ce: in the variety yttrofluorite, $(Ca,Y)F_{2-3}$, the YF_3 molecule may amount to 10–20 per cent with minor amounts of CeF_3. Some fluorites are reported to contain free fluorine, and on grinding these specimens may give a strong odour of ozone and HF: this variety is sometimes known as antozonite. Some dark purple fluorite may contain hydrocarbons, and in particular the Blue John fluorite from Treak Cliff, Castleton, Derbyshire, has yielded as much as 0·27 per cent carbon. Dark purple fluorites have also been reported to be relatively rich in strontium, containing up to 1 per cent Sr.

Fluorite can be prepared artificially by the evaporation of a solution of CaF_2 in HCl. Large synthetic crystals for optical purposes have been obtained by fusing precipitated CaF_2 in a graphite crucible in a vacuum furnace; PbF_2 may be added to act as a scavenger for impurities.

OPTICAL AND PHYSICAL PROPERTIES

The low refractive index, small dispersion and isotropic nature make colourless fluorite a suitable material for optical use. For fluorite with substantial substitution of Y for Ca, the refractive index is considerably increased.

The problem of colour in fluorite has been extensively discussed. The theories put forward include physical disturbance in the crystal structure, radioactive inclusions or emanations from nearby radioactive material, traces of rare-earths, and the presence of inclusions of carbonaceous material, MnO_2, etc. Purple fluorite found in association with radioactive minerals becomes colourless on heating above about 175°C: the colour is associated with an increase in refractive index and a decrease in specific gravity, and these phenomena are ascribed to the disruption of the structure by nuclear particles. The fluorescence (a phenomenon which derives its name from fluorite) is often strong and has been correlated with relatively high contents of the rare-earths Eu, La and Ce: Y and Sm may also be important in the green varieties. It seems most probable that the common blue colour of fluorite is associated with a defect structure: omission of fluorine ions results in the presence of excess Ca ions which become neutral by separation from their valency electrons, thus forming the so-called F centres: the thermal bleaching mentioned above is thus due to the release of the free electrons.

DISTINGUISHING FEATURES

In hand specimen fluorite may be distinguished by its perfect octahedral cleavage, its vitreous lustre and its cubic habit. The colour is so variable as to be of little help, but varying shades of purple and violet are common colours, as are green and yellow, while the colourless material is not rare. It is relatively soft, does not effervesce with acid like calcite, but is attacked by H_2SO_4. Under the microscope its isotropic character and very low refractive index are characteristic: purple varieties often have sufficient depth of colour to remain purple or violet in thin section. Cryolite has an even lower relief, is very weakly birefringent, and has a pseudocubic {001} cleavage. Halite has a perfect {001} cleavage and a higher refractive index.

PARAGENESIS

In igneous rocks fluorite may occur as a late-crystallizing, mainly hydrothermal product, especially in granites, syenites and greisen: it is a rather common accessory mineral in some granitic pegmatites. Examination of liquid inclusions in pegmatite fluorites by the decrepitation method has given a range of crystallization temperature of 450°–550°C. It is found in the Alnö Island alkaline complex where it occurs in calcite–fluorite dykes, and has been reported from nepheline-syenite, and from apatite-rich deposits in alkaline rocks in the Transvaal where it occurs in economically important quantities. Some Newfoundland deposits, in granite, consist of veins 5 to 20 feet thick, containing 75 to 95 per cent CaF_2. Fluorite has also been recorded in the drusy cavities of blocks ejected from volcanoes, and as a volcanic sublimate. In these igneous occurrences associated minerals include cassiterite, topaz, apatite, lepidolite, etc., for the pneumatolytic deposits, and calcite, pyrite, apatite, etc., for the hydrothermal product.

Fluorite is often found associated with typical hydrothermal minerals not known to be directly related to any igneous body. Such hydrothermal vein deposits may also carry barytes, sphalerite, galena, calcite and chalcedony or quartz. In the English Pennines purple and green fluorite occur towards the centre of the fluorite zone while in the outer portion yellow fluorite is found, often associated with barytes. The Illinois–Kentucky fluorite deposits are epigenetic and include vein deposits and bedding replacement deposits: physical guides were structural and stratigraphical. Dilution of mineralizing fluids by ground water, and the change in temperature gradient on contact with excess ground water, are considered to be the major chemical factors governing the formation of these fluorite deposits.

Fluorite is sometimes found as a cementing material in sandstone: violet grains of fluorite are fairly common as a detrital mineral in sands, being derived from acid igneous rocks and hydrothermal deposits. The mineral is known from geodes, with calcite, barytes, sphalerite, etc., in limestone, where it is probably hydrothermal in origin. The variety of fluorite known as Blue John occurs in spheroidal nodular masses with a radiating crystalline structure, and contains blue bands of varying intensity arranged concentrically, parallel to the nodular surface, and between these, colourless, yellow or paler blue bands: this variety is virtually restricted to an area near Castleton, Derbyshire.

REFERENCES

ALLEN, R. D. (1952) 'Variations in chemical and physical properties of fluorite,' *Amer. Min.*, vol. 37, p. 910.

DUNHAM, K. C. (1952) 'Fluorspar', *Mem. Geol. Surv. Gt. Britain: Special Rep. Min. Resources Gt. Britain*, vol. 4.

FORD, T. D. (1955) 'Blue John fluorspar', *Proc. Yorkshire Geol. Soc.*, vol. 30, p. 35.

Halite

CUBIC

n 1·544

Dispersion: Moderate.   D 2·16–2·17.   H 2½.
Cleavage: {100} perfect.
Twinning: On {111} for synthetic crystals.
Colour: Colourless or white when pure, more typically orange or red due to inclusions of iron compounds; it may also be grey, yellow or blue: colourless in thin section.

Soluble in water. Salty taste. Colours a flame deep yellow.

The structure of halite, the first to be analysed by X-rays, consists of Na and Cl ions arranged alternately along rows parallel to the edges of a face-centred cubic cell (a 5·64 Å; Z = 4). If ions of one type are taken at the corners and face centres of the cell, those of opposite sign lie at the mid-points of cell edges and at the cube centre. Thus each Na is octahedrally coordinated by six Cl and each Cl by six Na.

Carefully purified halite contains over 99 per cent NaCl; massive rock salt, however, may contain admixed clay, iron oxides, gypsum, etc. There is little replacement of Na by K, although sylvine (KCl) is isomorphous. Large single-crystals used for making lenses for ultra-violet or infra-red spectroscopes, etc., are prepared by the slow cooling of the fused salt for 7 to 10 days.

It is normally colourless, but material which is deeply coloured in hand specimen may show a faint colour in thin section. Although the reddish colours in some rock salt are due to iron compounds, certain yellow and blue halites owe their colour to the presence of F centres, i.e. structural sites where an electron is held in an anion vacancy. In hand specimen the perfect cubic cleavage, saline taste, solubility and relative softness are characteristic. In thin section the isotropic nature and the low relief are distinctive: sylvine has a refractive index (n 1·490) less than that of Canada Balsam.

Halite occurs chiefly in sedimentary rocks where it has been deposited by evaporation from sea water or salt lakes: associated minerals include gypsum, anhydrite, carnallite, sylvine, etc. NaCl represents 77·6 per cent of the salts evaporated from present day sea water: on evaporation, halite begins to crystallize when the volume of sea water has been reduced to about 10 per cent of its original volume. Deformation of stratified rocks with interbedded halite deposits may produce upthrusting of massive salt domes; these are usually circular in cross-section and may be several miles in diameter. Halite also occurs as a volcanic sublimate and as a surface efflorescence in arid regions.

Appendix 1

CALCULATION OF A CHEMICAL FORMULA FROM A MINERAL ANALYSIS

HORNBLENDE ANALYSIS

	(1) wt.% of oxides	(2) mol. prop. of oxides	(3) atom. props. of oxygen from each mol.	(4) Nos. of anions on basis of 24 (O, OH) i.e. col. (3) × 8·3743	(5) Nos. of ions in formula		
SiO_2	51·63	0·8593	1·7186	14·392	Si	7·20	0·80 } 8·00
Al_2O_3	7·39	0·0725	0·2175	1·821	Al	1·21	0·41
Fe_2O_3	2·50	0·0157	0·0471	0·394	Fe^{+3}	0·26	
FeO	5·30	0·0738	0·0738	0·618	Fe^{+2}	0·62	} 5·07
MnO	0·17	0·0024	0·0024	0·021	Mn	0·02	
MgO	18·09	0·4487	0·4487	3·758	Mg	3·76	
CaO	12·32	0·2197	0·2197	1·840	Ca	1·84	} 2·00
Na_2O	0·61	0·0098	0·0098	0·082	Na	0·16	
H_2O^+	2·31	0·1283	0·1283	1·074	OH	2·15	
Total	100·32		2·8659				

$$\frac{24}{2\cdot8659} = 8\cdot3743$$

The procedure for calculating a chemical formula is described by means of the above example, a hornblende.

Column 1 lists the composition of the mineral expressed in the usual manner as weight percentages of the constituent oxides.

Column 2 is derived by dividing each column 1 entry by the molecular weight of the oxide concerned. The figures so obtained therefore express the molecular proportions of the various oxides.

Column 3 is derived from column 2 by multiplying by the number of oxygen atoms in the oxide concerned. It thus gives a set of numbers proportional to the numbers of oxygen atoms associated with each of the elements concerned. At the foot of column 3 is its total (T).

If we require the amphibole formula based upon 24 oxygen atoms (this represents half the content of the unit cell) we need to re-cast the oxygen atom proportions so that they total 24. This is done by multiplying all of them by 24/T and the results are given in column 4.

Column 5 gives the number of cations associated with the oxygens in column 4. Thus for SiO_2 there is one silicon for 2 oxygens so the column 4 entry is divided by 2. For Al_2O_3 there are 2 aluminiums for every 3 oxygens so the column 4 entry is multiplied by $\frac{2}{3}$. For divalent ions the column 5 value is the same as that of column 4, and for monovalent ions (including hydrogen) the latter is doubled.

The numbers of ions on the basis of 24 oxygens given in column 5 can be grouped as shown to conform to a structural formula. In the present example it is assumed that the tetrahedral sites which are not filled by Si are occupied by Al, and the remaining Al atoms are in octahedral coordination.

It should be noted that a chemical analysis in itself can give only the ratios of atoms in the formula, and that the actual numbers of atoms given depends on an assumption about the actual number of one of them or of a group of them. A check of the correctness of the formula can be made if the cell volume and density are accurately known, since a calculated density can then be compared with that measured.

A check of charge balance, made by adding positive and negative charges in the formula, is a check only on arithmetic and not on the quality of the analysis. This is because any analysis expressed in terms of neutral oxides must lead to numbers of cations and oxygens which balance electrically.

In many silicates, as in the example above, the only anion in the mineral is oxygen (or OH). Each element is expressed (and generally directly determined) as a weight percentage of oxide, even though the oxides do not exist as such in the mineral. The calculation procedure outlined is justifiable, since each element can be thought of as associated with its appropriate share of the oxygen atoms in the crystal structure.

When oxygen is not the only anion present the calculation is somewhat more complicated, and an example (a clinohumite) is shown below.

CLINOHUMITE ANALYSIS

	(1) wt. % of oxides	(2) mol. prop. of oxides	(3) atom. props. of oxygen from each mol.	(4) Nos. of anions on basis of 18 (O, OH, F) *i.e.* col. (3) × 6·3961	(5) Nos. of ions in formula		
SiO_2	36·53	0·6079	1·2158	7·776	Si	3·88	
TiO_2	0·26	0·0033	0·0066	0·042	Ti	0·02	3·93
Al_2O_3	0·22	0·0022	0·0066	0·042	Al	0·03	
Fe_2O_3	0·56	0·0035	0·0105	0·067	Fe^{+3}	0·04	
FeO	5·04	0·0702	0·0702	0·449	Fe^{+2}	0·45	
MnO	0·34	0·0048	0·0048	0·031	Mn	0·03	9·11
MgO	54·16	1·3432	1·3432	8·591	Mg	8·59	
H_2O^+	1·52	0·0844	0·0844	0·540	OH	1·08	
H_2O^-	0·04	—	—	—	—		2·00
F	2·74	0·1442	0·1442	0·922	F	0·92	

	101·41		2·8863				
$-O \equiv F$	1·15		$-0·0721$ ($=\frac{1}{2} \times 0·1442$)				
Total	100·26		2·8142				

$$\frac{18}{2·8142} = 6·3961$$

Here fluorine is shown, as well as the oxides of all the cations, as a weight percentage. We may assume for simplicity that the fluorine atoms in the structure are bonded to magnesium atoms only, and yet the same atoms of magnesium are recorded as combined with oxygen in MgO. Thus an excess of oxygen is recorded and the total will exceed 100 per cent. To obtain a real total (which is a measure to some extent of the accuracy of the data), an oxygen equivalent of the fluorine atoms must be subtracted.

One excess oxygen atom is recorded for each two atoms of fluorine present, so that the oxygen equivalent of a fluorine by weight is obtained by multiplying the fluorine content by the factor

$$\frac{\text{atomic weight of oxygen}}{2 \times \text{atomic weight of fluorine}}, \text{ i.e. } \frac{16}{38}.$$

The oxygen equivalent of the fluorine weight is subtracted from the total of column 1 to give a true total.

The procedure for obtaining column 2 is as before, the fluorine content being divided by 19, the atomic weight of fluorine. For column 3 the number of fluorine atoms is inserted along with the oxygens and the total is again too high. It is necessary to subtract the oxygen equivalent of the fluorine atoms, i.e. half their number, to give a true total.

In the case of clinohumite, the number of anions (O,OH,F) assumed is 18, so that the total of column 3 is divided into 18 to give the multiplying factor which is applied to produce column 4. Column 5 is derived as before.

Appendix 2

Al_2O_3	101·94	H_2O	18·016	S	32·066
B	10·82	HfO_2	210·5	SO_3	80·066
B_2O_3	69·64	K_2O	94·20	Sc_2O_3	137·92
BaO	153·36	La_2O_3	325·84	SiO_2	60·09
BeO	25·013	Li_2O	29·88	SnO	134·70
CO_2	44·010	MgO	40·32	SrO	103·63
CaO	56·08	MnO	70·94	Ta_2O_5	441·90
CeO_2	172·13	MnO_2	86·94	ThO_2	264·05
Ce_2O_3	328·26	Mn_3O_4	214·42	TiO_2	79·90
Cl	35·457	Na_2O	61·982	UO_2	270·07
CoO	74·94	NiO	74·71	U_3O_8	842·21
Cr_2O_3	152·02	Nb_2O_5	265·82	V_2O_5	181·90
CuO	79·54	P_2O_5	141·95	Y_2O_3	225·84
F	19·00	PbO	223·21	ZnO	81·38
FeO	71·85	Rb_2O	186·96	ZrO_2	123·22
Fe_2O_3	159·70				

INDEX

Mineral names in **bold** type are those described in detail; page numbers in **bold** type refer to the principal descriptions or definition of the mineral. Entries other than mineral names are in *italic* type.

Acanthite, 460
Achroite, 91
Acmite, **132**, 183
Actinolite, 151, **163–6**, 239
Adularia, 20, 239, **282**, 289, 299, 301, 305, 312
Aegirine, 100, 107, **132–5**, 189
Aegirine-augite, 100, **132–5**
Aenigmatite, 191
Agate, 351
Age determination, 217, 461, 510
Åkermanite, 72–6, 141
Alabaster, 468
Albite, 20, 137, 138, 180, 181, 183, 214, 239, 282, 283, 288, **289**, **318–38**, 365, 389
Albite twins, **293**, 329, 331
Alexandrite, 406
Alkali amphibole sub-group, 155
Alkali Feldspars, 281, 282, **285–317**
Allanite, 61, 66, **68–9**
Allochroite, 26
Almandine, 21, **23**, **29**, 162
Alstonite, 503
Amblygonite, 218, 366
Amesite, 236, **241**
Amethyst, 346, 350
Amosite, 162
Amphibole Group, 148–90
Analcite, 363, 368, 370, 371, **389–92**, 393, 395, 400
Anatase, 18, 413, **418–19**
Andalusite, 35–7, **38–40**, 41–3
Andesine, 282, 283, 318
Andradite, 21, **25**, **30**, 432
Anglesite, 460–2, 503
Anhydrite, 467–9, **470–2**, 514
Ankerite, 473, 474, 489, **494–5**

Annite, 211, 212, 216
Anomalous interference colours, 32, 52, 72, 231
Anorthite, 30, 70, 169, 282, **318–38**, 388, 401
Anorthoclase, 282, 283, 285, 290, 291, 297, 298, 301, 306, 307
Anthophyllite, 57, 88, 149, 150, 151, 155, **156–9**
Anthophyllite–cummingtonite sub-group, 155
Antigorite, 5, 165, 183, **242–9**
Antiperthite, 284, **318**, 322, 324
Antozonite, 511
Apatite, 504–9
Apophyllite, 275–6, 400
Aquamarine, 82, 83
Aragonite, 469, 473, 474, 478, 481, 492, **497–501**
Arfvedsonite, 153, 155, 186, **187–90**
Arizonite, 413
Arsenopyrite, 446, 449, 451, 454
Asbestiform varieties, 162
Asbestos, 158, 162, **182**, **242**, 248
Ashcroftine, **393**, 396
Asterism, 209
Astrophyllite, 60, 78, **192**
Attapulgite, 250, 254
Augite, 99, 100, **120–8**
Augite–ferroaugite, 120–8
Augite lamellae, 130
Aventurine feldspar, 298, 321, 334, 410
Axinite, 97
Azurite, 455, 475

Baddeleyite, 15, 417

Balas ruby, 426
Barium bytownite, 339
Barium feldspars, 339
Barium oligoclase, 339
Barkevikite, 152, 155, **177–8**
Barytes, 449, 461, **462–4,** 465, 493, 495, 502, 503, 513
Barytocalcite, 503
Barytocelestine, 462
Basaltic ferrohastingsite, 175
Basaltic hornblende, 152, 154, 155, **175–6**
'Basic' sodalite, 375
Bassanite, 467
Bastite, 111
Bavenite, 82
Baveno twinning, 293, 294, 321
Bayerite, 439
'Beef', 482
Beidellite, 252, 264, **266,** 268, 272
Bentonite, 265, 268
Bertrandite, 82
Beryl, 48, **80–3,** 218, 219
Biotite, 197, 199, 208, **211–16,** 218, 238, 273, 417
Blue John, 511, **513**
Boehmite, 406, 436, 439, **440–1**
Bog iron ore, **444**
Bornite, 454
Bowlingite, 5, 6
Brammallite, 206, 254, **261**
Braunite, 486
Bravoite, 446
Brazilian 'ruby', 47
Bredigite, 58
Breunnerite, 484
Brewsterite, 393, 396
Brewsterlinite, 47
Brittle micas, 196, 197, **220–1**
Bronzite, 108, **112**
Brookite, 413, **420–1**
Brucite, 229, 247, 403, **434–5,** 493
Brunsvigite, **233,** 235, 237
Bustamite, 145, **146**
Bytownite, 282, 283, 318

Calciocelsian, 339

Calcite, 141, 165, 230, 239, 383, 388, 400, 465, 473, 474, **476–83,** 488, 490, 492–3, 495, 498–9, 500
Calcite II, 474
Calcite III, 474
Calcium amphibole sub-group, 154, 155
Calculation of a chemical formula, 515
Calderite, 23
Californite, 32
Cancrinite, 363, 376, **381–3**
Capillitite, 485
Carbonate apatite, 504
Carbonates, 473–503
Carlsbad twins, **293,** 294, 296, 318, 321, 331
Carnallite, 514
Carnegieite, 346, **356,** 358–60, 370
Cape ruby, 23
Cassiterite, 404
Catapleiite, 60, **78–9**
Cation exchange, 250, 257, 261, 264, **266,** 393, 394
Cattierite, 445
Cebollite, 74
Celadonite, 254
Celestine, 462, **465,** 469, 500, 502
Celsian, 281, 284, **339**
Cerussite, 460, 461, 475
Ceylonite, 426
Chabazite, 391, **393,** 395, 396, 399
Chalcedony, 341, **351,** 465, 513
Chalcocite, 454, 455, 460
Chalcopyrite, 446, 449, 451–2, **453–5,** 457–8, 460–1
Chalybite, 487
Chamosite, 232, **233,** 235, 237, **241,** 488
Cheralite, 510
Chert, 351
Chiastolite, 39, **40**
Chiklite, 185
Chlorapatite, 504–9
Chlorite, 165, 212, 214, **231–40,** 273, 421
Chloritoid, 52–5
Chondrodite, 11–12, 430

Chrome diopside, 105
Chromian augite, 106
Chromite, 424–33
Chromite series, 424, 429, 432
Chrysocolla, 455
Chrysolite, 4–6
Chrysotile, 242–9
Cinnamon stone, 25
Citrine, 350
Clay mica, 209
Clay Minerals, 250–74
Cleavelandite, 219, 321
Clinochlore, 159, **233**, 234, 237, 241
Clinochrysotile, 244
Clinoenstatite, 5, 99, 101, 102, 103, 104, **108**
Clinoferrohypersthene, 101
Clinoferrosilite, 99, 108, 140
Clinohumite, 11–12, 516
Clinozoisite, 61, 62, **63–7**, 71, 278
Clintonite, 197, 221
Coesite, **341**, 349, 351, 354
Collophane, 507, **509**
Common hornblende, 154, 155, **167– 174**, 175, 176, 177
Concentric twinning, 87
Cookeite, 93
Cordierite, 84–9, 158, 430
Corona, 173
Corundophilite, **233**, 234, 237, 239, 241
Corundum, 220, 334, **405–8**, 439
Cossyrite, 191
Covellite, 460
Cristobalite, 258, **340–55**, 370, 381
Crocidolite, 182, 183
Cronstedtite, 241
Crossed axial plane dispersion, 420
Crossite, 135, 179, **180**, 181, 182
Cryptoperthite, **283**, 291, 300, **312**
Cubanite, 454
Cummingtonite, 151, 155, 156, 157, **160–2**
Cummingtonite–grunerite, 154, **160– 162**
Cyprine, 32
Cyrtolite, 14

Dachiardite, **393**, 396
Dahllite, **505**, 509
Danalite, 380
Daphnite, **233**, 239
Datolite, 56, 97
Dead-burned nagnesite, 484
Dehydration, 257, 262
Delessite, **233**, 237, 239
Demantoid, **26**, 30
Desert roses, 463, 469
Deweylite, 496
Diabantite, **233**, 237, 241
Diaspore, 220, 406, 436, **438–9**, 440–2
Dickite, 250, 253, 255, **257**, 258, 259
Differential thermal analysis, 257, 262
Digenite, 454
Dioctahedral mica, 195, **196**, 197
Diopside, 99, 101, 102, 104, **115–19**, 123, 133, 137, 143, 150, 163, 164, 165, 169, 170, 483, 508
Diopside–hedenbergite, 100, **115–19**
Diopside lamellae, 110
Dipyre, 384
Distribution coefficient, 123
Dolomite, 7, 165, 210, 230, 403, 469, 473, 474, **489–93**, 494, 496
Dravite, 90–6
Dysanalyte, 423

Eastonite, **208**, 211, 212
Eckermannite, 153–5, **187–90**
Edingtonite, **393**, 395, 397
Edenite, 154, **155**, **167**, 168, 169, 173
Elbaite, 90–6
Emerald, 80, **82**, 83
Enantiomorphism, 349, 350
Endiopside, **99**, 115, 119
Enstatite, 101–3, 105, **108–14**, 116, 123, 150, 163, 164, 170, 180, 181, 229
Enstatite–orthoferrosilite, 100, **108– 114**
Epididymite, 82
Epidote, 20, 61, **63–7**, 71, 165, 166, 239, 401

Epidote Group, 61–9
Epistilbite, **393**, 396
Erionite, **393**, 395, 396
Eucolite, 59–60
Eudialyte, 59–60, 79
Eulite, 108, **112**
Exfoliation, 270, 272

Fassaite, 120, **121**, 127, 221
Faujasite, **393**, 395, 396
Fayalite, 1–8, 113, 162
Feldspar Group, 281–339
Ferrian wad, 147
Ferrierite, **393**, 396
Ferriferrous pigeonite, 99
Ferrimagnetism, 430
Ferririchterite, 185
Ferroactinolite, 155, **163–6**
Ferroaugite, 99, 100, 106, **120–8**, 129
Ferrobrucite, 434
Ferrodolomite, 494
Ferroedenite, 154, 167
Ferrogedrite, 154, **156**
Ferroglaucophane, 180
Ferrohastingsite, 152, 155, **167–74,**
  175, 178
Ferrohedenbergite, 99, 119, 126, 129
Ferrohortonolite, 6
Ferrohypersthene, 105, **112**
Ferropericlase, 403
Ferrorichterite, 185
Ferrosalite, **99**, 115
Ferrostilpnomelane, 222
Ferrotschermakite, 155, 168
Fibrolite, 35
Flame-fusion method, 416
Flint, 351
Fluor-apatite, 504–9
Fluorite, 449, 461, 464, 493, 495, 502,
  511–13
Fluor-muscovite, 202
Fluorphlogopite, 209
Fluor-tremolite, 163
Forsterite, 1–8, 11, 118, 143, 165,
  180, 181, 229, 247, 483, 493
Framboidal pyrite, 449
Francolite, **505**, 509

Franklinite, 424, 429, 432
Fuchsite, 202
Fuller's earth, 267, 268

Gahnite, 424, 426, 430
Gahnospinel, 426
Galaxite, 424, 426
Galena, 454, 458–9, **460–1,** 495, 503,
  513
Garnet Group, 21–31
Garnetoid, 26
Garnierite, 245
Garronite, 393, 396
Gedrite, 151, 155, **156–9**
Gehlenite, 72–6
Genthelvite, 380
Gibbsite, 305, 406, **436–7**
Gismondine, 376, **393,** 396
Glaucochroite, 1, 9
Glauconite, 197, 198, **207,** 254, 449
Glaucophane, 70, 71, 135, 138, 153,
  154, 155, **179–84,** 224
Glide twinning, 479, 491
Glycerol, 265
Glycol, 253, 259, 261, **265,** 273
Gmelinite, 393, 395, 396
Goethite, 5, 6, **437,** 439, **442,** 443,
  444, 488
Goldmanite, 26
Gonnardite, 393, 395, 397
Gonyerite, 236
Goslarite, 458
Greenalite, 224, 241
Grossular, 21, 24, **25, 30,** 32, 221,
  483
Grossularoid, 26
Grothite, 18
Grunerite, 113, 151, 155, 157, **160–2**
Gypsum, 466–9, 471, 500, 514

Hackmanite, 376, 377, 378
Haematite, 5, 175, 245, 247, 334,
  409–11, 412, 413, 426, 428, 429,
  437, 439, 442, 444, 449, 488
Halides, 511–514
Halite, 469, **514**

Halloysite, 250, 251, 253, **257**, 258, 305, 437
Hancockite, 64
Harmotome, 393, 395, 396
Hastingsite, **172**, 178
Hauerite, 446
Hausmannite, 485
Haüyne, 375
Hectorite, 254, 264, **266**, 268
Hedenbergite, 30, 99, 101, 105, 113, **115–19**, 122, 123, 140, 162, 432
Heliodor, 82
Helvite, 83, 380
Hemihydrate, 467
Hemimorphite, 458
Hepatite, 463
Hercynite, 54, **424**, 426, 430
Hessonite, 25
Heulandite, 391, 393, 395, 396, 398
Hibschite, 26
Hiddenite, 136
High-albite, 282, 283, **285**, **289**, 331
High-sanidine, 283, **285**, 306, 307, 308
Holmquistite, 155, **158**, 159
Hornblende, 151, 152, 155, 163, 165, **167–74**, 273, 388, 515
Hortonolite, 4, 6
Hour-glass structure, 55, 247, 277
Hour-glass zoning, 125, 133
Humite, 11–12
Humite Group, 11–12
Huntite, 473, 496
Huttonite, 510
Hyacinth, 16
Hyalophane, 284, 339
Hyalosiderite, 6
Hydralsite, 258
Hydrogarnet, 23, **26**
Hydrogrossular, 21, **26**, 30, 74
Hydromagnesite, 403, 435
Hydromica, 254
Hydromuscovite, **202**, 203, 251, 253, **261**
Hydroxides, 434–44
Hydroxyapatite, 504–9
Hydroxy-tremolite, 163

Hypersolvus granites, 313
Hypersthene, 108–14, 130

Iddingsite, **4, 5**
Idocrase, 32
Illite, 202, 203, 205, 212, 250, 251, 253, 254, **260–63**, 269
Ilmenite, 410, **412–14**, 417, 419, 428, 429
Ilmenorutile, 416
Indicolite, 93
Intermediate-albite, 282
Intermediate microcline, 282, **289**
Intermediate pigeonite, 99
Inverted pigeonite, 129, 131
Ion sieve, 394
Iron cordierite, 54, 86, 87
Iron-glance, 409
Iron-leucite, 304
Iron-mullite, 37
Iron-orthoclase, 299
Iron-sanidine, 304
Iron-wollastonite, 140, 141

Jacobsite, 424, 429
Jade, 137
Jadeite, 100, 107, 127, **137–9**, 183
Jargoon, 15
Jasper, 351
Johannsenite, 100, **115–19**

Kaersutite, 152, 154, 155, **176–7**
Kaliophilite, 356
Kalsilite, **356–65**
Kämmererite, 236
Kandites, 250, 253, **255–9**
Kaolinite, 203, 205, 212, 250, 251, 253, **255–9**, 269, 305, 326, 376, 437
Kaolinite Group, 255–9
Katophorite, 155, **186**
Keatite, **341**, 347, 349
Keilhauite, 18
Kidney ore, 409
Kimzeyite, 26
Kirschsteinite, 1, 10

Klementite, 237
Knebelite, 9
Knopite, 423
Kochubeite, 236
Kornerupine, 57
Kunzite, 136
Kupletskite, 192
Kutnohorite, 485, 489
Kyanite, 35, 36, 39, 40, **41–4**

Labradorescence, 283
Labradorite, 170, 173, **282, 283, 318–38**
Lamellar Twinning, 55, 58, 77, 86, 88, 277, 293, 297, 321, 329–34, 479
Lapis Lazuli, 376
Larnite, 58, 76
Larsenite, 1
Laumontite, 278, 391, **393,** 396, 399
Låvenite, 60, 78
Lawsonite, 70, 71, 138, 166, 183
Lazurite, 376, 377, 379
Lechatelierite, 341
Left-handed quartz crystal, 350
Lemberg's test, 492
Leonhardite, 396
Lepidocrocite, 437, 439, 440, 442, **443,** 444
Lepidolite, 136, 193, 197, 199, **217– 218,** 219, 366
Lepidomelane, 212
Leucite, 302, 303, **367–74,** 389, 391, 423
Leucoxene, 412, 413
Levyne, 393, 395, 396
Limonite, 444, 488
Lizardite, 242–9
Loparite, 423
Low-albite, 282, 283, **285, 289,** 319, **331**
Low-sanidine, 283, 307
Lustre mottling, 482

Maghemite, 409, **424,** 429, 432, 439, 443
Magnesian pigeonite, 99, 106

Magnesite, 5, 229, 403, 473, 474, 484, 493, 496
Magnesioarfvedsonite, 187–9
Magnesiochromite, 424, 429, 432
Magnesioferrite, 424, 426, 432
Magnesiokatophorite, 153, 155, **186**
Magnesioriebeckite, 155, **179–83**
Magnetite, 162, 245, 247, 410, **424–32,** 442, 451, 488
Magnetite series, 424, 426, 432
Malachite, 455, **475**
Malacon, 14
Manganandalusite, 39
Manganapatite, 506, 508
Manganite, 486
Manganophyllite, **209,** 210
Manganosiderite, 485
Marcasite, 446, 447, 449, 451, 452
Margarite, 197, **220,** 239
Marialite, 384–8
Martite, 409
Maximum microcline, 282, 289
Mboziite, 154, 155
Mechanical twinning, 480
Mediopotassic nepheline, 357
Meigen's reaction, 499
Meionite, 384–8
Melanite, **25,** 30
Melilite, 72–6, 365, 373, 423
Melnikovite, 448
Melnikovite pyrite, 448
Menaccanite, 414
Merwinite, 58
'*Mesh*' *structure,* 247
Mesolite, 393, 395, 397, 398
Meta-dickite, 253, **258**
Meta-halloysite, 250
Meta-kaolinite, 253, **258**
Metamict state, 13, **14**
Mica Group, 193–221
Micaceous haematite, 409
Microcline, 282, 283, **285–317**
Microcline microperthite, **283,** 285, 300, 311, 317
Microperthite, **283,** 291, 292, 300, 312
Microsommite, 382, **383**
Milarite, 82

Minnesotaite, 224
Mizzonite, **384**, 385
Molecular sieve, 394
Molecular weights, 518
Monazite, 510
Montasite, 162
Monticellite, 1, **10**, 76, 118, 141, 143, 403
Montmorillonite, 203, 205, 212, 232, 252, 254, 259, 262, **264–9**, 326, 366
Montmorillonite Group, **264–9**
Moonstone, 283, 292, 300, 321
Mordenite, **393**, 396
Morganite, 82
Mullite, 35, **37**, 39, 43, 86, 258
Muscovite, 193, 197, 198, **201–5**, 209, 210, 212, 217, 218, 261, 263
Myrmekite, **316**, 354

Nacrite, 250, 255, **257**, 258, 259
Natrolite, 363, 376, 389, **393**, 395, 397, 398
Nemalite, 434
Nepheline, 137, 169, 189, 346, **356–65**, 370, 373, 381, 383, 407, 423, 508
Nepheline Group, **356–65**
Nephrite, 137
Nontronite, 254, 264, **266**, 267, **268**, 269
Norbergite, **11–12**
Nosean, **375–9**, 395

O_1, **356**, 362
Obliquity, 282, **289**
Oligoclase, 282, **318**
Oligon spar, 487
Oligonite, 487
Olivine, **1–8**, 11, 169, 173, 244
Olivine Group, **1–10**
Omphacite, 120, **121**, 127, 174, 337
Opal, 269, **351**
Order–disorder relationship, 289
Ortho-chrysotile, 244
Orthoclase, 282, 283, **285–317**, 370
Orthoclase-microperthite, **285**, 300

Orthoenstatite, 103
Orthoferrosilite, 105, **108–14**
Orthopyroxene, **108–14**, 121, 124, 156, 157, 162, 173, 430
Ottrelite, 53
Oxides, **403–33**
Oxidized chlorite, **233**, 237

Palygorskite, 254
Paracelsian, 339
Paragonite, 197, 202, **206**, 261, 363
Parawollastonite, **140**, 141, 142
Pargasite, 152, 154, 155, **167–74**
Pargasite–ferrohastingsite series, 168
Parsettensite, 222
Pearls, 500
Pectolite, **144**, 189
Pencil ore, 409
Pennantite, 236, 237
Penninite, **233**, 237, 241
Pentlandite, **451**, 452
Percussion figure, 200
Periclase, 143, 229, **403**, 435, 484, 490, 493
Peristerite, 283, **319**, 320, **321**
Perovskite, **422–423**
Perpotassic nepheline, 357
Perthite, **283**, 292, 312, 315
Petalite, **366**, 380
Phenakite, 82
Phengite, **202**, 203, 254, **261**
Phillipsite, **393**, 395, 396, 399
Phlogopite, 193, 197, 198, 201, **208–10**, 211, 212, 216, 221, 430
Phosphates, **504–10**
Picotite, **426**, 431
Picrolite, 244
Piemontite, 61, **63–7**
Piezoelectric property, 347, **350**
Pigeonite, 99–101, 104, 107, 110, 121–3, 126, **129–31**
Pinite, 39, **86**
Pistomesite, 487
Plagioclase, 281, 282, 283, **318–38**
Plaster of Paris, 468
Plasticity of clays, 259

Plazolite, 26
Pleochroic haloes, **213**, 237
Pleonaste, **426**, 430, 431
Polar symmetry, 90
Pollucite, 366, 368
Polymorphs, 52, 55, 84, 103, 195, 255, 356, 382, 446, 457, 458
Ponite, 485
Prehnite, 71, 97, **277-9**, 391, 401
Protoenstatite, 5, 101, **103**, 109, 110, 116, 130
Pseudobrookite, 413, **421**, 428, 429
Pseudoleucite, 371, **373**, 374, 389, 391
Pseudothuringite, 233
Pseudowollastonite, 140-3
Pumpellyite, 70, **71**, 139, 166, 183, 279, 401
Pycnochlorite, 233, 235, 241
Pyralspite, 21
Pyrite, 442, **445-9**, 451, 452, 454, 455, 461, 469
Pyroelectric effect, 90
Pyrolusite, 145, 486
Pyromorphite, 460, 461
Pyrope, 21, **23**, **29**
Pyrophanite, 412
Pyrophyllite, 35, 41, 86, 205, **225-6**, 259, 266
Pyroxene Group, **99-139**, 142
Pyroxenes of Bushveld type, 110
Pyroxenes of Stillwater type, 110
Pyroxmangite, 142, **147**
Pyrrhotite, 446, 449, **450-2**, 454, 457, 460, 461

Quartz, 305, **340-55**, 469, 493
    Left-handed, 350
    Right-handed, 350
    Rose, 350
    Smoky, 350
    α-β Inversion, 353

Rankinite, 77
Rapakivi texture, 316
Red ochre, 409

Reddle, 409
Richterite, 153, 155, **185**
Riebeckite, 135, 153, 155, **179-84**
Right-handed quartz crystal, 350
Ripidolite, **233**, 234, 237, 241
Rhodochrosite, 145, 147, 473, 474, **485-6**
Rhodonite, 29, 142, **145**, 146, 147, 486
Rhombic section, **295**, 321
Roepperite, 9
Rose-muscovite, 198, **202**, 203
Rose quartz, 350
Rosenbuschite, **60**, 78
Rotary polarization, 349
Rubellite, **91**, 93, 95
Rubidium-microcline, 298
Ruby, 23, **405**, 406
Rutile, 18, 413, **415-17**

Salite, **99**, 113, 115
Sand-calcite, 481
Sanidine, 282, 283, **285**, 288, 291, 298, 307, 308, 312
Saponite, 252, 254, 264, **266**, **268**, 269, 272, 273
Sapphire, 405
Sapphirine, 57
Satin spar, 466, **468**
Sauconite, 254, 264, **266**, 268
Saussuritization, 62, 67
Scapolite, 326, **384-8**, 407, 508
Schiller, 111, 300
Schizolite, 144
Schorl, **90-6**
Schorlomite, **25**, 30
Scolecite, **393**, 395, 397, 398
Sector twinning, 21, 26
Sector zoning, 125
Selenite, 468
Sepiolite, **250**, 254
Septechamosite, 241
Septechlorite, 232, 236, **241**
Serandite, 144
Sericite, **202**, 204, 205, 212, 214, **261**, 305
Serpentine, 5, 229, 236, 241, **242-9**

Sheridanite, **233**, 234, 237, 241

Shortite, 183

Siderite, 410, 442, 473, 474, **487-8**, 493, 495

Siderophyllite, 208, 211, **212**, 316

Sideroplesite, 487

Silica Minerals, 340-55

Sillimanite, **34-6**, 37, 39, 40, 42, 43, 204, 334

Skemmatite, 147

Smectites, 250, 253, 254, **264-9**

Smithsonite, 475

Smoky quartz, 350

Soapstone, 227

Sodalite, 363, **375-9**, 395

Sodalite Group, 375-80

Sodium melilite, 74

Spandite, 25

Specular haematite, 409

Specularite, 409

Sperrylite, 454

Spessartine, 21, **23**, 24, **29**, 147, 486

Sphaerosiderite, **487**

Sphalerite, 446, 452, 454, **456-9**, 460, 495, 513

Sphene, **17-20**, 419, 421

Spinel, 169, 173, 221, 407, **424**, 426, 427, 430

Spinel Group, 424-33

Spinel series, **424**, 426, 430

Spodumene, 99, 100, 107, **136**, 218, 219, 366, 380

β-Spodumene, 136

Spurrite, **59**, 76, 141

Staining techniques, 311, 380, 390, 403, 481, 491, 499

Stannite, 404, 454, 458

Star sapphire, 406

Staurolite, **49-51**, 220

Steatite, 227

Stevensite, 144

Stilbite, **393**, 395, 396, 399

Stilpnomelane, 166, **222-4**

Stinkstein, 463

Stishovite, **341**, 349, 352, 355

Strontianite, 465, 473, **502**

Strontiobarytes, 462

Subcalcic augite, **99**, 106, 120, 121, 126

Subcalcic ferroaugite, **99**, 106, 120, 121, 126

Subpotassic nepheline, 357

Subsolvus granites, 313

Sulphates, 462-72

Sulphides, 445-61

Sulphur, 465, 469

Sylvine, 514

Systems

  $Al_2O_3-K_2O-SiO_2-H_2O$, 202

  $CaAl_2Si_2O_8-CaMgSi_2O_6$, 323

  $CaAl_2Si_2O_8-CaMgSi_2O_6-$ $NaAlSi_3O_8$, 323

  $CaAl_2Si_2O_8-KAlSi_3O_8-$ $NaAlSi_3O_8$, 281, 313, 314

  $CaAl_2Si_2O_8-KAlSi_3O_8-$ $NaAlSi_3O_8-H_2O$, 303, 305

  $CaAl_2Si_2O_8-Na_2Al_2Si_2O_8$, 360

  $CaAl_2Si_2O_8-NaAlSi_3O_8-H_2O$, 323

  $CaCO_3-MgCO_3$, 490

  $CaFeSi_2O_6-FeSiO_3$, 121

  $CaMgSi_2O_6-CaFeSi_2O_6$, 116

  $CaMgSi_2O_6-MgSiO_3$, 109, 121

  $CaSiO_3-FeSiO_3$, 117, 140

  $Fe-S$, 446

  $FeO-Fe_2O_3-TiO_2$, 428

  $KAlSi_3O_8-H_2O$, 369

  $KAlSi_2O_6-SiO_2$, 299

  $KAlSiO_4-NaAlSiO_4$, 362

  $KAlSiO_4-NaAlSiO_4-SiO_2$, 358, 359, 369, 370, 373

  $KAlSiO_4-NaAlSiO_4-SiO_2-H_2O$, 370, 372, 373

  $KAlSi_3O_8-NaAlSi_3O_8$, 303, 313

  $KAlSi_3O_8-NaAlSi_3O_8-H_2O$, 303, 304, 369

  $MgO-SiO_2$, 3, 5

  $MgO-SiO_2-H_2O$, 111, 229, 245

  $NaAlSiO_4-NaAlSi_3O_8$, 137, 360

  $NaAlSiO_4-NaAlSi_3O_8-H_2O$, 362

Talc, 143, 159, 165, **227-30**, 248, 268, 484, 493

Talc-chlorite, 233

Tantalo-rutile, 416

Tarnowitzite, 498
Tawmawite, 64
Teallite, 404
Tenebresence, 378
Tephroite, 1, 9, 29, 145, 147, 486
Tephroite-knebelite, 9
Tetrahedrite, 454, 459
Tetrakalsilite, 356, 358, 362
Thomsonite, 363, 376, 393, 395, 397, 398
Thulite, 61, 62
Thuringite, 233, 235, 237, 239
Tie-line intersection, 123
Tilleyite, 77
Tinzenite, 97
Titanaugite, 120, 125, 177
Titaniferous magnetite, 427, 428
Titanite (sphene), 17-20
Titanohaematite, 412
Titanomagnetite, 428
Topaz, 45-8, 218, 219
Topazolite, 26, 30
Tourmaline, 90-6, 220
Tourmaline suns, 96
Tourmaline tongs, 95
Tremolite, 117, 143, 149, 150, 154, 163-6, 168, 169, 483, 493
Tremolite-ferroactinolite, 163-6, 168
Trevorite, 424, 429
Tridymite, 340-55, 370
Trikalsilite, 356, 358, 362
Trioctahedral mica, 195, 196, 197
Troilite, 450-2
Tschermak component (of pyroxene), 127
Tschermakite, 154, 155, 168, 169, 174
Tsilaisite, 91, 93
Twin Laws, feldspars, 293
Twins, Albite, 293, 318, 329-34
  Baveno, 293, 294, 296, 321
  Carlsbad, 293, 294, 296, 318, 321, 331, 334
  Manebach, 293, 294, 296
  Pericline, 293, 295

Ugrandite, 21
Ulvöspinel, 424, 429
Undulatory extinction, 350
Unoxidized chlorite, 233, 237
Uralite, 111, 123, 166, 174
Uvarovite, 21, 26, 30

Vacant sites, 358, 360
Vaesite, 445
Vaterite, 474, 478
Verdelite, 93
Vermiculite, 212, 232, 239, 250, 252, 253, 254, 270-4
Verneuil process, 406, 426
Vesuvianite, 32-3, 74, 221, 483
Viridine, 39, 43
Vishnevite, 381-3

Wairakite, 389, 390, 391, 401
Wiluite, 32
Winchite, 185
Witherite, 463, 465, 473, 502, 503
Wollastonite, 30, 116, 140-3, 146, 482
Wood tin, 404
Wurtzite, 457, 458, 459

Xanthophyllite, 197, 221
Xenotime, 15
Xonotlite, 74, 140

Yellow ochre, 442
Yttrofluorite, 511
Yttrotitanite, 18
Yugawaralite, 393

Zeolite Group, 276, 278, 391, 393-402, 483
Zincian spinel, 426
Zinnwaldite, 48, 197, 218, 219
Zircon, 13-16
Zoisite, 61-2, 65, 97